THE GOSPEL
ACCORDING TO ST. JOHN

THE GOSPEL
ACCORDING TO ST. JOHN

THE GREEK TEXT
WITH INTRODUCTION AND NOTES

BY THE LATE

BROOKE FOSS WESTCOTT, D.D., D.C.L.

BISHOP OF DURHAM
SOMETIME REGIUS PROFESSOR OF DIVINITY, CAMBRIDGE

VOLUME ONE

Wipf & Stock
PUBLISHERS
Eugene, Oregon

Wipf and Stock Publishers
199 W 8th Ave, Suite 3
Eugene, OR 97401

The Gospel According to St. John, Volume 1
The Greek Text with Introduction and Notes
By Westcott, B. F.
Softcover ISBN-13: 978-1-6667-5367-7
Hardcover ISBN-13: 978-1-6667-5368-4
eBook ISBN-13: 978-1-6667-5369-1
Publication date 7/20/2022
Previously published by , 1908

This edition is a scanned facsimile of
the original edition published in 1908.

PREFATORY NOTE

BISHOP WESTCOTT had, as is generally known, in co-operation with his lifelong friends Bishop Lightfoot and Professor Hort, formed in early days a plan for a "tripartite" Commentary on the New Testament, in which the Pauline writings were assigned to Bishop Lightfoot, the historico-Judaic to Professor Hort, and the Johannine to himself. This plan was discussed in the years 1859 and 1860, when Bishop Westcott was already at work on St. John. In a letter written to Dr. Hort in the Easter holidays of the year 1859 he says: "I have been enjoying extremely some work on St. John. How, indeed, is it possible not to enjoy such work? Yet how hard it is to study the Gospel widely enough and yet minutely! Just now it strikes me as a great Hebrew epic. The Hebrew poetic character—in the highest sense of the word—is very remarkable, and I do not think that I was ever sufficiently conscious of it before." From that time forward the Gospel Commentary was amid many interruptions continually in progress. From time to time other more urgent work thrust it temporarily into the background. For example, the preparation of *The Bible in the Church* led Dr. Lightfoot, in 1863, to express a hope that St. John had not been forgotten; and the publication of *The Gospel of the Resurrection,* in 1865, called forth from Mr. Macmillan a declaration of his joy that the way was now clear for the Commentary on St. John's Gospel. But Mr. Macmillan and others were doomed to disappointment, for in 1869 Bishop Westcott, after some heart-searching, yielded to a pressing request to undertake the Gospel for the *Speaker's Commentary,* and in consequence was reluctantly compelled to substitute the Authorised Version for the Greek text as the basis of his work. He did not, however, abandon his original plan of a Commentary on the Greek text of the Gospel, and reserved his right to utilise his published notes for such an edition. Writing to Mr. Macmillan in 1878, he says that the notes which he has been working at for the past eight years will serve as the basis of the Commentary which was " the dream of undergraduate days." He continued to work at the Gospel after the publication of his notes in the *Speaker's Comment-ary,* and prepared considerable material for the Greek edition.* The mass of the revised Commentary which he has left with us was, I am inclined to think, compiled during the years 1883—1887, after the publication of his Commentary on the Epistles of St. John and before his work on the Epistle to the Hebrews took final shape. He lectured on the Gospel at Cambridge in 1885, and in Westminster Abbey in 1887. Other notes were subsequently added, and a few of the latest pencilled additions probably belong to the last years of his life.

During the years that he was engaged in this revision he was much embarrassed by the rival claims of Messrs. Murray and Macmillan for the publication of the Greek edition ; but in the end Mr. Macmillan resigned his claim, and arrangements were concluded with Mr. Murray. The work, however, was not completed, and the publication has been deferred till now.

* The portions of the Gospel which my father has re-annotated comprise practically the whole of Chapters III., IV., VI., VII., VIII., IX., X., XI. and XII., and considerable sections of Chapters I., XVI. and XX. In other parts of the Gospel he has only made occasional notes,

In his revised Commentary, Bishop Westcott has freely availed himself of quotations from patristic commentaries, which the scope of his former work, intended for readers who might be innocent of Greek and Latin, had forbidden. These I have verified, and trust that they will be found substantially correct.

A completely satisfactory transference of the Commentary from the basis of the Authorised Version to that of the Greek text would have involved the remodelling of many of the notes. To some extent Bishop Westcott had done this; but where he has not done so I have been cautious in the transposition of notes, and have carefully refrained from making any alterations but such as seemed of absolute necessity.

The Greek text is that of Westcott and Hort, with occasional preference for marginal readings. I have placed beneath the text the readings of select Greek uncial manuscripts * in the case of such variations as Bishop Westcott had nòticed in his Introduction, but have not attempted to cite other textual evidence, as all the more important readings have been treated in special critical notes.

It was judged expedient to furnish an English version of the Gospel to face the Greek. Unhappily Bishop Westcott had not himself provided a continuous translation ; but, inasmuch as most of his renderings were subsequently adopted by the Revised Version, it was found more convenient to use that translation as the basis of this English version. I have only altered the text (or marginal text where preferred) of the Revised Version in those cases where it seemed that its rendering would not have satisfied my father. In some places where the Revised Version is in substantial, but not

---

* I have derived these readings from Tischendorf's eighth edition (*Octava critica major*),

literal agreement with Bishop Westcott's rendering, I have left it unaltered, and there are consequently slight discrepancies between the renderings in the translation and in the notes, which I trust will not prove vexatious. In these cases I felt that my father, who was a member of the Revision Committee, would have been content with the Revised Version rendering, but at the same time I did not feel justified in altering what he had written. I have frequently omitted his renderings from the notes, as being now superfluous.

The presentation of an English version has not only relieved the notes of many translations, but has rendered obsolete several brief notes which were solely concerned with the correction of the Authorised Version and its underlying Greek text. These notes have therefore been omitted.

I have inserted some Latin Vulgate renderings in the notes, even in cases where they do not represent the same Greek text.* I have also added an Index to the Notes.

The Introduction remains practically unaltered; the only section of it which my father had revised being that on the Quotations from the Old Testament.

Fully conscious as I am that there are many others who could have done this work far better than I have done it, I am yet happy in the conviction that it would have been my father's wish that one of his sons should undertake this task; and I am deeply grateful to my brother, the Rev. Prebendary F. Brooke Westcott, and my brother-in-law, the Rev. Dr. E. G. King, for having permitted me the privilege of presenting my father's latest words on the Gospel of St. John to those who will value them.

A. WESTCOTT.

CRAYKE, *July* 27, 1908.

* For this purpose I have used Wordsworth and White's text.

THE GOSPEL ACCORDING TO ST. JOHN

INTRODUCTION

I. THE AUTHORSHIP OF THE GOSPEL

1. *Internal Evidence*

THE Gospel itself forms the proper starting-point for a satisfactory inquiry into its origin. Doubts may be raised as to the early history of the book, owing to the nature of the available evidence, but there can be no question that it is impressed with an individual character, and that it contains indications of the circumstances under which it was composed. These indications, therefore, must first

be examined : this character must first be defined so far
as it illustrates the relation of the writer to the religious
and social circumstances of the first century ; and when
this is done, we shall be in a position to consider with
a fair appreciation the value of the historical testimony
in support of the universal tradition of the Early Church
which assigned the work to the Apostle St. John.

What then is the evidence which the fourth Gospel
itself bears to its authorship, first indirectly, and next
directly ? These are the two questions which we have
to answer before we can go further.

i. *The indirect evidence of the Gospel as to its authorship*

In examining the indirect evidence which the fourth
Gospel furnishes as to its authorship, it will be most
convenient, as well as most satisfactory, to consider the
available materials in relation to successive questions
which become more and more definite as we proceed.
How far then can we infer from the book itself, with
more or less certainty, that the author was, or was not,
a Jew, a Jew of Palestine, an eye-witness, an Apostle,
and, last of all, St. John; the son of Zebedee ?

(*a*) *The Author of the Fourth Gospel was a Jew.* A candid
examination of the evidence appears to leave no room for
reasonable doubt on this point.   The whole narrative
shows that the author was a Jew.   He is familiar with
Jewish opinions and customs, his composition is impressed
with Jewish characteristics, he is penetrated with the spirit
of the Jewish dispensation. His special knowledge, his
literary style, his religious faith, all point to the same
conclusion. The few arguments which are urged on the
other side derive whatever force they have from the isolation of particular phrases which are considered without
regard to the general aspect of the life to which they
belong.

These statements must be justified in detail.

(*a*) The familiarity of the author of the fourth Gospel
with Jewish opinions is shown most strikingly by the
outline which he gives of the contemporary Messianic

expectations. This subject will be brought before us more in detail afterwards (III. § 2). For the present it will be enough to refer to the details which are given or implied in i. 21, iv. 25, vi. 14 f., vii. 40 ff., xii. 34, etc. In all these cases the points are noticed without the least effort as lying within the natural circle of the writer's thoughts. So again he mentions casually the popular estimate of women (iv. 27), the importance attached to the religious schools (vii. 15), the disparagement of "the Dispersion" (vii. 35), the belief in the transmitted punishment of sin (ix. 2), the hostility of Jews and Samaritans (iv. 9), the supercilious contempt of the Pharisees for "the people of the earth" (vii. 49).

The details of Jewish observances are touched upon with equal precision. Now it is the law of the sabbath which is shown to be overruled by the requirements of circumcision (vii. 22 f.): now the ceremonial pollution which is contracted by entering a Gentile court (xviii. 28). The account of the visit to the Feast of Tabernacles only becomes fully intelligible when we supply the facts at which the writer barely hints, being himself filled with the knowledge of them. The pouring of water from Siloam upon the altar of burnt sacrifice, and the kindling of the lamps in the court of the women, explain the imagery of the "living water" (vii. 38), and of "the light of the world" (viii. 12). And here, again, a Jew only who knew the festival would be likely to describe "the last day of the feast," which was added to the original seven, as "the great day" (vii. 37). The same familiar and decisive knowledge of the people is shown in glimpses which are opened on domestic life at the marriage feast (ii. 1—10), and at the burial of Lazarus (xi. 17—44). The tumultuary stoning of Stephen (Acts vii. 57 ff.), which could not but be a well-known incident in the early Church, would have hindered any one who had not clear information upon the point from recording the answer of the Jews "It is not lawful for us to put any one to death" (xviii. 31); and so in fact these words were afterwards misunderstood by the Greek fathers.

But, on the other hand, it is said that the author of

the fourth Gospel was so ignorant of Jewish affairs that he represents the high-priesthood as an annual office when he speaks of Caiaphas as "high-priest in that year" (xi. 49, 51, xviii. 13). It would be sufficient to reply that such ignorance could not be reconciled with the knowledge already indicated : but a consideration of the clause solemnly repeated three times shows that the supposed conclusion cannot be drawn from it. The emphatic reiteration of the statement forces the reader to connect the office of Caiaphas with the part which he actually took in accomplishing the death of Christ. One yearly sacrifice for atonement it was the duty of the high-priest to offer. In that memorable year, when all types were fulfilled in the reality, it fell to Caiaphas to bring about unconsciously the one sacrifice of atonement for sin. He was high-priest before and after, but it was not enough for the Evangelist's purpose to mark this. He was high-priest in that year—"the year of the Lord" (Luke iv. 19), —and so in the way of divine Providence did his appointed part in causing "*one man to die for the people*" (xi. 50).

(β) From the contents of the fourth Gospel we turn now to its form. And it may truly be affirmed that the style of the narrative alone is conclusive as to its Jewish authorship. The vocabulary, the structure of the sentences, the symmetry and numerical symbolism of the composition, the expression and the arrangement of the thoughts, are essentially Hebrew. These points will require to be discussed at greater length when we come to examine the composition of the Gospel (II. § 5). It must suffice now to call attention to such terms as "light," "darkness," "flesh," "spirit," "life," "this world," "the kingdom of God," and the like: to such images as "the shepherd," "the living water," "the woman in travail": to the simplicity of the connecting particles: to the parallelism and symmetry of the clauses. The source of the imagery of the narrative, to sum up all briefly, is the Old Testament. The words are Greek words, but the spirit by which they live is Hebrew.

(γ) The Old Testament is no less certainly the source of the religious life of the writer. His Jewish opinions

and hopes are taken up into and transfigured by his
Christian faith; but the Jewish foundation underlies
his whole narrative. The land of Judæa was "the home"
(τὰ ἴδια; comp. xvi. 32, xix. 27) of the Incarnate Word,
and the people of Judæa were "His own people" (i. 11).
This was the judgement of the Evangelist when the
Messiah had been rejected by those to whom He came;
and, on the other hand, Christ, when He first entered
the Holy City, claimed the Temple as being "the house
of His Father" (ii. 16). From first to last Judaism is
treated in the fourth Gospel as the divine starting-point
of Christianity. It is true that the author records discourses in which the Lord speaks to the Jews of the
Law as being "their Law"; and that he uses the name
"the Jews" to mark an anti-Christian body; but even
these apparent exceptions really illustrate his main
position. The Pharisees as a body strove to keep "the
Law" in its widest acceptation, the monument, that is,
of the various revelations to Israel (x. 34, xv. 25, notes),
for themselves alone, and to bar the progress of the life
which it enshrined. In the process it became "their Law."
With the same fatal narrowness they reduced the representatives and bearers of the ancient revelation to a
national faction; and "the Jews" embodied just that
which was provisional and evanescent in the system which
they misunderstood (comp. III. § 1). These two characteristic thoughts of the Gospel will become clear when we
consider the general development of the history. Meanwhile it must be noticed that the Evangelist vindicates
both for the Law and for the people their just historical
position in the divine economy. The Law could not but
bear witness to the truths which God had once spoken
through it. The people could not do away with the
promises and privileges which they had inherited. Side
by side with the words of Christ which describe the Law
as the special possession of its false interpreters (viii. 17,
x. 34, xv. 25), other words of his affirm the absolute
authority of its contents. It is assumed as an axiom that
The Scripture cannot be broken (x. 35; see v. 18, note).
That which *is written in the prophets* (vi. 45; comp. vi. 31)

is taken as the true expression of what shall be. *Moses wrote of Christ* (v. 46 ; comp. i. 45). The types of the Old Testament, the brazen serpent (iii. 14), the manna (vi. 32), the water from the rock (vii. 37 f.), perhaps also the pillar of fire (viii. 12), are applied by Christ to Himself as of certain and acknowledged significance. Abraham *saw His day* (viii. 56). It was generally to "the Scriptures" that Christ appealed as *witnessing of Him*. Even the choice of Judas to be an apostle was involved in the portraiture of the divine King (xiii. 18, note, *that the Scripture might be fulfilled*; comp. xvii. 12) ; and the hatred of the Jews was prefigured in the words *written in their Law, They hated me without a cause* (xv. 25).

Such words of Christ must be considered both in themselves and in the consequences which they necessarily carry with them, if we are to understand the relation of the fourth Gospel to the Old Testament. They show exclusively that in this Gospel, no less than in the other three, He is represented as offering Himself to Israel as the fulfiller, and not as the destroyer, of "the Law." And it follows, also, whatever view is taken of the authorship of the Gospel, that the Evangelist in setting down these sayings of Christ accepts to the full the teaching which they convey.

Nor is this all. Just as the words of the Lord recorded in the fourth Gospel confirm the divine authority of the Old Testament, so also the Evangelist, when he writes in his own person, emphasises the same principle. The first public act of Christ reminded the disciples, as he relates, of a phrase in the Psalms (ii. 17). The Resurrection, he says, confirmed their faith *in the Scripture, and the word which Jesus spake*, as if both were of equal weight. In the light of the same event they understood at last what they had done unconsciously in accordance with prophetic utterances (xii. 14 ff.). So again at the close of his record of Christ's public ministry, he points out how the apparent failure of Christ's mission was part of the great scheme of Providence foreshadowed by Isaiah. The experience, and the words of the prophet, made such a result inevitable (xii. 37 ff.). This fulfilment of the wider teaching of prophecy is further confirmed by examples of the fulfilment of its details. Special incidents of the Passion are connected with the language of the Old Testament. The division of the garments, and the casting lots for the seamless robe (xix. 23 f.) ; the expression of thirst (xix. 28), the limbs left unbroken (xix. 36), the side pierced (xix. 37) —significant parallels with the treatment of the paschal lamb—give occasion to quotations from the Law, the Psalms, and the Prophets ; and these fulfilments of the ancient Scriptures are brought forward as solid grounds of faith (xix. 35).

" The Law," in short, is treated by the writer of the fourth Gospel, both in his record of the Lord's teaching, and, more especially, in his own comments, as only a Jew could have treated it. It was misinterpreted by those to whom it was given, but it was divine. So far as it was held, not only apart from, but in opposition to, its true fulfilment, it lost its true character. This character the Evangelist unfolds. The object with which he wrote was to show that Jesus was not only the *Son of God*, but also *the Christ*, the promised Messiah of the Jews (xx. 31), just as Nathanael, the true representative of Israel (i. 47), had recognised Him at first under this double title.

The portraiture of the people in the fourth Gospel is no less indicative of its Jewish authorship, whatever false deductions may have been popularly drawn from the use of the characteristic title " the Jews " for the adversaries of Christianity. Writing as a Christian the Evangelist still records the central truth, true for all ages, which Christ declared : *We*—as Jews—*worship that which we know, for the salvation*—the salvation promised to the world—*is from the Jews* (iv. 22), rising by a divine law out of the dispensation intrusted to their keeping. Nothing which was said at a later time neutralised these words of the Lord in which He identified Himself with the old people of God, and signalised their inherent prerogatives. The knowledge which the Jews had was the result of their acceptance of the continuous revelation of God from age to age ; while the Samaritans who refused to advance beyond the first stage of His manifestation, worshipped the true Object of worship, but ignorantly. They worshipped *that which they knew not* (iv. 22).

This was the rightful position of the Jews towards Christ, which is everywhere presupposed in the Gospel, but they failed to maintain it, and when the Evangelist wrote their national failure was past hope. They received Him not. But the sources and the kinds of their unbelief were manifold, and the narrative reflects the varieties of their character.

For the people are not, as is commonly assumed to be the case, a uniform, colourless mass. On the contrary, distinct bodies reveal themselves on a careful examination of the record, each with its own distinctive marks. Two great divisions are portrayed with marked clearness, "the multitude," and "the Jews." *The multitude* (ὁ ὄχλος) represents the general gathering of the Jewish inhabitants of Palestine, Galilæans for the most part, who are easily swayed to and fro, with no settled policy, and no firm convictions. These, when they saw the signs which Jesus had wrought at Jerusalem, received Him in Galilee (iv. 45), and followed Him, and, at a later time, would have made Him King (vi. 15). When they went up to the feasts they gathered round Him in expectation and doubt, ignorant of the deadly hostility of their rulers to the new prophet (vii. 20), and inclined to believe (vii. 40; compare the whole chapter). On the eve of the Passion they brought Him in triumph into the city (xii. 12); and, in the last scene in which they are presented in the Gospel, listen in dull perplexity to Christ's final revelation of Himself (xi. 29, 34). In the fourth Gospel they do not appear in the narrative of the Trial and the Crucifixion. They may have been used as instruments, but the guilt of this issue did not belong to them as a body.

In contrast with "the multitude" stand "the Jews."[1] Both titles are general terms, including various elements; both have local centres; both express tendencies of religious feeling. Just as "the multitude" reflect the spirit of Galilee, "the Jews" reflect the spirit of Jerusalem

---

[1] The term occurs rarely in the discourses of the Lord: iv. 22, xiii. 33, xviii. 20, 36. See note on the last passage.

(i. 19), and this term is perhaps used exclusively of those who lived in the limited region of Judæa. "The multitude" have vague, fluent opinions; "the Jews" hold fast by the popular expectation of a national Messiah, and a national sovereignty. From first to last they appear as the representatives of the narrow finality of Judaism (ii. 18, xix. 38). They begin their opposition by a charge of the violation of the Sabbath (v. 10 ff.; comp. xix. 31). Those of them who are present at Capernaum give expression to "murmurings" at the teaching to which "the multitude" had apparently listened with awed respect (vi. 41, 52; comp. vi. 22–40). They reduce the wavering multitude to silence at Jerusalem (vii. 11–13). If they *believe Christ*, they do not at once *believe on Him*, and while they cling to their own prejudices yield themselves to the perils of fatal error (viii. 31 ff., note). In their zeal for the Law they would at once stone Christ (viii. 59, x. 31); and to them generally the Crucifixion is attributed (xviii. 12, 14, 31, 36, 38, xix. 7, 12, 14). Yet even these are struck with wonder (vii. 15) and doubt (vii. 35, viii. 22); they are divided (x. 19), and ask peremptorily for a clear enunciation of Christ's claim (x. 24); and the defection of many from among them to Him marks the last crisis in the history (xii. 10 f.; comp. xi. 45, 48, ix. 40, xii. 42).

"The Jews" thus presented to a writer who looked back from a Christian point of sight[1] upon the events which he described the aggregate of the people whose opinions were opposed in spirit to the work of Christ. They were not, as they might have been, "true Israelites" (i. 47; comp. *v.* 31). But at the same time he does not fail to notice that there were among them two distinct tendencies, which found their expression in the Pharisees and Sadducees respectively. The latter are not mentioned by name in the fourth Gospel, but the writer describes them more characteristically, and with a more direct knowledge, by their social position at the time. They were "the high-priests," the faction of Annas and Caiaphas (Acts v. 17), the reckless hierarchy, whose policy is sharply

---

[1] The phrase "the Passover of the Jews" evidently implies a familiar Christian Passover: ii. 13, note. Comp. ii. 6, v. 1, vii. 2, xix. 42.

b

distinguished in one or two lifelike traits from that of
the religious zealots, the Pharisees. Several times indeed
the two parties appear as acting together in the great
Council (vii. 32, 45, xi. 47, 57, xviii. 3; comp. vii. 26, 48,
xii. 42 *the rulers*), yet even in these cases the two are only
once so grouped as to form a single body (vii. 45 πρὸς τοὺς
ἀρχ. καὶ Φαρ.), and "the chief priests" always stand first
as taking the lead in the designs of violence. This is
brought out very vividly in the fatal scene in the
Sanhedrin after the raising of Lazarus (see xi. 47, note).

In other places when the two parties are mentioned
separately the contrast between them familiar to the
historian underlies the record. The Pharisees are moved
by the symptoms of religious disorder: the high-priests
(Sadducees) by the prospect of ecclesiastical danger. The
Pharisees are the true representatives of "the Jews"
(i. 19 ‖ i. 24, ix. 13 ‖ ix. 18, ix. 22 ‖ xii. 42). They send to
make inquiries about the mission of John (i. 24); they
hear, evidently as of something which deeply concerned
them, of baptism among the followers of the Lord (iv. 1);
they scornfully reject the opinion of the illiterate multitude (vii. 47); they question the authority of Christ
(viii. 13); they condemn His miracles as wrought on the
Sabbath (ix. 13 ff.); they excommunicate His followers
(xii. 42; comp. ix. 22); but at last they look with irresolute
helplessness upon the apparent failure of their opposition
(xii. 19). From this point they appear no more by
themselves. "The chief priests" take the direction of
the end into their own hands. Five times they are
mentioned alone, and on each occasion as bent on carrying
out a purpose of death and treason to the faith of Israel.
They plotted the murder of Lazarus because *many for his
sake believed on Jesus* (xii. 11). Pilate sees in them the
true persecutors of Christ: *Thy nation and the chief priests
delivered Thee up to me* (xviii. 35). Their voices first raise
the cry *Crucify, Crucify Him* (xix. 6). They make the
unbelieving confession, *We have no king but Cæsar* (xix. 15),
and utter a vain protest against the title in which their
condemnation was written (xix. 21, *the chief priests of the
Jews*).

This most significant fact of the decisive action of the
Sadducæan hierarchy in compassing the death of the
Lord, which is strikingly illustrated by the relative attitude of the Pharisees and Sadducees to the early Church
as described in the Acts, explains the prominent position
assigned to Annas in the fourth Gospel (xviii. 13). Annas
was the head of the party. Though he had ceased to be
high-priest for many years, he swayed the policy of his
successors. St. Luke in his Gospel significantly sets him
with Caiaphas as " high-priest " (ἐπ᾿ ἀρχιερέως not ἐπ᾿ ἀρχιε-
ρέων, iii. 2), as if both were united in one person ; and in
the Acts he, and not Caiaphas (iv. 6), is alone called " high-
priest." The coincidence is just one of those which reveal
the actual as distinguished from the official state of things.

One further remark must be made. The general use of
the term " the Jews " for the opponents of Christ not only
belongs necessarily to the position of an apostle at the
close of the first century, but it is even possible to trace
in the books of the New Testament the gradual change by
which it assumed this specific force. In the Synoptic
Gospels it occurs only four times except in the title " king
of the Jews " ; Matt. xxviii. 15 ; Mark vii. 3 ; Luke vii. 3,
xxiii. 51 ; and in the first of these, which is probably the
latest in date, the word marks a position of antagonism.
In the Acts the title oscillates between the notions of
privilege and of opposition, but the course of the history
goes far to fix its adverse meaning. The word is comparatively rare in the Epistles of St. Paul. It occurs most
commonly (twelve times out of twenty-four) in contrast
with " Greek," both alike standing in equal contrast with
the idea of Christianity ; and for St. Paul, " a Hebrew of
Hebrews," his countrymen, " Jews by nature " (Gal. ii. 15),
are already separated from himself. The name of a race
has become practically the name of a sect (Rom. iii. 9 ;
1 Cor. i. 22 ff., ix. 20, x. 32 ; comp. Gal. ii. 13, i. 13 f.).
The word is not found in the Catholic epistles, but in the
Apocalypse it is used twice (ii. 9, iii. 9), evidently to
describe those who insisted on their literal descent and
ceremonial position, and claimed the prerogatives of Israel
outside the Church. Such false-styled Jews were the

worst enemies of the Gospel; and a Christian writing at
the close of the century could not but speak of the people
generally by the title which characterised them to his
contemporaries.

(b) *The Author of the Fourth Gospel was a Jew of Palestine.*
The facts which have just been noticed carry us beyond
the conclusion which they were alleged to establish. They
show that the writer of the fourth Gospel was not only a
Jew, but a Palestinian Jew of the first century. It is inconceivable that a Gentile, living at a distance from the
scene of religious and political controversy which he
paints, could have realised, as the Evangelist has done,
with vivid and unerring accuracy the relations of parties
and interests which ceased to exist after the fall of
Jerusalem; that he could have marked distinctly the part
which the hierarchical class—the unnamed Sadducees—
took in the crisis of the Passion; that he could have caught
the real points at issue between true and false Judaism,
which in their first form had passed away when the
Christian society was firmly established; that he could
have portrayed the growth and conflict of opinion as to
the national hopes of the Messiah side by side with the
progress of the Lord's ministry. All these phases of
thought and action, which would be ineffaceably impressed upon the memory of one who had lived through
the events which the history records, belonged to a state
of things foreign to the experience of an Alexandrine, or
an Asiatic, in the second century.

For in estimating the value of these conclusions which
we have gained, it must be remembered that the old land-
marks, material and moral, were destroyed by the Roman
war: that the destruction of the Holy City—a true coming
of Christ—revealed the essential differences of Judaism
and Christianity, and raised a barrier between them: that
at the beginning of the second century the influence of
Alexandria was substituted for that of the Jewish schools
in the growing Church.

(a) And these considerations which apply to the arguments drawn from the religious and political traits of the

history, apply also in corresponding degrees to the more special indications that the author of the fourth Gospel was a Jew of Palestine. Among these, the most convincing perhaps is to be found in his local knowledge. He speaks of places with an unaffected precision, as familiar in every case with the scene which he wishes to recall. There is no effort, no elaborateness of description in his narratives : he moves about in a country which he knows. His mention of sites is not limited to those which are found elsewhere in Scripture, either in the Gospels or in the Old Testament. "Cana of Galilee" (Κανὰ τῆς Γαλιλαίας, ii. 1, 11, iv. 46, xxi. 2), thus exactly distinguished, is not noticed by any earlier writer. "Bethany beyond Jordan" (i. 28), a place already forgotten in the time of Origen, is obviously distinguished from the familiar Bethany "near Jerusalem," the situation of which is precisely fixed as "about fifteen furlongs" from the city (xi. 18). Ephraim, again, situated "near the wilderness" (xi. 54) may be identical with Ophrah (1 Sam. xiii. 17), but it is not otherwise named in Scripture. Once more, Ænon (iii. 23) is not known from other sources, but the form of the name[1] is a sure sign of the genuineness of the reference, and the defining clause, "near to Salim," even if the identification were as difficult now as it has been represented to be, shows that the place was clearly present to the writer.[2] Nothing indeed but direct acquaintance with the localities can account for the description added in each of these cases. A writer for whom these spots were identified with memorable incidents which were for him turning-points of faith, would naturally add the details which recalled them to his own mind : for

---

[1] This is true whether the word be taken as an adjectival form "abounding in springs" (comp. Ez. xlvii. 17), or as a corruption of a dual form "the two springs," but it is doubtful whether it can be so rendered. It is said that Ainan and Ainaim, "the two springs," are the names of several places in Arabia. The Syriac versions write the name as two words, "the spring of the dove."

[2] Lieut. Conder in the *Quarterly Statement* of the Palestine Exploration Fund (July, 1874, pp. 191 f.) identifies it with 'Aynún near to Salim, due east of Nablus. The use of the phrase *beyond Jordan* (iii. 26) implies that the country was on the West of the river.

another the exact definition could have no interest. Other indications of minute knowledge are given in the implied notice of the dimensions of the lake of Tiberias (vi. 19 ; comp. Mark vi. 47), and of the relative positions of Cana and Capernaum (ii. 12, *went down*).

One name, however, has caused much difficulty. *The city of Samaria named Sychar* (iv. 5) has been commonly identified with Shechem (Sychem, Acts vii. 16), and the changed form has been confidently attributed by sceptical critics to the ignorance of the Evangelist. The importance of Shechem, a city with which no one could have been unacquainted who possessed the knowledge of Palestine which the writer of the fourth Gospel certainly had, might reasonably dispose of such a charge. And more than this: the picture with which the name is connected is evidently drawn from life. The prospect of the corn-fields (*v.* 35), and of the heights of Gerizim (*v.* 20), are details which belong to the knowledge of an eye-witness. The notice of the depth of the well (*v.* 11) bears equally the stamp of authenticity. If then there were no clue to the solution of the problem offered by the strange name, it would be right to acquiesce in the belief that Sychar might be a popular distortion of Shechem, or the name of some unknown village. But the case does not stand so absolutely without help towards a decision. The earliest ancient authorities (4th cent.) distinguish Shechem and Sychar. Shechem could hardly have been described as *near to the plot of ground which Jacob gave to Joseph* (*v.* 5). There are, moreover, several references to *Sukra, Sukar, ain-Sukar* (עין סוכר סוכרא, סכר) in the Talmud ; and a village *'Askar* still remains, which answers to the conditions of the narrative. Some difficulty has been felt in identifying 'Askar with Sychar, since it is written at present with an initial *'Ain,* but in a Samaritan Chronicle of the 12th century the name appears in a transitional form with an initial *Yod* (יסכר), and the Arabic translation of the Chronicle gives 'Askar as the equivalent. The description [of St. John], Lieut. Conder writes, " is most accurately applicable to 'Askar. . . . It is merely a modern mud village, with no great indications of antiquity, but there are remains of ancient tombs near the road beneath it." (*Report of the Palestine Exploration Fund*, 1877, pp. 149 f., 1876, p. 197.)

The notices of the topography of Jerusalem contained in the fourth Gospel are still more conclusive as to its authorship than the notices of isolated places in Palestine. The desolation of Jerusalem after its capture was complete. No creative genius can call into being a lost site. And the writer of the fourth Gospel is evidently at home in the city as it was before its fall. He knows much that we learn from independent testimony, and he knows what is not to be found elsewhere. But whether he mentions spots known from other sources, or named only by himself, he speaks simply and certainly. As he recalls a familiar scene he lives again in the past, and forgets the desolation which had fallen upon the place which rises before his eyes. "*There is*," he writes, "*at Jerusalem a pool called Bethesda*" (v. 2), and by the form of the sentence carries us back to the time when the incident first became history. "Bethesda by the sheep-gate," "the pool of Siloam" (ix. 7), "the brook Kidron" (xviii. 1), which are not named by the other Evangelists (yet see Luke xiii. 4), stand out naturally in his narrative. What imagination could have invented a Bethesda (or Bethzatha) with its five porches, and exact locality (v. 2)? What except habitual usage would have caused the Kidron to be described as "the winter torrent [1]"? How long must the name Siloam have been pondered over before the perfectly admissible rendering "Sent" was seen to carry with it a typical significance? The *Prætorium* and *Golgotha* are mentioned by the other Evangelists; but even here the writer of the fourth Gospel sees the localities, if I may so speak, with the vividness of an actual spectator. The Jews crowd round the Prætorium which they will not enter, and Pilate goes in and out before them (xviii. 28 ff.). Golgotha is "*nigh to the city*," where people pass to and fro, and "*there was a garden there*" (xix. 17, 20, 41). And the fourth Evangelist alone notices the Pavement, the ·

---

[1] For the discussion of the reading see note on xviii. 1. If the reading "the torrent *of the Cedars*" be adopted, the argument is not affected.

raised platform of judgement, with its Hebrew title, Gabbatha (xix. 13). The places Bethesda and Gabbatha are not, in fact, mentioned anywhere except in the fourth Gospel, and the perfect simplicity with which they are introduced in the narrative, no less than the accuracy of form in the Aramaic titles (whatever be the true reading of Bethesda), marks the work of a Palestinian Jew, who had known Jerusalem before its fall.

The allusions to the Temple show no less certainly the familiarity of the writer with the localities in which he represents Christ as teaching. The first scene, the cleansing of the Temple, is in several details more lifelike than the similar passages in the Synoptists (ii. 14—16). It is described just as it would appear to an eye-witness in its separate parts, and not as the similar incident is summed up briefly in the other narratives. Each group engaged stands out distinctly, the sellers of oxen and sheep, the money-changers sitting at their work, the sellers of doves; and each group is dealt with individually. Then follows, in the course of the dialogue which ensues, the singularly exact chronological note, "*Forty and six years was this Temple in building*" (ii. 20).

The incidents of the Feast of Tabernacles (which are given in chapters vii. and viii.) cannot be understood, as has been already noticed, without an accurate acquaintance with the Temple ritual. The two symbolic ceremonies—commemorating the typical miracles of the wilderness—the outpouring of water on the altar of sacrifice, and the kindling the golden lamps at night, furnish the great topics of discourse. The Evangelist is familiar with the facts, but he does not pause to dwell upon them. Only in one short sentence does he appear to call attention to the significance of the events. "*These things*," he says, "*Jesus spake in the treasury, as He taught in the Temple*" (viii. 20). The mention of the exact spot carried with it to minds familiar with the Herodian Temple a clear revelation of what was in the Apostle's mind. For the treasury was in the court of the women where the great candelabra were placed, looking to which Christ said, "*I am the light*"—not of one people, or of one city, but—"*of the world.*" And there is still another thought suggested by the mention of the place. The meeting-hall of the Sanhedrin was in a chamber adjacent to it. We can understand therefore the hasty attempts of the chief priests and Pharisees to seize Christ, and the force of the words which are added, that even there, under the very eyes of the popular leaders, "*no man laid hands on Him.*"

The next visit to Jerusalem, at the Feast of Dedication, brings a new place before us. "*It was winter,*" we read, "*and Jesus was walking in Solomon's Porch*" (x. 22), a part of the great eastern cloister suiting in every way the scene with which it is connected.

Once again, as I believe, we have a significant allusion to the decoration of the Temple. On the eve of the Passion, at the close of the discourses in the upper chamber, the Lord said, "*Arise, let us go hence*" (xiv. 31). Some time after we read that when He had finished His High-priestly prayer, He went forth with His disciples over the brook Kidron. It seems to be impossible to regard this notice as the fulfilment of the former command. The house, therefore, must have been left before, as is clearly implied in the narrative, and the walk to the Mount of Olives might well include a visit to the Temple; and over the gate of the Temple was spread the great vine of gold, which was reckoned among its noblest ornaments. Is it then a mere fancy to suppose that the image of the vine and its branches was suggested by the sight of this symbolic tracery, lighted by the Paschal moon, and that the High-priestly prayer was offered under the shadow of the Temple walls?

However this may be, it is inconceivable that any one, still more a Greek or a Hellenist, writing when the Temple was rased to the ground, could have spoken of it with the unaffected certainty which appears in the fourth Gospel. It is monstrous to transfer to the second century the accuracy of archæological research which is one of the latest acquirements of modern art. The Evangelist, it may be safely said, speaks of what he had seen.

(β) The arguments which have been already drawn from the political, social, religious, and local knowledge of the author of the fourth Gospel, show beyond all doubt, as it appears, that he was a Palestinian Jew. A presumption in favour of the same conclusion may be derived from the quotations from the Old Testament which are contained in the Gospel. These show at least so much that the writer was not dependent on the LXX.; and they suggest that he was acquainted with the original Hebrew.

A rapid summary of the facts will enable the student to estimate the weight of this additional evidence.

The Quotations from the Old Testament in the Gospel[1]

1. The people, the Evangelist, and the Lord Himself equally assume the Messianic interpretation of the O.T. Comp. v. 39, 46.

(a) The people :
vii. 42. (οὐχ ἡ γραφ. εἰπ. . . . ;)
xii. 34. ('Ημεῖς ἠκουσ. ἐκ τ. νομ. . . .)
Comp. vi. 31 ; xii. 13.

(b) The Evangelist :
ii. 17. (ἐμνήσθησαν οἱ μαθ. ὅτι γεγραμ. ἐστ.)
xii. 14 f. (εὑρὼν δ. ὁ Ἰησ. ὀνάριον . . . καθ. ἐστ. γεγρ.)
xii. 38. (οὐκ ἐπίστευον . . . ἵνα ὁ λογ. 'Ησ. . . . πληρ.)
xii. 40. (οὐκ ἠδυν. πιστ. ὅτι παλ. εἰπ. 'Ησ. . . .)
xix. 24. (εἶπαν οὖν . . . ἵνα ἡ γρ. πληρ.)
xix. 36. (ἐγεν. γὰρ ταῦτα ἵνα ἡ γρ. πληρ.)
xix. 37. (πάλιν ἑτέρα γρ. λεγ.)
Comp. xx. 9. (οὐδέπω γ. ἤδεισαν τ. γραφ. . . .)

(c) The Lord :
vi. 45. (ἐστ. γεγρ. ἐν τ. προφ. . . .)
vii. 38. (καθὼς εἰπ. ἡ γρ. . . .)
x. 34. (Οὐκ ἐστ. γεγραμ. . . . ;)
xiii. 18. (ἀλλ' ἵνα ἡ γρ. πληρ. . . .)
xv. 25. (ἀλλ' ἵνα πληρ. ὁ λογ. . . . γεγραμ. . . .)
Comp. viii. 17 ; xvii. 12.

---

[1] What here follows is the only portion of the Introduction which Bishop Westcott has revised and expanded. He probably intended this revised section in connexion with the subsequent section on the Relation of the Gospel to the Old Testament to be a separate note, but it remains unfinished, and has been restored to its former place.—A. W.

To these express references must be added the allusive use of the O.T.:

i. 51. (Jacob's Ladder).   Gen. xxviii. 12.

x. 16. (One Shepherd).   Ezek. xxxvii. 24; xxxiv. 23.

xii. 27. (ἡ ψυχή μου τετάρακται).   Ps. vi. 3; xlii. 6.

xvi. 22. (καὶ χαρήσεται ὑμῶν ἡ καρδία).   Isa. lxvi. 14.

And express reference to incidents:

iii. 14. (The Brazen Serpent).   Num. xxi. 9.

viii. 56. (The exultation of Abraham).   Gen. xxii.

2. The quotations are distributed over the three divisions of the Hebrew Scriptures:

(a) The Law:

Gen. xxviii. 27; xxii.

Ex. xii. 46; xvi. 4 ‖ Ps. lxxviii. 24.

Num. xxi. 9.

Deut. xix. 15.

(b) The Prophets:

Isa. vi. 10; liii. 1; lxvi. 14.

Ezek. xxxiv. 23 ‖ xxxvii. 24.

Zech. ix. 9; xii. 10.

(c) The Psalms:

Ps. xii. 13; xxii. 18; xli. 9; lxix. 4 ‖ Ps. xxxv. 19; lxix. 9, 21; lxxxii. 6.

3. About half the quotations are peculiar to St. John, including, with one exception, all the quotations made in the Lord's discourses.

Others are common to St. John and the Synoptists:

Zech. ix. 9 ‖ Matt.

Isa. vi. 10 ‖ Synn. and Acts.

Ps. xxii. 18 ‖ Synn.

Isa. xl. 3 ‖ Synn.

Three peculiar quotations come from sections of which other parts are quoted in N.T.:

Ps. lxix. 9 (Synn., Acts, Rom.).

Isa. liii. 1 (Synn., Acts, Rom.); liv. 13 (Gal.).

The quotations peculiar to St. John are 6, 10, 11, 12, 14 (see below).

4. The use of the LXX. and of the Hebr. is unquestionable. The use of the Hebrew text is shown (1) by some of the direct quotations, and also (2) by phrases which

are rendered from the original in a form different from the LXX., as in the Apocalypse, and inwoven into the Gospel:

(1) (7) Zech. xii. 10; (8) Isa. liv. 13; (11) Ps. xli. 9. (2) i. 14 ‖ Ex. xxxiv. 6. The use of the LXX. is shown both by verbal coincidence in the rendering of the Hebr., and in one case by the adoption of a significant word which is added by the LXX. to the Hebrew (Isa. liii. 1).

5. The words are quoted in their simple direct meaning, but this is taken to have a far-reaching application. There is nothing like the allegorising of Philo, *e.g.*, Ps. lxxxii. 6 (x. 34).

Sometimes the fulfilment of the prophecy was presented as a design (ἵνα πληρωθῇ, ἵνα τελειωθῇ):

(a) by the Evangelist, xii. 38 [xii. 40]; xix. 24, 28 f.; xix. 36 [xix. 37]. (β) by Christ, xiii. 18; xv. 25 [xvii. 12].

Sometimes it is marked as a coincidence (καθώς ἐστιν γεγραμμένον):

(a) by the Evangelist, ii. 17; xii. 14 f. Comp. vi. 31. (β) by Christ, vi. 45 [vii. 38]; x. 34.

In this connexion we must notice the deeper sense attributed to the Lord's words:

ii. 21 f. (ἐκεῖνος δὲ ἔλεγ. περὶ τ. ναοῦ τ. σωμ. αὐτ.)

vii. 37—39. (τοῦτο δ. εἶπ. περὶ τ. πνευμ. οὖ ἔμελλ. . . . .)

In the record of the Passion several historic details are noticed in the Law, the Prophets, and the Psalms:

"They brake not His legs": Ex. xii. 46. "One of the soldiers pierced His side": Zech. xii. 10. "The soldiers . . . took His garments . . .": Ps. xxii. 18.

But generally the references to Scripture, and all those in the discourses of the Lord, with one partial exception, xiii. 18, are to moral (spiritual) characteristics of the Messianic age:

(a) Illumination: vi. 45. Καὶ ἔσονται πάντες διδακτοὶ θεοῦ. xii. 38.

(b) Unbelief: xii. 38. Κύριε, τίς ἐπίστευσεν . . .; xii. 40. τετύφλωκεν αὐτ. τ. ὀφθ. . . . .; xv. 25. Ἐμίσησάν με δωρεάν,

The Messiah :

ii. 17. ὁ ζῆλος τοῦ οἴκου σου καταφάγεταί με.

x. 34. Ἐγὼ εἶπα, Θεοί ἐστε.

6. Notice also the more general relation to O.T. :

(1) The privilege of Jews :

iv. 22. Ὑμεῖς προσκυνεῖτε ὃ οὐκ οἶδ. . . . ὅτι ἡ σωτηρία ἐκ τῶν Ἰουδαίων ἐστίν.

(2) Abraham, Moses, Isaiah :

viii. 56. Ἀβραὰμ ὁ πατ. ὑμ. ἠγαλλ. ἵνα ἴδ. . . . Comp. i. 51. (τ. ἀγγ. τ. θε. ἀναβαιν. κ. καταβαιν.)

iii. 14. καθὼς Μωυσῆς ὕψωσεν τὴν ὄφιν. . . .

xii. 37 ff. ἵνα ὁ λογ. Ἡσαίου τ. προφ. πληρ. . . .

(3) The typical teaching of Jewish history and law :

iii. 14; v. 17; vi. 31 ff.; vii. 22, 37 f.; viii. 12; xiii. 18; xix. 36.

(1) *Quotations by the Evangelist.*

ii. 17. . . . γεγραμμένον ἐστίν Ὁ ζῆλος τοῦ οἴκου σου κ α τ α-φάγ ε τ α ί με.

Ps. lxix. (lxviii.) 9. κατέφαγε (Symm. κατηνάλωσε) So Hebr. . . . . (1)

xii. 14, 15. καθώς ἐστιν γεγραμμένον Μὴ φοβοῦ, θυγάτηρ Σιών· ἰδοὺ ὁ βασιλεύς σου ἔρχεται, κ α θ ή μ ε ν ο ς ἐπὶ πῶλον ὄνου.

Zech. ix. 9. Χαῖρε σφόδρα, θύγατερ Σιών, . . . ἰδοὺ ὁ βασιλεύς σου ἔρχεται . . . ἐπιβεβηκὼς ἐπὶ . . . πῶλον νέον. (All the Greek versions have ἐπιβεβηκώς. Theodotion has ἐπὶ ὄνον καὶ πῶλον υἱὸν ὄνου.) Hebr. עַל־חֲמוֹר וְעַל־עַיִר בֶּן־אֲתֹנוֹת

(2)

xii. 38. . . . ἵνα ὁ λόγος Ἡσαίου . . . πληρωθῇ ὃν εἶπεν Κύριε, τίς ἐπίστευσεν τῇ ἀκοῇ ἡμῶν ; καὶ ὁ βραχίων κυρίου τίνι ἀπεκαλύφθη ;

Isa. liii. 1. (exact, except that Κύριε is added in the LXX.). . . . . (3)

xii. 40. . . . ὅτι εἶπεν Ἡσαίας Τετύφλωκεν αὐτῶν τοὺς ὀφθαλμοὺς καὶ ἐπώρωσεν αὐτῶν τὴν καρδίαν, ἵνα μὴ ἴδωσιν τοῖς ὀφθαλμοῖς καὶ νοήσωσιν τῇ καρδίᾳ καὶ στραφῶσιν, καὶ ἰάσομαι αὐτούς.

Isa. vi. 10. ἐπαχύνθη ἡ καρδία τοῦ λαοῦ τούτου . . . καὶ τοὺς ὀφθαλμοὺς ἐκάμμυσαν, μή ποτε ἴδωσι τοῖς ὀφθαλμοῖς

. . καὶ τῇ καρδίᾳ συνῶσι καὶ ἐπιστρέψωσι καὶ ἰάσομαι
αὐτούς. (The version of Symm. uses the same words
generally as LXX.) Comp. Matt. xiii. 13 ff.; Mark iv. 12.
(4)

xix. 24. ἵνα ἡ γραφὴ πληρωθῇ Διεμερίσαντο τὰ ἱμάτιά μου
ἑαυτοῖς καὶ ἐπὶ τὸν ἱματισμόν μου ἔβαλον κλῆρον.
Ps. xxii. (xxi.) 18 (exact) . . . . . . (5)
xix. 36. ἵνα ἡ γραφὴ πληρωθῇ Ὀστοῦν οὐ συντριβήσεται
αὐτοῦ.
Ex. xii. 46. ὀστοῦν οὐ συντρίψετε ἀπ' αὐτοῦ (al. συντρί-
ψεται). Num. ix. 12. ὀ. οὐ συντρίψουσιν ἀ. αὐ. (al. συντρί-
ψεται). Cf. Ps. xxxiv. (xxxiii.) 20 . . . . (6)
xix. 37. ἑτέρα γραφὴ λέγει Ὄψονται εἰς ὃν ἐξεκέντησαν.
Hebr. דקרו.
Zech. xii. 10. ἐπιβλέψονται πρός με ἀνθ' ὧν κατωρχήσαντο
(Theodot. εἰς ὃν ἐξεκέντησαν. Aq. Symm. ἐξεκέντησαν, ἐπεξε-
κέντησαν).
Comp. Rev. i. 7 . . . . (7)

(2) Quotations in the Lord's discourses.
vi. 45. ἔστιν γεγραμμένον ἐν τοῖς προφήταις Καὶ ἔσονται
πάντες διδακτοὶ θεοῦ.
Isa. liv. 13. καὶ (θήσω) πάντας τοὺς υἱούς σου διδακτοὺς θεοῦ.
The words are not connected as in LXX. with v. 12,
but treated as in the Hebrew, independently . (8)
vii. 38. καθὼς εἶπεν ἡ γραφὴ ποταμοὶ ἐκ τῆς κοιλίας αὐτοῦ
ῥεύσουσιν ὕδατος ζῶντος.
There is no exact parallel. The reference is probably
general . . . . (9)
x. 34. οὐκ ἔστιν γεγραμμένον . . . Ἐγὼ εἶπα Θεοί ἐστε ; . . .
οὐ δύναται λυθῆναι ἡ γραφή.
Ps. lxxxii. (lxxxi.) 6 (exact) . . . . . (10)
xiii. 18. ἵνα ἡ γραφὴ πληρωθῇ Ὁ τρώγων μου τὸν ἄρτον
ἐπῆρεν ἐπ' ἐμὲ τὴν πτέρναν αὐτοῦ.
Ps. xli. (xl.) 9 (10). . . . ὁ ἐσθίων ἄρτους μου ἐμεγάλυνεν
ἐπ' ἐμὲ πτερνισμόν. (Aq. Symm. Theodot. κατεμεγαλύνθη
μου). Hebr. הגדיל עלי עקב . . . . . . (11)
xv. 25. ἵνα πλ. ὁ λόγος . . . Ἐμίσησάν με δωρεάν.
Ps. xxxiv. (xxxv.) 19. οἱ μισοῦντές με δωρεάν. Ps. lxviii.
(lxix.) 5 . . . . (12)

(3) *Other quotations.*

By John the Baptist :

i. 23. ἐγὼ φωνὴ βοῶντος ἐν τῇ ἐρήμῳ Εὐθύνατε τὴν ὁδὸν Κυρίου.

Isa. xl. 3. ἑτοιμάσατε . . . εὐθείας ποιεῖτε τὰς τρίβους τοῦ θεοῦ ἡμῶν (Aq. Theodot. ἀποσκευάσατε. Symm. εὐτρεπίσατε) . . . . (13)

By Galilæans :

vi. 31. καθώς ἐστιν γεγραμμένον "Αρτον ἐκ τοῦ οὐρανοῦ ἔδωκεν αὐτοῖς φαγεῖν.

Ps. lxxviii. (lxxvii.) 24 . . . (μάννα φαγεῖν) καὶ ἄρτον οὐρανοῦ ἔδωκεν αὐτοῖς. Ex. xvi. 4, 15. . . . ὕω . . . ἄρτους ἐκ τοῦ οὐρανοῦ . . . οὗτος ὁ ἄρτος ὃν ἔδωκε Κύριος ὑμῖν φαγεῖν. (14)

The triumphal cry (xii. 13; Ps. cxviii. 25) can hardly be treated as a quotation. In preserving the Hebrew form *Hosanna* St. John agrees with the Synoptic Evangelists and differs from the LXX.

An examination of these fourteen[1] citations (1—7 by the Evangelist; 8—12 by the Lord; 13, 14 by others) shows that they fall into the following groups :

1. Some agree with the Hebrew and LXX., where these both agree;

(5), (10), (12).

2. Others agree with the Hebrew against the LXX. ;

(7), (8), (11).

3. One agrees with the LXX. against the Hebrew ;

(3).

4. One differs from the Hebrew and LXX. where these both agree ;

(1).

---

[1] To these fourteen citations Bishop Westcott subsequently added the following :

xix. 28 f. ἵνα τελειωθῇ ἡ γραφὴ Διψῶ λέγει. Ps. lxix. 21 . . (5*)

xx. 9. οὐδέπω ᾔδεισαν τὴν γραφήν ὅτι δεῖ αὐτὸν ἐκ νεκρῶν ἀναστῆναι (7*)

viii. 17. ἐν τῷ νόμῳ τῷ ὑμετέρῳ γέγραπται. Deut. xix. 15 . . (9*)

xvii. 12. οὐδεὶς . . ἀπώλετο εἰ μὴ ὁ υἱὸς τῆς ἀπωλείας ἵνα ἡ γραφὴ πληρωθῇ (12*)

vii. 42. οὐχὶ ἡ γραφὴ εἶπεν ὅτι ἐκ τοῦ σπέρματος Δαυείδ, καὶ ἀπὸ Βηθλεέμ . . . ἔρχεται ὁ χριστός; Ps. lxxxix. 3 ; Mic. v. 2. Comp. xii. 34, ἠκούσαμεν ἐκ τοῦ νόμου . . . . (14*)

5. Others differ from the Hebrew and LXX. where they do not agree ;

(2), (4).

6. Free adaptations ;

(6), (9), (13), (14).

(γ) There is yet another argument to be noticed in support of the Palestinian authorship of the fourth Gospel, which appears to be of great weight, though it has commonly been either passed over, or even regarded as a difficulty. The doctrine of the Word, as it is presented in the Prologue, when taken in connexion with the whole Gospel, seems to show clearly that the writer was of Palestinian and not of Hellenistic training.

In considering St. John's teaching on the Logos, " the Word," it is obvious to remark, though the truth is very often neglected in practice, that it is properly a question of doctrine and not of nomenclature. It constantly happens in the history of thought that the same terms and phrases are used by schools which have no direct affinity, in senses which are essentially distinct, while they have a superficial likeness. Such terms (*e.g.*, *idea*) belong to the common dialect of speculation; and it is indeed by the peculiar force which is assigned to them that schools are in many cases most readily distinguished. A new teacher necessarily uses the heritage which he has received from the past in order to make his message readily understood.

It may then be assumed that St. John, when he speaks of " the Word," " the Only-begotten," and of His relations to God and to the world, and to man, employs a vocabulary and refers to modes of thought which were already current when he wrote. His teaching would not have been intelligible unless the general scope of the language which he employed, without explanation or preparation, had been familiar to his readers. When he declares with abrupt emphasis that " the Word was in the beginning," and that "the Word became flesh," it is evident that he is speaking of " a Word " already known in some degree by the title, though he lays down new truths as to His

being. He does not speak, as in the Apocalypse (xix. 13;
comp. Heb. iv. 12) of "the Word of God," but of "the
Word" absolutely. Those whom he addressed knew of
Whom he was speaking, and were able to understand that
which it was his office to make known about Him In
this case, as in every other similar case, the thoughts of
men, moving in different directions under the action of
those laws of natural growth which are the expression
of the divine purpose, prepared the medium and provided
the appropriate means for the revelation which was to be
conveyed in the fulness of time.

In this respect the manifold forms of speculation,
Western and Eastern, fulfilled a function in respect to
Christian philosophy similar to that which was fulfilled in
other regions of religious experience by the LXX.; and
the results which were gained were embodied in Greek
modes of speech, which were ready at last for the declaration of the divine message.

It becomes then a question of peculiar and yet of
subordinate interest to determine from what source St.
John derived his language. It is admitted on all hands
that his central affirmation, "the Word became flesh,"
which underlies all he wrote, is absolutely new and unique.
A Greek, an Alexandrine, a Jewish doctor, would have
equally refused to admit such a statement as a legitimate
deduction from his principles, or as reconcileable with
them. The message completes and crowns "the hope of
Israel," but not as "the Jews" expected. It gives stability
to the aspirations of humanity after fellowship with God,
but not as philosophers had supposed, by "unclothing"
the soul. St. John had been enabled to see that Jesus
of Nazareth was "the Christ" and "the Son of God":
it remained for him to bring home his convictions to
others (xx. 31). The Truth was clear to himself: how
could he so present it as to show that it gave reality to
the thoughts with which his contemporaries were busied?
The answer is by using with necessary modifications the
current language of the highest religious speculation to
interpret a fact, to reveal a Person, to illuminate the
fulness of actual life. Accordingly he transferred to the

c

region of history the phrases in which men before him had spoken of "the Logos"—"the Word," "the Reason"—in the region of metaphysics.   St. Paul had brought home to believers the divine majesty of the glorified Christ: St. John laid open the unchanged majesty of "Jesus come in the flesh."

But when this is laid down it still remains to determine in which direction we are to look for the immediate source from which St. John borrowed the cardinal term *Logos*, a term which enshrines in itself large treasures of theological speculation.

The scantiness of contemporary religious literature makes the answer more difficult than it might have been if the great Jewish teachers had not shrunk from committing their lessons to writing.   And, in one sense, the difficulty is increased by the fact that a striking aspect of Jewish thought has been preserved in the copious writings of PHILO of Alexandria (born c. 20 B.C.), who is naturally regarded as the creator of teaching, of which he is in part only the representative.   However far this view may be from the truth, the works of Philo furnish at least a starting-point for our inquiry.   This typical Alexandrine Jew speaks constantly of "the divine Logos" (ὁ θεῖος λόγος) in language which offers striking, if partial, parallels with the Epistle to the Hebrews and St. Paul.   The divine Logos is "Son of God," "firstborn Son (πρωτόγονος, I. 414), "image of God" (εἰκὼν θεοῦ, I. 6), "God" (I. 655), "high-priest" (ἀρχιερεύς, I. 653), "man of God" (ἄνθρωπος θεοῦ, I. 411), "archetypal man" (ὁ κατ᾽ εἰκόνα ἄνθρωπος, I. 427), "the head of the body" (I. 640; comp. I. 121), "through whom the world was created" (II. 225).

At first sight it might seem that we have here beyond all doubt the source of St. John's language.   But the ambiguity of the Greek term *Logos*, which means both *Reason* and *Word*, makes it necessary to pause before adopting this conclusion.   When Philo speaks of "the divine Logos" his thought is predominantly of the divine Reason and not of the divine Word.   This fact is of decisive importance.   The conception of a divine Word, that is, of a divine Will sensibly manifested in personal

action, is not naturally derived from that of a divine
Reason, but is rather complementary to it, and characteristic of a different school of thought.   Is it then possible
to find any clear traces of a doctrine of a divine Logos
elsewhere than at Alexandria ?

The Targums furnish an instructive answer to the
question.   These paraphrases of the Hebrew Scriptures
have preserved, as it appears, the simplest and earliest
form in which the term "the Word" was employed in
connexion with God.   They were most probably not
committed to writing in the shape in which we now have
them, till some time after the Christian era; but all
evidence goes to show that they embody the interpretations
which had been orally current from a much earlier time.
In the Targum of Onkelos on the Pentateuch, which is
the oldest in date, the action of God is constantly though
not consistently referred to " His Word " (*Memra*, מימר,
מימרא).   Thus it is said that "the Lord protected Noah by
His Word, when he entered the ark " (Gen. vii. 16): that
He " made a covenant between Abraham and His Word "
(Gen. xvii. 2); that the Word of the Lord was with Ishmael
in the wilderness (xxi. 20).   At Bethel Jacob made a
covenant that "the Word of the Lord should be His
God" (Gen. xxviii. 21).   Moses at Sinai "brought forth the
people to meet the Word of God" (Exod. xix. 17).   And
in Deuteronomy the Word of the Lord appears as a
consuming fire talking to His people, and fighting for
them against their enemies (Deut. iii. 2, iv. 24).

Such examples might be multiplied indefinitely; and
it may be noticed that the term *Debura* (דבורא) occurs in
this sense as well as *Memra*.   Thus it is said in the
Jerusalem Targum on Numb. vii. 89, *the word* (דבורא) *was
talking with him*; and again, Gen. xxviii. 10, *the word* ("ד)
desired to talk with him.

In connexion with this usage it must also be observed
that " a man's word " is used as a periphrasis for " himself."   So we read Ruth iii. 8 (*Targ. Jon.*), " between
his word (*i.e.*, himself) and Michal " (Buxtorf and Levy,
s.v.).   The "word" is in fact the active expression of the
rational character, and so may well stand for the person

from whom it issues. As applied to God, the term was free from any rude anthropomorphism, while it preserved the reality of a divine fellowship for man.

One striking difference between the Aramaic and Greek terms will have been remarked. *Logos*, as we have seen, is ambiguous, and may signify either *reason* or *word*, but *Memra* (*Debura*) means *word* only. If now we return to Philo, the importance of this fact becomes obvious. With Philo the Palestinian sense of *word* sinks entirely into the background, if it does not wholly disappear. He has borrowed a term which was already current in the Greek Scriptures, and filled it with a new meaning.

Three currents of thought in fact meet in Philo's doctrine of " the Logos," the Stoic, the Platonic, and the Hebraic. He was nothing less than a creative genius. He felt rightly that the revelation of the Old Testament contained implicitly the harmony of the manifold speculations of men, and he therefore adopted boldly the thoughts of Greek philosophy for the interpretation of its language. He found a " Logos " in the Greek Bible which he accepted as the record of revelation, and he applied to that what Greek writers ʰad said of the " Logos," without thinking it necessary to inquire into the identity of the terms. At one time he borrows from Plato when he speaks of the Logos as " the archetypal idea " (*De Spec. Leg.* 36, ii. p. 333 f.), or as bearing " the idea of ideas " (*De Migr. Abr.* 18, i. p. 452 m.). More commonly he uses the Stoic conception of the Logos, as the principle of reason, which quickens and informs matter.

At the same time, while it appears that Philo borrowed both the title of the *Logos* as *Reason*, and the most prominent features of His office, from Hellenic sources, he sought the confirmation of his views in the Old Testament; and in doing this he shows that he was not unacquainted with Jewish speculations on the *Word*. But in spite of the unwavering faith with which he found in the letter of the law the germ and the proof of the teaching which he borrowed from Greece, he abandoned the divine position of the Jew. The whole scope of the writers of the Old Testament is religious. They move in a region of life and history. Their idea of God is that of the Lord who rules the world and His chosen people, not simply as the Author of existence, but as One who stands in a moral relation to men, "speaking" to them. The whole scope of Philo on the other hand is metaphysical. He moves in a region of abstraction and thought. His idea of God is pure being. With him the speculative aspect of the Logos-doctrine overpowers the moral. He does not place the Logos in connexion with the Messiah, nor even specially with Jewish history. It is perhaps of less significance that he speaks of it now as if it were personal, and again as if it were impersonal: now as an attribute, and now as "a second god."

If now we ask with which of these two conceptions of the Logos, current respectively in Palestine and Alexandria, the teaching of St. John is organically connected, the answer cannot be uncertain.

Philo occupied himself with the abstract conception of the divine Intelligence, and so laid the foundations of a philosophy. The Palestinian instinct seized upon the concrete idea of "the Word of God," as representing His personal action, and unconsciously prepared the way for a Gospel of the Incarnation. St. John started from the conception of "the Word"; and by this means in the end he gave reality to the conception of "the Reason."

The development of the action of the Logos, the Word, in the Prologue to the fourth Gospel places the contrast between Philo and the Evangelist in the broadest light. However wavering and complex Philo's description of the Logos may be, it is impossible not to feel that he has in every case moved far away from the idea of an Incarnation. No one, it is not too much to say, who had accepted his teaching could without a complete revolution of thought accept the statement "the Logos became flesh." The doctrine of the personality of the Logos, even if Philo had consistently maintained it, would not have been in reality a step towards such a fact. On the other hand, in the Prologue the description of the Logos is personal from the first (ἦν πρὸς τ. θ.), and His creative enery is at once connected with man. "The Life was the light of men." "The Light was coming into the world ($\mathring{\eta}\nu$ . . . $\overset{\mbox{\tiny '}}{\epsilon}\rho\chi.$).." And in due time "the Logos became flesh." Thought follows thought naturally, and the last event is seen to crown and complete the history which leads up to it.

Philo and St. John, in short, found the same term current, and used it according to their respective apprehensions of the truth. Philo, following closely in the track of Greek philosophy, saw in the Logos the divine Intelligence in relation to the universe: the Evangelist, trusting firmly to the ethical basis of Judaism, sets forth the Logos mainly as the revealer of God to man, through creation, through theophanies, through prophets, through the Incarnation. The Philonean Logos, to express the same thought differently, is a later stage of a divergent interpretation of the term common to Hebrew and Hellenist.

It is, however, very probable that the teaching of Philo gave a fresh impulse to the study of the complementary conception of the Logos as the divine Reason, which was shadowed forth in the Biblical doctrine of Wisdom ($\sigma o\phi\acute{\iota}a$). Nor is there any difficulty in supposing that the apostolic writers borrowed from him either directly or indirectly forms of language which they adapted to the essentially new announcement of an Incarnate Son of God. So it was that the treasures of Greece were made contributory to the full unfolding of the Gospel. But the essence of their doctrine has no affinity with his. The speculations of Alexandria or Ephesus may have quickened and developed elements which otherwise would have remained latent in Judaism. But the elements were there; and in this respect the evangelic message "the Word became flesh," is the complete fulfilment of three distinct lines of preparatory revelation, which were severally connected with "the Angel of the Presence" (Gen. xxxii. 24 ff.; Exod. xxxiii. 12 ff., xxiii. 20 f.; Hos. xii. 4 f.; Isa. vi. 1 [John xii. 41], lxiii. 9; Mal. iii. 1); with "the Word" (Gen. i. 1; Ps. xxxiii. 6, cxlvii. 15; Isa. lv. 11; comp. Wisd. xviii. 15); and with "Wisdom" (Prov. viii. 22 ff., iii. 19; Ecclus. i. 1—10, xxiv. 9 (14); Bar. iii. 37, iv. 1; comp. Wisd. vii. 7—11).

In short, the teaching of St. John is characteristically Hebraic and not Alexandrine. It is intelligible as the final co-ordination through facts of different modes of thought as to the divine Being and the divine action, which are contained in the Old Testament. And on the other hand it is not intelligible as an application or continuation of the teaching of Philo.

The doctrine of the Logos has been very frequently discussed. An excellent account of the literature up to 1870 is given by Dr. Abbot in his appendix to the article on "the Word" in the American edition of the *Dictionary of the Bible*. Several later works are included in the list given by Soulier, *La Doctrine du Logos chez Philon d'Alexandrie*, Turin, 1876. The works of Gfrörer, *Philo u. d. Jud.-Alex. Theosophie*, 1835; Dähne, *Jud.-Alex. Religions-Philosophie*, 1854; Dorner, *The Person of Christ* (Eng. Trans.); Jowett, *St. Paul and Philo (Epistles of St. Paul*, i. 363 ff.); Heinze, *Die Lehre v. Logos in Griech. Philosophie*, 1872; Siegfried, *Philo v. Alex.*, 1875, may be specially mentioned. Grossmann has given a complete summary of the word "Logos" in Philo, in his *Quæstiones Philoneæ*, 1829.

(c) *The Author of the Fourth Gospel was an eye-witness of what he describes.* The particularity of his knowledge, which has been already noticed summarily, leads at once to the next point in our inquiry. The writer of the Gospel was an eye-witness of the events which he describes. His narrative is marked by minute details of persons, and time, and number, and place and manner, which cannot but have come from a direct experience. And to these must be added various notes of fact, so to speak, which seem to have no special significance where they stand, though they become intelligible when referred to the impression originally made upon the memory of the Evangelist.

(a) *Persons.* The portraiture of the chief characters in the Gospel will be noticed afterwards. In this connexion it is sufficient to observe the distinctness with which the different actors in the history rise before the writer. There is no purpose, no symbolism to influence

his record.   The names evidently belong to the living
recollection of the incidents.   The first chapter is crowded
with figures which live and move : John with his disciples,
Andrew, Simon Peter, Philip, Nathanael.   Momentous
questions are connected with definite persons.   *He saith
unto Philip, Whence shall we buy bread, that these may eat ?
. . . Philip answered him . . .* (vi. 5, 7 ; comp. Matt. xiv.
14 ff. and parallels).   Certain Greeks said to Philip, *Sir,
we would see Jesus.   Philip cometh and telleth Andrew:
Andrew cometh and Philip and they tell Jesus* (xii. 21 f.).
*Thomas saith unto Him, Lord, we know not whither thou
goest ; how do we know the way ?* (xiv. 5).   *Philip saith, Lord,
shew us the Father, and it sufficeth us* (xiv. 8).   *Judas saith,
not Iscariot, Lord, how is it that thou wilt manifest thyself to
us, and not unto the world?* (xiv. 22).   *The disciple whom
Jesus loved . . . falling back upon His breast, saith, Lord,
who is it?* (xiii. 25 ; comp. xxi. 20).   Nicodemus (iii. 1 ff.,
vii. 50, xix. 39), Lazarus (xi. 1 ff., xii. 1 ff.), Simon the
father of Judas Iscariot [1] (vi. 71, xii. 4, xiii. 2, 26), and
Malchus (xviii. 10), are mentioned only in the fourth
Gospel.   The writer of this Gospel alone mentions the
relationship of Annas to Caiaphas (xviii. 13), and identifies
one of those who pointed to Peter as the kinsman of him
whose ear Peter cut off (xviii. 26).

(β) *Time.*   The details of time belong perhaps more
obviously to the plan of the narrative than the details
of persons.   The greater seasons, even though they are
not noted in the Synoptists, may be supposed to have
been preserved in tradition, as the first Passover (ii. 13, 23),
the Feast of the New Year (v. 1), the Second Passover
(vi. 4), the Feast of Tabernacles (vii. 2), the Feast of
Dedication (x. 22) ; but other specifications of date can
only be referred to the knowledge of actual experience.
Such are the indications of the two marked weeks at the
beginning and end of Christ's ministry (i. 29, 35, 43, ii. 1,
xii. 1, 12 (xiii. 1), xix. 31, xx. 1), of the week after the

---

[1] In this connexion it is interesting to notice that the writer of the
fourth Gospel knew that the title Iscariot was a local or family name.
He applies it both to Judas and to his father Simon : vi. 71, xiii. 2, 26,
xii. 4, xiv. 22.

Resurrection (xx. 26), the enumeration of the days before the raising of Lazarus (xi. 6, 17, 39), the note of the duration of Christ's stay in Samaria (iv. 40, 43; compare also vi. 22, vii. 14, 37). Still more remarkable is the mention of the hour or of the time of day which occurs under circumstances likely to have impressed it upon the mind of the writer, as *the tenth hour* (i. 40), *the sixth hour* (iv. 6), *the seventh hour* (iv. 52), *about the sixth hour* (xix. 14), *it was night* (xiii. 30), *in the early morning* (xviii. 28, xx. 1, xxi. 4), *the evening* (vi. 16, xx. 19), *by night* (iii. 2).

(γ) *Number.* The details of number, though fewer, are hardly less significant. It is unnatural to refer to anything except experience such definite and, as it appears, immaterial statements as those in which the writer of the fourth Gospel mentions the *two* disciples of the Baptist (i. 35), the *six* waterpots (ii. 6), the *five* loaves and *two* small fishes (vi. 9), the *five-and-twenty* furlongs (vi. 19), the *four* soldiers (xix. 23. Cf. Acts xii. 4), the *two hundred* cubits (xxi. 8), the *hundred and fifty and three* fishes (xxi. 11).

The number of the loaves and fishes is preserved in the Synoptic narrative, but this single parallel does not in any way lessen the value of the whole group of examples as a sign of immediate observation in the Evangelist. Other records of number show the clearness if not the directness of the writer's information, as the *five* husbands (iv. 18), the *thirty and eight* years' sickness (v. 5), the estimate of *three hundred* pence (xii. 5; comp. Mark xiv. 5), the weight of a *hundred* pounds (xix. 39).

(δ) *Place.* Many of the local details characteristic of the fourth Gospel have been already noticed. Here it is only necessary to observe that the manner in which the scenes of special acts and utterances are introduced shows that they belong to the immediate knowledge of the writer. We cannot naturally account for the particularity except on the supposition that the place was an integral part of the recollection of the incidents. Thus the scenes of John's baptism are given as at *Bethany* and *Ænon* (i. 28, iii. 23; comp. x. 40). The son of the nobleman was sick *at Capernaum* while Jesus was at *Cana* (iv. 46 f). Jesus found the paralytic whom He had healed *in the Temple* (v. 14). He gained many adherents when He went towards the close of His ministry *beyond Jordan to the place where John was at first baptizing* (x. 40 ff.). When Mary came to Him He had not yet come to the village, but *was in the place where Martha met Him* (xi. 30). He spent the interval between the raising of Lazarus and His return to Bethany on the eve of the Passion *in the country near the wilderness, in a city called Ephraim* (xi. 54). The people as they *stood in the Temple* speculated on His reappearance (xi. 56).

So again Christ spoke certain memorable words *in a solemn gathering* (ἐν συναγωγῇ) at *Capernaum* (vi. 59, note), in *the treasury* (viii. 20), in *Solomon's porch* (x. 23), before crossing the Kidron (xviii. 1).

(ε) *Manner.* More impressive still are the countless small traits in the descriptions which evince either the skill of a consummate artist or the recollection of an observer. The former alternative is excluded alike by the literary spirit of the first and second centuries and by the whole character of the Gospel. The writer evidently reflects whát he had seen. This will appear most clearly to any one who takes the record of a special scene and marks the several points which seem to reveal the impressions of an eye-witness, as (for example) the calling of the first disciples (i. 35—51), or the foot-washing, (xiii. 1—20), or the scene in the high-priest's court (xviii. 15—27), or the draught of fishes (xxi. 1—14). In each one of these narratives, and they are simply samples of the nature of the whole narrative, it is almost impossible to overlook the vivid touches which correspond with the actual experience of one who had looked upon what he describes. Thus, to take a single illustration from the first (i. 35—51), we cannot but feel the life (so to speak) of the opening picture. John is shown standing, in patient expectation of the issue, as the tense implies (ἱστήκει, comp. vii. 37, xviii. 5, 16, 18, xix. 25, xx. 11), with two of his disciples. As Christ moves away, now separate from him, he fixes his eyes upon Him (ἐμβλέψας, comp. v. 43), so as to give the full meaning to the phrase which he repeats, in order that his disciples may now, if they will, take the lesson to themselves. Each word tells; each person occupies exactly the position which corresponds with the crisis. And the description becomes more significant when contrasted with the notice of the corresponding incident on the former day (i. 29 ff.).

Not to dwell at length on these scenes, one or two detached phrases may be quoted which will serve to show the kind of particularity on which stress is laid. The loaves used at the feeding of the five thousand are *barley* loaves which a boy has (vi. 9; comp. *v.* 13); when Mary came to Jesus she *fell at His feet* (xi. 32; contrast *vv.* 20 f.); after the ointment was poured out *the house was filled from its fragrance* (xii. 3); the branches strewn in the way of Jesus were taken from *the palm-trees* which were by the roadside (xii. 13); *it was night* when Judas went forth (xiii. 30); Judas brings a band of Roman soldiers as well as officers of the priests to apprehend Jesus (xviii. 3); Christ's tùnic was *without seam, woven from the top throughout* (xix. 23); the napkin which had been about His head was *wrapped together in a place by itself* (xx. 7); Peter *was grieved* because Jesus said to him the third time, Lovest thou me? (xxi. 17).

Compare also xiii. 24, xviii. 6, xix. 5, xxi. 20. Each phrase is a reflection of a definite external impression. They bring the scenes as vividly before the reader as they must have presented themselves to the writer.

If it be said that we can conceive that these traits might have been realised by the imagination of a Defoe or a Shakespeare, it may be enough to reply that the narrative is wholly removed from this modern realism; but besides this, there are other fragmentary notes to which no such explanation can apply. Sometimes we find historical details given bearing the stamp of authenticity, which represent minute facts likely to cling to the memory of one directly concerned (i. 40), though it is in fact difficult for us now to grasp the object of the writer in preserving them. It is equally impossible to suppose that such details were preserved in common tradition or supplied by the imagination of the writer. Examples are found in the exact account of Andrew finding *first his own brother* Simon

(i. 41), of the passing visit to Capernaum (ii. 12), of John's baptism (iii. 23), of the boats from Tiberias (vi. 22 f.), of the retirement to Ephraim (xi. 54).

Sometimes the detail even appears to be in conflict with the context or with the current (Synoptic) accounts, though the discrepancy vanishes on a fuller realisation of the facts, as when the words *Arise, let us go hence* (xiv. 31) mark the separation between the discourses in the upper chamber and those on the way to the garden (compare i. 21 with Matt. xi. 14; iii. 24 with Matt. iv. 12).

Elsewhere a mysterious saying is left wholly unexplained. In some cases the obscurity lies in a reference to a previous but unrecorded conversation, as when the Baptist says to the disciples who had followed him, *Behold the Lamb of God* (i. 29; comp. vi. 36, xii. 34), or, perhaps, to unknown local circumstances (i. 46). In others it lies in a personal but unexpressed revelation, as in the words which carried sudden conviction to Nathanael, *Before Philip called thee, when thou wast under the fig-tree, I saw thee* (i. 48). Apparent contradictions are left without any comment, as v. 31 compared with viii. 14; xiii. 36 compared with xvi. 5; xiv. 19 compared with xvi. 19; and, on the other hand, an explanation is given which, though it might appear superfluous at a later time, becomes at once natural in one who in the process of narration is carried back to the scene itself with all its doubts and perplexities, as when it is said in interpretation of the words, *ye are clean, but not all;* "for He knew him that was betraying Him; for this reason He said, Ye are not all clean" (xiii. 11).

(d) *The Author of the Fourth Gospel was an Apostle.* Such touches as those which have been now enumerated, and every page of the Gospel will supply examples, show that the writer was an eye-witness of many at least of the scenes which he describes. The age of minute historical romance had not yet come when the fourth Gospel was written, even if such a record could possibly be brought within the category. A further examination of the narrative shows that the eye-witness was also an apostle. This follows almost necessarily from the character of the

scenes which he describes, evidently as has been shown from
his own knowledge, the call of the first disciples (i. 19—34),
the journey through Samaria (iv.), the feeding of the
five thousand (vi.), the successive visits to Jerusalem
(vii. ix. xi.), the Passion, the appearances after the Resurrection.   But the fact is further indicated by the intimate
acquaintance which he exhibits with the feelings of "the
disciples."   He knows their thoughts at critical moments
(ii. 11, 17, 22, iv. 27, vi. 19, 60 f., xii. 16, xiii. 22, 28, xxi. 12;
comp. Luke xxiv. 8; Matt. xxvi. 75).   He recalls their
words spoken among themselves (iv. 33, xvi. 17, xx. 25,
xxi. 3, 5) as to their Lord (iv. 31, ix. 2, xi. 8, 12, xvi. 29).

He is familiar with their places of resort (xi. 54, xviii. 2,
xx. 19).

He is acquainted with imperfect or erroneous impressions received by them at one time, and afterwards
corrected (ii. 21 f., xi. 13, xii. 16, xiii. 28, xx. 9, xxi. 4).

And yet more than this, the writer of the fourth Gospel
evidently stood very near to the Lord.   He was conscious
of His emotions (xi. 33, xiii. 21).   He was in a position to
be well acquainted with the grounds of His action (ii. 24 f.,
iv. 1, v. 6, vi, 15, vii. 1, xvi. 19).   Nor is this all; he speaks
as one to whom the mind of the Lord was laid open.
Before the feeding of the five thousand he writes, *This He*
(Jesus) *said trying him, for He Himself knew what He was
about to do* (vi. 6).   *Jesus knew in Himself* the murmurings
of the disciples (vi. 61); *He knew from the beginning who
they were that believed not, and who it was that should betray
Him* (vi. 64); *He knew the hour of His Passion* (xiii. 1, 3),
and who should betray Him (xiii. 11); *He knew* indeed *all
the things that were coming upon Him* (xviii. 4); He *knew*
when *all things were accomplished* (xix. 28).

(e)   *The Author of the Fourth Gospel was the Apostle John.*
Such statements when they are taken in connexion with
the absolute simplicity of the narrative necessarily leave
the impression that the Evangelist was conscious of having
had the opportunity of entering, more deeply even than
others, into the conditions of the Lord's life.   And this
reflection brings us to the last point.   If the writer of the
fourth Gospel was an apostle, does the narrative indicate

any special apostle as the writer? In the Epilogue
(xxi. 24) the authorship of the book is assigned, as we shall
see afterwards, to *the disciple whom Jesus loved* (ὃν ἠγάπα ὁ
'Ἰησοῦς). This disciple appears under the same title twice
in the narrative of the Passion (xiii. 23, xix. 26), as well as
twice afterwards (xxi. 90), and once in connexion with
St. Peter under a title closely resembling it (xx. 2, ὃν ἐφίλει
ὁ 'Ἰησοῦς). He is known to the high-priest (xviii. 15), and
stands in very close relationship with St. Peter (xiii. 24,
xx. 2, xxi. 7 ; comp. xviii. 15 ; Acts iii.). Though his name
is not mentioned, there is nothing mysterious or ideal
about him. He moves about among the other apostles
quite naturally, and from the enumeration (xxi. 2 ; comp.
i. 35 ff.) of those present at the scene described in the last
chapter, it follows that he must have been either one of
the sons of Zebedee, or one of *two other disciples* not described
more particularly.

If now we turn to the Synoptic narrative we find three
disciples standing in a special sense near to Jesus, Peter
and the sons of Zebedee, James and John. There is then
a strong presumption that the Evangelist was one of
these. St. Peter is out of the question. One of the two
sons of Zebedee, James, was martyred very early
(Acts xii. 2), so that he could not have been the author
of the Gospel. John therefore alone remains ; and he
completely satisfies the conditions which are required to
be satisfied by the writer, that he should be in close
connexion with St. Peter, and also one admitted to
peculiar intimacy with the Lord.

Does then this definite supposition that St. John was the
anonymous disciple who wrote the fourth Gospel find any
subsidiary support from the contents of the history ? The
answer cannot be doubtful. St. John is nowhere mentioned
by name in the Gospel; and while it appears incredible
that an apostle who stands in the Synoptists, in the Acts
(iii. 1, iv. 13, etc.), and in St. Paul (Gal. ii. 9), as a central
figure among the twelve, should find no place in the
narrative, the nameless disciple fulfils the part which
would naturally be assigned to St. John. Yet further,
in the first call of the disciples one of the two followers

of the Baptist is expressly named as Andrew (i. 40); the other is left unnamed. Andrew, it is said, found *first his own brother Simon* (i. 41). The natural interpretation of the words suggests that the brother of some other person, and if so, of the second disciple, was also found. A reference to the last scene at the sea of Galilee (xxi. 2) leads to the certain inference that these two brothers were the sons of Zebedee, and so that the second disciple was St. John. Another peculiarity of the Gospel confirms the inference.

The Evangelist is for the most part singularly exact in defining the names in his Gospel. He never mentions Simon after his call (i. 42 f.) by the simple name, as is done in the other Gospels, but always by the full name Simon Peter, or by the new name Peter. Thomas is three times out of four further marked by the correlative Greek name Didymus (xi. 16, xx. 24, xxi. 2), which is not found in the Synoptists. Judas Iscariot is described as the son of a Simon not elsewhere noticed (vi. 71, xii. 4, xiii. 2, 26). The second Judas is expressly distinguished from Iscariot even when the latter had left the eleven (xiv. 22). Nicodemus is identified as *he that came to Jesus by night* (xix. 39 [vii. 50]). Caiaphas on each of the two separate occasions where he is introduced is qualified by the title of his office as *the high-priest of that year* (xi. 49, xviii. 13).

But in spite of this habitual particularity the Evangelist never speaks of the Baptist, like the three other Evangelists, as "John the Baptist," but always simply as "John." It is no doubt to be noticed that in most places the addition of the title would have been awkward or impossible; but elsewhere such an identification might have been expected (i. 15 and ᴠ. 33, 36; comp. Matt. iii. 1, xi. 11 ff.). If, however, the writer of the Gospel were himself the other John of the Gospel history, it is perfectly natural that he should think of the Baptist, apart from himself, as John only.[1]

---

[1] It is also to be observed that the writer of the fourth Gospel does not give the name of Salome, the wife of Zebedee (xix. 25. Comp. Matt. xxvii. 56), or of James (xxi. 2), or of the Mother of the Lord.

But it is said that if it is admitted that the Apostle John is to identified with the nameless disciple of the fourth Gospel, the second of the two disciples of the Baptist, the companion of St. Peter, the disciple whom Jesus loved ; it is still impossible, in spite of the attestation of the Epilogue, that he could have written the Gospel. The Gospel, such is the contention, must have been written by some one else, for it is argued that the author could not have spoken of himself as *the disciple whom Jesus loved*, claiming in this way for himself, and not as he might reasonably have done for another whom he took as his hero, a pre-eminence over his fellow apostles ; and (it is further urged in particular) that St. John would not have " studiously elevated himself in every way above the Apostle Peter " as this writer does.

The last objection may be disposed of first. The notion that the author of the fourth Gospel wishes to present St. John as the victorious rival of St. Peter, is based mainly upon the incident at the Last Supper, where St. Peter beckoned to St. John to ask a question which he did not put himself (xiii. 24 ff.) ; and it is asserted that the same idea is supported by the scenes in the court of the High Priest, and by the Cross. It would be sufficient to reply that all these incidents belong to details of personal relationship, and not to official position, and St. John was (as it appears) the son of the sister of the Mother of the Lord. But if we go into details an examination of the narrative as a whole shows that it lends no support whatever to the theory of any thought of rivalry or comparison between St. Peter and St. John existing in the writer's mind. St. John stands, just as he stands in the Acts, silent by the side of the Apostle to whom the office of founding the Church was assigned (cf. xxi. 21 ; Acts iii. 1). And as for the incident at the Last Supper, the person who occupied the third and not the second place would be in a position to act the part assigned to St. John (John xiii. 23, note). Here then St. Peter takes the precedence ; and elsewhere he occupies exactly the same place with regard to the Christian Society in the fourth Gospel as in the other three. He receives the promise of his significant surname (i. 42); he gives utterance to the critical confession of Christ's majesty (vi. 68); he is placed first (as it seems) at the foot-washing during the Last Supper (xiii. 6); he is conspicuous at the betrayal in defence of his Lord (xviii. 10); he stands patiently without the high-priest's door till he is able to obtain admission (xviii. 16); the message of the Resurrection is brought to him and to " the other disciple " only as second to him (xx. 2); he first sees the certain signs that Christ had risen (xx. 7); he directs the action of the group of apostles during their time of suspense (xxi. 3); he is the first to join the Lord upon the seashore, and the chief in carrying out His command (xxi. 7, 11); he receives at last the Great Commission (xxi. 15 ff.).

The representative official precedence of St. Peter thus really underlies the whole narrative of the fourth Gospel. The nearness of St. John to the Lord is a relation of sympathy, so to speak, different in kind.

But this ascription of a special relation of the unnamed disciple to the Lord as *the disciple whom Jesus loved*, with a feeling at once general ($\dot{\eta}\gamma\dot{\alpha}\pi\alpha$) and personal ($\dot{\epsilon}\phi\dot{\iota}\lambda\epsilon\iota$, xx. 2), requires in itself careful consideration. And if it were true, as is frequently assumed, that St. John sought to conceal himself by the use of the various periphrases under which his name is veiled, there might be some difficulty in reconciling the use of this exact title with the modest wish to be unnoticed. But in point of fact the writer of the fourth Gospel evidently insists on the peculiarity of his narrative as being that of a personal witness. He speaks with an authority which has a right to be recognised. It is taken for granted that those whom he addresses will know who he is, and acknowledge that he ought to be heard. In this respect the fourth Gospel differs essentially from the other three. They are completely impersonal, with the exception of the short preface of St. Luke. We can then imagine that St. John as an eye-witness might either have written his narrative in the first person throughout, or he might have composed an impersonal record, adding some introductory sentences to explain the nature of the book, or he might have in-

d

dicated his own presence obliquely at some one or other of the scenes which he describes. There is no question of self-concealment in the choice between these alternatives; and there can be also no question as to the method which would be most natural to an apostle living again, as it were, in the divine history of his youth. The direct personal narrative and the still more formal personal preface to an impersonal narrative seem to be alien from the circumstances of the composition. On the other hand, the oblique allusion corresponds with the devout contemplation from a distance of events seen only after a long interval in their full significance. The facts and the actors alike are all separated from the Evangelist as he recalls them once more in the centre of a Christian Society.[1]

But if it be admitted that the oblique form of reference to the fact that the writer of the fourth Gospel was an eye-witness of what he describes was generally the most natural, does it appear that this particular form of oblique reference, to which objection is made, was itself natural? The answer must be looked for in the circumstances under which it is used. After the distinct but passing claim to be an eye-witness (i. 14), the Evangelist does not appear personally in the Gospel till the scenes of the Passion. He may be discovered in the call of the disciples (i. 41), but only by a method of exhaustion. So far there was nothing to require his explicit attestation. But in the review of the issue of Christ's work it may well be asked whether the treachery of Judas was indeed foreseen by Christ. St. John shows how deeply he felt the importance of the question (vi. 70, 71, xiii. 11 ; comp. xiii. 18 f.). It was then essential to his plan that he should place on

---

[1] In illustration of this view, reference may be made to Mr. Browning's noble realisation of the situation in his " Death in the Desert " :

> ". . . much that at the first, in deed and word,
> Lay simply and sufficiently exposed,
> Had grown (or else my soul was grown to match,
> Fed through such years, familiar with such light,
> Guarded and guided still to see and speak)
> Of new significance and fresh result ;
> What first were guessed as points I now knew stars."

record the direct statement of the Lord's foreknowledge on the authority of him to whom it was made. That communication was a special sign of affection. Can we then be surprised that, in recalling the memorable fact that it was made to himself, he should speak of himself as *the disciple whom Jesus loved* (ἠγάπα)? The words express the grateful and devout acknowledgement of something received, and contain no assumption of a distinction above others. Christ loved all (xiii. 1, 34, xv. 9); St. John felt, and confesses, that Christ loved him, and showed His love in this signal manner. The same thought underlies the second passage where the phrase occurs (xix. 26). The charge to receive the Mother of the Lord almost necessarily calls out the same confession. In the last chapter (xxi. 7, 20) the title seems to be repeated with a distinct reference to the former passages, and no difficulty can be felt at the repetition.

The remaining passage (xx. 2) is different, and ought not to have been confounded with those already noticed. There can be no doubt that if the words *she cometh to Simon Peter and the other disciple whom Jesus loved* had stood alone, the reader would have included St. Peter under the description ; the word " other " has no meaning except on this interpretation (contrast xxi. 7). But it has been assumed that the entirely different phrase used here (ὃν ἐφίλει) must be identical with that used elsewhere of St. John alone (ὃν ἠγάπα), and the passage has been accordingly misunderstood. Yet the contrast between the two words equally translated " love," gives the clue to the right meaning. St. Peter and St. John shared alike in that peculiar nearness of personal friendship to Christ (if we may so speak) which is expressed by the former word (φιλεῖν, see xi. 3, 36), while St. John acknowledges for himself the gift of love which is implied in the latter ; the first word describes that of which others could judge outwardly ; the second that of which the individual soul alone is conscious. The general conclusion is obvious. If that phrase (ὃν ἐφίλει ὁ Ἰησοῦς) had been used characteristically of St. John which is in fact used in relation to St. Peter and St. John, there might have been some ground

for the charge of an apparent assumption of pre-eminence
on the part of the Evangelist; as it is, the phrase which is
used is no affectation of honour; it is a personal thanksgiving for a blessing which the Evangelist had experienced,
which was yet in no way peculiar to himself.

As far, therefore, as indirect internal evidence is concerned, the conclusion towards which all the lines of
inquiry converge remains unshaken, that the fourth
Gospel was written by a Palestinian Jew, by an eye-
witness, by *the disciple whom Jesus loved*, by John the son
of Zebedee. We have now to consider the direct evidence
which the Gospel offers upon the question.

ii.   *The direct evidence of the Gospel as to its authorship*

Three passages of the Gospel appear to point directly
to the position and person of the author: i. 14, xix. 35,
xxi. 24. Each passage includes some difficulties and
uncertainties of interpretation which must be noticed
somewhat at length.

(a) Ch. i. 14. *The word became flesh and tabernacled among
us, and we beheld His glory* . . . (ὁ λόγος σὰρξ ἐγένετο,
καὶ ἐσκήνωσεν ἐν ἡμῖν, καὶ ἐθεασάμεθα τὴν δόξαν αὐτοῦ . . .).
The main question here is as to the sense in which the
words *we beheld* are to be taken. Are we to understand
this " beholding " of the historical sight of Christ, so that
the writer claims to have been an eye-witness of that
which he records? or can it be referred to a spiritual
vision, common to all believers at all times?

Our reply cannot but be affected by the consideration
of the parallel passage in the beginning of the first Epistle
of St. John, which was written, it may certainly be
assumed, by the same author as the Gospel: *That which
was from the beginning, which we have heard, which we have
seen with our eyes, which we beheld, and our hands handled,
concerning the Word of life* . . . (1 John i. 1, ὃ ἦν ἀπ' ἀρχῆς,
ὃ ἀκηκόαμεν, ὃ ἑωράκαμεν τοῖς ὀφθαλμοῖς, ὃ ἐθεασάμεθα καὶ αἱ
χεῖρες ἡμῶν ἐψηλάφησαν, περὶ τοῦ λόγου τῆς ζωῆς . . .). Now
there cannot be any doubt that the " beholding " here,
from the connexion in which it stands (*we have seen with*

our eyes, our hands handled), must be understood literally.
Language cannot be plainer. The change of tense moreover emphasises the specific historical reference (*we beheld*,
and not as of that which ideally abides, *we have beheld*
[1 John iv. 14, John i. 32, n.]). This being so, the same
word in the same tense and in the same general connexion
cannot reasonably be understood otherwise in the Gospel.
It may also be added further, that the original word
(θεᾶσθαι) is never used in the New Testament of mental
vision (as θεωρεῖν).[1] The writer then (such must be our
conclusion) claims to have *beheld* that *glory* which his
record unfolds.

But it is said that the phrase *among us* cannot be
confined to the apostles or immediate disciples of Christ
exclusively, and that it must be taken to include *all*
Christians (Luke i. 1), or even all men. If, however, this
interpretation of *among us* admits the wider interpretation
of the pronoun, it does not exclude the apostles, who are
in this connexion the representatives of the Church and
of humanity, and it does not therefore touch the meaning
of the following clause, in which the sense of *beheld* is fixed
independently. The whole point of the passage is that
the Incarnation was historical, and that the sight of the
Incarnate Word was historical. The words cannot without
violence be made to give any other testimony. The objection is thus, on a view of the context, wholly invalid; and
the natural interpretation of the phrase in question, which
has been already given, remains unshaken. The writer
professes to have been an eye-witness of Christ's ministry.[2]

(*b*) Ch. xix. 35. This second passage, which, like the
former one, comes into the narrative parenthetically, is
in some respects more remarkable. After speaking of
the piercing of the Lord's side, the writer adds, *And
forthwith came there out blood and water. And he that*

---

[1] The word occurs in John i. 32, 38, iv. 35, vi. 5, xi. 45 ; 1 John i. 1,
iv. 12, 14.

[2] The significant variation of language in *v.* 16 supports the view
which has been given. The Apostolic *we* is distinguished from the
Christian *we all*. The use of the direct form in these two cases (*we
beheld, we received*) is remarkable. Contrast xx. 30 (ἐνώπ. τῶν μαθ.).

*hath seen hath borne witness, and his witness is true: and
he knoweth that he saith true, that ye also may believe.
For these things came to pass that* . . . (καὶ ὁ ἑωρακὼς
μεμαρτύρηκεν καὶ ἀληθινὴ αὐτοῦ ἐστὶν ἡ μαρτυρία, καὶ ἐκεῖνος
οἶδεν ὅτι ἀληθῆ λέγει ἵνα καὶ ὑμεῖς πιστεύητε. ἐγένετο γάρ . . .
John xix. 35 ff.). One point in this passage, the contrast
between the two words rendered *true*, cannot be given
adequately in an English version. The witness is described as "fulfilling the true conception of witness"
(ἀληθινός), and not simply as being correct (ἀληθής); it is
true to the idea of what witness should be, and not only
true to the fact in this special instance (comp. viii. 16,
note) so far as the statement is true. There is, therefore,
no repetition in the original in the two clauses, as there
appears to be in the English version. This detail is not
without significance for the right understanding of the
whole comment. It brings out clearly the two conditions
which testimony ought to satisfy, the first that he who
gives it should be competent to speak with authority, and
the second that the account of his experience should be
exact. But the main question to be decided is whether
the form of the sentence either suggests or admits the
belief that the eye-witness to whose testimony appeal is
made is to be identified with the writer of the Gospel.

The answer to this question has been commonly made
to turn upon a false issue. It has been argued, with a
profusion of learning, that the use in the second clause
of the pronoun which expresses a remote, or rather an
isolated, personality (ἐκεῖνος), is unfavourable to the identification of the Evangelist and the eye-witness, or, at least,
lends no support to the identification. It has also been
asserted, as might have been expected, by less cautious
scholars, that the use of this pronoun is fatal to the
identification. On the other hand, it has been shown by
examples from classical authors and also from St. John's
Gospel (ix. 37) that a speaker can use this pronoun of
himself.[1] But in reality the problem contained in the

---

[1] The most complete discussion of this part of the problem is to be
found in a set of papers in the *Studien u. Kritiken*, 1859, 1860, by Steitz
on the one side, and by Ph. Buttmann on the other.

passage must be solved at an earlier stage. If the author
of the Gospel could use the first clause (*he that hath seen*,
etc.) of himself, there can be no reasonable doubt that
he could also use of himself the particular pronoun which
occurs in the second clause ; and to go even further, there
can be no reasonable doubt that according to the common
usage of St. John he would use this particular pronoun
to resume and emphasise the reference (i. 18, v. 39, 37).
No one, in other words, with any knowledge of St. John's
style can seriously dispute the fact that the " he " of the
second clause is the same as the " witness " of the first
clause.

This being so, only two interpretations of the passage
are possible. The Evangelist either makes an appeal to
an eye-witness separate from himself, but not more definitely described, who is said to be conscious of the truth
of his own testimony ; or he makes an appeal to his own
actual experience, now solemnly recorded for the instruction of his readers.

We are thus brought to the right issue. Is it the fact
that the second alternative is, as has been confidently
affirmed, excluded by the nature of the case ? Is it the
fact that we cannot suppose that St. John, if he were the
writer, would have referred to his own experience obliquely ? On the contrary, if we realise the conditions
under which the narrative was drawn up, it will be seen
that the introduction of the first person in this single
place would have been more strange. The Evangelist has
been already presented as a historical figure in the scene
(*vv.* 26, 27); and it is quite intelligible that an Apostle
who had pondered again and again, as it may well have
been, what he had gradually shaped, should pause at this
critical point, and, dwelling upon that which he felt to
be a crucial incident, should separate himself as the witness
from his immediate position as a writer. In this mental
attitude he looks from without upon himself (ἐκεῖνος) as
affected at that memorable moment by the fact which
he records, in order that it may create in others the present
faith (πιστεύητε) which it had created in his own soul.
The comment from this point is therefore perfectly com-

patible with the identification of the witness and the author.

We may, however, go further. The comment is not only compatible with the identification; it favours the identification, not indeed by the use of the particular pronoun, which tells neither one way nor the other, but by the whole construction of the passage. The witness is spoken of as something which abides after it has been given; *he hath borne witness*; and, more than this, the witness is given still; *he knoweth that he saith true*; and, yet again, the giver of the witness sets himself in contrast with his readers; *he hath given his witness . . . that ye may believe.* It is not possible then to doubt that the words taken in their context assert that the eye-witness was still living when the record was written [1]; and if so, it is most natural to suppose that his present utterance, to which appeal is made, is that contained in the Gospel itself. It is difficult to appreciate the evidential force of an appeal to the consciousness of an undefined witness.

In this connexion another point must be observed. If the author were appealing to the testimony of a third person he would almost necessarily have used an aorist and not a perfect, *he that saw bore witness*, and not *he that hath seen hath borne witness*. For the mere narrator the testimony centres in the moment at which it was rendered; for the witness himself it is a continuous part of his own life.

The conclusion to which these remarks converge will appear still more certain if the comment be reduced to its simplest elements. If it had stood, *He that hath seen hath borne witness, that ye also may believe*, no ordinary reader would have doubted that the writer was appealing to his own experience, recorded in the history, since no other testimony is quoted. But the intercalated clauses do not in any way interfere with this interpretation. They simply point out, as has been already noticed, the relation in which this special statement stands to its attestation. They show that this testimony satisfies the two conditions, which must be ratified for the establish-

---

[1] This conclusion holds good to whomsoever the comment be referred.

ment of its authority, that it is adequate in relation to
its source, and that it is correct in its actual details. For
a witness may give true evidence and yet miss the essential
features of that of which he speaks. Hence the writer
affirms the competency of the witness, while he affirms
also that the testimony itself was exact.

On the whole, therefore, the statement which we have
considered is not only compatible with the identity of the
eye-witness and the writer of the Gospel, but it also
suggests, even if it does not necessarily involve, the
identification of the two. On the other hand, the only
other possible interpretation of the passage is wholly
pointless. It supposes that an appeal is made with
singular emphasis to an unknown witness, who is said to
be conscious of the truthfulness of his own testimony.
Such a comment could find no place in the connexion in
which the words stand.

(c) Ch. xxi. 24. The third passage which occurs in the
appendix to the Gospel (ch. xxi.) is different in character
from the other two. After the narrative of the Lord's
saying with regard to "the disciple whom He loved," the
record continues: *this is the disciple who witnesseth concerning these things, and who wrote these things: and we
know that his witness is true* (οὗτός ἐστιν ὁ μαθητὴς ὁ μαρτυρῶν
περὶ τούτων καὶ ὁ γράψας ταῦτα, καὶ οἴδαμεν ὅτι ἀληθὴς αὐτοῦ
ἡ μαρτυρία ἐστίν). There can be no doubt as to the meaning
of the words. The writing of the Gospel is distinctly
assigned by them to "the beloved disciple" (*v.* 21). But
it is not at once obvious to whom the words are to be
assigned. Is the author of the Gospel himself the
speaker? or must the note be referred to others who
published his Gospel, as, for example, to the Ephesian
elders? Before we attempt to answer this question it
must be observed that whichever view be taken the
sentence contains a declaration as to the authorship of
the Gospel contemporaneous with its publication, for
there is not the least evidence that the Gospel was ever
circulated in the Church without the epilogue (ch. xxi.).
And yet further, the declaration extends both to the substantial authorship (*he that witnesseth concerning these things*)

and also to the literal authorship of the record (*he that wrote these things*). So much is clear; but perhaps it is impossible to press the present tense (*he that witnesseth*) as a certain proof that the author was still alive when the work was sent forth. The form as it stands here by itself may simply indicate the vital continuity of his testimony. However this may be, the note at least emphasises what was felt to be a real presence of the writer in the society to which he belonged.

If we now proceed to fix the authorship of the note, it will at once appear that the passage (xix. 35) which has been already considered practically decides the question. The contrast between the two notes is complete. In that the note is given in the singular and in the third person; in this it is given in the plural and in the first person. In that the witness is regarded as isolated and remote (*he that . . . and he . . .*); in this the witness is regarded as present (*this is . . .*). If we believe that the former is, as has been shown, a personal affirmation of the writer himself, it seems almost impossible to believe that this is a personal affirmation also. No sufficient reason can be given for the complete change of position which he assumes towards his own work. The plural (*we know*) by itself would be capable of explanation, but the transition from the historical singular (*this is . . .*) to the direct plural (*we know . . .*) is so harsh and sudden as to be all but inadmissible; and the difficulty is aggravated by the occurrence of the first person singular (*I suppose*) in the next sentence. On the other hand, if we bear in mind that the Gospel as originally composed ended with xx. 31, to which xxi. 25 may have been attached, and that the narratives in xxi. 1—23 were drawn up by the same author at a later time under circumstances which called for some authoritative interpretation of a mistaken tradition, we can readily understand how the note was added to the record by those who had sought for this additional explanation of the Lord's words, and preserved when the completed Gospel was issued to the Church. At the same time, if *v.* 25 formed the last clause of the original Gospel, it would naturally be transferred to the end of the enlarged record.

The general result of the examination of these passages is thus tolerably distinct. The fourth Gospel claims to be written by an eye-witness, and this claim is attested by those who put the work in circulation.

2. *External Evidence as to the Authorship*

In considering the external evidence [1] for the authorship of the fourth Gospel, it is necessary to bear in mind the conditions under which it must be sought. It is agreed on all hands that the Gospel was written at a late date, towards the close of the first century, when the Evangelic tradition, preserved in complementary forms in the Synoptic Gospels, had gained general currency, and from its wide spread had practically determined the popular view of the life and teaching of the Lord. And further, the substance of the record deals with problems which belong to the life of the Church and to a more fully developed faith. On both grounds references to the contents of this Gospel would naturally be rarer in ordinary literature than references to the contents of the other Gospels. Express citations are made from all about the same time.

Christian theological literature practically begins for us with Irenæus, Clement of Alexandria, and Tertullian, and these writers use the four Gospels as fully and decisively as any modern writer. The few letters and apostolic treatises and fragments which represent the earlier literature of the second century give very little scope for the direct use of the New Testament. But it is most significant that Eusebius, who had access to many works which are now lost, speaks without reserve of the fourth Gospel as the unquestioned work of St. John, no less than those

---

[1] The character of the present Introduction necessarily excludes detailed criticism of the authorities which are quoted. But it may be said, once for all, that the passages which are set down are used after a careful examination of all that has been urged against their validity. The original texts have been discussed in detail by Dr. Sanday (*The Gospels in the Second Century*, 1876) and by Dr. Lightfoot in the *Contemporary Review*, 1875, f., wh have noticed at length the most recent literature on the subject.

three great representative Fathers who sum up the teaching of the century. If he had known of any doubts as to its authorship among ecclesiastical writers, he would without question have mentioned these, as he has quoted the criticism of Dionysius of Alexandria on the Apocalypse.

We start then with the undeniable fact that about the last quarter of the second century, when from the nature of the case clear evidence can first be obtained, the Gospel was accepted as authoritative by heretical writers like Ptolemæus and Heracleon, and used by the opponents of Christ like Celsus, and assigned to St. John by Fathers in Gaul, Alexandria, and North Africa, who claimed to reproduce the ancient tradition of their churches, and this with perfect naturalness, there being evidently no trace within their knowledge of a contrary opinion. It is true that the Gospel was not received by Marcion, but there is no evidence to show that he was influenced by anything but subjective considerations in the formation of his collection of Scriptures. Irenæus also mentions an earlier sect, of doubtful affinity, which, claiming for itself the possession of prophetic gifts, rejected the Gospel of St. John and its characteristic promises of the Paraclete (Iren. c. Hær. III. 11. 9, " Alii ut donum Spiritus frustrentur quod in novissimis temporibus secundum placitum Patris effusum est in humanum genus, illam speciem non admittunt quæ est secundum Joannis evangelium, in qua Paracletum se missurum Dominus promisit; sed simul et evangelium et propheticum repellunt Spiritum "). But the language of Irenæus lends no support to the supposition that this sect questioned the authority of the Gospel on critical grounds. At the same time it must be noticed that Epiphanius (Hær. LI. 3) and Philastrius (Hær. 60) assert that a body of men whom they call Alogi assigned the authorship of the Gospel and of the Apocalypse to Cerinthus. The statement as it stands is scarcely intelligible; and it seems to have arisen from the mistaken extension to the authorship of the Gospel, by way of explaining its rejection, of a late conjecture as to the authorship of the Apocalypse.

Such an exception can have no weight against the uniform ecclesiastical tradition with which it is contrasted. This tradition can be carried still further back than Irenæus, who is its fullest exponent. The first quotation of the Gospel by name is made by THEOPHILUS of Antioch (c. A.D. 181): ". . . The holy Scriptures teach us, and all the inspired men (οἱ πνευματοφόροι), one of whom John saith: *In the beginning was the Word, and the Word was God.* . . . Afterwards he saith: *and the Word was God: all things were made through Him, and without Him was not even one thing made* (ad Autol. 11. 22). ATHENAGORAS (c. A.D. 176) paraphrases and combines the language of the Gospel in such a way as to show that it was both familiar and authoritative, and had been carefully weighed by him: "The Son of God is *the Word* of the Father in idea and actually (ἐν ἰδέᾳ καὶ ἐνεργείᾳ). For *all things were made* in dependence on Him and *through Him* (πρὸς αὐτοῦ [Acts xxvii. 34] καὶ δι' αὐτοῦ), the Father and the Son being One. But since *the Son is in the Father and the Father in the Son,* by unity and power of the Spirit (ἑνότητι καὶ δυνάμει πνεύματος), the Son of God is in the Mind and Word of the Father" (*Leg.* 10; comp. John i. 3, x. 30, xvii. 21). About the same time CLAUDIUS APOLLINARIS, bishop of Hierapolis, speaking of the different opinions as to the day of the Last Supper, evidently treats "the disagreements of the Gospels" (*i.e.,* the Synoptists and St. John) as something really out of the question (Routh, *Rell.* I. 167 ff.; comp. *Hist. of N. T. Canon,* p. 224); and he gives an explanation of John xix. 34 (see note), which shows that the incident had become a subject of deep speculation. Still earlier TATIAN, the scholar of Justin (c. A.D. 160), quotes words of the Gospel as well known: "This is in fact," he says, "that which has been said: *The darkness apprehendeth not the light*" (*Orat.* 13, τοῦτο ἔστιν ἄρα τὸ εἰρημένον [Acts ii. 16] ἡ σκοτία τὸ φῶς οὐ καταλαμβάνει, John i. 5; comp. John i. 3 with *Orat.* 19); and the latest criticism confirms the old belief that his *Diatessaron* was constructed from the texts of the four Canonical Gospels (Lightfoot, *Contemporary Review,* May, 1877).

So far the line of testimony appears to be absolutely beyond doubt. The traces of the use of the fourth Gospel in the interval between A.D. 100—160 are necessarily less clear ; but as far as they can be observed they are not only in perfect harmony with the belief in its apostolic origin, but materially strengthen this belief.

The EPISTLE OF CLEMENT to the Corinthians was probably written before the Gospel of St. John, but already this writing shows traces of the forms of thought which are characteristic of the book (cc. VII. XXXVI. *Hist. of N. T. Canon*, pp. 25 f.). The EPISTLE OF BARNABAS again offers some correspondences and more contrasts with the teaching of St. John in the common region of "mystical" religious thought. In the LETTERS OF IGNA-TIUS, which even if they are not authentic certainly fall within the first half of the century, the influence of the teaching, if not demonstrably of the writings, of St. John is more direct. The true meat of the Christian, for ex-ample, is said to be the " bread of God, *the bread of heaven, the bread of life,* which is *the flesh of Jesus Christ,*" and his drink is " *Christ's blood,* which is love incorruptible " (*ad Rom.* VII.; comp. John vi. 32, 51, 53). And again : " The Spirit is not led astray, as being from God. For it *knoweth whence it cometh and whither it goeth,* and *testeth* (ἐλέγχει) that which is hidden " (*ad Philad.* VII.; comp. John iii. 8, xvi. 8).

It is, however, with POLYCARP and PAPIAS[1] that the decisive testimony to the authenticity of St. John's writings really begins. Recent investigations, inde-pendent of all theological interests, have fixed the martyrdom of Polycarp in A.D. 155-6. (See Lightfoot, *Contemporary Review*, 1875, p. 838.) At the time of his death he had been a Christian for eighty-six years (*Mart. Polyc.* c. IX.). He must then have been alive during the greater part of St. John's residence in Asia, and there is no reason for questioning the truth of the statements that

[1] For a complete discussion of the historical positions of these two Fathers in regard to early Christian teaching and literature, see the articles of Dr. Lightfoot in the *Contemporary Review* for May, August, and October, 1875.

he "associated with the Apostles in Asia (*e.g.*, John, Andrew, Philip; comp. Lightfoot's *Colossians*, pp. 45 f.), and was entrusted with the oversight of the Church in Smyrna by those who were eye-witnesses and ministers of the Lord" (Euseb. *H. E.* III. 36; comp. Iren. *c. Hær.* III. 3. 4). Thus, like St. John himself, he lived to unite two ages. When already old he used to speak to his scholars of "his intercourse with John and the rest of those who had seen the Lord" (Iren. *Ep. ad Flor.* § 2); and Irenæus, in his later years, vividly recalled the teaching which he had heard from him as a boy (Iren. *l.c.*; comp. *c. Hær.* III. 3. 4). There is no room in this brief succession for the introduction of new writings under the name of St. John. Irenæus cannot with any reason be supposed to have assigned to the fourth Gospel the place which he gives to it unless he had received it with the sanction of Polycarp. The person of Polycarp, the living sign of the unity of the faith of the first and second centuries, is in itself a sure proof of the apostolicity of the Gospel. Is it conceivable that in his lifetime such a revolution was accomplished that his disciple Irenæus was not only deceived as to the authorship of the book, but was absolutely unaware that the continuity of the tradition in which he boasted had been completely broken ? One short letter of Polycarp, with which Irenæus was acquainted (Iren. *l.c.*), has been preserved. In this there is a striking coincidence with the language of 1 John : "Every one," he writes, "who doth not confess that Jesus Christ hath come in the flesh, is antichrist" (*ad Phil.* VII.; comp. 1 John iv. 2, 3). The sentence is not a mere quotation, but a reproduction of St. John's thought in compressed language which is all borrowed from him ($\pi\hat{a}\varsigma$, $\hat{o}\varsigma$ $\ddot{a}\nu$, $\dot{o}\mu o\lambda o\gamma\epsilon\hat{\iota}\nu$ 'I. X. $\dot{\epsilon}\nu$ $\sigma a\rho\kappa\dot{\iota}$ $\dot{\epsilon}\lambda\eta\lambda\upsilon\theta\dot{\epsilon}\nu a\iota$, $\dot{a}\nu\tau\dot{\iota}\chi\rho\iota\sigma\tau o\varsigma$). The words of St. John have, so to speak, been shaped into a popular formula. And if it be said that the reference to the Epistle shows nothing as to the Gospel, the reply is that the authorship of the two cannot reasonably be separated. A testimony to one is necessarily by inference a testimony to the other.

The testimony of PAPIAS to the Gospel of St. John is,

like that of Polycarp, secondary and inferential. Papias, according to Eusebius, " used testimonies from the former Epistle of John" (Euseb. *H. E.* III. 39). The mention of this fact, as the Epistle was universally received, is remarkable ; but the Catholic Epistles formed an exceptional group of writings, and it is perhaps on this account that Eusebius goes beyond his prescribed rule in noticing the use which was made even of those among them which were "acknowledged." At any rate the use of the Epistle by Papias points to his acquaintance with the Gospel. Several minute details in the fragment of the preface to his " Exposition of Oracles of the Lord" tend in the same direction. And there is a remarkable tradition found in a preface to a Latin MS. of the Gospel which assigns to Papias an account of the composition of the Gospel similar to that given in the Muratorian fragment (see *Hist. of N. T. Canon*, p. 76, n.).

But it is said that if Papias had used the Gospel Eusebius would not have neglected to notice the fact. The statement rests on a complete misunderstanding of what Eusebius professed to do. He did not undertake to collect references to " the acknowledged books " among which he placed the four Gospels, so that however often Papias might have quoted St. John's Gospel, Eusebius would not according to his plan have noticed the fact, unless something of special interest had been added to the reference (comp. *Hist. of N. T. Canon*, pp. 229 f.; Lightfoot, *Contemporary Review*, 1875, pp. 169 ff.).

The object of Papias was, as has been shown elsewhere, to illustrate the evangelic records by such information as he could gain from the earliest disciples ; and it is by no means unlikely that the " history of the woman taken in adultery," which has found a place in the Gospel of St. John, was recorded by him in illustration of John viii. 15 (see note *ad loc.*).

In close connexion with Papias stand "the elders" quoted by Irenæus, among whose words is one clear reference to St. John (Iren. v. 36. 2): "for this reason [they taught] the Lord said, *there are many mansions in my Father's home (ἐν τοῖς τοῦ πατρός μου μονὰς εἶναι πολλάς.*

John xiv. 2. Comp. Luke ii. 49). The quotation is anonymous, but it is taken from a writing and not from tradition; and the context makes it at least highly probable that the passage was quoted from Papias' "Exposition."

Whatever may be thought of the passing references of Polycarp and Papias to the writings of St. John, the main value of their testimony lies in the fact that they represent what can justly be called a school of St. John. Papias like Polycarp may himself have heard the Apostle (Iren. v. 33. 4). At least he studied with Polycarp (Iren *l.c.*). And he had still another point of connexion with the apostolic body. He conversed at Hierapolis with two daughters of the Apostle Philip (Euseb. *H. E.* iii. 39; Lightfoot, *Colossians*, 45 ff.). Nor were these two men alone. There were many about them, like the elders quoted by Irenæus, who shared in the same life. The succession was afterwards continued at Sardis through Melito, at Ephesus through Polycrates (comp. Euseb. *H. E.* v. 22), at Hierapolis through Claudius Apollinaris, at Lyons through Pothinus and Irenæus (compare also the *Epistle of the Churches of Vienne and Lyons, c.* 4, A.D. 177); and the concordant testimony of the latest witnesses in these different Churches is a sure proof that they preserved the belief which had been held from the first by the school to which they belonged (comp. Lightfoot, *Contemporary Review*, August, 1876).

The testimony of the Gospel of St. John is, as might have been expected on the assumption of its authenticity, most clear among the writers who stood in the closest connexion with his teaching. But it is not confined to them. JUSTIN MARTYR certainly appears to have been acquainted with the book. His evidence is somewhat obscure. All his references to the Gospels are anonymous; but at the same time his description of "the Memoirs" as written "by the *Apostles* and those who followed them" (*Dial.* 103), exactly answers to our present collection of four. And though the coincidences of language between Justin and St. John are not such as to establish beyond question Justin's dependence on the Evangelist,

e

this at least is the most natural explanation of the similarity (*Hist. of N. T. Canon,* p. 166, n.). And more than this, his acquaintance with the Valentinians (*Dial.* 35; comp. Iren. III. 11. 7, "qui a Valentino sunt eo [Evangelio] quod est secundum Iohannem plenissime utentes. . . .") shows that the fourth Gospel could not have been unknown to him.

Justin's teaching on the Word is perhaps a still more important indication of the influence of St. John. The teaching presupposes the teaching of St. John, and in many details goes beyond it. Thoughts which are characteristically Alexandrine, as distinguished from Hebraic, find a place in Justin; and he shows not only how little power there was in the second century to fashion such a doctrine as that of the fourth Gospel, but also how little Christian speculation was able to keep within the limits laid down by the Apostles.

The SHEPHERD OF HERMAS offers an instructive example of the precariousness of the argument from silence. The book contains no definite quotations from the Old or New Testament. The allusions which have been found in it to the characteristic teaching of St. John are I believe real, but they are not unquestionable. Yet it is certain from an independent testimony, that the Gospel was accepted as one of the four Gospels almost at the same date when the book was written, and probably in the same place. The Muratorian Fragment notices that the Shepherd was written " very lately (*c.* A.D. 170) in our times, in the city of Rome," and at the same time speaks of the Gospel according to St. John as "the fourth" Gospel in such a way as to mark its general recognition (*Hist. of N. T. Canon,* pp. 211 ff.; see below, II. § 2). To the same date also must be referred the two great translations of the East and West, the Syriac and Latin, in which the four Gospels stand without rivals.

Outside the Church the testimony to the general use of St. John's Gospel is both early and decisive. In the quotations from early heretical writers the references to it are comparatively frequent. In many cases its teaching formed the starting-point of their partial and erroneous conclusions. The first Commentary on the Gospel was written by Heracleon (c. A.D. 175); and his copy of the book had already been defaced by false readings. At an earlier date the Gospel was used by the author of the Clementine Homilies, by Valentinus and his school, by the Ophites, and by Basilides (*Hist. of N. T. Canon*, 282 ff., Sanday, *The Gospels in the Second Century*, pp. 292 ff.).

The testimony of Basilides is of singular interest. *The Refutation of Heresies*, attributed to Hippolytus, which was first published in 1851, contains numerous quotations from his writings and from the writings of his school. In one passage at least where there can be no reasonable doubt that the author of the *Refutation* is quoting Basilides himself (c. A.D. 130), a phrase from the Gospel of St. John is used as the authoritative basis for a mystical explanation (*Ref. Hær.* VII. 22).

In reviewing these traces of the use of the Gospel in the first three-quarters of a century after it was written, we readily admit that they are less distinct and numerous than those might have expected who are unacquainted with the character of the literary remains of the period. But it will be observed that all the evidence points in one direction. There is not, with one questionable exception, any positive indication that doubt was anywhere thrown upon the authenticity of the book. It is possible to explain away in detail this piece of evidence and that, but the acceptance of the book as the work of the Apostle adequately explains all the phenomena without any violence; and hitherto all the new evidence which has come to light has supported this universal belief of the Christian Society, while it has seriously modified the rival theories which have been set up against it.

II. The Composition of the Gospel

1. *The Author*

The facts bearing upon the life of St. John which are recorded in the New Testament are soon told. He was the son, apparently the younger son, of Zebedee and Salome (Mark xv. 40, xvi. 1, compared with Matt. xxvii. 56).

Salome, as it appears from John xix. 25 (see note), was the sister of "the Mother of the Lord," so that St. John was the cousin of the Lord "according to the flesh." He was probably younger than the Lord and than the other apostles. It is therefore easily intelligible that his near connexion by birth, combined with the natural enthusiasm of youth, offered the outward occasion for the peculiar closeness in which he stood to Christ.

Of his father Zebedee, a fisherman probably of Bethsaida or the neighbourhood (John i. 41 ff.), nothing is known except that he was sufficiently prosperous to have hired servants (Mark i. 20). At a later time Salome appears as one of the women who followed the Lord and "ministered to Him of their substance" (Mark xv. 40 f., compared with Luke viii. 3). And it is clear from John xix. 27 that the apostle had some means.

Like the other apostles, with the single exception of Judas Iscariot, St. John was a Galilæan. The fact has a moral value. When the rest of the Jewish nation was drawn partly to political intrigues, partly to speculations of the schools, the people of Galilee retained much of the simple faith and stern heroism of earlier times. It was made a reproach to them that they were unskilled in the traditions, and kept to the letter of the Law (comp. vii. 52, note). The rising of Judas "in the days of the taxing" (Acts v. 37) may have been a hopeless outburst of fanaticism, but at least it showed that there were many in Galilee who were ready to die for the confession that they had "no lord or master but God." The same spirit appears in the multitude who would have "taken Jesus by force" at the lake of Tiberias and made Him king (vi. 14 f.). They were ready to do and to suffer something for their eager if mistaken Messianic hope. It was amidst the memories of such conflicts, and in an atmosphere of passionate longing, that St. John grew up. And in some measure he shared the aspirations of his countrymen if he avoided their errors. When the Baptist proclaimed the advent of Christ, St. John was at once ranged among his disciples. And more than this: though "simple and unlettered" (Acts iv. 13), he appears to have grasped with exceptional power the spiritual import of the Baptist's message, who directed him immediately to Christ as "the Lamb of God." St. John obeyed the sign, and followed without delay the Master who was mysteriously pointed out to him. Thus from the first the idea of sovereignty was mingled with that of redemption, the issue of victory with the way of suffering, in the conception of the work of the Messiah whom he welcomed.

The ardour of the Galilæan temper remained in the apostle. St. John with his brother St. James received from the Lord (Mark iii. 17) the remarkable surname, Boanerges, "sons of thunder." Thunder in the Hebrew idiom is "the voice of God"; and the sons of Zebedee appear to have given swift, startling, vehement utterance to the divine truth which they felt within them. Theirs was not characteristically the decisive action, but the sudden moving word which witnessed to the inner fire. It may have been some stern voice which marked St. James as the first martyr among the apostles. Certainly the sayings of St. John which are recorded by St. Luke correspond with the prophetic energy which the title indicates (Luke ix. 49 ‖ Mark ix. 38; comp. Num. xi. 28; Luke ix. 54). His zeal was undisciplined, but it was loyal and true. He knew that to be with Christ was life, to reject Christ was death; and he did not shrink from expressing the thought in the spirit of the old dispensation. He learnt from the Lord, as time went on, a more faithful patience, but he did not unlearn the burning devotion which consumed him. To the last, words of awful warning, like the thundering about the throne, reveal the presence of that secret fire. Every page of the Apocalypse is inspired with the cry of the souls beneath the altar, "How long" (Rev. vi. 10); and nowhere is error as to the Person of Christ denounced more sternly than in his Epistles (2 John 10; 1 John iv. 1 ff.).

The well-known incident which occurred on the last journey to Jerusalem reveals the weakness and the strength of St. John's character. His mother, interpreting the desire of her sons, begged of Christ that they might sit, the one on His right hand and the other on His left,

in His Kingdom (Matt. xx. 20 ff., comp. Mark x. 35 ff.).
So far they misunderstood the nature of that especial
closeness to their Lord which they sought. But the reply
showed that they were ready to welcome what would be
only a prerogative of suffering. To be near Christ, even
if it was "to be near the fire" and "near the sword," was
a priceless blessing. And we can feel that the prayer
was already granted when Salome and St. John waited by
the Cross (John xix. 25 ff.).

This last scene reveals St. John nearest of all the
apostles to Christ, as "the disciple whom Jesus loved"
(ch. xiii. 23, note). Together with his brother St. James
and St. Peter, he was one of the three admitted to a closer
relationship with Christ than the other apostles (Luke viii.
51, ix. 28; Mark xiv. 33); and of the three his connexion
was the closest. He followed Christ to judgement and to
death (John xviii. 15, xix. 26), and received from Him the
charge of His Mother as her own son (xix. 27, note).

After the Ascension St. John remained at Jerusalem
with the other apostles. He was with St. Peter at the
working of his first miracle; and afterwards he went with
him to Samaria (Acts i. 13, iii. 1 ff., viii. 14). At the time
of St. Paul's first visit to Jerusalem he seems to have been
absent from the city (Gal. i. 18); but on a later occasion
St. Paul describes him as one of those accounted to be
"the pillars of the Church" (Gal. ii. 9). At what time
and under what circumstances he left Jerusalem is wholly
unknown. At the opening of the Apocalypse (i. 9) he
speaks of himself as "in the island called Patmos, for the
word and the testimony of Jesus." Beyond this there is
no further notice of him in the New Testament.[1]

When we pass beyond the limits of Scripture, St. John
is still presented to us under the same character, as the
Son of Thunder, the prophetic interpreter of the Old
Covenant. Now it is related that he refused to remain
under the same roof with Cerinthus (or according to

---

[1] This is not the place to discuss the authorship of the Apocalypse.
Its doctrinal relation to the Gospel of St. John, which will be discussed
afterwards, appears to be decisive in support of the early date of the
banishment.

another account " Ebion "), who denied the reality of the Incarnation : " Let us fly," he said, " lest the bath fall on us, since Cerinthus is within, the enemy of the truth " (Iren. III. 3. 4; comp. Epiph. *Hær.* xxx. 24). Now he is described as a " priest wearing the plate (or diadem) " prescribed by the law (Ex. xxxix. 30 f.) for the high-priest (Polycrates ap. Euseb. *H. E.* III. 31, v. 24 ; comp. ch. xviii. 15, note). Now he is shown, in one of the most beautiful of early histories, seeking out the lost and enforcing the obligation of ministerial duty (Euseb. *H. E.* III. 23, on the authority of Clement of Alexandria). Once again we read that " when he tarried at Ephesus to extreme old age, and could only with difficulty be carried to the church in the arms of his disciples, and was unable to give utterance to many words, he used to say no more at their several meetings than this, ' Little children, love one another.' At length," Jerome continues, " the disciples and fathers who were there, wearied with hearing always the same words, said, ' Master, why dost thou always say this ? ' ' It is the Lord's command,' was his worthy reply, ' and if this alone be done, it is enough.' " (Hieron. *Comm. in Ep. ad Gal.* vi. 10).[1]

These traditions are in all probability substantially true, but it is impossible to set them in a clear historical framework. Nothing is better attested in early Church history than the residence and work of St. John at Ephesus. But the dates of its commencement and of its close are alike unknown. It began after the final departure of St. Paul, and it lasted till about the close of the first century (Iren. II. 22. 5, μέχρι τῶν Τραιάνου χρόνων, A.D. 98—117). This may be affirmed with confidence ; but the account of his sufferings at Rome (Tert. *de Præscr. Hær.* 36 . . . " in oleum demersus nihil passus est "; comp. Hieron. *ad Matt.* xx. 23), and of the details of his death at Ephesus, are quite untrustworthy. One legend, which is handed down in various forms, is too remarkable to be wholly omitted. It was widely believed that St. John was not

[1] These traditions are collected in a very agreeable form in Dean Stanley's *Sermons and Essays on the Apostolic Age.* The later legends are given by Mrs. Jameson, in her *Sacred and Legendary Art.*

dead, but sleeping in his grave; and that he would so remain till Christ came. Meanwhile, it was said, "he showed that he was alive by the movement of the dust above, which was stirred by the breath of the saint." "I think it needless," Augustine adds, "to contest the opinion. Those who know the place must see whether the soil is so affected as it is said; since I have heard the story from men not unworthy of credence" ("revera non a levibus hominibus id audivimus." Aug. *In Joh. Tract. CXXIV.* 2).

These words of Augustine are part of his commentary on the mysterious saying of the Lord which, as is seen from the Gospel (xxi. 21 ff.), was perceived to mark in some way the future work of the apostle : "If I will that he tarry till I come, what is that to thee ?" St. John did most truly "tarry till the Lord came." It is impossible for us to realise fully what was involved in the destruction of the Holy City for those who had been trained in Judaism. It was nothing else than the close of a divine drama, an end of the world. The old sanctuary, "the joy of the whole earth," was abandoned. Henceforth the Christian Church was the sole appointed seat of the presence of God. When Jerusalem fell Christ came, and with His coming came also the work of St. John. During the period of conflict and fear and shaking of nations which preceded that last catastrophe, St. John had waited patiently; and we may believe that he had fulfilled his filial office to the Mother of the Lord in his own home in Galilee to the last, gaining by that a fuller knowledge of the revelation of the Son of God, and bringing into a completer harmony the works which he had seen, and the words which he had heard.

In these scattered traits we can gain a consistent if imperfect conception of St. John. The central characteristic of his nature is intensity, intensity of thought, word, insight, life. He 'regards everything on its divine side. For him the eternal is already : all is complete from the beginning, though wrought out step by step upon the stage of human action. All is absolute in itself, though marred by the weakness of believers. He sees the past and the future gathered up in the manifestation of

the Son of God. This was the one fact in which the hope
of the world lay. Of this he had himself been assured by
evidence of sense and thought. This he was constrained
to proclaim : ", We have seen and do testify." He had no
laboured process to go through : he saw. He had no con-
structive proof to develop : he bore witness. His source
of knowledge was direct, and his mode of bringing conviction was to affirm.

2. *The Occasion and Date*

An early and consistent tradition represents the Gospel
of St. John as written at the request of those who were
intimate with the Apostle, and had, as we must suppose,
already heard from his lips that teaching which they
desired to see recorded for the perpetual guidance of the
Church.   CLEMENT OF ALEXANDRIA has preserved the
tradition in its simplest form. He states on the authority
"of the elders of an earlier generation" (παράδοσις τῶν
ἀνέκαθεν πρεσβυτέρων) that "St. John, last [of the Evange-
lists], when he saw that the outward (bodily) facts had
been set forth in the [existing] Gospels, impelled by his
friends, [and] divinely moved by the Spirit, made a
spiritual Gospel" (Clem. Alex. ap. Euseb. *H. E.* VI. 14).
This general statement is given with additional details in
the MURATORIAN FRAGMENT on the Canon.   "The fourth
Gospel [was written by] John, one of the disciples (*i.e.*,
Apostles).   When his fellow disciples and bishops urgently
pressed (*cohortantibus*) him, he said, 'Fast with me [from]
to-day, for three days, and let us tell one another any
revelation which may be made to us, either for or against
[the plan of writing] (*quid cuique fuerit revelatum alteru-
trum*).' On the same night it was revealed to Andrew,
one of the Apostles, that John should relate all in his own
name, and that all should review [his writing]" (see *Hist.
of N. T. Canon*, p. 527).   There can be no doubt that
JEROME had before him either this fragment or, as appears
more probable, the original narrative on which it was
based, when he says that "ecclesiastical history records
that John, when he was constrained by his brothers to

write, replied that he would do so, if a fast were appointed and all joined in prayer to God; and that after this [fast] was ended, filled to the full with revelation (*revelatione saturatus*), he indited the heaven-sent preface: *In the beginning was the Word . . ."* (*Comm. in Matt.* Prol.) Eusebius, to whom we are indebted for the testimony of Clement, adds in another place, as a current opinion, that St. John wrote after the other Evangelists, to the truth of whose narrative he bore witness, in order to supply an account of the early period of the Lord's ministry which they omitted; and at the same time he implies, what is otherwise most likely, that the Apostle committed to writing what he had long delivered in unwritten preaching (Euseb. *H. E.* III. 24).

Other writers attempt to define more exactly the circumstances under which St. John was induced to compose his Gospel. Thus in the Scholia on the Apocalypse attributed to VICTORINUS of Pettau († c. 304), it is said that " he wrote the Gospel after the Apocalypse. For, when Valentinus and Cerinthus and Ebion and the others of the school of Satan were spread throughout the world, all the bishops from the neighbouring provinces came together to him, and constrained him to commit his own testimony to writing " (Migne, *Patrol.* v. p. 333). This statement appears to be an amplification of the Asiatic tradition preserved by Irenæus, which has been already noticed; and is only so far interesting as it shows the current belief that the fourth Gospel was written as an answer to the questionings of a comparatively advanced age of the Church. So much indeed seems to be historically certain; for, though it is impossible to insist upon the specific details with which the truth was gradually embellished, there can be no reason to question the general accuracy of a tradition which was widely spread in the last quarter of the second century. The evidence of Clement of Alexandria is independent of that of the Muratorian Canon, while both appear to point back to some common authority, which cannot have been far removed from the time of the Apostle. The fourth Gospel, we may thus conclude from the earliest direct evidence, was written after the other three, in Asia, at the request of the Christian churches there, as a summary of the oral teaching of St. John upon the life of Christ, to meet a want which had grown up in the Church at the close of the Apostolic age (comp. Epiph. *Hær.* XLI. 12).

The contents of the Gospel go far to support this view of its relatively late date. It assumes a knowledge of the substance of the Synoptic narratives. It deals with later aspects of Christian life and opinion than these. It corresponds with the circumstances of a new world.

(*a*) The first of these statements will come under examination at a later time, and will not be contested in its general shape. The two others can be justified by a few references to the Gospel, which will repay careful study.

(*b*) No one can read the fourth Gospel carefully without feeling that the writer occupies a position remote from the events which he describes. However clear it is that he was an eye-witness of the Life of the Lord, it is no less clear that he looks back upon it from a distance.[1] One plain proof of this is found in the manner in which he records words which point to the spread of the Gospel beyond the limits of Judaism. This characteristic view is distinctly brought out in the interpretation which he gives of the judgement of Caiaphas: *Now this he said not of himself, but being high-priest in that year, he prophesied that Jesus should die for the nation* (τοῦ ἔθνους, see note), *and not for the nation only, but in order that he might gather together in one the children of God that were scattered abroad* (xi. 51 f.). It is beyond question that when the Evangelist wrote these words, he was reading the fulfilment of the unconscious prophecy of Caiaphas in the condition of the Christian Church about him.

The same actual experience of the spread of the Gospel

---

[1] This is the impression which is conveyed by the notes which he adds from time to time in interpretation of words or facts : vii. 39, xii. 33, xviii. 9, 32, xix. 36, xxi. 19. These notes offer a remarkable contrast to those in which attention is called in the first Gospel to the present and immediate fulfilment of prophecy, Matt. i. 22, xxi. 4, etc. (γέγονεν ἵνα πληρωθῇ).

explains the prominent position which St. John assigns to those sayings of Christ in which He declared the universality of His mission : *other sheep I have which are not of this fold : them also must I lead. . . . and they shall become one flock, one shepherd* (x. 16). *I, if I be lifted up from the earth will draw all men unto myself* (xii. 32). The Son has *authority over all flesh* (xvii. 2). *All that which the Father giveth me*, He said, *shall come to me; and him that cometh to me I will in no wise cast out* (vi. 37). The knowledge of God and of Jesus Christ *is eternal life* (xvii. 3); and this knowledge, the knowledge of the truth, conveys the freedom, of which the freedom of the children of Abraham was only a type (viii. 31 ff.). The final form of worship is the worship of "the Father," in which all local and temporal worships, typified by Gerizim and Jerusalem, should pass away (iv. 21 ff.).

This teaching receives its final seal in the answer to Pilate : *Thou sayest that I am a king. To this end have I been born, and to this end am I come into the world, that I should bear witness unto the truth. Every one that is of the truth heareth my voice* (xviii. 37). The relation of the believer to Christ is thus shown to rest on a foundation which is of all most absolute. Christ, while He fulfilled "the Law," which was the heritage of the Jews, revealed and satisfied the Truth, which is the heritage of humanity.

There are indeed traces of the announcement of this universalism of the Gospel in the Synoptic narratives, and especially in that of St. Luke. It is taught there that Christ came as *the salvation prepared before the face of all the peoples, a light for revelation to Gentiles, and a glory to God's people Israel* (ii. 31, 32). *Repentance unto remission of sins* was to be preached *in His name unto all the nations beginning from Jerusalem* (xxiv. 47). It may be possible also to see in the fate of the Prodigal Son an image of the restoration of the heathen to their Father's home. But in these cases the truth is not traced back to its deepest foundations ; nor does it occupy the same relative position as in St. John. The experience of an organised Christian society lies between the two records.

This is plainly intimated by the language of the Evangelist himself. He speaks in his own person of the great crisis of the choice of Israel as over. *He came to His own home and His own people received Him not* (i. 11); and so in some sense, the choice of the world was also decided, *the light hath come into the world, and men loved the darkness rather than the light* (iii. 19). The message of the Gospel had already been proclaimed in such a way to Jew and Gentile that a judgement could be pronounced upon the general character of its acceptance.

This typical example serves to show how St. John brings into their true place in the completed Christian edifice the facts of Christ's teaching which were slowly realised in the course of the apostolic age. And while he does so, he recalls the words in which Christ dwelt upon that gradual apprehension of the meaning of His Life and work, which characterised in fact the growth of the Catholic Church. Throughout the last discourses of the Lord, the great charge to the apostolate, we seem to hear the warning addressed to St. Peter at the outset : *What I do thou knowest not now, but thou shalt come to know (γνώσῃ) afterwards* (xiii. 7). It is implied in the recital that the words of patient waiting had found their accomplishment by the mission of the new Advocate. *I have yet many things to say unto you, but ye cannot bear them now. Howbeit when He is come, even the Spirit of truth, He shall guide you into all the truth* (xvi. 12 ; comp. xv. 26). Even if Christ had already *made known all things* (xv. 15), there was need of the long teaching of time, that His disciples might master the lessons which they had implicitly received.

The record of these appeals to a future growth of knowledge can admit of only one interpretation. In dwelling on such aspects of Christ's teaching, it is clear that the Evangelist is measuring the interval between the first imperfect views of the Apostles as to the kingdom of God, and that just ideal, which he had been allowed to shape, under the teaching of the Paraclete, through disappointments and disasters. Now at length, on the threshold of a new world, he can feel the divine force of much that was before hard and mysterious. He had

waited till his Lord came; and he was enabled to recognise His Presence, as once before by the lake of
Galilee, in the unexpected victories of faith.

(c) In the last quarter of the first century, the world
relatively to the Christian Church was a new world; and
St. John presents in his view of the work and Person
of Christ the answers which he had found to be given
in Him to the problems which were offered by the changed
order. The overthrow of Jerusalem, carrying with it
the destruction of the ancient service and the ancient
people of God, the establishment of the Gentile congregations on the basis of St. Paul's interpretation of the
Gospel, the rise of a Christian philosophy (γνῶσις) from
the contact of the historic creed with Eastern and Western
speculation, could not but lead one who had lived with
Christ to go back once more to those days of a divine
discipleship, that he might find in them, according to
the promise, the anticipated replies to the questionings
of a later age. This St. John has done; and it is impossible not to feel how in each of these cardinal directions he points his readers to words and facts which
are still unexhausted in their applications.

(a) We have already touched upon the treatment of
the Jewish people in the fourth Gospel. They appear as
the heirs of divine blessings who have Esau-like despised
their birthright. The prerogatives of the people and their
misuse of them are alike noted. But in this respect there
is one most striking difference between the fourth Gospel
and the other three. The Synoptic Gospels are full of
warnings of judgement. Pictures of speedy desolation are
crowded into the record of the last days of the Lord's
ministry (Matt. xxiv., Mark xiii., Luke xxi.). His coming
to judgement is a central topic. In St. John all is changed.
There are no prophecies of the siege of the Holy City; there
is no reiterated promise of a Return; the judgement had
been wrought. Christ had come. There was no longer
any need to dwell upon the outward aspects of teaching
which had in this respect found its accomplishment. The
task of the Evangelist was to unfold the essential causes
of the catastrophe, which were significant for all time, and

to show that even through apparent ruin and failure the will of God found fulfilment.   Inexorable facts had revealed the rejection of the Jews.   It remained to show that this rejection was not only foreseen, but was also morally inevitable, and that it involved no fatal loss.   This is the work of St. John.   He traces step by step the progress of unbelief in the representatives of the people, and at the same time the correlative gathering of the children of God by Christ to Himself.   There was a divine law of inward affinity to good or evil in the obedience and disobedience of those who heard.   *I am the good shepherd; and I know mine own, and mine own know me, even as the Father knoweth me and I know the Father* (x. 14, 15).   *Ye believe not, because ye are not of my sheep.   My sheep hear my voice, and I know them, and they follow me* (x. 26, 27).   *This is the judgement, that the light is come into the world, and men loved the darkness rather than the light, for their works were evil* (iii. 19).

The fourth Gospel reveals in these and similar passages the innermost cause of the rejection of the Jewish people. The fact underlies the record, and the Evangelist lays open the spiritual necessity of it.   He reveals also the constitution of the Spiritual Church.   The true people of God survived the ruin of the Jews: the ordinances of a new society replaced in a nobler shape the typical and transitory worship of Israel.   When this Gospel was written, the Christian congregations, as we see from St. Paul's Epistles, were already organised, but the question could not but arise, how far their organisation was fitted to realise the ideal of the kingdom which Christ preached. The Evangelist meets the inquiry.   He shows from the Lord's words what are the laws of His service, and how they are fulfilled by the institutions in which they were embodied.   The absolute worship was to be in *spirit and truth* (iv. 23), as distinguished from letter and shadow; and the discourses with Nicodemus and at Capernaum set forth by anticipation how the sacraments satisfy this condition for each individual.   On the other hand, the general ministerial commission, which is contained only in the fourth Gospel (xx.), gives the foundation of the whole.

In that lies the unfailing assurance of the permanence of the new society.

(β) So far the fourth Gospel met difficulties which had not been and could not be realised till after the fall of Jerusalem. In like manner it met difficulties which had not been and could not be felt till the preaching of St. Paul had moulded the Christian Society in accordance with the law of freedom. Then first the great problems as to the nature of the object of personal faith, as to the revelation of the Deity, as to the universality of the Gospel, were apprehended in their true vastness; and the Evangelist shows that these thoughts of a later age were not unregarded by Christ Himself. The experience of the life of the Church—which is nothing less than the historic teaching of the Holy Spirit—made clear in due time what was necessarily veiled at first. Sayings became luminous which were riddles before their solution was given. Christ, in relation to humanity, was not characteristically the Prophet or the King, but the Saviour of the world, the Son of Man, the Son of God. In this connexion the fact of the Incarnation obtained its full significance. By the Incarnation alone the words which were partially interpreted through the crowning miracle of the Lord's ministry were brought home to all men; *I am the Resurrection and the Life* (xi. 25).

Thus by the record of the more mysterious teaching of the Lord, in connexion with typical works, St. John has given a historical basis for the preaching of St. Paul. His narrative is at once the most spiritual and the most concrete. He shows how Faith can find a personal object. The words *He that hath seen me hath seen the Father* (xiv. 9) mark an epoch in the development of religious thought. By them the idea of God receives an abiding embodiment, and the Father is thereby brought for ever within the reach of intelligent devotion. The revelation itself is complete (xvii. 6, 26), and yet the interpretation of the revelation is set forth as the work of the Holy Spirit through all ages (xiv. 26). God in Christ is placed in a living union with all creation (v. 17; comp. i. 3, note). The world, humanity and God are presented in the words

and in the Person of Christ under new aspects of fellowship and unity.

It will be evident how this teaching is connected with
that of St. Paul. Two special points only may be noticed :
the doctrine of the sovereignty of the divine will, and the
doctrine of the union of the believer with Christ. The
foundation of these two cardinal doctrines, which rise
supreme in the Pauline Epistles, lie deep in the fourth
Gospel.

The first, the doctrine of Providence, Predestination,
however it be called, not only finds reiterated affirmation
in the discourses of the Lord contained in the fourth
Gospel, but it is also implied as the rule of the progress
of the Lord's life. His " hour " determines the occurrence
of events from man's point of view; and the Evangelist
refers to it in connexion with each crisis of the Gospel
history, and especially with the Passion in which all crises
were consummated (ii. 4, vii. 30, viii. 20, xii. 23, 27, xiii. 1,
xvi. 4, xvii. 1 ; comp. vii. 6—8, ὁ καιρός). So also the will
or " the gift " of the Father is the spring of the believer's
power (iii. 27, vi. 37, 44, 65, xvii. 12); and Christ fulfils
and applies that will to each one who comes to Him (xv. 16,
5, v. 21).

Faith again assumes a new aspect in the narrative of
St. John. It is not merely the mediative energy in
material deliverances, and the measure (so to speak) of
material power; it is an energy of the whole nature, an
active transference of the whole being into another life.
Faith in a Person—in One revealed under a new " name "
—is the ground of sonship (i. 12), of life (xi. 25), of power
(xiv. 12), of illumination (xii. 36, 46). The keywords of
two complementary views of truth are finally combined :
this is the work of God, that ye believe—believe with a
continuous ever-present faith (πιστεύητε not πιστεύσητε)—
on Him whom He sent (vi. 29 ; comp. viii. 30, note).

(γ) Once again ; when the fourth Gospel was written
Christianity occupied a new intellectual position. In
addition to social and doctrinal developments, there were
also those still vaster questions which underlie all organisation and all special dogma, as to the function and stability

f

of knowledge, as to the interpretation and significance of life, as to the connexion of the seen and unseen. The new faith had made these questions more urgent than before, and the teaching of the Lord furnished such answers to them as man can apprehend. Knowledge was placed in its final position by the declaration *I am the Truth . . . The Truth shall make you free* (xiv. 6, viii. 31 ff.). Everything real is thus made tributary to religious service. Again, the eternal is revealed as present, and life is laid open in all its possible nobility. The separation which men are inclined to make arbitrarily between " here " and " there " in spiritual things is done away. *This is life eternal . . .* (xvii. 3); *He that heareth my word hath life eternal . . .* (v. 24). Once more, the essential unity and the actual divisions of the world are alike recognised. *All things were made (ἐγένετο) through Him* [in the Word] (i. 3); *. . . and the Light shineth in the darkness* (i. 5); and *the Word became (ἐγένετο) flesh.* Thus in Christ there is offered the historic reconciliation of the finite and the infinite, by which the oppositions of thought and experience are made capable of being reduced to harmony.

These internal indications of date completely accord with the historical tradition, and lead to the conclusion that the composition of the Gospel must be placed late in the generation which followed the destruction of Jerusalem. The shock of that momentous revolution was over, and Christians had been enabled to interpret it. There is no evidence to determine the date exactly. St. John, according to the Asiatic tradition recorded by Irenæus (II. 22. 5 ; III. 3. 4) lived " till the times of Trajan " (A.D. 98—117), and the writing of the Gospel must be placed at the close of his life. It is probable, therefore, that it may be referred to the last decennium of the first century, and even to the close of it.

Tradition is uniform in fixing St. John's residence at Ephesus (Iren. III. 3. 4; Polycr. ap. Euseb. *H. E.* III. 31 ; Clem. Alex. *Quis div. salv.* c. 42; Orig. ap. Euseb. *H. E.* III. 1, etc.), and naming that city as the place where he wrote his Gospel (Iren. III. 1. 1, etc.); and no valid objection has been brought against the belief which was preserved on the spot by a continuous succession of Church teachers.[1]

3. *The Object*

From what has already been said, it will be clear that the circumstances under which the fourth Gospel was written served to define its object. This is clearly expressed by St. John himself : *Many other signs did Jesus in the presence of His disciples which have not been written in this book; but these have been written that ye may believe* (πιστεύητε, cf. vi. 29) *that Jesus is the Christ, the Son of God, and that believing ye may have life in His name* (xx. 30 f.). The record is therefore a selection from abundant materials at the command of the writer, made by him with a specific purpose, first to create a particular conviction in his readers, and then in virtue of that conviction to bring life to them. The conviction itself which the Evangelist aims at producing is twofold, as corresponding with the twofold relation of Christianity to the chosen people and to mankind. He makes it his purpose to show that Jesus, who is declared by that human name to be truly and historically man, is at once *the Christ*, in whom all types and prophecies were fulfilled,[2] and also *the Son of God*,

[1] The denial of the Asiatic residence of St. John does not call for serious discussion. To suppose that the belief grew out of Irenæus' confusion of " John the presbyter " with " John the apostle," involves the further assumption that Polycarp himself led him into the error (Iren. *Ep. ad Flor.*). Comp. Steitz, *Stud. u. Krit.* 1868 ; Hilgenfeld, *Einl.* 394 ff.

[2] It is not without instruction to notice that writers of very different schools have unconsciously omitted the words " the Christ " in quoting this verse, and thereby obscured the full design of the Apostle. Among others I may quote as representatives :

Reuss, *Hist. de la Théologie Chrétienne*, ed. 2, II. 426, " Ceci, dit-il dans ses dernières lignes, ceci est écrit, afin que vous croyiez que Jésus est le Fils de Dieu, et afin que vous ayez la vie par cette croyance."

Weisz, *Lehrbuch d. Bibl. Theol.* Ausg. 2, s. 636, " Der Glaube, welcher die Bedingung des Heilsaneignung bildet . . . ist die zuversichtliche Ueberzeugung davon, dasz Jesus der Sohn Gottes ist."

Lias, *The Doctrinal System of St. John*, p. 2. [The purpose for which the Gospel was written] " is stated in express language by the author : ' These things have been written that ye might believe that Jesus is the Son of God, and that, believing, ye might have life through His name.' (John xx. 31)."

who is, in virtue of that divine being, equally near to all *the children of God*—His Father and their Father (xx. 17), —*scattered throughout the world* (xi. 52; comp. i. 49). The whole narrative must therefore be interpreted with a continuous reference to these two ruling truths, made clear by the experience of the first stage in the life of the Church; and also to the consequence which flows from them, that life is to be found in vital union with Him who is made known in this character (ἐν τῷ ὀνόματι αὐτοῦ). Each element in the fundamental conviction is set forth as of equal moment. The one (*Jesus is the Christ*) bears witness to the special preparation which God had made; the other (*Jesus is the Son of God*) bears witness to the inherent universality of Christ's mission. The one establishes the organic union of Christianity with Judaism; the other liberates Christianity from Jewish limitations.[1]

It will at once appear that this pregnant description of the object of the Gospel coincides completely with the view which has been given as to the date and occasion of its composition. To establish that *Jesus is the Christ* is to prove that Christianity is the true spiritual heir of Judaism, through which a divine society and a divine service have been established for all time. To establish that *Jesus is the Son of God* is to place the doctrine of St. Paul upon a firm basis, inasmuch as the Saviour is revealed in His essential relation of Creator to all the world. To establish that *life is* to be had *in His name*, is to raise all being, all thought, into a new region, where rests the hope (at least) of the reconciliation of the conflicts and contradictions of our present order.

So far then the fourth Gospel is distinguished from the other three in that it is shaped with a conscious design to illustrate and establish an assumed conclusion. If we compare the avowed purpose of St. John with that of St. Luke (i. 1—4), it may be said with partial truth that the inspiring impulse was in the one case doctrinal, and in the other case historical. But care must be taken not to exaggerate or misinterpret this contrast. Christian

---

[1] This definition of the object of the Gospel must be compared with the parallel definition of the object of the First Epistle, 1 John i. 1—4.

doctrine is history, and this is above all things the lesson
of the fourth Gospel. The Synoptic narratives are implicit dogmas, no less truly than St. John's dogmas are
concrete facts. The real difference is that the earliest
Gospel contained the fundamental facts and words which
experience afterwards interpreted, while the latest Gospel
reviews the facts in the light of their interpretation. But
in both cases the exactness of historical truth is para-
mount. The discovery of the law of phenomena does
not make the record of the phenomena less correct than
before in the hands of him who has ascertained it. On
the contrary, such knowledge keeps the observer from
many possibilities of error, while it enables him to regard
facts in new relations, and to present them in such a way
that they may suggest to others the general truth which
he has gained. The historic interest of St. John in the
substance of his narrative is, in other words, purified and
made more intense by the dogmatic significance with
which he feels that each incident is charged.

If the scope of the fourth Gospel is thus distinctly
apprehended in all its fulness according to the Evangelist's
own description, it becomes unnecessary to discuss at any
length the different special purposes which have been
assigned as the motive of his work. The narrative is not
in express design polemical, or supplementary, or didactic,
or harmonising; and yet it is all this, because it is the
mature expression of apostolic experience perfected by the
teaching of the Holy Spirit in the writer's own life and in
the life of the Church.

i. The Gospel is not specifically polemical (Iren. *Adv.*
Hær. iii. 11, Hieron. *Comm. in Matt.* Prol. ; comp. *De*
Virr. Ill. 9). It is quite true that many passages in the
Gospel of St. John are conclusive against particular points
of Ebionitic and Docetic error (comp. 1 John ii. 22, iv. 2)
and against false claims of the disciples of the Baptist
(comp. Acts xix. 3 f.) ; but it does not follow that it was
the particular object of St. John to refute these false
opinions. The full exhibition of the Truth was necessarily
their refutation ; and in this respect their existence may
have called attention to points which had been overlooked

or misunderstood before. But the first Epistle shows with what directness the Apostle would have dealt with adversaries if controversy had been the purpose immediately present to his mind.

ii. The same remark applies to the "supplemental" theory (Eusebius, *H. E.* iii. 24; comp. Hieron. *De Virr. Ill.* 9). As a matter of fact the fourth Gospel does supplement the other three, which it presupposes. It supplements them in the general chronology of the Lord's life, as well as in detailed incidents. But this is because the Gospel is the vital analysis of faith and unbelief. It traces in order the gradual development of the popular views of Christ among those to whom He came. As a natural consequence it records the successive crises in the divine revelation which happened in Jerusalem, the centre of the religious activity of the Jewish theocracy. The scope of the Gospel is from the nature of the case supplementary to that of the other three; and this being so, the history is also supplementary.

iii. But though the scope of the fourth Gospel is supplementary to that of the other three, it cannot rightly be said that the aim of the Evangelist was essentially didactic (comp. Clem. Alex. ap. Euseb. *H. E.* vi. 14) in such a sense that he has furnished an interpretation of the Gospel rather than a historical record. The substance of the narrative is distinctly affirmed to be facts (*these signs are written*); and the end contemplated is practical (*that ye may have life*), and speculative only so far as right opinion leads to right action.

iv. Once again: The conciliatory—irenical—effect of the Gospel cannot be questioned, but this effect is due to the teaching on Christ's Person which it discloses, and not to any conscious aim of the writer. Just as it rises above controversy while it condemns error, it preserves the characteristic truths which heresy isolated and misused. The fourth Gospel is the most complete answer to the manifold forms of Gnosticism, and yet it was the writing most used by Gnostics. It contains no formal narrative of the institution of sacraments, and yet it presents most fully the idea of sacraments. It sets forth with the strongest emphasis the failure of the ancient people, and yet it points out most clearly the significance of the dispensation which was committed to them. It brings together the many oppositions—antitheses—of life and thought, and leaves them in the light of the one supreme fact which reconciles all, *the Word became Flesh*; and we feel from first to last that this light is shining over the record of sorrow and triumph, of defeat and hope.

4. *The Plan*

The view which has been given of the Gospel enables us to form a general conception of what we must call its plan. This is, to express it as briefly as possible, the parallel development of faith and unbelief through the historical Presence of Christ. The Evangelist is guided in the selection, and in the arrangement, and in the treatment of his materials by his desire to fulfil this purpose. He takes a few out of the vast mass of facts at his disposal (xxi. 25, xx. 30), which are in his judgement suited to produce a particular effect. Every part of his narrative is referred to one final truth made clear by experience, that "Jesus is the Christ, the Son of God." He makes no promise to compose a life of Christ, or to give a general view of His teaching, or to preserve a lively picture of the general effect which He produced on average observers, or to compose a chapter on the general history of his own times, or to add his personal recollections to memoirs of the Lord already current; nor have we any right to judge his narrative by the standard which would be applicable to any one of such writings. He works out his own design, and it is our first business to consider how he works it out. When this is done we shall be in a position to consider fairly the historical characteristics of the Gospel.

The development and details of St. John's plan are considered at length elsewhere. Here it will be sufficient to indicate in a tabular form the outlines of the history.

THE PROLOGUE, i. 1—18.

The Word in His absolute, eternal Being; and in relation to Creation.

THE NARRATIVE, i. 19—xxi. 23.

The Self-revelation of Christ to the world and to the Disciples.

I.—THE SELF-REVELATION OF CHRIST TO THE WORLD (i. 19 —xii. 50).

    1. *The Proclamation* (i. 19—iv. 54).

        i. The testimony to Christ (i. 19—ii. 11)
        of *the Baptist*, i. 19—34,
           disciples, i. 35—51,
           signs (water turned to wine), ii. 1—11.

        ii. The work of Christ (ii. 13—iv. 54)
        in Judæa (Nicodemus), ii. 13—iii. 36,
           Samaria (the woman of Samaria), iv. 1—42,
           Galilee (the nobleman's son healed), iv. 43 —54.
           Unbelief as yet passive.

    2. *The Conflict* (v. 1—xii. 50).

        i. The Prelude (v., vi.),
        (a) *In Jerusalem* (the impotent man healed on the Sabbath), v.
        The Son and the Father.
        (b) *In Galilee* (the five thousand fed), vi.
        Christ and men.

        ii. The great Controversy (vii.—xii.).
        (a) *The Revelation of faith and unbelief*, vii. —x.
        The Feast of Tabernacles, vii., viii.
        The Feast of Dedication (the blind man healed on the Sabbath), ix., x.
        (b) *The decisive Judgement*, xi., xii.
        The final sign and its issues (the raising of Lazarus), xi.
        The close of Christ's public ministry, xii.

II.—THE SELF-REVELATION OF CHRIST TO THE DISCIPLES (xiii.—xxi.).

    1. *The last ministry of love* (xiii.—xvii.).
        i. The last acts of love (xiii. 1—30).

ii. The last discourses (xiii. 31—xvi. 33),
In the chamber, xiii. 31—xiv.,
On the way, xv., xvi.

iii. The prayer of consecration, xvii.

2. *The Victory through death* (xviii.—xx.).

i. The Betrayal (xviii. 1—11).

ii. The double Trial (xviii. 12—xix. 16).

iii. The end (xix. 17—42).

iv. The new life (xx.).

3. *The Epilogue*, xxi.

i. The Lord and the body of disciples (the miraculous draught of fishes), xxi. 1—14.

ii. The Lord and individual disciples (xxi. 15—23).

Concluding notes, xxi. 24, 25.[1]

Such in a rough outline appears to be the distribution of the parts of the Gospel. It will be felt at once how fragmentary the record is, and yet how complete. The incidents all contribute to the orderly development of the truths which it is the object of the Evangelist to commend to his readers. In developing the plan thus broadly defined he dwells on three pairs of ideas, witness and truth, glory and light, judgement and life. There is the manifold attestation of the divine mission: there is the progressive manifestation of the inherent majesty of the Son: there is the continuous and necessary effect which this manifestation produces on those to whom it is made; and the

---

[1] The data for fixing the chronology are very meagre. The following appears to be the best arrangement of the main events.

Early spring : the calling of the first disciples, i. 19—ii. 11.

First Passover (April), ii. 13—iii. 21 ;
iii. 22—iv. 54.

The Feast of the New Year (September), v. See Additional Note.

Second Passover (April), vi.

The Feast of Tabernacles (October), vii., viii.

The Feast of Dedication (December), ix., x. ;
xi., xii.

Third Passover (April), xiii.—xx.

narrative may be fairly described as the simultaneous
unfolding of these three themes, into which the great
theme of faith and unbelief is divided. A rapid survey of
their treatment will bring out many instructive features
in the composition.

(a) *The Truth and the Witness.* It is characteristic of
Christianity that it claims to be "the Truth." Christ
spoke of Himself as "the Truth" (xiv. 6). God is revealed
in Christ as "the only true (ἀληθινός) God" (xvii. 3). The
message of the Gospel is "the Truth." This title of
the Gospel is not found in the Synoptists, the Acts or the
Apocalypse; but it occurs in the Catholic Epistles (James
v. 19; 1 Pet. i. 22; 2 Pet. ii. 2), and in the Epistles of
St. Paul (2 Thess. ii. 12; 2 Cor. xiii. 8; Eph. i. 13, etc.).
It is specially characteristic of the Gospel and Epistles of
St. John.

According to the teaching of St. John, the fundamental
fact of Christianity includes all that "is" in each sphere.
Christ the Incarnate Word is the perfect revelation of the
Father: as God, He reveals God (i. 18). He is the perfect pattern of life, expressing in act and word the
absolute law of love (xiii. 34). He unites the finite and
the infinite (i. 14, xvi. 28). And the whole history of the
Christian Society is the progressive embodiment of this
revelation.

In the presence of Pilate, the representative of earthly
power, Christ revealed the object of His coming, as a
permanent fact, to be that He might "bear witness to the
truth" (γεγέννημαι, ἐλήλυθα, not ἦλθον, ἵνα μαρτυρήσω τῇ
ἀληθείᾳ, xviii. 37). This "Truth," it is implied, was already,
in some sense, among men even if it was unrecognised.
There were some who "were of the Truth," drawing, as it
were, their power of life from it (comp. 1 John ii. 21, iii. 19).
Over these Christ claimed the supremacy of a King.

Among the chosen people this testimony of conscience
was supplemented by the voice of the representative of the
prophets. The Baptist bore, and still bears, witness to
the Truth (v. 33, μεμαρτύρηκε).

But Christ came not only to maintain a Truth which
was present among men, but to make known a new fulness

of Truth. The "Truth came (ἐγένετο "was realised as the right issue of things") through Him" (i. 17; comp. v. 14 πλήρης . . . ἀληθείας). His teaching was "the Truth" (viii. 40; comp. xvii. 17, ὁ λόγος ὁ σός). He is Himself the Truth (xiv. 6).

And this work is carried out step by step by the Spirit (xvi. 13 ff.) who is sent in Christ's name by the Father (xiv. 26), as He also is sent by Christ Himself (xvi. 7). Under this aspect the Spirit, like Christ, is the Truth which He makes known (1 John v. 6).

And again, the whole sum of the knowledge of Christ and of the Spirit is "the Truth" (1 John ii. 21; 2 John 1), which can be recognised by man (John viii. 32, γνώσεσθε τὴν ἀλήθειαν), and become the object of fixed knowledge (1 John ii. 21, οἴδατε τὴν ἀλ.); though, on the other hand, men can withstand and reject its claims (viii. 44 f.; comp. Rom. i. 18).

So far the Truth is regarded as a whole without us (objectively), working and witnessing (3 John 8, 12). But at the same time the Spirit, as the Spirit of Truth, or rather of "the Truth," brings the Truth into direct communication with man's spirit (xiv. 17, xv. 26, xvi. 13; 1 John iv. 6, opposed to τὸ πν. τῆς πλάνης); and "the Truth" becomes an inward power in the believer (1 John i. 8, ii. 4; 2 John 2).

Truth therefore reaches to action. *We do* or *do not the Truth* (iii. 21; 1 John i. 6).[1] It follows that the reception of the Truth brings freedom (viii. 32), because the Truth corresponds with the law of our being. By the Truth we are sanctified (xvii. 17).

No one therefore can fail to see how inconsistent it is with the apostolic conception of Christianity to represent the Faith as antagonistic to any form of Truth. It is interpreted by every fragment of Truth. All experience is a commentary on it. And we must be careful to keep ourselves open to every influence of light.

The message which St. John has to convey in his

---

[1] This aspect of the Truth is brought out specially by St. Paul, who contrasts "unrighteousness" with "truth": Rom. i. 18, ii. 8; 1 Cor. xiii. 6; 2 Thess. ii. 12. Comp. Eph. iv. 24, v. 9.

Gospel is " the Truth," and this is commended to men by various forms of witness (μαρτυρία). There is nothing in the Synoptic Gospels to prepare for the remarkable development which he gives of this idea. It evidently belongs to a time when men had begun to reason about the faith, and to analyse the ground on which it rested. The end of the witness is the confirmation of the truth (xviii. 37); and the Evangelist, looking back upon his own experience, is able to distinguish the several forms which the witness assumed and still essentially retains.

The witness to Christ which he records is therefore manifold, and extends over the whole range of possible attestation of divine things. In due succession there is (1) the witness of the Father; (2) the witness of Christ Himself; (3) the witness of works; (4) the witness of Scripture; (5) the witness of the Forerunner; (6) the witness of disciples; and that which illuminates and quickens all, (7) the witness of the Spirit.

(1) The witness of the Father is that to which Christ appeals as the proper witness of Himself: *I (ἐγώ) receive not my witness from a man . . . the Father which sent me, He (ἐκεῖνος) hath borne witness concerning me* (v. 34, 37). *If I (ἐγώ) bear witness concerning myself, my witness is not true. There is another that beareth witness of me, and I know that the witness which He beareth concerning me is true* (v. 31 f.; contrast viii. 14). *I am he that beareth witness concerning myself, and the Father that sent me beareth witness concerning me* (viii. 18). This witness then is distinguished from the witness of a prophet (*e.g.*, John the Baptist), and from the witness of Christ standing (if we can so conceive) in the isolation of His Personality. It lies in the absolute coincidence between the will and words and works of Christ and the will of the Father, realised by Christ in His divine-human Person (*I know*, v. 32). Such witness carries conviction to men so far as they have themselves been brought into unity with God. Man can feel what is truly divine while he reaches after it and fails to attain to it. The sense of his own aspirations and of his own short-comings enables him to appreciate the perfection of Christ. Thus the witness of the Father is (what we speak

of as) the "character" of Christ. The witness is continuous, present and abiding (μαρτυρεῖ, μεμαρτύρηκε), and it reposes upon the general conception of God as Father (*the Father* not *my Father*), standing in this paternal relation to all men. As soon as the thought of "the Fatherhood of God" is gained, it is felt that "the Son" expresses it absolutely. The witness of this perfect coincidence therefore finds its cogency in the response which it calls out from the soul of man. Man recognises the voice as naturally and supremely authoritative (1 John v. 9).

(2) The witness of the Father finds a special expression in the witness of the Son concerning Himself. This witness is valid because it reposes on a conscious fellowship with God (comp. x. 30), in which no element of selfishness can find any place, and on a direct and absolute knowledge of divine things (iii. 11, 32 f.), and of a divine mission seen in its totality (viii. 14 ; comp. *v.* 55). In this sense Christ said, *Even if I bear witness concerning myself my witness is true, because I know whence I came and whither I go* (viii. 14). Such witness necessarily derives power from what can be seen of the witness of the Father in Christ's character. And more than this, Christ's claim to universal sovereignty lay in the fact that He came *into the world in order to bear witness to the truth* (xviii. 37). *Every one* therefore, He adds, *that is of the truth heareth my voice* (id.). Thus it is seen that the final power of the witness of Christ to Himself is derived from man's affinity to truth which is found perfectly in Him. *His sheep*, according to the familiar image, *know His voice* (x. 4 f.). And He has a special message for each : *He calleth (φωνεῖ) His own sheep by name* (x. 3). The end of this is that *he that believeth on Him hath the witness in himself* (1 John v. 10).

(3) This divine witness, the internal witness which is addressed to man's moral constitution, takes a special and limited form in the witness of works. Thus Christ said: *The witness which I have is greater than that of John ; for the works which the Father hath given me to accomplish, the very works that I do bear witness concerning me that the Father hath sent me* (v. 36, note). Within a narrow range, and in a concrete and sensible manner, His works revealed

His perfect communion with the Father (v. 17 ff.). Men
could see in them, if not otherwise, tokens of His real
nature and authority. *The works which I do in my Father's
name*, claiming a special connexion with Him, making
Him known as *my Father, these bear witness concerning me*
(x. 25; comp. xiv. 11, xv. 24). And this kind of witness
which was given in one form by Christ Himself during
His historical presence is still continued. His disciples
are enabled to perform *greater works* than those to which
He appealed (xiv. 12 ff.). The Christian Society has still
the living witness of " signs."

For in the record of the "works" of Christ, St. John draws
no line between those which we call natural and those
which we call supernatural. The separate " works " are
fragments of the one " work " (iv. 34, xvii. 4). Whether
they are predominantly works of power or of love, wrought
on the body or on the spirit, they have the same office and
end (comp. v. 20 f., 36, ix. 3 f., xiv. 10). They are "shown ":
they require, that is, a sympathetic interpretation (x. 32;
comp. v. 20). The earliest emotion which they produce
may be simply " wonder " (v. 20), but wonder is the first
step to knowledge. This follows both in its decisive
apprehension and in its progressive extension (x. 38, ἵνα
γνῶτε καὶ γινώσκητε).

Works therefore, according to St. John, are signs (vi. 26);
and their witness, from their want of directness and from
their outwardness of form, is secondary to that of " words "
(xiv. 11, xv. 22 ff.). The internal witness, according to
our mode of speaking, is placed above the external. The
former is an appeal to the spiritual consciousness, the
latter to the intellect.

(4) So far we have seen that the witness to Christ is
found in Himself, in what He is, and in what He did and
does through His disciples. But He stood also in a definite
relation to the past. Witness was borne to Him both by
the records of the ancient dispensation and by the last
of the prophets. *Ye search the Scriptures*, Christ said to
the Jews, *because ye think that in them ye have eternal life*—
that they are in themselves the end, and not the preparation for the end—*and they are they which witness*

concerning me; and ye will not come to me that ye may have life (v. 39, 40). Without Christ the Old Testament is an unsolved riddle. By the writings of Moses and the prophets (v. 46, i. 45) He was seen to be the goal and fulfilment of immemorial hopes, which became a testimony to Him in whom they were satisfied. The Old Testament was to the first age and is to all ages, if regarded in its broad and indisputable outlines, a witness to Christ.

(5) The witness of the Old Testament found a final expression in the latest of the prophets. John the Baptist occupied a position which was wholly peculiar. *He came for witness, to bear witness concerning the Light, that all men might believe through him* (i. 7). His own light was borrowed and kindled (v. 35, i. 8); yet it was such as to attract and arrest (v. 35), and served to prepare men for that which should follow. In this sense Christ appealed to it. *Ye have sent to John, and he hath borne witness to the truth. But I receive not my witness from a man, but these things I say that ye may be saved* (v. 33 f.). The witness was, so to speak, an accommodation to the moral condition of those for whom it was given. It was the attestation of a personal conviction based upon a specific proof. The Baptist realised his own character and office (i. 19 ff.); and he recognised Christ by the sign which had been made known to him (i. 32 ff.). He realised the sternest form of Judaism, and at the same time perceived the universality of that in which Judaism should be crowned. In a signal example he offered the witness of the leader of men who sways the thoughts of the multitude.

(6) The witness of the Baptist was to one decisive event. By this was revealed to him the relation of Christ to the Old Covenant of which he was himself the last representative. His was the individual witness of an exceptional man. To this was added the witness, so to speak, of common life. The witness of the disciples was in various degrees a witness to what they had experienced in their intercourse with Christ, a witness to facts. *Ye also*, Christ said to the eleven, *bear witness, because ye are with me from the beginning* (xv. 27). *He that hath seen hath*

borne witness (xix. 35).   *This is the disciple that witnesseth concerning these things and wrote these things* (xxi. 24; comp. 1 John i. 2, iv. 14).

(7) But in all these cases there was need of an interpreter. Neither the mission nor the Person of Christ could be understood at once. It was necessary that He should be withdrawn in order that the disciples might be able to receive the full revelation of His Nature.   This was their consolation in the prospect of persecution and hatred. *When the Paraclete is come whom I will send from the Father, even the Spirit of Truth, which proceedeth from the Father, He shall bear witness concerning me* (xv. 26).   In this witness lies the continual unfolding of the infinite significance of the Incarnation.   The Spirit takes of that which is Christ's, and declares it (xvi. 14). It is the Spirit, as St. John himself says elsewhere, *that beareth witness, because the Spirit is the truth* (1 John v. 6).

If now we look back over these seven types of witness to which St. John appeals in the Gospel, it will be seen that they cover the whole range of the possible proof of religious truth, internal and external.   The witness of the Father and of Christ Himself is internal, and rests on the correspondence of the Gospel with that absolute idea of the divine which is in man.   The witness of works and of Scripture is external and historical, and draws its force from the signs which the Gospel gives of fulfilling a divine purpose.   The witness of the prophets and of the disciples is personal and experiential, and lies in the open declaration of what men have found the Gospel to be. Lastly, the witness of the Spirit is for the believer the crown of assurance and the pledge of the progress of the Truth.

(b) *Light and Glory.* The second pair of words, Light and Glory, which characterise St. John's narrative, correspond to a certain extent with the Witness and the Truth. The Witness becomes effective through Light.   The Truth is revealed in Glory.

The description of God as Light (1 John i. 5) expresses in its final form that idea of self-communication which is realised in many ways.   The works of God are a revelation

of Him (i. 4 f., note); and among these man's own constitution, though this is not specially brought out by
St. John (comp. Matt. vi. 23; Luke xi. 35). The Word
as Light visited men (ix. 5, ὅταν) before the Incarnation
(i. 9 f.; comp. v. 38; Rom. ii. 15 f.), at the Incarnation
(viii. 12, xii. 46, iii. 19—21; comp. xi. 9 f.), and He still
comes (xiv. 21); even as the Spirit who still interprets His
" name " (xiv. 26, xvi. 13; comp. 1 John ii. 20 ff., 27).

St. John draws no distinction in essence between these
three different forms of revelation, in nature, in conscience,
in history: all alike are natural or supernatural, parts of
the same harmonious plan.   But man has not independently light in himself.   The understanding of the
outward revelation depends upon the abiding of the divine
word within (v. 37 f.).   Love is the condition of illumination (xiv. 22 ff.).   And the end of Christ's coming was that
those who believe in Him may move in a new region of
life (xii. 46), and themselves *become sons of light* (xii. 35 f.),
and so, as the last issue of faith, have *the light of life* (viii.
12).

Under the action of the Light the Truth is seen in Christ
as Glory.   Christ, " the light of the world," is seen by the
believer to be the manifested glory of God.

(1) Step by step the Gospel of St. John lays open the
progress of this manifestation.   The summary of its whole
course is given by the Apostle at the outset: *The Word
became flesh and tabernacled among us, and we beheld His
glory, glory as of an only son from a father* (i. 14), absolutely
representing, that is, Him from whom He came.   The
beginning of Christ's signs was a manifestation of His
glory (ii. 11), and that it might be so, it was shown only
when *the hour was come* (ii. 4).   For the glory of the Son
was not of His own seeking (viii. 50), but was wholly the
expression of His Father's will through Him (viii. 54).
And conversely the Son by His perfect conformity to the
Father's will *glorified the Father upon earth* in the fulfilment of His appointed work (xvii. 4), wherein He was
also glorified Himself (xvii. 10).

(2) The glory of Christ was therefore in a true sense the
glory of God.   *This sickness*, the Lord said in regard to

g

Lazarus, *is not unto death*, as its real issue, *but for the glory of God, that the Son of God may be glorified through it* (xi. 4). And so the restoration of Lazarus to life was a vision of *the glory of God* (xi. 40), as producing faith in Him whom He sent (xi. 42). The glorification of "the name" of the Father was the historic work of the Son (xii. 28). When the crisis was past, *Jesus saith, Now was the Son of man glorified* (ἐδοξάσθη), *and God was glorified in Him* (xiii. 31). At the end the correlation is not between the Son and the Father, but between the Son of man and God. In Him, little by little, under the conditions of human existence, the absolute idea of manhood was fulfilled.

(3) It follows that the thought of Christ's glory is extended beyond the Incarnation. The glory which was consummated through the Incarnation *he had with the Father before the world was* (xvii. 5); and when the prophet was allowed to look upon *the Lord, sitting upon a throne, high and lifted up* (Isa. vi. 1 ff.), what he saw was *the glory of Christ* (xii. 41).

(4) And on the other hand, as the glory of the Son is extended backward, so also the glory of *Jesus, the Son of man*, consummated on the divine side even in God (xiii. 32) at the Ascension (vii. 39, xii. 16), to which the way was opened by the Passion (xii. 23, xiii. 31), is to be realised by men little by little in the course of ages. The petitions of believers are granted *that the Father may be glorified in the Son* (xiv. 13): their fruitfulness, already regarded as attained, is a source of this glory (xv. 8). And one chief office of the Spirit is *to glorify Christ* by making Him more fully known (xvi. 14).

(c) *Judgement and Life.* The glory of Christ and of God in Christ, which is thus presented as the substance of revelation, belongs to a spiritual sphere. It can therefore only be perceived by those who have true spiritual vision. As an inevitable consequence, the revelation of the divine glory carries with it a judgement, a separation.

The fundamental notion of this Judgement lies in the authoritative and final declaration of the state of man as he is in relation to God and standing apart from God. It follows as a necessary consequence that Judgement in this sense is contrasted with "salvation," "life." *He that believeth* [on the Son] *is not judged* (iii. 18). He *hath passed out of death into life* (v. 24; comp. v. 29). For Christ has life (i. 4, v. 26), and His words are life (vi. 53; comp. vi. 68, xii. 50). He came to offer life to men (x. 28, xvii. 2), that they too may have it (iii. 15 f., v. 40, vi. 40, x. 10). He is indeed Himself "the Life" (xi. 25, xiv. 6) and the support of life (vi. 33, 35, 48, 51; comp. iv. 14). To know the Father and Him is eternal life (xvii. 3); and he that "believeth in Him," he that is united with Him by faith, hath the life as a present possession (iii. 36, v. 24, vi. 47, 54; comp. viii. 12), which otherwise he cannot have (vi. 53). The relation of the believer to Christ is made parallel with the relation of the Son to the Father (vi. 57). *Because I live*, Christ said to the eleven, *ye shall live also* (xiv. 19). Thus the believer, in virtue of the vital connexion which he has realised with God in His Son, is no longer considered apart from Him. Judgement therefore in his case is impossible.

This conception of judgement explains the apparent contradiction in the views which are given of the part of Christ in regard to it. On the one side judgement is realised as self-fulfilled in the actual circumstances of life. *This is the judgement, that the light is come into the world and men loved the darkness rather than the light, for their works were evil* (iii. 19); and by this contrast the unbeliever is convicted from within: *he hath one that judgeth him: the word that I spake*, Christ said, *shall judge him at the last day* (xii. 48). Hence it is said: *God sent not the Son into the world to judge the world, but that the world may be saved through Him* (iii. 17). *I came not to judge the world, but to save the world* (xii. 47).

And yet on the other side judgement belongs to Christ, and satisfies the utmost ideal of judgement because it reposes upon adequate knowledge. Thus we read: *the Father hath given all judgement unto the Son* (v. 22; comp. v. 27); and *for judgement* (κρίμα) *came I into this world....* (ix. 39; comp. viii. 26). *I judge no man; yea, and if I* (ἐγώ) *judge, my judgement is true*, ἀληθινή, viii. 15 f.). *As I hear I judge, and my judgement is just* (v. 30).

Striking as the contrast between these passages appears to be, it is only necessary to consider what the judgement is in order to feel their harmony. Spiritual judgement is a consequence involved in the rejection of the revelation which Christ made. His will was to unite men to Himself, so that they might have life and not be judged. So far then as they rejected Him, and stood away from Him, His Presence showed them as they truly were. He judged them; and judgement was equivalent to condemnation. Thus the exhibition of the contrast of the true and the false became one of the means for developing belief and unbelief according to the character of Christ's hearers (viii. 26). Whatever might be the result, His message must be delivered.

In one sense, therefore, judgement, like the gift of life, is immediate. It lies in the existence of an actual relation (iii. 18) which carries with it its final consequences. In another sense it is still future, so far as it will be realised in a spiritual order of being *in the last day* (xii. 48). There is *a resurrection of life* and *a resurrection of judgement* (v. 29), in which the issues of both begun here will be completely fulfilled. Meanwhile the process is going on upon earth. The manifestation of perfect holiness presented to the world in perfect self-sacrifice (v. 30) has set up a standard which cannot be put out of sight. Under this aspect Christ's coming was a sentence of judgement ($\kappa\rho\iota\mu\alpha$, ix. 39). The judgement of the sovereign power of the world in the Passion (xii. 31) has left men no excuse (see xvi. 11, note). In that they can see the mind of God, and according as they surrender themselves to it, or resist it, they find life or judgement.

So far the judgement is self-fulfilled. It cannot but be carried out. The word of Christ sooner or later must justify itself (xii. 48). There is no need that He should seek to assert and vindicate its supremacy. *There is one that seeketh and judgeth* (viii. 50), the eternal power of righteousness symbolised in the Law (v. 45), and expressed in the Gospel (xii. 48 ff.).

But though this is so, the idea of divine action is never lost in the Bible in an abstraction, however emphatic. And while the eternal necessity of judgement is thus set forth, the historical execution of judgement, both present and final, is recognised as a work of the Son ; and though it was not the purpose of His mission, yet it was committed to Him in virtue of His mission. *The Father doth not judge any man, but hath given all judgement to the Son* (v. 22). Even as the Father gave Him *to have life in Himself,* and so to be a spring of life to all who are united with Him, so also He *gave Him authority to execute judgement because He is a Son of man*—not *the* Son of man—(v. 27), because He is truly man, and not only the representative of humanity. His judgement, therefore (comp. Heb. iv. 14 ff.), is essentially united with His complete sympathy with man's nature, and extends to the fulness of human life. It finds place always and everywhere.

These contrasts bring out into full relief the conflict between faith and unbelief, which, as has been said, is the main subject of St. John's Gospel. In the Synoptic Gospels faith occupies a different position. It is in these almost exclusively relative to a particular object (Matt. viii. 10, ix. 2, 22, 29, etc. ; Mark ix. 23, etc.). Only once does the full expression for faith in the Person of Christ occur (πιστεύειν εἰς, Matt. xviii. 6, ‖ Mark ix. 42). In St. John, on the other hand, this is the characteristic form under which faith is presented. The simple noun is not found in his Gospel. Faith is the attitude of the whole believing man. Such faith in Christ is the condition of eternal life (i. 12, vi. 40). To produce it was the object of the Evangelist (xx. 31). And the history marks in typical crises the progress of its development.

The first sign is followed by an access of faith in the disciples (ii. 11). The first entrance into Jerusalem was followed by faith disturbed by preconceived ideas (ii. 23, iii. 12 ff.). The preaching in Samaria called out a complete confession of faith (iv. 39 ff.), which stands in contrast with the faith resting on signs which followed in Galilee (iv. 48 ff.).

From this point active unbelief appears side by side with faith. By claiming authority over the Sabbath, and "making Himself equal with God " (v. 17 f.), the Lord offered a test of devotion to those who followed Him :

He fulfilled that to which Moses pointed (v. 39, 45 ff.). The decisive trial in Galilee caused a fresh division between those who had hitherto been disciples. It was now revealed that life was to be gained by the personal appropriation of the virtue of Christ's Life and Death (vi. 53 ff.). Some turned aside, and St. Peter confessed the Apostolic faith even in the mysterious prospect of the Passion (vi. 66 ff.). At the Feast of Tabernacles the antagonism of the hierarchy was more decided (vii. 32, 47 ff.), and the Lord traced it to its source in an analysis of the spirit of those who believed Him with a view to the execution of their own designs (viii. 31, note). At the same time He revealed His pre-existence (viii. 31 ff., 58). The separation between the old Church and the new, which was implicitly included in these discourses, was openly shown in the scenes which followed. Christ offered Himself openly as the object of faith as " the son of man " (ix. 35 ff.), and declared the universality of His work (x. 16). The raising of Lazarus, which carried with it the condemnation of the Lord, showed Him to be the conqueror of death and through death (xi. 25 f., 50, xii. 23 ff.). So the public revelation was completed, and with it faith and unbelief were brought to their last issue (xii. 37 ff.).

The last discourses and the last prayer point to the future victories of faith ; and the narrative closes with the beatitude of the Risen Christ : *Blessed are they that have not seen, and yet have believed* (xx. 29), which crowned the loftiest confession of faith triumphant over doubt: *My Lord and my God* (xx. 28).

Even from this rapid summary it will be seen that the self-revelation of Christ became stage by stage the occasion of fuller personal trust and more open personal antagonism. In Him *thoughts from many hearts were revealed* (Luke ii. 35). And St. John lays open the course of the original conflict which is the pattern of all conflicts to the end of time.

5. *The Style*

The characteristic repetition and development of the three pairs of ideas, Witness and Truth, Glory and Light,

Judgement and Life, in the structure of St. John's Gospel, serve to indicate the peculiarities of the style of the book. There is both in the vocabulary and in the form of the sentences a surprising simplicity, which becomes majestic by its solemn directness.

(a) It is not necessary to dwell upon the vocabulary. Any one who will trace out the use of the six words already discussed will feel how the apparent monotony contains a marvellous depth and fulness. An examination of other words, as *sign* (σημεῖον), and *works* (ἔργα), and *name* (ἐν τῷ ὀνόματι, εἰς τὸ ὄνομα), *the Father* (ὁ πατήρ) and *my Father* (ὁ πατήρ μου), the *world* (κόσμος, not ὁ αἰὼν οὗτος and the like), to *love*, to *know* (εἰδέναι and γινώσκειν), will lead to the same conclusion (compare Additional Notes on i. 10, iv. 21). The apparent sameness of phraseology produces throughout an impressive emphasis.

(b) This emphatic monotony is still more observable in the form and in the combination of the sentences. The constructions are habitually reduced to the simplest elements. To speak of St. John's Gospel as "written in very pure Greek" is altogether misleading. It is free from solecisms, because it avoids all idiomatic expressions. The grammar is that which is common to almost all language. Directness, circumstantiality, repetition, and personality, are the characteristic marks of the separate sentences. And the sentences and thoughts are grouped together in a corresponding manner. They are co-ordinated and not subordinated. The sequence of the reasoning is not wrought out, but left for sympathetic interpretation.

The narrative is uniformly direct. Even the words and opinions of others are given directly and not obliquely. Any one of the detailed incidents in St. John's narrative will illustrate this characteristic of his style. Thus we read in the opening scene : *This is the witness of John when the Jews sent . . . to ask him, Who art thou ? and he confessed . . . I am not the Christ. And they asked him, What then ? Art thou Elijah ? And he saith, I am not . . .* (i. 19 ff.). And again, *Certain of the multitude therefore, when they heard these words, said, This is of a truth the Prophet. Others said,*

This is the Christ. But some said, What, doth the Christ come out of Galilee? (vii. 40 f.; comp. ii. 3 ff., iv. 27 ff., v. 10 ff., vi. 14, viii. 22, ix. 2 ff., etc.).[1]

It is a part of the same method that illustrative details are added parenthetically or as distinct statements, and not wrought in the texture of the narrative (vi. 10, iv. 6, x. 22, xiii. 30, xviii. 40).

The circumstantiality of St. John's style is a necessary result of this directness. Each element in the action is distinguished, as a general rule, and set out clearly. Thus while the other Evangelists write habitually according to the common Greek idiom, [*Jesus*] *answering said* (ἀποκριθεὶς εἶπε), St. John never uses this form, but writes instead [*Jesus*] *answered and said* (ἀπεκρίθη καὶ εἶπεν). He places the two parts of the act in equal prominence; and though it might appear at first sight that the phrases are exactly equivalent, yet the co-ordination of details brings a certain definiteness to the picture which fixes the thought of the reader. The same tendency is shown in St. John's analysis of other actions, *Jesus cried aloud and said* (xii. 44). *Jesus cried aloud in the temple, teaching and saying* (vii. 28). *John beareth witness of Him and hath cried, saying* . . . (i. 15). *They questioned him and said* (i. 25). In these and similar cases it will be found that the separation of the whole into its parts adds to the impressiveness, and to the meaning of the description.

One remarkable illustration of this peculiarity is found in the combination of the positive and negative expression of the same truth. *All things were made through Him, and without Him was not any thing made* (i. 3). *He confessed, and denied not* (i. 24). *Jesus did not trust Himself unto them, for that He knew all men, and because He needed not*

---

[1] This directness of construction is so universal in the Gospel that the only example (so far as I have observed) of an oblique sentence is in iv. 51, where the true reading appears to be *met him, saying that his son liveth*, in place of *met him and told him, saying, Thy son liveth* ; for, on the other hand, the common oblique reading in xiii. 24 is incorrect ; and the vivid phrase, *and saith to him, Say, who is it?* must be substituted for *that he should ask who it should be of whom he spake.*

This is in fact a characteristic of the New Testament style generally ; see Winer, § LX. 9 ; but in St. John it is most marked.

that any one should bear witness concerning man (ii. 24 f.).
*God . . . gave His only Son that whosoever believeth on Him
may not perish but have eternal life* (iii. 16). Comp. x. 5,
xvii. 20; 1 John i. 6, ii. 4, 27.

The circumstantiality of St. John's style leads to frequent
repetition of the subject or of the significant word in a
sentence (i. 1, *Word*; i. 7, *witness*; i. 10, *world*; iv. 22,
worship; v. 31 f., *witness*; vi. 27, *meat*; xi. 33, *weeping*).

Such repetitions are singularly marked in the record of
dialogues, in which the persons are constantly brought
into prominence. Sentence after sentence begins with
words, "Jesus said," "the Jews said," and the like, so that
the characters in the great conflict are kept clearly present
to the mind of the reader in sharp contrast (ii. 18 ff., iv.
7 ff., viii. 48 ff., x. 23 ff.).

This usage leads to what has been called above the
personality of St. John's narrative. This is shown by the
special frequency with which he introduces a demonstra-
tive pronoun to call back the subject, when a clause has
intervened between the subject and the verb. This he
does in two ways. Sometimes he employs the pronoun of
present reference: *He that abideth in me and I in him, this
man* (οὗτος) *beareth much fruit* (xv. 5; comp. vii. 18, etc.);
and sometimes, which is the more characteristic usage, the
pronoun of remote, isolated reference: *He that entereth not
by the door . . . that man* (ἐκεῖνος) *is a thief and a robber*
(x. 1; comp. i. 18, 33, v. 11, 37, 38, xii. 48, xiv. 21, 26,
xv. 26).

Another feature of the same kind is the frequency of
St. John's use of the personal pronouns, and especially
of the pronoun of the first person. In this respect much
of the teaching of the Lord's discourses depends upon
the careful recognition of the emphatic reference to His
undivided Personality. *Yea, and if I* (ἐγώ) *judge—I, who
am truly God, and truly man—my judgement is true; for I
am not alone, but I and the Father that sent me* (viii. 16).
In this case, as in most cases, the pronoun calls attention
to the nature of the Lord: elsewhere it marks the isolation
(so to speak) of His personality; so that we read two
sentences which, being in appearance directly contra-

dictory, are harmonised by giving due emphasis to the exact force of the pronoun (v. 31, viii. 14, note).

(c) The method of combining sentences in St. John corresponds completely with the method of their separate construction. The simplicity, directness, circumstantiality, repetition, which mark the constituent sentences, mark also whole sections of his work. Words, sentences, paragraphs follow one another in what must appear to an unreflecting reader needless iteration, though in fact it is by this means that the central thought is placed in varied lights, so that its fulness can at last be grasped. The multiplication of simple elements in this instance, as elsewhere, produces in the end an effect of commanding grandeur, and so the student learns to pause in order that he may carefully consider the parts which separately contribute to it. (See, for example, ch. xvii.)

The most obvious illustration of this feature lies in St. John's constant habit of framing his record of events and discourses without connecting particles. When the feeling is most intense clause follows clause by simple addition. No conjunction binds the parts together. The details are given severally, and the reader is left to seize them in their unity (iv. 7, 10 ff., xi. 34, 35, xiv. 15 ff., xv. 1—20).

At the same time St. John does in fact insist more than the other Evangelists upon the connexion of facts, even if he commonly leaves them in simple juxtaposition. His most characteristic particle in narrative (it is rare in the discourses) is *therefore* (οὖν), and this serves in very many cases to call attention to a sequence which is real, if not obvious. *There arose* therefore *a question on the part of John's disciples with a Jew about purifying* (iii. 25). *When* therefore *He heard that he was sick, He abode for the time two days in the place where He was* (xi. 6). Comp. iii. 29, iv. 46, vii. 28.

In like manner the unusual frequency of the phrase *in order that* (ἵνα), which marks a direct object, is a sign of the habitual tendency of St. John to regard things in their moral and providential relations. Even where the usage departs most widely from the classical standard, it is possible to see how the irregular construction springs out of a characteristic mode of thought (*e.g.*, iv. 34, v. 36, vi. 29, viii. 56, xii. 23, xiii. 34, xvii. 3); and frequently the particle suggests a profound interpretation of the divine counsel (v. 20, x. 17, xii. 38, xv. 8, xvi. 2).

The simple co-ordination of clauses is frequently assisted by the repetition of a marked word or phrase, such as occurs in separate sentences. In this way a connexion is established between two statements, while the idea is carried forward in a new direction. Sometimes the subject is repeated: *I am the good Shepherd. The good Shepherd layeth down his life for the sheep* (x. 11). Sometimes a word is taken up from a former clause and repeated with significant emphasis: *Greater love hath no man than this, that a man lay down his life for his friends. Ye are my friends . . . No longer do I call you servants . . . but I have called you friends . . .* (xv. 13 ff.). Sometimes a clause is repeated which gives (so to speak) the theme of the passage: *I am the door of the sheep . . . I am the door: by me if any man enter in, he shall be saved . . .* (x. 7 ff.). *I am the good Shepherd: the good Shepherd layeth down his life for the sheep . . . I am the good Shepherd . . . and I lay down my life for my sheep* (x. 11, 14). *I am the true vine . . . I am the vine: ye are the branches* (xv. 1, 5). Sometimes a clause is repeated which gives a closing cadence: *The world hated them because they are not of the world, even as I am not of the world . . . They are not of the world, even as I am not of the world . . . Sanctify them in the truth . . . that they themselves may be sanctified in truth* (xvii. 14 ff.). Three times in the sixth chapter the clause recurs: *I will (may) raise him up at the last day* (39, 40, 44). And even in the simple narrative of St. Peter's denial the scene is impressed upon the reader by the solemn repetition of the words: *Peter was standing and warming himself* (xviii. 18, 25).[1]

(*d*) This repetition in some cases leads to a perfect poetic parallelism (xiv. 26, 27).

And in fact the spirit of parallelism, the instinctive

---

[1] So also words are repeated through considerable sections of the Gospel: *love, to love* (xiii.—xvii.); *life* (v., vi.); *light* (viii.—xii.).

perception of symmetry in thought and expression, which
is the essential and informing spirit of Hebrew poetry,
runs through the whole record, both in its general
structure and in the structure of its parts. From first to
last the Truth is presented, so to speak, in ever-widening
circles. Each incident, each discourse, presupposes what
has gone before, and adds something to the result.

6.   *Historical Exactness*

Our inquiry up to this point has established beyond
doubt that the structure of the fourth Gospel corresponds
with the fulfilment of a profound purpose. It is composed
both generally and in detail with singular symmetry.
There is a growing purpose wrought out from stage to
stage in the great divisions of the record; and there are
subtle and minute traits in each separate narrative which
reveal to careful examination the presence of an informing
idea throughout it. The correspondences of part with
part may indeed be due as much to the one fundamental
conception of the whole work as to special and conscious
adaptation of details; but none the less we must feel that
the historical elements are means to an end; that the
narrative expresses distinctly (as it professes to do) the
writer's interpretation of the events with which he deals.
We must feel that it is not an exhaustive exposition (so
far as the Evangelist's knowledge went) of the incidents
of the Lord's life; that it does not preserve some features
of His work which were unquestionably prominent; that
we could not put together from it a complete picture of
Jesus of Nazareth as He *went about doing good, and healing
all that were oppressed of the devil* (Acts x. 38). We allow,
or rather we press, the fact that the fourth Gospel, so
far as it is regarded as a biography, or as a biographical
sketch, is confined to certain limited aspects of the Person
and Life and Work with which it deals. But while we
make the fullest acknowledgement of these truths, we
affirm also that the literal accuracy of the contents of
the Gospel is not in any way prejudiced by the existence
of this particular purpose. The historical illustrations
of the writer's theme—if we even so regard the incidents

which he relates—are no less historical because they are illustrations : the Evangelist's conception of the real significance of Christ's Presence is not to be set aside because it is his conception : the special traits which are given are in no degree upon to suspicion, because they are special traits emphasised with a definite object.   Neither the apostolical authorship nor the historical trustworthiness of the narrative is affected by the admission that the writer fulfils his work, according to his own words, with an express purpose in view.

The first point is not before us now ; but there is one argument directly bearing upon it, which underlies very much of the popular criticism of the Gospel though it is not very often put into a distinct shape, which may be most conveniently noticed here.   It is sometimes plainly said, and more often silently assumed, that an Apostle could not have spoken of One with whom he had lived familiarly, as the writer of the fourth Gospel speaks of the Lord.   In reply to this argument one sentence only is necessary.   In order to have any force the argument takes for granted all that is finally at issue, and implies that it is *not* true that "the Word became flesh."   If, on the other hand, this revelation is true, as we believe, then the fourth Gospel helps us to understand how the over-whelming mystery was gradually made known : how the divine Nature of Christ was revealed little by little to those with whom He had conversed as man.   Unless our faith be false, we may say that we cannot conceive any way in which it could have been historically realised except that which is traced out in the experience reflected in the writings of St. John.   The Incarnation is confessedly a great mystery, in every sense of the word, but no fresh difficulty is occasioned by the fact that in due time it was laid open to those among whom the Son of God had moved.

Moreover, it may be added, the difficulty of admitting that an Apostle came to recognise the true divinity of One with whom he had lived as man with man is not done away by denying the apostolic authorship of the Gospel. The most conspicuous critics who refuse to assign the

Gospel to St. John agree in assigning the Apocalypse to him ; and it is no easier for us to understand how (not to quote xxii. 13) an Apostle could speak of the Master whom he had followed to the Cross as being the Holy and the True, who has the key of David, " who openeth, and no man shutteth ; and shutteth, and no man openeth " (iii. 7), as joined with " Him that sitteth on the throne," in being " worthy to receive blessing, and honour, and glory, and might, for ever and ever " (v. 13), than to understand how he could look back upon His *life* as the life of the Incarnate Word.   The Christology of the Gospel and the Christology of the Apocalypse are alike, we may venture to say, historically inexplicable unless we take as the key to their interpretation the assertion of the fact, "the Word became flesh," apprehended under the action of the Spirit, in the consciousness of those who had known Christ "from the Baptism of John to the Resurrection."

These considerations, however, carry us away from our immediate subject; for we are not concerned at present with the apostolic authorship of the Gospel.   We have to inquire how far its trustworthiness is affected by the existence of a specific didactic design in the writing.   But before discussing this question one other topic must be referred to, only to be set aside, which will be examined in detail afterwards.   The arguments against the trustworthiness of the Gospel drawn from the fact that its contents do not for the most part coincide with the contents of the Synoptic Gospels may be dismissed, or, at least, held in suspense.   For this end it will be enough to insist on the obvious fact that a general difference in the contents of two narratives relating to a complex history, which are both avowedly incomplete, cannot be used to prejudice the accuracy of either.   And the most cursory consideration of the fragmentariness of the records of Christ's life will make it evident that the mere addition of the facts related by St. John to those preserved in the other Gospels cannot create any difficulty.   They do not differ in kind from incidents related by the Synoptists; and we have no external means for determining the principles by which the choice of incidents embodied in the Synoptic narratives was determined. There is certainly no reason for supposing that these narratives would have included the incidents peculiar to St. John, if they had been familiarly known at the time when the records were drawn up. The Synoptists indicate summarily cycles of events which they do not relate; and St. John refers definitely to "many other signs" with which he was personally acquainted.

Thus we are brought back to the proper subject of our inquiry. Does the author of the fourth Gospel forfeit his claim to observe accuracy of fact because the facts are selected with a view to a definite purpose? He professes to write, as we have seen, in the hope of creating in others the faith which he holds himself (xix. 35, xx. 31). Now that faith is in reality a special interpretation of all history drawn from a special interpretation of One Life. We may therefore modify our question and ask, Does the Evangelist forfeit his claim to be a truthful historian, because he turns his eye steadily to the signs of the central laws of being? The answer to the question must be sought finally in the conditions of the historian's work. These conditions include in every case choice, compression, combination of materials. And he fulfils his work rightly who chooses, compresses, combines his materials according to a certain vital proportion. In other words, the historian, like the poet, cannot but interpret the facts which he records. The truth of history is simply the truth of the interpretation of an infinitude of details contemplated together. The simplest statement of a result presents a broad generalisation of particulars. The generalisation may be true or false; it may be ruled by an outward or by an inward principle; but in any case it only represents a total impression of the particulars seen in one way. It does not represent either all the particulars or all the impressions which they are capable of producing. What is called pure "objective" history is a mere phantom. No one could specify, and no one would be willing to specify, all the separate details which man's most imperfect observation can distinguish as elements in any one "fact"; and the least reflection shows that there are other elements not less numerous or less important than those open to our observation, which cannot be observed by us, and which yet go towards the fulness of the " fact." The subjectivity of history is consequently a mere question of degree. A writer who looks at the outside of things, and reproduces the impression which this would convey to average men, is as far from the whole truth as the writer who brings his whole power to bear upon an individual realisation of it. Thus every record of a " fact" is necessarily limited to the record of representative details concerning it. The truthfulness of the historian as a narrator lies therefore in his power of selecting these details so as to convey to others the true idea of the fact which he has himself formed. In this respect the literal accuracy of any number of details is no guarantee for the accuracy of the impression conveyed by the sum of them regarded as a whole ; and it is no paradox to say that a " true " detail which disturbs the proportion of the picture becomes in the connexion false.

What has been said of separate " facts " is obviously true of the sequence of facts. It is impossible not to feel that a true conception of the character of a life (if such a phrase may be used) of the spirit of a social movement would illuminate the connexion and meaning of the external details in which they are manifested, and that many details regarded externally would be liable to the gravest misapprehension if the conception were either false or wanting. And further, it is no less clear that the necessity for this interpretative power becomes more urgent as the subject becomes more complex.

There is undoubtedly at present a strong feeling in favour of realistic, external, history ; but it may reason-ably be questioned whether this fashion of opinion will be permanent, and it is obviously beset by many perils. Realistic history often treats only of the dress and not of the living frame, and it can never go beyond the outward circumstances of an organisation which is inspired by one vital power. The photographer is wholly unable to supply the function of the artist ; and realism must be subordinated to the interpretation of the life, if history is to take its true place as a science. This is the thought which underlies the Hebrew type of historic record. In the Old Testament the prophet is the historian. The facts which he records are significant, if fragmentary, expressions of an inner divine law wrought out among men. His interest is centred in the life which is manifested in action, but not exhausted by it. His aim is to reveal this life to others through the phenomena which the life alone makes truly intelligible to him.

We are not now concerned to inquire whether the prophetic interpretation of the life of men and nations and humanity be true or false. All that needs to be insisted upon is that the historian must have some view of the life whereby the events which he chronicles are held together. This view will influence him both in the choice of incidents and in the choice of details. And he will be the best historian who grasps the conception of the life most firmly, and who shows the absolute and eternal in the ordinary current of events. For him each event will be a sign.

Now whatever debates may arise on other points it cannot be doubted that the writer of the fourth Gospel has a distinct conception of a spiritual law of the life of humanity which found its final realisation in the Incarnation. This conception is therefore his clue in the choice and arrangement of facts. He takes just so many events and so much of each as will illustrate the central truth which he finds in a particular view of the Person of Christ. If his view of Christ be right, it cannot be seriously questioned that the traits on which he chiefly dwells are intrinsically natural; and no other view appears to be able to explain the phenomena of the belief attested by the earliest Christian literature, the letters of St. Paul and the Apocalypse, and by the existence of the Christian Church. Thus the Gospel of St. John adds that express teaching on the relation of Christ to God—of the Son to the Father—which underlies the claims to exclusive and final authority made by Him in the Synoptists. And the definiteness of the Evangelist's aim does not diminish but rather increases his interest in the exact conditions and circumstances under which Christ acted and spoke; for

h

our historic interest must always vary directly with our sense of the importance of the history.

Some of these points will come before us again in greater detail, but so much at least is clear, that the " subjectivity " of the fourth Evangelist affords in itself no presumption against his historical accuracy. Every historian is necessarily subjective. And it must be shown that the Evangelist's view of the Person of Christ, which is established independently of his Gospel, is false, before any argument against his trustworthiness can be drawn from a representation of Christ's works and words which corresponds with that view.

It is then no disparagement of the strict historical character of the fourth Gospel that the writer has fulfilled the design which he set before himself, of recording such "signs" out of the whole number of Christ's works as he considered likely to produce a specific effect. But even if it is admitted that historical exactness is generally reconcilable in theory with the execution of a particular design in the selection and exhibition and combination of facts, and further that this particular design may be the interpretation of the innermost meaning of the life, while it includes only a small fraction of the outward events, yet it will be urged that this method of explanation does not apply to all the phenomena of St. John's Gospel; that the discourses of the Lord, in especial as given there, cannot be regarded otherwise than as free compositions of the Evangelist; that their contents are monotonous and without progress from first to last; that they are of the same character under different circumstances; that they have no individuality of style ; that, on the contrary, they are almost indistinguishable in form and substance from the first epistle in which the writer speaks in his own person, and from the speeches which he places in the mouth of other characters, as the Baptist. These objections, it will be seen, are quite independent of any supposed incompatibility of the accounts of St. John and of the Synoptists, and require a separate examination. They arise out of the study of the book itself, and must be considered first. The apparent contrasts between the records of the teaching of the Lord given in the first three Gospels and in the fourth will be noticed afterwards.

1. What has been already said as to the conditions which determine the selection of representative details and of representative incidents in a narrative of events applies with necessary limitations to the historical record of teaching. It is obvious that if a record of a debate of several hours' length is to be compressed into a few sentences, the value of the record will depend not upon the literal reproduction of the exact words used here and there or in a brief episode of the discussion, but upon the power of the historian to enter into the spirit of the debate and to sketch its outline in right proportion. The thoughts of the speakers are more important than the style of the speakers. And it is quite conceivable that the meaning and effect of a long discourse, when reduced to a brief abstract, may be conveyed most truly by the use of a different style, and even, to a certain extent, of different language from that actually employed.

Again : the style of a speaker enters in very various degrees into his teaching, according to his subject and his circumstances. At one time it is of the essence : at another time, it is wholly subordinate to the general drift of the exposition. The keen, pregnant saying, the vivid illustration must be preserved exactly, or their character is lost. The subtle argument may be just touched suggestively, so that the sympathetic reader can supply the links which cannot be given in full. A many-sided speaker will thus furnish materials for very different studies. But it would be wholly wrong to conclude that the sketch which preserves most literally those fragments of his words, which are capable of being so preserved, is more true than the sketch which gives a view of the ultimate principles of his doctrine. The former may give the manner and even the outward characteristics : the latter may reveal the soul.

Now to apply these principles to the discourses contained in the fourth Gospel, it is undeniable that the discourses of the Lord which are peculiar to St. John's

Gospel are, for the most part, very brief summaries of elaborate discussions and expositions in relation to central topics of faith. It is wholly out of the question that they can be literally complete reports of what was said. From the necessities of the case the Evangelist has condensed his narrative. He has not given, and he could not have given, consistently with the nature of this work, all the words which were actually spoken ; and this being so, it follows that he cannot have given the exact words or only the words which were spoken. Compression involves adaptation of phraseology. And when once we realise the inevitable conditions of condensation, we find ourselves constrained to trust (in this case as in others) to the insight and power of him who selects, arranges, emphasises words which are in his judgement best suited to convey the proportionate impression of discourses which he apprehends in their totality.

One or two illustrations will show how a conversation is compressed in St. John's narrative. A simple example is found in xii. 34. The question of the Jews turns upon the title "the Son of man," which has not been recorded in the context. But it is easy to see how the previous references to the sufferings of Christ in connexion with the universality of His mission gave a natural opportunity for the use of it. The Evangelist, however, has noticed only the fundamental facts. The reader himself supplies what is wanting for the explanation of the abrupt use of names. The idea of " elevation " is the key to the thought, and that word St. John has preserved in his record of what has gone before (v. 32): the title " Son of man " was already familiar, and he passes over the particular phrase in which it occurred.

In viii. 34 ff. there is a more complicated and still more instructive example of the compression of an argument. The recorded words do no more than give the extreme forms : the course which the spoken words must have followed can only be determined by careful thought, though it can be determined certainly. Men are sinners, and if sinners then slaves of sin. What, therefore, is the essential conception of slavery ? It is an arbitrary, an unnatural, relation: the opposite of sonship, which expresses a permanent, an absolute connexion answering to the very constitution of things. The communication of sonship to the slave is consequently the establishment of his freedom. And in spiritual things He alone can communicate the gift to whom the dispensation of it has been committed. If, therefore, "the Son"—the one absolute Son—give freedom, they who receive it are free indeed. The imagery of a whole parable lies implicitly in the brief sentence.

In other cases "answers" of the Lord evidently point to detailed expressions of feeling or opinion with which the Evangelist was familiar, and which yet he has not detailed: e.g., xii. 23, 35. At the close of his account of the public ministry of Christ he gives, without any connexion of place or time, a general summary of the Lord's judgement on His hearers (xii. 44—50). The passage is apparently a compendious record and not a literal transcription of a single speech.

And so elsewhere it is probable that where no historical connexion is given, words spoken at different times, but all converging on the illumination of one truth, may be brought together: e.g., x. (λόγοι, v. 19).

The force of these considerations is increased if, as seems to be surely established, most of the discourses recorded by St. John were spoken in Aramaic. Whatever may have been the case in some other parts of Palestine, a large and miscellaneous crowd gathered at Jerusalem was able to understand what was spoken to them "in the Hebrew tongue" (Acts xxi. 40), and the favour of the multitude was conciliated by the use of it. The divine voice which St. Paul heard was articulate to him in Hebrew words (Acts xxvi. 14). St. Peter evidently spoke in an Aramaic dialect in the court of the high-priest, and the bystanders not only understood him but noticed his provincialism (Matt. xxvi. 73; Mark xiv. 70). Aramaic, it is said, in the Acts (i. 19), was the proper language of "the dwellers in Jerusalem" (τῇ διαλέκτῳ αὐτῶν). And again, the title with which Mary addressed the risen Lord was "Hebrew" ('Ραββουνεί, John xx. 16). The phrase which

the Lord quoted from the Psalms upon the cross was
" Hebrew " (Mark xv. 34). These indications, though they
are not absolutely conclusive, are yet convergent, and
lead to the conclusion that at the Holy City and in intercourse with the inner circle of the disciples Christ used
the vernacular Aramaic dialect. As claiming to be the
fulfiller of the Law, He could hardly have done otherwise
without offering violence to the religious instincts of the
nation. If then He spoke in Aramaic on those occasions
with which St. John chiefly deals, the record of the
Evangelist contains not only a compressed summary of
what was said, but that also a summary in a translation.[1]

It may be remarked yet further that the providential
office of St. John was to preserve the most universal
aspect of Christ's teaching. His experience fitted him to
recall and to present in due proportions thoughts which
were not understood at first. In this way it is probable
that his unique style was slowly fashioned as he pondered
the Lord's words through long years, and delivered them
to his disciples at Ephesus. And there is nothing
arbitrary in the supposition that the Evangelist's style
may have been deeply influenced by the mode in which
Christ set forth the mysteries of His own Person. Style
changes with subject, according to the capacity of the
speaker; and St. John's affinity with his Lord, which
enabled him to reproduce the higher teaching, may
reasonably be supposed to have enabled him also to preserve, as far as could be done, the characteristic form in
which it was conveyed.

However this may have been, such a view of St. John's
record of the Lord's discourses as has been given derogates
in no respect from their complete authority and truthfulness. A complete reproduction of the words spoken
would have been impossible as a complete reproduction of
the details of a complicated scene. Even if it had been

---

[1] It may be sufficient to add, without entering further into the subject,
that the testimony of Josephus, *Ant.* xx. xi. 2, is explicit as to the
feeling with which Jews regarded Greek as a foreign language, and to
the fact that the Jews of Jerusalem habitually spoke Aramaic (c. *Apion.*
I. 9, μόνος αὐτὸς συνίην).

possible it would not have conveyed to us the right impression. An inspired record of words, like an inspired record of the outward circumstances of a life, must be an interpretation. The power of the prophet to enter into the divine thoughts is the measure of the veracity of his account.

Thus the question finally is not whether St. John has used his own style and language in summarising the Lord's teaching, but whether he was capable of so entering into it as to choose the best possible method of reproducing its substance. It may or may not be the case that the particular words, in this sentence or that, are his own. We are only concerned to know whether, under the circumstances, these were the words fitted to gather into a brief space and to convey to us the meaning of the Lord. We may admit then that St. John has recorded the Lord's discourses with "freedom." But freedom is exactly the reverse of arbitrariness, and the phrase in this connexion can only mean that the Evangelist, standing in absolute sympathy with the thoughts, has brought them within the compass of his record in the form which was truest to the idea.[1]

These considerations seem to be amply sufficient to meet the objections which are urged against the general form of the discourses in St. John. A more particular examination will show how far the more special objections which are based upon their alleged monotony are valid.

2. St. John, as we have seen, writes with the purpose of revealing to his readers the Person of the Lord, and shows Him to be "the Christ," and "the Son of God." As a natural consequence he chooses for his record those discourses which bear most directly upon his theme, and dwells on that side of those discourses which is most akin to it. It will be seen later that the Synoptists have preserved clear traces of this teaching, but it was not their

---

[1] In this connexion the notes which are given by the Evangelist in ii. 21, vii. 39, xii. 33, are of the greatest importance. If he had not kept strictly to the essence of what Christ said, he might easily have brought out in the saying itself the sense which he discovered in it at a later time.

object to follow it out or to dwell upon it predominantly. With St. John it was otherwise. He wished to lead others to recognise Christ as what he had himself found Him to be. There is therefore in the teaching which he preserves an inevitable monotony up to a certain point. The fundamental truths of the Gospel as an object of faith are essentially simple. They do not, like questions of practice and morals, admit of varied illustration from life. Christ is Himself the sum of all, and St. John brings together just those words in which on exceptional occasions (as it appears) He revealed Himself to adversaries and doubters and friends. For there is an indication that the discourses recorded by St. John are not (so to speak) average examples of the Lord's popular teaching, but words called out by peculiar circumstances. Nothing in the fourth Gospel corresponds with the circumstances under which the Sermon on the Mount or the great group of parables were spoken. On the other hand, the private discussions with Nicodemus and the woman of Samaria find no parallels in the other Gospels, and yet they evidently answer to conditions which must have arisen. The other discourses, with the exception of those in ch. vi., which offer some peculiar features, were all held at Jerusalem, the centre of the true and false theocratic life. And more than this: they were distinctively festival discourses, addressed to men whose religious feelings and opinions were moved by the circumstances of their meeting. On such occasions we may naturally look for special revelations. The festivals commemorated the crises of Jewish history ; and a closer examination of the discourses shows that they had an intimate connexion with the ideas which the festivals represented. As long as the Jewish system remained, this teaching would be for the most part unnoticed or unintelligible. When the old was swept away, then it was possible, as the result of new conditions of religious growth, to apprehend the full significance of what had been said.

Yet further: while there is so far a " monotony " in the discourses of St. John that the Lord, after the beginning of His public ministry, turns the thoughts of His hearers in each case to Himself, as the one centre of hope, yet the form in which this is done presents a large variety of details corresponding with the external circumstances under which the several discourses were held, and there is also a distinct progress in the revelation. The first point will be touched upon in the next section : the second becomes evident at once, if account be taken of the order of the successive utterances of the Lord, and of the limits of possible change in the variable element which they contain.

It is undoubtedly true that as we read St. John's Gospel in the light of the Prologue we transfer the full teaching which that contains into all the later parts of the narrative, and that they derive their complete meaning from it. But if the discourses are examined strictly by themselves, it will be seen that they offer in succession fresh aspects of the Lord's Person and work : that the appearances of repetition are superficial : that each discourse, or rather each group of discourses, deals completely with a special topic. Thus in ch. v. the Son and the Jews are contrasted in their relation to God, and from this is traced the origin of unbelief. In ch. vi. the Son is shown to be the Giver and the Support of life. In chs. vii., viii. He is the Teacher and the Deliverer : in chs. ix., x., the Founder of the new Society. The discourses of the eve of the Passion have, as will be seen afterwards, a character of their own.

3. There is, then, a clear advance and historical development in the self-revelation of Christ as presented by St. John. There is also an intimate correspondence between the several discourses and their external conditions. For the most part the discourses grew (so to speak) out of the circumstances by which they were occasioned. The festival discourses, for example, are coloured by the peculiar thoughts of the season. The idea of the Passover is conspicuous in ch. vi., that of the Feast of Tabernacles in chs. vii., viii., that of the Dedication in ch. x. The traits of connexion are often subtle and unemphasised, but they are unmistakable. There is a psychological harmony between the words and the hearers for the time being. Nothing less than a complete and careful analysis of the

Gospel can bring home the force of this argument, but
two illustrations will indicate the kind of details on which
it rests.   The scene by the well at Sychar illustrates one
type of teaching (iv. 4—42): the discourse after the healing
at Bethesda another (v. 19—47).

There can be no question as to the individuality of
the discourse with the woman of Samaria.   The scene,
the style, the form of opinion are all characteristic.   The
well, the mountain (v. 20), the fertile cornfields (v. 35),
form a picture which every traveller recognises.   The
style of the conversation is equally lifelike.   The woman,
with ready intelligence, enters into the enigmatic form of
the Lord's sentences.   She gives question for question,
and, like Nicodemus, uses his imagery to suggest her
own difficulties.   At the same time, her confession keeps
within the limits of her traditional faith.   For her the
Christ is a prophet.   And it is easy to see how the fuller
testimony of her countrymen unparalleled in the Gospels
was based upon later teaching (v. 42), which their position
enabled them to receive as the Jews could not have done.

The discourse in ch. v. is characteristic in other ways.
It is the recorded beginning of Christ's prophetic teaching.
He unfolds the nature of His work and of His Person in
answer to the first accusations of the Jews before some
authoritative body (see v. 19, note).   It is not a popular
discourse, but the outline of a systematic defence.   It
springs naturally out of the preceding act, and it appears
to refer to the circumstances of the Feast.   It is not so
much an argument as a personal revelation.   At the same
time it offers an analysis of the religious crisis of the
time.   It discloses the relation in which Jesus stood to the
Baptist (33—35), to Moses (46), to revelation generally
(37 f.), to Judaism (39 f.).   It deals, in other words, with
just those topics which belong to the beginnings of the
great controversy at Jerusalem.[1]

One other illustration may be given to show the inner

[1] It may be added also that the occasion and contents of the discourse
are in complete agreement with the Synoptic narrative.   In these no
less than in St. John the open hostility of the Jews starts from the
alleged violation of the Sabbath (Matt. xii. 2 ; Mark ii. 27 f.) ; and

harmony which underlies the progress of the self-revelation of the Lord as recorded by St. John. Without reckoning the exceptional personal revelations to the woman of Samaria (iv. 26), and to the man born blind (ix. 37), the Lord reveals Himself seven times with the formula "I am," five times in His public ministry, and twice in the last discourses. It must be enough here to enumerate the titles. Their general connexion will be obvious.

(1) vi. 35 ff. *I am the Bread of life.*
     viii. 12. *I am the Light of the world.*
     x. 7. *I am the Door of the sheep.*
     x. 11. *I am the good Shepherd.*
     xi. 25. *I am the Resurrection and the Life.*
(2) xiv. 6. *I am the Way, and the Truth, and the Life.*
     xv. 1 ff. *I am the true Vine.*

4. But it is said that the language attributed to the Baptist and that of the Evangelist himself are undistinguishable from that of the discourses of the Lord. What has been said already shows to what extent this must be true. St. John deals with one aspect of the truth, and uses the same general forms of speech to present the different elements which contribute to its fulness. But beneath this superficial resemblance there are still preserved the characteristic traits of the teaching of each speaker. There is, as has been pointed out, a clear progress in the Lord's revelation of Himself. The words of the Baptist, coming at the commencement of Christ's

they offer the following correspondences of thought with St. John's record :

     v. 14, Matt. xii. 45 (Luke xvii. 19).
     vv. 19 f., Matt. xi. 27 ; Luke x. 22.
     v. 20, Matt. iii. 17.
     v. 22, Matt. xxviii. 18.
     v. 23, Luke x. 16 (Matt. x. 40).
     vv. 22, 27, Matt. xvi. 27.
     v. 29, Matt. xxv. 32, 46.
     v. 30, Matt. xxvi. 39.
     v. 39, Luke xxiv. 27 (Matt. xxvi. 54).
     v. 43, Matt. xxiv. 5.
     v. 44, Matt. xii. 14 ff., xviii. 1 ff.
     v. 46, Luke xvi. 31.

work, keep strictly within the limits suggested by the
Old Testament. What he says spontaneously of Christ
is summed up in the two figures of the "Lamb" and
"the Bridegroom," which together give a comprehensive
view of the suffering and joy, the redemptive and the
completive work of Messiah under the prophetic imagery.
Both figures appear again in the Apocalypse; but it is
very significant that they do not occur in the Lord's
teaching in the fourth Gospel or in St. John's Epistles.
His specific testimony, again, *this is the Son of God* (i. 34), is
no more than the assertion in his own person of that which
the Synoptists relate as a divine message accompanying
the Baptism (Matt. iii. 17, and parallels). And it is worthy
of notice, that that which he was before prepared to recognise in Christ (i. 33) was the fulness of a prophetic office
which the other Evangelists record him to have proclaimed
as ready to be accomplished (Matt. iii. 11).[1]

Even in style too, it may be added, the language assigned
to the Baptist has its peculiarities. The short answers,
I am not; No; I am not the Christ (i. 20 f.), are unlike anything else in St. John, no less than the answer in the words
of prophecy (i. 23). Comp. iii. 29, note.

The correspondences of expression between the language
attributed to the Lord in the Gospel and the Epistles of
St. John are more extensive and more important. They
are given in the following table:

John iii. 11. *῞Ο οἴδαμεν*
λαλοῦμεν καὶ ὃ ἑωράκαμεν
μαρτυροῦμεν.

1 John i. 1—3. *῞Ο ἦν*
ἀπ' ἀρχῆς, . . . ὃ ἑωράκαμεν
τοῖς ὀφθαλμοῖς ἡμῶν . . . καὶ
ἡ ζωὴ ἐφανερώθη, καὶ ἑωρά-
καμεν καὶ μαρτυροῦμεν . . .
ὃ ἑωράκαμεν καὶ ἀκηκόαμεν
ἀπαγγέλλομεν καὶ ὑμῖν.

v. 32 ff. *῎Αλλος ἐστὶν ὁ*
μαρτυρῶν περὶ ἐμοῦ, καὶ οἶδα
ὅτι ἀληθής ἐστιν ἡ μαρτυρία
ἣν μαρτυρεῖ περὶ ἐμοῦ . . .

v. 9 ff. *Εἰ τὴν μαρτυρίαν*
τῶν ἀνθρώπων, λαμβάνομεν,
ἡ μαρτυρία τοῦ θεοῦ μείζων
ἐστίν, ὅτι αὕτη ἐστὶν ἡ μαρτυ-

---

[1] The passage, iii. 31—36, is to be attributed to the Evangelist and
not to the Baptist. See note.

ἐγὼ δὲ οὐ παρὰ ἀνθρώπου τὴν
μαρτυρίαν λαμβάνω.
v. 24. Ὁ τὸν λόγον μου
ἀκούων . . . μεταβέβηκεν ἐκ
τοῦ θανάτου εἰς τὴν ζωήν.

v. 38. . . . τὸν λόγον αὐτοῦ
οὐκ ἔχετε ἐν ὑμῖν μένοντα.
vi. 56. ὁ τρώγων μου τὴν
σάρκα καὶ πίνων μου τὸ αἷμα
ἐν ἐμοὶ μένει κἀγὼ ἐν αὐτῷ.
Comp. xiv. 17.

viii. 29. Ἐγὼ τὰ ἀρεστὰ
αὐτῷ ποιῶ πάντοτε.
viii. 44. Ἐκεῖνος (ὁ δια-
βόλος) ἀνθρωποκτόνος ἦν
ἀπ᾽ ἀρχῆς.
viii. 46. Τίς ἐξ ὑμῶν ἐλέγχει με περὶ ἁμαρτίας ;
viii. 47. Ὁ ὢν ἐκ τοῦ θεοῦ
τὰ ῥήματα τοῦ θεοῦ ἀκούει·
διὰ τοῦτο ὑμεῖς οὐκ ἀκούετε
ὅτι ἐκ τοῦ θεοῦ οὐκ ἐστέ.
x. 15. Τὴν ψυχήν μου
τίθημι ὑπὲρ τῶν προβάτων.
xii. 35. Ὁ περιπατῶν ἐν τῇ
σκοτίᾳ οὐκ οἶδεν ποῦ ὑπάγει.

xiii. 34. Ἐντολὴν καινὴν
δίδωμι ὑμῖν ἵνα ἀγαπᾶτε ἀλλήλους, καθὼς ἠγάπησα ὑμᾶς
ἵνα καὶ ὑμεῖς ἀγαπᾶτε ἀλλήλους.

ρία τοῦ θεοῦ ὅτι μεμαρτύρηκεν
περὶ τοῦ υἱοῦ αὐτοῦ. . . .
iii. 14. Ἡμεῖς οἴδαμεν ὅτι
μεταβεβήκαμεν ἐκ τοῦ θανάτου
εἰς τὴν ζωήν, ὅτι ἀγαπῶμεν
τοὺς ἀδελφούς.
ii. 14. . . . ὁ λόγος [τοῦ
θεοῦ] ἐν ὑμῖν μένει.
iv. 15. Ὃς ἐὰν ὁμολογήσῃ,
ὅτι Ἰησοῦς [Χριστός] ἐστὶν ὁ
υἱὸς τοῦ θεοῦ, ὁ θεὸς ἐν αὐτῷ
μένει καὶ αὐτὸς ἐν τῷ θεῷ.
Comp. v. 16 ; iii. 24.
iii. 22. . . . ὅτι . . . τὰ
ἀρεστὰ ἐνώπιον αὐτοῦ ποιοῦμεν.
iii. 8. . . . ὅτι ἀπ᾽ ἀρχῆς
ὁ διάβολος ἁμαρτάνει. Comp.
iii. 12, 15.
iii. 5. . . . ἁμαρτία ἐν αὐτῷ
οὐκ ἔστιν.
iv. 6. Ἡμεῖς ἐκ τοῦ θεοῦ
ἐσμέν, Ὁ γινώσκων τὸν θεὸν
ἀκούει ἡμῶν, ὃς οὐκ ἔστιν ἐκ
τοῦ θεοῦ, οὐκ ἀκούει ἡμῶν.
iii. 16. . . . ἐκεῖνος ὑπὲρ
ἡμῶν τὴν ψυχὴν αὐτοῦ ἔθηκεν.
ii. 11. Ὁ δὲ μισῶν τὸν
ἀδελφὸν αὐτοῦ . . . ἐν τῇ
σκοτίᾳ περιπατεῖ, καὶ οὐκ
οἶδεν ποῦ ὑπάγει . . .
iii. 23. Αὕτη ἐστὶν ἡ ἐντολὴ
αὐτοῦ, ἵνα πιστεύσωμεν τῷ
ὀνόματι τοῦ υἱοῦ αὐτοῦ Ἰησοῦ
Χριστοῦ καὶ ἀγαπῶμεν ἀλλήλους, καθὼς ἔδωκεν ἐντολὴν
ἡμῖν.
iv. 11. Ἀγαπητοί, εἰ οὕτως
ὁ θεὸς ἠγάπησεν ἡμᾶς, καὶ
ἡμεῖς ὀφείλομεν ἀλλήλους ἀγαπᾶν. Comp. ii. 7 ff., iii. 11, 16.

xv. 10. Ἐὰν τὰς ἐντολάς
μου τηρήσητε, μενεῖτε ἐν τῇ
ἀγάπῃ μου.

iv. 16. Ὁ θεὸς ἀγάπη ἐστίν,
καὶ ὁ μένων ἐν τῇ ἀγάπῃ ἐν τῷ
θεῷ μένει καὶ ὁ θεὸς ἐν αὐτῷ
[μένει].

xv. 18. Εἰ ὁ κόσμος ὑμᾶς
μισεῖ . . .

iii. 13. Μὴ θαυμάζετε,
ἀδελφοί μου, εἰ μισεῖ ὑμᾶς ὁ
κόσμος.

xvi. 24. Αἰτεῖτε καὶ λήμ-
ψεσθε, ἵνα ἡ χαρὰ ὑμῶν ᾖ
πεπληρωμένη.

i. 4. Ταῦτα γράφομεν ὑμῖν,
ἵνα ἡ χαρὰ ὑμῶν ᾖ πεπλη-
ρωμένη. Comp. 2 John 12.

xvi. 33. Ἐγὼ νενίκηκα τὸν
κόσμον.

v. 4 f. Αὕτη ἐστὶν ἡ νίκη
ἡ νικήσασα τὸν κόσμον, ἡ
πίστις ἡμῶν.

Compare also the following passages:

iv. 22 f.   viii. 35.   iv. 16.
vi. 69 (πεπιστ. κ. ἐγνωκ.)   v. 20.   ii. 17.

In addition to these phrases there are single terms,
more or less characteristic, which are common to the
Lord's discourses and the Epistle: ἀληθινός, ἀνθρωποκτόνος,
ἐρωτᾶν, μαρτυρίαν λαμβάνειν, ὁ υἱός; and the frequent use of
the final particle ἵνα is found in both (xv. 12, xvii. 3; compared with iii. 23).

An examination of the parallels can leave little doubt
that the passages in the Gospel are the originals on which
the others are moulded. The phrases in the Gospel have
a definite historic connexion: they belong to circumstances
which explain them. The phrases in the Epistle are in
part generalisations, and in part interpretations of the
earlier language in view of Christ's completed work and
of the experience of the Christian Church. This is true of
the whole doctrinal relation of the two books, as will be
seen later on. The Epistle presupposes the Gospel, and if
St. John had already through many years communicated
his account of the Lord's teaching orally to his circle of
disciples, it is easy to see how the allusions would be
intelligible to the readers of the Epistle if it preceded the
publication of the Gospel. If the Epistle was written after
the Gospel was published, the use of the Lord's words in

what is practically a commentary upon them can cause no difficulty.

The Prologue to the Gospel offers the real parallel to this Epistle. In this there is the same application of the teaching of the Gospel from the point of view of the advanced Christian society. The exposition of the truth assumes the facts and words which follow in the narrative, while it deals with them freely and in the Apostle's own phraseology.

This will appear from the following table :

v. 1. Ἐν ἀρχῇ ἦν ὁ λόγος.	i. 1. Ὃ ἦν ἀπ' ἀρχῆς . . . περὶ τοῦ λόγου τῆς ζωῆς . . .
. . . ὁ λόγος ἦν πρὸς τὸν θεόν. Contrast xvii. 5.	i. 2. . . . τὴν ζωὴν τὴν αἰώνιον ἥτις ἦν πρὸς τὸν πατέρα. v. 20.
. . . θεὸς ἦν ὁ λόγος. v. 9. τὸ φῶς τὸ ἀληθινόν . . . ἐρχόμενον εἰς τὸν κόσμον.	ii. 8. Ἡ σκοτία παράγεται καὶ τὸ φῶς τὸ ἀληθινὸν ἤδη φαίνει.
v. 5. τὸ φῶς ἐν τῇ σκοτίᾳ φαίνει. Comp. xii. 35.	
v. 12. Ὅσοι δὲ ἔλαβον αὐτόν, ἔδωκεν αὐτοῖς ἐξουσίαν τέκνα θεοῦ γενέσθαι . . .	iii. 1. Ἴδετε ποταπὴν ἀγάπην δέδωκεν ἡμῖν ὁ πατήρ ἵνα τέκνα θεοῦ κληθῶμεν, καὶ ἐσμέν.
v. 12. . . . τοῖς πιστεύουσιν εἰς τὸ ὄνομα αὐτοῦ.	v. 13. . . . ὑμῖν . . . τοῖς πιστεύουσιν εἰς τὸ ὄνομα τοῦ υἱοῦ τοῦ θεοῦ.
v. 13. οἳ . . . ἐκ θεοῦ ἐγεννήθησαν.	v. 1. Πᾶς ὁ πιστεύων ὅτι Ἰησοῦς ἐστὶν ὁ Χριστός, ἐκ τοῦ θεοῦ γεγέννηται.
v. 14. Ὁ λόγος σὰρξ ἐγένετο.	iv. 2. Πᾶν πνεῦμα ὃ ὁμολογεῖ Ἰησοῦν Χριστὸν ἐν σαρκὶ ἐληλυθότα, ἐκ τοῦ θεοῦ ἐστίν.
v. 14. . . . ἐθεασάμεθα τὴν δόξαν αὐτοῦ.	i. 1. Ὃ ἐθεασάμεθα.
v. 18. Θεὸν οὐδεὶς ἑώρακεν πώποτε. Comp. vi. 46.	iv. 12. Θεὸν οὐδεὶς πώποτε τεθέαται. Comp. v. 20.

These parallels, which are found in eighteen verses only,

offer, as it will be felt, a close affinity to the Epistle not in language only, but in formulated thought. And further, the Prologue and the Epistle stand in the same relation of dependence to the discourses. In this respect it is interesting to compare what is said in the Prologue on "the Life," and "the Light," and "the Truth," with the passages in the Lord's words from which the Evangelist draws his teaching.

(1) The Life.   Comp. v. 26, xi. 25, xiv. 6.

(2) The Light.   Comp. viii. 12, ix. 5, xii. 46.

(3) The Truth.   Comp. viii. 32, xiv. 6.

It will be remembered that the cardinal phrases "the Word," "born (begotten) of God," are not found in the discourses of the Lord.[1]

Elsewhere in the Gospel there are in the narrative natural echoes, so to speak, of words of the Lord (ii. 4 compared with vii. 30, *his hour was not yet come*); and correspondences which belong to the repetition of corresponding circumstances (iv. 12 || viii. 53; iii. 2 || ix. 33), or to the stress laid upon some central truth (vii. 28 || ix. 29 f. || xix. 9). Still the conclusion remains unshaken that the discourses of the Lord have a marked character of their own, that they are the source of St. John's own teaching, that they perfectly fit in with the conditions under which they are said to have been delivered.

7.   *The Last Discourses*

But it may be said that the last discourses, in which there may have been some compression yet not such as to alter their general form, offer peculiar difficulties: that they are disconnected, indefinite, and full of repetitions: that it is most improbable that thoughts so loosely bound together could have been accurately preserved in the memory for half a century: that we must therefore suppose that the Evangelist here at least has allowed his

---

[1] The remarks made upon the Prologue generally, including the brief comment on the Baptist's testimony (i. 16—18), apply also to the two comments of the Evangelist upon the conversation with "the teacher of Israel" (iii. 16—21), and on the Baptist's last testimony (iii. 31—36). See notes.

own reflections to be mingled freely with his distant recollections of what the Lord said.

It may be at once admitted that these discourses offer a unique problem. They belong to an occasion to which there could be no parallel, and it may be expected that at such a crisis the Lord would speak much which " the disciples understood not at the time," over which still some of them would untiringly reflect. Our modes of thought again follow a logical sequence; Hebrew modes of thought follow a moral sequence. With us, who trust to the instruction of books, the power of memory is almost untrained : a Jewish disciple was disciplined to retain the spoken words of his master.

Thus we have to inquire primarily whether the teaching really suits the occasion ? whether there is a discernible coherence and progress in the discourses? If these questions are answered in the affirmative, it will be easy to understand how a sympathetic hearer, trained as a Jew would be trained, should bear them about with him till his experience of the life of the Church illuminated their meaning, when the promised Paraclete " taught him all things and brought all things to his remembrance which Christ had spoken."

If the discourses are taken as a whole it will be found that their main contents offer several peculiarities. Three topics are specially conspicuous : the mission of the Paraclete, the departure and the coming of Christ, the Church and the world. And generally a marked stress is laid throughout upon the moral aspects of the Faith.

It is scarcely necessary to point out the fitness of such topics for instruction at such a time. If the Lord was what the Apostles announced Him to be it is scarcely conceivable that He should not have prepared them by teaching of this kind before His departure, in order that they might be fitted to stand against the antagonism of the Jewish Church, and to mould the spiritual revolution which they would have to face. The book of the Acts— " the Gospel of the Holy Spirit "—is in part a commentary upon these last words.

At the same time it is most important to observe

that the ideas are not made definite by exact limitations. The teaching gains its full meaning from the later history, but the facts of the later history have not modified it. The promises and warnings remain in their typical forms. At first they could not have been intelligible in their full bearing. The fall of Jerusalem at length placed them in their proper light, and then they were recorded.

The moral impress of the last discourses is clear throughout. They are a sermon in the chamber to the Apostles, completing the Sermon on the Mount to the multitudes. In this section only Christ speaks of His "commandments" (ἐντολαί, ἐντολή, xiv. 15, 21, xv. 10, xiii. 34, xv. 12; comp. xv. 14, 17), and by the use of the word claims for them a divine authority. The commandments are summed up in one, "to love one another." The love of Christian for Christian is at once the pattern and the foundation of the true relation of man to man. And as the doctrine of love springs out of Christ's self-sacrifice (xv. 13, xiii. 34), so is it peculiar to these discourses in the Gospel. The time had come when it could be grasped under the influence of the events which were to follow.

The successive forms under which the principle of love is inculcated illustrate the kind of progress which is found throughout the chapters (e.g., xiii. 34, xv. 12). The three following passages will indicate what is meant:

xiv. 15. *If ye love me, ye will keep* (τηρήσετε) *my commandments.*

xiv. 21. *He that hath my commandments, and keepeth them, he it is that loveth me: and he that loveth me shall be loved of my Father, and I will love him, and will manifest myself to him.*

xv. 10. *If ye keep my commandments, ye shall abide in my love; even as I have kept my Father's commandments, and abide in his love.*

At a first reading it might be easy to miss the advance from obedience resting on love to progressive knowledge, and then to a divine certainty of life. When the relation of the three connected texts is seen, it is difficult not to feel that what appears to be repetition is a vital movement.

A similar progress is noticeable in the four chief passages which describe the work of the Paraclete :

xiv. 16, 17.

I will ask the Father, and
he shall give you another Paraclete,
that he may be with you for ever ;
even the Spirit of truth,
whom the world cannot receive. . . .

xiv. 26.

The Paraclete, even the Holy Spirit,
whom the Father will send in my name,
he shall teach you all things, and
bring to your remembrance all
things that I said unto you.

xv. 26.

When the Paraclete is come
whom I will send unto you from the Father
even the Spirit of truth,
which proceedeth from the Father,
he shall bear witness of me.

xvi. 7 ff.

If I go not away, the Paraclete will not come to you ;
but if I go, I will send him unto you.
And he, when he is come, will convict the world . . .
. . . when he is come, even the Spirit of truth,
he will guide you into all the truth . . .

Step by step the relation of the Paraclete to Christ is made clear : (1) *I will ask, another Paraclete ;* (2) *the Father will send in my name ;* (3) *I will send ;* (4) *if I go I will send him.* And again His work is defined more and more exactly : (1) *be with you for ever ;* (2) *teach all things . . . that I said unto you ;* (3) *bear witness of me ;* (4) *convict the world, guide into all the truth.* Such subtle correspondences are equally far from design and accident : they belong to the fulness of life.

The teaching on the relation of the Church to the

world, which is peculiar to this section, moves forward
no less plainly. In xiv. 17, 22 ff., it is shown that the
world is destitute of that sympathy with the divine Spirit
which is the necessary condition of the reception of
revelation. Afterwards the hatred of the world is foretold
as natural (xv. 18 ff.); and then this hatred is followed out
to its consequences (xvi. 1 ff.). Yet, on the other hand,
it is promised that the Spirit shall convict the world; and
at last Christ declares that He Himself has already conquered the world (xvi. 33).

The same general law of progress applies to the notices
of Christ's departure and return in chs. xiv., xvi. In the
first passage the central thought is " I come "; attention
is concentrated on what Christ will do (xiv. 3, 18, 23). In
the second the thought is rather of the relation of the
disciples to Him (xvi. 16, 22).

These examples indicate at least the existence of a real
coherence and development of thought in the discourses.
It is unquestionably difficult to follow out the development
of thought in detail. In the notes an endeavour has been
made to do this. Here it must be sufficient to give a brief
outline of the general course which the addresses take.
These form two groups, the discourses in the chamber
(xiii. 31—xiv.) and on the way (xv., xvi.). The predominant thoughts in the first are those of separation from
Christ as He had been hitherto known, and of sorrow in
separation : in the second, of realised union with Christ
in some new fashion, and of victory after conflict.

I.   The Discourses in the Chamber (xiii. 31—xiv.)

1.   *Separation, its necessity and issue* (xiii. 31—38)

(*a*) Victory, departure, the new Society (31—35).
(*β*) The discipline of separation (St. Peter) (36—38).

2.   *Christ and the Father* (xiv. 1—11)

(*a*) The goal and purpose of departure (1—4).
(*β*) The way to the divine (St. Thomas) (5—7).
(*γ*) The knowledge of the Father (St. Philip) (8—11).

3. *Christ and the disciples* (xiv. 12—21)

(*a*) The disciples continue Christ's work (12—14).

(*β*) He still works for them (15—17).

(*γ*) He comes to them Himself (18—21).

4. *The law and the progress of revelation* (22—31)

(*a*) The conditions of revelation (St. Jude) (22—24).

(*β*) The mode of revelation (25—27).

(*γ*) Christ's work perfected by His return (28—31).

The teaching springs from the facts of the actual position, and then deals with successive difficulties which it occasions.

II.   THE DISCOURSES ON THE WAY (xv., xvi.)

1.   *The living union* (xv. 1—10)

(*a*) The fact of union (1, 2).

(*β*) The conditions of union (3—6).

(*γ*) The blessings of union (7—10).

2.   *The issues of union: the disciple and Christ* (11—16)

(*a*) Christ's joy comes from sacrifice (12, 13).

(*β*) The disciple's connexion with Christ is by love (14, 15).

(*γ*) It is stable as resting on His choice (*v.* 16).

3. *The issues of union : the disciples and the world* (17—27)

(*a*) Love of Christ calls out hatred of the world (17—21).

(*β*) With this inexcusable hatred the disciples must contend (22—27).

4.   *The world and the Paraclete* (xvi. 1—11)

(*a*) The last issues of hatred (1—4).

(*β*) The necessity of separation (4—7).

(*γ*) The conviction of the world (8—11).

5.   *The Paraclete and the disciples* (12—15)

(*a*) He completes Christ's work (12, 13),

(*β*) and glorifies Christ (14, 15).

6. *Sorrow turned to joy* (16—24)

(*a*) A new relation (16, 17).

(*β*) Sorrow the condition of joy (19—22).

(*γ*) Joy fulfilled (23, 24).

7. *Victory at last* (25—33)

(*a*) A summary (25—28).

(*β*) A confession of faith (29, 30).

(*γ*) Warning and assurance (31—33).

The form of the discourse is changed. The Lord reveals uninterruptedly the new truths, till the close, when the disciples again speak no longer separately, but, as it were, with a general voice. The awe of the midnight walk has fallen upon them.

It is not of course affirmed that this view of the development of the discourses is exhaustive or final; but at least it is sufficient to show that they are bound together naturally, and that the dependence of the parts is such as could be easily apprehended and retained by those who listened. There is novelty under apparent sameness: there is variety under apparent repetition: there is a spiritual connexion underneath the apparently fragmentary sentences. This is all that it is necessary to show. As far as we can venture to judge the words befit the occasion; they form a whole harmonious in its separate parts: they are not coloured by later experiences: they might easily have been preserved by the disciple who was in closest sympathy with the Lord.

III. Characteristics of the Gospel

1. *Relation to the Old Testament*

St. John recognises in his narrative the divine preparation for the advent of Christ which was made among the nations. Such a discipline is involved in the view which he gives of the general action of the Word before His Incarnation (i. 5), and particularly in his affirmation of His universal working (i. 9). Nor was this discipline wholly without immediate effect. At the time of the advent Christ had *other sheep*, which were not of the Jewish *fold* (x. 16). There were *children of God scattered abroad* (xi. 52): some who had yielded themselves to the guidance of the divine light which had been given to them, and who were eager to welcome its fuller manifestation (iii. 20 ff.): citizens of a kingdom of truth waiting for their king (xviii. 37).

But while these broader aspects of the divine counsel find a place in the fourth Gospel, St. John brings out with especial force that the discipline of Israel was the true preparation for the Messiah, though Judaism had been perverted into a system antagonistic to Christianity, and Christ had been rejected by His own people. If he affirms more distinctly than the other apostolic writers, from the circumstances of his position, that the Jews had proved to be ignorant of the contents and scope of the revelation which had been committed to them (v. 37 ff.), and of the nature of the Lord whom they professed to worship with jealous reverence (xvi. 3, vii. 28, viii. 19, 54 f., xv. 21); if he affirms that their proud confidence in the literal interpretation of the facts of their providential history was mistaken and delusive (v. 37; contrast Gen. xxxii. 30; Exod. xx. 18 ff., xxiv. 10; Deut. iv. 12, 36, v. 4, 22:—vi. 32, cf. Ps. lxxviii. 24); he affirms no less distinctly that the old Scriptures did point to Christ, and that the history was instinct with a divine purpose. This appears by (*a*) his general recognition of the peculiar privileges of the Jews; (*b*) his interpretation of types: (*c*) his application of prophecies; and particularly by his treatment of the Messianic expectations of the people.

(*a*) The words of the Prologue, *He came to His own home* (τὰ ἴδια), *and His own people* (οἱ ἴδιοι) *received Him not* (i. 11, note), place beyond question the position which the Evangelist assigned to his countrymen in the divine order. They were in a peculiar sense the subjects of the Christ. In this sense Christ claimed their allegiance, and sovereign authority in the centre of their religious life. His greeting to Nathanael was: *Behold an Israelite indeed* (i. 47): His command in the temple at His first visit: *Make not my Father's house a house of merchandise* (ii. 16). In answer to the questionings of the Samaritan woman, who placed the tradition of her fathers side by side with that of the Jews, He asserted the exceptional knowledge and the unique office of His people : *we worship that which we know* (iv. 22), and *salvation*—the promised salvation (ἡ σωτηρία)—*is from* (ἐκ) *the Jews* (iv. 22), two phrases which mark at once the progressive unfolding of the divine truth (Heb. i. 1), and the office of the old dispensation to furnish the medium out of which the new should spring. In the beginning of His conflict with official Judaism, Christ assigns to the Scriptures their proper function towards Himself (v. 39, 46 f.). From this point "the Jews" take up a position of antagonism, and their privileges perish in their hands (comp. pp. clxii, clxiii).

(*b*) It is a significant fact that three and three only of the old saints, Abraham, Moses, and Isaiah, are mentioned by the Lord or by the Evangelist in connexion with Messiah. These three cover and represent the three successive periods of the training of the people : so subtle and so complete are the harmonies which underlie the surface of the text. Christ claimed for Himself testimonies from the patriarchal, the theocratic, and the monarchical stages of the life of Israel.

viii. 56. *Your father Abraham rejoiced to see*—in the effort to see (ἵνα ἴδῃ)—*my day : and he saw it, and was glad.*

The point of the reference lies in the view which it gives of the first typical example of faith as reaching forward to a distant fulfilment. It was not stationary, but progressive. In that onward strain lies the secret of the Old Testament.

The second reference to the patriarchal history in the Gospel of St. John is the complement of this effort after the remote. Abraham looked onwards to that which was not yet revealed : Jacob rested in his present covenant with God. This aspect of faith also is recognised by the Lord.

i. 51. *Verily, verily, I say unto you, ye shall see heaven opened, and the angels of God ascending and descending upon the Son of man.*

The desire of Abraham was fulfilled in the universal

sovereignty of Christ: the vision of Jacob was fulfilled in the abiding presence of Christ. A greater than Abraham brought freedom for all through the Truth: a greater than Jacob opened a well whose waters sprang up within the believer unto eternal life.

The references to Moses are not less pregnant. It is shown that just as Christ was the object to whom the patriarch looked in the future and in the present, so He was the object in regard of whom all the discipline of the Law was shaped. Jesus said to the leaders of the Jews: *Had ye believed* (*Did ye believe*) *Moses, ye would have believed* (*would believe*) *me, for he wrote of me* (v. 46).

This thought is brought out by references both to details of the Law and also to the circumstances which accompanied the promulgation of the Law.

Twice the Lord defended Himself from the charge of violating the Sabbath. On each occasion He laid open a principle which was involved in this institution.

v. 17. *My Father worketh even until now, and I work.*

The cessation from common earthly work was not an end, but a condition for something higher: it was not a rest *from* work, but *for* work (see note *ad loc.*).

vii. 22. *For this cause*—by which I have been moved in my healing—*hath Moses given you circumcision* (*not that it is of Moses, but of the fathers*), *and on the sabbath ye circumcise a man.*

The Sabbath, therefore, was subordinate to the restoration of the fulness of the divine covenant. It was made to give way to acts by which men were "made whole."

The one reference to the idea of the Passover is equally significant. *These things*, the Evangelist writes in his record of the crucifixion, *were done that the Scripture should be fulfilled, A bone of him shall not be broken* (xix. 36, note). The words came like an after-thought. They are left without definite application, and yet in that single phrase, by which the Lord is identified as the true Paschal Lamb, the meaning of the old sacrifices is made clear. "The Lamb of God" is revealed as the one offering to whom all offerings pointed.

The two interpretations of facts in the history of the

Exodus which St. John has given are even more remarkable than these lights thrown upon the Mosaic discipline
and the Mosaic ritual.   The first is the interpretation of
the brazen serpent; the second the interpretation of the
manna.

Jesus said to Nicodemus : *As Moses lifted up the serpent
in the wilderness, even so must the Son of man be lifted up*
(iii. 14).   The Jews said : *Our fathers did eat the manna in
the wilderness ; as it is written, He gave them bread from
heaven to eat.   Jesus therefore said unto them, Verily, verily,
I say unto you, Moses gave you not that bread from heaven ;
but my Father giveth you the true bread from heaven. . . . I
am the bread of life. . . .* (vi. 31 ff.).   Thus the most
significant deliverance from the effects of sin, and the
most striking gift of divine Providence recorded in the
Pentateuch, are both placed in direct connexion with
Christ.   In each case that which was temporal is treated
as a figure of that which is eternal.   Great depths of
thought are opened.   The lifelong wanderings of the
Jews are shown to be an image of all life.[1]

(c) St. John's dealing with the later teaching of the
prophets, the interpreters of the kingdom, is of the same
character.   He does not deal so much with external
details as with the inner life of prophecy.   He presents
Christ as being at once the Temple (ii. 19) and the King
(xii. 13).   He makes it clear that the new dispensation
towards which the prophets worked was one essentially
of spiritual blessing.   The sense of complete devotion to
God, of the union of man with God in Christ, of the gift
of the Spirit through Him, were the thoughts in which he
found the stamp of their inspiration.   Thus it is that he
has preserved the words in which the Lord gives us the
prophetic description of the Messianic times : *They shall all
be taught of God* (vi. 45); and those again in which He
gathers up the whole doctrine of Scripture on this head :
*If any man thirst, let him come unto me and drink.   He that
believeth on me, as the scripture hath said, out of his belly
shall flow rivers of living water* (vii. 37 f., note); and those
in which He showed that the conception of the union of

---

[1] Compare also the notes on vii. 37, viii. 12, and above, p. xiii. f.

God and man was not foreign to the Old Testament, when it was said even of unjust judges, *Ye are gods*, because the Word of God, in which was a divine energy, came to them (x. 34 f., note).

On the other hand St. John has recorded how the Lord recognised in the hostile unbelief of the Jews the spirit of their fathers, *who hated* the Lord's Anointed *without a cause* (xv. 25), and pointed out how the treachery of Judas had its counterpart in that of Ahitophel, of whom it was written, *He that eateth bread with me hath lifted up his heel against me* (xiii. 18).

There is the same mysterious depth, the same recognition of a spiritual under-current in common life, in the references which the Evangelist himself makes to the later books of Scripture. Once at the beginning of the Gospel he tells how the disciples were enabled to see fulfilled in the Lord the words of the suffering prophet, *The zeal of thine house shall consume me* (ii. 17) ; and at the close of the account of the public ministry he points out how the unbelief of the Jews, the most tragic of all mysteries, had been foreshadowed of old. *These things*, he writes, *said Isaiah, because—because*, not *when* (ὅτι not ὅτε, see note)—*he saw* Christ's *glory, and spake of Him* in the most terrible description of the unbelief and blindness of Israel (xii. 37 ff.).

It seems to me impossible to study such passages without feeling that the writer of the fourth Gospel is penetrated throughout—more penetrated perhaps than any other writer of the New Testament—with the spirit of the Old. The interpretations which he gives and records, naturally and without explanation or enforcement, witness to a method of dealing with the old Scriptures which is of wide application. He brings them all into connexion with Christ. He guides his readers to their abiding meaning, *which cannot be broken* ; he warns the student against trusting to the letter, while he assures him that no fragment of the teaching of *the Word of God* is without its use. And in doing this he shows also how the scope of revelation grows with the growth of men. Without the basis of the Old Testament, without the fullest acceptance of the unchanging divinity of the Old Testament, the Gospel of St. John is an insoluble riddle.

2. *The unfolding of the Messianic idea*

The history of the Gospel of St. John is, as has been seen, the history of the development of faith and unbelief, of faith and unbelief in Christ's Person. It is therefore, under another aspect, the history of the gradual unfolding of the true Messianic idea in conflict with popular expectations. On the one side are the hopes and the preoccupations of the Jews: on the other side are the progressive revelations of the Lord. And there is nothing which more convincingly marks the narrative as a transcript from life than the clearness with which this struggle is displayed. A summary outline of the Gospel from this point of view will probably place the facts in a distinct light.

The opening scene reveals the contrasted elements of expectation as they had been called into activity by the preaching of the Baptist (i. 19 ff.). The Baptist's words and testimonies (i. 29, 33, 36) were fitted to check the popular zeal, and at the same time to quicken the faith of those who were ready to receive and to follow that greater One who should come after according to the divine promise (i. 29 f., 36). So it came to pass that some of his disciples found in Jesus, to whom he mysteriously pointed, the fulfilment of the old promises and of their present aspirations (i. 35—42). Others at once attached themselves to the New Teacher (*Rabbi*, i. 38); and He was acknowledged as *Messiah* (i. 41); *the Son of God, and King of Israel* (i. 49). The " sign " which followed confirmed the personal faith of these first followers (ii. 11); but so far there was nothing to show how the titles which had been at least silently accepted were to be realised.

The cleansing of the temple was in this respect decisive. Messiah offered Himself in His Father's house to His own people, and they failed to understand, or rather they misunderstood, the signs which He gave them. As a consequence, He *did not commit himself unto them, because*

He knew all men; and . . . what was in man (ii. 23 ff.).
The origin of this misunderstanding is shown in the imperfect confession of Nicodemus (iii. 2 ff.), and in the complaint of the disciples of the Baptist (iii. 26).   On the other
hand, the testimony of Christ and the testimony of the
Baptist set the real issue before men, as the Evangelist
shows in his comments on the words.   The Messiah of
those whom the Evangelist characterises as "the Jews"
had no place in the work of Jesus; and His work as
Messiah had no place in their hearts.

Such was the situation at Jerusalem.   It was otherwise
in Samaria.   There Jesus could openly announce Himself
to be the Christ, inasmuch as the claim was rightly though
imperfectly understood (iv. 25 f.); and the confession of
the Samaritans who had sought His fuller teaching showed
how far they were from resting in any exclusive or
temporal hopes (iv. 42, *the Saviour of the world*, according
to the true reading).

The next visit to Jerusalem (ch. v.) gave occasion for
a fundamental exposition of the nature and work of the
Lord, and of the manifold witness to Him, side by side
with an analysis of the causes of Jewish unbelief.   The
later history is the practical working out of the principles
embodied in this discourse.

The first decisive division between the followers of
Christ was in Galilee.   There superficial faith was more
prevalent and more eager.   The "multitude" wished to
precipitate the issue according to their own ideas (vi. 14 f.).
In answer to this attempt Christ turned the minds of those
who came to Him by most startling imagery from things
outward, and foreshadowed His own violent death as the
condition of that personal union of the believer with
Himself, to bring about which was the end of His work.
So He drove many from Him (vi. 60), while He called out
a completer confession of faith from the twelve (vi. 69).
Words which had been used before (ch. i.), have now a
wholly different meaning.   To believe in Christ now was
to accept with utter faith the necessity of complete self-
surrender to Him who had finally rejected the homage of
force.

The issue at Jerusalem was brought about more slowly. The interval between ch. v. and ch. vii. was evidently filled with many questionings (vii. 3 f., 11 f.); and when Jesus appeared at Jerusalem He created divisions among the multitude (vii. 30 f., 43). Some thought that He must be the Christ from His works (vii. 31), and from His teaching (vii. 26, 37 ff., 46 ff.). They even questioned whether possibly their leaders had reached the same conclusion (vii. 26, ἔγνωσαν). But they did not see that He satisfied the prophetic tests which they applied to Messiah (vii. 27, 42, 52).

In the midst of this uncertainty the rulers openly declared themselves (vii. 32, 48); and under their influence the mass of the people fell away when Christ set aside their peculiar claims and purposes (viii. 33, 58 f.). He still, however, continued to lay open more truths as to Himself, and revealed Himself to the outcast of the synagogue as "the Son of man" (ix. 35, note). Divisions spread further (ix. 16, x. 19); and at last the request was plainly put: *If thou art the Christ, tell us plainly* (x. 24). Again, the result of the answer was a more bitter hostility (x. 39), and wider faith (x. 42).

The end came with the raising of Lazarus. This was preceded by the confession of Martha (xi. 27), and followed by the counsel of Caiaphas (xi. 47 ff.). There was no longer any reason why Christ should shrink from receiving the homage of His followers. He accepted openly the title of King when He entered the Holy City to die there (xii. 13 ff.); and the public ministry closed with the questioning of the people as to "the Son of man," who seemed to have usurped the place of Him who should reign for ever (xii. 34).

Such a history of the embodiment of an idea, an office, carries with it its own verification. The conflict and complexity of opinion, the growth of character, the decisive touches of personal and social traits, which it reflects, stamp it not only as a transcript from life, but also as an interpretation of life by one who had felt what he records. The whole history moves along with a continuous progress. Scene follows scene without repetition and without anticipation. The revelation of doctrine is intimately connected with a natural sequence of events, and is not given in an abstract form. Thoughts are revealed, met, defined from point to point. We not only see individualised characters, but we see the characters change under intelligible influences as the narrative goes forward. And this is all done in the narrowest limits and in a writing of transparent simplicity. Art can show no parallel. No one, it may be confidently affirmed, who had not lived through the vicissitudes of feeling, which are indicated often in the lightest manner, could have realised by imagination transient and complicated modes of thought which had no existence in the second century.

It did not fall within the scope of the Synoptists to trace out the unfolding of the Messianic idea in the same way; but the teaching upon the subject which they record is perfectly harmonious with that of St. John.

The Synoptists and St. John agree in describing (a) the universal expectation at the time of the Advent (Matt. iii. 5, and parallels; John i. 41, 19, 20, iii. 26, iv. 25); (β) the signs by which the Christ should be heralded (Matt. xvi. 1; John vi. 30 f.); the preparation by Elijah (Matt. xi. 14, xvii. 10; John i. 21), and (none the less) the suddenness of His appearance (Matt. xxiv. 26 f.; John vii. 27); (γ) the readiness of some to welcome Him even as He came (Luke ii. 25 ff., Symeon; 36, Anna; John i. 45, Philip; 49, Nathanael).

They agree likewise in recording that the Lord pointed to His death under figures from an early time (Matt. ix. 15, and parallels; John iii. 14); and that open hostility to Him began in consequence of His claims to deal authoritatively with the traditional law of the Sabbath (Matt. xii. 13 ff.; John v. 16); and of His assumption of divine attributes (Mark ii. 6; John v. 18).

There is, however, one difference in this far-reaching agreement. All the Evangelists alike recognise the prophetic, royal, and redemptive aspects of Christ's work; but St. John passes over the special reference to the Davidic type, summed up in each of the two Synoptists by the title " Son of David " (yet see vii. 42 ; Rev. v. 5, xxii. 16).[1] The explanation is obvious. The national aspect of Messiah's work passed away when " the Jews " rejected Him. It had no longer in itself any permanent significance. The Kingdom of Truth (xviii. 37) was the eternal antitype of Israel. The Gospel was a message for the world. The fall of Jerusalem proclaimed the fact ; and that catastrophe which interpreted the earlier experience of the Apostle made the recurrence of like experience impossible.

Thus the fall of Jerusalem determined the work of St. John with regard to the conception of the Lord's office. The apprehension of the absolute office of Messiah corresponds with the apprehension of Christianity as essentially universal. These truths St. John established from Christ's own teaching ; and so by his record the title of " the Son of God " gained its full interpretation (xx. 31 ; 1 John iv. 15, v. 13, 20).

St. John shows in a word how Christ and the Gospel of Christ satisfied the hopes and destinies of Israel, though both were fatally at variance with the dominant Judaism. And in doing this he fulfilled a part which answered to his characteristic position. The Judaism in which the Lord lived and the early Apostles worked, and the Judaism which was consolidated after the fall of Jerusalem, represented two distinct principles, though the latter was, in some sense, the natural issue of the former. The one was the last stage in the providential preparation for Christianity : the other was the most formidable rival to Christianity.

3. *The Characters*

The gradual self-revelation of Christ which is recorded in St. John's Gospel carries with it of necessity the revelation of the characters of the men among whom He moved. This Gospel is therefore far richer in distinct personal types of unbelief and faith than the others.

Attention has been called already (p. xvi ff.) to the

[1] The title occurs twice only in the Epistles, but in important passages : Rom. i. 3 ; 2 Tim. ii. 8.

characteristic traits by which the classes of people who appear in the history are distinguished—"the multitude," "the Jews," "the Pharisees," "the high-priests." In them the broad outlines of the nature of unbelief are drawn. In the events of the Passion three chief actors offer in individual types the blindness, and the weakness, and the selfishness, which are the springs of hostility to Christ. Blindness—the blindness which will not see—is consummated in the high-priest: weakness in the irresolute governor: selfishness in the traitor apostle. The Jew, the heathen, the disciple become apostate, form a representative group of enemies of the Lord.

These men form a fertile study. All that St. John records of Caiaphas is contained in a single sentence; and yet in that one short speech the whole soul of the man is laid open. The Council in timid irresolution expressed their fear lest "the Romans might come and take away both their place and nation if Christ were let alone." They had petrified their dispensation into a place and a nation, and they were alarmed when their idol was endangered. But Caiaphas saw his occasion in their terror. For him Jesus was a victim by whom they could appease the suspicion of their conquerors: *Ye know nothing at all, nor consider that it is expedient for you that one man should die for the people, and that the whole nation perish not* (xi. 49 f.). The victim was innocent, but the life of one could not be weighed against the safety of a society. Nay rather it was, as his words imply, a happy chance that they could seem to vindicate their loyalty while they gratified their hatred. To this the divine hierarchy had come at last. Abraham offered his son to God in obedience to the Father whom he trusted: Caiaphas gave the Christ to Cæsar in obedience to the policy which had substituted the seen for the unseen.

Caiaphas had lost the power of seeing the Truth: Pilate had lost the power of holding it. There is a sharp contrast between the clear, resolute purpose of the priest, and the doubtful, wavering answers of the governor. The judge shows his contempt for the accusers, but the accusers are stronger than he. It is in vain that he tries

k

one expedient after another to satisfy the unjust passion of his suitors. He examines the charge of evil-doing and pronounces it groundless; but he lacks courage to pronounce an unpopular acquittal. He seeks to move compassion by exhibiting Jesus scourged and mocked and yet guiltless; and the chief-priests defeat him by the cry, *Crucify, Crucify* (xix. 6). He hears His claim to be a " King not of this world " and " the Son of God," and is " the more afraid "; but his hesitation is removed by an argument of which he feels the present power: *If thou let this man go, thou art not Cæsar's friend* (xix. 12). The fear of disgrace prevailed over the conviction of justice, over the impression of awe, over the pride of the Roman. The Jews completed their apostasy when they cried: *We have no king but Cæsar* (xix. 15); and Pilate, unconvinced, baffled, overborne, delivered to them their true King to be crucified, firm only in this, that he would not change the title which he had written in scorn, and yet as an unconscious prophet.

Caiaphas misinterpreted the divine covenant which he represented: Pilate was faithless to the spirit of the authority with which he was lawfully invested: Judas perverted the very teaching of Christ Himself. If once we regard Judas as one who looked to Christ for selfish ends, even his thoughts become intelligible. He was bound to his Master not for what he was, but for what he thought that he would obtain through Him. Others, like the sons of Zebedee, spoke out of the fulness of their hearts, and their mistaken ambition was purified; but Judas would not expose his fancies to reproof: St. Peter was called Satan—an adversary—but Judas was a devil, a perverter of that which is holy and true. He set up self as his standard, and by an easy delusion he came to forget that there could be any other. Even at the last he seems to have fancied that he could force the manifestation of Christ's power by placing Him in the hands of His enemies (vi. 70, xviii. 6, notes). He obeys the command to " do quickly what he was doing," as if he were ministering to his Master's service. He stands by in the garden when the soldiers went back and fell to the ground, waiting, as it were, for the revelation of Messiah in His Majesty. Then came the end. He knew the sovereignty of Christ, and he saw Him go to death. St. John says nothing of what followed ; but there can be no situation more overwhelmingly tragic than that in which he shows the traitor for the last time standing ($ἱστήκει$) with those who came to take Jesus.

The types of faith in the fourth Gospel are no less distinct and representative. It is indeed to St. John that we owe almost all that we know of the individual character of the disciples. St. Peter, it is true, stands out with the same bold features in all the Evangelists. St. Matthew and St. Mark have preserved one striking anecdote of the sons of Zebedee. St. Luke gives some traits of those who were near the Lord in His Infancy, of Zacchæus, of Martha and Mary. But we learn only from St. John to trace the workings of faith in Nathanael, and Nicodemus, and Andrew, and Philip, and Thomas, and "the disciple whom Jesus loved " ; in the woman of Samaria, and in Mary Magdalene. As in the case of Caiaphas, Pilate and Judas, a few words and acts lay open the souls of all these in the light of Christ's presence.

Of St. John it is not necessary to speak again. His whole nature, his mode of thought, his style of speech, pass by a continuous reflection into the nature, the thought, the style, of the Master for whom he waited. In the others there is a personality more marked because more limited. To regard them only from one point of view, in Nicodemus and the woman of Samaria we can trace the beginnings of faith struggling through the prejudice of learning and the prejudice of ignorance. In St. Philip and St. Thomas we can see the growth of faith overcoming the hindrances of hesitation and despondency. In St. Peter and St. Mary Magdalene we can see the activity of faith chastened and elevated.

The contrast between Nicodemus and the woman of Samaria, the two to whom Christ, according to the narrative of St. John, first unfolds the mysteries of His kingdom, cannot fail to be noticed. A rabbi stands side by side with a woman who was not even qualified in popular opinion to be a scholar: a Jew with a Samaritan: a dignified member of the Council with a fickle, impulsive villager. The circumstances of the discourses are not less different. The one is held in Jerusalem, the other almost under the shadow of the schismatical temple in Gerizim: the one in the house by night, the other in the daylight by the well-side. Christ is sought in the one case; in the other He asks first that so He may give afterwards. The discourses themselves open out distinct views of the kingdom. To Nicodemus Christ speaks of a new birth, of spiritual influence witnessed by spiritual life, of the elevation of the Son of man in whom earth and heaven were united: to the Samaritan He speaks of the water of life which should satisfy a thirst assumed to be real, of a worship in spirit and truth, of Himself as the Christ who should teach all things.

But with all this difference there was one thing common to the Jewish ruler and to the Samaritan woman. In both there was the true germ of faith. It was quickened in the one by the miracles which Jesus did (iii. 2); in the other by His presence. But both were drawn to Him and rested in Him. Both expressed their difficulties, half seizing, half missing His figurative language. Both found that which they needed to bring them into a living union with God. The pretensions of superior knowledge and discernment were cast down. The suspicions of rude jealousy were dispelled. The revelation of a suffering Redeemer scattered the proud fancies of the master of Israel: the revelation of a heavenly Father raised the conscience-stricken woman to new hope. Even after the Crucifixion Nicodemus, "who came by night at first," openly testified his love for Christ; and the Samaritan at once, forgetful of all else, hastened to bring her countrymen to Him whom she had found.

Here we see the beginning of faith: in St. Philip and in St. Thomas we see something of the growth of faith. It is an old tradition (Clem. Alex. *Strom.* iii. 4, § 25) that St. Philip was the disciple who asked the Lord that he might first go and bury his father, and received the stern reply, " Follow thou me, and let the dead bury their dead."

Whether this be true or not, it falls in with what St. John tells us of him. He appears to hang back, to calculate, to rest on others. "Jesus," we read, "findeth Philip" (i. 43). He had not himself come to Jesus, though the words imply that he was ready to welcome, or even waiting for, the call which was first spoken to him. So again, when the Lord saw the multitude in the wilderness, it was to Philip He addressed the question, to "prove him," "Whence shall we buy bread, that these may eat?" (vi. 5 ff.). And even then he could only estimate the extent of the want. He had no suggestion as to how it must be met. But if his was a slow and cautious and hesitating faith, it was diffusive. He had no sooner been strengthened by the words of Christ than he in turn found Nathanael. "We have found," he saith, "Him of whom Moses in the Law and the prophets wrote" (i. 45). He appealed, as we must believe, to the witness of their common search in the Scriptures in times gone by, and his only answer to his friend's doubt—the truest answer to doubt at all times—was simply "Come and see." Yet his own eyes were holden too in part. Even at the last he could say, "Lord, show us the Father, and it sufficeth us" (xiv. 8). But he said this in such a spirit that he received the answer which for him and for us gives faith an object on which it can rest for ever: "Jesus saith unto him, Have I been so long time with you, and yet hast thou not known me, Philip? he that hath seen me hath seen the Father" (xiv. 9 f.).

Philip believed without confidence. Thomas believed without hope. The whole character of Thomas is written in the first sentence which we hear him speak: "Let us also go, that we may die with Him" (xi. 16). He could love Christ even to the last, though he saw nothing but suffering in following Him. He knew not whither He went; how could he know the way? (xiv. 5). But even so, he could keep close to Him: one step was enough, though that was towards the dark. No voice of others could move him to believe that which of all he wished most. The ten might tell him that the Lord was risen, but he could not lightly accept a joy beyond all that for which he had looked. "Except I shall see in His hands the print of the nails, and put my finger into the print of the nails, and thrust my hand into His side, I will not believe" (xx. 24 ff.). But when the very test which he had laid down was offered, the thought of proof was lost in the presence of Christ. He saw at once what had not yet been seen. The most complete devotion found the most fervent expression in those last words of faith, "My Lord, and my God" (xx. 27 f.).

In this way disciples were led on little by little to know the Master in whom they trusted. Often they failed through want of enthusiasm or want of insight. Some there were also who failed by excess of zeal. Mary Magdalene, when the blindness of sorrow was removed, would have clung to the Lord whom she had again found, lest again He should be taken from her. She would have kept Him as she had known Him. She would have set aside the lesson that it was good that He should go away. Then came those words which at once satisfied and exalted her affection, "Go unto my brethren, and say to them, I ascend unto my Father and your Father, and my God and your God" (xx. 15 ff.). She, the tender, loving woman, is made the messenger of this new Gospel: she is first charged to declare the truth in which her own passionate desire was transfigured: she who would have chained down heaven to earth is commissioned to proclaim that earth is raised to heaven.

Something of the same kind may be noticed in the history of St. Peter. Unlike Philip he is confident, because he knows the strength of his love: unlike Thomas he is hopeful, because he knows whom he loves. But his confidence suggests the mode of his action: his hope fashions the form of its fulfilment. Peter saith unto Jesus, "Thou shalt never wash my feet," and then with a swift reaction, "Lord, not my feet only, but also my hands and my head" (xiii. 6 ff.). If he hears of a necessary separation, he asks, "Lord, why cannot I follow thee now? I will lay down my life for thy sake" (xiii. 36 ff.). He draws his sword in the garden (xviii. 10 f.): he presses into the courtyard of the high-priest (xviii. 16 ff.). He

dares all and doubts nothing. But when the trial came
he was vanquished by a woman. He had chosen his own
part, and the bitterness of utter defeat placed him for ever
at the feet of the Saviour whom he had denied. He knew,
though it was with grief, the meaning of the last triple
charge : he knew, though it was through falls, the meaning
of the answer to his last question : *If I will that he tarry
till I come, what is that to thee? Follow thou me* (xxi. 22).

There is one other character common to all four
Evangelists which cannot be altogether passed by.   St.
John's notices of the Baptist have little externally in
common with the Synoptic narratives, but they reveal a
character which answers to the stern figure of the preacher
of repentance. His last testimony to Christ (iii. 27—30)
completely corresponds with the position of one who is
looking forward to a future dimly seen. The herald must
fulfil his herald's work to the end. His glory is to accept
the necessity of decline (iii. 30).

It is needless to add any comments to this rapid
enumeration of the characters who people the brief
narrative of St. John. The vividness, the vigour, the
life, of their portraitures cannot be mistaken or gainsaid.
The different persons show themselves. They come
forward and then pass out of sight as living men, and
not like characters in a legendary history. They have an
office not only separately but in combination. They
witness, in other words, not only to the exactness but
also to the spiritual completeness of the record.

This fulness of characteristic life in the fourth Gospel
is practically decisive as to its apostolic authorship.
Those who are familiar with the Christian literature
of the second century will know how inconceivable
it is that any Christian teacher could have imagined
or presented as the author of the fourth Gospel has
done the generation in which the Lord moved. The
hopes, the passions, the rivalries, the opinions, by which
His contemporaries were swayed had passed away, or
become embodied in new shapes. A great dramatist
could scarcely have called them back in such narrow
limits as the record allows. Direct knowledge illuminated

by experience and insight, which are the human conditions
of the historian's inspiration, offer the only adequate
explanation of the dramatic power of the Gospel.

4. *Symbolism*

It will be evident from the illustrations which have been
already given that there is a subtle and yet unmistakable
harmony within the different parts of St. John's Gospel;
that each narrative which it contains is to be considered
not only in itself, but also in relation to the others with
which it is connected : that fact is interpreted by thought
and thought by fact : that the historical unity of the book
is completed by a moral and spiritual unity. Under one
aspect the lessons of the Old Testament are illuminated
by Christ's presence. Under another aspect the characters
which move about the Lord offer typical representations
of faith and unbelief in their trials and issues. And in
all this there is not the least violence done to the outward
history, but there is simply a practical recognition of the
necessary fulness which there was in the Life, in the
Words, and in the Works of the Son of man.

St. John himself is careful to explain that all which he
saw when he wrote his Gospel was not clear to the disciples
at once. The words of the Lord to St. Peter had a wider
application than to any one detail : *What I do thou knowest
not now, but thou shalt come to know* (γνώσῃ) *hereafter* (xiii.
7). The Resurrection was the first great help to this
advance in knowledge (ii. 22, xii. 16) ; and the meaning
of the Resurrection itself was extended when Christ
raised a new Temple in place of the old after the fall of
Jerusalem, and His Church was finally established (ii. 19,
note).

There can then be no cause for surprise if St. John,
looking back over the whole range of his experience,
selects just those parts of Christ's ministry for his record
which fit together with the most complete mutual correspondences. Such a selection would not be so much the
result of a conscious design as of a spiritual intuition. His
Gospel was in the truest sense of the word a " prophecy,"
a revelation of the eternal under the forms of time.

In this respect the miracles of the Lord which he has related form an instructive illustration of his method. Taken together they are a revelation of Christ, of " His glory." A very brief examination of them will be sufficient to establish by this one example that principle of a spiritual meaning in the plan and details of the Gospel which I have called the symbolism of St. John.

The two characteristic names which miracles bear in St. John's Gospel mark distinctly the place which he assigns to them in relation to the general course of the divine government. They are *signs* (ii. 11, note) and they are *works* (v. 20, note). They are " signs " so far as they lead men to look beneath the surface for some deeper revelations of the method and will of God, to watch for the action of that spiritual ministry—" the angels ascending and descending upon the Son of man "—which belongs to the new dispensation. They are " works " so far as they take their place among the ordinary phenomena of life (v. 17), differing from them not because they involve any more real manifestation of divine energy but simply because they are suited to arrest attention. They are " signs " in short, for they make men feel the mysteries which underlie the visible order. They are " works " for they make them feel that this spiritual value is the attribute of all life.

St. John has recorded in detail seven miracles of Christ's ministry and one of the risen Christ. Their general connexion with the structure of his Gospel (see p. lxxxviii) will appear from the following table:

1. *The water turned to wine*, ii. 1—11.
   The nobleman's son healed, iv. 46—54.
2. *The paralytic at Bethesda*, v. 1—15.
   The feeding of the five thousand, vi. 1—15.
   The walking on the sea, vi. 16—21.
   The restoration of the man born blind, ix. 1—12.
   The raising of Lazarus, xi. 17—44.
3. *The miraculous draught of fishes*, xxi. 1—12.

Of these the first two give the fundamental character of the Gospel, its nature and its condition: the next five are signs of the manifold working of Christ, as the restoration, the support, the guidance, the light and the life of men: the last is the figure of all Christian labour to the end of time.

The first two miracles, which the Evangelist significantly connects together as wrought at Cana, seem at first sight to have nothing in common. They are given without any comment except the record of their effects (ii. 11, iv. 53). But these two brief notes give the clue to the interpretation of the signs. They show from the beginning that Christianity is the ennobling of all life, and that its blessings are appropriated only by faith.

The change of the water into wine has always been rightly felt to be a true symbol of Christ's whole work. The point of the second miracle at Cana lies in the discipline of faith. The request to Christ (iv. 47) was itself a confession of faith, yet that faith was not accepted as it was. It was necessary at once to raise faith to the unseen. Whatever outward signs may be granted they do but point to something beyond. At the commencement of His ministry Christ declared in act what He repeated afterwards at its close : *Blessed are they that see not, and yet believe.*

The four chief miracles which are connected with Christ's conflict form the basis on each occasion of discourses in which their lessons are enforced. Here there can be no doubt of the symbolism: it is declared unmistakably that the works are "signs," charged with a divine purpose. In the case of the paralytic suffering is definitely connected with sin (v. 14). Christ removes the malady spontaneously and on a Sabbath. Such action is revealed to be after the pattern of God's action: *My Father worketh even until now, and I work* (v. 17). God seeks without ceasing to repair by tenderness and chastisement the ravages which sin has made in His creation, and to lead it onward to its consummation.

In the feeding of the five thousand the teaching is carried a step further. Man needs not restoration only but support. He has wants as well as defects : he has to struggle against material difficulties. Christ reveals

Himself as sufficient to supply every craving of man, and as sovereign over the forces of nature : *I am the bread of life. He that cometh to me shall never hunger ; and he that believeth on me shall never thirst* . . . (vi. 35). *What then if ye should behold the Son of man ascending where He was before? It is the spirit that quickeneth* (vi. 62 f.). So the works are invested with a permanent prophetic power.

Man needs support and he needs enlightenment also ; for we must go forward, and in one sense we are " blind from our birth." This is the next lesson of the miracles which John records. Before the blind regained his sight at Siloam Christ said : *When* (ὅταν) *I am in the world, I am the light of the world* (ix. 5). Sight was given to the obedient disciple. The Pharisees refused to read the sign which conflicted with their prejudices. And He then added : *For judgement I came into this world, that they which see not may see ; and that they which see may be made blind* (ix. 39).

But even if failings be remedied, if wants be satisfied, if light be given, there yet remains one more terrible enemy : death, physical death, comes at last. Here also Christ gave a sign of His power. In the very agony of apparent loss He said : *He that believeth in me, even though he die, shall live ; and whosoever liveth and believeth in me shall never die* (xi. 25 f.). And so far as any single fact offered to the senses can confirm the truth, the raising of Lazarus showed that there is a Life sovereign over physical life, a Life victorious over death.

The sequence of these " signs," these living parables of Christ's action, these embodiments of truth in deed, can hardly be mistaken. Nor is the meaning of the one miracle of the risen Lord less obvious. The narrative is the figure of the history of the Church. The long night passes in what seems to be vain effort. Christ stands in the dawn upon the shore, and at first His disciples know Him not. Even so in due time He is revealed in blessing ; and men are charged afresh to use the new gifts which He has enabled them to gather.

It would be easy to follow out these correspondences

and connexions of the different parts of St. John's Gospel
in other directions and in fuller detail; but enough has
been said to direct attention to the subject. If the
principle be acknowledged the application will follow.

IV. RELATION OF THE GOSPEL TO THE OTHER APOSTOLIC WRITINGS

1. *The Relation of the Fourth Gospel to the Synoptists*

It is impossible for any one to turn directly from the
first three Gospels to the fourth without feeling that he
has been brought in the later record to a new aspect of
the Person and Work of Christ, to a new phase of
Christian thought, to a new era in the history of the
Christian Church.   In this there is a halo of divine glory
always about the Saviour even in scenes of outward humiliation : the truths of the Gospel are presented in their
relations to the broadest speculations of men : the society
of believers, of " the brethren " (xx. 17, xxi. 23), stands
out with a clear supremacy above the world.   As we compare the pictures more carefully, and in this view they are
two and not four, we find that the general difference between the Gospels which is thus obvious reaches throughout their whole composition.   The Synoptists and St. John
differ in the general impression which they convey as to
the duration, the scene, the form, the substance of the
Lord's teaching.   They differ also in regard to the circumstances under which they were composed.   The latter
difference furnishes the final explanation of the former.
And here it may be well to make one remark on the total
effect which these differences produce upon the student of
the New Testament.   At first they are not realised in their
true weight and value.   The conception of the Lord which
is brought to the study of any Gospel includes elements
which are derived from all.   Contrasts are already reconciled.   So it was with the early Church.   No teacher found
the fourth Gospel at variance with the other three, though
they recognised its complementary character.   Then follows
in many cases an exaggerated estimate of the importance
of the differences which are apprehended upon a careful

comparison of the books. Fresh results impress us more in proportion as they are unexpected, and at variance with our preconceived opinions. Still later perhaps that comprehensive conception of the subject of the Gospel is regained by labour and thought, from which, as a tradition, the study began; and it is felt that a true and intelligible unity underlies external differences, which are now viewed in their proper position with regard to the records and to the subject.

Before considering the differences or the correspondences of the Synoptists and St. John, it is necessary to apprehend distinctly the fragmentary character of the documents which we have to compare. The narrative of St. John, and the narratives of the Synoptists, are alike partial, and alike recognise a large area of facts with which they do not deal.

(1) *Limited range of St. John's Gospel.*—The Gospel of St. John forms, as we have seen, a complete whole in relation to "its purpose"; but as an external history it is obviously most incomplete. It is a Gospel and not a Biography, an account of facts and words which have a permanent and decisive bearing upon the salvation of the world, and not a representation of a life simply from a human point of sight. The other Gospels, as based upon the popular teaching of the Apostles, include more details of directly human interest, but these also are Gospels and not Biographies. All the Gospels are alike in this: they contain in different shapes what was necessary to convey the message of redemption to the first age and to all ages in the unchangeable record of facts. Their completeness is moral and spiritual and not historical. The striking Jewish legend as to the Manna was fulfilled in Christ. He was to each true believer, from the absolute completeness of His Person, that which each desired; and the Evangelists have preserved for the society typical records of apostolic experience.

The fragmentariness of St. John's record is shown conclusively by his notice of periods of teaching of undefined length of which he relates no more than their occurrence:

iii. 22. *Jesus and his disciples came into the land of*

Judœa; and there he tarried (διέτριβεν) with them and baptized . . . (iv. 1—3) *making and baptizing more disciples than John.* Comp. iv. 54.

vii. 1. *After these things Jesus walked (περιεπάτει) in Galilee; for he would not walk in Judœa, because the Jews sought to kill him.*

x. 40—42. *And he went away again beyond Jordan into the place where John was at first baptizing; and there he abode* (the reading is uncertain, ἔμεινεν or ἔμενεν) . . . *and many believed on him there.*

xi. 54. *Jesus therefore walked no more openly among the Jews, but departed thence into the country near to the wilderness, into a city called Ephraim; and there he abode (ἔμεινεν) with the disciples.*

The last passage seems to describe a period of retirement, but the others imply action and continuous labour in Judæa, Galilee and Peræa, of which St. John has preserved no details. He passed these over (such is the obvious explanation) because they did not contribute materials necessary for the fulfilment of his special purpose. And so again the two days' teaching in Samaria, at which he was present, is represented only by the confession which it called out (iv. 42).

The same conclusion follows from the frequent general notices of "signs" and "works" which find no special recital:

ii. 23. *Many believed on his name beholding his signs which he did (ἐποίει).* Comp. iv. 45, *The Galilœans received him, having seen all the things that he did (ὅσα ἐποίησεν) in Jerusalem at the feast;* and iii. 2, *No man can do these signs that thou doest, except God be with him.*

vi. 2. *And a great multitude followed him, because they beheld the signs which he did (ἐποίει) on them that were sick.*

vii. 3. *His brethren therefore said unto him, Depart hence, and go into Judœa, that thy disciples also may behold thy works which thou doest.*

vii. 31. *But of the multitude many believed on him; and they said, When the Christ shall come, will he do more signs than those which this man hath done (ἐποίησεν)?*

x. 32. *Jesus answered them, Many good works have I*

shewed you from the Father; for which of those works do
ye stone me?

xi. 47. *The chief priests . . . said, What do we? for this*
man doeth many signs.

xii. 37. *Though he had done so many signs before them,*
yet they believed not on him.

xx. 30. *Many other signs therefore did Jesus in the*
presence of the disciples which are not written in this
book . . .

xxi. 25. *And there are also many other things which Jesus*
did, the which, if they should be written every one, I suppose
that even the world itself would not contain the books that
should be written.

A consideration of what the Lord's Life was, as it has
been made known to us, shows that this last summary
statement is only a natural expression of the sense of that
which we must feel to be its infinite fulness. And the
other passages open glimpses of a variety and energy of
action of which St. John's narrative itself gives no completer view. Of "all that the Lord did" at Jerusalem,
which moved the faith alike of "the teacher of Israel,"
and of "the Galilæans," he has noticed only the cleansing
of the temple. Of the healings of the sick in Galilee, he
has recorded only one. He tells us nothing of "the disciples in Judæa" (vii. 3), who might desire to see works
such as Christ wrought in other places. Of the "many
good works" shown at Jerusalem (x. 32), two only are
given at length. A fair appreciation of these facts will
leave no doubt that St. John omitted far more events
than he related out of those which he knew. The Gospel
of the Church, which it was his office to write, might be
expected to take shape in special festival discourses at
the centre of the Old Faith. He deals with aspects of
Christ's Life and teaching which were not clear at first,
but became clear afterwards. And in doing this he leaves
ample room for other accounts widely differing in character
from his own.

One other point deserves notice in this connexion. The
abrupt breaks in St. John's narrative show that he was
guided by something different from a purely historic aim

in his work. The simple phrase *after these things* (iii. 22, v. 1, vi. 1) is used to mark a decided interval in time and place ; and if the interpretation of x. 22 which has been adopted be correct, the transition in ix. 1 is not less sharp.[1]

(2) *Limited range of the Synoptists.* The Synoptic Gospels, no less than St. John, imply much more than they record. The commencement of the Galilæan ministry in their narratives not only leaves room for, but points to, earlier work.

Matt. iv. 12. *Now when he heard that John was delivered up, he withdrew (ἀνεχώρησεν) into Galilee.*

Mark i. 14. *Now after that John was delivered up, Jesus came into Galilee preaching the Gospel of God.*

The words have no force unless it be supposed that the Evangelists referred to an earlier ministry in Judæa which is deliberately passed over (comp. John ii. 3). Nor is there anything in Luke iv. 14 f. opposed to this view. The summary which is there given may include any period of time, and specifies a wide area of place (comp. *v.* 23).

Again, the Sermon on the Mount involves some previous teaching in Judæa in which the character of the Scribes and Pharisees had been revealed. It is most unlikely that their "righteousness" would have been denounced (Matt. v. 20) unless the Lord had met them in the seat of their power and proved them.

Still more instructive is the great episode in St. Luke (Luke ix. 51—xviii. 14), which shows how much material there was at hand of which no use was made in the oral Gospel of the Apostles. At the same time it is of interest to observe that this peculiar section has in one incident (x. 38 ff.) a point of connexion with St. John, and the notices of the Samaritans which it contains (x. 33, xvii. 16, [ix. 52]) offer in some respects a parallel to the fourth chapter of his Gospel.

(3) *The differences of the Synoptists and St. John.* Taking account of these characteristics of the Gospels we can form a juster estimate of their differences. The Synoptists

---

[1] It may be added that St. John nowhere notices *scribes* (viii. 3 is an interpolation), *taxgatherers* ("publicans"), *lepers*, or *demoniacs.*

and St. John differ at first sight (as has been already said) as to the time, the scene, the form, and the substance of the Lord's teaching.

If we had the Synoptic Gospels alone it might be supposed that the Lord's ministry was completed in a single year; that it was confined to Galilee till the visit to Jerusalem at the Passover by which it was terminated : that it was directed in the main to the simple peasantry, and found expression in parables, and proverbs, and clear, short discourses, which reach the heart of a multitude : that it was a lofty and yet practical exposition of the Law, by One who spake as man to men. But if we look at St. John all is changed. In that we see that the public ministry of Christ opened as well as closed with a Paschal journey: that between these journeys there intervened another Passover and several visits to Jerusalem : that He frequently used modes of speech which were dark and mysterious, not from the imagery in which they were wrapped, but from the thoughts to which they were applied : that at the outset He claimed in the Holy City the highest prerogatives of Messiah, and at later times constantly provoked the anger of His opponents by the assumption of what they felt to be divine authority. And beyond all these differences of arrangement and manner, the first three Gospels and the fourth have very few facts in common. They meet only once (at the feeding of the five thousand), before the last scenes of the Passion and Resurrection. And in this common section they are distinguished by signal differences. To mention only two of the most conspicuous : the Synoptists do not notice the raising of Lazarus, which marks a crisis in the narrative of St. John ; and, on the other hand, St. John does not mention the Institution of the Holy Eucharist, which is given in detail by each of the Synoptists (see notes on chs. xi., xiii.).

A student of the Gospels can have no wish to underrate the significance of phenomena like these, which must powerfully affect his view of the full meaning both of the documents and of their subject. But he will interrogate them, and not at once assume that they have only

l

to witness to discrepancies. From such questioning one result is gained at once. It is seen (to omit the question of time for the present) that differences of form and substance correspond with differences of persons and place. On the one side there is the discourse at Nazareth, the Sermon on the Mount, the groups of parables, words first spoken to the Galilæan multitudes with the authority of the Great Teacher, and then continued afterwards when they came up to the Feast full of strange expectations, which were stimulated by the Triumphal Entry. On the other side there are the personal communings with individual souls, with "the Master (Teacher) of Israel" and the woman of Samaria, unveilings of the thoughts of faithless cavillers, who had been trained in the subtleties of the Law, and rested on the glories of their worship: glimpses of a spiritual order opened at last to loving disciples, in which they were prepared to find, even through sorrow, the accomplishment of their early hopes. On the one side there is the Gospel of "the common people who heard gladly"; on the other side the Gospel of such as felt the deeper necessities and difficulties of faith. The lessons which appealed to broad sympathies are supplanted by those which deal with varieties of personal trial and growth. The cycle of missionary teaching is completed by the cycle of internal teaching: the first experience of the whole band of Apostles by the mature experience of their latest survivor.

These general remarks are supported by numerous minute details which indicate that the Synoptists do in fact recognise an early Judæan ministry and teaching similar to that of St. John, and that St. John recognises important work in Galilee and teaching similar to that of the Synoptists.

(a) *The scene of the Lord's teaching.* The general description of the Lord's following as including multitudes *"from Judæa and Jerusalem"* (Matt. iv. 25; comp. Mark iii. 7 f.) cannot be pressed as proving that He had Himself worked there. Similar language is used in connexion with the Baptist (Matt. iii. 5). But the reading of St. Luke iv. 44, *he was preaching in the synagogues of Judæa* (for *Galilee*), which is supported by very strong MS. authority (אBCLQR *Memph.*), taken in connexion with Luke v. 17, may fairly be urged in favour of such a view. Indeed, the feeling of the people of Jerusalem on the Lord's last visit is scarcely intelligible unless they had grown familiar with Him on former visits.   So again the well-known words of the lamentation over Jerusalem, *How often would I have gathered thy children . . . and thou wouldest not* (Matt. xxiii. 37 ff.), scarcely admit any other sense than that Christ had personally on many occasions sought to attach the inhabitants to Himself, as now when the issue was practically decided.   The visit to Martha and Mary (Luke x. 38 ff.) suggests previous acquaintance with them, and so probably previous residences in the neighbourhood of Jerusalem (John xi. 1 ff.).   The circumstances connected with the preparation for the last visit (Matt. xxi. 2 f., xxvi. 17 ff., and parallels) point to the same conclusion.   Compare Acts x. 37, 39.   On the other hand St. John, when he notices a brief sojourn of the Lord and His first disciples at Capernaum (ii. 12), seems to imply a longer abode there at another time ; and in a later passage he records words which show that Galilee was the ordinary scene of Christ's ministry (vii. 3).   It might indeed have been plausibly argued from these words that when they were spoken He had not wrought any conspicuous works in Judæa.

(β) *The manner of the Lord's teaching.*   It has been already shown that the form of the Lord's teaching could not but depend upon the occasion on which it was delivered ; and there is no scene in St. John which answers to those under which the Sermon on the Mount, or the chief groups of parables were delivered ; and conversely there are no scenes in the Synoptists like those with Nicodemus and the woman of Samaria.   The discourses at Jerusalem recorded by the Synoptists were spoken after Christ had openly accepted the position of Messiah by His triumphal entry : those recorded by St. John belong to earlier times, when He was gradually leading His hearers to grasp the truth of faith in Him. As the circumstances become more like in character there is a growing resemblance in style. In John x., xii., we have the implicit parables of the Sheepfold, the Good Shepherd, the Grain of Corn. In Matt. xi. 25 ff., Luke x. 21 ff., there is a thanksgiving spoken in regard to the disciples' work which in character is not unlike the last discourses.

(γ) *The duration of the Lord's teaching.* The data for determining the length of the Lord's ministry are singularly few. The time of its commencement is approximately fixed by the different elements given by St. Luke (iii. 1), as marking the Call of the Baptist. But there is nothing in the Gospels to connect its close with any particular year of Pilate's procuratorship. Pilate was recalled in A.D. 36, and Herod was banished in A.D. 39. They may therefore have met at Jerusalem in any year during Pilate's term of office. Caiaphas retained his office till the end of Pilate's procuratorship. The date of the death of Annas is not known, but he lived to old age. So far there is a wide margin of uncertainty; and this can only be removed by the assumption that the Gospels supply a complete chronology of the Ministry, for the earliest tradition is both late and conflicting. Here, however, we are left to probability. The Synoptists appear to include the events of their narrative in a single year; but it is very difficult to bring the development of faith and unbelief to which they witness, the Missions of the Twelve and of the Seventy, and the different circuits of the Lord, within so brief a space.[1] St. John, on the other hand, notices three Passovers, but he gives no clear intimation that he notices every Passover which occurred in the course of the Lord's work. In such a case the fragmentariness of the records is a conclusive answer to the supposed discrepancy.

(4) *The coincidences of the Synoptists and St. John.* So far we have dwelt upon the differences between the Synoptists and St. John. Their correspondences are less obvious and impressive, but they are scarcely less important.

---

[1] The reading and interpretation of Luke vi. 1 (δευτεροπρώτῳ) is too uncertain to be pressed.

The common incidents with which they deal are the following :

1. *The Baptism of John* (St. John adds the mention of *the Levites*, i. 19 : the questions, i. 20 ff. : the place, *Bethany*, i. 28 : the *abiding* of the Spirit on Christ, i. 32 f. : the after testimony to Christ, i. 26 ff.).

2. *The feeding of the five thousand* (St. John notices the time, *the Passover was near*, vi. 4 : the persons, *Philip* and *Andrew*, vi. 5, 8 : the command to collect the fragments, *v.* 12 : the issue of the miracle and the retirement of Jesus, *v.* 14 f.).

3. *The Walking on the Sea* (St. John mentions the distance, vi. 19 : the feeling of the disciples, *v.* 21 : the result, *ib.*).

4. *The Anointing at Bethany* (St. John mentions the time, xii. 1, *six days before the Passover :* the persons, *Mary*, *v.* 3 (comp. Matt. xxvi. 7 ; Mark xiv. 3), and *Judas*, *vv.* 4, 6 : the full details of the action, *v.* 3).

5. *The Triumphal Entry* (St. John mentions the time, *on the next day*, xii. 12 : the reference to Lazarus, *v.* 18 : the judgement of the Pharisees, *v.* 19).

6. *The Last Supper* (St. John records the feet-washing, xiii. 2 ff. : the question of St. John, *v.* 23 : the ignorance of the Apostles, *v.* 28 : the discourses in the chamber and on the way [1]).

7. *The Betrayal.* See notes on ch. xviii.

8. *The Trial.* Ib.

9. *The Crucifixion.* Ib.

10. *The Burial* (St. John notices the action of Nicodemus, xix. 39 : the garden, *v.* 41).

11. *The Resurrection.* See note on ch. xx.

Not to enter in detail upon an examination of the parallels, it may be said that in each case St. John adds details which appear to mark his actual experience ; and also that the facts in all their completeness form a natural

---

[1] The apparent difference between the Synoptists and St. John as to the day of the Last Supper is of importance in regard to the Synoptists and not in regard to St. John. The narrative of St. John is perfectly definite and consistent : it bears every mark of exact accuracy, and is in harmony with what seems to be the natural course of the events.

part of both narratives. They do not appear either in the
Synoptists or in St. John as if they were borrowed from
an alien source.

The passages in which St. John implies an acquaintance
with incidents recorded by the Synoptists are more
numerous.

i. 19 ff.	The general effect of John's preaching (Matt. iii. 5, etc.).
— 32 ff.	The circumstances of the Lord's Baptism (Matt. iii. 16 f.).
— 40.	Simon Peter is well known.
— 46.	Nazareth the early home of Christ (Matt. ii. 23, etc.).
ii. 12.	Capernaum the later residence of Christ.
—	The family of Christ. Comp. vi. 42, vii. 3, xix. 25 f.
— 19.	The false accusation; Matt. xxvi. 61.
iii. 24.	The date of John's imprisonment (Matt. iv. 12; comp. John iv. 43).
vi. 3.	Retirement to " the mountain."
— 62.	The Ascension.
— 67.	" The twelve." Comp. *vv.* 13, 70, xx. 24 (not in chs. i.—iv.).
xi. 1, 2.	Mary and Martha are well known.
xviii. 33.	The title " the King of the Jews."
— 40.	Barabbas suddenly introduced.
xix. 25.	The ministering women (Matt. xxvii. 55, etc.).

There are also several coincidences in the use of
imagery between St. John and the Synoptists, and not a
few sayings of which the substance is common to them.

Common imagery.

iii. 29.	The Bride and the Bridegroom. Matt. ix. 15, and parallels.
iv. 35 ff.	The harvest. Matt. ix. 37 f.
xiii. 4 ff.	Serving. Matt. x. 24; Luke xii. 37, xxii. 27.
xv. 1 ff.	The vine. Matt. xxi. 33.
— 2.	The unfruitful tree. Matt. vii. 19.

Common sayings.

iv. 44.	Comp. Matt. xiii. 57; Mark vi. 4; Luke iv. 24 (used in different connexions).

vi. 42.   Comp. *ll. cc.*
— 69.   Comp. Matt. xvi. 16, and parallels (corresponding confessions).
xii. 25.   Comp. Matt. x. 39, xvi. 25; Luke xvii. 33 (used in different connexions).
xiii. 16.   Comp. Luke vi. 40 ; Matt. x. 24 (used in different connexions).
— 20.   Comp. Matt. x. 40, (xxv. 40) ; Luke x. 16 (used in different connexions).
xvi. 2 f.   Comp. Matt. xxiv. 10 f.

In other parallels there are not a few verbal coincidences :

i. 23.   I am *the voice of one crying in the wilderness*, Make straight *the way of the Lord.*
— 26 f.   *I baptize in water . . . He that cometh after me, the latchet of whose shoe I am not worthy to unloose.*
— 32.   *. . . descending as a dove . . .*
— 43.   *Follow me.*   Matt. viii. 22, etc.
iii. 5.   *to enter into the kingdom of God.*
v. 8.   *Arise, take up thy bed and walk.*   Mark ii. 9.
vi. 20.   *It is I : be not afraid.*
viii. 52.   *taste of death.*   Mark ix. 1.
xii. 5.   *to be sold for three hundred pence and given to the poor.*   Mark xiv. 5.
— 13.   *Hosanna, blessed is he that cometh in the name of the Lord.*
xiii. 21.   *One of you shall betray me.*
— 38.   *The cock shall not crow till thou shalt deny me thrice.*
xix. 3.   *Hail, King of the Jews.*
xx. 19.   *He saith unto them, Peace be unto you.*

Coincidences more or less striking are found in the following passages.

i. 18.	Matt. xi. 27.	vi.	35.	Matt. v. 6.
— 33.	— iii. 11.	—	37.	— xi. 28.
iii. 18.	Mark xvi. 16.	—	39.	— xviii. 14.
iv. 44.	— vi. 4.	—	46.	— xi. 27.
v. 22.	Matt. vii. 22f.	—	70.	Luke vi. 13.
vi. 7, 10.	Mark vi. 37	vii.	45 f.	Matt. vii. 28.
	—39.	ix.	16.	— xii. 2.

x. 15.	Matt. xi. 27.	xvi. 1 f.	Matt. x. 17 ff; xiii. 21.
xi. 25.	— x. 39.		
xii. 8.	— xxvi. 11.	xvii. 2.	— xxviii. 18.
— 13.	Mark xi. 9.	xviii. 11.	— xxvi. 42, 52.
— 44.	Luke ix. 48.		
xiii. 1.	Mark xiv. 41.	— 15, 18, 22.	Mark xiv. 64 f.
— 3.	Matt. xi. 27.		
— 16.	— x. 24.	— 20.	Matt. xxvi. 55.
— 20.	— x. 40.	— 39.	Mark xv. 6.
— 21.	Mark xiv. 18 —21.	xix. 1—3, 17.	— — 16, 19, 22.
xiv. 18.	Matt. xxviii. 20.	— 6.	Luke xxiii. 21.
— 28.	Mark xiii. 32.	[— 19.	— — 38, an interpolation in St. Luke.]
xv. 8.	Matt. v. 16.		
— 14.	— xii. 49 f.	xx. 14.	Mark xvi. 9.
— 20.	— x. 25.	— 23.	Matt. xvi. 19.
— 21.	— x. 22.		

The connexion between St. John and St. Luke is of especial interest. From the relation of St. Luke to St. Paul it is natural to expect that the peculiarities of his Gospel would furnish indications of transition to the form of the Gospel which St. John has preserved. Instances of this relation have been already given in the notices of Samaritans, and of Martha and Mary (pp. clx, clxiii). The following coincidences in thought or language may be added :

i. 19 ff.	Luke iii.15f.	xiv. 30.	Luke iv. 13 (ἄχρι καιροῦ).
vi. 42.	— iv. 22.		
x. 27 ff.	— xii. 32.	xvi. 7.	— xxiv. 49 (ἐγὼ ἐξαποσ- τέλλω).
xiii. 1, xiv. 30.	— ix. 51 (ἀναλή- ψεως) ;		
	xxii. 53.	xviii. 36 f.	— xvii. 20 f.
— 4 ff.	— xxii. 27.	— 38.	— xxiii. 4.
— 17.	— xi. 28.	xx. 3, 6.	— xxiv.12 (the reading is doubt- ful).
— 22.	— xxii. 23.		
— 27.	— — 3.		
— 37.	— — 33.	— 19 ff.	— — 36 ff.

Such correspondences prove nothing as to the direct literary connexion of the two Gospels, nor do the few significant words which are common to St. Luke and St. John (*e.g.*, τὸ ἔθνος of Jews, μονογενής), but they do show the currency of a form of the apostolic Gospel with characteristic features proximating to characteristic features in St. John.

5. *The relation of the Synoptists to St. John in regard to the Lord's Person.* But it may be said that even if the considerations which have been urged establish the possibility of reconciling the apparent differences of the Synoptists and St. John as to the place, the manner, and the duration of the Lord's Teaching: if they show that there is theoretically room for the events and the discourses of both narratives: if they supply in both cases indications of a wider field and a more varied method than is habitually recorded in the two histories respectively; yet the fundamental differences between the first three Gospels and the fourth as to the general view of the Lord's Person practically exclude such a reconciliation.

This difficulty unquestionably underlies the other difficulties and gives force to them. It is not possible to do more here than to point out the main arguments by which it can fairly be met.

The Person of the Lord is as truly the centre of the teaching of the Synoptists as of the teaching of St. John. It is not His doctrine but Himself which is to redeem the world (Matt. xx. 28).

The narratives of the Nativity, though they did not form part of the apostolic oral Gospel, are completely harmonious with it. There is no contrast (for example) in passing from the history of the Nativity to that of the Baptism.

The claims of the Lord which are recorded by the Synoptists, if followed to their legitimate consequences, involve the claims recorded by St. John.

Matt. vii. 22.   *in my name.*
— ix. 2 ff.   *Thy sins be forgiven thee.*
— x. 1.   (Gives power to work signs.)
— — 39.   *he that loseth his life for my sake. . . .*

Matt. xi. 27.   *All things are delivered unto me. . . .*

— xiii. 41.   *The Son of man will send forth his angels.*
Comp. xvi. 27, xxv. 31.

— xviii. 20.   *Where two or three are gathered together in my name, there am I . . .* (as said of Shekinah).

— xx. 28.   *his life a ransom for many.*

— xxi. 37 ff.   *They will reverence my son.*

— xxii. 45.   *If David call him Lord.*

— xxv. 31.   *When the Son of man shall come in his glory.* Comp. xxvi. 64.

— xxvi. 28.   *My blood of the covenant.*

— xxviii. 20.   *I am with you alway.*

Luke xxi. 15.   *I will give you a mouth and wisdom.*

— xxiv. 49.   *I send the promise of my Father upon you.*

A careful estimate of these passages will make it clear that the Synoptists recognise in the Lord the power of judgement, of redemption, and of fellowship, which are the main topics of the teaching in St. John. In one respect only St. John adds a new truth to the doctrine of the Lord's Person which has no direct anticipation in the Synoptists. These do not anywhere declare His pre-existence. (Yet compare Luke xi. 49 with Matt. xxiii. 34 and John x. 35.)

The general conclusion, however, stands firm. The Synoptists offer not only historical but also spiritual points of connexion between the teaching which they record and the teaching in the fourth Gospel; and St. John himself in the Apocalypse completes the passage from the one to the other.

2. *The Apocalypse and the Fourth Gospel*

The Apocalypse is doctrinally the uniting link between the Synoptists and the fourth Gospel. It offers the characteristic thoughts of the fourth Gospel in that form of development which belongs to the earliest apostolic age. It belongs to different historical circumstances, to a different phase of intellectual progress, to a different theological stage, from that of St. John's Gospel; and yet it is not only harmonious with it in teaching, but in the order of thought it is the necessary germ out of which the Gospel proceeded by a process of life.

(1) *Affinities of the Apocalypse with the Gospel.* The points of connexion between the Apocalypse and the Gospel of St. John are far more numerous than are suggested by a first general comparison of the two books. The main idea of both is the same. Both present a view of a supreme conflict between the powers of good and evil. In the Gospel this is drawn mainly in moral conceptions; in the Apocalypse mainly in images and visions. In the Gospel the opposing forces are regarded under abstract and absolute forms, as light and darkness, love and hatred; in the Apocalypse under concrete and definite forms, God, Christ, and the Church warring with the devil, the false prophet, and the beast.

But in both books alike Christ is the central figure. His victory is the end to which history and vision lead as their consummation (see xvi. 33, note). His Person and Work are the ground of triumph, and of triumph through apparent failure (Rev. i. 5, vi. 16, vii. 14, xii. 11).

It follows that in both books the appearance of Christ is shown to issue in a judgement, a separation, of elements partially confused before. The " hatred " of evil gains a new intensity (Rev. ii. 6; 2 John 10). The Apocalypse gives, so to speak, in an ideal history the analysis of the course of unbelief which is laid open in John viii.

On man's part the conflict with evil is necessarily a conflict in action. The Apocalypse and the Gospel therefore lay stress on obedience and works. To " keep the commandments " is now the fulfilment of Christian duties (John xiv. 23, note; 1 John ii. 3 f.; v. 2 f.; 2 John 6; Rev. xii. 17, xiv. 12 [xxii. 14, a false reading]).

The universality of the Gospel is an immediate consequence of the proclamation of its moral character. And there is not the least trace in the Apocalypse of the doctrine of the permanent or general obligation of the Law or of circumcision. The particular injunctions which are enforced in ii. 14, 20 are combined in the Acts (xv. 28 f., xxi. 25) with the removal of such an obligation from the Gentiles. External ceremonies fall wholly into the background, as symbols only of that which is universal and spiritual (Rev. v. 8 ff., xiv. 6 f. ; comp. 1 John ii. 2).

At the same time the Apocalypse no less than the Gospel recognises the preparatory office of Judaism. In both it is assumed that "Salvation is of the Jews" (John iv. 22, 38). The Seer shows that the sovereignty which the prophets foretold was established in Jesus, "the Christ" (xii. 5, 10, xi. 15); and the imagery of the old Scriptures is used from first to last to foreshadow the conflict, the victory, and the judgement of the divine King (*e.g.*, Zech. xii. 10; John xix. 37; Rev. i. 7).

In correspondence with the universality of the Gospel is the office of personal "witness" on which the firmest stress is laid in all the writings of St. John. The experience of the believer finds expression in a testimony which is strong in the face of death. In the Apocalypse the characteristic form in which this "witness" appears is as "the testimony of Jesus" (i. 2, 9, xii. 17, xix. 10, xx. 4). The true humanity of the Saviour is that revelation on which faith reposes.

This testimony to the Incarnation leads to a final correspondence between the Apocalypse and the fourth Gospel which is of the highest importance. Both present the abiding of God with man as the issue of Christ's work. *If any man love me, he will keep my word, and my Father will love him, and we will come to him and make our abode with him* (John xiv. 23). *Behold I stand at the door and knock : If any man hear my voice and open the door, I will come in to him, and will sup with him and he with me* (Rev. iii. 20). *Behold the tabernacle of God is with men, and He will dwell* (σκηνώσει) *with them* (Rev. xxi. 3).

(2) *Contrasts of the Apocalypse with the Gospel.* Side by side with these coincidences of thought, which reach to the ruling conceptions of the books, there are also important contrasts in their subject-matter and their modes of dealing with common topics.

The most striking contrast lies in the treatment of the doctrine of Christ's Coming in the two books. This is the main subject of the Apocalypse, while it falls into the background in the Gospel and in the Epistles of

St. John. In the Apocalypse the thought is of an outward coming for the open judgement of men : in the Gospel of a judgement which is spiritual and self-executing. In the Apocalypse the scene of the consummation is a renovated world : in the Gospel " the Father's house." In the former the victory and the transformation are from without, by might, and the " future " is painted under historic imagery : in the latter, the victory and the transformation are from within, by a spiritual influence, and the " future " is present and eternal.

It is part of this same contrast that the progress of the conflict between good and evil is presented very differently in the Apocalypse and in the Gospel. In the Apocalypse it is portrayed under several distinct forms as a conflict of Christ with false Judaism, with idolatry, with the Roman empire allied with false prophecy : in the Gospel it is conceived in its essence as a continuous conflict between light and darkness. On the one side are outward persecutors ; on the other the spirit of falsehood : on the one side, the working of the revelation of Christ ; on the other the revelation of Christ itself. Or, to put the facts under another aspect, the Apocalypse gives a view of the action of God in regard to men, in a life full of sorrow, and partial defeats, and cries for vengeance : the Gospel gives a view of the action of God with regard to Christ who establishes in the heart of the believer a Presence of completed joy.

In regard to Judaism this contrast assumes a special form. In the Apocalypse the triumph of Christianity is described under the imagery of Judaism. The Church is the embodied fulfilment of Old Testament prophecy. The outlines are drawn of the universal, ideal Israel (vii. 4), the ideal Jerusalem (iii. 12, xxi. 2, 10), and the ideal worship (xx. 6, xxii. 3 ; comp. viii. 3, v. 8), yet so that there is no longer any temple (xxi. 22). In the Gospel Christianity is proclaimed as the absolute truth. Outward Judaism is shown in its opposition to Christ's word, not as fulfilled by it, standing without, isolated and petrified ; and not taken up with it, quickened and glorified (compare Rev. ii. 9, iii. 9, with John viii. 39 ff.).

The conception of God in the two books shows corresponding differences. The conception of God in the Apocalypse follows the lines of the Old Testament. He is "the Lord God, the Almighty" (i. 8, iv. 8, etc.), "which was and is" (xi. 17, xvi. 5. Comp. i. 4, 8, iv. 8), who executes righteous judgement on the world (xi. 18, xiv. 10, xvi. 19, xix. 15). Nothing is said of His love in sending His Son; nor of the Paraclete. In the Gospel God is revealed characteristically by Christ as "the Father" and not only as "my Father" (see iv. 21, note); and specially in connexion with the work of redemption. In the one case it may be said that His action is revealed in relation to the sinful history of the world: and in the other His being in relation to the purpose of the world.[1]

Besides these differences of substance there are also differences of language both in vocabulary and style. The difference in the scope of the books accounts in part for these. The irregularities of style in the Apocalypse appear to be due not so much to ignorance of the language as to a free treatment of it, by one who used it as a foreign dialect. Nor is it difficult to see that in any case intercourse with a Greek-speaking people would in a short time naturally reduce the style of the author of the Apocalypse to that of the author of the Gospel. It is, however, very difficult to suppose that the language of the writer of the Gospel could pass at a later time in a Greek-speaking country into the language of the Apocalypse.

Such, very briefly, are the coincidences and differences between the Apocalypse and the fourth Gospel. Several conclusions appear to follow from them.

The differences answer to differences in situation; and are not inconsistent with identity of authorship.

Of the two books the Apocalypse is the earlier. It is less developed both in thought and style. The material imagery in which it is composed includes the idea of progress in interpretation. The symbols are living. On the other hand, to go back from the teaching of the Gospel to

[1] The difference between the two books as to subordinate spiritual powers, angels and evil spirits, follows from the difference in their structure. Comp. i. 51, note.

that of the Apocalypse, to clothe clear thought in figures, to reduce the full expression of truth to its rudimentary beginnings, seems to involve a moral miracle, which would introduce confusion into life.

The Apocalypse is after the close of St. Paul's work. It shows in its mode of dealing with Old Testament figures a close connexion with the Epistle to the Hebrews (2 Peter, Jude). And on the other hand it is before the destruction of Jerusalem.

The crisis of the Fall of Jerusalem explains the relation of the Apocalypse to the Gospel. In the Apocalypse that " coming " of Christ was expected, and painted in figures : in the Gospel the " coming " is interpreted.

Under this aspect the Gospel is the spiritual interpretation of the Apocalypse. The materials of the Gospel were treasured up, pondered, illuminated as time went on. Meanwhile the active and manifold religious thought of Ephesus furnished the intellectual assistance which was needed to exhibit Christianity as the absolute and historical religion in contrast with Judaism and Heathenism. The final desolation of the centre of the old Theocracy was the decisive sign of the form which the new Faith must take. Then first, according to the divine law of order, the Spirit would guide the Apostle into all the Truth.

This is not the place to work out in detail the likeness and difference of the Apocalypse and the fourth Gospel on special points of doctrine; but the Christology of the two books illustrates very remarkably the position which has been assigned to the Apocalypse as connecting the Synoptists and St. John. It is necessary then to indicate shortly the teaching of the Apocalypse on Christ's work and being.

The work of Christ is presented summarily as the victory through death of One who was truly man. Christ was the representative of David (v. 5, xxii. 16), pierced (i. 7), crucified (xi. 8), and again quickened (i. 5; comp. Col. i. 18). So He " bought " the redeemed (v. 9, xiv. 3 f.); and His blood brings to them release (i. 5, λύσαντι ἀπὸ τ. ἁ.), cleansing (vii. 14), and victory (xii. 11). And in this He fulfilled the divine will for men (i. 1 [ἔδωκεν], ii. 26, 5, 10, 16, iii. 10, 5, 21, v. 5, xxi. 23).

The exaltation of Christ followed on the completion of His earthly work. The " Lamb slain " was raised to glory (v. 9, 12). The "seven spirits of God " are His (v. 6, iii. 1; comp. i. 4; John xv. 26). In the heavenly sanctuary He is revealed as the divine High Priest (i. 12—17; comp. ii. 9, x. 5 f.) "like a son of man " (i. 13, xiv. 14); truly man, and yet more than man, "the living One " (i. 17; comp. John v. 26). He possesses divine knowledge (ii. 2, 9, 13, 19, etc., ii. 23; comp. Jer. xi. 20, etc.); and divine power (xi. 15, xii. 10, xvii. 14, xix. 16). He receives divine honour (v. 8 ff., xx. 6); and is joined with God (iii. 2, v. 13, vi. 16 f., vii. 10, xiv. 4, xxi. 22, xxii. 1, 3; comp. John v. 20, 23), so that with God He is spoken of as one (xi. 15, βασιλεύσει, xx. 6, μετ᾽ αὐτοῦ, xxii. 3, οἱ δοῦλοι αὐτοῦ λατρεύσουσιν αὐτῷ); He shares also in part the divine titles (i. 7, iii. 7, xix. 11; comp. vi. 10, iii. 14; comp. Isa. lxv. 16, but not xxii. 13).

The full importance of these passages is brought out by the stern denunciations against every form of idolatry with which the book abounds (comp. 1 John v. 21). Christ therefore is wholly separated from creatures. And further, the passages show that the imagery which is used in the Old Testament to describe the revelation of God is trans- ferred by the writer to Christ (comp. John xii. 41, note).

One other point remains to be noticed. In the Synop- tists there is no direct statement of the pre-existence of Christ. The truth is recognised in the Apocalypse, but relatively rather than absolutely. Christ is spoken of as *the first and the last* (i. 17, ii. 8); *the beginning of the creation of God* (iii. 14; comp. Prov. viii. 22; Col. i. 15); and *the Word of God* (xix. 13). In these phrases we find the earliest form of the " Logos doctrine," which is still kept within the lines of the Old Testament ideas. But the later unfolding of the truth is included in this earliest confession. If an Apostle was enabled to see in the Master whom he had followed the Being to whom all creation pays homage in the spiritual world, there is no difficulty in apprehending how he could rise, without doing violence to the laws of human thought, to the enunciation of the fact on which the fourth Gospel is a commentary, *the*

Word became flesh and dwelt among us, and we beheld His glory.

In a word, the study of the Synoptists, of the Apocalypse, and of the Gospel of St. John in succession enables us to see under what human conditions the full majesty of Christ was perceived and declared, not all at once, but step by step, and by the help of the old prophetic teaching.

3. *The Gospel and the Epistles of St. John*

The relation of the Gospel of St. John to his Epistles is that of a history to its accompanying comment or application. The first Epistle presupposes the Gospel either as a writing or as oral instruction. But while there are numerous and striking resemblances both in form and thought between the Epistle and the Evangelist's record of the Lord's discourses and his own narrative, there are still characteristic differences between them. In the Epistle the doctrine of the Lord's true and perfect humanity (σάρξ) is predominant: in the Gospel that of His divine glory (δόξα). The burden of the Epistle is "the Christ is Jesus": the writer presses his argument from the divine to the human, from the spiritual and ideal to the historical. The burden of the Gospel is "Jesus is the Christ": the writer presses his argument from the human to the divine, from the historical to the spiritual and ideal. The former is the natural position of the preacher, and the latter of the historian.

The difference between the Epistle and the Gospel in their eschatological teaching follows from this fundamental difference. In the Gospel the doctrine of the "coming" of the Lord (xxi. 22, xiv. 3), and of "the last day" (vi. 40, 44), and of "the judgement" (v. 28 f.), are touched upon generally. In the Epistle "the manifestation" of Christ (ii. 28) and His "presence" stand out as clear facts in the history of the world. He comes, even as He came, "in flesh" (2 John 7); and "antichrists" precede His coming (1 John ii. 18 ff.).

Again, in the Epistle the doctrine of propitiation is more distinct and fully expressed than in the Gospel (ἱλασμός, 1 John ii. 2, iv. 10; comp. Heb. ii. 17; καθαρίζειν,

m

1 John i. 7, 9); and in connexion with this the duty of the confession of sins (1 John i. 9), and the office of the Lord as Paraclete (Advocate) (1 John ii. 1; comp. John xiv. 16, note). But it is most worthy of notice that no use is made in the Epistle of the language of the discourses in John iii. and vi. On the other hand, the conception of ·the " unction " of Christians (1 John ii. 20, 27; comp. Rev. i. 6) is a later interpretation of the gift of the Spirit which Christ promised.

Generally too it will be found on a comparison of the closest parallels, that the Apostle's own words are more formal in expression than the words of the Lord which he records. The Lord's words have been moulded by the disciple into aphorisms in the Epistle : their historic connexion has been broken. At the same time the language of the Epistle is in the main direct, abstract, and unfigurative. The Apostle's teaching, so to speak, is " plain " (παρρησία), while that of the Lord was "in proverbs " (ἐν παροιμίαις, John xvi. 25).

One or two examples will illustrate the contrast which has been indicated :

John viii. 12. *I am the Light of the world : he that followeth me shall not walk in darkness, but shall have the light of life.*

1 John i. 5, 7. *This then is the message we have heard of him, and declare unto you, that God is light, and in him is no darkness at all . . . If we walk in the light as he is in the light, we have fellowship one with another . . .*

John xv. 23. *He that hateth me hateth my Father also.*

1 John ii. 23. *Whosoever denieth the Son, the same hath not the Father; but he that acknowledgeth the Son hath the Father also.*

Compare also pp. cxxiv ff.

Generally it will be felt that there is a decisive difference (so to speak) in the atmosphere of the two books. In the Epistle St. John deals freely with the truths of the Gospel in direct conflict with the characteristic perils of his own time : in the Gospel he lives again in the presence of Christ and of the immediate enemies of Christ, while he brings out the universal significance of events and teaching not fully understood at the time.

V. THE HISTORY OF THE GOSPEL

1. *The Text*

The materials for determining the text of the Gospel of St. John are, as in the case of other Gospels, and of the books of the New Testament generally, ample and varied. It will be sufficient to notice the most important authorities in which the Gospel of St. John is preserved.

I. GREEK MANUSCRIPTS.

Cod. Sinaiticus (א).   The entire Gospel.

Cod. Alexandrinus (A).   Wants vi. 50—viii. 52.

Cod. Vaticanus (B).   The entire Gospel.

Cod. Ephraemi (C).   Eight considerable fragments. (1) i. 1—41.   (2) iii. 33—v. 16.   (3) vi. 38—vii. 3.   (4) viii. 34—ix. 11.   (5) xi. 8—46.   (6) xiii. 8—xiv. 7.   (7) xvi. 21—xviii. 36.   (8) xx. 26—end.

Cod. Bezæ (D).   Wants i. 16—iii. 26; and xviii. 13—xx. 13 has been supplied by a later hand, perhaps from the original leaves.

Cod. Paris. (L).   Wants xxi. 15—end.

There are besides eight other uncial MSS. containing the Gospel complete or nearly complete; and thirteen which contain more or less considerable fragments.[1]

---

[1] In addition to noting the readings of the six Greek uncial MSS. mentioned above I have also on occasion noted the readings of the following selected uncials :

E (*Cod. Basiliensis*).   The entire Gospel.

F (*Cod. Boreeli*).   Contains, with considerable lacunæ, i. 1—xiii. 34.

G (*Cod. Seidelii*).   Wants xviii. 5-19 ; xix. 4-27.

M (*Cod. Campianus*).   The entire Gospel.

N (*Cod. Purpureus*).   Contains xiv. 2-10 ; xv. 15-22.

P (*Cod. Guelferbytanus.* Sæc. VI.).   Contains i. 29-41 ; ii. 13-25 ; xxi. 1-11.

Q (*Cod. Guelferbytanus.* Sæc. V.).   Contains xii. 3-20 ; xiv. 3-22.

T (*Cod Borgianus*).   Contains vi. 28-67 ; vii. 6—viii. 32 (omitting the Adulteress Lection).

T^b (*Cod. Petropolitanus*).   Contains i. 25-42 ; ii. 9—iv. 50.

X (*Cod. Monacensis*).   Contains ii. 22 ; vii. 1—xiii. 5 ; xiii. 20—xv. 25 ; xvi. 23—xxi. 25 (ii. 23—vi. 71 has been supplied later).

Y (*Cod. Barberinus*).   Contains xvi. 3—xix. 41.

Γ (*Cod. Tischendorfianus* IV.).   The entire Gospel.

Δ (*Cod. Sangallensis*).   Wants xix. 17-35.—A. W.

The cursive mss., which are almost of every degree of excellence, are more than 600.[1]

II. ANCIENT VERSIONS.

(1) *The Old* (Curetonian) *Syriac* (*Syr. vt.*). Four fragments: (1) i. 1—42. (2) iii. 5—vii. 37. (3) vii. 37—viii. 53, omitting vii. 53—viii. 11. (4) xiv. 11—29.

The Vulgate Syriac (Peshito, *Syr. psh.*). The entire Gospel.

The Harclean Syriac (*Syr. hcl.*). The entire Gospel.

(2) *The Old Latin* (*Lat. vt.*). The entire Gospel in several distinct types.

The Vulgate Latin (*Vulg.*). The entire Gospel.

The Memphitic (Coptic, in the dialect of Lower Egypt). The entire Gospel.

The Thebaic (Sahidic, in the dialect of Upper Egypt). Very considerable fragments have been published in the Appendix to Woide's *Cod. Al. N. T.*, of which a collation is given in Schwartze's edition of the Memphitic Gospels.

III. FATHERS.

In addition to isolated quotations there remain, from early times: the Commentaries of CYRIL of ALEXANDRIA (nearly complete); the Explanatory Homilies of AUGUSTINE and CHRYSOSTOM; and large fragments of the Commentaries of ORIGEN and THEODORE of MOPSUESTIA.

This is not the place to enter in detail upon the methods of textual criticism. It must suffice to say that the problem is in the first stage essentially historical. The primary object of the critic is to discover in the case of variations the most ancient reading. When this has been done it remains to take account of any arguments which may be urged against the authenticity of the earliest text. Unless these are of great weight the prerogative of age must prevail. But this first process cannot be accomplished by simply taking the reading of the most ancient copies, or giving a fixed value, so to speak, to each copy according to its antiquity. The most ancient copy is *ceteris paribus* likely to give the most ancient text on the whole, and with

---

[1] I have occasionally noticed the readings of exceptionally good cursives, *e.g.,* 33. (See *WH*. Introduction, p. 154.).—A. W.

a less degree of probability in each particular case. But the ancient authorities often disagree. Hence it is a necessary condition for the determination of the most ancient text to study the chief authorities *as wholes* (1) separately, and (2) in their mutual relations. In this way it can be ascertained beyond doubt what MSS. (for example) preserve a distinctly ante-Nicene text. When this is done the mass of evidence can be reduced to manageable dimensions. If it cannot be shown that a reading has any ante-Nicene authority, it may in almost all cases be confidently set aside.

No one of the existing MSS. of the New Testament is older than the fourth century; but the earliest, which have been already enumerated, represent very different types of text, and are, as far as can be ascertained, of very different origin. To speak of them all as " Alexandrine " is in every way misleading.

(1) A most careful examination of B leaves it in possession of the title to supreme excellence. Its readings have no specific colouring. It is not unlikely that it represents the text preserved in the original Greek Church of Rome.

(2) The texts of ℵ and D, which have much in common, are of very high antiquity, dating from the end of the second century. Their common element is closely akin to an element in the Old Syriac and Old Latin versions, and shows much license in paraphrase and in the introduction of synonymous phrases and words. The characteristics of these MSS. are probably of Palestinian origin.

(3) The characteristic readings of C and L indicate the work of a careful grammatical revision. They seem to be due to Alexandria.

(4) In the Gospels A gives a revised (Antiochene) text which formed the basis of the later Byzantine texts. These texts were almost exclusively reproduced from the sixth century onwards.

The characteristic readings of B, of ℵD, and of C, L, have all more or less support in the ante-Nicene age. The characteristic readings of A, on the other hand, cannot be traced back beyond the fourth century, though it has also a valuable ancient element in common with BCL rather than with אD.

It follows, therefore (speaking generally), that a reading which is found in B and in a primary representative of one of the other groups has very high claims to be considered the original reading. On the other hand, a reading which is found only in the representatives of one of the last three groups is likely to be a correction; and the same may be said of a reading which is given only in representatives of the third and fourth groups. Very few readings in the Gospels will be found to stand the test of a comprehensive examination which are not supported by א or B or D.

These conclusions necessarily depend upon an exhaustive induction of particulars. No process can be more precarious than the attempt to settle each case of variation as it arises. A reading, which taken alone may appear to be plausible or even true, is often seen to be an ingenious correction from a consideration of the characteristics of the authorities by which it is supported taken as a group. No authority has an unvarying value. No authority is ever homogeneous. It is only by taking a wide view of the grouping of the authorities that a solid conclusion can be gained. And in this respect the evidence which is available for determining the text of the New Testament is so copious and varied that little final doubt can be left.

Very little has been said in detail on various readings in the notes, except on a few passages of unusual interest. It will therefore be useful to give a brief summary of the authorities for a selection of variations which have a critical interest. This may serve as a basis for further study to those who wish to pursue the subject; and at the same time it will illustrate the comparative value of the different authorities in their different combinations.[1]

[1] No attempt is made to give a complete summary of the evidence. "MSS." signifies many (or the remainder of) uncial and "mss." many (or the remainder of) cursive manuscripts. *Latt.* and *Syrr.* the Latin and Syrian versions in agreement; and verss. versions generally. If the title of an authority is enclosed in ( ), this indicates that the evidence is modified by some circumstance or other.

1. *Interpretative or Supplementary Glosses*

i. 24. καὶ ἀπεσταλμένοι ἦσαν ἐκ τῶν Φαρισαίων, ℵ*A* BC*L *Memph.* See note.

καὶ οἱ ἀπεσταλμένοι ἦσαν ἐκ τ. Φαρ., ℵ^{cb}A²C³X (MSS. mss.) *Latt. Syrr.*

— 27. ὁ ὀπίσω μου ἐρχόμενος, ℵ*B(C*LT^b), *Syr. vt. Memph.* Αὐτός ἐστιν ὁ ὀπίσω μου ἐρχόμενος, ὃς ἔμπροσθέν μου γέγονεν, AC³X (MSS. mss.) *Latt.* Comp. v. 15.

iii. 15. ἔχῃ ζωὴν αἰώνιον. μὴ ἀπόληται ἀλλ᾽ ἔχῃ ζω. αἰων. See note.

— 25. Ἰουδαίου ℵ^cABL (MSS. mss.) *Syr. psh.* Ἰουδαίων ℵ* (MSS. mss.) *Latt. Syr. vt. Memph.*

— 34. δίδωσιν, ℵBCLT^b 1 33 (*Lat. vt.*). δίδωσιν ὁ θεός, AC²D (MSS. mss.) Verss.

iv. 42. ὁ σωτὴρ τοῦ κόσμου, ℵBC*T^b *Latt. Syr. vt. Memph.* ὁ σωτ. τ. κοσμ. ὁ χριστός, ADL (MSS. mss.).

v. 4. See note.

— 16. ἐδίωκον, ℵBCDL 1 33 (*Latt.*) *Syr. vt.* ἐδίωκον . . . κ. ἐζήτουν αὐτὸν ἀποκτεῖναι, A (MSS. mss.). Comp. v. 18.

vi. 9. παιδάριον. παιδάριον ἕν. See note.

— 22. εἰ μὴ ἕν, ℵ^cABL 1 (*Latt.*). εἰ μὴ ἓν (or ἐκεῖνο ἕν) εἰς ὃ ἐνέβησαν οἱ μαθηταὶ αὐτοῦ (or οἱ μαθ. τ. Ἰησοῦ), ℵ*D (MSS. mss.) *Syrr.*

— 51. ἡ σάρξ μου ἐστὶν ὑπὲρ τῆς τοῦ κόσμου ζωῆς, BCDLT 33 *Latt. Syrr. vt. Theb.* (and ℵ in a changed order). ἡ σάρξ μ. ἐστ. ἣν ἐγὼ δώσω ὑπὲρ τ. τ. κοσ. ζωῆς, MSS. mss. (A is defective) (*Syrr.*) *Memph.* See note.

— 59. add σαββάτῳ, D (*Lat. vt.*).

vii. 46. οὐδέποτε οὕτως ἐλάλησεν ἄνθρωπος, ℵ^cBLT *Memph.* οὐδεπ. οὕτ. ἐλαλ. ἀνθρ. ὡς οὗτος ὁ ἄνθρωπος, ℵ* (D)X MSS. mss.

viii. 59. ἐκ τοῦ ἱεροῦ, ℵ*BD *Latt. Theb.*

ἐκ τοῦ ἱεροῦ καὶ διελθὼν διὰ μέσου αὐτῶν ἐπορεύετο καὶ παρῆγεν οὕτως, ℵ^{ca}CLX 33 *Memph.*

ἐκ τοῦ ἱεροῦ διελθὼν διὰ μέσου αὐτῶν καὶ παρῆγεν οὕτως, A (MSS. mss.) *Syrr.*

x. 13, 26. See notes.

xi. 41. τὸν λίθον, ℵBC*DLX 33 *Latt. Theb.* (*Syrr.*).

τ. λιθ. οὗ ἦν, A 1.

τ. λιθ. οὗ ἦν ὁ τεθνηκὼς κείμενος, C³ (MSS. mss.).

xii. 7. ἄφες αὐτὴν ἵνα . . . τηρήσῃ, ℵBDLQX 33 (*Latt.*) *Memph. Theb.*

ἄφες αὐτήν· . . . τετήρηκεν, A (MSS. mss.).

xiii. 14. καὶ ὑμεῖς ὀφείλετε.

πόσῳ μᾶλλον ὑμ. ὀφειλ., D (*Lat. vt.*).

— 32. καὶ ὁ θεὸς δοξάσει, ℵ*BC*DLX *Lat. vt.*

εἰ ὁ θεὸς ἐδοξάσθη ἐν αὐτῷ καὶ ὁ θε. δοξ., ℵ^cA (MSS. mss.) *Vg. Memph.*

xiv. 4. ὅπου ἐγὼ ὑπάγω οἴδατε τὴν ὁδόν, ℵBC*LQX *Memph.*

ὁπ. ἐγ. ὑπ. οἰδ. καὶ τὴν ὁδὸν οἴδατε, ADN (MSS. mss.) *Latt. Syrr.*

— 5. πῶς οἴδαμεν τὴν ὁδόν ; BC*D (*Lat. vt.*).

πῶς δυνάμεθα τὴν ὁδὸν εἰδέναι ; (ℵ)ALNQX *Vg. Syrr.*

xvi. 16. ὄψεσθέ με, ℵBDL (*Lat. vt.*).

ὀψ. με ὅτι ὑπάγω πρὸς τὸν πατέρα, A MSS. mss. (*Memph.*) *Syrr.* Comp. *vv.* 5, 10.

xvii. 21. ἵνα . . . ἐν ἡμῖν ὦσιν, BC*D (*Lat. vt.*) *Theb.*

ἵνα . . . ἐν ἡμῖν ἓν ὦσιν, ℵAC³LX MSS. mss. *Vg. Memph. Syrr.*

See also iii. 13, note.

In connexion with these explanatory additions, a few passages may be noticed in which an easy word has been substituted for a more difficult one.

i. 16.   Note.

vi. 63.   Note.

viii. 16. ἀληθινή, BDLTX 33.

ἀληθής, ℵ MSS. mss.

x. 38.   ἵνα γνῶτε καὶ γινώσκητε, BLX 1 33 *Theb. Memph.*

ἵνα γνῶτε καὶ πιστεύσητε, ℵA (MSS. mss.) *Latt.*

2. *Paraphrases*

The group ℵ D *Syr. vt.* and *Lat. vt.* are specially marked by paraphrastic variations.

i. 4.   ἐν αὐτῷ ζωή ἐστιν, ℵD *Syr. vt. Lat. vt.*   See note.

— 34.   ὁ ἐκλεκτὸς τοῦ θεοῦ, ℵ *Syr. vt.*   See note.

ii. 3.   οἶνον οὐκ εἶχον ὅτι συνετελέσθη ὁ οἶνος τοῦ γάμου, ℵ* (*Lat. vt.*).

iii. 5.   τὴν βασιλείαν τῶν οὐρανῶν, ℵ*.

— 6.   quia (quoniam) deus spiritus est et ex (de) deo natus est, *Syr. vt.* (*Lat. vt.*).

— 8.   ἐκ τοῦ ὕδατος καὶ τοῦ πνεύματος, ℵ *Lat. vt. Syr. vt.*

v. 13.   ἀσθενῶν, D (*Lat. vt.*).

— 19.   the Father doeth (ὁ πατήρ for ἐκεῖνος), *Syrr. Memph.*

vi. 15.   καὶ ἀναδεικνύναι βασιλέα, ℵ*.

— —   φεύγει πάλιν, ℵ* (*Latt.*) *Syr. vt.*   See note.

— 17.   κατέλαβεν δὲ αὐτοὺς ἡ σκοτία, ℵD.

— 51.   ἐκ τοῦ ἐμοῦ ἄρτου, ℵ (*Lat. vt.*).

x. 38.   θέλετε πιστεύειν, D *Latt.*

xi. 9.   . . . ὥρας ἔχει ἡ ἡμέρα ; D.

— 33.   ἐταράχθη τῷ πνεύματι ὡς ἐμβριμώμενος, D 1 *Theb.*

xii. 32.   πάντα, ℵ*D *Latt.*

xiv. 7.   καὶ τὸν πατέρα μου γνώσεσθε, ℵD (*Lat. vt.*).

xvii. 3.   add εἰς τοῦτον τὸν κόσμον, D.

— 10.   ἐδόξασας με, D.

xviii. 37. περὶ τῆς ἀληθείας, ℵ*.

Other examples of readings characteristic of this group will be found in the following passages:

i. 14 (πλήρη), 48.
ii. 15.
iv. 24, 42, 46, 51.
v. 9, 13, 25, 32, 42.
vi. 3, 23, 25, 27, 37, 46, 56 (note), 64, 66.
vii. 1, 6, 12, 26, 37, 47, 48, 50, 52
viii. 16, 21, 27.
ix. 35.
x. 11, 15, 25, 34, 39.
xi. 14.

xiv. 11.
xv. 20.
xvi. 13, 19.
xvii. 2, 7, 10, 23 (ἠγάπησα), 26.
xviii. 1 (note), 35.
xix. 4, 13, 33, 38.
xx. 1, 11, 15, 24 f.
xxi. 17, 18.

It is not probable that any one of these readings will commend itself to the student; but it must be added that in the case of omission it appears that the authority of this group is sometimes of greater weight. The omissions in St. John's Gospel which they support in the following passages are by no means unlikely to be correct:

iii. 25, 32, note.
iv. 9, οὐ γὰρ συνχρῶνται Ἰουδαῖοι Σαμαρείταις.

On the other hand their omissions in vi. 23, x. 8 (πρὸ ἐμοῦ), xxi. 23, are not to be admitted.

The readings of ℵ when they are unsupported are often quite arbitrary: e.g., iii. 36, vi. 10, 23, viii. 57, xi. 31, xiv. 16, xix. 13.

3. Passages in which the sense is considerably affected by the variation are not very numerous:

i. 16.   Note.
— 18.   Note.
— 28.   Note.
— 39 (40).   ὄψεσθε, BC*LTᵇ 1 33 (mss.) Syrr.
             ἴδετε, ℵAX MSS. (mss.) Latt. Memph.   Comp.
             v. 47.
— 51.   Note.
ii. 17.   καταφάγεται, ℵABLPTᵇ (MSS. mss.).
             κατέφαγε, a few mss.
iii. 15.   Note.
v. 1.   Note.
— 3 f.   Note.
vi. 69.   Note.
vii. 8.   οὔπω ἀναβαίνω, BLTX (MSS. mss.) Theb. Syrr.

οὐκ ἀναβαίνω, אD (some MSS. mss.) *Lat. vt. Syr. vt. Memph.* In such a case it is right to follow that combination of ancient authority which is elsewhere most trustworthy. For the combination in favour of οὐκ see note on vi. 15.

vii. 39. Note.

— 53—viii. 11. Note.

viii. 38. ἃ ἠκούσατε παρὰ τοῦ πατρός (or τοῦ πατρὸς ὑμῶν), אᶜBCLX 1 33 *Memph.*

ἃ ἑωράκατε παρὰ τ. πατ. ὑμ., א*D(T) (MSS. mss.) *Latt.*

— 44. Note.

ix. 35. Note.

x. 14. γινώσκουσί με τὰ ἐμά, אBDL *Latt. Memph. Theb.*

γινώσκομαι ὑπὸ τῶν ἐμῶν, AX MSS. mss. (*Syrr.*).

— 22. Note.

xii. 17. ὅτε . . . ἐφώνησεν, אABX (MSS. mss.) *Vg.*

ὅτι . . . ἐφων., DL *Lat. vt. Theb. Memph.*

— 41. ὅτι εἶδε, אABLX 1 33 *Memph. Theb.*

ὅτε εἶδε, D (MSS. mss.) *Latt. Syrr.*

— 47. φυλάξῃ, אABDLX 1 33 *Latt. Syrr. Theb. Memph.*

πιστεύσῃ, (MSS. mss.).

xiii. 2. δείπνου γινομένου, א*BLX.

δείπνου γενομένου, אᶜAD (MSS. mss.).

— 24. καὶ λέγει αὐτῷ, Εἰπὲ τίς ἐστι περὶ οὗ λέγει, (א)B CLX 33 *Latt.*

πυθέσθαι τίς ἂν εἴη περὶ οὗ λέγει, AD MSS. mss. *Syrr.*

— 25. ἀναπεσὼν οὕτως, (אᶜ) BCLX.

ἐπιπεσών, א*AD (MSS. mss.).

xiv. 10. ποιεῖ τὰ ἔργα αὐτοῦ, אBD.

αὐτὸς ποιεῖ τὰ ἔργα, AQ(LX) (MSS. mss.).

— 15. τηρήσετε, אBL *Memph.*

τηρήσατε, ADQX MSS. mss. *Latt. Syrr.*

xvii. 11. ᾧ δέδωκας, אABCL (MSS. mss.), *Syrr. Theb.* (ὅ D*X mss.).

οὓς δέδωκας, a few mss. *Vg. Memph.*

— 12. ᾧ δέδωκας, BC*L 33 (אᶜ *Theb. Memph.*).

οὓς δέδωκας, ADX (MSS. mss.) *Latt. Syrr.*

xviii. 15.   Note.

— 24.   Note.

xix. 3.   καὶ ἤρχοντο πρὸς αὐτὸν καὶ ἔλεγον, ℵBLX 33
(MSS. mss.) Latt. Theb. Memph.
καὶ ἔλεγον, A (MSS. mss.).

A careful examination of these passages will show how rarely A gives a certain ante-Nicene reading when authorities are divided. The relative lateness of its text compared with the texts of ℵBD and C, will be further apparent from the following passages : i. 26 (δέ), 39 (ἴδετε), 49 ; iv. 21 (πίστευσον), 46 (ὁ Ἰησοῦς) ; v. 3 (πολύ), 15 (καί) ; vi. 40 (τοῦ πέμψαντός με), 45 (οὖν) ; ix. 11, 41 (οὖν) ; x. 4 (τὰ ἴδια πρόβατα), 14 ; xi. 31 (λέγοντες).

In the case of proper names A seems to have adopted the later corrections, as in writing Καπερναούμ for Καφαρναούμ (ℵBCD, etc.) ; and Ἰωνᾶς for Ἰωάνης, as the name of the father of St. Peter (i. 43). This remark is not without weight in regard to the readings of A in v. 2 ; xviii. 1 (see notes).

On the other hand, it will be no less evident that in the examples given the readings of B are almost beyond question correct ; and further inquiry will tend to prove that no reading of B which is supported by independent authority, and certainly no reading of B which is supported by a primary uncial (e.g., ℵ, C, D, A), can be altogether set aside.

The following examples will repay study. Combination of Bℵ :

iv. 15.   διέρχωμαι.

v. 17.   om. Ἰησοῦς.

ix. 20.   ἀπεκρ. οὖν.

— 23.   ἐπερωτήσατε.

— 28.   καὶ ἐλοιδ.

xii. 4.   λέγει δέ.

xiv. 17.   om. αὐτό sec.

xvii. 11.   αὐτοί.

xix. 24.   om. ἡ λέγουσα.

— 35.   πιστεύητε.

— 39.   ἔλιγμα.

Such considerations carefully checked and followed out lead to conclusions which can be confidently accepted even where the most ancient evidence is unusually divided, e.g., i. 21, iii. 15, vii. 39, viii. 39, x. 29.[1]

Two general conclusions will follow from a careful study of the variations in all the passages where the text of St. John is in any way doubtful, (1) that the utmost extent of variation is comparatively unimportant; and (2) that the most ancient text adds in almost every case some minute touch which increases the vigour or clearness of the language. The criterion of apparent fitness which is most ambiguous when applied to separate readings becomes trustworthy when it is applied to a considerable group of readings.

2. *The interpretation of the Gospel*

The first commentary on the Gospel of St. John of which any distinct record has been preserved was written by HERACLEON, "the most esteemed (δοκιμώτατος) representative of the School of Valentinus" (Clem. Al. *Strom.* IV. 9. 73), whose friend he is said to have been. The work must therefore probably be assigned to the first half of the second century. The quotations preserved by Origen show that Heracleon dealt with long continuous passages of the Gospel (*e.g.*, c. iv.), but it is not certain that he commented on the whole. The text which he followed had one important various reading (iv. 18, ἕξ, *six*, for πέντε, *five*); and the manner in which he treats the book shows that he regarded it as of divine authority in the minutest details, though he frequently distorts its meaning by strange mystical interpretations.[2]

The Commentary of ORIGEN was written at the injunction of his friend Ambrosius (*In Joh. Tom.* 1. §§ 3, 6). The

---

[1] I have, as the A.V. is no longer the basis of this commentary, omitted a list of 179 passages where slight variations of the text from which A.V. was translated have " been silently corrected."—A. W.

[2] Part of the fragments of Heracleon are printed after Grabe and Massuet in Stieren's Irenæus, I. 938 ff. Jerome mentions a Commentary on the four Gospels attributed to Theophilus of Antioch, but questions its authenticity (*De Virr. Ill.* 25 ; *Præf. ad Matt.* Ep. CXXI. 6).

work was begun and the first five books were written at Alexandria (c. A.D. 225, Euseb. *H. E.* VI. 24), before his ordination at Cæsarea (A.D. 228). The troubles which followed this event interrupted the task and it seems not to have been completed, if indeed it ever was completed, till more than ten years after its commencement (comp. *Tom.* VI. § 1). Eusebius mentions that of the whole work "only twenty-two books" (*τόμοι*) had come down to his time. He does not say how many there were originally. Jerome, according to the common texts, speaks of "thirty-four" or "thirty-nine" books (*Præf. Hom. in Luc.*), but these readings are commonly altered to "thirty-two" on the authority of Rufinus (Huet, Orig. III. 2. 7). At present there remain Books I. II. (John i. 1—7 *a*), VI. (John i. 19—29), x. (John ii. 12—25), XIII. (John iv. 13—44), XIX. (part of John viii. 19—24), xx. (John viii. 37—52), XXVIII. (John xi. 39—57), XXXII. (John xiii. 2—33), with fragments of IV. V. At the beginning of the thirty-third book, which deals with ch. xiii., Origen speaks with doubt as to the completion of the whole Commentary, nor does he at the end of the book give, as he sometimes does, a promise of the immediate continuation of the work. It is possible therefore that his labours may have ended at this point. Certainly the whole Commentary would have occupied at least fifty books.

The work has Origen's faults and excellences in full measure. It is lengthy, discursive, fanciful, speculative; but it abounds with noble thoughts and intuitions of the truth. As a commentator Origen created a new form of theological literature.

Little remains of the works of the earlier Greek Commentators of the fourth century, THEODORUS of Heraclea (Perinthus), (Theodor. *H. E.* II. 3, Hieron. *De Virr. Ill.* 90), and DIDYMUS of Alexandria (Hieron. *De Virr. Ill.* 105). The *Homilies* of CHRYSOSTOM, composed while he was still at Antioch (before A.D. 398), form the foundation of a historical interpretation of the Gospel. His explanations and applications of the text are clear, vigorous, and eloquent. The reader will probably miss the signs of a spontaneous sympathy with the more mysterious aspects of the Gospel.

AUGUSTINE in his *Lectures on St. John (Tractatus in Joh. CXXIV.)* is strongest where Chrysostom is weakest. His ignorance of Greek constantly betrays him into the adoption of a false sense of the words, but his genius no less frequently enables him to enter with the fullest insight into the thought of a passage which may escape the verbal interpreter. I have ventured not infrequently to quote his terse and pregnant comments in their original form. No translation can do them justice.

The Commentaries of THEODORE of Mopsuestia were popularly considered the best of the Antiochene school. Considerable fragments of his Commentary on St. John remain.

At the opposite extreme to Theodore is CYRIL of Alexandria, whose Commentary on St. John remains nearly complete. In this dogmatic interests overpower all other considerations. It was natural that Cyril should read the Gospel in the light of the controversies in which he was absorbed; but under his treatment the divine history seems to be dissolved into a docetic drama. At the same time his speculations, like those of the other Alexandrines, abound in isolated thoughts of great subtlety and beauty.

The two distinct *Catenæ* of Corderius and Cramer contain extracts from other Greek Commentaries, Ammonius of Alexandria, Apollinaris of Laodicea, Severus of Antioch, Theodore of Heraclea, etc., but Cyril closes the series of the great patristic interpreters of St. John. The Greek Commentaries of THEOPHYLACT († 1107) and EUTHYMIUS († *c.* 1118) are mainly epitomes of Chrysostom, but both are clear and sensible. The Latin Commentaries of Beda and Walafrid Strabo (*Glossa ordinaria*) depend largely on Augustine.

RUPERT of Deutz (*Comm. in Joh.* Libb. xiv.) in this subject as in others showed original power. His Commentaries on St. John are marked by great fertility in subtle speculation, though he claims to deal more with humble details than Augustine. The fragments of the Commentary of JOHANNES SCOTUS ERIGENA are not less interesting, and he explains the text carefully.

More comprehensive, however, and serviceable than these commentaries is the *Golden Chain* (*Catena Aurea*) of THOMAS AQUINAS, which brings together a large selection of comments from Greek and Latin writers. It must, however, be used with great caution, for a considerable proportion of the quotations adduced from early writers are taken from spurious books.

Of the Commentaries of the sixteenth century it must be sufficient to mention a few which will serve as representatives. Those of Ferus (*i.e.*, Wild, of Mainz, 1536), Corn. a Lapide (*i.e.*, Van der Steen, Louvain and Rome, † 1637), and Maldonatus (Maldonato, of Salamanca and Paris, 1596; St. John is unfinished), among Roman Catholic scholars; of Brentius (*i.e.*, Brenz, *Homilies*, of Stuttgart, 1528), and J. Gerhard (of Jena, 1617), among Lutherans; of Musculus (*i.e.*, Meusslin of Berne, 1548), and R. Gualther (*Homilies*, of Berne, 1565), among the "Reformed," are all conspicuous for thought, research, and vigour. Lampe (of Utrecht, 1724) has given a very complete list of the Commentaries down to his own time; and his own work is a mine of learning, which it is, however, painful to work from the form in which he has arranged his materials.

The spread of idealism in Germany in the first quarter of the present (nineteenth) century gave a fresh impulse to the study of St. John. Fichte (1806, *Anw. z. sel. Leben*, VI.) and Schelling (1841, *Werke*, II. 4, pp. 302 f.), in different ways and with a partial conception of the scope of the Gospel, insisted upon its primary importance for the apprehension of Christian truth in relation to the present age. When Neander began his public work (1813), he lectured on the Gospel of St. John, and on his deathbed (1850) he announced as the subject of his next course "The Gospel of St. John considered in its true historical position." Meanwhile great light had been thrown upon the composition and contents of the Gospel. The commentaries of Lücke (1st ed. 1820—24), of Tholuck (1st ed. 1827), of Klee (1829), of Olshausen (1st ed. 1832), of Meyer (1st ed. 1834), and of De Wette (1st ed. 1837), contributed in various degrees to illustrate its meaning.

It does not fall within my scope to criticise these or later books.[1]

For obvious reasons I have thought it best to refrain from using modern English Commentaries, with one partial exception. Otherwise I have endeavoured to take account as far as possible of the writings of every school which seemed likely to contribute to the understanding of St. John. My one aim has been to express what seems to me the sense and teaching of his words. With this view I have, except in a few cases, simply given the conclusion at which I have arrived without reviewing rival opinions, or citing the authorities by which it is supported or opposed. I have not, however, consciously passed over or extenuated any difficulty which I have been able to feel: nor, again, have I called particular attention to details which happen to have come into undue prominence in modern controversy.

It would be an idle task to enumerate all the names of those from whose writings I have sought and gained help; and I should be unable to measure the debts which I owe to scholars who often teach much when they do not command assent. Yet there are some names which cannot be passed over in silence. When I began to work seriously at the Gospel of St. John more than twenty-five years ago I felt that I owed most to Origen, Neander, Olshausen, Luthardt, and, from a very different point of view, to F. C. Baur. In arranging my thoughts during the last eight years I feel that I owe most to Godet, whose Commentary, except on questions of textual criticism, seems to me to be unsurpassed. And on the other hand, Keim has continually offered criticisms and suggestions which have opened fresh sources of illustration for the text. But throughout this space of Cambridge work, the living voice of friends has been far more helpful to me than books. The fulness of sympathy in common labour brings light

---

[1] An admirable summary of the literature dealing with the authenticity of St. John's Gospel has been added by Dr. C. R. Gregory to the English translation of Luthardt's *St. John the Author of the Fourth Gospel*, Edinburgh, 1875.

and fresh power of vision, and not only materials for thought.

Throughout the notes I have quoted the renderings of the Latin Vulgate in the hope of directing more attention to the study of it. It seems to me that we have lost much in every way from our neglect of a Version which has influenced the Theology of the West more profoundly than we know.

One department of illustration, it must be added, still calls for systematic study. The didactic method and not only the language of St. John is essentially Hebraic; and very much has still to be learnt especially from the *Midrashim* before the full force of his record can be apprehended. The collections which Wetstein has made from Lightfoot and other early Rabbinic scholars, Delitzsch's *Horæ Hebraicæ* (in the *Ztschr. f. Luth. Theol.*); the recent work of Wünsche (*Neue Beiträge zur Erlauterung der Evangelien aus Talmud u. Midrash*, Göttingen, 1878), which is very useful, but by no means always exact; Siegfried's *Philon von Alexandria* (indirectly), and Mr. Taylor's excellent edition of the *Sayings of the Jewish Fathers (Pirke Aboth)*, rather point to the rich mine than exhaust it.[1]

There is a remarkable legend (*Shemoth R. c. v.*), that when the LORD gave the Law from Sinai He wrought great marvels with His voice (Job xxxvii. 5). "The voice sounded from the South; and as the people hastened to the South, lo! it sounded from the North. They turned to the North, and it came from the East. They turned to the East, and it came from the West. They turned thither, and it came from heaven. They lifted up their eyes to heaven, and it came from the depths of the earth. And they said one to another, Where shall wisdom be found? (Job xxviii. 12).

"And the Voice went forth throughout the world, and was divided into seventy voices, according to the seventy

---

[1] The *Kôl Kôré* of R. Soloweyczyk translated into French under the title *La Bible, le Talmud et l'Evangile*, Paris, 1875, St. Matthew and St. Mark, is of little value in this respect.

tongues of men, and each nation heard the Voice in its own tongue, and their souls failed them ; but Israel heard and suffered not.

" And each one in Israel heard it according to his capacity; old men, and youths, and boys, and sucklings, and women : the voice was to each one as each one had the power to receive it."

The student of St. John will find the parable fulfilled as he ponders the Apostle's words with growing experience, and unchanged patience. He himself limits the meaning which he finds in them.

" Omnes carnalium sordes affectuum ab oculis cordis abstergendæ sunt iis qui in scholâ Christi venerabilibus student litteris ; ut hanc aliquatenus valeant Aquilam prosequi, quam cordis munditia juvit ut claritatem solis æterni, plus ceteris divinæ visionis animalibus, irreverberata posset mentis acie contemplari" (Rupertus of Deutz).

ADDITIONAL NOTES IN VOLUME I

NOTES ON READINGS

ΚΑΤΑ ΙΩΑΝΗΝ

ΚΑΤΑ ΙΩΑΝΗΝ

1 Ἐν ἀρχῇ ἦν ὁ λόγος, καὶ ὁ λόγος ἦν πρὸς τὸν θεόν,
2 καὶ θεὸς ἦν ὁ λόγος. Οὗτος ἦν ἐν ἀρχῇ πρὸς τὸν θεόν.

Κατὰ Ἰωάνην] The title of the Gospel, which is found in very different forms in ancient authorities, is no part of the book itself. The earliest authorities, and those which represent the earliest text, give the simplest form: Κατὰ Ἰωάννην [-άνην] אBD; *Secundum Iohannem* (as the running heading) Lat. vt.; and so Syr. vt.: *Of John*. The word Εὐαγγέλιον, which is implied in this title, is supplied by the mass of MSS. (Εὐαγγέλιον κατὰ Ἰ. [without the article] ACLX, etc.; and so, as the initial heading, Lat. vt., Syr. vt.). Very many of the later MSS. add the definite article (Τὸ κατὰ Ἰ. εὐαγγ.), and very many also add an epithet: Τὸ κατὰ Ἰ. ἅγιον εὐαγγ. A few MSS. give the remarkable title: Ἐκ τοῦ κατὰ Ἰ. [ἁγίου] εὐαγγ. The printed texts of the Peshito give: *The holy Gospel of the preaching of John the preacher*. There is a similar variety in the titles given in the English Versions: Ðæt Godspell aefter Iohannes gerecednesse [narration] (Anglo-Saxon). *The Gospel (Euuangelie) of Joon* [or *Joon* simply] (Wycliffe). *The Gospel of Saint John* (Tyndale 1526, 1534, 1535, Coverdale, Matthew, Great Bible). *The Gospel after S. John* (Taverner 1539, with the running heading *The Gospel of S. John*). *The*

Gospel by Saint Iohn (Bishops' Bible 1568, 1572). *The Holy Gospel of Jesus Christ according to John* (Geneva 1560, Rheims 1582 with the running heading *The Gospel according to S. John*, Tomson 1583). *The Gospel according to S. John* (E.V.).

THE PROLOGUE (i. 1—18).

Though the narrative of St. John's Gospel is not marked off by any very distinct line from the introductory verses, it has been generally acknowledged that i. 1—18 forms an introduction to the whole work. This conclusion appears to be completely established by a careful analysis of the contents of the section, which present in a summary form the main truths that are illustrated by the records of the history. The first verse appears to stand by itself: the remaining verses give an outline of the relations of the Word to Creation. The connexion of the different parts, and the order of progress, will be best seen in a tabular form:

I. THE WORD IN HIS ABSOLUTE, ETERNAL BEING (*v.* 1).

1. His *Existence:* Beyond time.
2. His *Personal Existence:* In active Communion with God.
3. His *Nature:* God in Essence.

ST. JOHN

1 In the beginning was the Word, and the Word
2 was with God, and the Word was God. The same

II. The Word in relation to
Creation (vv. 2—18).
 1. *The essential facts* (vv. 2—5).
  i. The source of creation.
      In the divine counsel
      (v. 2).
  ii. The act of creation (v. 3).
      The Word the Agent
      (*through Him*).
      The Word the Quicken-
      ing Presence (*not apart
      from Him*).
  iii. The being of things created
      (vv. 4, 5).
      a. In the divine Idea
      (v. 4).
          As to the World.
          As to Man.
      b. In human history (v.
      5).
          The continuous con-
          flict of Light and
          Darkness follow-
          ing on a critical
          assault of Dark-
          ness.
 2. *The historic manifestation of
    the Word generally* (vv.
    6—13).
  i. The testimony of prophecy
      represented by John (vv.
      6—8).
      a. John's personality (v.
      6).
      b. The end of his mission
      (v. 7).
      c. His nature (v. 8).
  ii. The manifestations of the

Word (as Light) before
the Incarnation (vv. 9,
10).
      a. By special revelations
      (v. 9).
      b. By His immanent
      Presence (v. 10).
  iii. The Coming of the Word
      to the Chosen People
      consummated at the In-
      carnation (vv. 11—13).
      a. National unbelief (v.
      11).
      b. Individual faith (vv.
      12, 13).
 3. *The Incarnation as appre-
    hended by personal experi-
    ence* (vv. 14—18).
  i. The personal witness (v.
      14).
      a. The fact.
      b. The observation of the
      fact.
      c. The moral nature of
      the fact.
  ii. The witness of prophecy
      (John) (v. 15).
      a. The promised Christ.
      b. His essential dignity.
  iii. The nature of the revela-
      tion (vv. 16—18).
      a. In the experience of
      believers.
      b. In relation to the Law.
      c. In its final source.

Other arrangements of the
Prologue have been proposed
which bring out different aspects.

3 πάντα δι' αὐτοῦ ἐγένετο, καὶ χωρὶς αὐτοῦ ἐγένετο οὐδὲ¹
4 ἕν. ὃ γέγονεν ἐν αὐτῷ ζωὴ ἦν², καὶ ἡ ζωὴ ἦν τὸ φῶς

¹ οὐδέν ℵ*D ; οὐδὲ ἕν ℵᶜABCLOXΓ.   ² ἐστιν ℵD ; ἦν ABCLOXΓ. See note.

It has been divided into two parts: 1—5 (the essential nature of the Word), 6—18 (the historical manifestation of the Word); and again into three parts : 1—5, 6—13, 14—18, which have been supposed to present the progressive revelation of the Word, either in fuller detail from section to section, or in historical order, as He is essentially, as He was made known under the Old Covenant, as He was made known under the New ; and yet again into three parts : 1—4 (the activity of the Word before the Incarnation generally), 5—11 (the revelation of unbelief), 12—18 (the revelation of faith).

The detailed examination of the text will show how far these arrangements correspond with the structure of the whole passage.

I. THE WORD IN HIS ABSOLUTE, ETERNAL BEING (v. 1).

CHAP. I. 1. The first sentence of the Gospel offers a perfect example of the stately symmetry by which the whole narrative is marked. The three clauses of which it consists are set side by side: . . . καί . . . καί . . .; the subject (ὁ λόγος) is three times repeated ; and the substantive verb three times occupies the same relative position. The symmetry of form corresponds with the exhaustiveness of the thought. The three clauses contain all that it is possible for man to realise as to the essential nature of the Word in relation to time, and mode of being, and character : He was

(1) ἐν ἀρχῇ : He was (2) πρὸς τὸν θεόν : He was (3) θεός. At the same time these three clauses answer to the three great moments of the Incarnation of the Word declared in v. 14. He who " was God," σὰρξ ἐγένετο : He who "was with God," ἐσκήνωσεν ἐν ἡμῖν (comp. 1 John i. 2) : He who " was in the beginning," ἐγένετο (in time).

This revelation is the foundation of the whole Gospel of St. John. It sets aside the false notion that the Word became " personal " first at the time of Creation or at the Incarnation. The absolute, eternal, immanent relations of the Persons of the Godhead furnish the basis for revelation. Because the Word was personally distinct from "God" and yet essentially "God," He could make Him known. Compare an interesting passage of Irenæus : II. XXX. 9.

Ἐν ἀρχῇ] In principio v.; In the beginning. The phrase carries back the thoughts of the reader to Gen. i. 1, which necessarily fixes the sense of the beginning. Here, as there, " the beginning " is the initial moment of time and creation ; but there is this difference, that Moses dwells on that which starts from the point, and traces the record of divine action from the beginning (comp. 1 John i. 1, ii. 13), while St. John lifts our thoughts beyond the beginning and dwells on that which " was " when time, and with time finite being, began its course. Comp. Prov. viii. 23. Already

³ was in the beginning with God. All things were made through him; and apart from him not even ⁴ one thing was made. That which hath been made in him was life; and the life was the light of men.

when "God created the heaven and the earth," "the Word *was*." The "being" of the Word is thus necessarily carried beyond the limits of time, though the pre-existence of the Word is not definitely stated. The simple affirmation of existence in this connexion suggests a loftier conception than that of pre-existence; which is embarrassed by the idea of time. Pre-existence, however, is affirmed in a different connexion : ch. xvii. 5.

This force of ἐν ἀρχῇ is brought out by a comparison with the corresponding phrase in 1 John i. 1, ἀπ᾿ ἀρχῆς. The latter marks the activity of the Word in time from the initial point : the former emphasises the existence of the Word at the initial point, and so before time.

ἦν] The verb does not express a completed past, but rather a continuous state. The imperfect tense suggests in this relation, as far as human language can do so, the notion of absolute, supra-temporal, existence.

ὁ λόγος] *verbum* v. (though some early Latin authorities give *sermo*) ; *the Word.* This translation "the Word" ought undoubtedly to be kept. It is probable that there is a reference to the language of Gen. i. 3 ff. : "God said." For the history and meaning of the term Logos see Introduction. Here it will be sufficient to observe :

1. The personal title λόγος is used absolutely only in *vv.* 1, 14

(Rev. xix. 13 ; Heb. iv. 12—ὁ λόγος τ. θεοῦ). In 1 John i. 1 the phrase ὁ λόγος τ. ζωῆς is not personal, but equivalent to "the revelation of the life."

2. The term λόγος never has the sense of *reason* in the New Testament.

3. St. John introduces the term without any explanation. He assumes that his readers are familiar with it.

4. The theological use of the term appears to be derived directly from the Palestinian *Memra*, and not from the Alexandrine *Logos*.

5. Though the term is not used in the apostolic writings in the sense of *Reason*, yet the first verse deals with the divine relations independently of the actual revelation to men. Ὁ λόγος of *v.* 1 includes the conception of the immanent word (λόγος ἐνδιά-θετος) of Greek philosophy in thought though not in language. But the idea is approached from the side of historical revelation. He who has been made known to us as "the Word" *was* in the beginning. Thus the economic Trinity, the Trinity of revelation, is shown to answer to an essential Trinity. The Word as personal (ἐνυπόστατος) satisfies every partial conception of the *Logos*.

6. The personal titles ὁ λόγος and ὁ λόγος τοῦ θεοῦ must be kept in close connexion with the same terms as applied to the sum of the Gospel in the New Testament, and with the phrase "the

5 τῶν ἀνθρώπων· καὶ τὸ φῶς ἐν τῇ σκοτίᾳ φαίνει, καὶ
6 ἡ σκοτία αὐτὸ οὐ κατέλαβεν. Ἐγένετο ἄνθρωπος ἀπε-

word of the Lord" in the prophecies of the Old Testament.
The Word, before the Incarnation, was the one source of the
many divine words; and Christ,
the Word Incarnate, is Himself
the Gospel.

7. The Evangelist uses the title
λόγος and not υἱός here, because
he wishes to carry his readers to
the most absolute conceptions.

ἦν πρὸς τ. θεόν] erat apud
deum v.; was with God. This
remarkable phrase is found also
Matt. xiii. 56; Mark vi. 3, ix.
19, xiv. 49; Luke ix. 41;
1 John i. 2. The idea conveyed
by it is not that of simple co-
existence, as of two persons
contemplated separately in company (εἶναι μετά, iii. 26, etc.), or
united under a common conception (εἶναι σύν, Luke xxii. 56), or
(so to speak) in local relation
(εἶναι παρά, ch. xvii. 5), but of
being (in some sense) directed
towards and regulated by that
with which the relation is fixed
(v. 19). The personal being of
the Word was realised in active
intercourse with and in perfect
communion with God. Compare
Gen. i. 26, where the same truth
is expressed under distinct human
imagery. The Word "was with
God" before He revealed God.
The main thought is included
in the statement that ὁ θεὸς ἀγάπη
ἐστίν (1 John iv. 16; comp. ch.
xvii. 24); and it finds expression
in another form in the description
of "the life, the life eternal,
which was manifested to men."
This life ἦν πρὸς τὸν πατέρα (not
πρὸς τὸν θεόν, 1 John i. 2): it was
realised in the intercommunion

of the divine Persons when time
was not.

θεὸς ἦν ὁ λόγος] deus erat
verbum v.; the Word was God.
The predicate (θεός) stands emphatically first, as in iv. 24. It
is necessarily without the article
(θεός, not ὁ θεός), inasmuch as it
describes the nature of the Word
and does not identify His Person.
It would be pure Sabellianism to
say "the Word was ὁ θεός." No
idea of inferiority of nature is
suggested by the form of expression, which simply affirms the
true deity of the Word. Compare for the converse statement
of the true humanity of Christ
v. 27 (ὅτι υἱὸς ἀνθρώπου ἐστίν,
note).

On the other hand it will be
noticed that "the Word" is
placed in personal relation to
"God" (ὁ θεός) spoken of absolutely in the second clause; while
in the third clause "the Word"
is declared to be "God," and so
included in the unity of the
Godhead. Thus we are led to
conceive that the divine nature is
essentially in the Son, and at the
same time that the Son can be
regarded, according to that which
is His peculiar characteristic, in
relation to God as God. He is
εἰκὼν τοῦ θεοῦ, and not simply of
the Father.

II. THE WORD IN RELATION TO
    CREATION (vv. 2—18).

This main section of the Prologue falls into three parts:
1. The essential facts (vv. 2—5).
2. The historic manifestation of
   the Word generally (vv.
   6—13).

₅ And the light shineth in the darkness; and the
₆ darkness overcame it not.   There arose ¹ a man,

¹ *lit.* became.

3. *The Incarnation as apprehended by personal experience* (vv. 14—18).

The Evangelist having given
in the first verse such an idea as
man can receive of the Word in
Himself, next traces out step by
step the mode in which the Word
has entered into relation with
Creation.

1. *The essential facts* (vv. 2—5).
This sub-section lays open the
source of creation in the divine
counsel (v. 2), the act of creation
through the Word and by His
Presence (v. 3), the being of
things created in the divine idea
(v. 4), and as manifested in
history (v. 5).

2. In passing from the thought
of the Personal Being of the
Word in Himself to the revelation of the Word, the Evangelist
brings the revelation into the
closest connexion with the essential Nature of the Word by the
repetition in combination of the
three clauses of the first verse:
Οὗτος ἦν ἐν ἀρχῇ πρὸς τ. θεόν. At
the moment of creation that
relation, which *was* eternally,
was actually effective. Creation
itself was (in some sense) the
result of the eternal fellowship
expressed in the relation of the
Word to God.

Οὗτος] *Hoc* v.; *This* (*Word*),
He who has just been declared
to be God. The pronoun implies
and emphasises the whole previous definition. Comp. vi. 46,
vii. 18, etc.

3. πάντα] *omnia* v.; *all things*,
taken severally, and not all
things regarded as a defined whole

(τὰ πάντα, Col. i. 16). The
thought to be brought out is that
of the vast multiplicity of created
things (spirits, matter, etc.). Of
all these no one came into being
without the Word. For this
reason the term " the world " (ὁ
κόσμος, vv. 9, 10) is purposely
avoided.

δι᾽ αὐτοῦ] *per ipsum* v.; *through
him.* The Word is described as
the mediate Agent of Creation
(διά, not ὑπό). Comp. Col. i. 16 ;
Heb. i. 2. The Father is the
one spring, source (πηγή), and
end of all finite being, as He is
of the Godhead: εἰς θεὸς ὁ πατήρ,
ἐξ οὗ τὰ πάντα . . . εἰς κύριος Ἰ. Χ.
δι᾽ οὗ τὰ πάντα (1 Cor. viii. 6).
Thus in different relations creation can be attributed to the
Father and to the Son. Comp.
v. 17.

ἐγένετο] *facta sunt* v.; *were
made* (lit. *became*). Creation
itself is represented as a " becoming " in contrast with the "being"
emphasised before. The same
contrast recurs in vv. 6, 9.

Three distinct words are used
in the New Testament to convey
the conception of creation, (1)
κτίζειν, to *create*, and (2) ποιεῖν, *to
make*, in reference to the Creator ;
and (3) γίγνεσθαι, *to become*, in
reference to that which is created.
Κτίζειν (Rev. iv. 11, x. 6 ; Col. i.
16, etc.) suggests the idea of
design, plan, purpose ; ποιεῖν
(Rev. xiv. 7 ; Mark x. 6, etc.), of
an actual result or object produced (comp. Eph. ii. 10) ; γίγνεσθαι, of the law fulfilled in the
production of the object. The
use of ἐγένετο in vv. 14, 17 brings

7 σταλμένος παρὰ θεοῦ, ὄνομα αὐτῷ Ἰωάνης· οὗτος ἦλθεν
εἰς μαρτυρίαν, ἵνα μαρτυρήσῃ περὶ τοῦ φωτός, ἵνα πάντες

out its force as expressive of the
unfolding of a divine order.

χωρὶς αὐτοῦ] sine ipso v.; apart
from him (comp. xv. 5). Creation is set forth under a twofold aspect, as depending on the
divine Agency and on the divine
Presence. It is first called into
being by the Word, and then
sustained in being by Him (Heb.
i. 3). Compare the use of ἐν
αὐτῷ, Col. i. 16, 17; Acts xvii.
28.

οὐδὲ ἕν] not even one thing.
St. John emphasises the universality of the action of the Word.
The same thought is expressed in
detail by St. Paul: Col. i. 16.
For the combination of a
positive and negative expression
to express the fulness of truth,
see ch. iii. 16, vi. 50; 1 John i.
5, ii. 4, 27, v. 12.

3, 4. ὃ γέγονεν ἐν αὐτῷ ζωὴ ἦν]
These words admit two very distinct divisions. The last clause
of v. 3 may be taken either (1)
with the words which precede, as
E.V., or (2) with the words
which follow. It would be difficult to find a more complete
consent of ancient authorities in
favour of any reading, than that
which supports the second punctuation: χωρὶς αὐτοῦ ἐγένετο οὐδὲ
ἕν. ὃ γέγονεν ἐν αὐτῷ ζωὴ ἦν. See
note at the end of the chapter.

γέγονεν] hath been made. The
change of tense distinguishes the
act of creation (aor.) from the
continuance of things created
(perf.). Compare Col. i. 16
(ἐκτίσθη, ἔκτισται).

4. ἡ ζωὴ ἦν τὸ φῶς τ. ἀνθρ.] vita
erat lux hominum v.; the life was
the light of men. The works of

the Word supplied for a time,
from within and from without,
that which He supplied more
completely by His personal manifestations (ix. 5, note), and afterwards by His historical Presence
(viii. 12, xii. 46), and yet more
completely by His Presence
through the Spirit in the Church.
He is Himself, however revealed,
the Light of men and of the
world (viii. 12, ix. 5).

τὸ φῶς] the light, the one light.
It must be observed that the
Word is not here spoken of
directly as "the Light of men."
He is "the Light" through the
medium of "Life." In part and
according to the divine constitution of things He is made known,
and makes Himself known, in and
through the vital processes of
creation.

τ. ἀνθρώπων] of men, of men as
a class, and not of individuals
only. Comp. iii. 19, xvii. 6.
Man, as made in the image of
God, stood in a special relation to
the Word. "He saith not the
Light of the Jews only, but of all
men; for all of us, in so far as
we have received intellect and
reason from that Word which
created us, are said to be illuminated by Him" (Theophylact,
quoted by Thomas Aqu.).

5. In v. 4 the divine essence
and the divine purpose of creation are declared from the side
of God; in v. 5 the Evangelist
describes the actual state of
things from the side of man.
The description holds good generally. It embraces the experience
of Judaism and Heathendom, of
pre-Christian and post-Christian

7 sent from God; his name was John. The same
came for witness, that he might bear witness of
the light, that all men might believe through him.

times. The truth which found
its most signal fulfilment in the
historical Presence of Christ,
was established in various ways
both before and after it. The
conflict of Light and Darkness
which represents one aspect of
the history of the Gospel, represents also one aspect of all human
history.

τὸ φῶς] *the light.* It is probable that the word must be
taken in a somewhat wider sense
in this clause than in the last, so
as to include not only the manifestations of the Word (as "Life")
through "Nature" in the widest
sense of the term, but also the
Personal manifestations of the
Word. It is impossible for us to
judge how far the two series of
manifestations may be in fact
united. Comp. Ps. xxxvi. 9.

ἐν τῇ σκοτίᾳ] *in tenebris* v. ; *in
the darkness.* Side by side with
the light the darkness appears
suddenly, and without preparation. An acquaintance with the
history of the Fall is evidently
presupposed. The perfect fellowship of man and God has been
broken. Man, in his self-will,
has separated, isolated himself.
He has made for himself, so to
speak, an atmosphere of darkness, by seeking to sever his life
from the Source of life. For all
that is without God, apart from
Him, is darkness. Comp. 1 John
i. 5.

φαίνει] *lucet* v. ; *shineth.* Comp.
1 John ii. 8. The light does not
"appear" only; it "lightens,"
Gen. i. 17; Ps. lxxvii. 18, xcvii.

4 (LXX.). It is of the essence
of light to invade the realm of
darkness. Φαίνει describes that
which is the action of light in
itself, as distinguished from
φωτίζει (*v.* 9), its effect as "illuminating" men. This action of
the Light is not to be limited to
any one point. It is continuous
from the creation to the consummation of things, though
there have been times when it
has flashed forth with peculiar
splendour.

αὐτὸ οὐ κατέλαβεν] *eam non
comprehenderunt* v. ; *overcame it
not.* Κατέλαβεν has received two
very different renderings—*overcame* and *apprehended.* It is
found again in a parallel passage, xii. 35 : ἵνα μὴ σκοτία ὑμᾶς
καταλάβῃ; and also in an old
reading of vi. 17 : κατέλαβε δὲ
αὐτοὺς ἡ σκοτία (אD). In these
cases the sense cannot be doubtful. The darkness comes down
upon, enwraps men. As applied
to light, this sense includes the
further notion of overwhelming,
eclipsing. The relation of darkness to light is one of essential
antagonism. If the darkness is
represented as pursuing the light
it can only be to overshadow
and not to appropriate it. And
this appears to be the meaning
here. The existence of the darkness is affirmed, and at the same
time the unbroken energy of the
light. But the victory of the
light is set forth as the result of
a past struggle; and the abrupt
alteration of tense brings into
prominence the change which has

₈ πιστεύσωσιν δι᾽ αὐτοῦ. οὐκ ἦν ἐκεῖνος τὸ φῶς, ἀλλ᾽ ἵνα
₉ μαρτυρήσῃ περὶ τοῦ φωτός. ⸀Ἦν τὸ φῶς τὸ ἀληθινὸν
ὃ φωτίζει πάντα ἄνθρωπον ἐρχόμενον εἰς τὸν κόσμον.

passed over the world. It could
not but happen that the darkness
(when it came) should seek to
cover all; and in this attempt it
failed : *the light is shining in the
darkness ; and the darkness overcame it not.*

This general interpretation of
the word, which is completely
established by the usage of St.
John (comp. 1 Thess. v. 4), is
supported by the Greek Fathers;
but the Latin version gives the
rendering *comprehenderunt,* "took
hold of," "embraced." This
sense, however, and that of "understood" (expressed in the New
Testament by the middle voice
of the verb : Acts iv. 13, x. 34,
xxv. 25; Eph. iii. 18) seem to
be inconsistent with the image
and foreign to the context. The
darkness, as such, could not
"seize," "appropriate," the light.
In doing this it would cease to
exist. And yet further, the notion of the historical development of revelation is not at
present pursued. The great elements of the moral position of
the world are stated : their combinations and issues are outlined
afterwards. In this respect *v.* 5
is parallel with 9—13, indicating the existence and continuance
of a conflict which is there regarded in its contrasted issues.
The whole phrase is indeed a
startling paradox. The light
does not banish the darkness:
the darkness does not overpower the light. Light and
darkness coexist in the world
side by side.

2. *The historic manifestation of
the Word generally (vv.* 6—13).

In the former section the great
facts which issue in the spiritual
conflict of life have been set
forth. The Evangelist now traces
in outline the course of the conflict which is apprehended in its
essential character in the final
manifestation of the Light. This
manifestation was heralded by
prophecy, of which John the
Baptist was the last representative *(vv.* 6—8). It had been
prepared also by continuous revelations of the Word, as light,
at once through special commu-
nications *(v.* 9), and by His immanent Presence *(v.* 10). But
when He came to His own in
the fulness of time, He found, as
the Incarnate Saviour, national
unbelief *(v.* 11), relieved only by
individual faith *(vv.* 12, 13). The
conflict shadowed out before *(v.* 5)
still continued.

6—8. The office of prophecy
is shown through the work of
the Baptist; of whom the Evangelist speaks in regard to his
personality *(v.* 6), the end of his
mission *(v.* 7), his nature *(v.* 8).
The abrupt introduction of John
is explained by the fact that the
review of the revelation, preparatory to the Incarnation,
starts from the last, that is the
most intelligible, stage in it. The
Baptist—a priest and a Nazarite
—was the completed type of the
Prophet (Matt. xi. 9 f. and parallels); and it was by the Baptist,
an interpreter of the Old Dispensation and herald of the New,

8 He was not the light, but *came* that he might bear
9 witness of the light. There was the light, the true
light which lighteth every man, coming into the

that St. John himself was guided
to Christ (*vv.* 35 ff.).

6. Ἐγένετο] *Fuit* v.; *There
arose* (lit. *became*). Each of the
three words which describe the
advent of John is expressive.
His "becoming" is contrasted
with the "being" of the Word
(*v.* 9). He is spoken of as "a
man" with a significant reference
to the mystery realised in *v.* 14.
And at the same time he was
charged with a divine mission.

ἀπεσταλμ. παρὰ θεοῦ] *missus a
deo* v.; *sent from* (and not simply
" by ") *God* (comp. xv. 26). On
the word ἀποστέλλω, see xx. 21,
note. Comp. Mal. iii. 1; ch. iii.
28. The two words ἐγένετο . . .
ἀπεσταλμένος are not a mere periphrasis for "was sent": they fix
attention separately on the person
and on the mission of the Baptist.

ὄνομα αὐτῷ . . .] *cui nomen
erat* . . . v.; *his* (in accordance
with St. John's sharp brief style;
so iii. 1) *name was* . . . Possibly
an allusion to the meaning of the
name (Theodore, Gotthold, God's
gracious gift) underlies the clause.
Compare Luke i. 63.

Ἰωάνης] *John.* On the use of
the simple name without any
title in the fourth Gospel, see
Introd.

7. οὗτος] He who was of such
a nature, so commissioned, so
named. Comp. *v.* 2, and contrast
the pronoun in *v.* 8.

ἦλθεν εἰς μαρτυρίαν, ἵνα μαρτ. . . .
ἵνα πάντες] *venit in testimonium,
ut test. perhib.* . . . *ut omnes* v.;
*came for witness, that he might
bear* . . . *that all men* . . . John's

mission is first set forth under
its generic aspect: he came *for
witness*, not *for a witness;* and
then its specific object (ἵνα μαρτ.
περὶ τ. φ.) and its final object
(ἵνα π. πιστ.) are defined co-or-
dinately (ἵνα . . . ἵνα). This
combination of successive and
related ends under one form of
construction, is characteristic of
St. John's style: comp. xx. 31,
xv. 16, xvii. 21, 23 f. For the
phrase εἰς μαρτυρίαν compare the
kindred phrase Matt. viii. 4, x.
18, xxiv. 14 (εἰς μαρτύριον); Mark
vi. 11. The coming of the Baptist (ἦλθε) in the fulfilment of his
office is contrasted with his
personal coming (ἐγένετο, *v.* 6).

εἰς μαρτυρ.] On the idea of
" witness " see Introd. The office
of the prophet in the fullest
sense is to make known Another.
This office had been fulfilled
" in many parts and in many
fashions " by all God's messengers in earlier times, and at last
eminently by the Baptist (comp.
iii. 30). He came, as his prede-
cessors, but with a clearer charge,
ἵνα μαρτυρήσῃ περὶ τοῦ φωτός, to
interpret to men the signs of a
divine will and guidance without
them and within them, and then
to point to Him who was Himself the Life and the Light. In
this way provision was made for
leading men in human ways to
recognise the divine.

πάντες] *all men.* The prophets
had prepared the way for the
extension of the divine call beyond
Israel (comp. Isa. xlix. 6). The
Baptist at last delivered a message

10 ἐν τῷ κόσμῳ ἦν, καὶ ὁ κόσμος δι' αὐτοῦ ἐγένετο, καὶ
11 ὁ κόσμος αὐτὸν οὐκ ἔγνω. Εἰς τὰ ἴδια ἦλθεν, καὶ οἱ

which in its essence was universal.
As the last prophet, the last
interpreter of the Law, he carried
the preparatory discipline to its
final application. He spoke to
men as men; outward descent,
national privileges, disappeared
from their place in the divine
order from the time of his preaching. The basis of his preaching
was repentance — inner self-re-
nunciation—the end was faith.
In this connexion it is to be
noticed that the conception of
faith is sharpened by being left
in an absolute form: ἵνα πάντες
πιστεύσωσι (contrast v. 12) δι' αὐτοῦ (John). There can be but
one adequate object of faith,
even God made known in the
Son. Πιστεύειν is used similarly
v. 51, v. 44, xi. 15, xiv. 29, etc.,
iv. 41 f., 53, xix. 35, xx. 29, 31.

The character of the Baptist's
preaching is implied in its scope.
The phrase πάντες is unintelligible
except on the supposition that
the universal gospel was preceded
by a call to repentance. But it
is worthy of remark that St.
John does not notice explicitly
his call to repentance, nor do the
terms μετάνοια, μετανοεῖν find a
place in his Gospel or Epistles
(μετανοεῖν occurs frequently in
the Revelation). Thus the correspondence between St. John
and the Synoptists as to the
character of the Baptist's work
is complete without a correspondence of letter.

δι' αὐτοῦ] through him, that is
the Baptist, not the Light. The
message of the Baptist has an absolute and enduring power. He
still in spirit goes before Christ.

8. οὐκ ἦν ἐκεῖνος τὸ φῶς] non
erat ille lux v.; he was not the light.
From this passage and other
similar passages (v. 20, iii. 26 ff.)
it has been plausibly argued that
the Evangelist was familiar with
some who unduly exalted the
Baptist. Comp. Acts xix. 3 f.
John was ὁ λύχνος (v. 35), and not
the light. Ἐκεῖνος isolates and
so fixes attention upon the person
referred to. Comp. i. 18, note, ii.
21, note.

ἀλλ' ἵνα . . .] sed ut . . . v.;
but came that he might . . . The
ellipse is best filled up from v. 7.
Comp. ix. 3, xv. 25, note.

9, 10. The preparation of prophecy, represented by John, was
one part of the education of the
world. The Word Himself as
light (v. 5) visited the world which
He had made (v. 9), and was in
it still (v. 10).

9. Ἦν τ. φῶς τ. ἀληθινόν . . .
ἐρχόμενον εἰς τ. κόσμον] Erat lux
vera . . . venientem in mundum v.;
There was the true light . . . coming
into the world. The text is ambiguous. Ἐρχόμενον may agree
either (1) with man, or (2) with
light. Thus there are two distinct series of interpretations.
(1) If ἐρχόμενον be taken with
ἄνθρωπον, the sense will be either
(a) simply "every man," according to a common Hebrew idiom,
or (b) "every man at the moment
of his birth." But it is scarcely
possible that the words ἐρχόμενον
εἰς τὸν κόσμον can be without
distinct meaning; and, in spite
of Wordsworth's greatest ode, it
is hardly true to say that the
illumination of the Light, which
comes through Life, is most

10 world. He was in the world, and the world was
made through him, and the world recognised him
11 not. He came unto his own *home*, and his own

complete at man's entrance into
the world.

(2) If, on the other hand,
ἐρχόμενον be taken to agree with
φῶς, it may be directly connected
either (*a*) with φωτίζει, or (*b*)
with ἦν. In the first case (*a*) the
sense will be "lighteth every
man by coming"; but the context does not call for any statement as to the mode of the action
of the Light; and the Light
illuminates by "being" as well
as by "coming." If then (*b*)
ἦν . . . ἐρχόμενον be taken together, there is still some ambiguity remaining. The phrase
has been interpreted to mean (*a*)
"was destined to come," and (*β*)
"was on the point of coming,"
and (*γ*) "was in the very act of
coming."

But it seems best to take it
more literally, and yet more
generally, as describing a coming
which was progressive, slowly
accomplished, combined with a
permanent being, so that both
the verb ἦν and the participle
ἐρχόμενον have their full force,
and do not form a periphrasis for
an imperfect. The mission of
John was one and definite; but
all along up to his time "the
Light" of which he came to
witness continued to shine, being
revealed in many parts and in
many ways. *There was the Light,
the true Light which lighteth
every man;* that Light was, and
yet more, that Light was *coming
into the world.* The same idea
of a constant, continuous coming
of the Word to men is found

in vi. 33, 50, where ὁ καταβαίνων stands in marked contrast with ὁ καταβάς (*vv.* 51,
58). Taken in relation to the
context, the words declare that
men were not left alone to interpret the manifestations of the
Light in the Life around them
and in them. The Light from
whom that Life flows made
Himself known more directly.
From the first He was (so to
speak) on His way to the world,
advancing toward the Incarnation by preparatory revelations.
He came in type and prophecy
and judgement.

The identification of "the
Word" with "the Light" is
natural, and is prepared by *v.* 5.
But, at the same time, the titles
are not co-extensive. "The
Light" (as the other special titles,
the Bread of Life, etc.) describes
"the Word" only in special relation towards creation, and particularly towards men.

In this relation the Light is
characterised as (1) τὸ ἀληθινόν,
and (2) ὁ φωτίζει πάντα ἄνθρωπον. The former expression
(1) marks the essential nature of
the Light as that of which all
other lights are only partial rays
or reflections—as the archetypal
Light (see iv. 23, vi. 32, xv. 1).
The "true light" in this sense is
not opposed to a "false light,"
but to an imperfect, incomplete,
transitory light.

The latter (2) describes the
universal extent of its action.
The words must be taken simply
as they stand. No man is wholly

12 ἴδιοι αὐτὸν οὐ παρέλαβον. ὅσοι δὲ ἔλαβον αὐτόν, ἔδωκεν αὐτοῖς ἐξουσίαν τέκνα θεοῦ γενέσθαι, τοῖς πιστεύουσιν

destitute of the illumination of "the Light." In nature, and life, and conscience it makes itself felt in various degrees to all. The Word is the spiritual Sun: viii. 12 (xi. 9). This truth, it may be added, is recognised here by St. John, but he does not (like Philo) dwell upon it. Before the fact of the Incarnation it falls into the background. For the Jewish idea of "the light of Creation" (Isa. xxx. 26), see Taylor's *Sayings of the Jewish Fathers*, p. 72.

φωτίζει] *illuminat* v.; *lighteth.* Comp. Luke xi. 35, 36. The Light is contrasted in each particular with the witness to the Light. He "arose" (ἐγένετο); the Light "was" (ἦν). He guided his disciples away from himself; the Light illuminated in virtue of Its own nature. He came once for all; the Light was ever coming through the ages.

πάντα ἄνθ.] The idea is distinct from that of πάντες (v. 7). The relation is not collective, corporate, as it is here presented, but personal, and universal while personal. The reality of this relation furnished the basis for the crowning fact of the Incarnation. The world was made for this re-gathering.

ἐρχόμενον εἰς τ. κόσμ.] Comp. iii. 19, xii. 46.

10, 11. Verse 9, according to the interpretation which has been given, presents a comprehensive view of the action of the Light. This action is now divided into two parts. The first part (v. 10) gathers up the facts and issues of the manifestation of the Light

as immanent. The second part (v. 11) contains an account of the special personal manifestation of the Light to a chosen race. The two parts are contrasted throughout as to the mode (ἦν, ἐγένετο), the scene (τ. κόσμον, τ. ἴδια), the recipients (ὁ κόσμος, οἱ ἴδιοι), and the end (οὐκ ἔγνω, οὐ παρέλαβον) of the manifestation. The world failed to recognise Him who was doubly shown as its Creator and as its Preserver. The people of God failed to welcome Him whom they had been prepared to receive.

10. ἐν τ. κόσμῳ ἦν] Comp. v. 5, note. It is impossible to refer these words simply to the historical Presence of the Word in Jesus as witnessed to by the Baptist. The whole scope and connexion of the passage requires a wider sense. The Word acts by His Presence as well as by His special Advent. The continuance and progress of things, no less than their original constitution, are fitted to make Him known.

ὁ κόσμος] the sum of created being, which belongs to the sphere of human life as an ordered whole, considered apart from God, and in its moral aspect represented by humanity. See note at the end of the chapter.

αὐτόν] *him.* The personal character which has been already implied now finds expression, contrasted with the neuter in v. 5 (αὐτό). The previous pronoun (δι' αὐτοῦ) is ambiguous, but it is most natural to suppose that this also is masculine (as in E.V.).

ἔγνω] *cognovit* v.; *recognised.* Comp. ii. 25, note.

12 *people* received him not.   But as many as received
him, to them gave he right to become children of

The form of the sentence is peculiarly characteristic. The clauses are placed simply side by side (. . . καὶ ὁ κόσμος . . . καὶ ὁ κόσμος . . .). In this way the statement of the issue (καὶ ὁ κόσμος αὐτὸν οὐκ ἔγνω) gains in pathos. For a similar use of καί, see viii. 20, note.

11. The Evangelist now passes from the universal action of the Word as the Light to His special action. Creation and mankind were His, and not unvisited by Him ; but in "the world" and in humanity one spot and one people were in a peculiar sense devoted to Him. The land of Israel was τὰ ἴδια (His own home), and the children of Israel were οἱ ἴδιοι (His own people). The Word came to the holy land and to the holy nation, and they "received Him not."

ἦλθεν εἰς τ. ἴδ. . . . παρέλαβον] *in propria (sua) venit, et sui eum non receperunt* v. ; *He came unto his own home, and his own people received him not.*

Εἰς τὰ ἴδια] *to his own home.* Comp. xvi. 32, xix. 27 ; Acts xxi. 6 (Esther v. 10, vi. 22, LXX.). There can be no reasonable doubt that this phrase, and οἱ ἴδιοι (His own people) which follows, describe the land and the people of Israel as being, in a sense in which no other land and people were, the home and the family of GOD, of Jehovah. "The holy land" (Zech. ii. 12. Comp. 2 Macc. i. 7) was "the LORD's land" (Hos. ix. 3 ; Jer. ii. 7, xvi. 18. Comp. Lev. xxv. 23) ; and Israel was His portion (Exod. xix. 5 ; Deut. vii. 6, xiv. 2, xxvi. 18, xxxii. 9 ;

Ps. cxxxiv. (cxxxv.) 4. Comp. Ecclus. xxiv. 8 ff.). The development of the thought of the apostle is certainly destroyed by supposing that here the earth is spoken of as the Lord's home, and man as His people.

It must be noticed that by this appropriation of the Old Testament language, that which was before applied to Jehovah is now applied to Christ. Comp. xii. 41, note.

ἦλθεν] *came.* The word forms a climax when combined with those which precede: ἦν, ἐν τῷ κόσμῳ ἦν ; and in this connexion it appears to contain an allusion to the technical sense of ὁ ἐρχόμενος. Comp. ix. 39. The tense (comp. v. 7) seems necessarily to mark a definite advent, the Incarnation, which consummated the former revelations of the Word to Israel. It does not seem possible that the manifestations before the Incarnation and separate from it could be so spoken of. Nor is there anything in this interpretation which detracts from the force of v. 14. The Incarnation is regarded in the two places under different aspects. Here it is regarded in relation to the whole scheme of Redemption, as the crowning revelation to the ancient people of God ; in v. 14 it is regarded in its distinctive character as affecting humanity. Here it is seen from the side of national failure, there of individual faith.

παρέλαβον] *received.* Παρέλαβον, as distinguished from ἔλαβον in the next verse, suggests in this connexion the notion of

13 εἰς τὸ ὄνομα αὐτοῦ, οἳ¹ οὐκ ἐξ αἱμάτων οὐδὲ ἐκ θελήματος
σαρκὸς οὐδὲ ἐκ θελήματος ἀνδρὸς ἀλλ' ἐκ θεοῦ ἐγεν-

¹ qui . . . natus est b. Tert. Iren. See note.

" receiving that which has been handed down by another " (as opposed to παρέδωκα, comp. 1 Cor. xv. 1, 3, xi. 23), as distinct from that of "taking." The divine teachers of Israel, through John their representative, "offered" Christ to the people as Him whom the Lord had promised ; and the leaders of the people refused to acknowledge Him as their King.

12. The Jews as a nation did not receive Christ as Him for whose advent they had been disciplined ; but this national rejection was qualified by the personal belief of some. These however believed as *men*, so to say, and not as *Jews*. They became on an equality with those who believed from among the heathen. The Christian Church was not, as it might have been, the corporate transfiguration of the old Church, but was built up of individuals. To these, whether Jews or Gentiles by ancestry, ὅσοι ἔλαβον αὐτόν [Christ], ἔδωκεν ἐξουσίαν τέκνα θεοῦ γενέσθαι. The privilege of Israel (Exod. iv. 22) was extended to all the faithful.

The irregular construction ὅσοι δὲ ἔλαβον . . . ἔδωκεν αὐτοῖς . . . gives prominence to the act of personal faith which distinguishes the first-fruits of the new Israel. Thought is first fixed on the character of those who believed, and then by a change of subject on the Word, and what He did.

ἔλαβον] *received.* The word indicates the action of him who "takes" that which is within

reach, as anxious to make it his own. Comp. v. 43, xiii. 20, xix. 6. ἐξουσίαν] *potestatem* v. ; *right.* Ἐξουσία does not describe mere ability, but legitimate, rightful authority, derived from a competent source which includes the idea of power. Comp. v. 27, x. 18, xvii. 2, xix. 10, 11 ; Rev. ii. 26, etc. This right is not inherent in man, but "given" by God to him. A shadow of it existed in the relation of Israel to God. But that which was in that case outward and independent of the individual will was replaced in the Christian Church by a vital relationship.

As far as we can conceive of " this right to become children," it lies in the potential union with the Son, whereby those who receive Him are enabled to realise their divine fellowship. They are adopted—placed, if we may so speak, in the position of sons—that so they may become children actually. Comp. 2 Pet. i. 3, 4 ; Gal. iv. 6. The fruit is not given at once, but the seed. It is of God to give, but man must use His gift, which faith appropriates. It is thus important to observe how throughout the passage the divine and human sides of the realisation of Sonship are harmoniously united. The initial act is at once a " begetting " (ἐγεννήθησαν) and a " reception " (ἔλαβον). The growth follows from the use of a gift. The issue is complete on the part of God, but man must bring it to pass by continuous exertion (τέκνα γενέσθαι, τοῖς πιστεύουσιν).

13 God, *even* to them that believe on his name: which
were begotten, not of blood,[1] nor of the will of the

[1] *lit.* bloods.

τέκνα] *filios* v.; *children.* Comp.
xi. 52; 1 John iii. 1, 2, 10, v. 2;
Rom. viii. 16, 17, 21, ix. 8;
Phil. ii. 15. The idea of τέκνον,
as distinguished from υἱός, which
does not occur in this connexion
in St. John except Rev. xxi. 7,
is that of a community of nature
(*v.* 13), as distinguished from
that of a dignity of heirship. It
is an illustration of this limitation of the idea of spiritual
"childship," that in the divine
relation τέκνον is not found (as
υἱός is) in the singular (yet see
Tit. i. 4; 1 Tim. i. 2; Philem. 10).
It may be added that the divine
Sonship with which the New
Testament deals is always regarded in connexion with Christ.
Yet comp. Acts xvii. 28 ff.

γενέσθαι] *to become.* Comp.
Matt. v. 45.

τοῖς πιστεύουσιν . . .] *his qui
credunt* . . . v.; *even to them that
believe* . . . The words are in
apposition with the preceding
αὐτοῖς. The effective reception
of Christ is explained to be the
continuous energy of faith which
relies upon Him as being for the
believer that which He has made
Himself known to be. The faith
is regarded as present and lasting
(τοῖς πιστεύουσιν), and not simply
as triumphant in the crisis of
trial (τοῖς πιστεύσασιν, Heb. iv.
3); and its object is the revealed
Person of the Incarnate Word.
Comp. 1 John v. 13 (τοῖς πιστεύουσιν).

πιστ. εἰς τ. ὄν. αὐτ.] ii. 23;
1 John v. 13. Contrast πιστ. τῷ
ὄν. (1 John iii. 23). See v. 24,
note, viii. 30 f., note.

τὸ ὄνομα αὐτοῦ] *his name.* The
revealed name gathers up and
expresses for man just so much
as he can apprehend of the divine
nature. Comp. iii. 18, xx. 31.
From these passages it is clear
that the "name" to the believer
is that which describes the Incarnate Word as "the Christ,
the Son of God." For the use of
"the name" as applied to the
Father in St. John, see v. 43,
x. 25, xii. 13, 28, xvii. 6, 11, 12,
26; Rev. iii. 12, xi. 18, xiii. 6,
xiv. 1, xv. 4, 9, xvii. 4; as applied
to the Son, ii. 23, iii. 18, xiv. 13,
14, 26, xv. 16, xvi. 23, 24, 26,
xx. 31; 1 John ii. 12, iii. 23,
v. 13; Rev. ii. 3, 13, iii. 12, xiv.
1. Comp. 3 John 7 (τοῦ ὀνόματος).
Comp. ii. 23, note.

13. The spring of the new
life to which the believer has
"right" lies solely in God. The
beginning of it cannot be found
in the combination of the material
elements, by which physical life
is represented, nor in the natural
instinct, in obedience to which
beings are reproduced, nor in the
will of the rational man. This
appears to be the meaning of
the threefold negation. The progress is from that which is lowest
in our estimate of the origin of
life to that which is highest. At
the same time the three clauses
naturally admit a moral interpretation. The new birth is not
brought about by descent, by
desire, or by human power.

ἐξ αἱμάτων] *ex sanguinibus* v.;
of blood (lit. *bloods*). The use of
the plural appears to emphasise
the idea of the element out of

2

14 νήθησαν. Καὶ ὁ λόγος σὰρξ ἐγένετο καὶ ἐσκήνωσεν
ἐν ἡμῖν, καὶ ἐθεασάμεθα τὴν δόξαν αὐτοῦ, δόξαν ὡς

which in various measures the body is framed.

σαρκός . . . ἀνδρός . . .] These two clauses differ from the former by referring the beginning of life to purpose; and they differ from one another in that the first marks the purpose which comes from the animal nature, and the second that which comes from the higher human nature.

ἐγεννήθησαν] nati sunt v.; were begotten, as 1 John ii. 29, iii. 9, iv. 7, v. 1, 4, 18. The thought is of the first origin of the new life, and not of the introduction of the living being into a new region. The phrase appears to be parallel with ὅσοι ἔλαβον. The act of reception coincided with the infusion of the divine principle, by which the later growth became possible.

It is important to notice generally that St. John dwells characteristically upon the communication of a new life, while St. Paul dwells upon the gift of a new dignity and relation (υἱοθεσία, Rom. viii. 15; Gal. iv. 5; Eph. i. 5). When St. Paul brings out the newness of the Christian's being he speaks of him as a new "creation" (κτίσις, Gal. vi. 15; 2 Cor. v. 17). The language of St. James (i. 18) and of St. Peter (1 Pet. i. 3, 23) corresponds with that of St. John.

The statement as to the fact of the new birth is made quite generally, but it is natural to see in it the contrast between the spiritual birth which makes " a child of GOD," and the fleshly descent in which the Jews trusted, and which had been recognised

under the Old Dispensation. Comp. Matt. iii. 9.

3. The Incarnation as apprehended by personal experience (14—18).

This section, like the former, falls into three parts. St. John gives first the substance of the apostolic witness (v. 14); and then the witness of prophecy, represented by the Baptist (v. 15); and thirdly, a general account of the nature of the revelation (vv. 16—18).

14. The construction of the verse is somewhat irregular. It consists of a main clause, which describes the fact and the character of the Incarnation (ὁ λόγος σὰρξ ἐγένετο κ. ἐσκήνωσεν ἐν ἡμῖν, πλήρης χάριτος κ. ἀληθείας), broken by a parenthesis (κ. ἐθεασάμεθα τ. δοξ. . . . παρὰ πατρός), which records the observation of the fact, so that it presents in succession the Incarnation, the witness to the Incarnation, the character of the Incarnate Word.

The Incarnation, which has been touched upon in v. 11 in its relation to the whole course of revelation, is now presented in its essential character. In the former place the Advent was considered in reference to particular promises (ἦλθεν) and to a chosen people: now it is revealed in its connexion with humanity. Thus there is no retrogression or repetition, but a distinct progress in the development of thought. The special aspect of Messiah's coming, followed by the national failure to recognise His coming, prepares the way for the universal aspect of it.

14 flesh, nor of the will of man, but of God. And the Word became flesh, and tabernacled among us (and we beheld his glory, glory as of the [1] only begotten

[1] or an.

The general scope of the whole verse may be briefly summed up under four heads :

1. The nature of the Incarnation. Ὁ λόγος σὰρξ ἐγένετο.

2. The historical life of the Incarnate Word. Ἐσκήνωσεν ἐν ἡμῖν.

3. The personal apostolic witness to the character of that human-divine Life. Ἐθεασάμεθα τὴν δόξαν αὐτοῦ.

4. The character of the Incarnate Word as the Revealer of God. Πλήρης χάριτος καὶ ἀληθείας.

It may be added that the fact of the miraculous Conception, though not stated, is necessarily implied by the Evangelist. The coming of the Word into flesh is presented as a Creative act in the same way as the coming of all things into being was.

Καὶ ὁ λόγος . . .] And the Word . . . The conjunction carries the reader back to v. 1, with which this verse is closely connected by this repetition of the title ὁ λόγος, which is now at length resumed. All that has intervened is in one sense parenthetical. The Incarnation presupposes and interprets the Creation and the later history of man, and of man's relation to God. Thus the thoughts run on in perfect sequence: Ἐν ἀρχῇ ἦν ὁ λόγος . . . καὶ θεὸς ἦν ὁ λόγος . . . Καὶ ὁ λόγος σὰρξ ἐγένετο. This connexion is far more natural than that which has been supposed to exist between v. 14 and v. 9 or v. 11.

The announcement of the mystery of the Incarnation, embracing and completing all the mysteries of revelation, corresponds (as has been already noticed) to the declaration of the absolute Being of the Word in v. 1. " He was God "; and " He became flesh " : eternity and time, the divine and the human, are reconciled in Him. " He was with God "; and " He tabernacled among us " : the divine existence is brought into a vital and historical connexion with human life. " He was in the beginning "; and " we beheld His glory " : He who " was " beyond time was revealed for a space to the observation of men.

σὰρξ ἐγένετο] verbum caro factum est v. (Tert. sermo caro factus est); became flesh. Owing to the inherent imperfection of human language as applied to the mystery of the Incarnation, both these words are liable to misinterpretation. The word ἐγένετο must not be so understood as to support the belief that the Word ceased to be what He was before; and the word σάρξ must not be taken to exclude the rational soul of man. The clear apprehension of the meaning of the phrase, so far as we can apprehend it, lies in the recognition of the unity of the Lord's Person, before and after the Incarnation. His Personality is divine. But at the same time we must affirm that His humanity is real and complete. He,

μονογενοῦς παρὰ πατρός, πλήρης¹ χάριτος καὶ ἀληθείας·
15 (Ἰωάνης μαρτυρεῖ περὶ αὐτοῦ καὶ κέκραγεν λέγων Οὗτος
¹ πλήρη D; πλήρης ℵABCL.

remaining the same Person as before, did not simply assume humanity as something which could be laid aside: σὰρξ ἐγένετο. He did not simply become "a man": He became "man." The mode of the Lord's existence on earth was truly human, and subject to all the conditions of human existence; but He never ceased to be God. And the nature which He so assumed He retains in its perfection (1 John iv. 2, ἐν σαρκὶ ἐληλυθότα. 2 John 7, ἐρχόμενον ἐν σαρκί). As compared with the corresponding phrase ἔρχεσθαι ἐν σαρκί (1 John, l.c.), the phrase σὰρξ ἐγένετο brings out especially one aspect of the Incarnation. The former marks the unchanged continuity of the Lord's Personality, and the latter the complete reality of His Manhood.

How this "becoming" was accomplished we cannot clearly grasp. St. Paul describes it as an "emptying of Himself" by the Son of God (Phil. ii. 6 f.), a laying aside of the mode of divine existence (τὸ εἶναι ἴσα θεῷ); and this declaration carries us as far as we can go in defining the mystery.

Thus briefly the following main truths must be held as expressed in the words when they are fairly interpreted:

1. The Lord's humanity was complete, as against various forms of Apollinarianism, according to which the divine Logos supplied the place of part of that which belongs to the perfection of Manhood. (The Word became flesh, and not a body or the like.)

2. The Lord's humanity was real and permanent, as against various forms of Gnosticism, according to which He only assumed in appearance, or for a time, that which was and remained foreign to Himself. (The Word became flesh, and did not clothe Himself in flesh.)

3. The Lord's human and divine natures remained without change, each fulfilling its part according to its proper laws, as against various forms of Eutychianism, according to which the result of the Incarnation is a third nature, if the humanity has any real existence. (The Word became flesh, both terms being preserved side by side.)

4. The Lord's humanity was universal and not individual, as including all that belongs to the essence of man, without regard to sex or race or time. (The Word became flesh, and not a man.)

5. The Lord's human and divine natures were united in one Person, as against various forms of Nestorianism, according to which He has a human personality and a divine personality, to which the acts, etc., belonging to the respective natures must be referred. (The Word became flesh, and tabernacled, etc., without any change of the subject to the verb.)

6. The Word did not acquire personality by the Incarnation. He is spoken of throughout, not as a principle or an energy, but,

15 from the ¹ Father), full of grace and truth. John beareth witness of him, and crieth, saying, This was

¹ or a father.

whatever may be the inherent imperfection of such language, as a Person.

So far, perhaps, we can see generally a little of the Truth, but the attempt to express the Truth with precision is beset with difficulty and even with peril. Thus in using the words "personality" and "impersonal" in relation to Christ, it is obviously necessary to maintain the greatest reserve. For us "personality" implies limitation or determination, *i.e.* finiteness in some direction. As applied to the divine nature therefore the word is not more than a necessary accommodation required to give such distinctness to our ideas as may be attainable. The word "impersonal" again, as applied to the Lord's human nature, is not to be so understood as to exclude in any way the right application of the word "man" (ἄνθρωπος) to Him, as it is used both by Himself (viii. 40) and by St. Paul (1 Tim. ii. 5).

The phrase ὁ λόγος σὰρξ ἐγένετο is absolutely unique. The phrases which point towards it in St. John (1 John iv. 2), in the Epistle to the Hebrews (ii. 14), and in St. Paul (Rom. viii. 3; Phil. ii. 7; 1 Tim. iii. 16) fall short of the majestic fulness of this brief sentence, which affirms once for all the reconciliation of the opposite elements of the final antithesis of life and thought, the finite and the infinite.

σάρξ] *flesh.* Humanity from the side of its weakness and de-

pendence and mortality is naturally described as "flesh." In this respect "flesh" expresses here human nature as a whole regarded under the aspect of its present corporeal embodiment, including of necessity the "soul" (xii. 27), and the "spirit" (xi. 33, xiii. 21, xix. 30), as belonging to the totality of man (comp. Heb. ii. 14). At the same time the word marks the points of connexion between man and the material world, so that it has a further significance as presenting in a familiar contrast the spiritual and the material (ὁ λόγος, σάρξ). Thus several ante-Nicene Fathers speak of the Word, or the Son, as Spirit with reference to this passage (Tert. *de Carne Christi*, 18; Hippol. *c. Noet.* 4; Hermas, *Sim.* v. 6, ix. 1; Theoph. *ad Autol.* ii. 10; Clem. II. *ad Cor.* ix., with Lightfoot's note).

ἐγένετο] *became.* This term forms a link between this verse and verse 3. As "all things *became* through the Word," so He Himself "*became flesh.*" The first creation and the second creation alike centre in Him.

ἐσκήνωσεν] *habitavit* v.; *tabernacled.* Σκηνόω describes properly the occupation of a temporary habitation. The σκηνή (tent or tabernacle) was easily fixed and easily removed, and hence it furnished a natural term for man's bodily frame. Yet apparently the original idea of "tent" (σκηνή) was lost in the form σκῆνος, which expresses the idea of "frame" apart from any further

ἦν ὃν¹ εἶπον· ὁ ὀπίσω μου ἐρχόμενος ἔμπροσθέν μου
16 γέγονεν, ὅτι πρῶτός μου ἦν·) ὅτι² ἐκ τοῦ πληρώματος

¹ ὃν εἶπον אᵇABᵃDL ; ὁ εἰπών א*B*C*. See note.
² ὅτι אBCDLX 33; καὶ ACᶜEFG. See note.

figurative meaning: Wisd. ix.
15 ; 2 Cor. v. 1, 4 ; 2 Pet. i. 13 f.
(σκήνωμα). And so also σκηνόω
is used without any reference to
the notion of transitoriness: Rev.
vii. 15, xii. 12, xiii. 6, xxi. 3.

Whether, however, the thought
of the temporariness of Christ's
sojourn upon earth is indicated
by the term or not, there can
be no doubt that it serves to
contrast the Incarnation with
the earlier "Christophanies,"
which were partial, visionary,
evanescent, and at the same time
to connect the Personal Presence
of the Lord with His earlier
Presence in the Tabernacle which
foreshadowed it, Exod. xxv. 8;
Lev. xxvi. 11. The Lord in old
times *walked in a tent and in a
tabernacle* (2 Sam. vii. 6 ; cf. Ps.
lxxviii. 67 ff.), as now. He dwelt
among men according to the promises expressed after that type
(Joel iii. 21 ; Ezek. xxxvii.). The
parallelism becomes more striking
if we accept the current view
that the Tabernacle was a symbol
of the world.

Many also have found in the
word itself a distinct reference to
the *Shekinah*; but before any
stress can be laid upon the coincidence of form, it is necessary
that the history of the term
Shekinah should be examined far
more carefully than it has been
examined at present, with a view
to determining : 1. The earliest
use of the term. 2. The comparative use of the word in the
different Targums. 3. The exact

senses in which it is used in relation to (a) the Word, and (β) the
Glory.

ἐν ἡμῖν] *in our midst*. Among
those who, like the Evangelist,
were eye-witnesses of His life.
Comp. Gen. xxiv. 3 (LXX.).

The supposition that the plural
marks the dwelling of the Word
as being realised in the nature or
in the race, as distinguished from
the individual, is quite inconsistent with the historical purport
of the whole phrase. Moreover
this truth has been already stated
by the use of the term σάρξ.

κ. ἐθεασάμεθα . . . πατρός] The
breaking of the construction by
this parenthetical clause, marks
the pause which the Evangelist
makes to contemplate the mystery which he has declared. He
looks, as it were, from without
upon the record and comments
upon it. The same phenomenon
in different forms recurs *v.* 16,
iii. 16, 31, xix. 35 ; 1 John i. 2.

ἐθεασάμεθα] *vidimus* v. ; *we
beheld* (1 John i. 1). The abode
of the Word among men was
only for a brief space, but yet
such that those near Him could
contemplate His glory at leisure
and calmly. His historical Presence was real if transitory. And
while the appearance of the Lord
was in humility, yet even under
the limitations of His human
form, those who looked patiently
could see the tokens of the divine
revelation made through Him.
Comp. Luke ix. 32 ; 2 Pet. i. 16 ff.;
John iv. 14 (τεθεάμεθα).

he of whom I spake; he that cometh after me is come to be before me: because he was before me. 16 Because out of his fulness we all received, and grace

τ. δόξαν αὐτοῦ] *his glory*. The word δόξα carries on the parallel between the divine Presence in the Tabernacle and the divine Presence by the Word Incarnate among men. From time to time the Lord manifested His glory in the wilderness (Exod. xvi. 10, xxiv. 16, xl. 34, etc.); in the Temple of Solomon (1 Kings viii. 11); and to the prophets (Isa. vi. 3. Comp. ch. xii. 41; Ezek. i. 28, etc.; Acts vii. 55); and even so Christ's glory flashed forth at crises of His history. It is not possible for us to define exactly in what way this majesty was shown, by signs, by words, by events. Comp. Luke ix. 31 f. It is enough that the Evangelist records his own experience. The Son of man had a glory which corresponded with His filial relation to the Father, even when He had laid aside His divine glory (xvii. 5).

For the general idea of δόξα in St. John, see Introd.

δόξαν ὡς] *glory as of* . . . This glory of the Incarnate Word is described as being " glory as of an only son from his father," a glory, that is, of one who represents another, being derived from him, and of the same essence with him. The particle of comparison and the absence of articles in the original show that the thought centres in the abstract relation of father and son; and yet in the actual connexion this abstract relation passes necessarily into the relation of "the Son " to " the Father."

ὡς] Comp. Rev. v. 6, xiii. 3.

μονογενοῦς] *unigeniti* v.; *only begotten*. Comp. iii. 16; 1 John iv. 9. The rendering " only begotten " somewhat obscures the exact sense of μονογενής, which is rather " only-born." That is, the thought in the original is centred in the personal Being of the Son and not in His generation. Christ is the One only Son, the One to whom the title belongs in a sense completely unique and singular, as distinguished from that in which there are many children of God (*vv.* 12 ff.). The use of the word elsewhere in the New Testament to describe an only child (Luke vii. 12, viii. 42, ix. 38; Heb. xi. 17) brings out this sense completely. The ideas of the Son as " begotten " of the Father, and as " the only Son," are expressed separately in the ancient Creeds (*e.g. Ep. Syn. Ant.* Routh, *Rell.* iii. 290, γεννητόν, μονογενῆ υἱόν. *Symb. Nic.* γεννηθ. ἐκ τ. π. μονογενῆ, etc.).

In the LXX. the word occurs seven times: Tobit iii. 15 (vi. 11), viii. 17 (of only children); Wisd. vii. 22; and (as a translation of יחיד) Ps. xxii. (xxi.) 21, xxxv. (xxxiv.) 17 (of the soul, the one single, irreparable life of man), xxv. (xxiv.) 16 (of the sufferer left alone and solitary). The Hebrew word thus translated is in seven other places represented by ἀγαπητός, which carries with it also the notion of an only child (Gen. xxii. 2, 12, 16; Judges xi. 34; Jer. vi. 26; Amos viii. 10; Zech. xii. 10).

αὐτοῦ ἡμεῖς πάντες ἐλάβομεν, καὶ χάριν ἀντὶ χάριτος·
17 ὅτι ὁ νόμος διὰ Μωυσέως ἐδόθη, ἡ χάρις καὶ ἡ ἀλήθεια

Christian writers from early times have called attention to the connexion of the two words applied in the New Testament to Christ, μονογενής and πρωτότοκος (Col. i. 15), which present the idea of His Sonship under complementary aspects. The first marks His relation to God as absolutely without parallel, the other His relation to creation as pre-existent and sovereign. Comp. Lightfoot on Col. i. 15.

παρὰ πατρός] from the Father, or, from a father. The idea conveyed is not that of sonship only, but of a mission also. Christ was a Son, and a Son sent to execute a special work (comp. v. 6, ἀπεστ. παρὰ θεοῦ, vi. 46, vii. 29, xvi. 27, xvii. 8). The converse thought is expressed in v. 18 (ὁ ὢν εἰς τ. κ. τ. π.).

πλήρης χαρ. κ. ἀληθ.] full of grace and truth. The phrase is connected with the main subject of the sentence, the Word . . . tabernacled among us . . . full of grace. For a moment the Evangelist had rested upon the glorious memories of that which he had seen (comp. 1 John i. 1, 2). Now he goes on to characterise Christ's Presence by its inward marks. Each of the two elements is laid open in vv. 16, 17. The combination recalls the description of Jehovah, Exod. xxxiv. 6 (Ps. xxv. 10); and is not infrequent in the Old Testament: Gen. xxiv. 27, 49, xxxii. 10; Ps. xl. 10, 11, lxi. 7 (חסד ואמת). As applied to the Lord, the phrase marks Him as the Author of perfect Redemption and perfect Revelation. Grace corresponds

with the idea of the revelation of God as love (1 John iv. 8, 16) by Him who is Life; and Truth with that of the revelation of God as light (1 John i. 5) by Him who is Himself Light.

15. The testimony of John is introduced in the same manner as before, as representing the final testimony of prophecy. John gave not only a general witness to "the Light," but also pointed out the true position which Christ occupied towards himself in virtue of His nature.

μαρτυρεῖ . . . κ. κέκραγεν . . .] beareth witness . . . and crieth (hath cried) . . . The witness of John is treated as present and complete; present because his mission was divine, complete because it was directed to a special end which was reached (μαρτυρεῖ, κέκραγεν). Comp. v. 34. The words of John are given here in a form different from that in which they appear in v. 30, and with a different scope. Οὗτος ἦν ὃν εἶπον (Vulg. quem dixi), to whom my teaching pointed generally; and not "in behalf of whom (ὑπὲρ οὗ, all. περὶ οὗ, Vulg. de quo) I made a special statement." The words which follow are therefore most probably to be taken as an independent statement: "This is the Christ of whom I spake; and He has now entered on His office. He that cometh after me is come to be (become) before me . . ."

κέκραγεν] clamat v.; crieth, vii. 28, 37, xii. 44. The voice of the Baptist was more than that of a witness. It was the

17 for grace. Because the law was given through Moses ; grace and truth came through Jesus Christ.

loud, clear voice of the herald who boldly proclaimed his message so that all might hear it.

ἦν] *was he.* The Baptist throws himself backward in thought to the time when he looked forward to the Christ who had not yet appeared, and proclaimed His coming.

ὁ ὀπίσω μου ἐρχ. ἔμπροσθέν μου γέγονεν] *qui post me venturus est, ante me factus est* v. ; *he that cometh after me is come to be before me.* The words express the Baptist's witness to Christ from the moment when His Messiahship was signified. As soon as He was manifested He took up a position in advance of His forerunner, though the forerunner had already been long labouring. The witness of the Baptist before Christ's Baptism was simply in general terms, " He that cometh after me is mightier than I " (Matt. iii. 11 ; Luke iii. 16); but St. John gives his recognition of the actual present majesty of his successor. " After " and " before " are both used in a metaphorical sense from the image of progression in a line. He who comes later in time comes " after " ; and he who advances in front shows by that his superior power. The supposed reference to the pre-existence of the Word, as if the Baptist said, " He that cometh after me in respect of my present mission hath already been active among men before I was born," seems to be inconsistent with the argument which points to a present consequence (γέγονεν) of an eternal truth (πρῶτός μου ἦν).

ὅτι πρῶτός μου ἦν] *because he was before me.* The precedence in dignity (iii. 33) which Christ at once assumed when He was manifested, was due to His essential priority. He *was* in His essence (viii. 58) before John, and therefore at His revelation He took the place which corresponded with His nature.

πρῶτός μου] *prior me* v. ; *before me.* This phrase is very remarkable. It expresses not only relative, but (so to speak) absolute priority. He was first altogether in regard to me, and not merely former as compared with me. Comp. xv. 18.

16. ὅτι ἐκ τ. πληρ.] *because out of his fulness* . . . The words depend on v. 14, πλήρης χάριτος κ. ἀληθείας, so that the sense is, We have knowledge of His character as " full of grace and truth " because . . . The intercalated witness of the Baptist, pointing to the true nature of Christ, marks the source of this spiritual wealth.

These words, and those which follow, are certainly words of the Evangelist and not of the Baptist. This is shown not only by their general character, but by the phrase *we all.*

ἐκ] *out of,* as a copious source of blessing.

πλήρωμα—*plenitudo* v. ; *fulness* —the plenitude, the full measure of all the divine powers and graces which were concentrated absolutely in Christ, the Incarnate Word. The term occurs here only in St. John's writings ; but it is found five times in the two Epistles of St. Paul to the Colossians and Ephesians, which

18 διὰ ᾽Ιησοῦ Χριστοῦ ἐγένετο.   θεὸν οὐδεὶς ἑώρακεν πώποτε·
μονογενὴς¹ θεὸς ὁ ὢν εἰς τὸν κόλπον τοῦ πατρὸς ἐκεῖνος
ἐξηγήσατο.

¹ ὁ μονογενὴς υἱός AX ; μονογενὴς θεός א*BC*L ; ὁ μονογενὴς θεός אᶜ. See note.

form the connecting link between the writings of St. Paul and St. John (Col. i. 19, ii. 9 ; Eph. i. 23, iii. 19, iv. 13). Of these passages the two in the Epistle to the Colossians illustrate most clearly the meaning of St. John. St. Paul says that πᾶν τὸ πλήρωμα dwelt in Christ (i. 19), and more definitely, that ἐν αὐτῷ κατοικεῖ πᾶν τὸ πλήρωμα τῆς θεότητος σωματικῶς, "and ye," he continues, addressing the Christians to whom he is writing, ἐστὲ ἐν αὐτῷ πεπληρωμένοι . . . (ii. 9 f.). Here St. Paul's thought is evidently that the whole sum of the divine attributes exists together in Christ, and that each Christian in virtue of his fellowship with Him draws from that πλήρωμα whatever he needs for the accomplishment of his own part in the great life of the Church. And so, from another point of sight, the Church itself, made up of the many parts, thus severally perfected, is " the body of Christ," His "fulness" realising in actual fact that which answers to the whole divine power in its Head (Eph. i. 23). St. John's idea in the present passage is the same : Christians receive from Christ, as from a spring of divine life, whatever they severally require according to their position and work. All is in Him, and all in Him is available for the believer. Comp. v. 20, xv. 15, xvii. 22. For a complete discussion of the word, see Lightfoot, *Colossians*, pp. 323 ff.

ἡμεῖς πάντες] *we all.* The addition of πάντες here (as compared with *v.* 14) appears to place us in a new company. The circle of the eye-witnesses passes into the larger fellowship of the Christian Church. Speaking from the centre of the new Society the apostle can say " *We all*— whether we saw Christ's glory or not—can attest the reality of His gifts. *We all received of His fulness,* when we were admitted into His fold, and at each succeeding crisis of our spiritual life." The essential universality of the blessing excludes the special claims of every select body. Comp. iii. 34.

ἐλάβομεν] *received.* The verb is without any direct object, since ἐκ τοῦ πληρώματος is not partitive. The conception of " the fulness " however at once suggests one : " *we all received* that which answered to our wants."

χάριν ἀντὶ χάριτος] *gratiam pro gratia* v. ; *grace for grace.* Each blessing appropriated became the foundation of a greater blessing. To have realised and used one measure of grace was to have gained a larger measure (as it were) in exchange for it. Thus this clause is not an explanation of that which has preceded, but a distinct addition to it. The phrase is illustrated by a saying in *Aboth,* iv. 5, " the reward of a precept is a precept."

17. ὅτι ὁ νόμος . . .] *because the law* . . . The clause is parallel with *v.* 16, and not the ground of it.

18 No man hath ever yet seen God; *one who is* God only begotten, which is in the bosom of the Father, he declared *him*.

ὁ νόμος διὰ Μωνσέως ἐδόθη, ἡ χάρ. κ. ἡ ἀληθ. . . .] *the law was given through Moses; grace and truth came through* . . . The Law is represented as an addition to the essential scheme of redemption. Comp. Gal. iii. 19 ; Rom. v. 20. It was "given" for a special purpose. On the other hand, the Gospel "came" (ἐγένετο), as if, according to the orderly and due course of the divine plan, this was the natural issue of all that had gone before. Judaism was designed to meet special circumstances ; Christianity satisfies man's essential nature.

ἡ χάρις καὶ ἡ ἀληθ.] *gratia et veritas* v.; *grace and truth*. Grace and Truth are now presented under the aspect of their complete embodiment (comp. *v.* 14, χ. καὶ ἀλ.). The Gospel is spoken of as ἡ χάρις, so far as it is the revelation of God's free love, and as ἡ ἀλήθεια, so far as it presents the reality and not the mere images or shadows of divine things. Comp. iv. 23. In both respects it was contrasted with the Law. The Law had a reward for obedience (Gal. iii. 12), and consequently brought a knowledge of sin (Rom. iii. 20 ; comp. vi. 14) ; and on the other hand, it had only the shadow of the good things to come (Heb. x. 1 ; Col. ii. 17). This exact and subtle correspondence of St. John's teaching with that of the other apostolic writings is to be noticed. The word χάρις does not occur elsewhere in his writings

except in salutations (2 John 3 ; Rev. i. 4, xxii. 21).

For the idea of Truth, see Introd.

διὰ Ἰησ. Χρ.] *through Jesus Christ.* The Person who has been present to the Evangelist throughout is now at last fully named. Comp. xvii. 3, xx. 31. The "name" thus given includes the declaration of the true humanity of the Saviour (*Jesus*), and of His relation to the earlier dispensation (*Christ*). His divine nature is set forth in the next verse. Comp. 1 John i. 3.

18. This last verse justifies the claim of the Gospel to be the Truth, while it lays down the inherent limitations of human knowledge. It is impossible, so far as our experience yet goes, for man to have direct knowledge of God as God. He can come to know Him only through One who shares both the human and divine natures, and who is in vital fellowship both with God and with man. In Christ this condition is satisfied. He who as the Word has been declared to be God, who as the Son is one in essence with the Father, even He set forth that which we need to know. It is tacitly assumed throughout, as it will be observed, that "the Truth" and "the knowledge of God" are identical terms.

θεὸν οὐδεὶς ἑώρακεν πώποτε] *no man hath ever yet seen God.* Comp. 1 John iv. 12. In both places θεόν is without the article. By this manner of expression

19   Καὶ αὕτη ἐστὶν ἡ μαρτυρία τοῦ Ἰωάνου ὅτε ἀπέστειλαν
πρὸς αὐτὸν οἱ Ἰουδαῖοι ἐξ Ἱεροσολύμων ἱερεῖς καὶ

thought is turned to the divine Nature rather than to the divine Person : " God as God " (comp. i. 1, note). The Theophanies under the Old Dispensation did not fall under this category. Comp. Exod. xxxiii. 12 ff. (xxxii. 30). Even Christ Himself was not " seen " as God. The perception of His true divine Nature was not immediate, but gained by slow processes (xiv. 9). The words set aside the false views of Judaism and Heathenism (v. 37 ; 1 John v. 20 f.). They do not deny the possibility of a true knowledge of God, but of a natural knowledge of God, such as can be described by "sight." The sight of God is the final transfiguration of man (1 John iii. 2). The simple act of vision is marked here (ἑώρακεν), while in the Epistle it is the calm sight of beholding (τεθέαται). Comp. xiv. 9, xii. 45.

By the use of the word πώποτε the Evangelist perhaps points forward to that open vision of the Divine which shall be granted hereafter (1 John iii. 2 ; Matt. v. 8).

μονογενὴς θεός] one who is God only begotten. The remarkable variation of reading in this place, μονογενὴς θεός for ὁ μονογενὴς υἱός (see additional note), makes no difference in the sense of the passage; and, however strange the statement may appear, does not seriously affect the form in which it is conveyed to us. " One who is God only begotten," or " God the only Son " (μονογενὴς θεός), One of whom it can be predicated that He is unique in His

Being, and God, is none other than " the only begotten Son " (ὁ μονογενὴς υἱός). The word Son—"the only begotten Son"—carries with it the identity of essence. The article in the one case defines as completely as the predicate in the other. But the best-attested reading (μονογενὴς θεός) has the advantage of combining the two great predicates of the Word, which have been previously indicated (v. 1 θεός, v. 14 μονογενής).

ὁ ὢν εἰς τ. κόλπ.] which is in (or into) the bosom. The image is used of the closest and tenderest of human relationships, of mother and child (Num. xi. 12), and of husband and wife (Deut. xiii. 6), and also of friends reclining side by side at a feast (comp. xiii. 23), and so describes the ultimate fellowship of love. The exact form of the words is remarkable. The phrase is not strictly " in the bosom," but "into the bosom." Thus there is the combination (as it were) of rest and motion, of a continuous relation, with a realisation of it (comp. i. 1, ἦν πρός). The " bosom of the Father " (like heaven) is a state, and not a place.

The words, as used by the Evangelist, may point to the exaltation of the ascended Christ ; but in connexion with " God the only Son " (μονογ. θεός) it is more natural to take them as an absolute description of the nature of the Son, so that the participle will be timeless. In fact the Ascension of Christ is essentially connected with the divine glory

19   And this is the witness of John, when the Jews
sent unto him from Jerusalem priests and Levites

which he had "before the foundation of the world" (xvii. 5).

τοῦ πατρός] *of the Father.* The choice of this title in place of God (τοῦ θεοῦ) serves to mark the limits of the revelation made through Jesus Christ. Even this was directed to one aspect (so to speak) of the Godhead. The Son made God known not primarily as God, but as the Father. At the same time this title lays the foundation of revelation in the essential relation of the Persons of the Godhead. Comp. 1 John i. 2.

In this connexion the description of the relation of the Word to God (*v.* 1, ὁ λόγος ἦν πρὸς τὸν θεόν) is seen to be complementary to that of the relation of the Son to the Father. The one marks an absolute relation in the Godhead. The other a relation apprehended with regard to creation. Hence in the latter the form of expression is borrowed from human affection.

ἐκεῖνος] *ipse* v.; *he.* This pronoun emphasises the attributes of the person already given, and isolates Him for the distinct contemplation of the reader. Comp. *v.* 33. This usage finds an interesting illustration in the fact that in 1 John ἐκεῖνος is used distinctively for the Lord: 1 John ii. 6, iii. 3, 5, 7, 16, iv. 17.

ἐξηγήσατο] *enarravit* v.; *declared him,* once and for ever. The verb ἐξηγέομαι is constantly used in classical writers of the interpretation of divine mysteries. Cf. Gen. xli. 8, 24; Lev. xiv. 57. The absence of the object in the original is remark-able. Thus the literal rendering is simply, *he made declaration.* Comp. Acts xv. 14.

The position of the object of the former clause (God) at the beginning of the sentence, leads naturally to the supplying of it in thought here; or rather suggests that which corresponds with it in connexion with the new verb, "the truth concerning Him, revealed as a Father, as man could bear the revelation." The knowledge of God, which Christ had as God, He set forth to men as man. Comp. Matt. xi. 27. Men *hear* from Him that which He *saw.* Comp. vi. 45 f., note.

Several important reflections follow from the consideration of the Prologue.

1. The writer occupies a distinct historical position. He speaks as one (i) who was originally a Jew, (ii) who had been an eye-witness, (iii) who is surrounded by a Christian society.

(i) His Jewish descent appears to be marked by the use of τὰ ἴδια and οἱ ἴδιοι (*v.* 11); by the mode in which creation is spoken of (ἐν ἀρχῇ); by the implied reference to the Fall (*v.* 5).

(ii) It is impossible to interpret *v.* 14 (ἐθεασάμεθα) without violence otherwise than as containing a direct statement of the writer's experience, and that too given in a form which is strikingly natural.

(iii) The phrase ἡμεῖς πάντες (*v.* 16) can only be an appeal to the experience of the Christian body in which the writer was living.

20 Λευείτας ἵνα ἐρωτήσωσιν αὐτόν Σὺ τίς εἶ; καὶ ὡμολόγησεν καὶ οὐκ ἠρνήσατο, καὶ ὡμολόγησεν ὅτι Ἐγὼ

2. There is no effort on the part of the writer to establish, or to enforce, or to explain. He sets forth what is matter of experience to him with complete conviction and knowledge. Nothing can be farther from the appearance of introducing any new teaching. The Evangelist takes for granted that his readers understand perfectly what he means by "the Word," "the Father." He does not expressly affirm but assumes the identification of the Word with Jesus Christ (v. 17).

3. There is no trace of any purely speculative interest in the propositions which are laid down. The writer at once passes to life and history from the contemplation of the divine in itself (v. 1). After the first verse everything is set down with a view to the revelation of God through the Word to men; and this revelation is treated historically in its different elements, and from the side of man. Moreover the Person of the Revealer is one from first to last, though He is regarded successively as the Word, the Life, the Light, the Word made flesh, even Jesus Christ. And the last term under which God is spoken of is "the Father," in which the abstract idea is lost in the personal.

4. Though the purely speculative is absent from the Prologue, as it is from the Gospel generally, the treatment of the subject is such that the Evangelist supplies the clues for the prosecution of the highest problems so far as man can pursue them. This he

does (1) By opening a momentary vision of the Godhead itself in which can be seen the Immanent Trinity, (2) by showing the relation of Creation to the Creator as Preserver, (3) by the declaration of the fact of the Incarnation, in which the Unity of the Finite and the Infinite is realised. And the more the Prologue is studied under these aspects, the more conspicuous become its originality and exhaustiveness.

5. The Prologue does in fact define the scope of the Gospel and interpret it. In this respect it corresponds with the close (xx. 31), which expresses in other terms vv. 14, 18.

And while the phraseology is peculiar, this section contains nothing which is not either directly affirmed in the Lord's discourses, or directly deducible from them.

1. The Pre-existence of Christ, vi. 62, viii. 58, xvii. 5, 24.

2. His Creative energy, v. 17.

3. The Universality of His work, viii. 12, x. 16.

The main subject of the Gospel which has been prepared by the Prologue is THE SELF-REVELATION OF CHRIST TO THE WORLD AND TO THE DISCIPLES. Under this aspect the Gospel falls into two great divisions, THE SELF-REVELATION OF CHRIST TO THE WORLD (i. 19—xii. 50); and THE SELF-REVELATION OF CHRIST TO THE DISCIPLES (xiii. 1—xxi. 23).

The first of these two great divisions falls also into two parts, THE PROCLAMATION (i. 19—iv. 54), and THE CONFLICT (v. 1—xii. 50).

20 to ask him, Who art thou? And he confessed, and denied not; and he confessed, I am not the Christ.

The Proclamation
(i. 19—iv. 54).

The record of the beginning of the Gospel contained in the first four chapters presents in act and word the main elements of the Message which Christ claimed to bring and to be, and typical examples of the classes of men to whom it was offered. So far He meets with misunderstanding, but with no active hostility. Principles and tendencies are laid open, but they await their development.

The Proclamation consists of two parts, which are marked distinctly in the construction of the narrative (ii. 11, iv. 54). The first part deals with (i) The Testimony to Christ (i. 19—ii. 11), and the second with (ii) The Work of Christ (ii. 13—iv. 54).

i. The Testimony to Christ
(i. 19—ii. 11).

This section consists of three divisions, which deal with three forms of witness, three typical relations of Christ, three modes of revelation. The first gives the witness of the prophet, the relation of Christ to the preparatory dispensation, the revelation by direct divine communication (i. 19—34). The second gives the witness of disciples, the relation of Christ to individual men, the revelation through spiritual insight (i. 35—51) The third gives the witness of acts, the relation of Christ to nature, the revelation through signs (ii. 1—11). In each case there is an activity of faith in recognising the divine message, half-veiled,

half-open; and the section closes characteristically with the joyful confirmation of believers (ii. 11).

The period covered by the incidents is marked as a week (i. 29, 35, 43, ii. 1), which corresponds with the week at the close of the Lord's ministry.

The incidents are peculiar to St. John, and he writes as an eye-witness throughout: i. 35, 41, ii. 2.

1. The Testimony of the Baptist (i. 19—34).

The narrative of St. John starts from the same point as the original Apostolic Gospel (comp. Acts i. 22, x. 37, xiii. 24; Mark i. 1); but, as belonging to a later period in the growth of the Church, it distinguishes more exactly than did the relation of the Baptist both to the Old Covenant and to Christ.

The first part of the Baptist's testimony is concerned with the popular expectations to which his preaching had given fresh life, and contains the announcement of the Christ (19—28). The second part gives his personal recognition of the Christ who had now entered on His work (29—34). The verses which follow (35—37) form a transition, but belong most properly to the next section.

The circumstances of the Baptism of Christ are evidently presupposed as known; and the Baptism itself had already taken place before the mission from Jerusalem. This follows both from the record of time (vv. 29, 35, etc.), and from the fact that

*21 οὐκ εἰμὶ ὁ χριστός. καὶ ἠρώτησαν αὐτόν Τί οὖν; [σὺ] Ἠλείας εἶ; καὶ λέγει Οὐκ εἰμί. Ὁ προφήτης

the Baptist already "knew" Jesus as the Christ (v. 26, "whom ye know not." Comp. v. 33). See note at the end of the section.

St. John says nothing of the Baptist's preaching of repentance, though it is implied in the words by which the Baptist described his office (v. 23). This did not fall within the scope of the Evangelist, which was confined to the direct relations of the herald and the Christ. How fully these relations are defined will appear from the following analysis of the Baptist's testimony as given by the Evangelist:

The Testimony of John.
a. In answer to the mission of the Jews with relation to popular expectations.

The presence of the Christ announced (i. 19—28).
a. The person of the herald (vv. 19—23).
  (1) Negatively (vv. 19—21).
  Not the Christ (v. 20).
  Not the promised forerunner of the day of the Lord (v. 21).
  Not the prophet, of undefined mission (v. 21).
  (2) Positively (vv. 22, 23). "A voice."
β. His office (vv. 24—28).
  To baptize (v. 25) with a preparatory baptism of water (v. 26), before the coming of One of greater dignity (v. 27).
b. Spontaneously in the presence of Christ, as the result of divine revelation.

The nature of the Christ revealed (vv. 29—34).
a. The fulfilment of prophecy (vv. 29—31).
  The Person and the work (v. 29).
  The herald's earlier testimony (v. 30).
  The fulfilment of the herald's work (v. 31).
β. The sign of the fulfilment (vv. 32—34).
  The sign itself (v. 32).
  The sign in relation to the promise (v. 33).
  The sign interpreted (v. 34).

The Christ announced in answer to the official inquiries of the Jews (19—28).

This mission from Jerusalem, which is not mentioned by the Synoptists, took place, as has been seen, after the Baptism, and was probably caused by some rumours which arose from that event. It may be regarded as being, in some sense, a Temptation of John corresponding to the (simultaneous) Temptation of Christ. John refused the titles in which the hierarchical party expressed their false views, even as Christ refused to satisfy their expectations by the assumption of external power. At the same time there does not appear to be sufficient reason for supposing that the mission was sent with evil purpose. Various motives probably combined to lead different parties to seek from John a clear statement of his position with regard to the national hope. In this respect the place which

21 And they asked him, What then? Art thou Elijah?
And he saith, I am not.   Art thou the prophet?

John occupies relatively to the Jewish teachers on the one side, and to the Christ on the other, offers a remarkable picture of the religious circumstances of the time. Both negatively and positively the scene is a living picture of a crisis of transition. The answer of the Baptist to the people (Luke iii. 15 ff.; Matt. iii. 11) is distinct from, and yet perfectly harmonious with, St. John's record.

19. Καὶ αὕτη . . .] *And this is the witness* . . . The conjunction (*And*) takes up the references already made to John's testimony: *vv.* 15, 6, 7. Thus the history is bound up with the dogmatic Prologue, the transition lying in *v.* 17 (*Jesus Christ*); and so the loftiest thoughts pass at once and naturally into simple facts. It may be noticed also that the narrative evidently begins with the immediate, personal knowledge of the writer; and perhaps from the fact to which he referred the beginning of his own faith.

For μαρτυρία, compare i. 7, iii. 11, v. 31, and notes. For *John*, *v.* 6, note.

οἱ Ἰουδαῖοι] *the Jews*, specifically *the Pharisees* as the representative class (*v.* 24). On the use of the term generally, see Introd. In this case the envoys were probably despatched by the Sanhedrin. They came directly from the religious centre of the people (*from Jerusalem*; cf. *Erub.* 43 *b* (*Ab.* 337): "Elijah would make known his coming first to the Great Council"),

and included the two classes which represented the ecclesiastical side of the nation. The compound phrase (*priests and Levites*) is nowhere else used in the New Testament; and "Levite" occurs only in Luke x. 32 (with "priest" in significant connexion), and Acts iv. 36. The exact description of those sent marks the special knowledge of the Evangelist. It may be added that he nowhere uses the titles *scribes* and *elders* found in the other Gospels (viii. 3 is unauthentic).

On the popular expectation of the Messiah see vii. 41, note. For the incident compare v. 33.

Σὺ τίς εἶ;] The pronoun is emphatic, "As for thyself—thou that excitest the people and stirrest vague hopes (Luke iii. 15)—who art thou?" Contrast *v.* 22, Τίς εἶ; The inquirers do not put their question definitely by "Art thou the Christ?" (comp. *v.* 25). They throw upon the Baptist the responsibility of expressing what was in their mind.

20. ὡμολ. κ. οὐκ ἠρνήσ. . . .] *he confessed, and denied not* . . . For the combination compare *v.* 3, note. The first term (*confessed*) marks the ready self-devotion of the testimony; the second (*denied not*) the completeness of it. Both terms are used absolutely. A similar phrase is quoted from Josephus, *Ant.* VI. vii. 4.

The use of the word ὁμολογεῖν recognises that the question of the Jews called for boldness and self-denial in the answerer. The word is comparatively frequent

3

22 εἶ σύ; καὶ ἀπεκρίθη Οὔ. εἶπαν οὖν αὐτῷ Τίς εἶ; ἵνα
ἀπόκρισιν δῶμεν τοῖς πέμψασιν ἡμᾶς· τί λέγεις περὶ
23 σεαυτοῦ; ἔφη Ἐγὼ φωνὴ βοῶντος ἐν τῇ ἐρήμῳ Εὐθύνατε τὴν ὁδὸν Κυρίου, καθὼς εἶπεν Ἡσαίας ὁ

in St. John, and suggests in each case a victory of faith or love (ix. 22, xii. 42; 1 John ii. 23, iv. 2, 3, 15; 2 John 7; comp. Rev. iii. 5; 1 John i. 9). We can feel what the trial was to take the lower place in the crisis of highest popularity.

καὶ ὡμολ. ...] *and he confessed* ... The substance of the confession is added to the statement of the fact of the confession.

Ἐγὼ οὐκ εἰμί ...] The position of the pronoun, according to the true reading, is emphatic. " *I* am not the Christ for whom perhaps some of you take me (Acts xiii. 25; Luke iii. 15), but the Christ is indeed among you." Thus the answer is addressed rather to the spirit than to the form of the question.

The emphatic insertion of the pronoun (ἐγώ) throughout the section is remarkable : *I* am the voice (*v.* 23); *I* baptize (*v.* 26); *I* am not worthy (*v.* 27); of whom *I* said (*v.* 30); *I* knew him not (*vv.* 31, 33); *I* came (*v.* 31); *I* have seen (*v.* 34). The relation of the Baptist to Christ is suggested everywhere.

21. Τί οὖν;] *What then* are we to think? This construction is not found elsewhere in St. John, though it occurs in St. Paul (Rom. vi. 15, xi. 7). The words can also be rendered, *What then* (not *Who*) *art thou?* What is the function which thou hast to discharge? *Art thou Elias?* Comp. Acts xiii. 25 (Τί ἐμὲ ὑπονοεῖτε εἶναι;).

Ἡλείας] Mal. iv. 5, the forerunner of the day of the Lord. Comp. Ecclus. xlviii. 10 f.; Matt. xi. 14, xvii. 10 — 13. In a spiritual sense John was Elijah (comp. Luke i. 17), yet not so as the Jews literally understood the promise. Thus the denial of the Baptist is directed to the Jewish expectation of the bodily return of Elijah, of which Lightfoot has collected interesting notices on Matt. xvii. 10. And at the same time the mission of the Baptist did not exhaust the promise of the coming of Elijah ; beyond that coming there was yet another : Matt., *l.c.* (ἔρχεται καὶ ἀποκαταστήσει). Οὐ λέγουσιν Προφήτης εἶ σύ; ἕνα τῶν πολλῶν αἰνιττόμενοι· ἀλλὰ μετὰ τοῦ ἄρθρου Ὁ προφήτης εἶ σύ; ... διὰ τοῦτο καὶ οὗτος ἠρνήσατο οὐ τὸ προφήτης εἶναι ἀλλὰ τὸ ἐκεῖνος ὁ προφήτης (Chrys.). Comp. Luke ix. 30.

Ὁ προφήτης] *The prophet.* The abruptness of the form of the question is remarkable (*The prophet art thou?*). The reference is probably to Deut. xviii. 15, interpreted not of the Christ (Acts iii. 22, vii. 37), but in some lower sense. Comp. vii. 40, vi. 14. The general expectation often took a special shape, Matt. xvi. 14; as in the widespread expectation of Jeremiah: 2 Macc. ii. 4 ff. and Grimm *ad loc.*

ἀπεκρίθη Οὔ] *he answered, No.* The replies grow shorter from time to time : "I am not the Christ," "I am not," "No."

22. εἶπαν οὖν ...] *they said*

22 And he answered, No. They said therefore unto him, Who art thou? that we may give an answer to them that sent us. What sayest thou of thyself? 23 He said, I am a voice of one crying in the wilderness, Make straight the way of the Lord, as said Isaiah

therefore . . . The first question was a consequence of the former answer.

Τίς εἶ; ἵνα . . .] The same natural ellipse occurs ix. 36. The slight difference of the form of this question from that of the question in *v.* 19 is significant. There the thought centres in the person of one who acts with strange authority (σύ . . .) : here in doubt as to his office (τίς . . .).

23. 'Εγὼ φωνή . . .] *Ego vox* . . . v. ; *I am a voice* . . . The Baptist answers in the words of Isaiah (xl. 3). Of himself he says nothing. He refers his questioners to the teaching of the prophets for the solution of their difficulty.

The quotation carries with it far more than directly meets the ear. The words are the opening call in the great gospel of Isaiah (xl. ff.) : the first of those calls (*vv.* 3, 6, 9) which claim man's service in preparation for the fulfilment of the counsels of Jehovah for His people.

A Jew on hearing the words would necessarily think of the description of the Lord's Coming which was thus heralded, and of the mysterious portraiture of "the Servant of the Lord" (lii. 13 ff.—liii.) which followed. Here then lies the germ of the Baptist's later testimony.

The image is that of the material preparation for the advance of a triumphant con-

queror. The Lord comes with His people from their exile by the shortest, not by the common and circuitous route ; as once before in the triumphal march from Egypt (comp. Ps. lxviii. 7).

The spiritual application of the words (Luke iii. 4, ‖[s]; comp. Luke i. 17) is natural or even necessary. The return of Jehovah to "His own home" can only be conceived of as a spiritual fact.

The prophecy is applied to the Baptist by the Synoptists (Matt. iii. 3, Οὗτός ἐστιν ; Mark i. 3 ; Luke iii. 4), who also connect a second prophecy with the mission of the Baptist (Mark i. 2 ; Luke i. 76, vii. 27 ; Matt. xi. 10) : the announcement of the coming of the messenger before the terrible day of the Lord (Mal. iii. 1, iv. 5). Thus the two pictures taken together combine to bring out the fulness of the double work of John : to make a way for the deliverance of exiles, and for the judgement of unfaithful servants. The one Advent of Christ brought with it eventually both results.

St. John does not notice specially the heralding of judgement. The omission corresponds with his omission of the prophecy of the destruction of Jerusalem and of the Coming of Christ. For him in its outward shape that Coming was past.

In the language of Isaiah the

24 προφήτης. Καὶ ἀπεσταλμένοι¹ ἦσαν ἐκ τῶν Φαρισαίων.
25 καὶ ἠρώτησαν αὐτὸν καὶ εἶπαν αὐτῷ Τί οὖν βαπτίζεις
εἰ σὺ οὐκ εἶ ὁ χριστὸς οὐδὲ Ἠλείας οὐδὲ ὁ προφήτης;
26 ἀπεκρίθη αὐτοῖς ὁ Ἰωάνης λέγων Ἐγὼ βαπτίζω ἐν
27 ὕδατι· μέσος ὑμῶν στήκει ὃν ὑμεῖς οὐκ οἴδατε, ὀπίσω
μου ἐρχόμενος, οὗ οὐκ εἰμὶ [ἐγὼ] ἄξιος ἵνα λύσω αὐτοῦ

¹ ἀπεστ. א*ABC*; οἱ ἀπεστ. אᵇᶜA²C³XΓ.   See note.

Baptist was simply "a voice of one crying," not invested with a distinct personality ("thou art to me No bird, but an invisible thing, A voice, a mystery").

The verb βοᾶν, which is comparatively rare in the New Testament, occurs here only in the writings of St. John. It describes the cry which answers to strong feeling.

In the original (Hebrew) the words in the wilderness are joined with the verb which follows, and it may be so here, make straight in the wilderness . . . The transposition can be explained by the fact that only one member of the sentence is quoted here, yet see Matt. iii. 3. In either case the moral application of the words is obvious.

Cf. Pesichta, 103 b (Weber, 334): "If Israel repented for one day."

Patristic commentators dwell on the relation of "the Voice" to "the Word": "Sicut ad hoc fit vox ut verbum audiatur, sic ego ad hoc vel natus sum ut per ministerium meum Christus, qui est incarnatum verbum Patris presens agnoscatur" (Rupert). So Irenæus, fragm. 46 (50): Φωνὴ δὲ καὶ λύχνος Λόγου καὶ φωτὸς πρόδρομος. Origen, In Joh. tom. vii. p. 110: Φωνὴ διδακτικὴ καὶ παραστατικὴ ἐκείνου τοῦ λόγου [τοῦ ἐν ἀρχῇ] ὁ Ἰωάννης. So

Theophylact : "When the voice has been uttered it dies into the air, and is known no more."

24. Καὶ ἀπεσταλμένοι . . . Φαρ.] And they had been sent from—out of the body of—the Pharisees. They were Pharisees themselves, and therefore men whose attention would be fixed on the solemn and startling rite with which the new movement was inaugurated. Comp. iii. 1, vii. 48 ; Matt. xv. 1.

25. Τί οὖν βαπτίζεις;] Why then baptizest thou? They wished to condemn him from his own admission. The Christ, and His authoritative herald as representing Him (Elijah or the prophet), might indeed baptize, for so it was suggested by the prophets : Ezek. xxxvi. 25; Isa. lii. 15; Zech. xiii. 1; comp. Heb. x. 22. But who else could presume to treat the chosen peopled as defiled?

It is uncertain how far baptism was already in use at this time in the admission of proselytes, but the obvious significance of the rite was unmistakable.

26. Ἐγὼ βαπτίζω ἐν ὕδατι . . .] I baptize in water. . . The answer of the Baptist is given in the briefest possible form. He turns the thoughts of his questioners from himself to Another, who is already present, though unre-

24 the prophet. And they had been sent from the
25 Pharisees. And they asked him, and said unto him,
Why then baptizest thou, if thou art not the Christ,
26 neither Elijah, neither the prophet? John answered
them, saying, I baptize in water: in the midst of
27 you standeth one whom ye know not, coming after
me, the latchet of whose shoe I am not worthy to

cognised. "Do not," he seems
to say, "mistake the value
of my work or of my baptism.
I baptize, because the form of
this baptism in water shows
that, however striking outwardly,
it does not belong to the work of
the Christ; and still it is designed
to prepare for the recognition of
the Christ actually present in the
midst of you. My work is the
work of a servant, and the work
of a herald. There is therefore
nothing to condemn in my conduct, if you consider what my
baptism is, and what the Christ's
baptism is, and know that He is
among you; so that the preparatory outward rite has a just
place." These two facts are made
clear: (1) That He whom the
Baptist came to announce is now
among His people, and (2) that
He is of immeasurably greater
dignity than the Baptist himself.
The order of the words (ἐγὼ βαπτ.
ἐν ὕδ.; contrast v. 31, ἐν ὕδ.
βαπτ.) shows that the first
thought is of the baptism as such
and next of its special character.
Comp. Acts i. 5.

It is significant that the
Baptist does not now use the
term ὁ ἰσχυρότερος (Matt. iii. 11,
‖ˢ) of the Christ. It may
have been that as the conception of "the Lamb of God" was
revealed to him, this term

seemed liable to misunderstanding.

μέσος ὑμῶν στήκει . . .] in the
midst of you standeth one . . .
The absence of the conjunction,
and the position of the adjective
at the beginning of the sentence,
bring out sharply the opposition
between the Baptist (I baptize)
and his Successor; just as the
ὑμεῖς (ὑμ. οὐκ οἴδατε) marks the
contrast between the Baptist and
the Pharisees. St. John had at
this time recognised Jesus; he
knew Him, but his questioners
did not.

The word στήκει, as distinguished from "is," marks the
dignity and firmness of the
position which Christ was shown
to hold (Mark xi. 25; 1 Thess.
iii. 8, etc.).

27. ὀπίσω μου ἔρχ.] coming
after me, which is to be taken
closely with the words which
precede.

τ. ἱμάντα τ. ὑποδήμ.] the shoe's
lachet. To loose this, or to
"carry the shoes" (Matt. iii. 11),
was the business of a slave.
Compare Mark i. 7, note.

The Pharisees hear words
which might well move them to
deeper questionings; but for this
they had no heart. It is enough
to have discharged their specific
duty.

28. ἐν Βηθανίᾳ] in Bethany.

23 τὸν ἱμάντα τοῦ ὑποδήματος. Ταῦτα ἐν Βηθανίᾳ¹ ἐγένετο
29 πέραν τοῦ Ἰορδάνου, ὅπου ἦν ὁ Ἰωάνης βαπτίζων. Τῇ
ἐπαύριον βλέπει² τὸν Ἰησοῦν ἐρχόμενον πρὸς αὐτόν, καὶ
λέγει Ἴδε ὁ ἀμνὸς τοῦ θεοῦ ὁ αἴρων τὴν ἁμαρτίαν

¹ Βηθανίᾳ ℵABC*EFGHL; Βηθαβαρᾷ C²KT. See note.
² Insert ὁ Ἰωάννης C³EFG.

Bethabara (Judges vii. 24 ?) is a correction, made as early as the end of the second century (*Syr. vt.*). The site has been identified by Conder. *Bethany* was probably an obscure village in Peræa, and not to be confounded with the Bethany (xi. 18) on the Mount of Olives. According to a possible derivation, Bethany may mean " the house of the boat," as Bethabara " the house of the passage," both equally marking the site of a ferry or ford across the Jordan.

The mention of the locality adds to the force of the preceding recital (compare Chrysostom: Οὐ γὰρ ἐν οἰκίᾳ, οὐδὲ ἐν γωνίᾳ, [οὐδὲ ἐν ἐρημίᾳ,] ἀλλὰ τὸν Ἰορδάνην καταλαβὼν ἐν μέσῳ τῷ πλήθει . . . τὴν θαυμαστὴν ἐκείνην ἀνεκήρυξεν ὁμολογίαν), and incidentally shows that the date of the mission falls after the first stage of the ministry of the Baptist, when he had " left the wilderness of Judæa " (Matt. iii. 1) and retired " beyond Jordan." Compare x. 40, iii. 23.

The form of expression (ἦν βαπτίζων) is characteristic of the New Testament writers, and serves to emphasise the idea of continued action. Compare viii. 18, v. 39, xi. 1.

The Christ revealed as the fulfilment of the forerunner's work (29—34).

The inquiries made from Jerusalem would naturally create fresh expectation among John's disciples. At this crisis (Τῇ ἐπαύριον) the Lord, who had retired for a time after His Baptism (Luke iv. 1), returned, and John solemnly marked Him out, not by name, but by implication, as the promised Saviour. He does not call Him " the Christ."

29. βλέπει . . . ἐρχόμενον] Compare v. 36. Christ was probably coming directly from the Temptation. It was fitting that His active ministry should begin with the solemn recognition by His herald. The omission of the Temptation by St. John can cause no difficulty, except on the irrational supposition that he was bound to relate all he knew, and not that only which belonged to his design.

λέγει] No one is directly addressed. The words (as in v. 36) are spoken for those who " had ears to hear them."

Ἴδε] *Ecce* v.; *Behold.* " Lo, here is before you . . ." Compare v. 47, iii. 26, xix. 5, 14 ; 1 John iii. 1 ; and contrast Luke xxiv. 39. Chrysostom says of ἴδε: Δηλῶν ὅτι οὗτός ἐστιν ὁ πάλαι ζητούμενος.

ὁ ἀμνὸς τοῦ θεοῦ] *agnus dei* v.; *the Lamb of God.* It seems likely, from the abrupt definiteness of the form in which the phrase is introduced, that it refers to some conversation of

28 unloose.   These things were done in Bethany beyond Jordan, where John was baptizing.

29   The next day he seeth Jesus coming unto him, and saith, Behold, the Lamb of God, which taketh

the Baptist with his disciples, springing out of the public testimony given on the day before. The reference which he had made to Isaiah might naturally lead to further inquiries as to the general scope of the prophet; and there can be no doubt that the image is directly derived from Isaiah liii. 7 (comp. Acts viii. 32). But the idea of vicarious suffering endured with perfect gentleness and meekness, which is conveyed by the prophetic language (compare Jer. xi. 19), does not exhaust the meaning of the image. The language of Isaiah rests on the old sacrificial system of Judaism. The lamb was the victim offered at the morning and evening sacrifice (Exod. xxix. 38 ff.), and thus was the familiar type of an offering of self-devotion to God. And yet more, as the Passover was not far off (ii. 12, 13), it is impossible to exclude the thought of the Paschal Lamb, with which the Lord was afterwards identified (xix. 36. Comp. 1 Pet. i. 19). The deliverance from Egypt was the most conspicuous symbol of the Messianic deliverance (Rev. xv. 3; Heb. iii. 3 ff.; Ezek. xx. 33 ff.); "the lamb" called up all its memories and its promises. And it has been plausibly conjectured that this thought may have been brought home to the Baptist, who was of priestly descent, by the sight of the flocks of lambs passing by to Jerusalem as offerings at the coming Feast.

According to this view, two ideas from the Levitical system, self-surrender and redemption, are raised to their highest significance by the prophetic thought of the suffering "Servant of the Lord." That which was symbol becomes fact.

Thus it appears that the title, as applied to Christ, under the circumstances of its utterance, conveys the ideas of vicarious suffering, of patient submission, of sacrifice, of redemption, not separately or clearly defined, but significant according to the spiritual preparation and character of those before whom the words were spoken.

A corresponding glimpse of Christ's sufferings is given by Symeon in Luke ii. 25 ff.; and there can be no difficulty in believing that at this crisis the forerunner had a prophetic insight into a truth which was afterwards hidden from the disciples (Matt. xvi. 21 ff.).

It must be further noticed that the Lamb which the Baptist recognises was not one of man's providing. Christ is ὁ ἀμνὸς τοῦ θεοῦ—that is, the Lamb which God Himself furnishes for sacrifice (Gen. xxii. 8), while the accessory notions of "fitness for," "belonging to," are also necessarily included in the genitive. And it is not simply one of many, but the one in whom all the teaching of the typical ritual was realised.

This Lamb is absolutely "with-

30 τοῦ κόσμου. οὗτός ἐστιν ὑπὲρ οὗ ἐγὼ εἶπον Ὀπίσω
μου ἔρχεται ἀνὴρ ὃς ἔμπροσθέν μου γέγονεν, ὅτι πρῶτός

out blemish and without spot"
(1 Pet. i. 19), as the sacrificial
lambs were outwardly (Lev. xiv.
10, xxiii. 18, etc.).

The explanation which has
been given of the definite article
appears to be the most simple;
but it is possible that the article
may represent some earlier and
well-known use of the phrase, as
in "the prophet" (v. 21), "the
root of David" (Rev. v. 5). Nor
can any stress be laid upon the
fact that the application of the
title to Christ is strange and
unprepared. The title *the Lion
of the tribe of Judah* (Rev. v. 5;
comp. Gen. xlix. 9) is not less
singular; and, according to many
(but see note on v. 51), the title
"the Son of man" rests upon the
single passage of Daniel (vii. 13)
in the Old Testament.

The figure is found again in
Rev. v. 6 ff. (ἀρνίον) and in 1
Pet. i. 19 f.

ὁ αἴρων] *qui tollit* v.; *which
taketh away*. It seems to be
most in accordance with St.
John's usage to take this phrase
as defining the character of
"the Lamb of God," and not as
presenting Christ under a new
aspect, "even He that taketh
away the sin of the world."
The majority of the Old and
Vulgate Latin copies, the Old
Syriac, and other early authorities, however, adopt the latter
rendering by repeating "behold" (Vulg. *Ecce agnus dei,
ecce qui tollit* . . .).

The word αἴρειν may mean
either (1) *to take upon him*, or
(2) *to take away*. But the usage
of the LXX. and the parallel

passage, 1 John iii. 5, are
decisive in favour of the second
rendering (Vulg. *qui tollit*, all.
qui aufert); and the Evangelist
seems to emphasise this meaning
by substituting another word for
the unambiguous word of the
LXX. (φέρει, *beareth*). It was
however by "taking upon Himself our infirmities" that Christ
took them away (Matt. viii. 17);
and this idea is distinctly suggested in the passage of Isaiah
(liii. 11). The present tense
marks the future result as
assured in the beginning of the
work, and also as continuous
(comp. 1 John i. 7). So Chrysostom observes : Οὐκ εἶπεν Ὁ
ληψόμενος ἢ Ὁ ἄρας, ἀλλ' Ὁ αἴρων
τὰς ἁμαρτίας [sic] τοῦ κόσμου ὡς
ἀεὶ τοῦτο ποιοῦντος αὐτοῦ.

τ. ἁμαρτίαν τ. κόσμου] *peccatum
mundi* v.; *the sin of the world.*
The singular (as contrasted with
the plural, 1 John iii. 5) is
important, so far as it declares
the victory of Christ over *sin*
regarded in its unity, as the
common corruption of humanity,
which is personally realised in
the *sins* of separate men. Comp.
1 John i. 7, note. The parallel
passage in the Epistle (*l.c.*) shows
that the redemptive efficacy of
Christ's Work is to be found in
His whole Life (*He was manifested*) crowned by His Death.
Of the two aspects of the Atonement, as (1) The removal of the
consequences of sin, and (2) the
removal of sin, St. John dwells
habitually on the latter. Yet
see iii. 36; 1 John ii. 2.

The plural (*sins*), which has
been transferred into our own

30 away the sin of the world! This is he of whom[1]
I said, After me cometh a man which is come to

[1] *lit.* in behalf of whom.

Prayer-Book from the early Western Service-Books (*O Lamb of God : that takest away the sins of the world*), occurs in Latin quotations from the time of Cyprian (*qui tollis peccata*), but it is not found in any of the best MSS. of the Old Latin or of the Vulgate. It occurs also in the Morning Hymn of the Alexandrian Church (*Gloria in excelsis*): Ὁ ἀμνὸς τοῦ θεοῦ, ὁ υἱὸς τοῦ πατρός, ὁ αἴρων τὰς ἁμαρτίας τοῦ κόσμου, ἐλέησον ἡμᾶς· ὁ αἴρων τὰς ἁμαρτίας τοῦ κόσμου πρόσδεξαι τὴν δέησιν ἡμῶν, and this is probably the source of the liturgical use which slightly influenced the Latin texts.

In Isa. liii. 6 the Hebrew text has the plural, but sing. in *v.* 4. The LXX. has plural in both cases (see Heb. ix. 28, note).

τ. κόσμου] *the world.* Creation summed up in humanity considered apart from (viii. 12, ix. 5; 1 John iv. 9), and so at last hostile to God (xiv. 17, xv. 18). Yet potentially the work of Christ extends to the whole world (vi. 33; 1 John ii. 2). Compare Euthymius : Ὁ μὲν ἀμνὸς τοῦ νόμου θυόμενος ἁμαρτίαν ἑνὸς γένους ἀφήρει τοῦ Ἰσραηλιτικοῦ ὡς τύπος καὶ προχάραγμα καὶ σκιὰ τῆς ἀληθείας· ὁ δὲ ἀμνὸς τοῦ θεοῦ σφαγιασθεὶς τὴν ἁμαρτίαν τοῦ κόσμου παντὸς ἀφαιρεῖ καὶ καθαίρει τοὺς ἐν τῷ κόσμῳ ὡς ἀλήθεια· ἐκεῖνος μὲν γὰρ ἄλογος οὗτος δὲ λογικός, καὶ οὐ τοῦτο μόνον ἀλλὰ καὶ θεῖος. Compare additional note on *v.* 10.

The Synoptists have preserved a trace of this extension of the work of the Messiah from the Jews to mankind in the teaching of the Baptist (Matt. iii. 9). His call to confession and repentance included the idea of the universality of his message. He addressed men as sinful men, declaring their common failures and common needs, and indicating the source of common help. Comp. *v.* 7, note.

30. After the recognition of the Christ in a new and fuller light, the Baptist recalls his earlier words. He might have stirred other hopes. But now at least he is clear as to the Person and the Work. The Temptation is over—his Temptation and Christ's—and he can see "the strong one" in the Lamb of God.

ὑπὲρ οὗ] *in behalf of whom, i.e.* vindicating whose glorious office, as compared with my own.

ἐγὼ εἶπον] *I said.* The pronoun is purposely expressed : *I*, the prophetic messenger of His advent, declared His superior majesty, even when at the time I could not define it.

Ὀπίσω . . . γέγονεν] See *v.* 15, note.

a man] The word chosen (ἀνήρ, Vulg. *vir*) is emphatic, and here serves to ;ive dignity to the person described (contrast ἄνθρωπος, *v.* 6). Elsewhere, except in the sense of "husband," it occurs in St. John only in vi. 10, where the two terms (ἀνήρ, ἄνθρωπος) are contrasted. (See viii. 40, note.)

In Acts ii. 22, xvii. 31, ἀνήρ is used of Christ.

31 μου ἦν· κἀγὼ οὐκ ᾔδειν αὐτόν, ἀλλ᾽ ἵνα φανερωθῇ τῷ
32 Ἰσραὴλ διὰ τοῦτο ἦλθον ἐγὼ ἐν ὕδατι βαπτίζων. Καὶ
ἐμαρτύρησεν Ἰωάνης λέγων ὅτι Τεθέαμαι τὸ πνεῦμα
καταβαῖνον ὡς περιστερὰν ἐξ οὐρανοῦ, καὶ ἔμεινεν

31. κ. οὐκ ᾔδειν αὐ] and I knew
him not. I (emphatic), his pre-
cursor, trained for my work in
the deserts (Luke i. 80) till the
day for my mission came, knew
Him not as Messiah, and knew
not what the Messiah would be
(v. 26) (comp. Matt. xi. 27). But
apart from such special knowledge I had a distinct charge;
and I knew that my mission was
to lead up to the present manifestation of the Christ to the
chosen people.

From the narrative in St.
Luke it appears to be doubtful
whether the Baptist had any
personal knowledge of Jesus.

The Baptist still seems to
dwell on the contrast between
the dimension which he had
fashioned and the reality which
he had found. Yes, he seems to
say, it was He of whom I spoke;
and while I was sure of my duty
I knew Him not till the hour
came. Comp. 1 Sam. xvi.

The end of John's Baptism
was that the Christ should be
"manifested" (not baptized), that
the thoughts of hearts should
be revealed, and the sign made
intelligible. The deepening of
the sense of sin prepared the
conception of Christ's atoning
and redeeming work. The confessions of the people were completed by the self-surrender of
Christ.

"Hanc autem [the work of
Christ] veram et summam esse
pœnitentiam pro omni mundo
celebratam res ipsa ostendit, ratio

sentit, fides sancta confitetur"
(Rupert).

So it is that the revelation of
Christ as "the Son of God"
gives the divine answer to the
confession of sin, the call to repentance.

Ἰσραήλ] The term is always
used with the idea of the spiritual
privileges attaching to the race,
i. (50) 49, iii. 10, xii. 13. Comp.
Gal. vi. 16; Eph. ii. 12.

The popular belief that Messiah
would be unknown till He was
anointed by Elijah, is given in a
very remarkable passage of
Justin's Dialogue, cap. viii. (Rev.
vii. 4, xxi. 12.)

ἵνα ... διὰ τοῦτο ...] that ...
therefore ... The tense suggests that the work is done. So
with ὅτι, xv. 19; διὰ τοῦτο ...
ἵνα, Philem. 15; 2 Tim. ii. 10,
etc. The order of the words
differs from that in vv. 26, 33,
so that the subordinate character of his baptism is here the
predominant idea.

Chrysostom remarks:

Οὐκ ἄρα τοῦ βαπτίσματος ἐδεῖτο
ὁ Χριστός ... ἀλλὰ μᾶλλον τὸ
βάπτισμα ἔχρηζε τῆς δυνάμεως τοῦ
Χριστοῦ.

Augustine says of the Lord's
baptism:

"Et opus erat Domino bapti-
zari? Et ego interrogans cito re-
spondeo: Opus erat Domino
nasci? opus erat Domino cruci-
figi? opus erat Domino mori?
opus erat Domino sepeliri? Si
ergo tantam pro nobis suscepit
humilitatem, baptismum non

31 be before me : for he was before me. And I knew
him not ; but that he should be made manifest to
32 Israel, for this cause came I baptizing in water. And
John bare witness, saying, I have beheld the Spirit
descending as a dove out of heaven ; and it abode

erat suscepturus? Et quid pro-
fuit quia suscepit baptismum
servi? Ut tu non dedignareris
suscipere baptismum Domini."
ἦλθον ἐγώ . . . βαπτ.] *came I
baptizing in water*, fulfilling my
initiatory work.

32. How, then, it may be asked,
was this knowledge gained, this
revelation of Christ's nature communicated? The answer is given
in a final summary of the
Baptist's testimony given separ
ately. Comp. xii. 44 ff.

ἐμαρτύρησεν] *bare witness*. It is
important to preserve the identity
of language throughout : *vv.* 7, 8,
15, 19, 34.

Τεθέαμαι] *I have beheld*, "gazed
on," with calm, steady, thoughtful gaze, as fully measuring what
was presented to my eyes (1 John
i. 1). The perfect is found elsewhere in N.T. only 1 John iv.
12, 14. The aorist occurs frequently, i. 14, 38, etc. The verb
in *v.* 34 is different (ἑώρακα).

τὸ πνεῦμα καταβαῖνον] *the Spirit
descending.* This communication
of the Spirit to Christ belongs to
the fulfilment under human conditions of His whole work.
Hitherto that work had been
accomplished in the perfection of
individual Life. Messiah now
enters on His public office, and
for that receives, as true Man,
the appropriate gifts. The Spirit
by whom men are subjectively
united to God descends upon the
Word made Flesh, by whom

objectively God is revealed to
men.

ὡς περιστερὰν ἐξ οὐρ.] *as a
dove out of heaven.* This definite
revelation may be compared
with that of the "tongues of
fire," Acts ii. 3. The word used
of the Spirit "moving on the
face of the waters," in Gen. i. 2,
describes the action of a bird
hovering over its brood, and
the phrase is explained in the
Talmud, "The Spirit of God was
borne over the water, as a dove
which broods over her young"
(*Chagigah*, 15 a). To those who
had not "eyes to see" the outward phenomenon may not have
appeared anything extraordinary
(Τὰ τοιαῦτα οὐχὶ τῶν τοῦ σώματος
ὀφθαλμῶν δεῖται μόνον ἀλλὰ πρὸ
τούτων τῆς κατὰ διάνοιαν ὄψεως ὥστε
μὴ φαντασίαν περιττὴν τὸ πρᾶγμα
νομίσαι (Chrys.)), just as the articulate voice of God was said by
such to be thunder (xii. 29). But
Christ Himself, who "saw" this
visible manifestation in its divine
fulness (Matt. iii. 16 ; Mark i.
10), heard also the divine words as
a definite message. The dove, as
a symbol here, suggests the notion
of (1) Tenderness, (2) Innocence,
Matt. x. 16, (3) Gentle and
tranquil movement.

"Ergo ne Spiritu sanctificati
dolum habeant in columba de-
monstratum est ; ne simplicitas
frigida remaneat in igne demon-
stratum est " (Aug.).

ἔμειν. ἐπ' αὐτόν] *it abode upon*

33 ἐπ᾽ αὐτόν· κἀγὼ οὐκ ᾔδειν αὐτόν, ἀλλ᾽ ὁ πέμψας με
βαπτίζειν ἐν ὕδατι ἐκεῖνός μοι εἶπεν ᾽Εφ᾽ ὃν ἂν ἴδῃς
τὸ πνεῦμα καταβαῖνον καὶ μένον ἐπ᾽ αὐτόν, οὗτός
34 ἐστιν ὁ βαπτίζων ἐν πνεύματι ἁγίῳ· κἀγὼ ἑώρακα, καὶ
μεμαρτύρηκα ὅτι οὗτός ἐστιν ὁ¹ υἱὸς τοῦ θεοῦ.

35   Τῇ ἐπαύριον πάλιν ἱστήκει ᾽Ιωάνης καὶ ἐκ τῶν μαθητῶν
¹ ὁ ἐκλεκτός ℵ*.   See note.

him. The transition to the finite verb gives emphasis to this
fact. The phrase occurs in iii.
36 and Isa. xi. 2. The Spirit came
to the prophets only from time
to time (comp. 2 Kings iii. 15),
but with Christ it remained un-
changeably.

33. κἀγὼ οὐκ ᾔδειν] *and I
knew him not.* The phrase is
solemnly repeated from *v.* 31.
The mission and the sign of the
fulfilment of the mission¹ are
treated in the same way.

ὁ πέμψας με . . . ἐκεῖνος εἶπ.]
he that sent me . . . he said.
The sign was not left to the Baptist's interpretation. This detail is peculiar to St. John. In
what form this revelation was
conveyed to the Baptist we
cannot tell. He was conscious
of a direct personal charge. This
is brought out prominently by
the repetition of the pronoun
ἐκεῖνος. Comp. *v.* 18.

᾽Εφ᾽ ὃν ἄν] *Upon whomsoever,*
so that the dependence of the
Baptist's knowledge on the
divine sign is placed in a stronger
light.

μένον] *abiding,* as *v.* 32. Both
elements (the descent and the
resting) in this sign are obviously
significant. The Spirit "descended" for the fulfilment of a
ministry on earth ; He "abode"
on Christ so that from henceforth
that which was immanent in the

"Word" — His "glory" — was
continuously manifested to be-
lievers. The Son became the
Giver of the Spirit who revealed
Him, even as the Spirit enabled
Him to reveal the Father. He
Himself received the Spirit, as it
was His office to baptize with the
Spirit.

The "abiding" no less than
the "descent" of the Spirit was
an object of "sight" to the
herald of Christ. He was enabled to discern in the Lord after
His return from the Temptation
the permanence of His divine
endowment.

βαπτ. ἐν πνεύμ. ἁγ.] *baptizeth in
the Holy Ghost,* the atmosphere,
the element of the new life.
Comp. iii. 5 ; Matt. iii. 11, ἐν
πνεύματι ἁγίῳ κ. πυρί. The inward and outward purification
are thus combined. The transference of the image of baptism
to the impartment of the Holy
Spirit was prepared by such
passages as Joel ii. 28 (Acts
ii. 17).

The "descent" and "abiding"
of the Spirit upon Him "who
was in the beginning with God"
illustrates the perfect order with
which the divine counsel is
accomplished. As "the Son of
man" (comp. *v.* 51), Christ was
thus "consecrated" to His public
Work. Such a consecration is
spoken of as wrought by the

33 upon him. And I knew him not : but he that sent me to baptize in water, he said unto me, Upon whomsoever thou shalt see the Spirit descending and abiding upon him, the same is he that baptizeth in 34 the Holy Spirit. And I have seen, and have given my witness that this is the Son of God.

35   Again the next day John was standing, and two

Father before the Incarnation (x. 36), and by the Son before the Passion (xvii. 19).

34. ἐγὼ ἑώρακα, κ. μεμαρτύρηκα] *I* (emphatic) *have seen* as a fact, without the accessory notion of attentive observation (*v.* 32), *and have given my witness that* . . . So far my experience and my work are now completed. The sign for which I waited has been given ; the Messiah whom I was sent to herald has been revealed.

ὁ υἱὸς τ. θεοῦ] Dan. iii. 25. No one less could bestow the gift of the Spirit. The phrase is to be interpreted according to the context in which it occurs of those who are in each case regarded as the direct representatives of God, as sometimes of kings, etc. (Ps. lxxxii. 6) ; and so here it is used in the highest sense (comp. Ps. ii. 7). Some very early authorities (א, *Syr. vt.*, etc.) read *the chosen one of God.*

The Baptist does not mention the Voice while he affirms its Substance.

2. THE TESTIMONY OF DISCIPLES (i. 35—51).

The work of the Baptist passed naturally into the work of Christ. His testimony found a true interpretation from some of his disciples, and they first

attached themselves to the Lord. Christ who had been announced and revealed was welcomed and followed.

The whole section consists of a series of examples of spiritual insight. Christ reveals His power by showing His knowledge of men's thoughts (*vv.* 42, 48) ; and the disciples recognise their Master by their experience of what He is (*vv.* 39, 41, 49). The incidents are a commentary on the words " Come, and ye shall see " (*v.* 39)—this is the Master's promise—and " Come and see " (*v.* 46)—this is the disciple's appeal ; and the assurance with which the section closes opens the prospect of a more perfect divine vision (*v.* 51).

The very mixture of Hebrew (Simon, Nathanael) and Greek (Andrew, Philip) names seems to indicate the representative character of this first group of disciples ; and there is a progress in the confessions which they make : " *We have found the Messiah* " (*v.* 41) : " *We have found him, of whom Moses in the law, and the prophets, did write* . . ." (*v.* 45) : " *Rabbi, thou art the Son of God ; thou art King of Israel* " (*v.* 49).

The history falls into two parts, and deals with two groups of disciples. First, John's work

36 αὐτοῦ δύο, καὶ ἐμβλέψας τῷ Ἰησοῦ περιπατοῦντι λέγει
37 Ἴδε ὁ ἀμνὸς τοῦ θεοῦ. καὶ ἤκουσαν οἱ δύο μαθηταὶ

is crowned (35—42); and then
Christ's work is begun (43—51).
This will be seen in the subjoined
table.

The Testimony of Disciples.
  a. The first group. The first
       day. John's teaching
       crowned (vv. 35—42).
    a. John's word understood
         and obeyed (35—39).
       (1) John's disciples and
            John (35—37).
       (2) John's disciples and
            Christ (38, 39).
    β. The new message pro-
         claimed (40—42).
       (1) The announcement
            (40, 41).
       (2) The blessing on
            obedient discipleship
            (42).
  b. The second group. The
       second day. Christ's
       teaching begun (vv. 43—
       51).
    a. The call (43—46).
       The Master's call (43, 44).
       The disciple's call (45, 46).
    β. The spiritual revelation
         (47—51).
       Personal (47—49).
       General (50, 51).

*The work of the first day of
Christ's Ministry. John's
teaching crowned (35—42).*

On this first day of His teaching Christ is recognised by those
who have been already prepared
to receive Him. The disciples
of John are shown in their true
position towards him and his
Successor. Christ is not said to
have called any one to Himself.
Two pairs of brothers, as it

appears, form the first group of
disciples, of whom the first pair
are named, Andrew and Simon;
and the second pair, John and
James, are only faintly indicated.
The first disciples become the
first preachers.

The date is shortly before the
Passover (ii. 1, 12); and in
accordance with this an early
tradition fixed the beginning of
Christ's Ministry at the vernal
equinox (*Clem. Hom.* i. 16).

35. Τῇ ἐπαύρ. πάλ. ἱστήκ. Ἰωάν.]
Altera die iterum stabat v.; *Again
the next day John was standing.*
The picture is one of silent
waiting. The hearts of all were
full with thoughts of some great
change. Ἱστήκει: compare vii.
37, xviii. 5, 16, 18, xix. 25, xx.
11; and Zech. iii. 6 f. (εἱστήκει
...διεμαρτύρατο). Rupert says of
stabat: "Juxta altiorem sensum
[*stabat*] magnam ac semper sus-
pensam ejus intentionem insinuat
qua videlicet ei, quem supradicto
modo cognoverat Domino nostro,
non solum exterius officio suæ
præcursionis deserviebat sed et
interius erecto mentis affectu
jugiter adstabat . . . Nec vero
dubium est quin ad reditum
Domini nostri idem Joannes toto
affectu tetenderit, ut iterum
videret eum quem videre salus
agnoscentis, gloria prædicantis,
gaudium erat demonstrantis.
Stabat ergo in altitudine cordis
speculator vitæ et salutis, nun-
tius redemptionis et pacis, judex
gratiæ et caritatis."

ἐκ τ. μαθητῶν αὐτοῦ δύο] *two
of his disciples.* Compare viii.
17. One of them is identified
(*v.* 40) as Andrew; and the

³⁶ of his disciples; and he having looked on Jesus as
³⁷ he walked, saith, Behold, the Lamb of God! And
the two disciples heard him speak, and they followed

other was evidently the Evangelist. This appears from the absence of all further designation, and from the fact that the narrative bears the marks of having been written by an eyewitness for whom each least detail had a living memory.

36. ἐμβλέψας] *respiciens* v.; *having looked on.* The word describes one penetrating glance, as again in *v.* 42, the only other place where it is found in St. John. Comp. Mark x. 21, 27; Luke xx. 17, xxii. 61.

περιπατοῦντι] *as he walked*, no longer "coming unto him" (*v.* 29), but evidently (37, 38) going away. So for the last time the Baptist and the Christ were together; and the Baptist gave by anticipation a commentary on his own sublime words (iii. 30) when he pointed his scholars to their true Lord.

Ἴδε ὁ ἀμν. τ. θεοῦ] *Behold, the Lamb of God!* The words are not at this time a new revelation (as *v.* 29), and therefore the explanatory clause is omitted. The title alone is sufficient to recall what has been made known of the work. The words are a suggestion by the Baptist to those who had hitherto faithfully followed him, that now they were called away to a greater Master. The first disciples of Christ naturally came from among the Baptist's disciples. So the divine order was fulfilled, and the preparatory work had fruit. The new Church grew out of the old Church, as its proper consumma-

tion. The revelation of Christ as He was (*v.* 29) showed to those whose souls were rightly disciplined that He would complete what the Baptist had begun. At the same time the disciples of the Baptist could leave their teacher only in obedience to his own guidance as he interpreted their thoughts. And the direction came not as a command, but in a form which tested their faith. The words spoken answered to their inmost thoughts, and so they could understand and obey them. But without this spiritual correspondence the decisive sentence could have no power of constraint, for it does not appear that St. John even addressed them, but rather he spoke indefinitely (*v.* 29), and the message came home to them: *He saith . . . and the two disciples heard him speak* (as he spoke, ἤκουσαν λαλοῦντος), *and followed Jesus.*

37. ἠκολ.] *followed.* The word expresses the single act, as their choice was made once for all. The circumstance has a significance for all time. Christ's first disciples were made by the practical interpretation of a phrase which might have been disregarded.

They were attracted to Him, not by a work of power, but by a word—a thought—a spiritual fellowship. The title of tender compassion first drew them. They both obeyed. Chrysostom says:

Ὅρα τὴν σπουδὴν μετὰ αἰδοῦς γινομένην, οὐδὲ γὰρ εὐθέως προσελθόντες

38 αὐτοῦ λαλοῦντος καὶ ἠκολούθησαν τῷ Ἰησοῦ. στραφεὶς
δὲ ὁ Ἰησοῦς καὶ θεασάμενος αὐτοὺς ἀκολουθοῦντας λέγει
αὐτοῖς Τί ζητεῖτε; οἱ δὲ εἶπαν αὐτῷ Ῥαββεί, (ὃ λέγε-
39 ται μεθερμηνευόμενον Διδάσκαλε,) ποῦ μένεις; λέγει
αὐτοῖς Ἔρχεσθε καὶ ὄψεσθε. ἦλθαν οὖν καὶ εἶδαν ποῦ
μένει, καὶ παρ' αὐτῷ ἔμειναν τὴν ἡμέραν ἐκείνην· ὥρα
40 ἦν ὡς δεκάτη. Ἦν Ἀνδρέας ὁ ἀδελφὸς Σίμωνος Πέτρου
εἷς ἐκ τῶν δύο τῶν ἀκουσάντων παρὰ Ἰωάνου καὶ ἀκο-
41 λουθησάντων αὐτῷ· εὑρίσκει οὗτος πρῶτον τὸν ἀδελφὸν

ἐπηρώτησαν τὸν Ἰησοῦν ὑπὲρ ἀν-
αγκαίων καὶ μεγίστων πραγμάτων
οὐδὲ δημοσίᾳ παρόντων ἁπάντων
ἁπλῶς καὶ ὡς ἔτυχεν ἀλλ' ἰδίᾳ
διαλεχθῆναι αὐτῷ ἐσπούδαζον.

38. στραφεὶς δέ . . .] *conversus
autem* . . . v.; *Jesus turned* as
He was going away. This action
hindered the two disciples from
following Him silently and unperceived, as they might have
done (*they . . . followed . . .
but Jesus . . .*). Rupert says:
" Faciem suam . . . Jesus, id
est majestatis suæ divinam præ-
sentiam, secundum quam nus-
quam ambulat, non statim in
initio conversionis sequentibus
aperit . . ."

θεασ. αὐτ.] *beheld them*. Comp.
vi. 5.

Τί ζητεῖτε;] *What seek ye?* Not
whom? They certainly sought
Christ, but for what purpose and
with what hope? Christ asks,
as Euthymius (after Chrys.) says:
οὐκ ἀγνοῶν . . . ἀλλ' ἵνα διὰ τῆς
ἐρωτήσεως οἰκειώσηται τούτους.
It is of interest to compare the
first words of Christ recorded in
the several Gospels. *Suffer* it
be so *now ; for thus it becometh
us to fulfil all righteousness* (Matt.
iii. 15). *The time is fulfilled, and
the kingdom of heaven is at hand :*

repent ye and believe the gospel
(Mark i. 15). *How is it that ye
sought me? wist ye not that I
must be about my Father's business?* (Luke ii. 49). The first
words in the text followed by
Come, and ye shall see, the searching question and the personal
invitation are a parable *of* the
message of faith.

οἱ δὲ εἶπ. . . . Ῥαββεί] *and they
said . . . Rabbi.* The title (see iii.
2, note) shows reverent respect,
but it does not in this connexion
imply that the Lord had disciples already. The fresh recollection of the incident seems to
bring back the original terms
which had almost grown to be
foreign words (*vv.* 41, 42). The
English *Master* is to be taken in
the sense of " Teacher." Comp.
iii. 2, note.

ὃ λέγεται] Cf. xx. 16, "which is
expressed by." Comp. Acts ix.
36.

ποῦ μένεις;] *where abidest thou ?*
as *v.* 39 (ἔμειναν).

The answer implies that if
they could be with Christ, that,
and nothing less than that,
would satisfy their want. For
a thing (Τί; *v.* 38) these first
disciples substituted a Person.
They were in need of Christ

38 Jesus.   But Jesus turned, and beheld them following, and saith unto them, What seek ye? And they said unto him, Rabbi (which is to say, being interpreted, 39 Teacher), where abidest thou? He saith unto them, Come, and ye shall see. They came therefore and saw where he abode; and they abode with him that 40 day: it was about the tenth hour. One of the two that heard from John, and followed him, was Andrew, 41 Simon Peter's brother.   He findeth first his own

first and not of any special gift of Christ. They desired a quiet place for converse. As Chrysostom comments : Μετὰ ἡσυχίας ... καὶ εἰπεῖν τι πρὸς αὐτὸν καὶ ἀκοῦσαι τί παρ᾽ αὐτοῦ καὶ μαθεῖν ἤθελον.

39. Ἔρχεσθε κ. ὄψεσθε] *Come, and ye shall see.* The present imperative (comp. *v.* 47, vii. 37, xi. 34, and on the other hand iv. 16, ἐλθέ) describes an immediate act contemplated as already begun. The act of faith goes first : knowledge is placed definitely after. The double repetition, *So they came and saw*, must be noticed.

On the reply of Christ Cyril Al. remarks : Οὐ σημαίνει τὴν οἰκίαν καίτοι τοῦτο ποιεῖν ἐξαιτούμενος ἰέναι δὲ μᾶλλον εἰς αὐτὴν παράχρημα κελεύει . . . διδάσκων . . . ὅτι τῶν ἀγαθῶν τὴν ζήτησιν οὐκ εἰς ὑπερθέσεις ἀναριπτεῖσθαι καλόν.

τ. ἡμέρ. ἐκείνην] *that day*, that memorable day, from which the Christian society took its rise. Compare xx. 19, note.

ὥρα . . . δεκάτη] *the tenth hour*, *i.e.* 10 a.m. Compare iv. 6, note, and additional note on Chapter xix. An early hour seems to suit best the fulness of the day's events : The conviction—the finding of Peter—the

finding of James. The mention of the time is one of the small traits which mark St. John. He is here looking back upon the date of his own spiritual birth.

The absence of connecting particles in this passage is noteworthy.

40. Ἀνδρέας] Compare vi. 8, xii. 22 ; Mark xiii. 3, where the same four disciples appear together as here.

ἀδ. Σίμ. Πέτ.] *Simon Peter's brother.* Thus Peter is treated as the better known.

εἷς ἐκ τ. δύο] *one of the two*, the other being St. John ; *v.* 35, note.

ἀκουσάντ. παρὰ Ἰωάν.] *heard from John*, heard the great tidings from him, *i.e.* that Jesus was the Lamb of God. For the construction see vi. 45.

The same spiritual insight which was found in the Baptist is now seen in his disciples. Their attachment to Christ was spontaneous. They were not sent by John, nor called by Christ.

41. εὑρ. οὗτ. πρῶτ. τ. ἀδ. τ. ἴδ.] *he findeth first his own brother.* The words imply that someone else was afterwards found ; and from the form of the sentence we may conclude that this was

4

τὸν ἴδιον Σίμωνα καὶ λέγει αὐτῷ Εὑρήκαμεν τὸν Μεσ-
42 σίαν (ὅ ἐστιν μεθερμηνευόμενον Χριστός). ἤγαγεν αὐτὸν
πρὸς τὸν Ἰησοῦν. ἐμβλέψας αὐτῷ ὁ Ἰησοῦς εἶπεν Σὺ
εἶ Σίμων ὁ υἱὸς Ἰωάνου¹, σὺ κληθήσῃ Κηφᾶς (ὅ ἑρμη-

¹ Ἰωάνου אB*L 33 ; Ἰωνᾶ AB³X. See note.

the brother of the second disciple, that is James the brother
of John. All this evidently took
place on the same day (vv. 35,
43).

εὑρίσκει] The use of the word
in this chapter is most remarkable. It occurs again in this
verse and in 43 (44), and twice
in v. 45 (46). The search and
the blessing go together.

Εὑρήκαμεν] We have found.
This was the result of their intercourse with Christ. The verb
stands first, thus giving prominence to the search (v. 38) now
joyously ended. It is otherwise
in v. 45.

Of the word εὑρήκαμεν Chrysostom says truly : Τοῦτο τὸ ῥῆμα
ψυχῆς ἐστιν ὠδινούσης τὴν παρουσίαν
αὐτοῦ καὶ προσδοκώσης τὴν ἄφιξιν
ἄνωθεν καὶ περιχαροῦς γεγενημένης
μετὰ τὸ φανῆναι τὸ προσδοκώμενον.
And so below (v. 45): Τὸ
εὑρήκαμεν ζητούντων πῶς ἐστιν ἀεί.
The plural shows the sympathy
but not the presence of St. John.
Andrew identifies himself with
his friend. Neither he nor
Philip (v. 45) could say " I have
found " in the consciousness of a
common search.

Μεσσίαν (ὅ ἐστιν μεθερ. Χρ.)]
Messias (which is, being interpreted, Christ). The Hebrew
name is found only here and
iv. 25. Compare v. 38 (Rabbi),
note, v. 42 (Cephas) ; and contrast vv. 20, 25. On the form
(Μεσσίας or Μεσίας) as repre-

senting the Aramaic (מְשִׁיחָא)
see Delitzsch, Ztschr. f. Luth.
Theol., 1876, s. 603.

The announcement was an interpretation of the disciples' own
experience. It does not appear
that the title was used by the
Baptist. The prerogatives of
the Christ, the works of the
Christ, were laid open, and it
was the office of faith to recognise Him in whom they were
found.

The title " the Christ " is
found in the narrative of St.
John's Gospel, just as in the
Synoptists. It is not infrequently used by the people
doubting and questioning (vii.
26 f., 31, 41 f., x. 24, xii. 34.
Comp. ix. 22) ; and by the
Baptist in answer to them (i. 20,
25, iii. 28) ; but very rarely in a
confession of faith, as here and
xi. 27. Comp. iv. 25, 29. The
word is introduced wrongly in
iv. 42, vi. 69. For the usage of
St. John himself see xx. 31 ; 1
John ii. 22, v. 1 ; 2 John 9 ;
Rev. xi. 15, xii. 10, xx. 4. Comp.
i. 17, note. Perhaps the Hebrew
form is definitely preserved in
order to connect the Lord with
the Jewish hope, and to exclude
Gnostic speculations on the Æon
Christ.

41, 42. εὑρίσκει . . . λέγει . . .
ἤγαγεν] The change of tense
gives vividness to the narrative.
42. ἤγαγεν . . . ἐμβλέψας αὐτ.
ὁ Ἰησ. εἶπ.] he brought . . . Jesus

brother Simon, and saith unto him, We have found
42 the Messiah (which is, being interpreted, Christ).   He
brought him unto Jesus.   Jesus looked on him, and
said, Thou art Simon the son of John: thou shalt
be called Cephas (which is by interpretation, Peter).

looked on him and said.   Comp.
v. 36, note.

Σύ . . . σύ] *Thou . . . thou.*
This is a unique form of address.

Σὺ εἶ . . .] *Thou art* . . . This
is not necessarily a prophetic declaration by divine knowledge.
It rather means simply "this is
your natural name."   Some take
the phrase interrogatively: *Art
thou . . . ?* placing the old and
the new in sharper contrast.

ὁ υἱὸς Ἰωάνου] *filius Johanna* v.;
son of John.   Here and in ch. xxi.
this is the reading of the best
text.

σὺ κληθήσῃ Κηφᾶς] *thou shalt
be called Cephas*—hereafter thou
shalt win the name of Cephas.
This promise received its fulfilment, Matt. xvi. 18 (σὺ εἶ Πέτρος),
where the earlier naming is
implied.   The title appears to
mark not so much the natural
character of the apostle as the
spiritual office to which he was
called.

Κηφᾶς] *Cephas.*   The Aramaic
name (כֵּיפָא) is found in the New
Testament elsewhere only in 1
Cor. i. 12, iii. 22, ix. 5, xv. 5;
Gal. i. 18, ii. 9, 11, 14.

ὁ ἑρμηνεύ. Πέτρος] *quod inter-
pretatur Petrus* v.; *by interpretation, A stone.*   The sense would
perhaps be given better by
keeping the equivalent proper
name: *by interpretation Peter,
that is A stone,* or rather *a mass
of rock* detached from the living
rock.

Augustine's comment is:
" Non a Petro petra, sed Petrus
a petra; sicut non Christus a
Christiano, sed Christianus a
Christo vocatur. . . . Petra enim
erat Christus, super quod fundamentum etiam ipse ædifica-
tus est Petrus.   Fundamentum
quippe aliud nemo potest ponere
præter id quod positum est quod
est Christus Jesus" (*In Joh.*
cxxiv. 5).

Rupert says:
" Hac de causa Petrum a
seipso prima petra denominavit,
utpote in quo post seipsum tota
constituta erat fabrica spiritualis
ædificii . . .
" Igitur Simon, quod interpre-
tatur *Obediens,* quia primus petræ
illi erat superimponendus, super
quam ecclesia ædificatur, pulcre
mutato nomine Petrus ab ipsa
petra denominatur."

As to the *relation* of this
meeting with St. Peter to the
call recorded in Matt. iv. 18—
22; Mark i. 16—20; Luke v. 1
—11, it may be observed that

1. All the features are different.

   (*a*) Place—Judæa: Galilee.
   (*b*) Time — Close on the
        Baptism: Some time
        after.
   (*c*) Persons—Philip and Na-
        thanael are not named by
        Synoptists.
   (*d*) Circumstances — A
        simple meeting: A mi-
        racle.

43 νεύεται Πέτρος). Τῇ ἐπαύριον ἠθέλησεν ἐξελθεῖν εἰς τὴν
Γαλιλαίαν. καὶ εὑρίσκει Φίλιππον καὶ λέγει αὐτῷ ὁ
44 Ἰησοῦς Ἀκολούθει μοι. ἦν δὲ ὁ Φίλιππος ἀπὸ Βηθσαιδά,
45 ἐκ τῆς πόλεως Ἀνδρέου καὶ Πέτρου. εὑρίσκει Φίλιππος
τὸν Ναθαναὴλ καὶ λέγει αὐτῷ Ὃν ἔγραψεν Μωυσῆς ἐν

2. The narrative in the Synoptists implies some previous connexion.

3. This was the establishment of a personal relationship : that was a call to an official work. The former more naturally belongs to St. John's scope, as giving the history of the growth of faith. The latter falls in with the record of the organisation of the Church.

4. The teaching in Galilee to which the call recorded in the Synoptists belongs was really the beginning of a new work, distinct from the Lord's first work at Jerusalem, which followed on this.

5. The occupation of the disciples with their ordinary work after the first call finds a complete parallel in John xxi.

The work of the second day of Christ's ministry. Christ's own work begun (43—51).

The record of the fulfilment of John's work in the attachment of his disciples to Christ is followed by the record of the beginning of Christ's work. Jesus now "seeks" and commands (*v.* 43), and reveals both His authority and His insight.

43. Τῇ ἐπαύριον ἠθέλ. ἐξελθ. . . . κ. εὑρίσκ. . . . λέγ. αὐ. ὁ Ἰησ. . . .] *The next day (vv.* 29, 35) *he was minded to go forth . . . and he findeth . . . and Jesus saith . . .* The transposition of the subject

by the best authorities creates no real ambiguity. Compare xix. 5. The purpose is evidently spoken of as in accomplishment.

The co-ordination of the two clauses (ἠθέλησεν, καὶ λέγει), which would commonly be placed in dependence, is characteristic of St. John's style. Comp. ii. 13 ff.

ἐξελθεῖν εἰς τ. Γαλιλαίαν] "His hour was not yet come" for a public manifestation at Jerusalem, and therefore He returned for a time to His usual place of abode.

εὑρίσκει] How and where "Jesus found Philip" must remain unknown ; but the word implies that the meeting was not accidental. Compare *vv.* 43, 45 (41, 46), v. 14, ix. 35. The Lord "found" those who were "given" to Him : xvii. 6 ff., vi. 37. Comp. iv. 23.

Chrysostom remarks: Πρὶν αὐτῷ τινα κολληθῆναι οὐδένα καλεῖ . . . εἰ μὲν γὰρ μηδενὸς αὐτομάτου προσελθόντος αὐτὸς αὐτοὺς ἐφειλκύσατο κἂν ἀπεπήδησαν ἴσως· νῦν δὲ ἀφ' ἑαυτῶν ἑλόμενοι τοῦτο βέβαιοι λοιπὸν ἔμενον.

Rupert says : "Invenit utpote quem quæsivit : ipsum enim cum omnibus sanctis præscivit et prædestinavit."

Φίλιππον] See vi. 5, 7, xii. 21 ff., xiv. 8, 9. These passages throw light on the character of the disciple whom Christ sought. The name Philip is pure Greek. Comp. xii. 20 f.

43 The next day he was minded to go forth into
Galilee, and he findeth Philip: and Jesus saith unto
44 him, Follow me. Now Philip was from Bethsaida,
45 of the city of Andrew and Peter. Philip findeth
Nathanael, and saith unto him, We have found him,

Ἀκολούθει μοι] *Follow me*, as a
disciple bound to my service. The
words are here first pronounced
by Christ. Comp. Matt. viii. 22,
ix. 9, xix. 21, and parallels;
ch. xxi. 19, 22. The phrase in
Matt. iv. 19 is different.

44. ἦν . . . ἀπὸ Βηθσαι., ἐκ τ.
πολ. . . .] *erat . . . a Bethsaida, civitate . . .* v.; *was from Bethsaida,
of the city* . . . The Synoptists
mention that Simon and Andrew
had a house at Capernaum
(Mark i. 21, 29; comp. Matt.
viii. 5, 14; Luke iv. 31, 38).

Βηθσαιδά] Defined as Βηθσαιδὰ
τῆς Γαλιλαίας, xii. 21; and identified by Dr. Thomson with *Abu
Zany* on the west of the entrance
of the Jordan into the lake, and
by Major Wilson with *Khan
Minyeh* (Wilson, *Sea of Galilee,*
in Warren's *Recovery of Jerusalem*, pp. 342, 387). Comp.
Matt. xiv. 22, note; Mark viii.
22, note.

The notice of the home of
Philip explains how he was prepared to welcome Christ. He
knew and was in sympathy with
Andrew and Peter; and probably
he too with them had followed
the Baptist.

Rupert comments: "Hoc opus
divinam maxime commendat gratiam quod de civitate peccatrice
(Matt. xi. 21) tres isti vocati
sunt, magni patres justorum atque credentium."

The Lord finds in answer to
man's finding, and again man

finds in response to the Lord's
finding.

45. εὑρίσκ. Φίλ.] *Philip findeth.*
Probably on the journey. Nathanael was "of Cana in Galilee"
(xxi. 2). The first disciple who
"found Christ," and the first
disciple whom Christ "found,"
became alike evangelists at once.

Ναθαναήλ] *Nathanael* = Theodore. He is probably to be
identified with Bartholomew, for
the following reasons:

(1) The mention of him in
this place and in xxi. 2,
shows that he occupied a
prominent position among
the disciples. Those with
whom he is classed in each
place are apostles.

(2) No mention is made of
Nathanael in the Synop-
tists, or of Bartholomew
in St. John; while the
name Bartholomew is a
patronymic (Son of Tolmai)
like Barjona (Matt. xvi.
17), and Barjesus (Acts
xiii. 6).

(3) In the list of apostles
Bartholomew is coupled
with Philip by St. Matthew
(x. 3), St. Luke (vi. 14),
St. Mark (iii. 18), so that
the first six are the six
first called. In xxi. 2
Thomas is added, as in
Acts i. 13.

Ὃν ἔγραψεν M.] *Whom Moses
wrote*, a form of expression
apparently unique in the New

τῷ νόμῳ καὶ οἱ προφῆται εὑρήκαμεν, Ἰησοῦν υἱὸν τοῦ
46 Ἰωσὴφ τὸν ἀπὸ Ναζαρέτ. καὶ εἶπεν αὐτῷ Ναθαναήλ
Ἐκ Ναζαρὲτ δύναταί τι ἀγαθὸν εἶναι; λέγει αὐτῷ ὁ
47 Φίλιππος Ἔρχου καὶ ἴδε. εἶδεν Ἰησοῦς τὸν Ναθαναὴλ
ἐρχόμενον πρὸς αὐτὸν καὶ λέγει περὶ αὐτοῦ Ἴδε ἀληθῶς

Testament (false reading in Rom. x. 5). The use of the sing. (ἔγραψεν) is noteworthy. All the Scriptures are actually the voice of Moses. Comp. Matt. xxii. 40. Μωυσῆς ἐν τ. νόμ.] By types (ch. iii. 14 f.) and by more distinct words (Deut. xviii. 15. Comp. Acts iii. 22, vii. 37). Comp. v. 46. Μων. . . . κ. οἱ προφ.] the whole collection of the Old Testament Scriptures. Matt. v. 17, vii. 12, xi. 13, xxii. 40; Luke xvi. 29, 31, xxiv. 27; Acts xxiv. 14, xxviii. 23; Rom. iii. 21. A new stage has been reached: Philip has found not the Christ (41) merely, but Him of whom all the Scriptures of the Old Testament spoke. Philip confesses that He who had lived among them (vi. 42) satisfied the manifold promise of Lawgiver and Prophets.
. . . εὑρήκα.] . . . we have found. Note that the verb stands last. "Him of whom Moses wrote and the prophets, we have found." This form of the sentence (contrast v. 41) seems to imply that Philip and Nathanael had often dwelt on the Old Testament portraiture of the Messiah. So Euthymius remarks: Εὑρήκαμεν ὃν ἐζητοῦμεν, ὃν προσεδόκωμεν ἥξειν, ὃν αἱ γραφαὶ κατήγγελλον. By the use of the plural, Philip unites himself to the little group of disciples, and his words show that he had been before in communication with them.

Ἰησ. υἱ. τ. Ἰωσ. τ. ἀπ. Ναζ.] i.e. in Jesus of Nazareth. Philip describes the Lord by the name under which He appears to have been already known (Acts x. 37). Comp. Matt. xxi. 11; and ch. vi. 42 (vii. 42). The description is important, as showing that Philip recognised in One whom he knew as truly man, the fulfilment of all the promises of Scripture. Contrast ch. vi. 42.

46. Ἐκ Ναζ. δύν. τι ἀγ. εἶναι;] A Nazareth potest aliquid boni esse ? v.; From Nazareth can any good thing be ? i.e. can any blessing, much less such a blessing as the promised Messiah, arise out of a poor village like Nazareth, of which not even the name can be found in the Old Testament? Contrast Isa. ii. 3 (Zion). There is no evidence, unless the conduct of the Nazarenes to the Lord be such (Luke iv. 16 ff.), that Nazareth had a reputation worse than other places in Galilee (Matt. xiii. 58; Mark vi. 6). It was proverbial, however, that "out of Galilee ariseth no prophet" (vii. 52); and the candour of Nathanael would not hide a misgiving even when it was to the dishonour of his own country. The Messiah, moreover, was to be of David's seed and from David's city (vii. 42). The phrase εἶναι ἐκ denotes more than the simple home. It expresses the ideas of derivation and dependence, and so of moral correspondence.

of whom Moses in the law, and the prophets, did write, Jesus, the son of Joseph, the man from Nazareth. 46 And Nathanael said unto him, From Nazareth can any good thing be? Philip saith unto him, Come 47 and see. Jesus saw Nathanael coming to him, and

Comp. iii. 31, note, iv. 22. It should be remarked that some of the Fathers take the phrase as affirmative, i.e. "something good can come out of Nazareth."

Ἔρχου κ. ἴδε] *Veni et vide* v. ; *Come and see.* Compare v. 39. The words contain the essence of the true solution of religious doubts. The phrase is common in Rabbinic writers (בוא וראה), in a secondary sense, where attention is specially called to some peculiar teaching. See Wetstein on v. 40.

Ἔρχου] Comp. vii. 37, ἐρχέσθω, and contrast iv. 16 (ἐλθέ).

47—51. As the Lord had showed His power by the call of Philip, He now reveals His spiritual insight, and evokes the response of faith ; which becomes in turn the occasion of a larger promise.

47. εἶδεν . . . ἐρχ.] Nathanael at once accepted the challenge.

λέγει] The Lord was evidently accompanied by His disciples. In their presence He gives this testimony (comp. v. 36) *of him* (not *to him*, as reading the soul of the man approaching Him.

It will be noticed how the Lord interprets the thoughts of all whom He meets in these opening chapters of St. John : St. Peter (v. 42), St. Philip (v. 43), Nathanael (v. 47), the Blessed Virgin (ii. 4), Nicodemus (iii.), the Woman of Samaria (iv.). Compare ii. 25.

For Ἴδε see v. 29, note.

ἀληθ. Ἰσρ.] *an Israelite indeed* —one, that is, who answers in character to the name which marks the spiritual privileges of the chosen nation—"soldiers of God." There is already here a reference to Jacob's victories of faith (v. 51), which is made yet clearer by the second clause.

The adverb ἀληθῶς is characteristic of St. John : iv. 42, vi. 14, vii. 40, viii. 31 ; 1 John ii. 5.

For Ἰσρ. see v. 31, note; 2 Cor. xi. 22 ; Rom. ix. 4, xi. 1. The force of the title appears by comparing Acts ii. 14 with Acts ii. 22 (iii. 12, v. 35, xiii. 16, xxi. 28).

ἐν ᾧ δ. οὐκ ἔστιν] who is frank, simple, with no selfish aims to hide, no doubts to suppress, who dares to speak out his difficulties and yet readily accepts the call to bring them to the test of experience, one in whom the spirit of Jacob—the supplanter— has been wholly transformed to the type of Israel. Theophylact says justly of Nathanael's expressed difficulty : Οὐκ ἀπιστίας ἦσαν τὰ ῥήματα ἀλλὰ ἀκριβείας καὶ νομομαθοῦς διανοίας.

The future growth of St. Peter had formed the main topic of Christ's welcome to him (v. 42), as here the present character of Nathanael.

There is a close correspondence between the title and the indication which Philip's invitation

48 Ἰσραηλείτης ἐν ᾧ δόλος οὐκ ἔστιν. λέγει αὐτῷ Ναθαναήλ
Πόθεν με γινώσκεις ; ἀπεκρίθη Ἰησοῦς καὶ εἶπεν αὐτῷ
Πρὸ τοῦ σε Φίλιππον φωνῆσαι ὄντα ὑπὸ τὴν συκῆν
49 εἶδόν σε. ἀπεκρίθη αὐτῷ Ναθαναήλ Ῥαββεί, σὺ εἶ ὁ
50 υἱὸς τοῦ θεοῦ, σὺ βασιλεὺς εἶ τοῦ Ἰσραήλ. ἀπεκρίθη
Ἰησοῦς καὶ εἶπεν αὐτῷ Ὅτι εἶπόν σοι ὅτι εἶδόν σε

gives of Nathanael's character.
The invitation of Philip was
based on the testimony of "Moses
and the prophets," and Nathanael
is recognised as one in whom the
training of the nation had found
a pure expression.

48. Πόθεν με γινώσκεις;] Nathanael must have overheard the
words spoken about him, and
found in them some clear discernment of his thoughts (comp. ii.
25), which roused him to this
question of surprise uttered without reserve. He questions only
the source (πόθεν;) and not the exactness of the Lord's knowledge.

Πρὸ τοῦ . . .] The love of Christ
had anticipated the love of the
friend in finding Nathanael.

ὄντα ὑπὸ τ. συκῆν εἶδόν σε]
*when thou wast under the fig
tree, I saw thee.* This sentence,
like the former one, points to
some secret thought or prayer,
by knowing which the Lord
showed His divine insight into
the heart of man. He *saw* not
that which is outward only, but
that which was most deeply
hidden. Compare iv. 19. There
is nothing to show whether Nathanael was still in meditation
when Philip found him or not.

τὴν συκῆν] *the fig tree,* which
would be in leaf about this time
(Matt. xxi. 19 ff.; ch. ii. 13). The
definite article calls up the exact
scene. Comp. Mic. iv. 4; Zech. iii.
10, etc. The form of the phrase

(ὑπὸ τὴν συκῆν, contrasted with
ὑποκάτω τῆς συκῆς, v. 50, *underneath*) implies that Nathanael
had *withdrawn* under the fig tree,
for thought or prayer. This
meditation turned (as we must
suppose) upon the ideas recognised in the Lord's words—the
hope of the people, shown in
light and darkness by the effects
of the preaching of the Baptist.

Augustine's narrative of the
crisis of his own conversion is a
singular commentary on the
scene. He, too, had retired
(Sept. A.D. 386) beneath a fig
tree for solitary thought when
the voice "Tolle, lege" decided
his choice. " Ego sub quadam
fici arbore stravi me nescio
quomodo . . . et flebam amarissima contritione cordis mei.
Et ecce audio vocem de vicina
domo cum cantu dicentis et
crebro repetentis, quasi pueri an
puellæ nescio : Tolle, lege : tolle,
lege . . . Repressoque impetu lacrimarum surrexi, nihil aliud
interpretens nisi divinitus mihi
juberi ut aperirem codicem et
legerem quod primum caput invenissem " (*Confessiones,* viii. 12).

A passage is also quoted from
Bereshith R. lxii. (p. 294, Wünsche), in which Jewish Rabbis, according to some R. Akiva and his
scholars, are described as studying the law under a fig tree.

49. Ῥαββεί] All prejudice and
doubt is laid aside, and the title

saith of him, Behold, an Israelite indeed,[1] in whom
48 is no guile! Nathanael saith unto him, Whence
knowest thou me ? Jesus answered and said unto
him, Before Philip called thee, when thou wast under
49 the fig tree, I saw thee. Nathanael answered him,
Rabbi, thou art the Son of God; thou art King of
50 Israel. Jesus answered and said unto him, Because
I said unto thee, I saw thee underneath the fig tree,

[1] *lit.* in truth.

is given by instinct which before
(*v.* 48) he had withheld.

σὺ εἶ ὁ υἱ. τ. θεοῦ, σὺ βασιλεὺς εἶ
τ. Ἰσραήλ] *thou art the Son of
God; thou art King of Israel.*
Thus Messiah was described in
relation to (1) His divine origin,
(2) His human sovereignty.
Both attributes are implied in
the conception of a kingdom of
God. "The 'true Israelite,'" as
it has been well said, "acknowledges his king." Compare
Peter's confession in Matt. xvi.
16, and in ch. vi. 68, 69, and
that of Thomas in xx. 28.

ὁ υἱὸς τοῦ θεοῦ] The words are
an echo of the testimony of the
Baptist (*v.* 34). Nothing can
be more natural than to suppose
that the language of John had
created strange questionings in
the hearts of some whom it had
reached, and that it was with
such thoughts Nathanael was
busied when the Lord "saw"
him. If this were so, the confession of Nathanael may be, as
it were, an answer to his own
doubts.

βασιλεὺς τοῦ Ἰσραήλ] As here
at the beginning, so once again
this title is given to Christ at
the close of His ministry, xii. 13.
Compare Matt. xxvii. 42 ; Mark

xv. 32, where the mockery is
made more bitter by the use of
this theocratic phrase in place of
the civil title, "King of the
Jews." See xviii. 33, note.

The addition of this title
here shows that Nathanael had
not felt the full depth of his
words.

Chrysostom observes this : Ὁ
τοῦ θεοῦ υἱὸς οὐ τοῦ Ἰσραήλ ἐστι
βασιλεὺς μόνον ἀλλὰ καὶ τῆς οἰκου-
μένης ἁπάσης.

50. πιστεύεις;] *credis?* v. ; *believest thou?*] The words can also be
taken affirmatively; but the same
sense is given more forcibly by the
question (comp. xvi. 31, xx. 29),
which conveys something of surprise that the belief was accorded
so readily, and something of
warning that even this expression
of belief did not exhaust the
power of faith.

μείζω τούτων ὄψῃ] *see greater
things than these,* actually experience greater proofs of My
divine mission than are shown in
these revelations of thy thoughts.
The plural (τούτων) marks the
class and not the special incident.
Comp. 3 John 4. Euthymius
says on these words: Ἵνα καὶ
μεῖζον πιστεύσῃς· ἔτι γὰρ μικρὰ
ἀκούσας μικρὰ ἐπίστευσε.

51 ὑποκάτω τῆς συκῆς πιστεύεις; μείζω τούτων ὄψῃ. καὶ
λέγει αὐτῷ ᾿Αμὴν ἀμὴν λέγω ὑμῖν, ¹ ὄψεσθε τὸν οὐρανὸν
ἀνεῳγότα καὶ τοὺς ἀγγέλους τοῦ θεοῦ ἀναβαίνοντας καὶ
καταβαίνοντας ἐπὶ τὸν υἱὸν τοῦ ἀνθρώπου.

¹ Insert ἀπ᾽ ἄρτι AX. See note.

51. λέγ. αὐτ. . . . λέγ. ὑμῖν] he
saith unto him . . . I say unto
you. The word is for Nathanael,
but the blessing is for all believers.
"Unus et idem Dominus . . .
donat hominibus . . . suam præ-
sentiam et resurrectionem a mor-
tuis, sed non Deum immutans . . .
sed eundem ipsum qui semper
habet plura metiri domesticis,
et, proficiente eorum erga Deum
dilectione, plura et majora do-
nans " (Iren. IV. ix. 2).
"Hoc plane de seipso sperare
potest quisque fidelis. Cum
enim parva quæ sentit de Verbo
Dei fideliter et intentione bona
depromit dignum se exhibet cui
revelet majora Pater qui est in
cælis quæ revelare non potest
caro et sanguis " (Rupert).
᾿Αμὴν ἀμήν] The phrase is
found in the New Testament only
in the Gospel of St. John (who
never gives the simple Amen),
and (like the simple Amen in the
Synoptists) it is used only by
Christ. The word Amen is represented by in truth or truly
in Luke iv. 25, ix. 27. In the
LXX. the original word is retained only in responsive phrases
(Neh. v. 13, vii. 6). Elsewhere
it is translated "be it so "
(γένοιτο), Ps. xli. 13, lxxii. 19,
lxxxix. 52. The word is properly
a verbal adjective, "firm," "sure."
Cp. Isa. lxv. 16 (God of the Amen,
LXX. ὁ θεὸς ὁ ἀληθινός); Rev. iii.
14 (the Amen). See Delitzsch,

Ztschr. f. Luth. Theol., 1856, 11.
422 ff.
ἀπ᾽ ἄρτι (from henceforth) must
be omitted according to decisive
authority. If it were genuine it
would describe the communion
between earth and heaven as
established from the time when
the Lord entered on His public
ministry.
τ. οὐρ. ἀνεῳγ.] heaven opened.
The phrase is the symbol of free
intercourse between God and man.
Comp. Isa. lxiv. 1.
ἀγγ. . . . ἀναβαίν. κ. καταβαίν.]
angelos . . . ascendentes et de-
scendentes v.; angels . . . ascending
and descending. The order is remarkable. The divine messengers
are already on the earth, though
we see them not ; and they first
bear the prayer to God before
they bring down the answer from
Him. So it was in the vision of
Jacob (Gen. xxviii. 12), which
furnishes the image here ; and
by the Incarnation that vision
was made an abiding reality.
That which was a dream to the
representative of Israel was a
fact for the Son of man. Thus
the reference is to the continuing
presence of Christ (Matt. xxviii.
20), in whom believers realise the
established fellowship of the seen
and the unseen, and not to the
special acts of angelic ministration
to Christ alone during His earthly
life. There is an interesting discussion of Jacob's vision in Philo,
De Somn., §§ 22 ff., pp. 640 ff.

believest thou? thou shalt see greater things than
51 these. And he saith unto him, Verily, verily, I say
unto you, Ye shall see the heaven opened, and the
angels of God ascending and descending upon the
Son of man.

The connexion of the promise with the sign appears to lie in this, that the knowledge of the Lord was a proof of His perfect spiritual insight into the soul of Nathanael, and He shows that this fellowship of soul with soul shall be consummated in the uninterrupted intercourse of God and man.

The locality of the conversation may have been near Bethel or the ford Jabbok, so that the references to Jacob's history were forcibly suggested by the places made famous through the patriarch.

τοὺς ἀγγ. τοῦ θεοῦ] *the angels of God*, not simply *angels of God*, beings of this nature, but the whole host of heaven busy with their ministry of love. Compare ch. xx. 12 (comp. xii. 29). There are no other references (v. 4 is a gloss) to the being and ministry of angels in the Gospel or Epistles of St. John.

τ. υἱ. τ. ἀνθ.] By the use of this title the Lord completes the revelation of His Person, which has been unfolded step by step in the narrative of this chapter, in which He has been acknowledged as the greater Successor of the Baptist (*vv.* 26 f.), the Lamb of God (*vv.* 29, 36), the Son of God (*vv.* 34, 49), the Messiah (*vv.* 41, 45), the King of Israel (*v.* 49). These titles had been given by others. He chooses for Himself that one which definitely presents His work in relation to humanity in itself, and not primarily in relation to God or to the chosen people, or even to humanity as fallen. If, as appears probable, the title was now first adopted, it is to be noticed that it was revealed in answer to a signal confession of faith (Matt. xiii. 12). See additional note.

There is an evident fitness that the title should be made known here, for by it the words of Philip ("the son of Joseph, him of Nazareth") are transfigured. The true manhood of the Lord is revealed in its full majesty and power.

ADDITIONAL NOTES ON CHAP. I

3, 4. The last words of *v.* 3 (ὃ γέγονεν, [*that*] *which hath been made*) can be taken either (1) with the words which follow, or (2) with the words which go before. In the former case the text will run . . . χωρὶς αὐτοῦ ἐγένετο οὐδὲ ἕν. ὃ γέγονεν ἐν αὐτῷ ζωὴ ἦν . . . *without him was* not anything made: *that which hath been made was life in him (in him was life)*; in the latter case . . . χωρὶς αὐτοῦ ἐγένετο οὐδὲ ἓν ὃ γέγονεν. ἐν αὐτῷ ζωὴ ἦν . . . *without him was not anything made that hath been made. In him was life.* . . .

The former (to speak generally)

was the punctuation of the ante-Nicene age : the latter is that of the common texts, and of most modern versions and popular commentaries.

The evidence in greater detail is as follows :

(1) . . . χωρὶς αὐτοῦ ἐγένετο οὐδὲ ἕν. ὃ γέγονεν ἐν αὐτῷ ζωὴ ἦν . . . This punctuation is supported by overwhelming ancient authority of MSS., versions, and Fathers.

(a) *Manuscripts.* A C (first-hand) D place a distinct point before ὃ γέγονεν, and no point after it.[1] The remaining two (א B) of the five most ancient MSS. make no punctuation. Other important but later MSS. give the same stopping, as *e.g.* L.

(β) *Versions.* One of the most important of the *Old Latin* copies (*b*) inserts *autem*, so that the connexion is unquestionable : *Quod autem factum est, in eo vita est.* Others (*a*, *e*, *f*, *ff*[2], etc.) give the same connexion by punctuation. But in themselves the words are ambiguous ; and therefore it is not surprising that in *c* and in MSS. of the Vulgate generally (as in the editions) the *quod factum est* is connected with the words which go before.

[1] A careful and repeated examination of D satisfies me completely that this MS. has no stop after γέγονεν. There is a slight flaw in the vellum, which extends towards γέγονεν from the top of the following ε, of which the upper boundary is above the level of the writing ; but this is certainly not the vestige of a stop. The stops are below the level of the writing. And again, there is no increased space between γέγονεν and ἐν, such as is found where a stop occurs, as between οὐδέν and δ. On holding the leaf to the light, the point of a C falls within the flaw, and gives the semblance of a stop.

The *Old Syriac* (Curetonian), like *b*, introduces a conjunction, so as to leave no doubt as to the punctuation which it follows : *But that which was* . . . The Thebaic and Æthiopic versions support the same connexion.

(γ) *Fathers.* The same connexion is supported by Clem. Alex., Orig., (Euseb.), Cyr. Alex., Hil., Aug., and by the earliest heretical writers quoted by Irenæus, Hippolytus, Clem. Alex.

Ambrose gives both readings, but he adopts the reading *quod factum est in ipso vita est*, and evidently implies that this was known to be the oldest reading, though it was felt to be ambiguous in sense. Jerome's quotations appear to recognise both punctuations.

(2) χωρὶς αὐτοῦ ἐγένετο οὐδὲ ἕν ὃ γέγονεν. ἐν αὐτῷ ζωὴ ἦν. This punctuation is supported by

(a) *Manuscripts.* The mass of secondary uncials and later manuscripts.

(β) *Versions.* The Memphitic and the printed Latin texts. But the clause "which hath been made" is omitted in one MS. of the Memphitic.

(γ) *Fathers.* The modern stopping was due to the influence of the Antiochene School, who avowedly adopted it to make it clear that the former words applied only to "things created," and not, as had been alleged, to the Holy Spirit.

So Chrysostom (*in loc.*): "Without Him was made not even one thing which hath been made," "that is of things made (τῶν γενητῶν), both visible and mental (νοητῶν) ; none has been brought into being without the power of Christ. For we shall not put the full point at 'not even one thing,' as the heretics do (κατὰ τοὺς αἱρετικούς); for they say thus: 'that which hath become in Him was life,' wishing to speak of the Holy Spirit as a creation (κτίσμα)." At the same time he takes the next clause, ἐν αὐτῷ ζωὴ ἦν, as meaning "that in Him all things live and are in Him providentially ordered (προνοεῖται), so that that which has been said of the Father might properly be said also of Him, that in Him we live and move and have our being."

The punctuation thus recommended was supported also by Theodoret and Theodore of Mopsuestia, and prevailed in later times.

Epiphanius, in his *Ancoratus* (cap. lxxv.), written in A.D. 374, after quoting the passage according to the old punctuation (cap. lxxiv.), goes on to say that the words have been used by some to derogate from the honour of the Holy Spirit. The true way of reading the passage is, he continues, *All things were made through Him, and without Him was nothing made that hath been made in Him.* Nothing can be said for this division of the words, and it may be fairly concluded that Epiphanius is simply hazarding a hasty judgement. In *Hær.* lxix., § 56 (p. 779), he treats the words ὃ γέγονεν as the subject of ζωὴ ἦν, while he connects them with the words which go before (ἐπειδὴ ἦν καὶ ἦν καὶ ἦν (v. 1) καὶ τὰ ἐν αὐτῷ ζωὴ ἦν).

The interpretation of the passage is undoubtedly most difficult, but it does not seem that the difficulty is increased by the ancient punctuation. The difficulty in either case

centres in the use of the imperfect ("*was* life . . ." "*was* the light . . . "), for which several ancient authorities read *is* in the first place, a substitution which can only be regarded as an arbitrary correction. It is indeed by no means clear in what sense it can be said: *Life was in the Word, and the Life* [thus spoken of as in the Word] *was the Light of men*; or again: *That which hath been made was Life in the Word, and the Life* [thus enjoyed by creation in the Word] *was the Light of men.* Yet the second conception will be seen upon consideration to fall in with the scope of St. John's view of the nature and action of the Word.

The apostle deals with the two main aspects of finite being, origin and continuance. As to the first, he says exhaustively that *all things became through the Word* as Agent; and *Nothing, no not one thing, became without —apart from—Him.* At this point, then, the view of the act of creation is completed. But the continuance of created things has yet to be noticed. That which "became" still lasts. And as Creation (on one side) was "in the Word," so too continuance is in Him. The endurance of the universe is due to its essential relation to the Creator. Creation has not "life in itself" (v. 26), but it had and has life in the Word.

It will, however, be objected that the phrase of the apostle is "was life in Him," and not "has life in Him." At first sight the objection appears to be strong. The latter phrase would no doubt be far simpler than that which is actually used, and it would express part of the truth more clearly ; but at the same time it would fall short of the fulness of what is written. As it is, the thought of the reader is carried away from the present, and raised (so to speak) to the contemplation of the essence of things. For a moment we are taken from phenomena—"that which hath become "—to being, to the divine "idea" of things. From this point of sight the Life of the world was included in the Word, and with the Life also the destination of the Life. Even in that which is fleeting there is that which " was," something beyond time, of which particular issues are shown in time. In regard to God, things " were " in their absolute, eternal perfection ; in regard to men, " they have become." The thought occurs once again in the writings of St. John. There is the same contrast between the "idea" and the temporal realisation of the idea, in the Hymn of the Elders in the Revelation (iv. 11) : *Thou art worthy, our Lord and our God, to receive glory and honour and power, for thou didst create all things, and for thy pleasure (θέλημα) they were (ἦσαν, according to the true reading), and were created.*

Human language is necessarily inadequate to express distinctly such a conception as has been faintly indicated ; but at least it will be seen that the early punctuation of the passage suggests a view of the relation of the Creation to the Creator which claims to be reverently studied. That which was created and still continues, represents to us what was beyond time (if we dare so speak) in the Divine Mind. In its essence it was not only living, but *life* in the Word, in virtue, that is, of its connexion with Him (comp. chap. v. 17, note). And through it— through the finite — the Word made Himself known ; so that Creation was essentially a manifestation of the Word to men who were able to observe and to interpret in part the phenomena of life.

According to this view, the word *life* is used both times in the same sense to express the divine element in creation, that in virtue of which things " are," each according to the fulness of its being. It is the sum of all that *is* physically, intellectually, morally, spiritually in the world and in man. This " life " is for rational beings a manifestation of God through the Word ; and it was the Divine Will that it should be so : *the life was the light of men.* Comp. Rom. i. 19, 20, ii. 14, 15 ; Acts xiv. 17, xvii. 23 ff.

It will be seen that in this explanation the words *in him* are connected with *was life*, and not with *that which hath been made.* The unusual but emphatic order finds a parallel in the true reading of iii. 15. The other combination, however, has very early authority (comp. Iren. I. viii. 5). Thus Clement of Alexandria applies the words to the Christian reborn in Christ. " He that hath been baptized (ὁ πεφωτισμένος) is awake unto God, and such a one lives. For that which hath been made in Him is life" (*Pæd.* II. ix. § 79 ; comp. *Pæd.* I. vi. § 27).

Cyril of Alexandria, who grasps with singular vigour the double relation of Creation to the Word as Creator and Preserver of all things, which is conveyed in the passage, appears to invert the description of the continuous vital connexion of the Word and the world. "As for that which hath come into being"—so he paraphrases — "the Life, the Word that is the Beginning and Bond (σύστασις) of all things, was in it " . . . "The Word, as Life by nature, was in the things which have become, mingling Himself by participation in the things that are" (*Comm., ad loc.*). This construction seems to be quite impossible; and the meaning suffers, inasmuch as things are not referred to their one centre of living unity, but on the contrary this one life is regarded as dispersed.

Augustine (*Comm., in loc.*) has illustrated the meaning well. "*Quod factum est ;* hic subdistingue [he has just set aside the punctuation *quod factum est in illo, vita est*] et deinde infer, *in illo vita est.* Quid est hoc ? . . . Quomodo possum dicam. . . . Faber facit arcam. Primo in arte habet arcam : si enim in arte arcam non haberet, unde illam fabricando proferret ? . . . In arte invisibiliter est, in opere visibiliter erit. . . . Arca in o- pere non est vita, arca in arte vita est ; quia vivit anima artificis, ubi sunt ista omnia antequam proferantur. Sic ergo, fratres carissimi, quia Sapientia Dei, per quam facta sunt omnia, secundum artem continet omnia antequam fabricat omnia, hinc quæ fiunt per ipsam artem non continuo vita sunt, sed *quidquid factum est, vita in illo est.* Terram vides . . . cælum vides . . . fo- ris corpora sunt, in arte vita sunt."

Thus the ancient division of the clauses gives a consistent if mysterious sense to every phrase. If however the other punctuation, that of the E.V., be adopted, the addition of the words "that hath been made" adds nothing to the sense, and the harmony of the rhythm of the original is spoiled, especially if the true reading (οὐδὲ ἕν for οὐδέν) be taken. Then further, there is a certain abruptness in the begin- ning, *In him was life,* unlike the repetition of the subject in the adjacent clauses (*vv.* 1, 2, . . . *the Word . . . the same was, vv.* 4, 5, *the light . . . the light shineth . . .*). It is a still further objection to this arrange- ment of the passage, that nothing is said of the means by which the Life became the Light of men. The third verse naturally prepares the way for the announcement of the revelation of the Word through and in His works.

But still, even in this arrange- ment of the clauses, the sense, though less clearly expressed, will remain substantially the same. The mention of "life" in the Word must be made in reference to finite being and not in reference to Himself. He was the centre and support of all things, according to their several natures ; and the life thus derived from Him was the light of men. According to this view, the verb *was* describes what was the historical relation of things at the moment after crea- tion, and not what was the archetypal idea of things. Still even so that which "was" when God pronounced all things "very good," represents the essential law of being.

4. *in him* was (ἦν) *life*] An important and well-marked group of ancient authorities, which represent a text of the second century, א D, MSS. of Orig., *Lat. vt.*, *Syr. vt.*, read *in him* is (ἐστίν) *life.* The variant is without doubt a very early gloss ; and it may be observed, once for all, that these authorities, both separately and collectively, are characterised by a tendency to introduce interpretative readings. In such cases, where they stand alone against the other authorities, their reading, though of great antiquity and once widely current, is very rarely to be received.

10. *the world* (ὁ κόσμος.)

1. The conception of the "world" (κόσμος) is eminently characteristic of the writings of St. John. He nowhere uses αἰών (ὁ νῦν αἰών, ὁ αἰὼν οὗτος, etc.) for the moral order ; and conversely κόσμος is very rarely used with a moral sense, as the sphere of revelation, by the Synoptists (comp. Matt. v. 14, xiii. 38, xviii. 7, xxvi. 13 ; [Mark xvi. 15]), though it occurs more frequently in St. Paul (Rom. iii. 19 ; 1 Cor. i. 21, etc.).

2. The fundamental idea of κόσμος in St. John is that of the sum of created being which belongs to the sphere of human life as an ordered whole, considered apart from God (xvii. 5, 24). The whole is relative to man as well as to God. So far as it includes the material creation, this is regarded as the appointed medium and scene of man's work (comp. Wisd. ix. 2 f., x. 1). Spiritual existences (angels, etc.) are not included in this conception of the world :

they are "of the things above" as contrasted with "the things below" (viii. 23).

In this widest sense "the world was made through (διά)" the Word (i. 10). Comp. Rev. xiii. 8, xvii. 8.

3. More specially the world is that system which answers to the circumstances of man's present life. At birth he "comes into the world" (vi. 14, xvi. 21), and "is in the world" till death (xiii. 1, xvii. 11), comp. xvii. 15. The Lord during His earthly Life, or when He submits to its conditions, is "in the world" (ix. 5, xvii. 11, 13) in a more definite manner than that in which He is "in the world" from creation (i. 10), "coming into the world" (i. 9, xi. 27, xii. 46, xvi. 28, xviii. 37), and being "sent into the world" by the Father (x. 36, xvii. 18 ; 1 John iv. 9), and again "leaving the world" (xvi. 28). Comp. Rev. xi. 15.

4. So far "the world" represents that which is transitory and seen as opposed to the eternal (1 John ii. 15 ff., iii. 17). And these particular ideas of the transitoriness, the externality, the corruption of "the world" are emphasised in the phrase "this world" (ὁ κόσμος οὗτος, viii. 23, xi. 9, xii. 25, 31, xiii. 1, xviii. 36, xvi. 11 ; 1 John iv. 17. Comp. xiv. 30). So far as it is regarded under this aspect, the "world" has no direct connexion with God (comp. 1 John v. 19).

5. It is easy to see how the thought of an ordered whole relative to man and considered *apart* from God passes into that of the ordered whole *separated* from God. Man fallen impresses his character upon the order

which is the sphere of his activity. And thus the "world" comes to represent humanity in its present state, alienated from its Maker, and so far determining the character of the whole order to which man belongs. The world, instead of remaining the true expression of God's will under the conditions of its creation, becomes His rival (1 John ii. 15—17). St. John says little as to the cause or process of this alienation. It is referred however to the action of a being without, who is the source and suggestor of evil (viii. 44, xiii. 2 ; 1 John iii. 8).

6. Through this interruption in its normal development, the world which was made by the Word recognised Him not (i. 10; comp. xvii. 25 ; 1 John iii. 1). It became exposed to destruction (ἀπώλεια, iii. 16, viii. 24 ; 1 John v. 19 ff., ii. 2). Still it was the object of God's love (iii. 16 f.), and Christ took on Him its sin (i. 29). He was "the light" (viii. 12, ix. 5, xii. 46) ; "the Saviour of the world" (iv. 42, xii. 47 ; 1 John iv. 14), giving life to it (vi. 33, 51). He spoke not to a sect or to a nation, but to the world (xviii. 20, viii. 26). He is a propitiation "for the whole world" (1 John ii. 2).

7. The coming of Christ into the world was necessarily a judgement (ix. 39). Out of the whole, regarded as a system containing within itself the spring of a corresponding life (xv. 19, xvii. 14, 16 ; 1 John iv. 5, ii. 16), some were chosen by (xv. 19) or "given" to Him (xvii. 6). Thus the whole has become divided. Part attaches itself to God in answer to His call : part still stands aloof from Him. In con-

trast with the former, the latter is called the "world." In this sense the "world" describes the mass of men (comp. xii. 19) distinguished from the people of God, characterised by their peculiar feelings (vii. 7, xiv. 27, xv. 18 f., xvi. 20, xvii. 14 ; 1 John iii. 13, iv. 5) and powers (xiv. 17 ; 1 John iii. 1), hostile to believers, and incapable of receiving the divine spirit. The disciples and "the world" stand over against one another (xiv. 19, 22). On the one side are the marks of "light" and "love" and "life"; on the other, "darkness" and "hatred" and "death." The world has its champions (1 John iv. 1 ff.), its inspiring power (1 John iv. 4, v. 19), its prince (xiv. 30, xvi. 11). In the world the disciples have tribulation, though Christ has conquered it (xvi. 33) ; and His victory is repeated by them through the faith (1 John v. 4 f.).

8. But even this "world" is not uncared for, though for a time it was left (xvii. 9). The disciples are sent into it (xvii. 18). The Paraclete's Mission is to convict it (xvi. 8), the self-surrender of Christ (xiv. 31), the unity (xvii. 21) and the glory of the disciples (xvii. 23), are to the end that the world may come to knowledge and faith.

9. From this analysis of St. John's usage of the term it will be seen how naturally the original conception of an order apart from God passes into that of an order opposed to God : how a system which is limited and transitory becomes hostile to the divine : how the "world," as the whole scene of human activity, is lost in humanity : how humanity ceases to be "of the world" by its union with God in Christ.

5

13. In some of the early Latin copies (*b*, Tertullian, and perhaps the translator of Irenæus) a very remarkable variation was introduced into this verse, by which it was referred to the Word as subject, *Who . . . was born.* The variation arose from the ambiguity of the relative in Latin, which was taken with the nearest antecedent (*ejus, qui . . . natus est*).

15. ὃν εἶπον] The variations in a few of the most ancient authorities here suggest the possibility of some very early corruption of the text. The original hand of א gives, *This was he that cometh after me* who *is become before me* (οὗτος ἦν ὁ ὀπ. μ. ἐρχ. ὃς ἔμ. μ. γ.). This insertion of the relative (ὅς) finds some support in one Old Latin copy. The first hands of B and C and a very early corrector of א read *who spake* (ὁ εἰπών for ὃν εἶπον); and this reading gives an intelligible sense by emphasising the reference to the Baptist's testimony : " this John, and no other, was he who spake the memorable words."

16. ὅτι ἐκ . . .] The reading καὶ ἐκ, which is supported by A, the secondary uncials, almost all the cursives, three Syriac versions, and the Vulgate, is a good example of a change introduced, probably by the unconscious instinct of the scribe, for the sake of smoothness and (as it was supposed) of clearness. At a very early time (second century) verse 16 was regarded as a continuation of the words of the Baptist, so that the true reference of the second *because* (ὅτι) was lost, and the repetition of the conjunction in two consecutive clauses was felt to be very harsh. The true

reading, *because of* . . . (ὅτι ἐκ . . .), is supported by an overwhelming concurrence of the representatives of the most ancient texts (B, אD, CLX, 33, *Lat. vt., Memph.*), though it practically disappeared from later copies.

18. ὁ μονογενὴς υἱός] Two readings of equal antiquity, as far as our present authorities go, though unequally supported, are found in this passage. Of these the first, followed by E.V., *the only begotten Son* (ὁ μονογενὴς υἱός), is found in AX, the secondary uncials, all known cursives except 33, the *Lt. vt., Syr. vt., Syr. Hcl. and Hier.*, the *Vulgate, Arm.*

The second, *one who is God only begotten* (μονογενὴς θεός), is found in א*BC*L, *Peshito, Syr. Hcl. mg.* [D is defective.]

A third reading, *the only begotten God* (ὁ μονογενὴς θεός), which is found in אᶜ, 33 (the reading of the Memphitic version is ambiguous : it *may* express *the only begotten of God*, but it is more probable that it expresses *the only begotten God* (ὁ μονογενὴς θεός). Schwartze rejects the former rendering, which is that of Wilkins, too peremptorily), probably arose from a combination of the two readings, and may be dismissed at once. The strangely inaccurate statement of many commentators that ὁ μον. θεός is the reading of " אBCL, etc.," shows a complete misapprehension, not only of the facts but of the significance of the readings. The tempting reading of one Latin copy, *the only begotten*, has still less real claim to be taken into account in the face of the facts of the case. In considering this evidence it will appear that

1. The most ancient authorities for the reading *the only begotten Son*, the *Old Latin* and *Old Syriac* versions, are those which are inclined to introduce inter-pretative glosses (see note on *v.* 4), and on this occasion their weight is diminished by the opposition of א.

2. The reading *God only begotten*, in the Peshito, can hardly have been a correction of the original text, because this reading is not found in the type of text (*e.g.* AX) by the help of which the version appears to have been revised.

3. There is no ancient Greek authority for the reading *the only begotten Son*, while the Greek authorities for *God only begotten* represent three great types, B, א, CL.

4. The universal agreement of the later copies in the reading *the only begotten Son*, shows that there was no tendency in scribes to change it, while the correction of א (*the only begotten God*) shows us the reading *God only begotten*, modified under the influence of the common reading.

5. The substitution, intentional or accidental, of *God* (θ͞ς) for *Son* (υ͞ς) does not explain the omission of the article in the reading *God only begotten*; while, on the contrary, the substitution of *Son* for *God* would naturally carry with it the addition of the article (ch. iii. 16, 18).

6. The occurrence of the word "Father" in the context would suggest the use of the word "Son," while the word "God" would appear at first sight out of place in the relation described.

Thus the testimony of the direct documentary evidence for the text very decidedly prepon-derates in favour of the reading *God only begotten*.

The patristic testimony is complicated, and it is impossible to discuss it at length. It must be enough to say that

1. The phrase *God only begotten* (μονογενὴς θεός) is found from very early times in Greek writers of every school. By Clement, Irenæus, and Origen it is connected with this passage. [The Latin writers, almost without exception, have *unicus* or *unigenitus filius*.]

2. It is very unlikely that a phrase in itself most remarkable should have obtained universal and unquestioned currency among Greek writers if it were not derived from apostolic usage.

It may further be added that the Valentinian writers, the earliest writers by whom the text is quoted, could have had no reason for introducing the reading *God only begotten*, which they give. While on the other hand the substitution of *the only begotten Son* for *God only begotten* is not unlike the style of "Western" paraphrase (*e.g.* *vv.* 4, 34; Mark i. 20, vi. 36, 56, etc.; Luke xxiii. 35).

On the whole, therefore, the reading *God only begotten* must be accepted, because (1) it is the best attested by ancient authority; (2) it is the more intrinsically probable from its uniqueness; (3) it makes the origin of the alternative reading more intelligible.

An examination of the whole structure of the Prologue leads to the same conclusion. The phrase, which has grown foreign to our ears, though it was familiar to early Christian writers, gathers up the two thoughts of sonship and deity, which have been separately affirmed of the Word (vv. 14, 1).

The reading has been discussed in detail by Dr. E. Abbot (*Bibliotheca Sacra*, Oct. 1861 ; *Unitarian Review*, June, 1875) ; and by Dr. Hort (*Two Dissertations. . .*, Camb. 1875). The conclusion of Dr. Hort in favour of μονογενὴς θεός, after a full examination of Prof. Abbot's arguments for ὁ μονογενὴς υἱός, is pronounced by Prof. Harnack in an elaborate review of his essay in *Theol. Lit. Zeit.*, 1876, pp. 541 ff., to have been " established beyond contradiction."

24. All the most ancient MSS. (א*A*BC*, D is defective), with Origen (and *Memph.*) read ἀπεσταλμένοι ἦσαν in place of οἱ ἀπεστ. ἦσαν. This reading can be rendered either : *they had been sent from . . .* , or *certain had been sent from among . . .* Origen expressly distinguishes two missions, the first in *v.* 19, and the second here.

28. *Bethabara*] The great preponderance of authorities is in favour of the reading *Bethany*. Origen implies that a diversity of reading existed here in his time. " Almost all the copies," he says, " have *Bethany* ; but I am convinced that we ought to read *Bethabara*," which probably was the reading of the minority. His reasons are simply geographical ; and it is a striking fact that even his authority thus boldly exerted was unable to induce scribes to alter the reading which they found in their archetypes ; so that *Bethabara* still remains the reading only of a small minority. The oldest authority which gives *Bethabara* is *Syr. vt.*, but this very early

translation frequently admits glosses (see next note).

34. For the words *the Son of God* a group of authorities characteristically " Western " (see *v.* 4, note), א, *e*, *Syr. vt.*, Ambr., read *the chosen of God.* The two readings are combined curiously in several early Latin authorities (*electus Dei filius*).

42. There is no doubt that Ἰωάνου (אBL, *Lat. vt.*, *Memph.*) should be read for Ἰωνᾶ. Comp. xxi. 15, 16, 17. Both words are used as Greek representatives of יְהוֹחָנָן *Johanan.* Comp. 2 Kings xxv. 23 (LXX.).

51. The words ἀπ᾿ ἄρτι (*from henceforth*) must be omitted on the authority of the witnesses which preserve the purest ancient text (אBL, *Latt.*, *Memph.*, Orig.). They were probably added from Matt. xxvi. 64, where the words are undisturbed.

GENERAL IDEA OF THE PERSON AND WORK OF THE BAPTIST [1]

1. The work of Christ connected by all the Evangelists with that of the Baptist.

2. Connexion and contrast of the Old and New.

3. The testimony of Josephus : importance, significance, omissions.

4. The general view of St. John (i. 6 ff.).

[1] This note is the first section of an unfinished note on THE WITNESS OF THE BAPTIST. The scheme of the full note was apparently :

i. The position and work of the Baptist.
ii. Messianic expectations.
iii. The sign : the divine glory.
iv. (1) The Lamb of God ; (2) the Son of God ; (3) the Bridegroom ; (4) the title "the Christ" recognised (iii. 28). —A. W.

The Baptist was

5. the epitome: sacerdotal, ascetic, prophetical,
6. the interpreter : "Repent . . . kingdom of God,"
7. the close of the Old.
8. The significance of his baptism : socially, personally.
9. The work of John preparatory.
10. The Lord's judgement upon him.
11. The new Elijah.
12. He accepts eclipse, iii. 27—30.

1. All the Evangelists agree in definitely connecting the New Dispensation with the Old. Their account of the work and witness of the Lord is preceded by an account of the work and witness of a herald. The beginning of the Gospel of Jesus Christ is, in the language of St. Mark, the mission of John the Baptist. And all the Evangelists see in John the fulfilment of the prophecy which spoke of one who should prepare the way for the triumphal advent of Jehovah (Isa. xl. 3, 4 ; Matt. iii. 3 ; Mark i. 3 ; Luke iii. 4 [most fully]; John i. 23 [as used by John himself]).

2. The fact is full of significance. Not only does it present Christianity as the accomplishment of the promises of Judaism, but it also offers the best results of Judaism itself in a striking form (John v. 35). The contrast between John and Christ, which was keenly felt at the time (Matt. xi. 16 ff. ; Luke vii. 31 ff.), was in fact the contrast between the Old and the New, between that which had a natural origin in the circumstances of the time

and that which was a new creation. John could be recognised as a product of the old faith, and therefore he had a wide, if transient, welcome, and found a place in the history of Josephus. Christ stood in another region : only those who were "born anew" could "see the kingdom of God" (John iii. 3).

3. The notice of the Baptist in Josephus is of deep interest, both from what it says and from what it does not say. The historian has related the disastrous failure of Herod's expedition against Aretas (*Ant.* XVIII. v. 1). He then continues (§ 2):

"Some of the Jews thought that Herod's army was destroyed by the action of God, as a most just punishment for the death of John, who was surnamed the Baptist. For Herod put John (τοῦτον) to death, a good man, and one who bade (κελεύοντα) the Jews to practise virtue and follow justice towards one another and piety towards God (τῇ πρὸς ἀλλ. δικαι. καὶ πρὸς τὸν θ. εὐσεβείᾳ χρωμένος), and so to accept baptism (βαπτισμῷ συνιέναι). For [he said] that thus the act of baptism (βάπτισιν) itself would appear acceptable to Him [God], if they adopted it (χρωμένων), not to escape the consequences of any sins (ἐπί τινων ἁμαρτάδων παραιτήσει), but to obtain purity of body, on the supposition of course (ἅτε δή) that the soul also had been previously purified by righteousness. And when the rest [of the Jews who did not submit to baptism] were banding together — for they were very greatly excited (ἤρθησαν) by hearing his words—Herod feared lest his singular power of influencing men shown in this way (τὸ ἐπὶ τοσόνδε πιθανὸν αὐτοῦ τοῖς ἀνθρώποις) might issue in some form of revolt, for the people seemed likely to do anything at his [John's] counsel. He therefore thought it better to adopt precautionary measures (προλαβών) before any revolutionary movement took rise from him, than to have cause for repenting if an insurrection (μεταβολῆς) broke out, and he fell into trouble. So John was sent a prisoner to Machærus through Herod's suspicion, and put to death there; and the Jews thought that ruin befel the host in vengeance for him, since God was displeased with Herod."

Several points in this passage deserve attention. Josephus writes with a view to Gentile readers. He dwells characteristically on the moral and practical aspect of John's teaching — on its breadth and earnestness— and leaves its spiritual bearings in the background. He says nothing directly of the call to repentance, or of the proclamation of a kingdom of heaven. Yet his account is unintelligible till these elements in his preaching are recognised. When he points out that his baptism was not a magical lustration, but the sign and seal of an inward change; that it marked the consecration of the whole man to righteousness and piety, whereby the cleansed body was to be made the organ of a purified soul; that the bond of his society was not fanatical devotion to national independence, as with Judas of Galilee (*Ant.* XVIII. i. 6), but the resolute fulfilment of duty to God and man; he really writes out at length John's appeal for a complete change in the religious attitude and temper of his hearers. And so again the consequences which he attributes to the preaching, the widespread excitement beyond the circle of the Baptist's immediate followers, the apprehension of political risings, imply that John must have stirred expectations wholly different from those of personal reformation. There is an obvious break between the cause and the effect. And here the Gospels supply exactly what is required to explain the apparent inconsequence in the account of Josephus. All is clear when we introduce the announcement of "the One stronger," of "the coming kingdom," which suggested to the people hopes answering to their desires.

4. So the Baptist appeared to the Jewish historian writing for Gentiles.

To St. John he appears as the sufficient representative of all the Old Dispensation (John i. 6 ff., v. 33).

It is therefore necessary to understand the position of the Baptist in order to understand the position of Christ. In John, as has been said, we can see what Judaism was able to do: in Christ, what was further required to satisfy the wants which Judaism laid open. John's work, wrought "in the way of righteousness" [Matt. xxi. 32; cf. Luke xi. 1 (prayer); Matt. ix. 14 (fasting); John x. 41 (no sign)], carried its immediate justification with it. The worst condemnation of the Pharisees lay in the fact that when they "saw" the results of his teaching they did not repent (Luke vii. 29 f.).

5. John was the epitome of the Old. Judaism as a religion had three distinct manifestations: sacerdotal, ascetic, and prophetical. Of these two were effectively represented in the apostolic age by the Pharisees and the Essenes. Prophecy, as a power, was a thing of the past. But John united all three in his own person. By birth he was a priest (Luke i. 5), by divine appointment he was a Nazarite (Luke i. 15), by calling he was a prophet (Luke iii. 2, ἐγέν. ῥ. θ. ἐπί; cf. 1 Kings xvii. 2, ἐγ. ῥ. Κ. πρός (Elijah); Jer. i. 2). The combination is most remarkable; and perhaps it helps to explain his wide though short-lived influence with the hierarchy (John v. 33; cf. Matt. xxi. 25 and ‖[s]) no less than with the common people.

6. John was also the interpreter of the Old. His simple message, *Repent, for the kingdom of heaven is at hand*, gives the twofold lesson of the preparatory teaching of the people of God.[1] "Repent": that is to say, change your whole manner of thinking of God, the world, and man—the Law has failed as a guide to life, but it has been effectual to convince of sin. "The kingdom of heaven is at hand": that is to say, the prophets have pointed to a glorious future which shall now be realised. On the one side moral claims are urged with fresh intensity, on the other side

[1] Peculiar to St. Matt. iii. 2. In Mark i. 4, Luke iii. 3, βάπτισμα μετανοίας εἰς ἄφεσιν ἁμαρτιῶν; comp. Acts xiii. 24, xix. 4 (β. μ.). The phrase β. μ. is preserved in Just. *Dial.* § 88 ; Evang. Eb. (Epiph. *Hær.* xxx. 13 f.). (Μεταν., and this aspect of John's mission not in St. John : he dwells on his relation to Christ.)

the divine promises are brought forward with renewed confidence. Man's effort has been shown to be unavailing : God's gift is provided to compensate for the failure. As John looks back he sees only cause for self-abasement : as he looks forward he sees that Advent of the Lord which shall at once purify and quicken.

7. As John interpreted the Old, he also marked the close of it. His preaching foreshowed the cessation of the exclusive privilege of Israel. The judgement which he announced was to be executed according to actions and not according to race. The same words were spoken to the multitudes (Luke iii. 7 ff.), and to the Pharisees and Sadducees (Matt. iii. 7 ff.). Outward descent from Abraham, which was the common boast of the people, was of no avail to them. In this way John claimed for himself no more than a transitional work (Luke iii. 15 f.). His baptism in water was to be followed by a baptism in the Holy Ghost and in fire (Matt., Luke, *not* Mark); cf. Acts xi. 16. Cf. Acts i. 22 (x. 37, xiii. 24 f.), Luke xvi. 16, "The law and the prophets until John" (cf. Matt. xi. 12).

8. Under this aspect the baptism of John—a baptism of repentance — appointed by God (John i. 33) is shown in its true light. The Jews rightly felt that to administer it was to claim extraordinary power (John i. 25). The rite had a social and a personal meaning. Socially it placed the Israelite in the position of the Gentile proselyte. He too had to lay aside his special prerogatives and submit

to the acknowledgement of his uncleanness. The idea of uncleanness remains whether the custom of baptizing the proselytes was ancient or not. He too had to seek a new dedication. Another tribe of Levi, so to speak, had to be set apart for a spiritual office by another sprinkling of water (Numbers viii. 7). Personally again it brought sin home to the individual conscience. Confession became a preparation for the Divine Presence. For those only who are cleansed could the Day of the Lord rise with a blessing. In the sight of widespread corruption, therefore, the message of John was mainly of "the wrath to come" (Matt. iii. 7; Luke iii. 7; cf. Luke xxi. 23; 1 Thess. i. 10; Rom. v. 9 (τῆς ὀρ.), ii. 5; Eph. v. 6; Apoc. vi. 16, 17). But even so chastisement is one function of love, and St. Luke, who dwells most fully on the severe side of the Baptist's preaching, alone describes his tidings as a "gospel" (Luke iii. 18).[1]

9. The work of the Baptist was therefore preparatory. While he closed the Old he pointed distinctly to a personal beginning afterwards, to "One stronger" than himself, and not simply to a fuller doctrine. The first description of his Successor which he gave was expressed in general terms, but it was sufficient to mark Him as the ful-

filler of prophecy (ὁ ἐρχ., ὁ ἰσχ.), as One immeasurably raised above His forerunner, who was not worthy even to be His slave— One commissioned to dispense the highest gift of God. After the Baptism[1] of Jesus, John's language became more explicit, and he foreshadowed the twofold dignity of Christ as Son of man and Son of God (John i. 29, 34). But from first to last he presented himself as the herald of an immediate revelation, as "a prophet, and more than a prophet."

10. For what has been already said enables us to enter into the meaning of the judgement which the Lord pronounced upon John (Matt. xi. 7 ff.; Luke vii. 24 ff. (not Mark)). John was not, if in some sense the growth of the desert, a mere reed swayed to and fro by gusts of feeling, without a steady moral purpose. He was not, if in some sense the herald of the Great King, a mere courtier, arrayed according to the fashion of the times. He was the last and greatest representative of that order which was to pass away. He was a prophet, for his thoughts were fixed upon the eternal not yet recognised. He was more than a prophet, for prophets (1 Pet. i. 10; John i. 34) looked forward to a future which was still far off, but he had seen their hope realised.[2] Like Moses and Elijah (Exod. xxxiii. 11; 1 Kings xix. 9 ff.), and with a more abiding vision, he had spoken with the Lord "face to face." He refused

---

[1] The Baptism of the Lord answers to the Circumcision, presents the real assumption of humanity, with all its consequences (2 Cor. v. 21). He is made a new priest, and men in Him are consecrated anew (Exod. xxix. 4, xl. 12; Lev. viii. 6; Heb. x. 22).

[1] Note the importance of this crisis for the explanation of St. John.

[2] Hi futurum, hic præsentem; Hi venturum, venientem Monstrat iste filium.

the title of Elijah (John i. 21),
and yet he was Elijah. He fulfilled in one form the promise of
Malachi, but he pointed forward
by the mode of the fulfilment
to Another, of whom he was the
image (Matt. xvii. 11, ἔρχεται κ.
ἀποκατα.). Among those " born
of women" there was none
greater; but the least in the
kingdom of heaven was greater
than he (John i. 12 f.). A
spiritual birth, not of flesh or
of blood, gave a life essentially
higher than the highest life of
earth (comp. John iii. 31). The
actual enjoyment of the divine
gift, even in the humblest measure, was more than the clearest
prospect of its glory afar off.

11. John was and was not
Elijah. Popular expectation
looked for a literal return of
Elijah (Matt. xvii. 10; cf. xvi.
14); but the Evangelists, while
they dwell on the traits of resemblance in appearance and
teaching, make it clear that the
mission of the old prophet was
renewed " in spirit and power"
and not in a personal presence
(Luke i. 17; cf. Matt. xi. 14
(Mark)).

But at the same time this
identification of John the Baptist with Elijah, in respect of
the general character of his
work, gave a peculiar force to
his denunciations of coming
judgement. It was almost necessary that he should look for
some signal manifestation of
divine power. There was much in
the history of Israel to encourage
the expectation of the establishment of a kingdom through
avenging might. His natural
ideal of Messiah could not but
include a triumphal vindication
of God's righteousness. In this

connexion we can understand
the full intensity of the Temptation of the Lord. The whole
current of popular feeling was
towards some signal effort
through which the King of Israel should make Himself known.
Once again, therefore, the lesson
had to be learnt, not without
suffering, that the Lord was not
in the earthquake or the fire,
but in the still, small voice. For
the time the Baptist learnt it.
The revelation by which he recognised in the Christ "the
Lamb of God" opened to him
the true vision of the divine
way. But it can cause little
surprise if, in the solitude of his
prison, he seemed to think that
the Christ lingered in the fulfilment of His work (Matt.
xi. 2 ff.).

And here again it is not
fanciful to see an identity of
natural temperament in the two
great preachers of a religious re-
vival. John was like Elijah, not
only in his manner of life and in
his power of moral awakening,
but also in his weakness. The
same stern nature in each, concentrated upon the sight of triumphant evil, seems to have given
way to momentary doubt or misgiving when the issue for which
they looked appeared to tarry.
There is a pathos of supplication
and a call to decisive action in
the words *Art thou he that
cometh, or look we for another?*
The herald was sure that the
Christ whose works he recognised
must fulfil the spiritual ideal
which he had seen; and yet Jesus
seemed outwardly to shrink from
the assertion of His power. In
this light we come to understand
the full meaning of the crowning
sign of His work which the

Lord gave: *the poor have glad tidings preached to them.*

12. One further remark must be made upon the work of John. He remained to the end constant in his own place. He directed his disciples to Christ (John i. 35), but he did not become Christ's disciple himself. He accepted the divine sentence which gave him a subordinate office, and regarded with joy the certainty of his own eclipse (John iii. 30). The example has a permanent importance both for men and for churches. It is not in every case a duty to press upon others or to hasten to accept the fullest confession of the Truth. Each church, each nation, each believer has an appropriate charge, in one case complete and final, in another imperfect and preparatory. But whatever the charge may be, to recognise it and to keep to it is the truest fulfilment of the divine will.

THE SON OF MAN

1. The title "the Son of man" stands in significant contrast with the other titles which are assigned to the Lord, and particularly with that title which in some respects is most akin to it, "the Son of David." It was essentially a new title; it was used, so far as we know, with one exception only, by the Lord and of Himself; it expresses a relationship not to a family or to a nation, but to all humanity.

2. The title was a new one. It is common to regard it as directly derived from the Book of Daniel. But in reality the passage (vii. 13) in which the title is supposed to be found has only a secondary relation to it.

The vision of Daniel brings before him not "the Son of man," but one "like a son of man." The phrase is general (Ezek. ii. 1), and is introduced by a particle of comparison. The Greek represents the original exactly: ὡς υἱὸς ἀνθρώπου ἐρχόμενος ἦν, and the true parallel is found in Rev. i. 13, xiv. 14. The thought on which the seer dwells is simply that of the human appearance of the being presented to him (comp. Dan. x. 16; Ezek. i. 26). The force of this comparison comes out more plainly if the context be taken into account. The divine kingdom is being contrasted with the kingdoms of the world. These are presented under the images of beasts. The brute forces symbolised them, just as man, to whom originally dominion was given, symbolised the rightful sovereignty which was to be established. "I saw," the seer writes, "in my vision by night . . . and four great beasts came up from the sea. The first was like a lion, . . . and . . . a second . . . like a bear, . . . and lo another like a leopard. . . . I saw in the night visions, and behold one like a son of man came with the clouds of heaven. . . ." (vii. 2 ff.). The dominion which had been exercised by tyrants was henceforward to be entrusted to "the saints of the Most High" (vii. 17 f., 27). The former rulers had come forth from the sea— the symbol of all confusion and instability—the divine ruler came from heaven.

3. It is true that the image of Daniel found fulfilment in the sovereignty of Christ, and so the words of the seer, with the substitution of "the Son of man"

for " one like a son of man," were applied by the Lord to Himself (Matt. xvi. 27, xxiv. 30, xxvi. 64). But He was not only " like a son of man," He was " the Son of man." The less is of necessity included in the greater ; but in itself the language of Daniel furnishes no parallel to the language of the Gospels.

4. The same may be said of all the other passages in which the phrases " the sons of men " or " son of man " occur in the Old Testament. They describe man as dependent, limited, transitory. The singular, except in Ezekiel, as addressed to the prophet, is of rare occurrence ; and (as I believe) it is never found with the article (*e.g.* Ps. viii. 5, lxxx. 17).

5. But there can be no doubt that the image in Daniel exercised some influence upon later apocalyptic writings. The remarkable use of the title " Son of man " in reference to the Messiah in the Book of Henoch is directly based upon it. The sense of the title, however, remains equally limited as before. The Messiah is " a Son of man," and not properly " the Son of man " (c. 46, §§ 1, 2, 3, 4 ; c. 48, § 2). In these places the chosen messenger of the Most High is described simply as a man, and not as one who stands in any special relation to the human race.

6. There is very little in the Gospels to show how far the fuller applications of the title found in the Apocalypse of Henoch obtained currency, or how the people commonly understood the title. There is at least nothing to show that the title

was understood to be a title of the Messiah. On the contrary, " the Son of man " and " the Messiah " are, as it were, set one against the other, Matt. xvi. 13, 16 (the parallels, Mark viii. 27, Luke ix. 18, give simply *me*) ; John xii. 34. And it is inconceivable that the Lord should have adopted a title which was popularly held to be synonymous with that of Messiah, while He carefully avoided the title of Messiah itself.

7. The title, then, as we find it in the Gospels, *the Son of man* absolutely, was a new one. It is out of the question to suppose that the definite article simply expressed " the prophetic Son of man." The manner in which the title is first used excludes such an interpretation. The title is new, and the limits within which its usage is confined serve to fix attention on its peculiarity. In the Gospels it is used only by the Lord in speaking of Himself ; and beyond the range of His discourses it is found only in Acts vii. 56.

8. In the Lord's discourses the title is distributed generally. It is found both in the earlier and in the later discourses in about equal proportions. It is not, however, found in the discourses after the Resurrection. The title occurs many times in St. John's Gospel, but less frequently than in the other three ; and in the last discourses which St. John gives at length it occurs only once, in the opening sentence, xiii. 31. [In St. Matthew 30 times ; in St. Mark 13 ; in St. Luke 25 ; in St. John 12.]

9. The passages in which the title is found in the Synoptic Gospels may be grouped into two

great classes: (1) Those which refer to the earthly work of the Lord in the time of His humility; and (2) those which refer to His future coming in glory. The usage in St. John is strictly parallel, but the occurrence of the title in his Gospel will be considered more in detail on ix. 35.

(1) The earthly presence of the Lord as the Incarnate Son presented a series of startling contrasts. (a) He was to outward eyes despised, and yet possessing supreme authority; (β) He lived as men live, and yet He was at all times busy with His Father's work; (γ) His true nature was veiled, and yet not wholly hidden; (δ) His mission was a mission of love, and yet it imposed on those to whom He came heavy responsibility; (ε) to misinterpret Him was to incur judgement, and yet the offence was not past forgiveness; (ζ) He foresaw the end from the beginning, with its sorrows and glory.

The following passages in which the title occurs illustrate these different thoughts:

(a) Matt. viii. 20 ‖ Luke ix. 58. Matt. ix. 6 ‖ Mark ii. 10 ‖ Luke v. 24.

(β) Matt. xi. 19 ‖ Luke vii. 34. Matt. xiii. 37. Matt. xii. 8 ‖ Mark ii. 28 ‖ Luke vi. 5.

(γ) Matt. xvi. 13.

(δ) Luke xix. 10, xvii. 22.

(ε) Mark viii. 38 ‖ Luke ix. 26. Comp. Luke xii. 8. Matt. xii. 32 ‖ Luke xii. 10. (Mark iii. 28, τοῖς υἱ. τῶν ἀνθρ.).

(ζ) Mark viii. 31 ‖ Luke ix. 22. Comp. xxiv. 7. Matt. xvii. 12 ‖ Mark ix. 12. Matt. xvii. 22 ‖ Mark ix. 31 ‖ Luke ix. 44. Matt. xx. 18 ‖ Mark x. 33 ‖ Luke xviii. 31. Matt. xxvi. 2.

Matt. xxvi. 24 ‖ Mark xiv. 21 ‖ Luke xxii. 22. Matt. xxvi. 45 ‖ Mark xiv. 41. Matt. xii. 40 ‖ Luke xi. 30. Matt. xvii. 9 ‖ Mark ix. 9. Matt. xx. 28 ‖ Mark x. 45. Luke xxii. 69 (ἀπὸ τοῦ νῦν). Matt. xxvi. 64 (ἀπ' ἄρτι) ‖ Mark xiv. 62. Luke xxii. 48.

(2) Side by side with these traits of the human life of the Son of man, visions are opened of another life of glory, sovereignty, judgement. (a) Though He had come, yet He still spoke of His coming as future. (β) Meanwhile men are left on their trial, to which an end is appointed in a swift and unexpected catastrophe. This "presence" of the Son of man at "the consummation of the age" is to be followed by a (γ) judgement of men and nations, and (δ) by the gathering of the elect into a divine kingdom.

These thoughts are illustrated by the following passages in which the title occurs:

(a) Matt. x. 23, xvi. 27 f., xxiv. 44. Comp. Luke xii. 40.

(β) Luke vi. 22, xvii. 30, xviii. 8, xxi. 36; Matt. xxiv. 27, 37 (comp. Luke xvii. 24, 26), 39.

(γ) Matt. xiii. 40 f., xix. 28, xxv. 31 ff., Matt. xxiv. 30 ‖ Mark xiii. 26 ‖ Luke xxi. 27.

10. A consideration of these passages will enable us to seize the outlines of the teaching which is summed up in the title. The idea of the true humanity of Christ lies at the foundation of it. He was not only "like a son of man," but He was "a Son of man": His manhood was real and not apparent. But He was not as one man among many (yet the title ἄνθρωπος occurs John viii. 40, 1 Tim. ii. 5). He was the representative of the whole race: "*the* Son of man '

in whom all the potential powers of humanity were gathered.

11. Thus the expression which describes the self-humiliation of Christ raises Him at the same time immeasurably above all those whose nature He had assumed. Of no one, simply man, could it be said that he was " the man," or " the Son of man," in whom the complete conception of manhood was absolutely attained.

12. The teaching of St. Paul supplies a striking commentary upon the title when he speaks of Christ as the " second Adam " (1 Cor. xv. 45; comp. Rom. v. 14), who gathers up into Himself all humanity, and becomes the source of a higher life to the race.

13. As a necessary conclusion from this view of Christ's humanity which is given in the title "the Son of man," it follows that He is in perfect sympathy with every man of every age and of every nation. All that truly belongs to humanity—all therefore that truly belongs to every individual in the whole race— belongs also to Him. (Compare a noble passage in Goldwin Smith's *Lectures on History*, pp. 134 ff.)

14. The thought is carried yet further. We are allowed to see, and it can only be as it were " by a mirror in a riddle " (1 Cor. xiii. 12), that the relation which exists in the present order of things between every man and Christ, is continued in another order. As " the Son of man " He is revealed to the eyes of His first martyr, that Christians may learn that that which is begun in weakness shall be completed in eternal majesty (Acts vii. 56).

15. It may well be admitted that the early disciples did not at first apprehend all that the later history of the race enables us to see in the title. Perhaps it may have been from some sense of the mysterious meaning of the term, which had not yet been illuminated by the light of a Catholic Church, that they shrank themselves from using it. But we cannot be bound to measure the interpretation of Scripture by that which is at once intelligible. The words of the Lord are addressed to all time. They stand written for our study, and it is our duty to bring to their interpretation whatever fulness of knowledge a later age may have placed within our reach.

THE TESTIMONY OF THE BAPTIST
(i. 19—34)

In comparing this section with the corresponding passage in the Synoptists, we notice:

1. The Baptism and Temptation must precede *v.* 19. John knew Jesus as Messiah (*v.* 26), of which he was first assured at His Baptism (*v.* 33). And the succession of time (29, 35) leaves no interval for the Temptation, of which the Baptist would naturally have no knowledge. It is probable that *v.* 29 marks the return of the Lord from the Temptation.

2. The testimony of John given in the Synoptists belongs to the time before the Baptism, and is addressed to a popular audience: that in St. John, to special messengers (as it seems) from the Sanhedrin, and to the immediate disciples of the Baptist. The substance of the testimonies corresponds to these differences

of circumstances. The former is general, and combined with the idea of judgement; the latter is carefully defined with regard to current belief, and stimulative to faith. Moreover, the testimony recorded by St. John distinctly refers to the earlier testimony (v. 30).

3. The particularity and exactness of St. John's narrative, preserving the exact marks of time, and place, and look, and position, mark the work of an eye-witness.

4. The testimony of John, which was the first recognition and the first manifestation of Christ, is the natural beginning of St. John's Gospel, whose design is to give the historic development of faith and unbelief. Comp. xx. 31. In this incident faith in Christ was first shown and first tried. The testimony of John was a word of inspiration answering to the faith which regarded outward facts in a divine light.

5. The descent of the Holy Spirit upon Christ at His Baptism is presented by St. John simply as an objective sign to the Baptist. He does not speak of any communication of the Holy Spirit to Christ. The " abiding " is part of the sign, the completion of the " descent." By a comparison of the other Gospels we see that the manifestation was a sign to Christ also as well as to the Baptist; just as the words which contained the divine revelation (*My beloved Son*) were heard in their twofold application, as addressed to others, *This is my beloved Son* (Matt.), and as addressed to the Lord, *Thou art my beloved Son* (Mark, Luke). To the Baptist the sign showed that his work

was consummated by the open advent of Him whose way he was himself sent to prepare : to Christ, that the hour of His public ministry was come, a ministry commenced by an act of self-humiliation. At the same time we cannot but believe (so far as we realise the perfect humanity of Christ) that Christ at this crisis first became conscious as man of a power of the Spirit within Him corresponding to the new form of His work. See v. 33, note.

For the rest it will be seen that the narratives of this event lend no support to the Ebionitic view that the Holy Spirit was first imparted to Christ at His Baptism ; or to the Gnostic view that the Logos was then united to the man Jesus. And at the same time this event enables us to apprehend the different spheres of the Word and of the Spirit. By the Word God is revealed objectively to man : by the Spirit man is subjectively brought into fellowship with God. We could not, without destroying the essential ideal of the Christian Faith, suppose either that the spirit was made flesh or that the Word descended upon Christ.

THE CONFESSIONS OF CHRIST IN ST. JOHN'S GOSPEL [1]

We are all familiar with the broad fact that the Gospel of St. John brings before us a vivid picture of the growth of spiritual life, of the parallel development of faith and unbelief in the presence of Christ, of the Light and

[1] This is a fragment from a course of lectures delivered at Cambridge in the Lent Term of 1885, and in Westminster Abbey, 1887.—A. W.

its witness. The Evangelist selects out of the vast mass of the materials which were at his command such incidents as he judged most fitting to produce in his readers the conviction that "*Jesus is the Christ, the Son of God*" (xx. 30 f.). In this respect the experience of the first disciples is typical for later times. Humanity remains essentially the same. If then we can trace the successive stages through which true knowledge as to Christ was once gained and expressed, we shall have a lesson for ourselves. By observing such traces of a "natural" progress as may be disclosed, we shall gain a clue to the method by which divine mysteries are revealed to men and appropriated by them.

This then is what I desire to do in one limited field. We find in the Gospel of St. John a series of passages in which those who came into contact with Christ declare what they had learnt as to His Nature.

I shall endeavour, therefore, to examine these confessions as far as possible in their original aspect: to see what they meant for those who were first moved to utter them, and only afterwards what they mean for us: to watch, as it were, the dawn brightening into the noontide in which we live.

In pursuing such an inquiry we are dealing with that which nearly concerns ourselves.

No one, I believe, who seeks to give historical reality to his Creed can fail to ask himself, not without some anxiety, how the full faith as to Christ's Person was gained by those who companied with Him ; how those who had followed Him in His earthly wanderings rose to the conviction that in Him *the Word, through whom all things were made*, was indeed Incarnate. St. John, looking back from the midst of the Christian Church, which he had seen grow round him to its mature independence, to the life which he had known in his early manhood, in part answers the question. This answer we have to examine.

Successive confessions.

I. The Baptist :
> The Lamb of God: i. 29, 37.
> The Son of God : i. 34.
> The Bridegroom : iii. 29 f.
> The First Disciples :
> The Messiah : i. 41. He of whom Moses and the prophets wrote : i. 45.
> The Son of God : i. 49.
> The King of Israel : i. 49.

II. Nicodemus :
> A teacher come from God : iii. 2.
> Samaritans :
> The Christ: iv. 26, 29.
> The Saviour of the world : iv. 42.
> The Multitude :
> The prophet which should come into the world : vi. 14.
> Simon Peter :
> The holy One of God : vi. 69.
> The blind man :
> The Son of man : ix. 35, 38.
> Martha :
> The Christ, the Son of God, that cometh into the world : xi. 27.
> The Multitudes :
> He that cometh.
> The King of Israel.
> The earliest confessions repeated after the trial of manifold experience.
> The Apostles : xvi. 25—33.

III. The Triumph :
> St. Thomas : xx. 24—31.

2 Καὶ τῇ ἡμέρᾳ τῇ τρίτῃ γάμος ἐγένετο ἐν Κανὰ τῆς
2 Γαλιλαίας, καὶ ἦν ἡ μήτηρ τοῦ Ἰησοῦ ἐκεῖ· ἐκλήθη δὲ
3 καὶ ὁ Ἰησοῦς καὶ οἱ μαθηταὶ αὐτοῦ εἰς τὸν γάμον. καὶ
ὑστερήσαντος¹ οἴνου λέγει ἡ μήτηρ τοῦ Ἰησοῦ πρὸς αὐτόν

¹ ὑστερήσαντος οἴνου ℵªABLXΓΔ; οἴνον οὐκ εἶχον ὅτι συνετελέσθη ὁ οἴνος
τοῦ γάμου· εἶτα ℵ*.

3. THE TESTIMONY OF SIGNS (ii. 1—11).

The manifestation of the glory of Christ (ii. 11) follows naturally upon the recognition of His claims in virtue of testimony and experience. He shows by a significant sign, spontaneously offered in the presence of an acknowledged want and significant only to disciples (v. 11), the nature of the new order which He has already described (i. 51). He has been announced, and followed; He is now believed in. The scene still lies in the circle of the family, and not among "the people" or in "the world."

The narrative proceeds in a simple and exact sequence. The Evangelist describes the time and scene (vv. 1, 2), the occasion (vv. 3—5), the manner (vv. 6—8), the result (vv. 9, 10), and the effect (v. 11) of Christ's first sign.

CHAP. II. 1, 2. The details of time, place, and persons contribute to the meaning of "the beginning of signs." It was shown in close connexion with the faith of the first disciples (the third day), at the village where one at least of them dwelt (xxi. 2), at a festival of the highest natural joy.

1. τῇ ἡμέρᾳ τῇ τρίτῃ] the third day, i.e. from the last day mentioned, i. 43. The distance from the place where John was baptizing to Nazareth was about sixty miles, three days' journey.

γάμος ἐγένετο] nuptiæ factæ sunt v.; there was a marriage or a marriage feast. Such a feast was frequently celebrated for several (seven) days, Gen. xxix. 22 ff.; Judges xiv. 12. It is wholly unknown in whose honour the feast was held.

Κανὰ τ. Γαλ.] Cana of Galilee, so called each time when it is mentioned in the Gospel, to distinguish it from a Cana in Cœlo-Syria (Jos. Ant. xv. v. 1, etc.). This village is mentioned in the N. T. (comp. Jos. Vita, § 16) only by St. John here and iv. 46, xxi. 2. It has been traditionally identified (from the eighth century) with Kefr Kenna, about 4½ miles north-west of Nazareth. Recently the site has been sought at a village about nine miles north of Nazareth, Khurbet-Cana, which is said (though this is doubtful) to have retained the name Kana-el-Jelil. The Syriac versions agree in inserting a -t- in the name (Katna). This may point to local knowledge; and it has been conjectured that Kana may be identified with Katana, a place about four miles from Nazareth.

2 And the third day there was a marriage[1] in Cana
2 of Galilee; and the mother of Jesus was there: and
Jesus also was bidden, and his disciples, to the
3 marriage. And when the wine failed, the mother

[1] *or a marriage feast.*

ἡ μήτηρ τ. Ἰησ.] In St. John
alone the name of "the mother
of Jesus" is not mentioned, even
when Joseph is named (vi. 42).
Comp. xix. 25 ff., note.

ἦν . . . ἐκεῖ] *was there.* From
v. 5 it is evident that the Virgin
Mary was closely connected with
the family; and so she was already at the house when Jesus
arrived at Cana with His disciples.
The absence of all mention of
Joseph here and elsewhere (see
xix. 27) has been reasonably
supposed to imply that he was
already dead. See Mark vi. 3,
note.

2. ἐκλήθη δὲ καὶ ὁ Ἰησ. καί . . .]
vocatus est autem et Jesus et . . .
v.; *and Jesus also was bidden,
and . . .* (iii. 23, xviii. 2, 5, xix.
39).

ἐκλήθη] *was bidden, i.e.* on His
return from the Baptist, and not
had been bidden.

οἱ μαθ. αὐτ.] *his disciples.* This
is the first distinct mention of
the relation in which the little
group gathered from "the disciples of John" (i. 35, 37) now
stood to the greater Teacher
("Rabbi," i. 49).

3—5. The depth, obscurity,
and (at the same time) naturalness of this conversation witness
to the substantial truth of the
record. The words only become
intelligible when the exact re-

lation between the mother of
Jesus and her divine Son is
apprehended. As soon as this is
grasped the implied request, the
apparent denial, the persistence
of trust, the triumph of faith,
are seen to hang harmoniously
together.

3. ὑστερή. οἴνου] *deficiente vino*
v.; *when the wine failed*, as it
might be expected to do from
the unexpected addition of seven
guests to the party already
gathered. The fact that the
arrival of Jesus had brought the
difficulty, made it more natural
to apply to Him for the removal
of it. There is a Jewish saying,
"Without wine there is no joy"
(*Pesachim*, 109 *a*, Wünsche), and
the failure of the wine at a
marriage feast would be most
keenly felt. The reading of
some early authorities (‭א‬* and
copies of *Lat. vt.*) is a remarkable example of the paraphrases
which are characteristic of the
"Western" text: οἶνον οὐκ εἶχον,
ὅτι συνετελέσθη ὁ οἶνος τοῦ γάμου.

Οἶν. οὐκ ἔχ.] *They have no wine.*
It is enough to state the want.
To describe the circumstance is
in such a case to express a silent
prayer. Compare xi. 3, and
contrast that passage with iv. 47.

The Mother of the Lord
having heard of the testimony

6

4 Οἶνον οὐκ ἔχουσιν. καὶ¹ λέγει αὐτῇ ὁ Ἰησοῦς Τί ἐμοὶ
5 καὶ σοί, γύναι ; οὔπω ἥκει ἡ ὥρα μου. λέγει ἡ μήτηρ
6 αὐτοῦ τοῖς διακόνοις Ὅτι ἂν λέγῃ ὑμῖν ποιήσατε. ἦσαν
δὲ ἐκεῖ λίθιναι ὑδρίαι ἓξ κατὰ τὸν καθαρισμὸν τῶν
Ἰουδαίων κείμεναι, χωροῦσαι ἀνὰ μετρητὰς δύο ἢ τρεῖς.

¹ Omit καί Ν*ΕΓΓ.

of the Baptist, and seeing the disciples gathered round her Son, the circumstances of whose miraculous birth she treasured in her heart (Luke ii. 19, 51), must have looked now at length for the manifestation of His power, and thought that an occasion only was wanting. Yet even so she leaves all to His will. Contrast Luke ii. 48.

4. καὶ λέγει . . .] *and Jesus saith.* These two clauses are joined together closely, just as *vv.* 7, 8, while *vv.* 5 and 7 are not connected with what immediately precedes.

Note that here γύναι stands last. It is otherwise in xix. 26. Here the contrast comes first ; there the personality.

γύναι] *mulier* v. ; *woman.* In the original there is not the least tinge of reproof or severity in the term. The address is that of courteous respect, even of tenderness. See xix. 26. Comp. iv. 21, xx. 13, 15. At the same time it emphasises the special relation which it expresses ; as here the contrast between the divine Son and the human Mother.

Τί ἐμοὶ καὶ σοί;] *Quid mihi et tibi est?* v. ; *What have I to do with thee?* or, *What hast thou to do with me?* Literally, *What is there to me and thee?* "Leave me to myself ; let me follow out my own course." The phrase

occurs not infrequently in the Old Testament, 2 Sam. xvi. 10 ; 1 Kings xvii. 18 ; 2 Chron. xxxv. 21 (Judges xi. 12). It is found also in the New Testament : Matt. viii. 29, and parallels. Comp. Matt. xxvii. 19. Everywhere it marks some divergence between the thoughts and ways of the persons so brought together. In this passage it serves to show that the actions of the Son of God, now that He has entered on His divine work, are no longer dependent in any way on the suggestion of a woman, even though that woman be His Mother. Henceforth all He does springs from within, and will be wrought at its proper season. The time of silent discipline and obedience (Luke ii. 51) was over. Comp. Matt. xii. 46 ff.

οὔπω ἥκει ἡ ὥρα μου] *nondum venit hora mea* v. ; *mine hour is not yet come,* the due time for the fulfilment of my work. The words are here used of that part of Christ's work which was shown in the first revelation of His glory ; but more commonly they refer to the consummation of it in the Passion. See viii. 20, note, xvii. 1, note. Mary may have believed that the first manifestation of Christ would lead at once to full triumph ; and to that fancy the words are a pregnant answer,

⁴ of Jesus saith unto him, They have no wine. And Jesus saith unto her, Woman, what have I to do ⁵ with thee?¹ mine hour is not yet come. His mother saith unto the servants, Whatsoever he saith unto ⁶ you, do it. Now there were six waterpots of stone set there after the Jews' manner of purifying, con-

¹ *or* what hast thou to do with me?

There is no inconsistency between this declaration of Christ that " His hour was not yet come," and the fulfilment of the prayer which followed immediately. A change of moral and spiritual conditions is not measured by length of time. Comp. xiii. 1, note.

5. The Lord's reply left the faith which rests absolutely in Him unshaken. Nowhere else perhaps is such trust shown. Whether divine help was given through Him or not, so much at least could be provided, that if the right moment came—and it is impossible to use a temporal measure for moral changes—all should be ready for His action. *Whatsoever he saith unto you, do it;* the command is wholly unlimited : all is left to Christ.

6—8. The manner of working the miracle is described with singular minuteness and yet with singular reserve. The wine is found to be present ; the water shows the contents of the source from which it was drawn.

6. ἐκεῖ] *there*, in the court of the house, as it seems (*v.* 8), and not in the guest-chamber.

λίθ. ὑδρ. ἓξ] *lapideæ hydriæ sex* v.; *six waterpots of stone.* The large number would be required in consequence of the many guests assembled at the feast. They

were *of stone* — as our canon directs fonts to be—since that material is less liable to impurity. Vessels of stone or earthenware were prescribed by Jewish tradition for the washings before and after meals (*Sota,* 4, Wünsche). The " purifying" extended not only to the " washing of hands," but also to " the washing of cups and brasen vessels and couches" (Mark vii. 3, 4). For the washing of vessels, which were immersed and not only sprinkled, later tradition prescribed a receptacle holding " forty Sata," about five times as large as one of these.

Dr. E. D. Clarke gives a remarkable illustration of the passage : " . . . walking among these ruins [at Cana] we saw large, massy stone water-pots. . . not preserved nor exhibited as reliques, but lying about, disregarded by the present inhabitants . . . From their appearance and the number of them, it was quite evident that a practice of keeping water in large stone pots, each holding from eighteen to twenty-seven gallons, was once common in the country." (*Travels,* ii. p. 445, referred to by Van Lennep, *Bible Customs,* p. 45, note.)

τ. καθ. τ. Ἰουδ.] *the purifying of the Jews.* See *v.* 13. The words seem to contain an allusion

7 λέγει αὐτοῖς ὁ Ἰησοῦς Γεμίσατε τὰς ὑδρίας ὕδατος· Καὶ
8 ἐγέμισαν αὐτὰς ἕως ἄνω. καὶ λέγει αὐτοῖς Ἀντλήσατε
9 νῦν καὶ φέρετε τῷ ἀρχιτρικλίνῳ· οἱ δὲ ἤνεγκαν. ὡς δὲ
ἐγεύσατο ὁ ἀρχιτρίκλινος τὸ ὕδωρ οἶνον γεγενημένον,
καὶ οὐκ ᾔδει πόθεν ἐστίν, οἱ δὲ διάκονοι ᾔδεισαν οἱ
ἠντληκότες τὸ ὕδωρ, φωνεῖ τὸν νυμφίον ὁ ἀρχιτρίκλινος
10 καὶ λέγει αὐτῷ Πᾶς ἄνθρωπος πρῶτον τὸν καλὸν οἶνον
τίθησιν, καὶ ὅταν μεθυσθῶσιν τὸν ἐλάσσω· σὺ τετήρηκας

to a Christian purification. Comp.
iii. 25; Heb. i. 3; 2 Pet. i. 9.

μετρητ. δύο ἢ τρεῖς] *two or three
firkins apiece.* The μετρητής probably corresponds with the Bath,
which was equivalent to three
Sata (*measures*, Matt. xiii. 33),
about 8¾ gallons. It is reasonable to suppose that the vessels
provided for this extraordinary
gathering were of different sizes,
but all large.

7. λέγει αὐτ.] The sixth verse
is substantially parenthetical, and
in thought *v.* 7 follows *v.* 5
directly.

ἐγέμ. αὐτ. ἕως ἄνω] *impleverunt
usque ad summum* v.; *they filled
them up to the brim.* This preliminary work was done completely,
so that the contents of the vessels
were obvious to all.

8. Ἀντλήσατε] *Draw.* There
is considerable obscurity as to
the meaning of this word. According to the current interpretation the water in the vessels
of purification was changed into
wine, and the servants are bidden
to draw from these. There is
nothing in the text which definitely points to such an interpretation; and the original word
is applied most naturally to drawing water from the well (iv. 7,
15), and not from a vessel like

the waterpot. Moreover the
emphatic addition of νῦν seems to
mark the continuance of the
same action of drawing as before,
but with a different end. Hitherto they had drawn to fill the
vessels of purification: they were
charged *now* to "draw and bear
to the ruler of the feast." It
seems most unlikely that water
taken from vessels of purification
could have been employed for
the purpose of the miracle. On
the other hand, the significance
of the miracle comes out with
infinitely greater force if the
change is wrought through the
destination of the element. That
which remained water when kept
for a ceremonial use became wine
when borne in faith to minister
to the needs, even to the superfluous requirements, of life. This
view, that the change in the
water was determined by its
destination for use at the feast,
can be held equally if the water
so used and limited to that which
was used were "drawn" from the
vessels, and not from the well.

If, however, the traditional
view of the miracle be retained no
real difficulty can be felt in the
magnitude of the marriage gift
with which Christ endowed the
house of a friend,

7 taining two or three firkins apiece. Jesus saith unto them, Fill the waterpots with water. And they filled
8 them up to the brim. And he saith unto them, Draw now, and bear unto the ruler of the feast.
9 And they bare it. And when the ruler of the feast tasted the water now that it had become wine (and he knew not whence it was, but the servants which had drawn the water knew), the ruler of the feast
10 calleth the bridegroom, and saith unto him, Every man setteth on first the good wine; and when *men* have drunk freely, that which is poorer [1]: thou hast

[1] *lit.* smaller.

τ. ἀρχιτρικ.] *architriclino* v. ; *to the ruler of the feast.* Some have supposed this "ruler" to be the chief servant, "steward," to whose care all the arrangements of the feast were entrusted, and not one of the guests. This is the classical usage of the term employed, and hence Juvencus speaks of *summus minister.* But on the other hand, in Ecclus. xxxv. 1, 2, one of the guests is described as ἡγούμενος, and there is no certain evidence that the Jews had any such officer among their servants, who certainly would not in any case be likely to be found in such a household as this.

9, 10. The independent witness to the two parts of the miracle establishes its reality. The ruler of the feast declares what the element *is*, the servants knew what it *was.*

9. φωνεῖ . . . ὁ ἀρχ.] *vocat . . . architriclinus* v. ; *the ruler . . . calleth.* See xviii. 33.

γεγεν.] *when it had become,* or *after it had become.* The clause

is predicative, and not simply descriptive.

καὶ οὐκ ᾔδ. . . . ᾔδ.] *and he knew not . . . knew.* This clause is most probably to be taken as a parenthesis: *When the ruler tasted . . . (and he knew not . . . but . . . knew) he calleth . . .* Comp. i. 14, note. His ignorance of the source from which the wine came did not lead to his inquiry, but rather gave weight to his spontaneous testimony to its excellence.

10. The words are half playful, and fall in with the character of the scene. The form of the first part of the sentence is proverbial, and there is nothing to offend in the strong term, μεθυσθῶσιν (*inebriati fuerint* v.) (comp. Gen. xliii. 34, LXX.), "drunk freely," which has no immediate application to the guests present. The last clause seems to be one of those unconscious prophecies in which words spoken in recognition of a present act reveal the far deeper truth of which it is a sign.

11 τὸν καλὸν οἶνον ἕως ἄρτι. Ταύτην ἐποίησεν ¹ ἀρχὴν τῶν
σημείων ὁ Ἰησοῦς ἐν Κανὰ τῆς Γαλιλαίας καὶ ἐφανέρωσεν
τὴν δόξαν αὐτοῦ, καὶ ἐπίστευσαν εἰς αὐτὸν οἱ μαθηταὶ
αὐτοῦ.

12 Μετὰ τοῦτο κατέβη εἰς Καφαρναοὺμ αὐτὸς καὶ ἡ

¹ Insert τήν ΑΧΓΔ.

τ. καλ. οἶν.] *the good wine* from
his store. The definite article is
made pointed by the end of the
verse.

τετήρ.] *servasti* v. ; *hast kept.*
The idea of τηρεῖν is that of
watchful care rather than of
safe custody (φυλάσσειν). Comp.
ch. xii. 7.

11. . . . τ. σημείων] Hoc fecit
initium *signorum* v. ; . . . *signs.*
The value of the work was
rather in what it indicated than
in what it was. Miracles, in this
aspect which is commonest in
the New Testament, are revelations of truth through the symbolism of the outward acts.
The A. V. has always preserved
the translation *signs* in the
Synoptists except Luke xxiii. 8
(see Matt. xvi. 3) ; but in St.
John we frequently find the
rendering *miracles*, even where
the point of the teaching is lost
by this translation, *e.g.* John vi.
26, *not because ye saw signs,
but* . . . , where the motive was
not the prospect of something
yet nobler to be revealed, but
acquiescence in the gross satisfaction of earthly wants. Vhen-
ever the word is used of Christ's
works it is always with distinct
reference to a higher character
which they indicate. Those who
call them "signs" attach to Him
divine attributes in faith, ii. 23,
iii. 2, etc., or fear, xi. 47 ; and
each sign gave occasion to a

growth of faith or unbelief according to the spirit of those who
witnessed it. The word was
adopted into the Aramaic dialect
(סִימָן) in the general sense of
"sign."

It may be added that the
word δύναμις for *miracle* never
occurs in St. John, while he
very commonly includes miracles
under the term ἔργα, xiv. 11,
etc.

In this passage the twofold
effect of the sign is described by
St. John, first as a manifestation
of Christ's glory, and next as a
ground of faith in those who
were already disciples. The
office of miracles towards those
who do not believe is wholly left
out of sight.

ἐφανέρ.] *manifestavit* v. ; *manifested.* The word φανεροῦν is
frequent in St. John, ch. i. 31,
vii. 4, xxi. 1, etc.

τ. δόξ. αὐτ.] *gloriam suam* v.;
his glory. The glory (comp. i.
14, note) is truly, inherently,
Christ's glory. A prophet would
manifest the glory of God. The
manifestation of His glory in
this "sign" must not be sought
simply in what we call its
"miraculous" element, but in
this taken in connexion with the
circumstances, as a revelation of
the insight, the sympathy, the
sovereignty of the Son of man,
who was the Word Incarnate
See additional note.

11 kept the good wine until now. This as a beginning of his signs did Jesus in Cana of Galilee, and manifested his glory; and his disciples believed on him.

12 After this he went down to Capernaum, he, and

ἐπίστ. εἰς αὐτ. οἱ μαθ.] crediderunt in eum discipuli ejus v. ; *his disciples believed on him.* Testimony (i. 36) directs those who were ready to welcome Christ to Him. Personal intercourse converts followers into disciples (ii. 2). A manifestation of power, as a sign of diviner grace, converts discipleship into personal faith.

The phrase πιστεύειν εἰς is peculiarly characteristic of St. John. It is found in one place only in the Synoptic Gospels (Matt. xviii. 6 ‖ Mark ix. 42), and but rarely in St. Paul's Epistles (Rom. x. 14; Gal. ii. 16; Phil. i. 29). The idea which it conveys is that of the absolute transference of trust from oneself to another.

As the beginning of Christ's signs, this miracle cannot but have a representative value. We may observe

1. Its essential character. A sign of sovereign power wrought on inorganic matter, not on a living body.

2. Its circumstantial character. The change of the simpler to the richer element. In this respect it may be contrasted with the first public miracle of Moses, with whose history the record of miracles in the Old Testament commences.

3. Its moral character. The answer of love to faith, ministering to the fulness of human joy in one of its simplest and most natural forms. Contrast this feature with the action of the Baptist, Matt. xi. 18, 19.

In each respect the character of the sign answers to the general character of Christ as a new creation, a transfiguration of the ceremonial Law into a spiritual Gospel, the ennobling of the whole life. It may be added also that the scene of the "sign" —a marriage feast—is that under which the accomplishment of Christ's work is most characteristically prefigured, ch. iii. 29; Matt. xxii. 2 ff., xxv. 1 ff.; Rev. xix. 7, xxi. 2.

This miracle alone of those recorded by St. John has no parallel in the Synoptists; and we cannot but conclude from the minuteness of the details of the history that the Mother of the Lord made known some of them to the Apostle to whose care she was entrusted. Moreover in this miracle only does she occupy a prominent place.

12. This verse forms a transition. As yet the family life was not broken. Till " His hour was come " in a new sense the Lord still waited as He had hitherto lived.

Καφαρναούμ] *Capharnaum* v. ; *Capernaum.* Caphar-nahum, according to the most ancient authorities (Καφαρναούμ, כפר נחום. Josephus gives both Κεφαρναούμ and Κεφαρνώμη). This town was on the shores of the lake, so that Christ *went down* thither from Nazareth or Cana, which were on the table-

μήτηρ αὐτοῦ καὶ οἱ ἀδελφοὶ καὶ οἱ μαθηταὶ αὐτοῦ, καὶ
ἐκεῖ ἔμειναν οὐ πολλὰς ἡμέρας.

13 Καὶ ἐγγὺς ἦν τὸ πάσχα τῶν Ἰουδαίων, καὶ ἀνέβη εἰς

land above. Caphar (a *hamlet*, cf. Luke ix. 12, *Syr.*) is found in late names of places not infrequently, answering to the Arabic *Kefr*. The site of Capernaum has now been identified beyond all reasonable doubt with *Tell-Hûm* (Wilson, *Sea of Galilee*, in Warren's *Recovery of Jerusalem*, pp. 342 ff.; Tristram, *Land of Israel*, pp. 428 ff. ed. 3). Compare Matt. iv. 13, note.

From the mention of "his brethren," who are not noticed *vv.* 1, 2, it appears likely that the Lord had returned to Nazareth from Cana. The passing reference to a sojourn at Capernaum falls in with what is said in the Synoptists (Matt. iv. 13) of the Lord's subsequent removal thither from Nazareth at the commencement of His Galilæan ministry, though this fact is not expressly mentioned by St. John. Comp. vi. 24 ff.

οἱ ἀδελφ. . . . αὐτ.] *his brethren.* Most probably the sons of Joseph by a former marriage. See an exhaustive essay by Dr. Lightfoot, *Galatians*, Essay ii.

οὐ πολλ. ἡμ.] *non multis diebus* v.; *not many days.* This is perhaps mentioned to show that at present Capernaum was not made the permanent residence of the Lord, as it became afterwards.

ii.   THE WORK OF CHRIST
       (ii. 13—iv. 54).

The formation of a small group of disciples inspired by true faith (*v.* 11) was followed by the commencement of the Lord's public

work. This is presented in three forms as undertaken in three distinct scenes : Judæa, Samaria, Galilee.

Hitherto the Revelation of Christ has been given mainly through the confession of disciples (i. 51, note). The Evangelist now, as he traces the sequence of events, crowns the record of the testimony rendered to Christ by the record of His first self-revelation. He shows how He satisfied anticipations and wants; how He was misunderstood and welcomed. Unbelief is as yet passive, though it is seen by Christ (ii. 25).

The narrative deals still for the most part with representative individuals, and not with the masses of the people.

The general contents of the section are thus distributed :

1. The work in Judæa (ii. 13—iii. 36).

   a. At Jerusalem in the temple (ii. 13—22).

      i. The symbolic act (13—16).
         Effect on the disciples (*v.* 17).

      ii. The promised sign (18—21).
          Effect on the disciples (*v.* 22).

   b. At Jerusalem with Jews (ii. 23—iii. 21).

      i. Generally (23—25).
      ii. Specially (iii. 1—21).

   c. In Judæa generally (iii. 22—36).

his mother, and *his* brethren, and his disciples: and there they abode not many days.

13   And the passover of the Jews was at hand, and

2. The work in Samaria (iv. 1 —42).
  iv. 1—3, transitional.
  a. Specially (4—38).
  b. Generally (39—42).
3. The work in Galilee (iv. 43 —54).
  a. Generally (43—45).
  b. A special sign (46—54).

  1. THE WORK IN JUDÆA (ii. 13—iii. 36).

It was fitting that the Lord's public work should commence in Judæa and in the Holy City. The events recorded 'in this section really determined the character of His after ministry. He offered Himself by a significant act intelligible to faith as the Messiah : His coming was either not understood or misunderstood ; and, after a more distinct revelation of His Person in Samaria, He began his work afresh as a prophet in Galilee. Henceforward He appeared no more openly as Messiah at Jerusalem till His final entry.

Christ's work at Jerusalem in the temple (ii. 13—22).

It is impossible not to feel the change which at this point comes over the narrative. There is a change of place, of occasion, of manner of action. Jerusalem and Cana, the passover and the marriage feast, the stern Reformer and the sympathising Guest. So too the spiritual lessons which the two signs convey are also complementary. The first represents the ennobling of common life, the second

the purifying of divine worship. Or, to put the truth in another light, the one is a revelation of the Son of man, and the other a revelation of the Christ, the Fulfiller of the hope and purpose of Israel.

The history falls into two parts, the symbolic act (13—17), the promised sign (18—22). The contents of the section are peculiar to St. John, who was an eye-witness, ii. 17.

13—17. The record is a commentary on Mal. iii. 1 ff. Comp. Zech. xiv. 20 f. The first step in the Messiah's work was the abolition of the corruptions which the selfishness of a dominant and faithless hierarchy had introduced into the divine service. Origen (*In Joh.* tom. x. § 16) justly points out the spiritual application of this first act of Christ's ministry to His continual coming both to the Church and to individual souls.

13. τὸ πάσχα τῶν Ἰουδ.] *the passover of the Jews,* ch. xi. 55. Comp. vi. 4. The phrase appears to imply distinctly the existence of a recognised " Christian Passover " at the time when the Gospel was written. Compare *v.* 6. Origen (*In Joh.* tom. x. § 14) thinks that the words mark how that which was " the Lord's Passover" had been degraded into a merely human ceremonial.

For the general sense in which the term οἱ Ἰουδαῖοι is used in St. John, see Introd.

ἀνέβη] *ascendit* v. ; ch. v. 1, vii. 8, 10, xi. 55, xii. 20. Comp. Luke ii. 41 f.

14 Ἱεροσόλυμα ὁ Ἰησοῦς. καὶ εὗρεν ἐν τῷ ἱερῷ τοὺς
πωλοῦντας βόας καὶ πρόβατα καὶ περιστερὰς καὶ τοὺς
15 κερματιστὰς καθημένους, καὶ ποιήσας φραγέλλιον ἐκ
σχοινίων πάντας ἐξέβαλεν ἐκ τοῦ ἱεροῦ τά τε πρόβατα
καὶ τοὺς βόας, καὶ τῶν κολλυβιστῶν ἐξέχεεν τὰ κέρματα
16 καὶ τὰς τραπέζας ἀνέτρεψεν¹, καὶ τοῖς τὰς περιστερὰς
πωλοῦσιν εἶπεν Ἄρατε ταῦτα ἐντεῦθεν, μὴ ποιεῖτε τὸν

¹ ἀνέτρεψεν BX; ἀνέστρεψεν ALΓΓΔ; κατέστρεψεν א.

14. καὶ εὗρεν] *and he found.*
There is a pause at the end of *v.*
13, which must be marked by the
commencement of a new sentence.
The visit to the Holy City is
recorded first, and then the visit
to the temple. It was natural
that the Lord's work should begin not only at Jerusalem but
also at the centre of divine worship—the sanctuary of the theocracy. He now comes in due time
to try the people in His Father's
house, and to judge abuses which
He must have seen often on
earlier visits. The event is to
be placed before the passover
(*v.* 23), and probably on the eve
of the feast, when leaven was
cleared away, Exod. xii. 15; 1
Cor. v. 7.

ἐν τῷ ἱερῷ] *in the temple, i.e.*
in the outer court, the court of
the Gentiles, where there was a
regular market, belonging to the
house of Hanan (Annas).

The two words translated
"temple" in E.V. require to be
distinguished carefully, (1) Ἱερόν,
the whole sacred enclosure, with
the courts and porticoes, which
is never used metaphorically;
and (2) Ναός, the actual sacred
building, used below of the body
of the Lord (*v.* 21), and of
Christians who form His spiritual

body (1 Cor. iii. 16, 17, vi. 19;
2 Cor. vi. 16). The distinction
is often very interesting. Contrast Matt. iv. 5, xii. 6, xxiv. 1;
Luke ii. 37, 46; John x. 23;
Acts iii. 10, xxi. 28 (Ἱερόν, the
temple-courts), with Matt. xxiii.
17, 35, xxvii. 5, note, 51; Luke
i. 21; John ii. 20 (Ναός, the
sanctuary).

τοὺς πωλοῦντας] *those that
sold.* Not simply men engaged
in the traffic, but those who
were habitually engaged in it.

βό. . . . πρόβ. . . . περιστ.]
oxen . . . sheep . . . doves. Comp.
Matt. xxi. 12. Caspari, *Ein.
in d. L. J.* s. 102.

κερματιστάς] *nummularios* v.;
changers of money. Κερματιστής
indicates properly the changer of
large into smaller coins; κολλυ-
βιστής (*v.* 15) is derived from
the fee paid for the exchange
(κόλλυβος), which appears in the
vernacular Aramaic (Buxtorf,
Lexicon, s. v. קלבון). Obviously
no coins bearing the image of
the Emperor or any heathen
symbol could be paid into the
temple treasury, and all offerings
of money would require to be
made in Jewish coins. The
yearly payment of the half-
shekel, which could be made in
the country (Matt. xvii. 24), was

14 Jesus went up to Jerusalem. And he found in the temple those that sold oxen and sheep and doves, 15 and the changers of money sitting: and he made a scourge of cords, and cast all out of the temple, both the sheep and the oxen; and he poured out the changers' money, and overthrew their tables; 16 and to them that sold the doves he said, Take these things hence; make not my Father's house a house

also received at the temple, and the exchange required for this gave abundant business to the exchangers. Lightfoot has collected an interesting series of illustrations on Matt. xxi. 12.

15. φραγ. ἐκ σχοιν.] *flagellum de funiculis* v.; *a scourge of small cords*, as a symbol of authority and not as a weapon of offence. The "cords" (σχοινία, properly of twisted rushes) would be at hand. No corresponding detail is mentioned in the parallel narratives. Jewish tradition (*Sanhed.* 98 *b*, Wünsche) figured Messiah as coming with a scourge for the chastisement of evil-doers. On this occasion only, when He came to claim authority by act, did the Lord use the form of force. For the effect compare xviii. 6.

πάντας] apparently the sellers as well as the animals, though the next clause must be translated, *both the sheep and* . . . (τά τε πρόβατα καί . . .).

κ. . . . ἐξ. . . . κ. . . . εἶπ. . . .] *and he poured . . . and . . . he said* . . . Each stage in the action is to be distinguished.

κολλυβ.] See v. 14.

16. Ἄρατε ταῦτα ἐντ.] *Auferte ista hinc* v.; *Take these things hence*, since these could not be

driven. There is no reason to think that those who sold the offerings of the poor were, as such, dealt with more gently than other traffickers.

τ. οἶκ. τ. πατ. μου] *my Father's house.* Compare Luke ii. 49 (ἐν τοῖς τοῦ πατρός μου). The speciality of the title (*my* Father's house, not *our* Father's house) must be noticed. When Christ finally left the temple (Matt. xxiv. 1) He spoke of it to the Jews as *your house* (Matt. xxiii. 38); the people had claimed and made their own what truly belonged to God. It must be observed also that the Lord puts forth His relation to God as the fact from which His Messiahship might be inferred. This formed the trial of faith.

οἶκ. ἐμπ.] *house of merchandise.* Contrast Matt. xxi. 13 (σπήλαιον λῃστῶν). Here the tumult and confusion of worldly business are set over against the still devotion which should belong to the place of worship.

ἐμπορίου] *negotiationis* v. Ἐμπόριον means the place of traffic, the mart, and not the subject or the art of trafficking (ἐμπορία). Comp. Ezek. xxvii. 3 (LXX.). Thus the "house" is here regarded as having become a

17 οἶκον τοῦ πατρός μου οἶκον ἐμπορίου. Ἐμνήσθησαν ¹ οἱ
μαθηταὶ αὐτοῦ ὅτι γεγραμμένον ἐστίν Ὁ ζῆλος τοῦ
18 οἴκου σου καταφάγεταί ² με. Ἀπεκρίθησαν οὖν οἱ Ἰουδαῖοι
καὶ εἶπαν αὐτῷ Τί σημεῖον δεικνύεις ἡμῖν, ὅτι ταῦτα
19 ποιεῖς; ἀπεκρίθη Ἰησοῦς καὶ εἶπεν αὐτοῖς Λύσατε τὸν

¹ Insert δέ ΑΡΓΔ.   ² καταφάγεται ΝΑΒLΡΤᵇΧΓΔ; κατέφαγε 69.

market-house, no longer deriving
its character from Him to whom
it was dedicated, but from the
business carried on in its courts.

17. οἱ μαθ.] We notice here,
on the occasion of the first public
act of Christ, as throughout St.
John, the double effect of the
act on those who already believed,
and on those who were resolutely
unbelieving. The disciples *remembered* at the time (contrast
v. 22) that this trait was characteristic of the true prophet of
God, who gave himself for his
people. The Jews found in it
an occasion for fresh demands of
proof.

γεγραμ. ἐστ.] *it is written,* i.e.
stands recorded in Scripture.
Compare vi. 31, 45, x. 34, xii.
14. St. John prefers this resolved form to the simple verb
(γέγραπται), which prevails almost
exclusively in the other books.
Comp. iii. 21.

The words occur in Ps. lxix. 9.
The remainder of the verse is
applied to the Lord by St. Paul,
Rom. xv. 3. Other passages
from it are quoted as Messianic,
John xv. 25 (*v.* 4), xix. 28 and
parallels (*v.* 21); Rom. xi. 9, 10
(*v.* 22); Acts i. 20 (*v.* 25).

For a general view of the
quotations from the Old Testament in St. John see Introd.

Ὁ ζῆλος τ. οἰκ. σ.] *The zeal of
thine house,* the burning jealousy
for the holiness of the house of

God, and so for the holiness of
the people who were bound by
service to it, as well as for the
honour of God himself. Comp.
Rom. x. 2; 2 Cor. xi. 2.

καταφάγεται] *will eat* (devour)
me. The reference is not to the
future Passion of the Lord, but
to the overpowering energy and
fearlessness of His present action.
It is not natural to suppose that
the disciples had at the time any
clear apprehension of what the
issue would be. They only felt
the presence of a spirit which
could not but work.

18 ff. The act in which the
Lord offered a revelation of
Himself called out no faith in
the representatives of the nation.
Thereupon, in answer to their
demand, He takes the temple,
which he had vainly cleansed, as
a sign, having regard to the
destruction which they would
bring upon it. The end was now
visible, though far off. Comp.
Matt. ix. 15.

The words are an illustration
of Luke xvi. 31. To those who
disregarded the spirit of Moses,
the Resurrection became power-
less.

18. Ἀπεκ. οὖν οἱ Ἰουδ.] *Respon-
derunt ergo Judæi* v.; *The Jews
therefore answered.* See i. 22,
note. The connexion is with *v.*
16 directly.

Ἀπεκρίθησαν] The term is not
infrequently used when the word

17 of merchandise. His disciples remembered that it is written, The zeal of thine house shall eat me up. 18 The Jews therefore answered and said unto him, What sign showest thou unto us, seeing that thou 19 doest these things? Jesus answered and said unto them, Destroy this temple, and in three days I will

spoken is a reply to or a criticism upon something done, or obviously present to the mind of another : *e.g.* v. 17, xix. 7 ; Matt. xi. 25, xvii. 4, xxviii. 5 ; Mark x. 51, xii. 35 ; Luke i. 60, xiii. 14 ; Acts iii. 12, v. 8 ; Rev. vii. 13. And once even in reference to the significant state of the barren fig tree, Mark xi. 14.

Τί ση. δεικ. . . . ;] *What sign showest thou . . .?* By what clear and convincing token (comp. 1 Cor. i. 22) can we be made to see that thou hast the right to exercise high prophetic functions, *seeing that* (ὅτι, comp. ix. 17) *thou doest these things* which belong to a great prophet's work ? Comp. Matt. xxi. 23.

The same demand for fresh evidence in the presence of that which ought to be decisive is found ch. vi. 30 ; Matt. xii. 48 f., xvi. 1 ff.

ποιεῖς] The work was not past only, but evidently charged with present consequences.

19. Λύσατε τὸν ναόν . . .] *Solvite templum hoc . . .* v. ; *Destroy this temple . . .* The phrase here placed in its true context appears twice as the basis of an accusation, (1) Matt. xxvi. 61, note ; Mark xiv. 57, 58, and (2) Acts vi. 14. In both cases the point of the words is altered by assigning to Christ the work of destruction, which he leaves to the Jews. (*I am able to* (*I will*)

destroy, as contrasted with *Destroy*.)

In the interpretation of the words two distinct ideas have to be brought into harmony, (1) The reference to the actual temple which is absolutely required by the context, and (2) the interpretation of the Evangelist (*v.* 21). At the same time the "three days" marks the fulfilment as historical and definite. The point of connexion lies in the conception of the temple as the seat of God's presence among His people. So far the temple was a figure of the Body of Christ. The rejection and death of Christ, in whom dwelt the fulness of God, brought with it necessarily the destruction of the temple, first spiritually, when the veil was rent (Matt. xxvii. 51), and then materially (observe ἀπ' ἄρτι, Matt. xxvi. 64). On the other hand, the Resurrection of Christ was the raising again of the temple, the complete restoration of the tabernacle of God's presence to men, perpetuated in the Church, which is Christ's body.

In this connexion account must be taken of the comparison of the temple with Christ, Matt. xii. 6. Comp. ch. i. 14 (ἐσκήνωσεν).

The Resurrection of Christ was indeed the transfiguration of worship, while it was the transfiguration of life.

20 ναὸν τοῦτον καὶ [ἐν] τρισὶν ἡμέραις ἐγερῶ αὐτόν. εἶπαν

οὖν οἱ Ἰουδαῖοι Τεσσεράκοντα καὶ ἒξ ἔτεσιν οἰκοδομήθη

ὁ ναὸς οὗτος, καὶ σὺ ἐν τρισὶν ἡμέραις ἐγερεῖς αὐτόν;

21 ἐκεῖνος δὲ ἔλεγεν περὶ τοῦ ναοῦ τοῦ σώματος αὐτοῦ.

22 Ὅτε οὖν ἠγέρθη ἐκ νεκρῶν, ἐμνήσθησαν οἱ μαθηταὶ

In the Synoptic Gospels Christ connects the destruction of the temple with the faithlessness of the people: Matt. xxiv. 2 ff., xxiii. 38.

It may be noticed that on a similar occasion the Lord referred to the "sign of the prophet Jonah," as that alone which should be given (Matt. xii. 39, xvi. 4). Life through death; construction through dissolution; the rise of the new from the fall of the old—these are the main thoughts.

The imperative λύσατε is used as in Matt. xxiii. 32, πληρώσατε. Comp. xiii. 28. Thus in the first clear antagonism Christ sees its last issue. The word itself is a very remarkable one. It indicates a destruction which comes from dissolution, from the breaking of that which binds the parts into a whole, or one thing to another. Comp. 2 Pet. iii. 10 ff.; Acts xxvii. 41; Eph. ii. 14; and also v. 18, note; 1 John iii. 8.

ἐγερῶ...] *excitabo*... v.; *I will raise* . . . The Resurrection is here assigned to the action of the Lord, as elsewhere to the Father (Gal. i 1; see *v.* 22, note).

20. Τεσσ. κ. ἐξ ἔτ. οἰκοδ.] *In forty and six years was this temple built* as we now see it. The work is regarded as complete in its present state, though the reparation of the whole structure was not completed till thirty-six years afterwards. Herod the Great

began to restore the temple in 20 B.C. (Jos. *B. J.* i. xxi. (xvi.) 1): compare *Ant.* xv. xi. (xiv.) 1, and the design was completed by Herod Agrippa A.D. 64. The tense of the verb marks a definite point reached; that point probably coincided with the date of the Lord's visit; but the form of expression makes it precarious to insist on the phrase as itself defining this coincidence.

ἐγ. αὐ. ;] *wilt thou raise it up?* That which Christ raises (x. 18) is that which was (raise *it* up) and not another. The old Church is transfigured and not destroyed. The continuity of revelation is never broken.

ἐν τρισ. ἡμ.] Comp. Hos. vi. 2.

21. ἐκεῖνος δέ . . .] The pronoun (i. 18, note) is emphatic, and marks a definite contrast, not only between the Lord and the Jews, but also between the Lord and the apostles. St. John seems to look back again upon the far distant scene as interpreted by his later knowledge, and to realise how the Master foresaw that which was wholly hidden from the disciples.

περί . . .] *concerning* . . . This was the general topic of which He was speaking, not the direct object which He indicated, as in vi. 71 (ἔλεγεν τὸν Ἰ.), from which usage it must be carefully distinguished. Compare Eph. v. 32 (λέγω εἰς), where the ultimate application is marked.

₂₀ raise it up. The Jews therefore said, In forty and six years was this temple built, and wilt thou raise ₂₁ it up in three days? But he spake of the temple ₂₂ of his body. When therefore he was raised from the

τ. να. τ. σώμ. αὐτ.] *the temple of his body, i.e.* the temple defined to be His body, as in the phrase " the cities of Sodom and Gomorrah " (2 Pet. ii. 6). Compare Acts iv. 22 ; 2 Cor. v. 1 ; Rom. iv. 11 (*v. l.*). For the usage see 1 Cor. vi. 19 ; Rom. viii. 11.

St. John notices on other occasions the real meaning of words of the Lord not understood at first : vii. 39, xii. 33, xxi. 19 ; and in each case he speaks with complete authority. This trait of progressive knowledge is inexplicable except as a memorial of personal experience.

22. ἠγέρθη] *resurrexisset* v. ; *was raised* : so also xxi. 14. The full phrase would be, " was raised by God from the dead," as in the corresponding expression, " whom God raised from the dead " (Acts iii. 15, iv. 10, v. 30, x. 40, xiii. 30, 37 ; Rom. iv. 24, viii. 11, x. 9 ; 1 Cor. xv. 15, etc.). In all these cases the resurrection is regarded as an awakening effected by the power of the Father. Much less frequently it is presented simply as a rising again, consequent on the awakening, in reference to the manifestation of the power of the Son, Mark viii. 31, ix. 9 ; Luke xxiv. 7. Comp. John xi. 23, 24 and *v.* 19, note.

ἐμνήσθ.] *v.* 17. The repetition of the word seems to mark the facts of Christ's life as a new record of revelation, on which the disciples pondered even be- fore the facts were committed to writing. Compare xii. 16.

ἔλεγεν] *spake.* The tense implies either a repetition of or a dwelling upon the words. Comp. v. 18, vi. 6, 65, 71, viii. 27, 31, xii. 33, iv. 33, 42, etc.

ἐπίστ. τῇ γραφῇ] *believed the scripture.* A different construction is used here from that in *v.* 11 : they trusted the Scripture as absolutely true. Comp. iv. 50, v. 46, 47, xx. 9.

τῇ γραφῇ] The phrase ἡ γραφή occurs elsewhere ten times in St. John : vii. 38, 42, x. 35, xiii. 18 (xvii. 12), xix. 24, 28, 36, 37 (xx. 9), and in every case, except xvii. 12 and xx. 9, the reference is to a definite passage of Scripture given in the context, according to the usage elsewhere, Mark xii. 10 (xv. 28) ; Luke iv. 21 ; Acts i. 16, viii. 35, etc. (though St. Paul appears also to personify Scripture), while the plural is used for Scripture generally, v. 39 ; Luke xxiv. 32 ; 1 Cor. xv. 3, 4, etc. In xvii. 12 the reference appears to be to the words already quoted, xiii. 18, so that the present and the similar passage, xx. 9, alone remain without a determinate reference. According to the apostle's usage, then, we must suppose that here also a definite passage is present to his mind, and this, from a comparison of Acts ii. 27, 31, xiii. 35, can hardly be any other than Ps. xvi. 10.

τῷ λόγῳ ὃν εἶπεν ὁ Ἰησ., the revelation which St. John has

αὐτοῦ ὅτι τοῦτο ἔλεγεν [1], καὶ ἐπίστευσαν τῇ γραφῇ καὶ
τῷ λόγῳ ὃν [2] εἶπεν ὁ Ἰησοῦς.

23 Ὡς δὲ ἦν ἐν τοῖς Ἱεροσολύμοις ἐν τῷ πάσχα ἐν τῇ

[1] Insert αὐτοῖς K.   [2] ὃν εἶπεν אBLTᵇ ; ᾧ εἶπεν AΧΓΔ.

just recorded, not as an isolated
utterance (ῥῆμα), but as a comprehensive message (τῷ λόγῳ).

The Synoptists narrate a cleansing of the temple as having
taken place on the day of the
triumphal entry into Jerusalem
before the last passover (Matt.
xxi. 12 ff. ; Mark xi. 15 ff. ;
Luke xix. 45 ff.). Of such an
incident there is no trace in St.
John (xii. 12 ff.), and conversely
the Synoptists have no trace of
an earlier cleansing. It has been
supposed that the event has been
transposed in the Synoptic narratives owing to the fact that they
give no account of the Lord's
ministry at Jerusalem before the
last journey ; but a comparison
of the two narratives is against
the identification.

1. The exact connexion of the
event in each case is given in
detail.

2. There is a significant difference in the words used to justify
the act, Mark xi. 17 ; John ii. 16.

3. The character of the two
acts is distinct. The history of
St. John presents an independent
assumption of authority : the
history of the Synoptists is a
sequel to the popular homage
which the Lord had accepted.

4. The cleansing in St. John
appears as a single act. The
cleansing in the Synoptists seems
to be part of a continued policy
(Mark xi. 16).

5. In the record of the later
incident there is no reference to
the remarkable words (ii. 19)

which give its colour to the
narrative of St. John, though
the Synoptists show that they
were not unacquainted with the
words (Matt. xxvi. 61 ; Mark
xiv. 58).

Nor, on the other hand, is
there any improbability in the
repetition of such an incident.
In each case the cleansing was
effected in immediate connexion
with the revelation of Jesus as
the Messiah. This revelation
was twofold : first, when He
claimed His royal power at the
entrance on His work, and then
when He claimed it again at the
close of His work. In the interval between these two manifestations He fulfilled the office
of a simple prophet. In the
first case, so to speak, the issue
was as yet doubtful ; in the
second, it was already decided ;
and from this difference flows
the difference in the details
of the incidents themselves. For
example, there is a force in the
addition " a house of prayer *for
all nations*," in the immediate
prospect of the Passion and of
the consequent rejection of the
Jews, which finds no place at the
beginning of the Lord's ministry,
when He enters as a Son into
" His Father's house." And
again, the neutral phrase, " a
house of merchandise," is in the
second case represented by its
last issue, " a den of robbers."

Assuming that the two cleans-
ings are distinct, it is easy to see
why St. John records that which

dead, his disciples remembered that he spake this; and they believed the scripture, and the word which Jesus had said.

23 Now when he was in Jerusalem at the passover,

occurred at the beginning, because it was the first crisis in the separation of faith and unbelief; while the Synoptists necessarily, from the construction of their narratives, recorded the later one. This, on the other hand, was virtually included in the first, and there was no need that St. John should notice it.

Christ's work at Jerusalem with the people (ii. 23—iii. 21).

The record of the great Messianic work (ii. 14—16), which was the critical trial of the representatives of the theocracy, is followed by a summary notice of the thoughts which it excited among the people generally, and also in one who was fitted to express the feelings of students and teachers. The people imagined that they had found the Messiah of their own hopes: the teacher acknowledged the presence of a prophet who should continue, and probably reform, what already existed. In both respects the meaning of Christ's work was missed: the conclusions which were drawn from His "signs" (ii. 23, iii. 2) were false or inadequate.

The section falls into two parts: Christ's dealing with the people (ii. 23—25) and with "the teacher of Israel" (iii. 1—21).

The contents are peculiar to St. John. It is probable that he writes from his own immediate knowledge throughout (comp. iii. 11).

23—25. *Christ's dealing with the people generally.* In this brief passage the false faith of the people is contrasted with the perfect insight of Christ. The people were willing to accept Him as the Messiah, but He knew that it would be on their own terms and for the fulfilment of their own desires. Comp. vi. 14 f. (*Galilee*).

The explanation which St. John gives of the reserve of Christ shows a characteristic knowledge of the Lord's mind. It reads like a commentary gained from later experience on what was at the time a surprise and a mystery.

The words reveal to us a fresh Temptation of Christ, and this Temptation at Jerusalem corresponds with the Temptation in the wilderness. The Lord puts aside the offer of help and discipleship which would have secured outward success at the cost of some compromise with falsehood.

ἐν τ. Ἱεροσολύμοις] The Lord's work was continued, if not in the temple, yet still in the Holy City. It may be noticed that of the two Greek forms of the name, that which is alone found (in a symbolic sense) in the Revelation (iii. 12, xxi. 2, 10, Ἱερουσαλήμ) is not found in the Gospel, in which (as in St. Mark) the other form (Ἱεροσόλυμα) is used exclusively (twelve times).

The triple definition of place (*in Jerusalem*), time (*at the pass-*

7

ἑορτῇ, πολλοὶ ἐπίστευσαν εἰς τὸ ὄνομα αὐτοῦ, θεωροῦντες
24 αὐτοῦ τὰ σημεῖα ἃ ἐποίει· αὐτὸς δὲ Ἰησοῦς οὐκ ἐπίστευεν
25 αὐτὸν αὐτοῖς, διὰ τὸ αὐτὸν γινώσκειν πάντας καὶ ὅτι οὐ
χρείαν εἶχεν ἵνα τις μαρτυρήσῃ περὶ τοῦ ἀνθρώπου, αὐτὸς
γὰρ ἐγίνωσκεν τί ἦν ἐν τῷ ἀνθρώπῳ.

over), circumstance (during the feast), is remarkable. The place was the city which God had chosen : the time was the anniversary of the birth of the nation : the circumstances marked universal joy.

ἐν τῇ ἑορτῇ] at the feast, i.e. of unleavened bread, kept on the seven days which followed the actual passover (Lev. xxiii. 5, 6). It has been conjectured, not unreasonably, that the purifying of the temple (vv. 13, 17) took place on the eve of the passover, when the houses were cleansed of leaven.

πολλοί] Among these there may have been some Galilæans, who had come to the feast, as "the Jews" (v. 20) are not distinctly mentioned. Comp. viii. 30 f., iv. 45.

ἐπίστ. εἰς τὸ ὄν.] believed on his name. Comp. i. 12 and viii. 30, note ; 1 John v. 13, note. In this place the phrase seems to imply the recognition of Jesus as the Messiah, but such a Messiah as Him for whom they looked, without any deeper trust (for the most part) in His Person (v. 24). They believed not on Him (iii. 18), but on His name, as Christ (comp. Matt. vii. 22). Origen rightly dwells upon the phrase : Διαφέρει τοῦ πιστεύειν εἰς αὐτὸν τὸ πιστεύειν εἰς ὄνομα αὐτοῦ . . . αὐτοῦ τοίνυν μᾶλλον ἢ τοῦ ὀνόματος ἔχεσθαι δεῖ, ἵνα μὴ τῷ ὀνόματι αὐτοῦ δυνάμεις ποιοῦντες ἀκούσωμεν

τὰ ἐπὶ [τῶν] τῷ ὀνόματι μόνῳ καυχησαμένων αὐτοῦ εἰρημένα (In Joh. tom. x. § 28).

The phrase occurs again in connexion with the title "Son of God," 1 John v. 13, where there is no limitation of the fulness of the meaning. For the use of "believe on" (πιστεύειν εἰς) with other than a personal object, see 1 John v. 10, note.

θεωροῦντες] when they beheld, with the secondary notion of a regard of attention, wonder, reflection. The word (θεωρεῖν) is so used in vii. 3, xii. 45, xiv. 19, xvi. 16 ff., etc. In this place it connects the imperfect faith of the people with the immediate effect of that which arrested their attention. Contrast iv. 45 (ἑωρακότες).

αὐτοῦ τὰ σ.] his signs which he did time after time (ἃ ἐποίει). Here the Evangelist dwells on the works as still going on : in iv. 45 he regards the same works in their historical completeness (ὅσα ἐποίησεν). The conviction was wrought not at once, nor on a survey of all the works, but now by one, now by another. The same idea is given by the present participle (θεωροῦντες) in combination with the aorist (ἐπίστευσαν). The incidental notice of these "signs" (compare vii. 31, xi. 47, xx. 30) is an unquestionable proof that St. John does not aim at giving an exhaustive record of all he knew.

during the feast, many believed on his name, behold-
24 ing his signs which he did. But Jesus did not trust
25 himself unto them, for that he knew all men, and
because he needed not that any one should bear
witness concerning man; for he himself knew what
was in man.

Similar references to cycles of unrecorded works are found in the Synoptists : Mark iii. 10, vi. 56. Chrysostom, and others after him, contrast the effects of outward signs and moral evidence : Ἐκεῖνοι ἀκριβέστεροι ἦσαν οἱ μαθηταὶ ὅσοι μὴ ἀπὸ σημείων προσῄεσαν μόνον ἀλλὰ καὶ ἀπὸ τῆς διδασκαλίας· τοὺς μὲν γὰρ παχυτέρους τὰ σημεῖα ἐφείλκετο τοὺς δὲ λογικωτέρους αἱ προφητεῖαι καὶ αἱ διδασκαλίαι . . . οὓς καὶ ὁ Χριστὸς ἐμακάριζε λέγων μακάριοι οἱ μὴ ἰδόντες καὶ πιστεύσαντες.

24. αὐτὸς δὲ ʼI.] *but Jesus himself.* The contrast is emphasised by the preceding pronoun : comp. iv. 44 ; Matt. iii. 4 ; Mark vi. 17, xii. 36 f. ; Luke iii. 23, xxiv. 15.

ἐπίστευεν] The word recalls the ἐπίστευσαν in *v.* 23. Compare Luke xvi. 11. The kind of repetition would be in some degree, though inadequately, expressed in English by "many trusted on His name . . . but Jesus did not trust Himself to them." There is at the same time a contrast of tenses. The first verb marks a definite, completed act ; the second an habitual course of action. A partial commentary on this reserve of Christ is found in vi. 14 f., where He refuses to accept the homage of the people which is offered with false beliefs and hopes. Comp. Matt. vii. 21 ff.

24, 25. διὰ τό . . . καὶ ὅτι . . .] *eo quod . . . et quia . . .* v.; *owing to the fact that—for that . . . and because . . .* The ultimate reason lay in His knowledge of all men : the immediate reason in the fact that He needed no testimony to the character of any man.

24. διὰ τὸ αὐτὸν γιν.] The pronoun is emphatic. Christ knew " by Himself," " in virtue of His own power."

It is of great importance to distinguish in the narrative of St. John the knowledge (1) of discernment and recognition from that (2) of intuition and conviction. The one word (γινώσκειν) implies movement, progress : the other (εἰδέναι) satisfaction, rest. For the contrast between the words compare (1) i. 49 (48), iii. 10, vi. 69, xiii. 12 (γινώσκειν) ; (2) i. 26, 31, iii. 2, 11, ix. 29 (εἰδέναι). See additional note.

25. ἵνα τις μαρτ. π. τ. ἀ.] *bear witness concerning man* generically. Τοῦ ἀνθρώπου may mean also "the man with whom from time to time he had to deal," as it appears to do in the second case. Compare vii. 51 (τὸν ἄνθρωπον) ; Matt. xii. 43, xv. 11 ; 1 Cor. ii. 11 ; Rom. vii. 1.

αὐτὸς γὰρ ἐγ.] *for he himself knew,* by His own power on each occasion, *what was in man* (ἐγίνωσκεν, not ἔγνω). The pronoun is repeated a third time (αὐτός . . . αὐτόν . . . αὐτός), and the knowledge which has been described generally is now presented in its individual application.

This knowledge of the heart is elsewhere attributed to Jehovah (Jer. xvii. 10, xx. 12). Christ's knowledge, as it is here described, was immediate (*of Himself*), universal (*all men*), complete (*what was in man, i.e.* the thoughts and feelings as yet unexpressed). It is natural, therefore, that Chrysostom should see in it the knowledge which belongs to the Creator : Τὸ τὰ ἐν τῇ καρδίᾳ τῶν ἀνθρώπων εἰδέναι τοῦ πλάσαντος κατὰ μόνας τὰς καρδίας ἐστὶ θεοῦ ... οὐκ ἐδεῖτο τοίνυν μαρτύρων ὥστε τῶν οἰκείων πλασμάτων μαθεῖν τὴν διάνοιαν.

ADDITIONAL NOTES ON CHAP. II. 11, 24.

11. This passage brings forward very vividly one feature of St. John's Gospel which has been overlooked by one school of critics and exaggerated by another. It represents the whole human life of Christ, under its actual conditions of external want and suffering and of internal conflict and sorrow, as a continuous and conscious manifestation of divine glory. He shows from first to last how "the eternal life was manifested which was with the Father" (1 John i. 2) in the works, and in the words of Christ, in what He did and in what He suffered. (Compare Introd.) Such a view, it has been argued, is inconsistent with the portraiture of the Saviour in the other Gospels, and with the teaching of St. Paul upon the "exinanition" (ἑαυτὸν ἐκένωσεν) of Christ (Phil. ii. 5—11).

This objection appears to rest upon a totally inadequate conception of human life. If life is potentially the expression of a divine purpose, it is evident that all the circumstances which it includes are capable of ministering to the divine end. A want or a sorrow cannot be regarded in itself. It has a relation to a whole, and is interpretative at once and preparatory. A perfect human life—a life lived, that is, in absolute harmony with the divine—will therefore in every point reveal to those who have the eyes to see, something of God, of His "glory." And further, a human consciousness, which has complete insight into the true order of things, or so far as it has insight, will be able to realise at any moment the actual significance of each detail of experience. This being so, it is clear that all the acts and sufferings of "the Son of man" were essentially revelations of glory, and become so to us so far as we are enabled to apprehend their meaning. They are at the same time to be regarded externally, but that external realisation is only a condition for their spiritual understanding. From the nature of the case each fact in the life of Christ was the vehicle for conveying some eternal truth. It could not be otherwise. St. John lays open in some representative instances what this truth was, and while he does so he shows how the knowledge of it was present to the mind of·Christ. Humiliation, shame, death are thus not regarded outwardly, as they may rightly be in suitable connexions, but as the appointed—and so the best—means for the attainment of the highest end, and recognised as such. In this light they become "glories" (1 Peter i. 11).

These remarks hold true in regard to each event in the Lord's life ; but St. John, from his point of view, regards the whole work of Christ as one—as the complete fulfilment of the divine counsel. All is present at each moment, "one act at once," while we " as parts can see but part—now this, now that." The Passion *is* the Victory ; and this not only in relation to divine knowledge but also in relation to perfect human knowledge, which from point to point is in accordance with the divine.

St. John, therefore, while from time to time he dwells on Christ's glory and on Christ's assertion of His glory, is not recording, as has been said, that which can be understood only of the Eternal Word, but that which properly belongs to the Son of man, who at each stage, in each fragment of His life, recognised the perfect fulfilment through Himself of the purpose of the Father towards the world. Compare i. 51, viii. 28, xi. 40 ff., xiii. 31, xvii. 4.

24. All the Evangelists agree in representing the Lord as moving among men with a complete and certain knowledge of their characters and needs. Only on very rare occasions does He ask anything, as if all were not absolutely clear before His eyes (*e.g.* Mark viii. 5 ; comp. Mark xi. 13 ; John xi. 34). But St. John exhibits this attribute of complete human knowledge most fully, and dwells upon it as explaining Christ's action at critical times. He describes the

knowledge both as relative, acquired (γινώσκειν), and absolute, possessed (εἰδέναι). In some cases the "perception" (γνούς, ἔγνω, γινώσκει) is that which might be gained "naturally" by the interpretation of some intelligible sign (v. 6, vi. 15, xvi. 19, iv. 1). At other times it appears to be the result of an insight which came from a perfect spiritual sympathy, found in some degree among men (i. 42, 47, ii. 24 f., v. 42, x. 14 f., 27 : comp. xxi. 17), which reaches from the knowledge of the heart even to the knowledge of God (xvii. 25). The absolute knowledge (εἰδώς, εἰδέναι) is shown in connexion with divine things (iii. 11, v. 32, vii. 29, viii. 55, xi. 42, xii. 50), and with the facts of the Lord's being (vi. 6, viii. 14, xiii. 1, 3, xix. 28), and also in relation to that which was external (vi. 61, 64, xiii. 11, 18, xviii. 4). A careful study of these passages seems to show beyond doubt that the knowledge of Christ, so far as it was the discernment of the innermost meaning of that which was from time to time presented to Him, and so far as it was an understanding of the nature of things as they are, has its analogues in human powers. His knowledge appears to be truly the knowledge of the Son of man, and not merely the knowledge of the divine Word, though at each moment and in each connexion it was, in virtue of His perfect humanity, relatively complete. Scripture is wholly free from that Docetism —that teaching of an illusory manhood of Christ—which, both within the Church and without it, tends to destroy the historic character of the Gospel.

3 Ἦν δὲ ἄνθρωπος ἐκ τῶν Φαρισαίων, Νικόδημος ὄνομα
2 αὐτῷ, ἄρχων τῶν Ἰουδαίων· οὗτος ἦλθεν πρὸς¹ αὐτὸν
νυκτὸς καὶ εἶπεν αὐτῷ Ῥαββεί, οἴδαμεν ὅτι ἀπὸ θεοῦ
ἐλήλυθας διδάσκαλος· οὐδεὶς γὰρ δύναται ταῦτα τὰ

¹ πρὸς αὐτόν ℵABKLTᵇΔ; πρὸς τὸν Ἰησοῦν EFGHΓ.

*Christ's dealing with the repre-
sentative teacher* (iii. 1—21).

This first conversation is, together with the Evangelist's
comment, the personal application of the general call to
repentance, with which the
other Gospels open. It is, like
the public message of the Baptist or of Christ, a proclamation of the kingdom of heaven,
but given under new circumstances.

Under another aspect the
history is complementary to the
passage which precedes. Christ
was unwilling to commit Himself
—His Person—to those who had
false views; and in the same
spirit He laid open the truth
to one who sought it. By re-
fusal and by compliance alike
He showed His knowledge of
men.

The record consists of two
parts. The first part (1—15)
contains a summary of the actual
conversation; the second gives
the commentary of St. John
(16—21).

It is interesting to notice that
according to the Sarum Use, fol-
lowing the old Roman Use, the
section *vv.* 1—15 is read as the
Gospel for Trinity Sunday. This
Gospel is retained in our Prayer
Book, while the modern Roman
Use gives Matt. xxviii. 18 ff.
The fitness of the selection is
obvious. The narrative shows

how the Lord deals with the
difficulties of the thoughtful man,
reproving presumption and ele-
vating faith.

CHAP. III. 1—15. The general
outline of the discourse can be
marked with fair distinctness,
and places the relation in which
the new order—the kingdom of
God, established through Christ
—stands to the old in a clear
light.

Nicodemus comes as the representative of the well-instructed
and thoughtful Jew who looked
for the consummation of national
hope to follow in the line along
which he had himself gone, as
being a continuation and not a
new beginning (*v.* 2).

The Lord at once checks this
anticipation. The kingdom of
God cannot, He says, be seen—
outwardly apprehended — without a new birth. The right
conception of it depends upon
the possession of corresponding and therefore fresh powers
(*v.* 3).

But the obvious answer is,
Such a change in man is impossible. He is physically, morally, spiritually, one—the result
of all the past (*v.* 4).

This objection would be valid
if the change belonged to the
same order as that to which we
naturally belong. But the Lord
replies that the birth which He
reveals is an entrance to a new

3 Now there was a man of the Pharisees, named
2 Nicodemus, a ruler of the Jews: the same came
unto him by night, and said to him, Rabbi, we know
that thou art a teacher come from God: for no man

order, and wrought by a new power. It has an external element, because it belongs to men now in life: it has an internal element, because it carries men into a new world (v. 5).

No change of man in himself, so far as the life of sense is concerned, would be adequate (v. 6).

But none the less the change, though wrought by a mysterious and unseen Power—coming we know not whence, going we know not whither—in the interspace of earthly life, is manifested by its results (7 f.).

Such ideas were strange to Nicodemus, and to the traditional Judaism of the time (v. 9).

Yet even already there were some with the Lord who had known and seen the reality of the teaching and facts by which these ideas were established. (10 f.).

And, beyond these " earthly things " of which sensible experience was possible, the new kingdom included in its principles " heavenly things," still farther removed from current beliefs (v. 12).

Such was the doctrine of the Person of the Lord ; and flowing from it the doctrine of the Redemption through His Cross (13 ff.).

The circle of thought is thus complete. Christianity—in consideration of the completed work of Christ, which is presupposed—

stands contrasted with Judaism both as an organisation and as a divine economy. The entrance to the Church is through a sacrament, not outward only but spiritual also. The facts on which it rests, and which it proclaims, belong essentially to heaven, not to earth. Viewed in these relations, the discourse expands, and explains the truth stated generally in its outward form in the Sermon on the Mount : 'Εὰν μὴ περισσεύσῃ ὑμῶν ἡ δικαιοσύνη πλεῖον τῶν γραμματέων καὶ Φαρισαίων, οὐ μὴ εἰσέλθητε εἰς τὴν βασιλείαν τῶν οὐρανῶν (Matt. v. 20).

1. Ἦν δὲ ἄνθρ. . .] *Now there was a man*. . . The word ἄνθρωπος is repeated to emphasise the connexion with ii. 25. Nicodemus offered at once an example of the Lord's inward knowledge of men, and an exception to the general rule which He observed in not trusting Himself to them.

ἐκ τῶν Φαρ.] i. 24, note.

Νικόδημος] Comp. vii. 50, xix. 39. The name was not uncommon among the Jews. Nicodemus ben Gorion (Bunai), who lived till the siege of Jerusalem, has been identified (falsely, v. 4 γέρων) with this one. The traditions as to Bunai, which are very vague and untrustworthy, have been collected by Lightfoot on this place, and by Delitzsch, *Zeitschr. f. Luth. Theol.*, 1854.

σημεῖα ποιεῖν ἃ σὺ ποιεῖς, ἐὰν μὴ ᾖ ὁ θεὸς μετ᾽ αὐτοῦ.
3 ἀπεκρίθη Ἰησοῦς καὶ εἶπεν αὐτῷ Ἀμὴν ἀμὴν λέγω σοι,
ἐὰν μή τις γεννηθῇ ἄνωθεν, οὐ δύναται ἰδεῖν τὴν βασιλείαν

ἄρχων] *princeps* v., *i.e.* a member of the Sanhedrin : vii. 50. Comp. vii. 26, xii. 42 ; Luke xxiii. 13, 35, xxiv. 20 ; Acts iv. 8. The word, however, is used in Rabbinic literature (אַרכון) generally for a "great man" or "prince." See Buxtorf, *Lex. s. v.*; Matt. ix. 18 ; Luke xii. 58, xiv. 1, xviii. 18.

2. νυκτός] *by night.* This detail is noticed again in xix. 39 (but not according to the true reading in vii. 50). On each occasion where Nicodemus is mentioned we may see other traces of the timidity to which it was due. He defended Jesus without expressing any personal interest in Him : he brought his offering only after Joseph of Arimathæa had obtained the Body from Pilate.

It is interesting to find Rupert of Deutz dwelling on the bright traits in his character. Thus he contrasts him with the Pharisees to whom he belonged : " Miserunt illi nocte ut comprehenderent Jesum sine turba ; venit hic ipse nocte ut audiret Jesum sine turba cui Jesus semetipsum non credebat. Illi hora sua male usi sunt et potestate tenebrarum ; hic doctrinæ aptum, nocturni silentii bene captavit otium."

And again : " Jure beatificamus rationabile studium hominis quod deposito supercilio Pharisæorum, ex quibus erat, Dominum nostrum audiens magistrum illum vocavit vera intentione discendi."

Ῥαββεί] Such a style of address in the mouth of Nicodemus (*v.* 10) is significant (comp. i. 38). The title was one of late date, not having come into use till the time of Herod the Great, with the schools of Shammai and Hillel. It corresponds closely with " Master " (*Magister*), and was used in three forms, •Rab, Rabbi, Rabban (Rabbun, John xx. 16). According to the Jewish saying, " Rabbi was higher than Rab, Rabban than Rabbi, but greater than all was he who [like the prophets] was not called by any such title." The Aramaic form is retained i. 38 (with the interpretation Διδάσκαλε : comp. xx. 16), 49, iv. 31, vi. 25, ix. 2, xi. 8, and, of the Baptist, iii. 26. The corresponding Greek term, Διδάσκαλε, which is not infrequent in the Synoptic Gospels, is not found, except as an explanation, in St. John (yet notice viii. 4).

οἴδαμεν] Comp. Mark xii. 14. There is a symptom of latent presumption in the word. Nicodemus claims for himself and for others like him the peculiar privilege of having read certainly the nature of the Lord's office in the signs which He wrought. So much at least he and they could do, if the common people were at fault. Comp. ix. 24. It is natural to connect such a recognition of the divine mission of Jesus with the report of the envoys sent to John :

can do these signs that thou doest, except God be
3 with him. Jesus answered and said unto him, Verily,
verily, I say unto thee, Except one be born anew,

i. 19. Contrast Matt. xii. 24;
ch. ix. 29.

ὅτι ἀπὸ θεοῦ ἐλ.] The order is
expressive : " we know that it is
from God, not from man, thy
title to teach is derived." Jesus
had not studied in the schools,
but possessed the right of a
Rabbi from a higher source.
Comp. vii. 15, 16.

διδάσκαλος] magister v. ; a
teacher, not different in kind
from other teachers. In this
conception lay the essence of the
error of Nicodemus. Ἔτι κάτω
στρέφεται ὁ Νικόδημος, ἔτι ἀνθρωπίνην ἔχει περὶ αὐτοῦ διάνοιαν
καὶ ὡς περὶ προφήτου διαλέγεται,
οὐδὲν μέγα ἀπὸ τῶν σημείων
φανταζόμενος . . . Ἀλλ' ὁ φι-
λάνθρωπος θεὸς οὐδὲ οὕτως αὐτὸν
ἀπώσατο οὐδὲ διήλεξεν . . . τί
οὖν νυκτὸς ἔρχῃ καὶ λανθάνων πρὸς
τὸν τὰ τοῦ θεοῦ λέγοντα ; (Chrysostom).

The address of Nicodemus is
incomplete, but he evidently
wishes to invite the Lord to give
a fuller view of His teaching,
and that, it may reasonably be
supposed, with regard to the
kingdom of God of which John
had spoken.

ἐὰν μή . . . αὐτ.] Comp. Acts x.
38 ; 1 Sam. xviii. 14 ; c. ix. 31 f.
So St. Peter starts from signs,
Acts ii. 22.

ἀπεκρίθη] The Lord answered
not his words, but his thoughts.
The Lord's answers to questions
will be found generally to reveal
the true thought of the questioner, and to be fitted to guide
him to the truth which he is

seeking. Nicodemus implied that
he and those like him were prepared to understand and welcome
the Lord's teaching. Ἐνόμισεν ὁ
Νικόδημος γνῶναι αὐτὸν καὶ ὀρθὰ
φρονεῖν περὶ αὐτοῦ (Theophylact).
This appeared to him to be of
the same order as that with
which he was already familiar.
He does not address the Lord as
if he were ready to welcome
Him as "the Christ" or "the
prophet." On the other hand,
the Lord's reply sets forth distinctly that His work was not
simply to carry on what was
already begun, but to recreate.
The new kingdom of which He
was the founder could not be
comprehended till after a new
birth.

There was, however, a germ of
truth in the positive confession
of Nicodemus, and Christ revealed Himself "quia tantum
ore confessus est quantum corde
intelligere poterit" (Rupert).

Ἀμὴν ἀμήν] i. 51, note. The
words by their emphasis generally presuppose some difficulty or
misunderstanding to be overcome;
and at the same time they mark
the introduction of a new thought
carrying the divine teaching
farther forward, vv. 5, 11. Comp.
v. 19, vi. 47, 53. They are found
with a direct personal address
vv. 5, 11, xiii. 38, xxi. 18.

λέγω σοι] unto thee. The address
was general : the reply is personal. Comp. xiv. 8, 9.

γενν. ἄνωθεν] renatus fuerit denuo v. ; be born again. See additional note.

4 τοῦ θεοῦ. λέγει πρὸς αὐτὸν [ὁ] Νικόδημος Πῶς δύναται
ἄνθρωπος γεννηθῆναι γέρων ὤν; μὴ δύναται εἰς τὴν
κοιλίαν τῆς μητρὸς αὐτοῦ δεύτερον εἰσελθεῖν καὶ γεν-
5 νηθῆναι; ἀπεκρίθη [ὁ] Ἰησοῦς Ἀμὴν ἀμὴν λέγω σοι,
ἐὰν μή τις γεννηθῇ ἐξ ὕδατος καὶ πνεύματος, οὐ δύναται

οὐ δύν. ἰδεῖν . . .] Without this
new birth—this introduction into
a vital connexion with a new order
of being, with a corresponding
endowment of faculties—no man
can see—can outwardly apprehend—the kingdom of God. Our
natural powers cannot realise
that which is essentially spiritual.
The impossibility lies in the moral
characteristics of the man, and
not in any external power. Comp.
vi. 44, note. A new vision is
required for the objects of a new
world (comp. v. 36). Elsewhere
there are references to the change
required (Matt. xviii. 3 ; 1 Cor.
ii. 14) in order that we may
observe that which, though about
us, is unregarded (Luke xvii.
20, 21).

The sense which is commonly
given to " see " in this passage,
as if it were equivalent to "enjoy," "have experience of" (Luke
ii. 26, see death ; Acts ii. 27, see
corruption ; 1 Pet. iii. 10, see
good days), entirely sacrifices
the marked contrast between
"seeing" and "entering into"
the kingdom. Part of the same
thought is found in Luke xvii.
20.

In the Shepherd a sharp distinction is drawn between " seeing" and "entering into" the
kingdom of God: Ταῦτα τὰ ὀνόματα
[Λύπη, Πονηρία . . .] ὁ φορῶν τοῦ
θεοῦ δοῦλος τὴν βασιλείαν μὲν
ὄψεται τοῦ θεοῦ εἰς αὐτὴν δὲ οὐκ
εἰσελεύσεται (Sim. ix. 15).

τὴν βασ. τοῦ θ.] the kingdom of
God. The phrase occurs only
here and in v. 5 in St. John's
Gospel (yet compare xviii. 36,
37 ; Rev. i. 6, 9, v. 10, xii. 10,
xx. 4, 6, xxii. 5), while it is
frequent in the Synoptists. St.
Matthew alone uses, in addition,
the phrase " the kingdom of
heaven," which is found as an
early variant in v. 5 (in ‭א‬, etc.).
The phrase " the kingdom of
God " is found in the Acts, and
in each group of St. Paul's
Epistles ; but it does not occur in
the Epistle to the Hebrews or in
the Catholic Epistles (comp. 2 Pet.
i. 11). It has always a twofold
application, external and internal ; and the immediate application in each case leads on to a
more complete fulfilment in the
same direction. Thus under the
old dispensation the visible Israel
was the kingdom of God as
typical of the visible catholic
church, the spiritual Israel as
typical of the true spiritual
church. And now again the
visible church is the type of the
future universal reign of Christ,
as the spiritual church is of the
consummation of Christ's reign
in heaven.

The abrupt introduction of the
phrase, which finds no direct
preparation in the words of Nicodemus, appears to be designed
to lift the thoughts of the Rabbi
beyond the limit of the schools.
Even if popular teachers spoke

4 he cannot see the kingdom of God. Nicodemus
saith unto him, How can a man be born when
he is old? can he enter a second time into his
5 mother's womb, and be born? Jesus answered,
Verily, verily, I say unto thee, Except a man be
born of water and the [1] Spirit, he cannot enter

[1] or spirit.

of a kingdom of God, they could not " see " it.

4. It is commonly supposed that Nicodemus either misunderstood the general scope of the Lord's answer, or half-mockingly set it aside. But in fact he employs the image chosen by the Lord in sober earnest to bring out the overwhelming difficulties with which the idea suggested by it was encompassed. It is one indication of the point of his argument that he substitutes for the indefinite phrase used by the Lord (ἐὰν μή τις . . .) the definite title (πῶς δύναται ἄνθρωπος . . .;).

Πῶς δύναται . . .;] *How can a man . . . ?* How is it possible for a man whose whole nature at any moment is the sum of all the past, to start afresh ? How can he undo, or do away with, the result which years have brought and which goes to form himself ? His " I " includes the whole development through which he has passed ; and how then can it survive a new birth ? Can the accumulation of boyhood, youth, maturity be removed and the true " self " remain ?

γέρων ὤν] *cum senex sit* v. Nicodemus evidently applies the Lord's words to his own case. The trait is full of life.

μὴ δύναται . . .;] *can he enter a second time* (*iterato introire* v.)

into his mother's womb, and be born ? Nicodemus takes one part of a man's complex personality only. Is it possible to conceive physical birth repeated ? And if not, Nicodemus seems to say to Christ, how then can there be any such moral new birth as you claim ? For all life from its first beginning has contributed to the moral character which belongs to each person. The result of all life is one and indivisible.

This thought is one which cannot but occur to every one. It goes to the very root of faith. The great mystery of religion is not the punishment, but the forgiveness, of sin : not the natural permanence of character, but spiritual regeneration. And it is one aspect of this mystery which Nicodemus puts forth clearly.

5. Christ meets the difficulty urged by Nicodemus by an enlarged repetition of the former statement. As before He had insisted on the fact of the new birth, He now reveals the nature of the birth. This involves an outward and an inward element, which are placed side by side.

ἐὰν μή τις γενν. ἐξ ὕδ. κ. πν.] *nisi quis renatus fuerit ex aqua et spiritu* v. ; *except a man be*

⁶ εἰσελθεῖν εἰς τὴν βασιλείαν τοῦ ¹ θεοῦ. τὸ γεγεννημένον
ἐκ τῆς σαρκὸς σάρξ ἐστιν, καὶ τὸ γεγεννημένον ἐκ τοῦ
⁷ πνεύματος πνεῦμά ἐστιν. μὴ θαυμάσῃς ὅτι εἶπόν σοι

¹ τοῦ θεοῦ ℵ^cΑΒΛΓΔ; τῶν οὐρανῶν ℵ*.

born of water and spirit. The
preposition ἐξ recalls the phrase
" baptize—plunge—*in* water, *in*
spirit" (Matt. iii. 11), so that
the image suggested is that of
rising, reborn, out of the water
and out of that spiritual element,
so to speak, to which the water
outwardly corresponds. Comp.
Chrys. xxv. (xxiv.) 2.

The combination of the words
water and *spirit* suggests a remote parallel and a marked
contrast. They carry back the
thoughts of hearer and reader to
the narrative of creation (Gen.
i. 2), and to the characteristics
of natural birth, to which St.
John has already emphatically
referred (i. 13). The water and
the spirit suggest the original
shaping of the great Order out
of Chaos, when the Spirit of God
brooded on the face of the
waters ; and at the same time
this new birth is distinctly separated from the corruptible element
(blood) which symbolises that
which is perishable and transitory in human life.

These distant references serve
in some degree to point to the
true sense of the passage. If
further we regard the specific
Biblical ideas of *water* and *spirit*,
when they are separated, it will
be seen that *water* symbolises
purification (comp. i. 25, note)
and *spirit* quickening : the one
implies a definite external rite,
the other indicates an energetic
internal operation. The two are
co-ordinate, correlative, com-

plementary. Hence all interpretations which treat the term
water here as simply figurative
and descriptive of the cleansing
power of the Spirit are essentially defective, as they are also
opposed to all ancient tradition.

The phrase γεννᾶσθαι ἐκ is
found in the New Testament
only in the Gospel and First
Epistle of St. John. Comp. ch. i.
13, note ; 1 John iii. 1, additional
note.

This being so, we must take
account of the application of
these ideas of cleansing and
quickening to the circumstances
under which the words were first
spoken, and of their application
to the fulness of the Christian
economy. The words had an
immediate, if incomplete, sense,
as they were addressed to Nicodemus : they have also a final
and complete sense for us. And
yet more, the inceptive sense
must be in complete harmony
with the fuller sense, and help
to illustrate it.

It can, then, scarcely be questioned that as Nicodemus heard
the words, *water* carried with it
a reference to John's baptism,
which was a divinely appointed
rite (i. 33), gathering up into
itself and investing with a
new importance all the lustral
baptisms of the Jews (comp.
Heb. vi. 2, βαπτισμῶν διδ.) : the
spirit, on the other hand, marked
that inward power which John
placed in contrast with his own

6 into the kingdom of God. That which is born of the flesh is flesh ; and that which is born of 7 the ¹ Spirit is spirit. Marvel not that I said unto

¹ *or* spirit.

baptism. Thus the words, taken in their immediate meaning as intelligible to Nicodemus, set forth, as required before entrance into the kingdom of God, the acceptance of the preliminary rite divinely sanctioned, which was the seal of repentance and so of forgiveness, and following on this communication of a new life, resulting from the direct action of the Holy Spirit through Christ. The Pharisees rejected the rite, and by so doing cut themselves off from the grace which was attached to it. They would not become as little children, and so they could not enter into the kingdom of heaven.

But the sense of the words cannot be limited to this first meaning. Like the corresponding words in ch. vi., they look forward to the fulness of the Christian dispensation, when (after the Resurrection) the baptism of water was no longer separated from, but united with, the baptism of the spirit in the "laver of regeneration" (Titus iii. 5 ; comp. Eph. v. 26), even as the outward and the inward are united generally in a religion which is sacramental and not only typical. Christian baptism, the outward act of faith welcoming the promise of God, is incorporation into the Body of Christ, and so the birth of the Spirit is potentially united with the birth of water. The general inseparability of these two is

indicated by the form of the expression, *born of water and spirit* (ἐξ ὕδ. καὶ πν.), as distinguished from the double phrase, *born of water and of spirit* (comp. iv. 24, ἐν πνεύματι καὶ ἀληθείᾳ).

According to this view the words have a distinct historical meaning, and yet they have also a meaning far beyond that which was at first capable of being apprehended. They are in the highest sense prophetic, even as the following words, in which the Lord speaks of His Passion ; and at the same time they contemplate the fulness of the organised life of the Christian society (*enter into the kingdom of heaven . . . not see life, v.* 36).

εἰσελθεῖν εἰς . . .] *introire in . . . v.* ; *enter into*, become a citizen of the kingdom, as distinguished from the mere intelligent spectator (see *v.* 3) of its constitution and character. The image suggested by the words *enter into* is that of entering into the promised land —the type of the kingdom of heaven—as in Ps. xcv. 11.

The phrase εἰσελθεῖν εἰς τὴν βασ. τοῦ θεοῦ (τῶν οὐρ.) occurs Matt. v. 20, vii. 21, xviii. 3, xix. 23 ; Mark ix. 47, x. 23 ff. ; Luke xviii. 17, 25 ; Acts xiv. 22. In every case it is connected with thoughts of difficulty, effort, change.

6. A new birth is necessary to gain a true conception of the divine kingdom : a new birth,

8 Δεῖ ὑμᾶς γεννηθῆναι ἄνωθεν. τὸ πνεῦμα ὅπου θέλει
πνεῖ, καὶ τὴν φωνὴν αὐτοῦ ἀκούεις, ἀλλ᾽ οὐκ οἶδας πόθεν
ἔρχεται καὶ ποῦ ὑπάγει· οὕτως ἐστὶν πᾶς ὁ γεγεννημένος

distinctly specified as having an
outward fulfilment as well as
an inward, is necessary for
admission into the kingdom,
which is itself at once outward
and spiritual. This conclusion
follows from a very simple consideration. No principle can
produce results superior to itself.
If man is to enjoy a spiritual
life, that by which he enters it
—his birth—must be of a corresponding character. The flesh
(i. 13, see note) can only gener-
ate flesh. Spiritual life cannot
come forth from it. Comp.
1 Cor. xv. 50.

The fact which the Lord
affirms is at once more marvellous and more natural than that
by which Nicodemus typified it.
A mere repetition of the natural
birth would not bring that which
man requires. It would be alto
gether unavailing, even if it were
possible.

τὸ γεγενν.] The tense conveys
an idea which can only be reproduced by a paraphrase: "that
which hath been born, and at
present comes before us in this
light." There is an important
difference observed in the narrative between the *fact* of the
birth (*aorist, vv.* 3, 4, 5, 7) and
the *state* which follows as the
abiding result of the birth (*perfect, vv.* 6, 8). In 1 John v. 18
the true interpretation depends
upon the contrast between the
one historic Son of God (ὁ γεν-
νηθείς, opposed to *the evil one*)
and the sons of God, who live in
virtue of their new birth (ὁ

γεγεννημένος). Compare also
Gal. iv. 23, 29 for a fainter
representation of a corresponding
difference of tenses.

The neuter (τὸ γεγενν. . . .)
states the principle in its most
abstract form. In *v.* 8 a transition is made to the man (πᾶς ὁ
γεγενν. . . .). There is a similar
contrast in 1 John v. 4 (neuter)
and 1 John v. 1, 18 (masc.).

σάρξ . . . πνεῦμα] *caro . . . spiritus* v. ; *flesh . . . spirit.* The
words describe the characteristic
principles of two orders. They
are not related to one another as
evil and good ; but as the two
spheres of being with which man
is connected. By the "spirit"
our complex nature is united to
heaven, by the "flesh" to earth.
Comp. vi. 63, note.

The term *flesh* probably includes all that belongs to the life
of sensation, all that by which
we are open to the physical
influences of pleasure and pain,
which naturally sway our actions.
Thus, though it does not of itself
include the idea of sinfulness
(i. 14 ; 1 John iv. 2), it describes
human personality on the side
which tends to sin, and on which
actually we have sinned.

It must also be noticed that
that which is born of flesh and
spirit is described not as "fleshly"
and "spiritual," but as "flesh"
and "spirit." In other words,
the child, so to speak, is of the
same nature as the parent, and
does not only partake of his
qualities. The child also occupies
in turn the position of a parent,

8 thee, Ye must be born anew. The wind bloweth where it listeth, and thou hearest the voice thereof, but knowest not whence it cometh, and whither it goeth : so is every one that is born of the Spirit.

from which a progeny springs like to himself. Compare the corresponding usage, 1 John i. 5 (light), iv. 8 (love).

ἐκ τοῦ πν.] The primary sense seems to be *of spirit*, not *of the* [Holy] *Spirit*. But while the term is essentially abstract and expresses spirit as spirit, the quickening power is the Spirit. The idea of nature passes into that of Person. The *water* is not repeated, because the outward rite draws its virtue from the action of the Spirit.

Many early authorities (*Lat. vt., Syr. vt.*) add the gloss, *quia Deus spiritus est et de (ex) Deo natus est.* Ambrose (*De Spir.* iii. § 59) accuses the Arians of having removed the words *quia Deus spiritus est* from their MSS. The charge is an admirable illustration of the groundlessness of such accusations of wilful corruption of Scripture. The words in question have no Greek authority at all, and are obviously a comment.

7. μὴ θαυ. . . .] *non mireris . . .* v. ; *marvel not . . .* If then this is a necessary law—such is the force of the Lord's words—that the offspring must have the essential nature of the parent, and if the kingdom of God is spiritual and its citizens therefore spiritual, while the nature of man, as all experience it to be, is fleshly, swayed by powers which belong to earth, *Marvel not that I said unto thee, Ye must be born again*, not " Man

generally " must be born again, but " Ye must be born again "— even " you," the elect representatives of the chosen people, who think that you have penetrated to the true conception of Messiah's work, and prepared yourselves adequately for judging it and entering into it.

There appears also to be in the emphatic *ye* an implied contrast between the Lord, who needed no re-birth, and all other men. He does not say, as a human teacher, " *We* must be born again."

The passage from the singular (εἶπόν σοι) to the plural (δεῖ ὑμᾶς) ought not to be overlooked, comp. i. 51 ; and especially Luke xxii. 31, 32.

8. There is indeed ground for wonder at first sight in the prospect of such a change ; but this spiritual change falls in part under the test of experience. The very word which is used to describe it as " spiritual " suggests an image which finds fulfilment in life.

With μὴ θαυμάσῃς contrast ch. v. 28 ; 1 John iii. 13, Μὴ θαυμάζετε (Luke x. 4).

τὸ πνεῦμα . . . τοῦ πν.] *spiritus . . . ex spiritu* v. ; *the wind . . . the spirit.* In Hebrew, Syriac, Latin, the words are identical (as properly *Geist* and *Ghost*), and Wiclif and the Rhemish Version keep " spirit " in both cases, after the Latin. But at present the retention of one word in both places could only create confusion,

9 ἐκ¹ τοῦ πνεύματος. ἀπεκρίθη Νικόδημος καὶ εἶπεν αὐτῷ
10 Πῶς δύναται ταῦτα γενέσθαι; ἀπεκρίθη Ἰησοῦς καὶ εἶπεν
αὐτῷ Σὺ εἶ ὁ διδάσκαλος τοῦ Ἰσραὴλ καὶ ταῦτα οὐ
11 γινώσκεις; ἀμὴν ἀμὴν λέγω σοι ὅτι ὃ οἴδαμεν λαλοῦμεν
καὶ ὃ ἑωράκαμεν μαρτυροῦμεν, καὶ τὴν μαρτυρίαν ἡμῶν

¹ Insert τοῦ ὕδατος καὶ ℵ.

since the separation between the material emblem and the power which it was used to describe is complete. The use of the correlative verb (πνεῖ, ch. vi. 18; Rev. vii. 1; Matt. vii. 25, 27; Luke xii. 55; Acts xxvii. 40), and of the word *sound* (voice), is quite decisive for the literal sense of the noun (πνεῦμα); and still at the same time the whole of the phraseology is inspired by the higher meaning. Perhaps also the unusual word (πνεῦμα, 1 Kings xviii. 45, xix. 11; 2 Kings iii. 17) is employed to suggest this. The comparison lies between the obvious physical properties of the wind and the mysterious action of that spiritual influence to which the name "spirit," "wind," was instinctively applied. The laws of both are practically unknown; both are unseen; the presence of both is revealed in their effects.

ὅπου θέλει] The phrase is not to be pressed physically. The wind obeys its own proper laws, which depend on a complication of phenomena which we cannot calculate, and consequently for us it is a natural image of freedom. For a similar phrase applied to the Spirit, see 1 Cor. xii. 11.

τὴν φ....] *the voice* ... The word commonly implies an articulate, intelligible voice, as even in a passage like 1 Cor. xiv. 7 ff.;

yet in the Revelation the word is used more widely, *e.g.* ix. 9, xiv. 2, etc.

ἀλλ' οὐκ οἶδ.] *but* thou *knowest not.* "Nemo videt Spiritum; et quomodo audimus vocem Spiritus? Sonat Psalmus; vox est spiritus. Sonat Evangelium; vox est spiritus. Sonat sermo divinus; vox est spiritus" (Aug. *ad loc.*). Comp. Eccles. xi. 5.

οὕτως ἐ....] *so is every one* ... The form of the comparison is irregular. The action of the Spirit on the believer is like the action of the wind in the material world. As the tree (for example) by waving branches and rustling leaves witnesses to the power which affects it, *so is every one that hath been born of the Spirit.* The believer shows by deed and word that an invisible influence has moved and inspired him. He is himself a continual sign of the action of the Spirit, which is freely determined, and incomprehensible by man as to source and end, though seen in its present results.

It is not unreasonable to suppose that this image of the wind was suggested by the sound of some sudden gust sweeping through the narrow street without. Thus the form of the Lord's teaching corresponds with the teaching by parables in the Synoptists (Matt. xiii. 4, note).

ὁ γεγενν. ἐκ τοῦ πνεύ.] *born of*

9 Nicodemus answered and said unto him, How can
10 these things come to pass? Jesus answered and
said unto him, Art thou the teacher of Israel, and
11 perceivest not these things? Verily, verily, I say
unto thee, We speak that we do know, and bear
witness of that we have seen; and ye receive not

the Spirit: v. 6. An important group of ancient authorities (א, *Lat. vt.*, *Syr. vt.*) read ἐκ τοῦ ὕδατος καὶ τοῦ πνεύματος. The gloss is a good example of a natural corruption by assimilation.

9. Πῶς... γεν.;] *Quomodo... fieri?* v.; *How can these things come to pass?* Τὸ γὰρ Πῶς τοῦτο τῶν οὐ σφόδρα πιστευόντων ἐστὶν ἐπαπόρησις, τῶν ἀπὸ γῆς ὄντων ἔτι (Chrys.). How can this new birth, issuing in a new life, be realised? The idea is of change, transition, not of essence, repose. The emphasis lies on *can*. Compare the other similar question (πῶς δύναται ...;), v. 4, vi. 52, (xi. 16), and, on the other side, v. 44.

10. Σὺ εἶ ὁ διδ....] *Art thou the teacher of Israel?* the authorised teacher of the chosen people of God. The definite article (ὁ διδάσκαλος) marks the recognised official relation of Nicodemus to the people generally. Compare for a use of the article not unlike this Luke xviii. 13 (τῷ ἁμ.); 1 Cor. xv. 8 (τῷ ἐκτρ.).

καὶ ... γιν.] *and perceivest not* by the knowledge of progress, recognition. Though Nicodemus had previously been ignorant of that which the Lord declared, he ought to have recognised the teaching as true when he heard it. Contrast iv. 10; and compare xiv. 7, and ii. 24, note.

The Greek Fathers think that there is a reference to the spiritual meaning of the record of the passage through the Red Sea, but Rupert, with deeper insight, refers to Ezek. xxxii. 15 ff., xlvii. 1 ff.; Zech. xiii. 1 ff.

ταῦτα] the reality of character of the spiritual influence shown in the actions of man, which yet is not of man, but comes from another region.

11. ὃ οἴδ. λαλοῦμεν. The plural contrasted with the singular *vv.* 3, 5, 7, 12 (all are unemphatic) is remarkable. It has been explained as a simple rhetorical plural, or as containing an allusion to John the Baptist, to the Prophets, to the Holy Spirit, to the Father (viii. 16, 18); but all these explanations appear to fail when taken in connexion with the *you* and *ye*. The Lord and those with Him, of whom some, including the Evangelist, may have been present at the interview, appear to stand in contrast to the group represented by Nicodemus. Compare iv. 22. There were already gathered round Christ those who had had personal (ἑωράκαμεν) and immediate (οἴδαμεν) knowledge of the divine wonders which He announced. Their witness is indeed distinguished from His afterwards (*v.* 13), but so far it reached as to meet the difficulties, and fill up the shortcomings of the faith which Nicodemus had attained

8

12 οὐ λαμβάνετε. εἰ τὰ ἐπίγεια εἶπον ὑμῖν καὶ οὐ πιστεύετε,
13 πῶς ἐὰν εἴπω ὑμῖν τὰ ἐπουράνια πιστεύσετε; καὶ οὐδεὶς
ἀναβέβηκεν εἰς τὸν οὐρανὸν εἰ μὴ ὁ ἐκ τοῦ οὐρανοῦ

to. The plural, it will be noticed, is used in connexion with "the things on earth," but the singular only (εἶπω) of "the things in heaven." Rupert associates the plural with the μαρτυρία, referring to viii. 18: "In hoc duntaxat versiculo pluraliter loqui maluit . . . Videlicet quia testari se profitetur . . . testimonium autem unius legitimum non est, sed in ore duorum vel trium testium stat omne verbum."

ὃ οἶδ. . . . ὃ ἑωρ. . . .] The words answered to actual knowledge; the witness declared actual experience. The object in each clause stands first: "That which we know, we speak; and that which we have seen, we witness." On ἑωράκαμεν Chrysostom says: Ἐπειδὴ καὶ παρ' ἡμῶν ἡ ὄψις ἐστὶ τῶν ἄλλων αἰσθήσεων πιστοτέρα κἂν βουληθῶμέν τινα πιστώσασθαι οὕτω λέγομεν ὅτι τοῖς ὀφθαλμοῖς ἡμῶν ἑωράκαμεν οὐκ ἐξ ἀκοῆς οἴδαμεν, διὰ τοῦτο καὶ ὁ Χριστὸς ἀνθρωπινώτερον πρὸς αὐτὸν διαλέγεται τὸν λόγον κἀντεῦθεν πιστούμενος.

καὶ τὴν μαρτ.] The stress lies on our witness. "What we have seen we witness, and our witness ye receive not." Comp. v. 27, n. For the use of the simple and in this connexion of sad contrast see i. 10, v. 32, vii. 28, 30, xiv. 24, xvi. 32.

12. εἰ . . . εἶπον . . .] si dixi . . . v.; if I told . . . As, for example, in what He had just said to Nicodemus of the spiritual birth, though this was but as a sample of the teaching which He had already addressed to men (you, not thee)

such as Nicodemus. Comp. Wisd. ix. 16.

τὰ ἐπίγεια] terrena v., the things which have their sphere and place on earth. This is the uniform sense of ἐπίγειος, and it must be so interpreted in the other places where it occurs: 1 Cor. xv. 40 (bodies for life on earth). Comp. Col. iii. 2; 2 Cor. v. 1; Phil. ii. 10, iii. 19 (whose thoughts rest on earth); James iii. 15 (wisdom which finds its consummation on earth, and reaches no higher). Thus the strictly local meaning (1 Cor. xv. 40; Phil. ii. 10) passes insensibly into a meaning predominantly moral (Phil. iii. 19; James iii. 15).

Here the phrase "earthly things" will mark those facts and phenomena of the higher life as a class (τὰ ἐπίγεια) which have their seat and manifestation on earth: which belong in their realisation to our present existence: which are seen in their consequences, like the issues of birth: which are sensible in their effects, like the action of the wind: which are a beginning and a prophecy, and not a fulfilment.

πῶς . . . πιστεύσετε;] how shall ye believe? The words are spoken with a view to the future already realised. The question is not abstract (How can ye?), but framed with regard to actual circumstances.

ἐὰν εἴπω . . . τὰ ἐπουρ.] si dixero cœlestia v.; if I tell you heavenly things, those truths which belong to a higher order, which are in heaven (τὰ ἐπουράνια), and

12 our witness. If I told you earthly things, and ye believe not, how shall ye believe, if I tell you 13 heavenly things? And no man hath gone up into heaven, but he that came down out of heaven,

are brought down thence to earth as they can *become* to men. Such was the full revelation of the Son, involving the redemption of the world and the reunion of man with God, which is indicated in the three following verses. The reality of these truths finds no outward confirmation, as the new birth in its fruits. The difference thus indicated between the "earthly" and the " heavenly " elements of the Lord's teaching serves to show the ground of the contrast between St. John and the earlier Evangelists. The teaching of the Lord was on one side, like the teaching of the Baptist, a preparation for the kingdom of heaven (Mark i. 15); and on the other a revelation of the kingdom both in its embodiment and in its life. (Comp. Heb. vi. 1 f., στοιχεῖα, τελειότης.) On ἐπουράνιος see Heb. viii. 5, note.

13. καὶ οὐδείς . . .] The transition by " and " is completely according to the Hebrew idiom, which adds new thoughts without defining the exact relation in which they stand to what has gone before. That must be determined by the thoughts regarded in juxtaposition. Men might be unprepared to receive the teaching of heavenly things, yet side by side with this fact were two others : that Christ alone could teach them, and that His mission was but for a time. While also these facts included

the two great mysteries of the spiritual life : the truths as to the Person and as to the Work of the Son of man. Chrysostom thus traces the connexion : Ποία αὕτη ἡ ἀκολουθία . . .; μεγίστη μὲν οὖν καὶ σφόδρα τοῖς ἔμπροσθεν συνᾴδουσα. ἐπειδὴ γὰρ ἐκεῖνος εἶπεν ὅτι οἴδαμεν ὅτι ἀπὸ θεοῦ ἐλήλυθας διδάσκαλος, τοῦτο αὐτὸ διορθοῦται μονονουχὶ λέγων μὴ νομίσῃς με οὕτως εἶναι διδάσκαλον ὡς τοὺς πολλοὺς τῶν προφητῶν ἀπὸ γῆς ὄντας.

ἀναβέβηκεν . . .] *hath gone up to heaven.* Comp. Deut. xxx. 12 ; Prov. xxx. 4. No man hath risen into the region of absolute and eternal truth, so as to look upon it face to face, and in the possession of that knowledge declare it to men ; but the Son of man, He in whom humanity is summed up, has the knowledge which comes from immediate vision. And His elevation is yet more glorious than a mere ascent. He did not mount up to heaven, as if earth were His home, but came down thence *out of heaven,* as truly dwelling there ; and therefore He has inherently the fulness of heavenly knowledge. Comp. Plato's myth in the *Phædrus.*

εἰ μή . . .] The particles do not imply that Christ had ascended to heaven, as though He were one of a class, and contrasted with all the others (*no man except*), but simply that He in fact enjoyed that directness of knowledge by nature which another could only attain to by such an

14 καταβάς, ὁ υἱὸς τοῦ ἀνθρώπου ¹. καὶ καθὼς Μωυσῆς
ὕψωσεν τὸν ὄφιν ἐν τῇ ἐρήμῳ, οὕτως ὑψωθῆναι δεῖ τὸν
15 υἱὸν τοῦ ἀνθρώπου, ἵνα πᾶς ὁ πιστεύων ἐν αὐτῷ ² ἔχῃ

¹ Insert ὁ ὢν ἐν τῷ οὐρανῷ (A). See note.
² Insert μὴ ἀπόληται, ἀλλ' ΑΓΔ. See note.

ascension. The exception is to
the whole statement in the preceding clause, and not to any
part of it. Comp. Luke iv. 26 f. ;
Matt. xii. 4 ; Gal. i. 7.

ὁ . . . καταβάς] *he that came
down out of heaven*—that is, at
the Incarnation. Compare vi. 32,
33 ff., 42, etc. The phrase is used
of the manifestation of God in the
Old Testament : Exod. xix. 11 ff.,
Num. xi. 17, 25, xii. 5.

The exact form of expression
is very remarkable. It preserves
the continuity of the Lord's
personality, and yet does not
confound His natures : " He that
came down from heaven, even He
who being Incarnate is the Son of
man, without ceasing to be what
He was before." Compare i. 14,
vi. 38. So Theophylact says :
Υἱὸν δὲ ἀνθρώπου ἀκούσας καταβῆναι
ἐξ οὐρανοῦ μὴ νομίσῃς ὅτι ἡ σὰρξ ἐκ
τοῦ οὐρανοῦ κατέβη . . . ἀλλ' ἐπεὶ
μία ἡ ὑπόστασις ἤγουν ἓν πρόσωπον
ἦν ὁ Χριστὸς ἐκ δύο φύσεων σύνθετος,
τὰ τοῦ ἀνθρώπου ὀνόματα λέγονται
ἐπὶ τοῦ λόγου καὶ πάλιν τὰ τοῦ
λόγου τῷ ἀνθρώπῳ προστίθενται.

ὁ ὢν ἐν . . .] *qui est in cælo*
v. ; *which is in heaven.* These
words are omitted by many very
ancient authorities, and appear
to be an early gloss bringing out
the right contrast between the
ascent of a man to heaven and
the abiding of the Son of man
in heaven. See additional note
at the end of the chapter.

Augustine comments on the
Lord's two natures : " Ecce hic

erat et in cælo erat : hic erat
carne, in cælo erat divinitate :
immo ubique divinitate. Natus
de matre non recedens a Patre.
Duæ nativitates Christi intelli-
guntur : una divina per quam
efficeremur, altera per quam re-
ficeremur . . ."

14. The character of the revelation through the Son of man
has been set forth in the former
verse, and in this the issue of
that revelation in the Passion is
further indicated. This mystery
is shadowed forth under the
image of an Old Testament
symbol (Num. xxi. 7 ff.), just as
the Resurrection had been half
veiled, half declared, under the
figure of a restored temple (ii.
19). In the last miracle of
Moses, on the borders of the
promised land, the serpent had
been "lifted up," and made a
conspicuous object to all the
stricken people ; and so too was
Christ to be "lifted up," and
with the same life-giving issue.
How this "lifting up" should be
accomplished is not yet made
clear. See additional note. The
point of connexion between *v.* 13
and *v.* 14 lies in the repetition
of the title "the Son of man."
The Incarnation, under the actual circumstances of humanity,
carried with it the necessity of
the Passion.

οὕτως ὑψ. δεῖ . . .] *ita exaltari
oportet* . . . v. ; *so must the Son
of man be lifted up.* The order
of the words throws a significant

₁₄ *even* the Son of man. And as Moses lifted up the
serpent in the wilderness, even so must the Son of
₁₅ man be lifted up: that every one that believeth

emphasis on ὑψωθῆναι. The same
phrase (ὑψωθῆναι) occurs viii. 28,
xii. 32, note, 34, in reference to
the Passion; and elsewhere (Acts
ii. 33, v. 31; [Phil. ii. 9]) in
reference to the Ascension consequent upon it. Thus the words
imply an exaltation in appearance far different from that of
the triumphant king, and yet in
its true issue leading to a divine
glory. This passage through the
elevation on the cross to the
elevation on the right hand of God
was a necessity (δεῖ) arising out
of the laws of the divine nature.
Two divine necessities are
marked. "Men must be born
again" (*v.* 7), and "the Son of
man must be lifted up" (*v.* 14,
xii. 34). There is need of a personal regeneration; there is need
of a common atonement.

It is of interest to observe the
other facts of which St. John has
recorded the same moral necessity (δεῖ).

Of Christ—

x. 16, κἀκεῖνα δεῖ με ἀγαγεῖν.

xx. 9, δεῖ αὐτὸν ἐκ νεκρῶν ἀναστῆναι. Comp. iii. 30, ἐκεῖνον δεῖ
αὐξάνειν.

Of men—

iv. 24, ἐν πνεύματι καὶ ἀληθείᾳ
δεῖ προσκυνεῖν.

ix. 4, ἡμᾶς δεῖ ἐργάζεσθαι τὰ
ἔργα τοῦ πέμψαντός με.

If we look at the revelation of
the Son of man given in *vv.*
13—15 we shall see that it covers
all the circumstances of human
life. Union with God through
His Son is the fulfilment of the
creation of man: the Atonement

by the cross is required in consequence of man's Fall.

It is important to notice that
similar figurative references to
the issue of the Lord's work in His
Death are found in the Synoptic
record: Matt. ix. 14 ff., x. 38;
Mark viii. 34; Luke xiv. 27.

15. π. ὁ πιστ. ἐν αὐ. . . .] *every
one that believeth may have in
Him eternal life,* according to the
familiar formula of St. Paul, ἐν
Χριστῷ. To "believe" is used
absolutely *v.* 12, i. 50, iv. 42, 53,
vi. 36, xi. 15, xx. 29; and the
exceptional order of the words
(ἐν αὐτῷ ἔχῃ) finds a justification
in v. 39, xvi. 33.

ζωὴν αἰών.] *vitam æternam* v.;
eternal life. As the wounded
who looked on the brazen serpent were restored to temporal
health, so in this case *eternal life*
follows from the faith of the
believer on the crucified and
exalted Lord.

The exact phrase, *have eternal
life,* as distinguished from *live
for ever,* is characteristic of St.
John. It occurs *vv.* 16, 36, v.
24, vi. 40, 47, 54; 1 John iii.
15, v. 12 f. (x. 10, xx. 31, *hath
life*). Comp. Matt. xix. 16. The
use of the auxiliary verb marks
the distinct realisation of the life
as a personal blessing (*have* life),
as being more than the act of
living. Compare xvi. 22, *have
sorrow.* So too the gift is not
future but present (v. 24).

The word αἰώνιος is found in
St. John's Gospel and Epistles
only in connexion with ζωή
(Rev. xiv. 6, εὐαγγέλιον αἰών.).

16 ζωὴν αἰώνιον. Οὕτως γὰρ ἠγάπησεν ὁ θεὸς τὸν κόσμον
ὥστε τὸν υἱὸν τὸν μονογενῆ ἔδωκεν, ἵνα πᾶς ὁ πιστεύων

On the connexion again Chrysostom says:

Πάλιν καὶ τοῦτο δοκεῖ ἀπηρτῆσθαι τῶν ἔμπροσθεν πολλὴν δὲ καὶ αὐτὸ τὴν συνάφειαν ἔχει, εἰπὼν γὰρ τὴν μεγίστην εἰς ἀνθρώπους γεγενημένην εὐεργεσίαν διὰ τοῦ βαπτίσματος ἐπάγει καὶ τὴν ταύτης αἰτίαν καὶ ἐκείνης οὐκ ἐλάττονα τὴν διὰ τοῦ σταυροῦ.

The record of the conversation comes to an end without any formal close. There is nothing surprising in this. The history is not that of an outward incident, but of a spiritual situation. This is fully analysed; and the issue is found in the later notices of Nicodemus, so far as it has an immediate personal value.

Several observations are suggested by the narrative, which will be illustrated by later passages of the Gospel.

1. The account of the conversation is evidently compressed. The Evangelist does little more than indicate the great moments of the discussion. The full meaning and connexion of the parts can only be gained by supplying what he merely indicates.

2. In spite of the compression there is a distinct progress and completeness in the record. The order of thought is real and natural.

3. The thoughts are not obvious, but when they are understood they deal with critical difficulties; and with difficulties which belong to the first stage of the preaching of the Gospel.

4. The form and substance of the discussion keep completely within the line of Jewish ideas.

All that is said belongs to a time before the full declaration of the nature of Christ's work, while the language is fitted to move a hearer to deeper questionings, and is in perfect harmony with later and plainer revelations.

5. The occurrence of the phrase "kingdom of God" here only in St. John's Gospel belongs to the exact circumstances of the incident.

6. If the narrative were a free composition of a late date, it is inconceivable that the obscure allusions should not have been made clearer; and if it were composed for a purpose, it is inconceivable that the local colouring of opinion and method should have been what it is.

7. The recorded circumstances, the meeting of Christ, at the time of His first public appearance, with one in whom pride of descent and pride of knowledge were united, explains the subject and manner of the discourse. And the essential principles involved in it explain why the Evangelist was guided to report it. The narrative belongs to one definite point in the history of religious development and also to all time.

16 — 21. This section is a commentary on the nature of the mission of the Son, which has been indicated in Christ's words (vv. 13, 14), and unfolds its design (16, 17), its historic completion (18, 19), the cause of its apparent failure (20, 21). It adds no new thoughts, but brings out the force of the revelation already given in outline (1—15) by the light of Christian experience.

16 may in him have eternal life. For God so loved the world, that he gave his only begotten Son, that whosoever believeth on him may not perish, but

It is therefore likely (from its secondary character, apart from all other considerations) that it contains the reflections of the Evangelist, and is not a continuation of the words of the Lord. This conclusion appears to be firmly established from details of expression.

1. The tenses in v. 19 (ἐλήλυθεν, ἦν) evidently mark a crisis accomplished, and belong to the position which St. John occupied, but not to that in which the Lord stood, when the revelation of His Person and Work had not been openly presented to the world.

2. The phrase ὁ υἱὸς ὁ μονογενής (vv. 16, 18) is used of Christ elsewhere only in i. 14, 18; 1 John iv. 9; and in each case by the Evangelist.

3. The phrase πιστεύειν εἰς τὸ ὄνομα (v. 18) is not found in the recorded words of Christ, while it occurs in St. John's narrative, i. 12, ii. 23; 1 John v. 13.

4. ποιεῖν τὴν ἀλήθειαν occurs elsewhere in the New Testament only in 1 John i. 6.

The addition of such a comment finds a parallel in i. 16—18. There is also an obvious fitness in the apostolic exposition of the Lord's words at this crisis, as in that of the Baptist's words which follows (vv. 31—36). The questionings of Nicodemus and the testimony of John give, so to speak, the last utterances of Judaism, the last thoughts of the student, and the last message of the prophet. They show the difference and the connexion of the Old and New Dispensations. This difference and this connexion appeared under a changed aspect after Jerusalem had fallen, and it was of importance for the Evangelist to show that from the first the crisis was foreseen.

The succession of thoughts appears to be the following :—

1. The divine purpose in the Incarnation (16, 17).
This is set forth negatively and positively in relation to
(a) Man himself (personal),
  that he may
    not perish, but
    have everlasting life.
(β) The Son (general)
    not to judge the world,
    but that
    the world through
      Him may be saved.
2. The actual result (18, 19).
A judgement.
  (a) The application of the judgement.
    Those whom it reaches not,
    Those whom it has reached.
  (β) The nature of the judgement.
    Light offered,
    Darkness chosen.
3. The cause of the result in man (20, 21).
A twofold moral condition.
  (a) Those who do ill
    shrink from the light
    in fear of testing.
  (β) Those who do the Truth
    come to the light
    that their deeds may
    be made manifest

17 εἰς αὐτὸν μὴ ἀπόληται ἀλλὰ ἔχῃ ζωὴν αἰώνιον. οὐ γὰρ
ἀπέστειλεν ὁ θεὸς τὸν υἱὸν εἰς τὸν κόσμον ἵνα κρίνῃ τὸν
18 κόσμον, ἀλλ’ ἵνα σωθῇ ὁ κόσμος δι’ αὐτοῦ. ὁ πιστεύων
εἰς αὐτὸν οὐ κρίνεται. ὁ ¹ μὴ πιστεύων ἤδη κέκριται, ὅτι

¹ Insert δέ ALTᵇΓΔ.

16 ff. The pregnant declaration of the character and issue of the Lord's work given by Him to Nicodemus, as the representative of the old wisdom, leads the Evangelist to unfold its meaning more fully in relation to the actual circumstances in which he was himself placed. The issue of the proclamation of the Gospel had not in appearance corresponded with its promise and its power. But this issue did not modify its essential character.

16, 17. The divine purpose in the Incarnation was a purpose of universal love, even though it was imperfectly realised by man: a purpose of life to the believer, of salvation to the world.

16. Οὕτως γάρ . . .] *Sic enim . . .* v. Short explanatory remarks are frequently added in the same way (γάρ): ii. 25, iv. 44, vi. 6, 64, vii. 39, xiii. 11, xx. 9.

ἠγάπ. . . . τὸν κόσμ.] *dilexit . . . mundum* v.; *loved the world*, loved all humanity considered as apart from Himself. See i. 29, note. The love of God shown in the surrender and gift of His Son for men, is thus set forth as the spring of Redemption. The Father gave the Son even as the Son gave Himself.

Οὕτως . . . ὥστε] The supreme act serves as a measure of the love. Comp. 1 John iv. 11.

τὸν υἱὸν τ. μονογ. ἔδωκ.] *filium suum unigenitum daret* v.; *gave his only begotten Son*. The word

ἔδωκεν, not ἀπέστειλεν, as in v. 17, brings out the idea of sacrifice and of love shown by a most precious offering. The title "only begotten" is added to enhance this conception, and the exact form in which the title is introduced (τὸν υἱὸν τὸν μονογενῆ), which is different from that in v. 18 (τοῦ μονογενοῦς υἱοῦ) further emphasises it: "His Son, His only Son." Compare 1 John iv. 9; and Matt. iii. 17, etc. (ὁ υἱὸς ὁ ἀγαπητός). There is an obvious reference to Gen. xxii. 2.

ἵνα . . . μὴ ἀπόλ. ἀλλὰ ἔχῃ ζω. αἰών.] *ut . . . non pereat, sed habeat vitam æternam* v.; *may not perish* once for all, *but have* with an abiding present enjoyment *eternal* (as in v. 15) *life*. In this verse and in the next the negative and positive aspects of the truth as regards individuals and the race (*every one, the world*) are definitely opposed; and there is a striking parallelism in the related clauses: *perish, judge; have eternal life, be saved*. The addition of the clause, μὴ ἀπόληται ἀλλά, in this verse, as distinguished from v. 15, is explained naturally by the actual state of things which St. John saw in the Church and the world about him.

τ. κόσμ. . . . πᾶς ὁ πιστ.] The love of God is without limit on His part (v. 17, note), but to appropriate the blessing of love, man must fulfil the necessary condition of faith.

17 have eternal life. For God sent not the Son
into the world to judge the world; but that the
18 world may be saved through him. He that believeth on him is not judged: he that believeth
not hath been judged already, because he hath

17. οὐ γ. ἀπέστ. ὁ θεὸς τ. υἱ.]
non enim misit deus filium suum
v.; *for God sent not the Son.*
A transition is here made from
the notion of sacrifice, love, gift
(*v.* 16), to that of work and
authority. (Yet see 1 John iv.
9, ἀπέσταλκεν, not ἀπέστειλεν.)
There are two words equally
translated "send," which have
different shades of meaning:
ἀποστέλλειν suggests the thought
of a definite mission and a representative character in the envoy;
πέμπειν marks the simple relation
between the sender and the sent.
See xx. 21, note. It will be
observed also that the title *Son*
(*the Son*, not *his Son*), which is
that of dignity, takes the place
of *only begotten Son*, which is
the title of affection.

κρίνῃ] *judicet* v.; *judge* (and
so in verses 18, 19), as in the
exact parallel, xii. 47. It is
worthy of notice that St. John
does not use the compound verb
κατακρίνω, commonly translated
condemn, nor its derivatives,
though they occur in the history
of the woman taken in adultery
(viii. 10, 11).

In the later Jewish Messianic
anticipations the judgement of
the nations by the Messiah is the
most constant and the most
prominent feature.

ἵνα σωθῇ ὁ κόσμ.] *ut salvetur
mundus* v.; *that the world may
be saved.* The divine purpose is,
like the divine love, without any

limitation. The true title of the
Son is "the Saviour of the
world" (ch. iv. 42; 1 John iv.
14. Comp. ch. i. 29; 1 John ii.
2). The sad realities of present
experience cannot change the
truth thus made known, however little we may be able to
understand in what way it will
be accomplished. The thought
is made more impressive by the
threefold repetition of "the
world." Compare i. 10, xv. 19.
The general result is given here
(σωθῇ); in 1 John iv. 9 the individual appropriation of the
blessing (ζήσωμεν).

18, 19. But though judgement
was not the object of Christ's
mission, judgement is in fact the
necessary result of it. This
judgement is self-executed, and
follows inevitably from the revealed presence of Christ. (Comp.
Luke ii. 34, 35.)

18. οὐ κρίν. . . . ἤδη κέκριται]
*non judicatur . . . jam judicatus
est* v.; *is not judged . . . hath been
judged already.* The change of
tense is most significant. In the
case of the believer there is no
judgement. His whole life is *in*
Christ. In the case of the unbeliever, the judgement is completed; he is separated from
Christ, because he hath not
believed on the revelation made
in the person of Him who alone
can save. The epithet τοῦ μονογενοῦς, applied here again to the
Son, brings out in relation to

μὴ πεπίστευκεν εἰς τὸ ὄνομα τοῦ μονογενοῦς υἱοῦ τοῦ
19 θεοῦ. αὕτη δέ ἐστιν ἡ κρίσις ὅτι τὸ φῶς ἐλήλυθεν εἰς
τὸν κόσμον καὶ ἠγάπησαν οἱ ἄνθρωποι μᾶλλον τὸ σκότος
20 ἢ τὸ φῶς, ἦν γὰρ αὐτῶν πονηρὰ τὰ ἔργα. πᾶς γὰρ
ὁ φαῦλα πράσσων μισεῖ τὸ φῶς καὶ οὐκ ἔρχεται πρὸς
21 τὸ φῶς, ἵνα μὴ ἐλεγχθῇ τὰ ἔργα αὐτοῦ· ὁ δὲ ποιῶν τὴν

God (as has been seen) the idea
of the Father's love (v. 16); in
relation to man the singleness of
our hope.

ὅτι μὴ πεπίστ. εἰς τ. ὄν. . . .]
hath not believed in the name
of . . . , hath not acknowledged
Christ as being the only Son of
God, such as He is revealed to
be. Comp. ii. 23, note, i. 12,
note. The belief in Christ under
this one cardinal aspect leads to
the full faith in His Person.
Comp. 1 John v. 10, 13. The
tense (πεπίστευκεν) is emphatic,
and corresponds with κέκριται :
he is not in the state of one who
believed when it was open to
him to do so.

19. αὕτη δέ . . . ὅτι] hoc est
autem . . . quia v. The reality—
the necessity—of the judgement
of the unbelieving is involved in
the recognition of the character
of Christ's coming. Judgement
is not an arbitrary sentence, but
the working out of an absolute
law.

The form of expression is characteristic of St. John. Comp.
1 John i. 5, v. 11, 14.

ἡ κρίσις] judicium v.; judgement. But more exactly the
process (κρίσις), and not the result
(κρίμα) : the judging rather than
the judgement. The manifestation of Christ was in fact both a
process of judgement and also a
sentence of judgement upon man.

Compare ix. 39, note. For the
idea of "judgement," see Introd.

ὅτι . . . ἐλήλ. . . . καί . . .] The
two facts are placed simply side
by side (compare i. 10, 11, etc.),
each in its independent completeness.

τὸ φῶς ἐλήλ. . . .] the light, not
simply light. Comp. i. 4. And
so again, men loved the darkness
rather than the light. The alternatives were offered to men in
their most absolute form ; the
contrast of "the light" and "the
darkness" was complete ; and so
men made their choice.

καί . . . οἱ ἄνθρ.] et . . . homines
v. This was the immediate and
general issue on which the apostle
looked. Men as a class (οἱ
ἄνθρωποι, ch. xvii. 6) passed sentence on themselves in action.
Comp. xii. 48.

ἠγάπ. . . . ἦν] The past tenses
are used in the retrospect of the
actual reception of the revelation
of Christ made to men. Men
loved (ἠγάπησαν) the darkness at
the time when the choice was
offered, because their works were
habitually (ἦν) evil.

τὸ σκότ.] tenebras v.; the darkness. Comp. i. 5. There are two
words thus translated : σκότος,
which occurs here, and 1 John i.
6, only in St. John's writings,
expresses darkness absolutely as
opposed to light ; σκοτία, which
is found i. 5, viii. 12, xii. 35, 46 ;

not believed on the name of the only begotten
19 Son of God. And this is the judgement, that the
light is come into the world, and men loved the
darkness rather than the light; for their works were
20 evil. For every one that doeth ill hateth the light,
and cometh not to the light, that his works may not
21 be reproved. But he that doeth the truth cometh
to the light, in order that his works may be

1 John i. 5, ii. 8, 9, 11, darkness realised as a state.

μᾶλλον . . . ἤ . . .] *i.e.* choosing it in preference to. The decision was final. Comp. xii. 43.

ἦν γὰρ αὐτ. πον. τ. ἔργ.] *erant enim eorum mala opera* v.; *for their works were evil.* The order is very remarkable. Its force might be suggested in English by the inversion, "for evil were their works." It is best to keep the usual rendering of ἔργα, "works" not "deeds," here and in the following verses (*vv.* 20, 21).

20, 21. The tragic issue of Christ's coming, the judgement which followed it, was due to the action of a moral law. All that has affinity with the light comes to it, all that is alien from it shrinks from it. Men's works were evil, and therefore they sought to avoid conviction under the darkness.

20. ὁ φαῦλα πράσ.] *qui mala agit* v.; . . . *that doeth ill.* The word φαῦλος occurs v. 29; Rom. ix. 11; 2 Cor. v. 10 (in each case contrasted with ἀγαθός); Tit. ii. 8; James iii. 16; and corresponds to the English *bad,* as expressing that which is poor, mean, worthless, of its kind, and so unfit for careful scrutiny.

Πράσσειν expresses the scope

and general character of a man's activity: ποιεῖν (*v.* 21) the actual result outwardly shown. There is a similar contrast in Rom. i. 32, ii. 3, vii. 15, 19, 20. Bad actions have a moral weight, but no real and permanent being like the Truth.

μισεῖ τὸ φῶς] He both hates the light in itself and shrinks from it in consideration of its effects.

ἵνα μή . . . τὰ ἔργα αὐτοῦ] *in order that his works may not* . . . The particle marks the direct object of the evil-doer.

ἐλεγχθῇ] *arguantur* v.; *be reproved.* Properly "sifted, tried, tested," and then, if need be, "convicted," "shown faulty and reproved," as by one having authority and aptitude to judge. Comp. xvi. 8, note; Rev. iii. 19, and especially Eph. v. 13.

21. ὁ δὲ ποιῶν . . .] In addition to the contrast of the verbs already noticed (*v.* 20), there is a further contrast in the forms of the two expressions "doing ill" and "doing the truth." In the one case action is represented by the many separate bad works (φαῦλα πράσσων), in the other by the realisation of the one Truth (ποιῶν τὴν ἀλήθειαν), which includes in a supreme unity all right deeds.

ἀλήθειαν ἔρχεται πρὸς τὸ φῶς, ἵνα φανερωθῇ αὐτοῦ τὰ
ἔργα ὅτι ἐν θεῷ ἐστιν εἰργασμένα.

22 Μετὰ ταῦτα ἦλθεν ὁ Ἰησοῦς καὶ οἱ μαθηταὶ αὐτοῦ εἰς
τὴν Ἰουδαίαν γῆν, καὶ ἐκεῖ διέτριβεν μετ᾽ αὐτῶν καὶ
23 ἐβάπτιζεν. ἦν δὲ καὶ [ὁ] Ἰωάνης βαπτίζων ἐν Αἰνὼν
ἐγγὺς τοῦ Σαλείμ, ὅτι ὕδατα πολλὰ ἦν ἐκεῖ, καὶ παρε-

ὁ δὲ ποι. τ. ἀλήθ.] *qui autem
facit veritatem* v.; *but he that doeth
the truth.* The phrase is a remarkable one. Right action is
true thought realised. Every
fragment of right done is so
much truth made visible. The
same words occur in 1 John i. 6.
Comp. Neh. ix. 33; Gen. xxiv.
49, xlvii. 29. The phrase is not
infrequent in Rabbinic writings.
St. Paul gives emphasis to the
same thought by contrasting
"the truth" with "unrighteousness": 2 Thess. ii. 12; 1 Cor.
xiii. 6; Rom. i. 18, ii. 8. Comp.
Eph. iv. 24, v. 9.

ἔρχεται πρός . . .] It is not said
even of him that "he loveth the
light." This perhaps could not
be said absolutely of man. Action
is for him the test of feeling.
It must be noticed that the
words recognise in man a striving
towards the light. Comp. vii.
37 (διψᾷ), xi. 52, xviii. 37.

φανερωθῇ . . . ὅτι . . .] *be
made manifest, that* . . . Whatever may be the imperfection of
the deeds of the Christian in
themselves, he knows that they
were wrought in virtue of his
fellowship with God. He is not
therefore proudly anxious that
they may be tested, and that so
the doer may have praise since
they abide the test; but looks
simply to this that their spring
may be shown.

Hence it follows that the E.V.

is right in the rendering *that.*
The other rendering *because* introduces a thought foreign to the
argument. For the construction,
see 1 John ii. 19.

φανερωθῇ] *manifestentur* v., for
they have a character which bears
the light. Comp. Eph. v. 13.

ἐν θεῷ ἐστιν εἰργ.] *have been
wrought in God,* in union with
Him, and therefore by His
power. The order lays the emphasis on *God*: "that it is in
God, and not by the man's
own strength, they have been
wrought." The perfect participle
has its full force. The works of
the believer are wrought in God,
and as they have been once
wrought they still abide. St.
John elsewhere adopts the same
resolved form. Compare ii. 17,
note (γεγραμμένον ἐστίν).

*Christ's teaching in Judæa gener-
ally (vv. 22—36).*

This section forms the natural
sequel to the visit of Christ to
Jerusalem. He had offered Himself there with a significant sign
as Messiah. The sign was generally not interpreted or misinterpreted; and leaving the Holy
City, He began His work (so to
speak) again as a prophet, following in part the method of the
Baptist. Thus slowly by act and
word He prepared a body of
disciples to recognise Him, and

made manifest, that they have been wrought in God.

22 After these things came Jesus and his disciples into the land of Judæa; and there he tarried with 23 them, and baptized. And John also was baptizing in Ænon near to Salim, because there was much water there : and they came, and were baptized.

to believe in Him, and to accept the true conception of the Messiah's nature and work.

The section falls into three parts. There is a summary notice of Christ's work (22—24). This is followed by John's testimony (25—30); which is drawn out at a greater length by the Evangelist (31—36).

The contents of the section are peculiar to St. John, who writes as a companion of the Lord.

22—24. For a time Christ and the Baptist worked side by side, preaching " repentance " (Mark i. 15), and baptizing. The Messiah took up the position of a prophet in Judæa, as afterwards in Galilee. (See *v.* 24.)

22. Μετὰ ταῦτα] The phrase does not indicate immediate connexion. Comp. v. 1, note. The first preaching of Christ was in the temple. When He found no welcome there He spoke in the Holy City ; then in Judæa ; afterwards in Galilee, which thenceforth became the centre of His teaching.

ὁ Ἰησ. κ. οἱ μαθ. αὐτ.] Comp. ii. 2, 12.

The phrase occurs also in Matt. ix. 10 (Mark ii. 15), 19 ; Mark viii. 27. In each case there is a special force in the vivid representation of the great Teacher and of the accompanying

disciples as two distinct elements in the picture.

τὴν Ἰουδαίαν γῆν] *the land of Judæa*, as distinguished from Jerusalem itself. The exact phrase occurs here only in the New Testament. Comp. Mark i. 5 ; Acts xxvi. 20, where τὴν χώραν τῆς Ἰουδαίας is similarly contrasted with the capital.

διέτριβεν] *demorabatur* v.; *tarried*. The stay was probably prolonged for some time. See additional note on v. 1.

ἐβάπτ.] This baptism, actually administered by the disciples, iv. 2, would belong to the preparation for the kingdom, like John's baptism. It was not (and indeed could not be) an anticipation of the Christian Sacrament which it foreshadowed. Comp. Matt. iv. 17 ; Mark i. 14, 15. At this point then the work of Christ and of His forerunner met. Christ had not been acknowledged as king in the chief seat of the theocracy : therefore He began His work afresh on a new field and in a new character.

23. καὶ ὁ Ἰωάνης . . .] The Baptist continued to fulfil his appointed work, though he had acknowledged Christ.

ἐν Αἰν. ἐγγ. τ. Σαλ.] *in Ænon near to Salim*. The word Ænon is probably an adjectival form from the familiar· *ain* (eye,

24 γίνοντο καὶ ἐβαπτίζοντο· οὔπω γὰρ ἦν βεβλημένος εἰς
25 τὴν φυλακὴν Ἰωάνης. Ἐγένετο οὖν ζήτησις ἐκ τῶν
26 μαθητῶν Ἰωάνου μετὰ Ἰουδαίου¹ περὶ καθαρισμοῦ. καὶ
ἦλθαν πρὸς τὸν Ἰωάνην καὶ εἶπαν αὐτῷ Ῥαββεί, ὃς ἦν
μετὰ σοῦ πέραν τοῦ Ἰορδάνου, ᾧ σὺ μεμαρτύρηκας, ἴδε
27 οὗτος βαπτίζει καὶ πάντες ἔρχονται πρὸς αὐτόν. ἀπεκ-

¹ Ἰουδαίου ℵᶜABLΓΔ; Ἰουδαίων ℵ*G.

spring), meaning simply "abounding in springs" (fountains). The
situation of Salim is disputed.
In the time of Eusebius Salim
was identified with a place on
the confines of Galilee and
Samaria on the west of Jordan,
six or eight miles south of
Scythopolis (*Bethshan*). A place
bearing the name of *Aynûn* has
been found not far from a valley
abounding in springs to the north
of the *Salim* which lies not far to
the east of *Nablous* (*Palestine Exploration Report*, 1874, pp. 141 f.,
comp. 1876, p. 99). Comp. Introd.

ὕδ. πολ.] *aquæ multæ* v.; *much
water*. The form of the phrase
probably indicates many fountains or streams or pools of
water : Mark ix. 22; Matt.
xvii. 15. Elsewhere the plural
is used of the gathered or troubled waters : Matt. viii. 32, xiv.
28, 29; Rev. i. 15, etc.

παρεγίν.] *adveniebant* v. There
is no antecedent: "Men continued to come to him (the Baptist) and . . ." Compare xv. 6,
xx. 2; Mark x. 13; Acts iii. 2.

24. οὔπω γὰρ ἦν βεβλημ. . . .
Ἰωάνης] *nondum enim missus
fuerat Joannes* v.; *for John had
not yet been cast*. This note of
time must be taken in connexion
with Matt. iv. 12, 13, 17; Mark
i. 14. The public ministry of
the Lord in Galilee did not begin

till after this time, after John
was cast into prison, as the
Synoptists record. The events in
Galilee, which the Evangelist has
already related (ii. 1—12), were
preparatory to the manifestation at Jerusalem, which was the
real commencement of Christ's
Messianic work. St. John records the course and issue of
this manifestation : the other
Evangelists start with the record of the Galilæan ministry,
which dates from the imprisonment of the Baptist. Comp.
Mark i. 14, note.

25—30. The outward similarity of the work of Christ and
of the Baptist gave an occasion
(25, 26) for the last testimony
of the Baptist to Christ. In
the eyes of some, Christ appeared
as his rival. To these the Baptist himself showed what his own
work was, and then he left his
hearers to recognise Christ.

25. Ἐγένετο οὖν . . .] *There
arose therefore . . .*, as a consequence of this double work of
baptizing. The particle is one
not of time, but of consequence.

ζήτ. ἐκ τ. μαθ. Ἰωάν. . . .] *quæs-
tio ex discipulis Joannis* . . . v.; *a
questioning* (a discussion, disputa-
tion) *on the part of John's disciples*
. . . For the word ζήτησις see
Acts xv. 2; 1 Tim. vi. 4; 2 Tim.
ii. 23; Tit. iii. 9.

²⁴₂₅ For John had not yet been cast into prison. There arose therefore a questioning on the part of John's ₂₆ disciples with a Jew about purifying. And they came unto John, and said to him, Rabbi, he that was with thee beyond Jordan, to whom thou hast borne witness, behold, the same baptizeth, and all ₂₇ men come to him.   John answered and said, A man

μετὰ 'Ιουδαίου] *cum Judæis* v. ; *with a Jew,* according to the most probable reading, which gives a definiteness to the incident otherwise wanting.

περὶ καθαρ.] *de purificatione* v. ; *about purifying*—that is, as we may suppose, about the religious value of baptism, such as John's. We cannot but believe that Christ, when He administered a baptism through His disciples, explained to those who offered themselves the new birth which John's baptism and this preparatory baptism typified. At the same time He may have indicated, as to Nicodemus, the future establishment of Christian Baptism, the sacrament of the new birth. In this way nothing would be more natural than that some Jew, a direct disciple, should be led to disparage the work of John, contrasting it with that of which Christ spoke ; and that thereupon John's disciples, jealous for their master's honour, should come to him complaining of the position which Christ had taken up.

26. 'Ραββεί . . .] The title of reverence is emphatic. The speakers first contrast the new Teacher with their own, and then describe his present action. *Rabbi, he that was with thee,* in thy company as one of thy dis-

ciples, *beyond Jordan,* in the most conspicuous and successful scene of thy ministry, *to whom thou (σύ) hast borne witness,* as the authoritative judge, *behold he is baptizing . . .*

ᾧ] *to whom,* i.e. in whose favour, to support whose claims. Comp. v. 33, xviii. 37 ; 3 John 12 ; Luke iv. 22 ; Acts x. 43 (xiii. 22), xiv. 3, xv. 8 ; Rom. x. 2 ; Gal. iv. 15 ; Col. iv. 13. Elsewhere from the context *against,* Matt. xxiii. 31. Cf. James v. 3.

σὺ μεμαρτύρ.] *tu testimonium perhibuisti* v. The perfect marks the testimony as being yet effective : ch. i. 34.

ἴδε] A characteristic word of St. John. Comp. i. 29, note, xix. 5, 14.

βαπτίζει] This appeared to be an invasion of John's work.

πάντες] The natural exaggeration (*v.* 23) of angry zeal. Contrast *v.* 32.

27—30. The words of the Baptist meet the jealous zeal of his disciples. He (1) lays down the principle of revelation (*v.* 27) ; and then (2) applies it to his own work, both as to (*a*) The past witness (*v.* 28), and as to (*β*) the present fulfilment (*v.* 29) ; and then (3) draws the main conclusion (*v.* 30).

27. Every contrast of teacher with teacher is harmonised by

ρίθη Ἰωάνης καὶ εἶπεν Οὐ δύναται ἄνθρωπος λαμβάνειν
28 οὐδὲν ἐὰν μὴ ᾖ δεδομένον αὐτῷ ἐκ τοῦ οὐρανοῦ. αὐτοὶ
ὑμεῖς μοι μαρτυρεῖτε ὅτι εἶπον [ἐγώ] Οὐκ εἰμὶ ἐγὼ
ὁ χριστός, ἀλλ᾽ ὅτι Ἀπεσταλμένος εἰμὶ ἔμπροσθεν
29 ἐκείνου. ὁ ἔχων τὴν νύμφην νυμφίος ἐστίν· ὁ δὲ φίλος
τοῦ νυμφίου, ὁ ἑστηκὼς καὶ ἀκούων αὐτοῦ, χαρᾷ χαίρει

the truth that each has only
that which God has given him.

ἀπεκρίθη] The answer lies in
the simple explanation of the
essential relation between the
Forerunner and the Christ, drawn
from the universal truth. When
this is once apprehended, all
possibility of rivalry is gone.
The message which was brought
to John by his disciples as a
complaint, in his eyes crowns his
proper joy.

Οὐ δύν. . . . τ. οὐρ.] The principle is general, and must not be
interpreted either of Christ or
of the Baptist alone. It has
an application to both. The
Baptist says in fact: "I cannot claim any new authority
which has not been directly assigned to me; He, of whom you
speak, cannot effectually exercise
His power unless it be of divine
origin."

ἄνθρωπος] The word has force
(compare v. 4). It is the law of
human existence, as dependent
upon God, to which even Messiah
is subject. The Fathers are
wrong in supposing that a contrast between John and Christ
is intended.

λαμβ.] accipere v.; receive. The
word λαμβάνειν includes the conceptions of "receiving" and "taking." Comp. v. 32, note. The
thought here is that there is but
one source of spiritual power,

and that opened by God's love,
and not by man's own will.

ᾖ δεδομένον] fuerit datum v.;
have been given. The divine gift,
already complete in itself, makes
the human appropriation possible.

ἐκ τοῦ οὐρανοῦ] The phrase is
not the same as "from God":
out of the treasury, so to speak,
of all true and abiding blessings.
Comp. xix. 11.

28, 29. The principle stated in
v. 27 is applied directly by the
Baptist to himself, according to
his earlier definition of his work,
and, under a figure, to Christ.

28. αὐτοὶ ὑμεῖς] ye yourselves.
You need no teacher to meet your
difficulty. The zeal which you
display is shown to be mistaken
if you only recall what I said.
When I announced my mission I
declared it to be provisional. No
word of mine can have given occasion to the error whereby you
claim for me the highest place.

This emphatic phrase (αὐτοὶ
ὑμεῖς) occurs 1 Thess. iv. 9 (Mark
vi. 31 is different). Comp. Acts
xxiv. 15.

ἔμπρ. ἐκείνου] before that Jesus
of whom you speak. The direct
reference appears to be to the
Lord personally, as "He to
whom John had borne witness"
(comp. v. 30), and not to "the
Christ" generally (iv. 25). At
the same time the emphatic pronoun and the renewed descrip-

can receive nothing, except it have been given him
28 from heaven. Ye yourselves bear me witness, that
I said, I am not the Christ, but, that I am sent before
29 him. He that hath the bride is the bridegroom: but
the friend of the bridegroom, which standeth and
heareth him, rejoiceth greatly [1] because of the bride-

¹ *lit.* with joy rejoiceth.

tion of his own office point to the identification which is not made explicitly.

It is of interest to observe that the Baptist in his last message, when he had heard of "the works of the Christ," does not use the title, but asks "Art thou he that cometh?" (Matt. xi. 2 ff.).

29. The Baptist spoke plainly of himself, but he speaks of Christ's office and position in mysterious language, answering exactly to the situation. That position must be recognised in order that He may be known, as the Baptist knew Him.

τ. νυμφ. νυμφίος] *sponsam, sponsus* v.; *the bride . . . the bridegroom.* The image of the Bride and Bridegroom, used to describe the relation between Jehovah and His people, is found in the Old Testament:

(*a*) in the Law—
 Exod. xxxiv. 15 (זנה);
 Deut. xxxi. 16.

(*b*) in the Prophets—
 Hos. ii. 19 f. ; Ezek. xvi. ;
 Mal. ii. 11.

(*c*) in the Psalms—lxxiii. 27.

In the New Testament the same image (Christ and the Church) is found:

(*a*) Matt. ix. 15, xxii. 1 ff.,
 xxv. 1 ff.
 Rev. xix. 7, xxi. 2, 9,
 xxii. 17.

(*β*) Eph. v. 32 ff. ; 2 Cor. xi. 2 ;
 (James iv. 4).

The relation of Jehovah to Israel is fulfilled in that of Christ to the Church.

In all these titles, "the Lamb of God," "the Son of God," "the Bridegroom," we stand on this the arch of Old Testament imagery, and see how all finds fulfilment:

 the typical system,
 the national constitution,
 the divine relation.

The testimony of the Baptist is the interpretation of the system which he closes.

ὁ φιλ. τ. νυμφ.] *the friend of the bridegroom,* to whom it fell to demand the hand of the bride, and to prepare everything for the due reception of the bride and bridegroom. Comp. Buxtorf, *Lex. Rabb.,* or Levy, *Chald. Wörterbuch, s.v.* שׁושׁבינא. The Baptist had fulfilled his office in preparing and bringing the representatives of the spiritual Israel—the new Bride—to Christ —the Bridegroom.

ὁ ἑστηκώς] *which standeth* in the attitude of expectation and ready service, *and heareth him* (καὶ ἀκούων) not only as cognisant of his presence, but as waiting to fulfil his commands. Comp. xii. 29 (Mark ix. 1, τῶν ἑστηκότων ; Matt. xxvi. 73 ;

9

διὰ τὴν φωνὴν τοῦ νυμφίου. αὕτη οὖν ἡ χαρὰ ἡ ἐμὴ
30 πεπλήρωται. ἐκεῖνον δεῖ αὐξάνειν, ἐμὲ δὲ ἐλαττοῦσθαι.
31 ὁ ἄνωθεν ἐρχόμενος ἐπάνω πάντων ἐστίν. ὁ ὢν ἐκ

Acts xxii. 25; Heb. x. 11, note).
A different image Isa. lxi. 5
(LXX. otherwise).

χαρᾷ χαίρει] *gaudio gaudet* v.;
with joy rejoiceth. In this re-
joicing there is no alloy. Comp.
Luke xxii. 15 (so A.V.); Acts
iv. 17, v. 28, xxiii. 14; James v.
17. The idiom is common in
the LXX. as the representative
of the Hebrew construction with
the inf. abs., but it is found
also in classical writers. Comp.
LXX. construction with participle, Winer, p. 445. It is significant that it is found here only
in St. John's writings.

διὰ τ. φων. τ. νυμφ.] *because of
the bridegroom's voice,* when he
has entered his new home, bringing his bride with him, and there
first spoken with her at the
marriage feast. The full, clear
voice of the bridegroom's love is
contrasted with all the words of
those who have prepared for His
coming.

αὕτη . . . ἡ χαρὰ ἡ ἐμή] *this
joy,* the joy of seeing a work
happily consummated, *which is
mine.* Comp. xv. 9, note.

πεπλήρωται] *hath been fulfilled*
already, when, as you announce,
the Christ is gathering round
Him the disciples who are the
beginnings of His Church. Comp.
i. 34; comp. Philo, *Quod det.
potiori,* § 33.

30. ἐκεῖνον δεῖ . . .] *illum oportet
. . .* v.; *he must . . .* That lies in
the divine law of things. Comp.
vv. 7, 14, ix. 4, x. 16, xx. 9,
note; Rev. i. 1, iv. 1, xx. 3, etc.

ἐλαττ.] *minui* v.; *decrease* in

imprisonment, suspense, martyrdom. These last words of St.
John are the fulness of religious
sacrifice, and fitly close his work,
and with it the Old Dispensation.
At the same time, they have an
ever-germinant fulfilment. The
progress from the Law to the
Gospel, from the fulness of self
to the fulness of Christ, is the
law of Christian life. For the
later mission from the Baptist
to Christ in relation to this
testimony, see Matt. xi. 3.

31—36. This section contains
reflections of the Evangelist on
the general relation of the Son
to the forerunner, and to the
teachers of the earlier Dispensation generally. The Baptist had
spoken figuratively in the language of the Old Testament of
what Christ was, and so directed
his disciples to acknowledge Him.
The Evangelist, looking over the
long interval of years, reaffirms
in clearer words the witness of
the herald, and shows how it
has been fulfilled.

The passage is distinguished
from the answer of the Baptist by
(1) A marked contrast of style.
Verses 27 — 30 are in form
clear and sharp, with echoes of
the abrupt prophetic speech.
These (31—36) have a subtle
undertone of thought, which
binds them together closely, and
carries them forward to the
climax in *v.* 36.

(2) Parts of it contain clear
references to words of the Lord,
e.g. vv. 31, 32 refer to *vv.* 11 ff.,
v. 35 to x. 28, 29.

groom's voice : this my joy therefore hath been
30 fulfilled. He must increase, but I must decrease.

31   He that cometh from above is above all : he that

(3) The use of the title "Son"
absolutely (*vv.* 35, 36) appears
to be alien to the position of the
Baptist.

(4) The historical position
marked in *v.* 32 (οὐδείς) is strikingly different from that marked
in *v.* 29.

(5) The aorists in *v.* 33
describe the later experience of
Christian life. Comp. i. 16.

On the other hand, the use of
the present tense, *v.* 32 (μαρτυρεῖ,
λαμβάνει), *vv.* 31, 34 (λαλεῖ), is
not inconsistent with the position
of the Evangelist.

The section falls into the
following divisions :

1. The contrast of the earthly
   and the heavenly teacher
   (*vv.* 31, 32).
2. The experience and the
   endowment of the Church
   (33—35).
   (α) The experience of faith
       (*v.* 33).
   (β) Christ the perfect and
       abiding Teacher (*v.*
       34).
   (γ) The Son the supreme
       King (*v.* 35).
3. The issues (36).
   (α) Of faith—life.
   (β) Of disobedience—wrath.

31, 32. The earthly teacher,
and such were all who came
before Christ, is contrasted with
the One Teacher from heaven,
(1) in origin (ἐκ τῆς γῆς, ἄνωθεν,
ἐκ τοῦ οὐρανοῦ), (2) in being (ἐκ
τῆς γῆς, ἐπάνω πάντων), (3) in
teaching (ἐκ τῆς γῆς, ὃ ἑώρακεν κ.
ἤκουσεν in the kingdom of truth).
Comp. Matt. xi. 11.

31. Ὁ . . . ἐρχ.] *He that cometh
. . .* The work of Christ is regarded not as past nor as future,
but as ever-present (vi. 33).

ἄνωθεν] *desursum* v. ; *from
above,* from a higher region.
The same word is used in *v.* 3
(*again, anew*) ; see note. It
seems to be chosen from its connexion with the ἐπάνω which
follows.

ἐπάνω πάντων] *supra omnes*
v. ; *above all* — that is, *sovereign
over all things* (v. 35), and not
over all men only (as Vulg.),
though this is the prominent
idea here, where the Son is compared with former teachers.

ἐκ τ. γῆς . . .] *de terra . . .* v. ;
of the earth . . . The same phrase
is thrice repeated. The rendering "earthly" (of the A.V.) in the
second case obscures the thought,
and introduces confusion with
the "earthly," *i.e.* realised on the
earth, and not springing out of
the earth, in *v.* 12 (ἐπίγειος, see
note). The "earth," as distinguished from the "world,"
expresses the idea of the particular limitations of our being,
without any accessory moral
contrast with God. Its opposite
is heaven. Contrast 1 John iv.
5 (ἐκ τοῦ κόσμου). The term
does not occur elsewhere in St.
John's writings in this sense.
Comp. 1 Cor. xv. 47.

ὁ ὢν ἐκ τ. γῆς] *he that is of
the earth.* He who draws his
origin from the earth, a child of
earth, a man of men (comp.
Matt. ix. 11), *is of the earth,*
draws likewise the form and

32 τῆς γῆς ἐκ τῆς γῆς ἐστὶν καὶ ἐκ τῆς γῆς λαλεῖ· ὁ ἐκ
τοῦ οὐρανοῦ ἐρχόμενος¹ ὃ ἑώρακεν καὶ ἤκουσεν τοῦτο
μαρτυρεῖ, καὶ τὴν μαρτυρίαν αὐτοῦ οὐδεὶς λαμβάνει.
33 ὁ λαβὼν αὐτοῦ τὴν μαρτυρίαν ἐσφράγισεν ὅτι ὁ θεὸς

¹ Insert ἐπάνω πάντων ἐστὶν ℵᶜABLTᵇΔ. See note.

manner of his life from the earth, *and speaketh of the earth.* His birth, his existence, his teaching, are all of the same kind. The phrase εἶναι ἐκ, expressing a moral connexion, is characteristic of St. John. It includes the ideas of derivation and dependence, and therefore of a moral correspondence between the offspring (issue) and the source. Thus, according to the essential affinity of their character, men are said to be ἐκ τῆς ἀληθείας, xviii. 37; 1 John ii. 21, iii. 19; or ἐκ τοῦ κόσμου, xv. 19, xvii. 14, 16, xviii. 36; 1 John ii. 16, iv. 5; and again, with a personal relation, ἐκ τοῦ θεοῦ, vii. 17, viii. 47; 1 John iii. 10, iv. 1—7, v. 19; 3 John 11, and ἐκ τοῦ πατρός, 1 John ii. 16; or, on the other side, ἐκ τοῦ διαβόλου, 1 John iii. 8 (comp. John viii. 44), and ἐκ τοῦ πονηροῦ 1 John iii. 12. So Christ describes Himself as being ἐκ τῶν ἄνω, and "the Jews" as being ἐκ τῶν κάτω, viii. 23. The phrase is comparatively rare in the other writings of the New Testament, but when it occurs it is deserving of notice : Matt. i. 20, xxi. 25 f., and parallels; Luke ii. 4; Acts v. 38 f.; Rom. ix. 5; 1 Cor. i. 30, xi. 12 (2 Cor. v. 18); 2 Cor. iv. 7; Gal. iii. 10, 20; Col. iv. 11. The phrase γεγεννῆσθαι ἐκ has a kindred meaning. Εἶναι ἐκ expresses the essential, permanent relation ; γεγεννῆσθαι ἐκ refers to

the initial moment of the relation : i. 13, iii. 5, 6, 8, viii. 41; 1 John ii. 29, iii. 9, iv. 7, v. 1, 4, 18. It is not said of any that "they are born of the evil one." Compare iv. 22, note.

ἐκ τ. γῆς λαλεῖ] *speaketh of the earth.* The earth is the source from which he draws his words. Even divine things come to him through the earth. He has not looked on truth absolute in the heavenly sphere. But this "speaking of the earth" is not of necessity a "speaking of the world" (1 John iv. 5). On the contrary, *he that cometh from heaven* is not only supreme over all creation, and therefore unlimited by the earth, but, *v.* 32, *witnesseth*—testifieth with solemn authority (μαρτυρεῖ), in this connexion perhaps in contrast with λαλεῖ—*what he hath seen and heard* in heaven.

ὁ . . . ἐρχ.] *that cometh,* as on a conspicuous mission. In this case the thought is not of the source of being (ὁ ὢν ἐκ τῆς γῆς), but of the source of authority.

ἐκ τ. οὐρ.] *from heaven.* This phrase, as contrasted with ἄνωθεν, gives the exact correlative to ἐκ τῆς γῆς.

ἐπάνω πάντων ἐστίν] *supra omnes est* v. ; *is above all.* It is not improbable that these words should be omitted. See Additional Note.

32. ἑώρ. κ. ἤκ.] *hath seen and heard.* The change of tense appears to mark a contrast between

is of the earth is of the earth, and of the earth
32 he speaketh: he that cometh from heaven beareth
witness of what he hath seen and heard; and no
33 man receiveth his witness.   He that hath received

that which belonged to the existence (ἑώρακεν) and that which
belonged to the mission (ἤκουσεν)
of the Son. Comp. viii. 26, 40,
xv. 15 (vi. 45), and viii. 38 with
varr. lectt.

μαρτυρεῖ] *testatur* v.; *witnesseth.*
Even after the historical manifestation of Christ on earth has
ended, He still speaks through
His Church. The present here
is co-ordinate with the plural in
v. 11. In that passage the Lord
connects the testimony of the
disciples with His own; and so
here St. John regards the testimony of the disciples as being
truly the testimony of Christ.

καί . . . οὐδείς] The issue, as
elsewhere (*v.* 11, vii. 30, viii. 20),
is simply added to the description
of the revelation. For the time
the testimony of Christ through
His Church found no acceptance.
The close of the apostolic age
was a period of singular darkness
and hopelessness. Comp. 1 John
v. 19 (2 Tim. i. 15). It was possible then for St. John to say *no
man is receiving his witness.* This
sad judgement stands in sharp
contrast with *v.* 29 and *v.* 26.

τ. μαρτ. . . . λαμβ.] *receiveth
his witness.* Of the two words
which are translated *receive,*
λαβεῖν marks that something is
taken, δέξασθαι (ch. iv. 45 only
in St. John) adds the notion of
welcoming or receiving from
another (Luke xvi. 6, 7). Λαβεῖν
includes also the idea of retain-
ing that which is taken, while
δέξασθαι presents only the act of

reception. Hence St. John uses
the former of "receiving the
Word" (i. 12; comp. v. 43, xiii.
20). The phrase "receive the
witness" is peculiar to St. John:
vv. 11, 33, v. 34; 1 John v. 9.
(Comp. xii. 48, xvii. 8.) The
witness is not welcomed only, but
kept. It becomes an endowment,
a possession.

33—35. But even so, though
the current of faith was checked,
the Church was in existence.
There were disciples who had
received the testimony at an
earlier time, and found that in
so doing they had been solemnly
united with God; and this experience of faith is still assured
by the fact of Christ's absolute
knowledge and absolute power.

33. ὁ λαβών] *qui accipit* v.;
he that received. The reference
appears to be directly historic,
going back to the time when the
disciples were first gathered
round the Lord.

ἐσφράγισεν] *signavit* v.; *hath
set his seal to this,* hath confirmed
in the most solemn manner the
statement which follows, *that
God is true.* The term *seal* is
used here only in this sense.
Elsewhere the word is used of
marking as reserved for a special
destination: vi. 27; Rev. vii. 3.
Comp. Eph. i. 13, iv. 30. There
is a noble Jewish saying, quoted
by Lightfoot (*Hor. Hebr.*, John
vi. 27), that "the seal of God is
Truth." See xviii. 37, note.

ὅτι ὁ θεὸς ἀληθ. ἐ.] *quia deus verax est* v.; *that God is true.* This

34 ἀληθής ἐστιν. ὃν γὰρ ἀπέστειλεν ὁ θεὸς τὰ ῥήματα
τοῦ θεοῦ λαλεῖ, οὐ γὰρ ἐκ μέτρου δίδωσιν ¹ τὸ πνεῦμα.
35 ὁ πατὴρ ἀγαπᾷ τὸν υἱόν, καὶ πάντα δέδωκεν ἐν τῇ χειρὶ
αὐτοῦ. ὁ πιστεύων εἰς τὸν υἱὸν ἔχει ζωὴν αἰώνιον·
36 ὁ δὲ ἀπειθῶν τῷ υἱῷ οὐκ ὄψεται ζωήν, ἀλλ' ἡ ὀργὴ
τοῦ θεοῦ μένει ἐπ' αὐτόν.

¹ Insert ὁ θεός AC²DΓΔ.

affirmation admits of two senses.
(1) It may mean that in accepting the teaching of Christ the
believer accepts the teaching of
God, for the words of Christ are
in truth the words of God. The
believer therefore, by receiving
these, really attests what is a
direct message of God ; and in
so doing he feels that he enters
into a certain fellowship with
Him, than which man can have
no higher glory. The rejection
of the testimony of Christ is,
according to this interpretation,
spoken of as "making God a
liar" (1 John i. 10, v. 10). (2)
The statement may also be taken
in a wider sense. The believer
finds in Christ the complete fulfilment of every promise of God.
By his experience of what Christ
is and what Christ says to him
he gladly confesses that "God is
true," that He has left nothing
unsatisfied of the hope which He
has given to man. Comp. viii. 26.
The first explanation appears
at first sight to fall in best with
v. 34, but the second in fact embraces the first in a larger thought.

34. The proof of God's truth
is found in the absolute fulness
of Christ's spiritual endowment.

ὃν . . . ἀπεστ. ὁ θ.] he whom
God sent, the one heavenly messenger, as contrasted with all
the earthly.

τὰ ῥήματα . . .] the words . . .
Not "words" only (vi. 68), but the
complete, manifold expression of
the divine message.

οὐ γ. ἐ. μ. διδ.] non enim ad men-
suram dat deus v. ; for he giveth
not . . . by measure. It is doubtful whether the subject of the
sentence is "God" or "Messiah."
The object in any case must be
general.

If, as in the common interpretation, God be taken as the
subject, the sense appears to be :
"Christ speaks the words of
God, for God giveth not the
Spirit by measure, only in a definite degree, to all, but He gives
it completely."

If, on the other hand, Messiah
is the subject (as Cyril takes it),
the sense will be : "Christ speaks
the words of God, for His words
are attested by His works, in
that He giveth the Spirit to His
disciples as dispensing in its fulness that which is His own."

The second interpretation,
which appears to have been
neglected in later times, owing
to the false text, has much to
recommend it (xv. 26).

35. The ground of what has
been said lies in the actual relation of God to Messiah, as the
Father to the Son.

πάντα] v. 31. The term is not
to be limited in any way.

his witness hath set his seal to *this*, that God is true. 34 For he whom God sent speaketh the words of God: 35 for he giveth not the Spirit by measure. The Father loveth the Son, and hath given all things into his 36 hand. He that believeth on the Son hath eternal life; but he that disobeyeth the Son shall not see life, but the wrath of God abideth on him.

δέδωκ.] *hath given.* Contrast δίδωσιν (v. 34).

36. The absolute supremacy of the Christian revelation, as compared with all that went before, is seen in its final issues of life and incapacity for life.

ὁ πιστεύων] *he that believeth,* with a faith which is continuous, not momentary.

ἔχει ζω. αἰών.] *hath eternal life.* To believe and confess that Jesus *is the Son of God* (1 John iv. 15) is the pledge of new and abiding life. By that belief our whole relation to the world, to man, and to God is changed, and changed already: αὕτη δέ ἐστιν ἡ αἰώνιος ζωή . . . (xvii. 3, note).

ὁ ἀπειθῶν] *qui incredulus est,* v.; *he that disobeyeth.* Disbelief is regarded in its activity. The same word occurs 1 Pet. iv. 17; Rom. ii. 8, xi. 30, 31, etc. Nothing is said of those who have no opportunity of coming to the true knowledge of Christ. Comp. Mark xvi. 16 (πιστεύσας, ἀπιστήσας).

οὐκ ὄψ. ζωήν] *shall not see life,* shall be unable to form any true conception of life, much less enjoy it. Compare *v.* 3. The future is contrasted with the present (ἔχει . . . ὄψεται . . .): the simple idea of ζωή with the full conception ζωὴ αἰώνιος. Comp. v. 24, 39 f.

ἡ ὀργὴ τοῦ θεοῦ] *ira dei* v.; *the wrath of God.* The phrase is commonly used of a distinct manifestation of the righteous judgement of God (Rom. i. 18, iii. 5, ix. 22, xii. 19), and especially of "the coming wrath" (ἡ μέλλουσα ὀργή, Matt. iii. 7; Luke iii. 7; ἡ ὀργὴ ἡ ἐρχομένη, 1 Thess. i. 10; comp. Luke xxi. 23, ὀργὴ τῷ λαῷ τούτῳ; 1 Thess. ii. 16; Rom. ii. 5 (v. 9); Eph. v. 6; Col. iii. 6).

In this sense it is not infrequent in the Revelation (xi. 18, xiv. 10, xvi. 19, xix. 15), where "the wrath of God" is set side by side with "the wrath of the Lamb" (vi. 16 f.).

The phrase is very common in the Old Testament. (Comp. Heb. iii. 11.)

Here "the wrath of God" describes the general relation in which man as a sinner stands towards the justice of God. Compare Eph. ii. 3. St. John goes back from the revelation of God as Father to the original idea of God as God.

μένει ἐπ᾽ αὐτ.] The natural law is inexorable. Only faith in the revelation through Christ can remove the consequences of sin which must otherwise bring God's wrath upon the sinner. Comp. 1 John iii. 14.

ADDITIONAL NOTES ON CHAP. III

3. The word ἄνωθεν properly means "from the top," "from the beginning," "from above." Thus it is used literally of the rending of the vail of the temple "from the top" (Matt. xxvii. 51 ; Mark xv. 38 ; compare John xix. 23), and temporally of knowledge possessed from an early date (Acts xxvi. 5) or traced from the source (Luke i. 3), and locally, with a spiritual application, of the wisdom which cometh "from above" (James iii. 15, 17; comp. James i. 17). The word occurs in a sense similar to this last in John iii. 31, xix. 11. In Gal. iv. 9 it is combined with the simple term for "again" (πάλιν ἄνωθεν), as implying the complete repetition of an entire process, starting, as it were, afresh, so as to obliterate every trace of an intermediate change.

Two interpretations of the word, derived from distinct applications of the fundamental idea, have found favour in the present place from early times : (1) "from the beginning," "over again," "anew," and (2) "from above," "from heaven." The Syriac (Peshito), Memphitic, Æthiopic, and Latin versions give the rendering "anew" (Vulgate, "renatus (natus) denuo") ; the Greek writers (from Origen) generally adopt the sense, "from heaven"; the Harclean Syriac, Armenian, and Gothic versions translate "from above." The English versions have vacillated strangely. Tyndale and Coverdale, agreeing with Vulgate, Luther ("von neuen"), and Erasmus, ed. i., gave "anew"; but Coverdale, in the Great Bible, with the Zurich

version ("von oben herab"), and Erasmus, in his later editions ("e supernis"), gave "from above." The Bishops' Bible of 1568 reads "born again," but this is changed back again in 1572 to "born from above."

It has been urged in favour of the second rendering that St. John constantly speaks of "being born of God" (γενν. ἐκ τοῦ θεοῦ), i. 13 ; 1 John iii. 9, iv. 7, v. 1, 4, 18, while he does not speak (as St. Paul) of a "new creation." But it may be questioned whether the phrase used here (γενν. ἄνωθεν) could be used to convey this idea of being "born of God," and it would be most strange under any circumstances that the usual mode of expressing it should be abandoned. It is further of great importance to notice that in the traditional form of the saying (e.g. Just. M. Ap. i. 61) a word is used (ἀναγεννᾶσθαι) as equivalent to the ambiguous phrase of St. John (γεννηθῆναι ἄνωθεν), which unquestionably can only mean "to be reborn" (comp. 1 Pet. i. 3, 23). And, once again, the idea of "a birth from God" (i. 13) does not suit the context. The reality of the new birth has to be laid down first, and then its character (v. 5). The emphasis lies on "to be born." This too was evidently the sense in which Nicodemus understood the sentence (a second time). If he had found a reference to the divine action in the Lord's words he could not have left it unnoticed. There seems then to be no reason to doubt that the sense given by the Vulgate and E.V. is right, though the notion is not that of mere repetition (again, A.V.), but of an analogous process (*anew*, R.V.).

14. The narrative of the setting up of the brazen serpent (Num. xxi. 4 ff.) presents at first sight several difficulties. The use of an image in spite of the general prohibition, and that image the image of a serpent, is mysterious. Justin Martyr presses his Jewish opponent with this apparent violation of the divine law, and asks for an explanation. "We cannot give one," is the answer: "I have often asked my teachers about this, and no one could account for it" (*Dial.* § 94, p. 322 B).

The earliest reference to the incident is in the Book of Wisdom. "[The murmuring people] were troubled for a little while, for warning, having a symbol (σύμβολον, not σύμβουλον) of salvation, to remind them of Thy commandments; for he that turned to it was saved, not by reason of that which he beheld (διὰ τὸ θεωρούμενον), but by reason of the Saviour of all" (Wisd. xvi. 6 f.). This explanation of the efficacy of the symbol is commonly given by Jewish writers. So the Targum of Jonathan: "it shall come to pass that if [one bitten] look upon it, he shall live, if his heart be directed to the Name of the Word (*Memra*) of the Lord."

Philo interprets the serpent as the antithesis of the serpent of the Temptation, an idea which is found also in Rabbinic writings. "The serpent of Eve," he says, "was pleasure: the serpent of Moses was temperance (σωφροσύνη) or endurance (καρτερία). It is only by this spirit of self-denial that the allurements of vice are overcome" (*De Leg.*

Alleg. ii. tom. i. pp. 80 ff.; *De Agric.* tom. i. p. 315 f.).

This interpretation found some currency among the Christian Fathers. Ambrose, evidently following some earlier authority, speaks of "my serpent, the good serpent (comp. Matt. x. 16), who sheds not poison but its antidotes from his mouth . . . The serpent which, after the winter is past, puts off his fleshly dress (*exuit se corporis amictu*), that he may appear in fair beauty" (*In Ps.* cxliii. serm. vi. § 15).

The belief that the serpent was the emblem of healing and life (Knobel on Num. xxi.) according to the heathen conception, which was developed among the Ophite sects (comp. Tertull. *De Præscr. Hær.* 47), carries out this conception to a more extravagant form.

There can, however, be little doubt that the serpent in Scripture is the symbol of the personal power of evil (Rev. xii. 9 ff.; 2 Cor. xi. 3; Gen. iii. 1 ff.); and that the central thought in the Mosaic narrative is that of the evil by which the people suffered being shown openly as overcome (compare Col. ii. 15). He who, looking upon the symbol, recognised in it the sign of God's conquering power, found in himself the effects of faith. The evil was represented as overcome in a typical form (*a brazen serpent*) and not in an individual form (*a natural serpent*), and therefore the application of the image was universal.

If now we consider the immediate application of the symbol, it is at once clear that by transferring the image of the elevation of the serpent to Himself Christ foreshowed that He was to be presented in some way conspicuously to men, and that being so presented He was to be the source of life to those who looked to Him with faith. So much Nicodemus would be able to gather. Can we now, after the event, follow out the parallel yet further?

The elevation of the serpent on the pole, and the serpent itself, have been supposed to be directly significant of the circumstances of the death of Christ upon the cross. As to the first point, it seems to be reasonable to say that the mode in which the brazen serpent was shown to the eye of faith aptly prefigured the mode in which Christ was presented to men with redemptive power (comp. xii. 32). The second point presents greater difficulty, but it is frequently pressed by early writers. Thus the author of the Epistle of Barnabas supposes Moses to address the people in these words: " Whenever any one of you is bitten, let him come to the serpent which is placed upon the tree (ἐπὶ τοῦ ξύλου), and let him hope in faith, that he [the symbolic serpent] being dead can make alive, and immediately he shall be saved" (Barn. *Epist.* xii.). In this aspect the harmlessness of the typical serpent was naturally dwelt upon. So Origen writes: " A brazen serpent was a type of the Saviour," for He was not a serpent truly; but "represented (*imitabatur*) a serpent . . ." (*Hom.* XI. *in Ezech.* § 3). Others follow out this idea more in detail. For example, Gregory of Nyssa, explaining the history at some length, says: " The Law shows us that which is seen upon the

tree (τὸ ἐπὶ ξύλου φαινόμενον), and this is the likeness of a serpent and not a serpent, as also the divine Paul saith, ' in likeness of flesh of sin ' (Rom. viii. 3). The true serpent is sin; and he that deserts to sin puts on the nature of the serpent. Man therefore is freed from sin by Him who assumed (ὑπελθόντος) the form (εἶδος) of sin, and was made after our fashion (γενομένου καθ᾽ ἡμᾶς), who were changed to the form of the serpent " (*De Vita Mos.* i. pp. 414 f. (Migne). Compare Chrys. and Theoph. *ad loc.*).

Epiphanius, adopting the same view, that the serpent represented Christ, explains the connexion quite differently. " The Jews," he writes, " treating Christ as a serpent, were wounded by the wiles of the serpent (that is the devil), and then healing came to those who were bitten, as by the lifting up of the serpent" (*Hær.* xxxvii. § 7, pp. 273 f.).

Tertullian, on the other hand, saw in the serpent the image of the devil slain, though he implies that the figure was variously interpreted in his time (*De Idol.* v. Comp. *Adv. Jud.* x.).

Justin Martyr dwells only upon the figure of the cross (σημεῖον, LXX.), on which the serpent was raised, and not on the serpent itself, as the emblem of the Lord's saving Passion (*Apol.* i. 60, *Dial.* 94).

In the face of these and other differences of interpretation in detail, it seems to be far best to compare the two acts together as wholes, the elevation of the serpent, and the elevation of Christ on the cross, without attempting to follow out the comparison of the parts separately. The lifting up of the serpent, as Augustine says, is the death of Christ, the cause being signified by the effect (Aug. *De Pecc. Mer. et Remiss.* i. 32). In Christ sin was slain, and he who had the power of sin (Rom. vi. 6; Col. ii. 14). Christ lifted up upon the cross " draws all men unto Him for eternal salvation " (Ign. interpol. *Ad Smyrn.* 2). Looking to Him, the believer finds life. (Comp. Bas. *De Sp. S.* xiv.)

In the type and the antitype the same great ideas are conspicuous. There is in both the open manifestation of a source of healing to those smitten, effectual by faith, and that under the form of a triumph over the cause of suffering when it has been allowed to do its worst.

The Jewish writers are singularly silent as to the incident of the Brazen Serpent. "The thing was done by God's command, and it is not for us to inquire into the why and wherefore of the serpent form " (Aben Ezra, quoted by Taylor, *The Gospel in the Law*, pp. 119 ff.). They discuss, however, the manner in which the symbol was efficacious, and commonly agree in supposing that it was by directing men to lift up their eyes to their Father in heaven, and to see in Him the conqueror of their enemy. The chief passages bearing upon the question are collected by the younger Buxtorf in his treatise *De Serpente Æneo* (*Exercitationes*, pp. 458 ff., Basileæ, 1659). The general interpretation of the history has been frequently discussed at length. Two essays may be mentioned: Menken, *Ueber die eherne Schlange*, 1812 (*Schriften*,

vi. 351 ff., 1858), and Erskine, *The Brazen Serpent, or Life coming through Death*, 1831.

NOTES ON READINGS IN CHAP. III

There are three readings of considerable interest in ch. iii. which require to be noticed in some detail, as they involve important principles of textual criticism. They are the omission of the words

(1) *v.* 15, μὴ ἀπόληται ἀλλ'.
(2) *v.* 13, ὁ ὢν ἐν τῷ οὐρανῷ.
(3) *vv.* 31, 32, ἐπάνω πάντων ἐστί, καί.

(1) Of these *v.* 15 is the simplest case, and may be taken first. The words in question are omitted by

  (*a*) MSS. : אBLTᵇ 1, 33 and a few mss.

  (β) *Versions :* (*Old Lat.,* some), *Old Syr., Jerus. Syr., Memph.,* (*Æth.*), (*Arm.*).

  (γ) *Fathers :* Cyr. Al., Cypr., Lcfr.

They are found in

  (*a*) MSS. : A 99 and nearly all other MSS. and mss. (CD are defective).

  (β) *Versions :* (*Old Lat.,* some), *Vulg., Syr. P.* and *Hcl.,* (*Arm.*), (*Æth.*).

  (γ) Chr., Theodt., Victorin.

The same words occur in *v.* 16, where they are omitted by no early authority except *Old Syr.*

The consideration of this evidence shows that

1. The only ancient (ante-Nicene) evidence for the words is that of some Old Latin texts (represented among the Greek MSS. by 69).

2. The words were adopted by the Antiochene School in the

fourth century, and thence passed into the current Greek text.

3. The origin of the insertion is obvious; while there was no cause for omission.

The words, therefore, must be omitted without doubt.

In connexion with this omission, it must be observed that the primary authorities are greatly divided as to the preposition and pronoun which precede. We find εἰς αὐτόν ℵ and mass of MSS., (*Vulg.*), etc., ἐπ᾽ αὐτῷ L, ἐπ᾽ αὐτόν A, ἐν αὐτῷ BT, some Latin copies. In *v.* 16 L reads ἐπ᾽ αὐτῷ.

The common phrase πιστ. εἰς αὐτόν evidently could not have given rise to these variations, and it can only be regarded as an early correction. Of the other readings, ἐν αὐτῷ is at once the best attested, and by its difficulty explains the tendency to change.

(2) The problem in *v.* 13 is more difficult.

The words are omitted by
- (α) MSS.: ℵBLT^b 33.
- (β) *Versions:* (*Memph.*), (*Æth.*).
- (γ) *Fathers:* Eus., Cyr. Al. (constantly: 12 times. See Pusey, *Cyril*, vii. 1, Pref. p. xx), Orig. *int.*

They are found in
- (α) MSS.: (A) and apparently in all other MSS. and mss. (CD are defective).

In A the words ων εν τω ουνω have been written over an erasure, and it is supposed that the original reading was o εν τω ουνω. The o by the first hand is unaltered.

- (β) *Versions:* Old Lat., Old *Syr.,Vulg.,Syr. Pesh.* and *Hcl.*, *Arm.*, (*Memph.*), (*Æth.*).

- (γ) *Fathers:* Hippol., Dion. Alex., Did., (Orig. *int.*), Novat., Hil., Lcfr.

Here it will be seen that the ancient MSS. are on the side of omission, and the ancient versions on the side of retention. But it is obvious that an interpretative gloss in a version is easier of explanation than an omission in a copy of the original text. Such glosses are found not infrequently in the Old Latin and Old Syriac copies (*e.g.* iii. 6, 8), though they are commonly corrected in the revised Latin and Syriac texts of the 4th (5th) cent. (*Vulg.*, *Pesh.*). In this case, however, the words are contained in the Syrian Greek text (A), and so, even if they were a gloss, they would be left undisturbed (compare *v.* 25). And the omission of the words by ℵ, which is the Greek correlative of the *Old Lat.* and *Old Syr.*, greatly detracts from their weight here. In regard to the Patristic evidence, the constant usage of Cyril balances the quotations of Dionysius and Didymus. On the whole, therefore, there seems to be no reason for deserting the Greek authorities, which have been found unquestionably right in (1); the words being thus regarded as a very early (2nd cent.) insertion. There was no motive for omission; and the thought which they convey is given in i. 18.

(3) The third case, *vv.* 31, 32, is of a different kind. Of the words in question, καί is omitted by overwhelming authority, and may be set aside at once.

The words ἐπάνω πάντων ἐστί are omitted by
- (α) MSS.: ℵ¹D 1 and a few mss.

(β) *Versions:* (*Old Lat.*), *Old Syr.*, *Arm.*

(γ) *Fathers:* Orig., Eus., (Tert.), Hil.

They are found in

(a) MSS.: אᶜABLTᵇ and all others (C is defective).

(β) *Versions:* (*Old Lat.,* some), *Vulg.*, *Memph.*, *Syr. P.* and *Hcl.*, *Æth.*

(γ) *Fathers:* (Orig.), Chrys., (Tert.), (Orig. *int.*).

The authorities for omission represent the most ancient element (*Old Lat.*, *Old Syr.*, with א and D) of the authorities for the insertion of the disputed words in (2). It appears, however, from an examination of all the cases of omission by this group (*e.g.* iv. 9), that its weight is far greater for omission than for the addition or the substitution of words. In this case the motive (1) for the repetition of ἐπάνω πάντων ἐστίν, and then (2) for the addition of καί is sufficiently clear. The words, therefore, cannot but be regarded with great suspicion; and the sense certainly does not lose by their absence. On the contrary, the opposition of ὁ ὢν ἐκ τῆς γῆς ἐκ τῆς γῆς λαλεῖ to ὁ ἐκ τοῦ οὐρανοῦ ἐρχόμενος ὃ ἑώρακεν καὶ ἤκουσεν τοῦτο μαρτυρεῖ becomes far more impressive if the words in question are omitted.

4 Ὡς οὖν ἔγνω ὁ¹ κύριος ὅτι ἤκουσαν οἱ Φαρισαῖοι
ὅτι Ἰησοῦς πλείονας μαθητὰς ποιεῖ καὶ βαπτίζει [ἢ²]
2 Ἰωάνης,—καίτοιγε Ἰησοῦς αὐτὸς οὐκ ἐβάπτιζεν ἀλλ᾽ οἱ
8 μαθηταὶ αὐτοῦ,—ἀφῆκεν τὴν Ἰουδαίαν καὶ ἀπῆλθεν πάλιν
4 εἰς τὴν Γαλιλαίαν. Ἔδει δὲ αὐτὸν διέρχεσθαι διὰ τῆς

¹ ὁ κύριος ABCLTᵇ; ὁ Ἰησοῦς אD.   ² Omit ἢ ABGLΓ.

2. THE WORK IN SAMARIA
(iv. 1—42)

This section consists of three
parts. The opening verses (1—3)
form the historical transition
from the notice of the teaching
in Judæa (iii. 22 ff.). This is
followed by the detailed account
of the Lord's conversation with
the Samaritan woman (4—38),
and by a summary of His intercourse with the people (39—42).
The whole section is peculiar
to St. John, and bears evident
traces of being the record of an
eye-witness. Other notices of the
Lord's dealing with Samaritans
are found Luke ix. 52 ff., xvii.
16. Comp. Luke x. 33.

CHAP. IV. 1—3. The Lord
changes the scene of His ministry
that He may avoid a premature
collision with the Pharisaic
party. Comp. vii. 1, x. 39 f.

These verses serve as a transition passage. The Lord left
Judæa, as He had left Jerusalem, and went again to Galilee,
there to carry on His prophet's
work.

1. Ὡς οὖν ἔγνω ὁ κυρ.] Ut ergo
cognovit Jesus v.; When therefore
the Lord knew. The word οὖν
carries back the reader to the
narrative, iii. 22 ff. The action
which roused controversy was
necessarily notorious. Nothing
implies that the knowledge of

the Lord was supernatural (see
ii. 24, note). It could not but
be that, as Christ's work spread,
He should become acquainted
with the thoughts which it revealed outside the circle of His
disciples.

ὁ κύριος] The absolute title
occurs in the narrative of St.
John, vi. 23, xi. 2, xx. 20. Comp.
xx. 2, 13, 18, 25, xxi. 7. It is
found also not infrequently in
the narrative of St. Luke, x. 1,
xvii. 5 f., xxii. 61, etc.

οἱ Φαρισαῖοι] If the Pharisees
heard of the success of Christ's
teaching—and the word perhaps
implies that they continued to
observe the new Prophet who had
appeared at Jerusalem—there
could be no doubt how they
would regard Him. It is worthy
of notice that St. John never
notices (by name) the Sadducees
or the Herodians. The Pharisees
were the true representatives of
the unbelieving nation.

The direct form of the sentence
reproduces the message which
was brought to them: *Jesus*
[whose name they knew] *is making and baptizing more disciples
than John.*

ἢ Ἰωαν.] *than John* had done,
as by this time he was probably
thrown into prison. Though
John had more points of contact
with the Pharisees than Christ,
coming as he did *in the way of*

4 When therefore the Lord knew how that the
Pharisees had heard that Jesus is making and bap-
2 tizing more disciples than John (and yet Jesus himself
3 baptized not, but his disciples), he left Judæa, and
4 departed again into Galilee.   And he must needs

righteousness, even he had excited their apprehensions.   Cf.
Matt. xxi. 32.

2. καιτ. Ἰησ. . . .] *and yet Jesus*
. . . The words are a correction
of the report which has just
been quoted. Compare iii. 26.
Christ did not personally baptize
(comp. iii. 22), because this Judaic
baptism was simply a symbolic
act, the work of the servant and
not of the Lord. The sacrament
of baptism presupposes the Death
and Resurrection of Christ. This
is very well set forth by Tertullian, *De Bapt.* ii.

3. ἀφ.] *reliquit* v. ; *he left.* The
use of ἀφίημι is very remarkable
(καταλείπω might have been expected, Matt. iv. 13, Heb. xi.
27) ; and there is no exact
parallel in the New Testament
to this usage (yet compare ch.
xvi. 28). The general idea which
it conveys seems to be that of
leaving anything to itself—to its
own wishes, ways, fate; of with-
drawing whatever controlling
power was exercised before.
Christ had claimed Jerusalem as
the seat of His royal power, and
Judæa as His kingdom. That
claim He now in one sense gave
up.

πάλιν] *iterum* v. ; *again.* The
reference is to i. 43. There was
a danger of confusing these two
visits to Galilee in the Synoptic
accounts. St. John therefore
sharply distinguishes them.

εἰς τ. Γαλ.] Where His preaching would excite less hostility on
the part of the religious heads of
the people, while they would also
have less power there.

*The Conversation with the
Woman of Samaria* (4—38)

The record of the conversation
consists of two main parts, (1)
the account of the conversation
itself (4—26), and (2) the account
of its issues (27—38), both immediately (27—30), and in its
spiritual lessons (31—38).

The whole passage forms a
striking contrast and complement to iii. 1—21. The woman,
the Samaritan, the sinner, is
placed over against the Rabbi,
the ruler of the Jews, the
Pharisee. The nature of worship takes the place of the necessity of the new birth ; yet so
that either truth leads up to the
other. The new birth is the
condition for entrance into the
kingdom : true worship flows
from Christ's gift.

There is at the same time a
remarkable similarity of method
in Christ's teaching in the two
cases. Immediate circumstances,
the wind and the water, furnished
present parables, through which
deeper thoughts were suggested,
fitted to call out the powers and
feelings of a sympathetic listener.

The mode in which the Lord
dealt with the woman finds a

5 Σαμαρίας. ἔρχεται οὖν εἰς πόλιν τῆς Σαμαρίας λεγο-
μένην Συχὰρ πλησίον τοῦ χωρίου ὃ ἔδωκεν Ἰακὼβ [τῷ]
6 Ἰωσὴφ τῷ υἱῷ αὐτοῦ· ἦν δὲ ἐκεῖ πηγὴ τοῦ Ἰακώβ.
ὁ οὖν Ἰησοῦς κεκοπιακὼς ἐκ τῆς ὁδοιπορίας ἐκαθέζετο

parallel in the Synoptic Gospels, Luke vii. 37 ff. Compare Matt. xxvi. 6 ff. The other scattered notices of the Lord's intercourse with women form a fruitful subject for study, ch. xi., xx. 14 ff. ; Matt. ix. 20 and parallels, xv. 22 ff. and parallels, xxvii. 55 and parallels, xxviii. 9 f. ; Luke viii. 2 f., x. 38 ff., xi. 27 f., xiii. 11 ff.

4—26. The order of thought in the conversation is perfectly natural. A simple request (4—8) raises the question of the difference of Jew and Samaritan (9). The thought of this difference gives occasion to the suggestion of a unity springing from a gift of love greater than that of "a cup of cold water" (v. 10). How can such a gift be conceived of? how can a poor wayfarer provide it (v. 11 ff.)? The answer lies in the description of its working (vv. 13 f.). Then follows the personal petition (v. 15), followed by the personal conviction (vv. 16 ff.), and confession (v. 19). This leads to the expression of a central religious difficulty (v. 20), which Christ resolves (21—24). Hereupon the word of faith (v. 25) is crowned by the self-revelation of Christ (v. 26).

4. Ἔδει δέ . . .] he must needs i.e. probably this was the natural route from Jerusalem to Galilee. Josephus (Antiq. xx. v. 1) speaks of it as that usually adopted by Galilæan pilgrims ; and in one place uses the same phrase as St.

John : "Those who wish to go away quickly [from Galilee to Jerusalem] must needs (ἔδει) go through Samaria, for in this way it is possible to reach Jerusalem from Galilee in three days" (Vita, § 52). Sometimes travellers went on the other side of Jordan. Comp. Luke ix. 52 f. Or we may see in the phrase an indication of spiritual necessity (ix. 4). There was at least a fitness that Christ should lay the foundation of the Church outside Israel.

This " passing through " gave occasion for a prophetic revelation of the future extension of the Gospel (comp. Acts i. 8), and stands in no opposition to the special charge to the apostles, Matt. x. 5.

5. ἔρχεται οὖν . . .] so he cometh to a city . . . called Sychar (xi. 54 ; Matt. ii. 23). The term " city " is used widely, as in the passages quoted, and does not imply any considerable size, but rather one of the " little walled villages with which every eminence is crowned."

Συχάρ] This name has been commonly regarded as an intentional corruption of Sichem (Acts vii. 16, Shechem, Neapolis, Nablous) as signifying either " drunken-town " (Isa. xxviii. 1, שֵׁכָר) or " lying-town " (Hab. ii. 18, שֶׁקֶר). But the earlier writers (e.g. Eusebius, Onom. s. v.) distinguish Shechem and Sychar ; and the latter is said to lie " in front of Neapolis." Moreover, a

5 pass through Samaria. So he cometh to a city of Samaria, called Sychar, near to the parcel of ground that Jacob gave to his son Joseph: and Jacob's spring 6 was there. Jesus therefore, being wearied with his journey, sat thus by the spring. It was about the

place called Sychar (עין סוכר ,סוכר, סוכרא) is mentioned several times in the Talmud; and it is scarcely possible that so famous a place as Shechem would be referred to as Sychar is referred to here. There is at present a village, 'Askar, which corresponds admirably with the required site. The name appears in a transitional form in a Samaritan Chronicle of the 12th cent. as Iskar (Conder, in *Palestine Exploration Report*, 1877, p. 150). Compare Delitzsch, *Ztschr. f. Luth. Theol.*, 1856, pp. 240 ff., who has collected the Talmudic passages.

χωρίου] *prædium* v.; *the parcel of ground* (compare Matt. xxvi. 36). For the history see Gen. xxxiii. 19, xlviii. 22 (xxxiv. 25); Joshua xxiv. 32. The blessing of Jacob treated the purchase which he had made, and the warlike act of his sons in the district, as a pledge of the future conquests of the sons of Joseph, to whom he gives the region as a portion (שְׁכֶם). The LXX. play upon the word, and introduce *Shechem* (Σίκιμα) as the substantial (not literal) rendering. In recognition of the promise, the bones of Joseph were deposited at Shechem on the occupation of Palestine (Joshua xxiv. 32; Acts vii. 15, 16).

As the "parcel of ground" had been the earnest of future possession of the land, so the Lord's gathering of believers here was an earnest of His kingdom over the Gentiles.

6. πηγὴ τοῦ 'I.] *Jacob's spring.* The word "spring" (πηγή, עַיִן, Vulg. *fons*) is used here (twice) and in *v.* 14. Comp. James iii. 11 (βρύει); Rev. vii. 17, xxi. 6, and *well* (φρέαρ, בְּאֵר, *puteus*) in *vv.* 11, 12. Comp. Rev. ix. 1, 2. Both names are still given to the well, *Ain Yakûb* and *Bir-el-Yakûb*, but it is said to be really a tank and not a spring. The labour of constructing the well in the neighbourhood of abundant natural springs, shows that it was the work of a "stranger in the land." Comp. Gen. xxvi. 19. Lieut. Anderson, who descended to the bottom in May, 1866, found it then seventy-five feet deep and quite dry. "It is," he says, "lined throughout with rough masonry, as it is dug in alluvial soil" (Warren's *Recovery of Jerusalem*, pp. 464 f.).

An unsuccessful attempt to restore the well was made in 1877. An exact account of its state, with a drawing of the mouth-stone, is given in the *Report of the Palestine Exploration Society*, 1881, pp. 212 ff.

[The LXX. of Deut. xxxiii. 28 wanders from the Hebrew, or we might suppose that there was a reference to the mysterious title of God's people there.]

κεκοπιακώς] *fatigatus* v. It is important to notice in St. John

10

7 οὕτως ἐπὶ τῇ πηγῇ· ὥρα ἦν ὡς ἕκτη. ἔρχεται γυνὴ ἐκ
τῆς Σαμαρίας ἀντλῆσαι ὕδωρ. λέγει αὐτῇ ὁ Ἰησοῦς
8 Δός μοι πεῖν· οἱ γὰρ μαθηταὶ αὐτοῦ ἀπεληλύθεισαν εἰς
9 τὴν πόλιν, ἵνα τροφὰς ἀγοράσωσιν. λέγει οὖν αὐτῷ
ἡ γυνὴ ἡ Σαμαρεῖτις Πῶς σὺ Ἰουδαῖος ὢν παρ᾽ ἐμοῦ

the clearest traces of the Lord's perfect manhood. He alone preserves the word "I thirst" in the account of the Passion, xix. 28.

For other indications of the Lord's human feelings see xi. 3 ὃν φιλεῖς, 33 ἐνεβριμήσατο, ἐτάραξεν ἑαυτόν, 35 ἐδάκρυσεν, 38 ἐμβριμ. ἐν ἑαυτῷ, 41 f. Thanksgiving, xii. 27 ἡ ψυχή μου τετάρακται, xiii. 21 ἐταράχθη τῷ πν., xix. 28 διψῶ.

The word κοπιάω occurs again in the Gospel only v. 38 (comp. Apoc. iii. 3). The bodily weariness was a true symbol of the weary labour in Judæa (Isa. xlix. 4).

ἐκαθέζετο] The narrative describes the position (xi. 20), and not the act (ἐκάθισεν, xii. 14, xix. 13). "The Lord was sitting thus on the well"; the οὕτως, thus, may mean (1) either "thus wearied as He was," or (2) simply, just as He was, without preparation or further thought. Comp. 2 Pet. iii. 4. In the former sense it would have been natural that the adverb should precede the verb (οὕτως ἐκαθέζετο), as in Acts vii. 8, xx. 11, xxvii. 17.

Chrysostom remarks: Τί ἐστιν οὕτως; οὐκ ἐπὶ θρόνου, φησίν, οὐκ ἐπὶ προσκεφαλαίου ἀλλ᾽ ἁπλῶς καὶ ὡς ἔτυχεν ἐπ᾽ ἐδάφους.

ὥρα ἦν] The clause it was ... stands by itself. The time indicated is probably six in the evening. The night would not

close so rapidly as to make the subsequent description (v. 35) impossible. Compare Additional Note on ch. xix.

7. γυνὴ ἐκ τ. Σ.] A woman, and as such lightly regarded by the popular doctors (compare v. 27): a Samaritan, and as such despised by the Jews. Thus prejudices of sex and nation were broken down by this first teaching of the Lord beyond the limit of the chosen people. Yet more, the woman was not only an alien, but also poor; for to draw water was no longer, as in patriarchal times (Gen. xxiv. 15, xxix. 9 ff.; Exod. ii. 16 f.; compare Tristram, Land of Israel, pp. 25 f.), the work of women of station.

The exact form of the description is unusual: "a woman sprung from Samaria" (comp. i. 44, 46; Acts xxiii. 34, xiii. 21).

The later legends give the woman the significant name of Photina.

Δός μοι πεῖν] The request must be taken in its literal and obvious meaning (v. 6); but at the same time to ask was in this case to give. The Teacher first met His hearer on the common ground of simple humanity, and conceded to her the privilege of conferring a favour. Yet we cannot forget v. 34. "Ille qui bibere quærebat fidem ipsius mulieris sitiebat" (Aug.).

8. οἱ γὰρ μαθ. . . .] If His

7 sixth hour. There cometh a woman of Samaria to draw water: Jesus saith unto her, Give me to drink. 8 For his disciples were gone away into the city to 9 buy food. The Samaritan woman therefore saith unto him, How is it that thou, which art a Jew, askest

disciples had been present they could have supplied the want. "Something to draw with" (*v.* 11), a "bucket" of skin, often found by the well sides, would form naturally part of the equipment of the little travelling party. This seems to be a better explanation of the reason than to suppose that the absence of the disciples gave the opportunity for the conversation.

ἀπεληλύθεισαν] Perhaps St. John remained with Christ. The narrative is more like that of an eye-witness than a secondary account derived from the woman, or even from the Lord Himself. Yet it may be urged that *v.* 33 naturally suggests that the Lord had been left alone.

τροφάς] *cibos* v.; *food*, as commonly (Matt. iii. 4, vi. 25, etc.), but here only in the New Testament in the plural. Eggs, fruit, and the like might be purchased from Samaritans, as they could not contract defilement. Compare Lightfoot on *v.* 4. The later rules, however, were stricter. "To eat the bread of a Samaritan," it was said, "was as eating the flesh of swine."

9. ἡ γυν. ἡ Σαμαρ. . . .] *the Samaritan woman* . . . The stress is here laid on character, as implied in national descent, and not on mere local connexion (*v.* 7).

The strangeness of the request startles the woman; "What

further," she seems to ask, "lies behind this request?" The original is perfectly symmetrical (*thou which art a Jew . . . of me which am a Samaritan woman . . .*). There is force also in the distinct addition of the word *woman* (γυναικός). That the request was made not only of a Samaritan, but of a woman, completed the wonder of the questioner.

Ἰουδ. ὤν] Some peculiarity of dress or dialect or accent would show this (comp. Mark xiv. 70).

οὐ . . . Σαμαρ.] *for Jews . . . with Samaritans.* These words, which are omitted by an important group of ancient authorities, are, if genuine, an explanatory note of the Evangelist. In this relation the present form (συγχρῶνται) is remarkable. The origin of the hostility of the two peoples, which lasts to the present day, may be traced to the Assyrian colonisation of the land of Israel (2 Kings xvii. 24). From this followed the antagonism of the Samaritans to the Jews at the Return (Ezra iv., Neh. vi.), which led to the erection of a rival temple on Mount Gerizim. Comp. Ecclus. l. 25, 26. *Dict. of Bible*, iii. p. 1117.

συνχρῶνται] *coutuntur* v. The word suggests the relations of familiar intercourse and not of business. Compare Ignatius, *Magn.* 3: Πρέπει μὴ συνχρᾶσθαι τῇ ἡλικίᾳ τοῦ ἐπισκόπου (to treat

πεῖν αἰτεῖς γυναικὸς Σαμαρείτιδος οὔσης; [οὐ³ γὰρ συνχρῶνται Ἰουδαῖοι Σαμαρείταις.] ἀπεκρίθη Ἰησοῦς καὶ
10 εἶπεν αὐτῇ Εἰ ᾔδεις τὴν δωρεὰν τοῦ θεοῦ καὶ τίς ἐστιν
ὁ λέγων σοι Δός μοι πεῖν, σὺ ἂν ᾔτησας αὐτὸν καὶ

³ Omit οὐ γὰρ συνχρῶνται Ἰουδαῖοι Σαμαρείταις אD.

with undue familiarity). Offices of kindness were not expected between Jews and Samaritans. The spirit of religious bitterness still lingers on the spot. " On asking drink from a woman [near Nablous], who was filling her pitcher, we were angrily and churlishly refused :—' The Christian dogs might get it for themselves'" (Tristram, *Land of Israel*, p. 134, ed. 3). Comp. Luke ix. 53.

10. Εἰ ᾔδεις . . .] The words are, as commonly in St. John's Gospel, an answer to the essential idea of the foregoing question. The woman had sought an explanation of the marvel that a Jew should ask a favour of a Samaritan woman. This, however, as she dimly guessed, was only a part of the new mystery. The frank appeal to a human charity deeper than religious antagonism did indeed indicate a possibility of union greater than hope. Christ, reading the woman's heart, had confidently begged for that which might relieve a bodily want; if she could have read His heart, she would have prayed for help in her spiritual perplexity. Had she known what God had now done for men, and who that Jewish Teacher was whom she saw, she would herself have boldly asked of Him a favour far greater than He had asked of her, and would have received it at once; she would have become

the petitioner, and not have wondered at the petition : her present difficulty would have been solved by her apprehension of the new revelation which had been made, not to Jew or Samaritan, but to man. Had she known *the gift of God* (not *love* only in potentiality, but in exercise), the gift of His Son (iii. 16), in which was included all that man could want, she would have felt that needs of which she was partly conscious (*v.* 25) could at length be satisfied. Had she known *who it was that said to her, Give me to drink*, she would have laid open her prayer to Him without reserve or doubt, assured of His sympathy and help.

For a similar pregnant use of ἀπεκρίθη see *v.* 13, v. 19, vi. 26, vii. 21, x. 32, xii. 23, xiv. 23.

ᾔδεις] This knowledge is treated as something complete and fundamental (contrast iii. 10).

δωρεάν] *donum* v. The word occurs only in this place in the Gospels. It carries with it something of the idea of bounty, honour, privilege; and is used of the gift of the Spirit (Acts ii. 38, viii. 20, x. 45, xi. 17), and of the gift of redemption in Christ (Rom. v. 15 ; 2 Cor. ix. 15), manifested in various ways (Eph. iii. 7, iv. 7 ; Heb. vi. 4). This usage shows that there is here a general reference to the blessings given to men in the revelation of the Son, and not

drink of me, which am a Samaritan woman? (For
10 Jews have no dealings with Samaritans.) Jesus answered and said unto her, If thou hadst known the
gift of God, and who it is that saith to thee, Give
me to drink; thou wouldest have asked of him, and

a simple description of what was
given to the woman in the fact
of her interview with Christ.
"The gift of God" is all that is
freely offered in the Son.
Comp. Philo, *De Char.* § 25
(i. 154): Τῶν ὄντων τὰ μὲν χάριτος
μέσης ἠξίωται ἢ καλεῖται δόσις, τὰ
δὲ ἀμείνονος ἧς ὄνομα οἰκεῖον δωρεά.

σὺ ἂν ᾔτησας] The pronoun is
emphatic. If thou hadst known,
our places would have been re-
versed. *Thou* wouldest have been
the petitioner. Τάχα γὰρ δόγμα
τί ἐστι μηδένα λαμβάνειν θείαν
δωρεὰν τῶν μὴ αἰτούντων αὐτήν
(Orig. tom. xiii. 1, referring to
Ps. ii. 7 f.).

ὕδωρ ζῶν] *aquam vivam* v.;
living water, that is perennial,
springing from an unfailing
source (Gen. xxvi. 19), ever flowing fresh (Lev. xiv. 5). The
request which Christ had made
furnished the idea of a parable;
the bodily want whereby He suffered suggested an image of a
universal spiritual need, and of
the spiritual blessing which He
was ready to bestow.

The Jews were already familiar with the application of the
phrase (*living water*) to the
quickening energies which proceed from God (Zech. xiv. 8;
Jer. ii. 13, xvii. 13; comp. v. 14,
note), though it may be doubtful
how far the prophetic language
would be known to Samaritans
[who accepted only the Pentateuch in the Jewish canon].

Here the words indicate that
which on the divine side answers
to the spiritual thirst, the aspirations of men for fellowship
with God. This, under various
aspects, may be regarded as the
Revelation of the Truth, or the
gift of the Holy Spirit, individually or socially, or whatever,
according to varying circumstances, leads to that eternal life
(*v.* 14) which consists in the
knowledge of God and His Son
Jesus Christ (xvii. 3).

In the *Doctrine of the Apostles*
(i. 7) it is directed that, if possible, Baptism shall be administered "in living water." Chrysostom remarks: Τοῦ πνεύματος
τὴν χάριν ἡ γραφὴ ποτὲ μὲν πῦρ
ποτὲ δὲ ὕδωρ καλεῖ, δεικνῦσα ὅτι
οὐκ οὐσίας ἐστὶ ταῦτα παραστατικὰ
τὰ ὀνόματα ἀλλ' ἐνεργείας.

Euthymius has a striking
passage (based on Chrys.) concerning the various actions of
rain and fire: Διὰ μὲν τῆς τοῦ
πυρὸς προσηγορίας τὸ διεγεγερμένον
καὶ θερμὸν τῆς χάριτος καὶ δαπα-
νητικὸν ἁμαρτημάτων αἰνιττόμενος
διὰ δὲ τῆς τοῦ ὕδατος τόν τε καθαρ-
μὸν τὸν ἐξ αὐτοῦ καὶ τὴν πολλὴν
παραψυχὴν ταῖς ὑποδεχομέναις αὐτὸ
διανοίαις . . . Water and life
are naturally connected in the
East.

11, 12. The woman's answer
is in spirit exactly like the first.
Her thoughts reach forward to
some truth which she feels to be
as yet far from her. How can

11 ἔδωκεν ἄν σοι ὕδωρ ζῶν. λέγει αὐτῷ [1] Κύριε, οὔτε ἄντ-
λημα ἔχεις καὶ τὸ φρέαρ ἐστὶν βαθύ· πόθεν οὖν ἔχεις
12 τὸ ὕδωρ τὸ ζῶν; μὴ σὺ μείζων εἶ τοῦ πατρὸς ἡμῶν
Ἰακώβ, ὃς ἔδωκεν ἡμῖν τὸ φρέαρ καὶ αὐτὸς ἐξ αὐτοῦ
13 ἔπιεν καὶ οἱ υἱοὶ αὐτοῦ καὶ τὰ θρέμματα αὐτοῦ; ἀπεκρίθη Ἰησοῦς καὶ εἶπεν αὐτῇ   Πᾶς ὁ πίνων ἐκ τοῦ
14 ὕδατος τούτου διψήσει πάλιν· ὃς δ' ἂν πίῃ ἐκ τοῦ

[1] Insert ἡ γυνή א^cACDLT^b.

she conceive of the gift? The
well of Jacob is, in one sense, a
well of "living water," yet it
cannot be that which supplies
the Speaker with His gift, for
"the well is deep," and He has
"nothing to draw with." He
offers in word that for which
He asks. How again can she
conceive of Him who speaks to
her? He is wearied and thirsty,
and yet professes to command
resources which were sealed to
the patriarchs.

11. Κύριε] The title marks
growing respect (compare i 49).
Οὐχ ἁπλῶς ἐνταῦθα καλεῖ Κύριον
ἀλλὰ πολλὴν ἀπονέμουσα τὴν τιμήν
(Chrys.).

οὔτε . . . καί . . .] Cf. 3 John
10, οὔτε . . . ἐπιδέχεται . . . καί . . .
ἐκβάλλει . . . The construction
is not found elsewhere in the
New Testament.

τὸ φρε. . . . βαθ.] puteus altus
est v. The well is at present
partially choked up with rubbish.
See v. 6, note. In Maundrell's
time (March, 1697) it was 105
feet deep, and had fifteen feet of
water in it. Dr. Tristram found
in it only "wet mud" in December (Land of Israel, p. 143, ed.
3), but towards the end of February it was "full of water"
(id. p. 401).

12. μὴ σύ . . .;] numquid tu

. . . v. The pronoun is emphatic: "Art thou, a poor
wearied traveller, of more commanding power than the patriarch who gained by labour what
he gave us?" The interrogation
suggests the unlikelihood of the
thought (iii. 4, vii. 41, etc.).

πατ. ἡμ. Ἰακ.] The Samaritans
claimed descent from Joseph, as
representing the ancient tribes
of Ephraim and Manasseh
(Jos. Ant. XI. viii. 6).

ἔδωκ. ἡμ.] gave us, left, that
is, to his descendants as a precious heritage. The tradition is
independent of the Old Testament.

οἱ υἱοί] sons, the special representatives of his house.

θρέμματα] pecora v.; cattle.
The word may mean slaves, but
the sense given in E.V. is more
natural. The well was sufficient for large wants. Τὸ δὲ
καὶ τὰ θρέμματα αὐτοῦ πιεῖν ἐνδεικ-
τικόν ἐστι τῆς ἀφθονίας τοῦ ὕδατος
(Theophylact). The word occurs
here only in the New Testament,
and is not found in the LXX.

Origen sees in the enumeration
a sign of the different uses which
may be made of the same gift:
Οὐκ ὁμοίως πᾶς ἀντλεῖ ἀπὸ τῆς
πηγῆς τοῦ Ἰακώβ (tom. xiii. 6).

13, 14. The words of Christ
carry on the parable of the

11 he would have given thee living water. The woman
saith unto him, Sir, thou hast nothing to draw with,
and the well is deep: from whence then hast thou
12 the living water? Art thou greater than our father
Jacob, which gave us the well, and drank thereof
13 himself, and his sons, and his cattle? Jesus answered
and said unto her, Every one that drinketh of this
14 water shall thirst again: but whosoever drinketh of

tenth verse, and in doing so still
answer the thought and not the
words of the woman. They
imply that she had felt rightly
that it was some other water
than that for which Christ asked
which He was waiting to give:
that One greater than Jacob was
there. The water which the
patriarch had drunk and given
satisfied a want for the moment:
the living water satisfied a want
for ever, and in such a way that
a fresh and spontaneous source
supplied each recurrent need of
refreshment.

The mode in which the new
thought is developed corresponds
exactly with vi. 49 f.

13. ἀπεκρίθη] Οὐκ εἶπεν Ναί,
μείζων εἰμί· ἔδοξε γὰρ ἂν κομπάζειν
μόνον, τῆς ἀποδείξεως μηδέπω φαι-
νομένης· δι' ὧν δὲ λέγει τοῦτο
κατασκευάζει . . . εἰ γὰρ θαυμάζεις,
φησί, τὸν Ἰακὼβ ὅτι τοῦτο ἔδωκε
τὸ ὕδωρ, ἂν πολὺ τούτου βέλτιον
δῶ σοι, τί ἐρεῖς; (Chrys.).

Πᾶς ὁ πίνων] *Every one that*
. . . The form of expression is
contrasted with the hypothetical
ὃς ἄν in *v*. 14. With this change
of form follows also a change of
tense (ὁ πίνων = habitual; ὃς ἄν
πίῃ = once for all).

τοῦ ὑδ. τουτ.] pointing to the
well.

14. οὗ ἐγὼ δώσω] *that I shall
give.* The pronoun in the first
case is emphatic, and carries the
answer to the contrast which
the woman had drawn between
Jacob and Christ. The gift,
consequent in its realisation
upon the fulfilment of Christ's
work, is still future (δώσω).

οὐ μή . . . εἰς τὸν αἰῶνα] *non
. . . in æternum* v.; *never.* The
phrase is a very remarkable one,
and recurs viii. 51, 52 x. 28, xi.
26, xiii. 8.

Elsewhere it is found in the
New Testament in 1 Cor. viii.
13, where the translation "I
will eat no flesh while the world
standeth" expresses the literal
force of the words.

διψήσει] *sitiet* v.; *thirst*, in the
sense of feeling the pain of an
unsatisfied want, Rev. vii. 16.
But the divine life and the divine
wisdom bring no satiety, Ecclus.
xxiv. 21; Isa. xlix. 10. New
wants are met by new supplies
of divine grace. Even the Lord
said "I thirst" (xix. 28). Comp.
vi. 35.

γενησ. . . . πηγ. ὑδ. . . . ζω.
αἰων.] *shall become . . . a spring
of water . . . eternal life.* It
shall not serve for the moment
only, but shall also preserve
power to satisfy all future wants

ὕδατος οὗ ἐγὼ δώσω αὐτῷ, οὐ μὴ διψήσει εἰς τὸν αἰῶνα,
ἀλλὰ τὸ ὕδωρ ὃ δώσω αὐτῷ γενήσεται ἐν αὐτῷ πηγὴ
16 ὕδατος ἁλλομένου εἰς ζωὴν αἰώνιον. λέγει πρὸς αὐτὸν
ἡ γυνή Κύριε, δός μοι τοῦτο τὸ ὕδωρ, ἵνα μὴ διψῶ
16 μηδὲ διέρχωμαι¹ ἐνθάδε ἀντλεῖν. λέγει αὐτῇ Ὕπαγε

¹ διέρχομαι א°BEFGHKL ; διέρχωμαι א*ACDΓΔ.

if it be appropriated by the receiver (cf. vii. 38). The communication of the divine energy, as a gift of life, necessarily manifests itself in life. The blessing welcomed proves a spring of blessing, which rises towards and issues in *eternal life*; for this is as the infinite ocean in which all divine gifts find their end and consummation. The life comes from the Source of life and ascends to Him again.

The image is developed in three stages. Christ's gift is as a spring of water — of water leaping up in rich abundance, and that not perishing or lost, but going forth to the noblest fulfilment.

ἁλλομένου εἰς] *salientis in* v. The word describes the "leaping" of a thing of life, and not the mere "gushing up" of a fountain (cf. vi. 27, μεν. εἰς).

Οὐκ ἀπιθάνως τό "ἁλλομένου" διηγήσατο [ὁ Ἡρακλέων] καὶ τοὺς μεταλαμβάνοντας τοῦ ἄνωθεν ἐπιχορηγουμένου πλουσίως καὶ αὐτοὺς ἐκβλύσαι εἰς τὴν ἑτέρων αἰώνιον ζωὴν τὰ ἐπικεχορηγημένα αὐτοῖς (Orig. tom. xiii. 10).

There is a Jewish saying that "when the Prophets speak of water they mean the Law" (Wünsche, *ad loc.*). The Incarnate Word was what the Scribes wished to make the Scriptures (v. 39). Compare also *Aboth*, i. 4, 12.

"Aqua hæc Spiritus Sanctus est, aqua hæc Deus est, aqua hæc in corde Dei Patris fons vitæ est, in ore Dei Filii gratiæ et pacis flumen est, in beatis angelis torrens gloriæ est, in electis hominibus inundatio vitæ est. Quæ a quocunque bibita fuerit ad matricem suam, æternæ divinitatis abyssum resilit, inferno profundior, terra longior, mari latior, et cælo altior. Illuc in quem resilit, inde venit, pariterque bibentis animam etiamsi in infirmum descenderit saliendo in vitam æternam sustollit" (Rup.).

εἰς ζ. αἰ.] The image is obscure. "Eternal life" appears to be presented under the form of a loftier order towards which the highest power given to man now strives, and which God's great gift will reach. It is not simply an ocean, into which the divine stream will flow by a natural descent, but the original fountain, to which the current returns (ἄνω χωροῦσι παγαί).

Under this aspect the "water" which Christ gives and is, is like the "bread" which He gives and is. As it comes down out of heaven, it returns thither. "Omnia ex Deo *in* Deum" (Beng.).

15. The relation of the persons is now changed. A greater want supersedes the less. The woman is no longer able to follow the thoughts which lie before her in their mysterious

the water that I shall give him shall never thirst;
but the water that I shall give him shall become in
him a spring of water leaping up unto eternal life.
15 The woman saith unto him, Sir, give me this water,
that I thirst not, neither come all the way hither to
16 draw.   He saith unto her, Go, call thy husband, and

depth ; but at least she can ask
for the gift which has already
been assured to her (*v.* 10). She
seeks a favour in turn before she
has granted that which was
sought of her. *Sir, give me
this water, that I thirst not,
neither come hither to draw.* The
gift appeared to her to have two
virtues, corresponding with the
twofold description just given of
it. It would satisfy her own
personal wants : and it would
also, as being a source of blessing
no less than a blessing, enable
her to satisfy the wants of those
to whom she had to minister.
Compare the corresponding request in vi. 34, Κύριε.

λέγει πρὸς αὐτόν] *dicit ad eum*
v. The phrase occurs here only
in the conversation (comp. *vv.*
33, 48, 49), for the more common
λέγει αὐτῇ (*dicit ei* v.).
The slight shade of difference
may be expressed in English by
" saith unto," " saith to." In the
former case there is the suggestion of attention (look, thought)
specially directed to the person
addressed.

δός μοι . . .] Πολὺ οὖν συνετωτέρα
τοῦ Νικοδήμου ἡ γυνή . . . φησὶ
Κύριε, Δός μοι . . . ἐκεῖνος γὰρ
μυρίων τοιούτων ἀκούων ἔλεγε Πῶς
δύναται . . . (Chrys.).
Ἵνα μή occurs here only in St
John with the *pres. subj.* The
tense expresses vivid, immediate
feeling.

διέρχωμαι ἐνθάδε] *veniam huc*
v. ; *come all the way hither,*
across the intervening plain.
Compare Luke ii. 5 ; Acts ix. 38,
xi. 19.

16. λέγει . . .] The apparently
abrupt transition seems to be
suggested by the last words of *v.*
15. In those the speaker passed
beyond herself. She confessed
by implication that even the
greatest gift was not complete
unless it was shared by those to
whom she was bound. If they
thirsted, though she might not
thirst, her toilsome labour must
be fulfilled still. According to
this interpretation, Christ again
reads her thoughts ; and bids
her summon him to whom it
was her duty to minister. The
gift was for him also, and to be
given personally. We cannot receive the highest blessings alone.
The command was at the same
time a test of the woman's
awakening faith.

ἐνθάδε] Origen, who sees in the
well of Jacob, under one aspect, the spring of Scripture interpreted by human thought, adds
significantly : Παρατηρητέον οὖν
ὅτι καὶ αἰτούσῃ τὸ ὕδωρ τῇ Σαμαρεί-
τιδι τὸν Ἰησοῦν οἰονεὶ ἐπηγγέλλετο
παρέξειν αὐτὸ οὐκ ἐν ἄλλῳ τόπῳ
ἀλλ' ἢ παρὰ τῇ πηγῇ (tom. xiii. 4).
The woman had wished to be relieved from an irksome duty
(*neither come . . . hither*). The
Lord says *come hither.*

17 φώνησόν σου τὸν ἄνδρα καὶ ἐλθὲ ἐνθάδε. ἀπεκρίθη
ἡ γυνὴ καὶ εἶπεν [αὐτῷ] Οὐκ ἔχω ἄνδρα. λέγει αὐτῇ
18 ὁ Ἰησοῦς Καλῶς εἶπες ὅτι Ἄνδρα οὐκ ἔχω· πέντε
γὰρ ἄνδρας ἔσχες, καὶ νῦν ὃν ἔχεις οὐκ ἔστιν σου ἀνήρ·
19 τοῦτο ἀληθὲς εἴρηκας. λέγει αὐτῷ ἡ γυνή Κύριε, θεωρῶ
20 ὅτι προφήτης εἶ σύ. οἱ πατέρες ἡμῶν ἐν τῷ ὄρει τούτῳ

17. Οὐκ ἔχω ἄνδρα] *I have no husband.* The words are half sad, half apologetic, as of one who shrinks from the trial, conscious of weakness, and who seeks further assurance of power before rendering complete obedience. The command might disprove the knowledge and claims of the mysterious Teacher. The exact form of the Lord's answer suggests that a pause for a brief space followed. *Jesus saith to her, Thou saidst well, I have no husband . . . in that thou hast said truly.* The plea had been left, as it were, to be solemnly pondered, and the transposition of the words in the repetition of it, by which the emphasis is thrown on ἄνδρα which lay before on οὐκ ἔχω, at once reveals how the thoughts of the woman were laid bare.

Καλῶς εἶπες] It is possible that there is something of a sad irony in the words, as there is in Mark vii. 9; 2 Cor. xi. 4.

" Non expectavit aut exegit ut totum diceret, sed clementiæ manum porrigens pepercit pudori subvenit conscientiæ fluctuanti " (Rupert).

18. πέντε . . . ἄνδρας] Though the facilities for divorce are said to have been fewer among the Samaritans than among the Jews, there is no reason to suppose that the woman's former

marriages were illegally dissolved. That which was true in her statement pointed the rebuke. Her present position, though dishonourable, was not expressly forbidden by the Mosaic Law.

The singular details which are given of the woman's life have led many commentators to regard her as offering in her personal history a figure of the religious history of her people, which had been united to and separated from " five gods " (Jos. *Ant.* IX. xiv. 3; 2 Kings xvii. 29 ff.), and was at last irregularly serving the true God.

19. Κύριε] Τρίτον ἤδη ἡ Σαμαρεῖτις Κύριον ἀναγορεύει τὸν Σωτῆρα ἡμῶν (Orig. *ad loc.*).

θεωρῶ] The word marks contemplation, continued progressive vision, not immediate perception. It is used of a mental conclusion vividly realised: ch. xii. 19; Acts xxvii. 10; Heb. vii. 4. See ii. 23. Οἱονεὶ ἀναβλέψασά πως καὶ ἐν θεωρίᾳ νομίσασα γεγονέναι [φησὶ θεωρῶ . . .] (Orig.).

We cannot tell in what way the Lord's words were more significant to the woman than to us (see i. 48, 49), but they evidently bore with them to her a complete conviction that her whole life was open to the eyes of the speaker (*v.* 29).

προφήτης εἶ σύ] The emphasis lies on the title and not on the

17 come hither. The woman answered and said unto
him, I have no husband. Jesus saith unto her, Thou
18 saidst well, I have no husband : for thou hast had
five husbands ; and he whom thou now hast is not
19 thy husband : this hast thou said truly. The woman
saith unto him, Sir, I perceive that thou art a prophet.
20 Our fathers worshipped in this mountain ; and ye

pronoun. The first thought in
the Samaritan's mind is that the
connexion of man with God has
been authoritatively restored;
and if so, then, she argues, it
may be that discrepancies as to
local worship will be solved.
The order recalls i. 21. Comp.
viii. 48, xviii. 37.

" Una eademque responsione
et de se confessa est quod erat
et de illo quod eum esse intelligere poterat" (Rupert). Contrast
Luke vii. 39.

The title (προφήτης) is applied
to the Lord (1) by popular
rumour :

Mark vi. 15, προφήτης ὡς εἷς
τῶν προφητῶν.
Mark viii. 28, εἷς τῶν προφητῶν.
Comp. Luke ix. 8, 19, προφήτης
τις τῶν ἀρχαίων ἀνέστη.
Luke vii. 39, οὗτος εἰ ἦν προφήτης, ἐγίνωσκεν ἄν. Comp.
Luke xxii. 64, προφήτευσον,
τίς ἐστιν ὁ π., and parallels :
and more specifically (2) by the
multitudes :

Matt. xxi. 11, οὗτός ἐστιν ὁ
προφήτης Ἰησοῦς ὁ ἀπὸ Να-
ζαρὲθ τῆς Γαλιλαίας :
(3) by the two disciples :
Luke xxiv. 19, τὰ περὶ Ἰησοῦ
τοῦ Ναζαρηνοῦ, ὃς ἐγένετο ἀ-
νὴρ προφήτης δυνατὸς ἐν ἔργῳ
καὶ λόγῳ.
and (4) in definite confessions :
John iv. 19,

John vi. 14, οὗτός ἐστιν ἀληθῶς
ὁ προφήτης ὁ ἐρχόμενος εἰς
τὸν κόσμον.
John vii. 40, οὗτός ἐστιν ἀληθῶς ὁ προφήτης.
John ix. 17, προφήτης ἐστίν.
Comp. Acts iii. 22.

The central idea of the word
is that of the authoritative announcement of the will of God.
The prophet is the deliverer or
the interpreter of a divine message in a form intelligible to men
(1 Cor. xiv. 3). This is the classical sense of the word.

Διὸς προφήτης δ' ἐστὶ Λοξίας
πατρός, Eum. 19.

Compare
ἐπεὶ σὺ φέγγος, Τειρεσία, το-
δ' οὐχ ὁρᾶς,
ἐγὼ προφήτης σοι λόγων γε-
νήσομαι, Bacch. 210.

So in Exod. vii. 1
Prediction of the future is an
accident of the prophet's office ;
but so far included in it as he
deals with eternal truth. Comp.
Deut. xviii. 15 ff.

He " sees " God and declares
what he has seen (comp. 1 Sam.
ix. 9). So in the highest sense
John i. 18, iii. 11 ff.

Notice also the New Testament
prophets : Luke xi. 49, προφ. καὶ
ἀπ.; Eph. ii. 20, iii. 5, iv. 11.

20. To the student of the law,
the exclusive establishment of
worship at Jerusalem must have

προσεκύνησαν· καὶ ὑμεῖς λέγετε ὅτι ἐν Ἱεροσολύμοις
21 ἐστὶν ὁ τόπος ὅπου προσκυνεῖν δεῖ. λέγει αὐτῇ ὁ Ἰησοῦς
Πίστευέ μοι, γύναι, ὅτι ἔρχεται ὥρα ὅτε οὔτε ἐν τῷ ὄρει
τούτῳ οὔτε ἐν Ἱεροσολύμοις προσκυνήσετε τῷ πατρί.
22 ὑμεῖς προσκυνεῖτε ὃ οὐκ οἴδατε, ἡμεῖς προσκυνοῦμεν

been a great difficulty. To a Samaritan no question could appear more worthy of a prophet's decision than the settlement of the religious centre of the world. Thus the difficulty which is proposed is not a diversion, but the natural thought of one brought face to face with an interpreter of the divine will.

Οὐδὲν βιωτικὸν αὐτὸν ἐρωτᾷ, οὐ περὶ σώματος ὑγιείας, οὐ περὶ χρημάτων, οὐ περὶ πλούτου, ἀλλὰ περὶ δογμάτων εὐθέως . . . εἶδες πῶς ὑψηλοτέρα τῇ διανοίᾳ γέγονε; (Chrys.).

οἱ πατ. ἡμῶν] that is, either simply our ancestors from the time of the erection of the Samaritan temple after the Return, or, more probably, the patriarchs (comp. vi. 31). See below. The Samaritan temple was destroyed by John Hyrkanus c. 129 B.C. (Jos. Ant. XIII. ix. 1).

ἐν τ. ὄρ. τουτ. . . .] pointing to Mount Gerizim, at the foot of which the well lies. According to the Samaritan tradition, it was on this mountain that Abraham prepared the sacrifice of Isaac, and here also that he met Melchisedek (. . . Ἀβραὰμ λέγουσα καὶ γὰρ ἐκεῖ φασὶ τὸν υἱὸν ἀνηνέχθαι (Chrys. ad loc.)). In Deut. xxvii. 12 f. Gerizim is mentioned as the site on which the six tribes stood who were to pronounce the blessings for the observance of the law. And in the Samaritan Pentateuch, Geri-

zim and not Ebal is the mountain on which the altar was erected, Deut. xxvii. 4.

The natural reference to the unnamed mountain is an unmistakable trait from the life.

A striking passage is quoted from Bereshith Rabbi, § 32, by Lightfoot and Wünsche: "R. Jochanan, going to Jerusalem to pray, passed by [Gerizim]. A certain Samaritan seeing him asked him, Whither goest thou? I am, saith he, going to Jerusalem to pray. To whom the Samaritan, Were it not better for thee to pray in this holy mountain than in that cursed house?" Compare Bereshith R. § 81.

προσεκύνησαν] adoraverunt v. For this absolute use of προσκυνεῖν see xii. 20; Rev. v. 14 (true reading); Acts viii. 27, xxiv. 11; Heb. xi. 21 (LXX.).

καὶ ὑμεῖς] and ye, on your side . . . The whole problem is stated in its simplest form. The two facts are placed side by side (καί): traditional practice, Jewish teaching. No question is asked. The woman leaves the difficulty as she has put it before the prophet's eye. He will know best how to deal with it.

ὁ τοπ.] the place, that is, the one temple.

προσκ. δεῖ.] must worship (v. 24), according to a divine obligation. Compare iii. 30, note.

21. The rival claims of Gerizim and Jerusalem are not deter-

say, that in Jerusalem is the place where men must
21 worship.   Jesus saith unto her, Woman, believe me,
an hour cometh, when neither in this mountain, nor
22 in Jerusalem, shall ye worship the Father.   Ye worship

mined by the Lord, for they vanish in the revelation of an universal religion. At the same time He approaches the question from the side of the Samaritans. They had read of a spiritual worship. "Ye shall worship," He says at first, and not " Men shall worship."

γύναι] See ii. 4, xix. 26, xx. (13), 15. The address occurs elsewhere in the New Testament, Luke xiii. 12, xxii. 56; ὦ γύναι, Matt. xv. 28. In each case there appears to be some emphasis on the womanly character, either in tender sympathy or correction.

Πίστευέ μοι] marks the present beginning of faith, which is to grow to something riper. Compare x. 38, xii. 36, xiv. 1, 11. On the other hand, the single act of faith is marked (πίστευσον) in Acts xvi. 31. In the two parallel narratives, Mark v. 36, Luke viii. 50 (πίστευσον), the two forms are used : that which is general and continuous in the first passage is concentrated into a special act in the second by the addition of, " and she shall be saved." In the present connexion the unique phrase (πίστευέ μοι) corresponds with the familiar " Verily, verily " (which is not used in this chapter), as introducing a great truth.   Comp. Mal. i. 11.

ἔρχ. ὥρα] an hour cometh. This consummation was still future. The temple still claimed the reverent homage of believers (ii. 16).   Contrast v. 23.

ὥρα] There is a divine order in accordance with which each part of the whole scheme of salvation is duly fulfilled. Comp. v. 25, 28, xvi. 2, 4, 25, 32. So Christ had " His hour," ii. 4, note.

οὔτε . . . οὔτε] The two centres of worship are spoken of in the same terms (προσκυνήσετε) in the prospect of the future. "Non dicit : et istic et hic ; sed, neque istic neque hic " (Beng.).

προσκυν. τῷ πατ.] The word προσκυνεῖν was used indefinitely in v. 20: here it finds its true complement. The saying is addressed to the Samaritans, and not generally (v. 23). The object of worship determines its conditions. He who is known as the Father finds His home where His children are.   This absolute use of the title, " the Father," which occurs here for the first time, is characteristic of St. John, and almost peculiar to him. Other examples are found : Matt. xi. 27, and parallels ; Acts i. 4, 7 ; Rom. vi. 4 ; Eph. ii. 18. See Additional Note, and Additional Note on 1 John i. 2. The revelation of God as the Father sums up the new tidings of the Gospel. In this place the title stands in a significant relation to the boast of a special descent (our fathers, v. 20).

22. ὑμεῖς . . . οἴδατε] adoratis quod nescitis v. ; ye worship that which ye know not. The question of the place of worship resolves itself into one which is much

23 ὃ οἴδαμεν, ὅτι ἡ σωτηρία ἐκ τῶν Ἰουδαίων ἐστίν· ἀλλὰ
ἔρχεται ὥρα καὶ νῦν ἐστίν, ὅτε οἱ ἀληθινοὶ προσκυνηταὶ
προσκυνήσουσιν τῷ πατρὶ ἐν πνεύματι καὶ ἀληθείᾳ, καὶ
γὰρ ὁ πατὴρ τοιούτους ζητεῖ τοὺς προσκυνοῦντας αὐτόν·

larger. Your worship, that is, is directed to One with whose character, as He has revealed Himself through the prophets and in the history of His people, you are really unacquainted. You know whom to worship, but you do not know Him. By confining your faith to the law, you condemn yourselves to ignorance of the God of Israel. *We* Jews, on the other hand (the pronoun again is emphatic), *worship that which we know; because* the promised *salvation is of the Jews.* The power of Judaism lay in the fact that it was not simple deism, but the gradual preparation for the Incarnation. The Jew therefore *knew that which he worshipped,* so far as the will, and in that the nature, of God was gradually unfolded before him. Contrast viii. 54.

The truth thus declared makes it clear why a Jewish prophet must reveal the last expression of the divine will.

For ὃ οὐκ οἴδατε see *v.* 32.

ὑμ. . . . ἡμ. . . .] The sharp contrast between Samaritans and Jews which runs through the narrative (*vv.* 9, 20, *ye say*), and the pointed reference to "the Jews" which follows, fix beyond all reasonable doubt the interpretation of the pronouns.

Cyril discusses the question how the Lord can speak of Himself as worshipping the Father. He answers rightly: Πρᾶγμα ἀνθρώποις πρεπωδέστατον ἡ προσκύνησις . . . οὐκοῦν προσκυνεῖ μὲν

ὡς ἄνθρωπος ὅτε γέγονεν ἄνθρωπος προσκυνεῖται δὲ ἀεὶ μετὰ τοῦ πατρός . . .

ὃ . . .] The abstract form suggests the notion of God, so far as His attributes and purposes were made known, rather than of God as a Person, revealed to men at last in the Son: xiv. 9. Compare Acts xvii. 23 (ὃ οὖν).

The Samaritans, in a remarkable letter to Antiochus Epiphanes, in which they repudiate a Jewish origin, say that their fathers ἱδρυσάμενοι ἀνώνυμον ἐν τῷ Γαριζεὶν λεγομένῳ ὄρει ἱερὸν ἔθνον ἐπ᾽ αὐτοῦ τὰς καθηκούσας θυσίας, and go on to ask προσαγορευθῆναι τὸ ἀνώνυμον ἱερὸν Διὸς Ἑλληνίου, a request which was granted (Jos. *Ant.* XII. v. (vii.) 5).

ἡ σωτ. ἐ. τ. Ἰ.] *salus ex Judæis est* v.; *the* promised and expected *salvation,* to be realised in the mission of Messiah, is *from,* has its rise out of, *the Jews.* For ἡ σωτηρία see Acts iv. 12. Compare Acts xiii. 26. See also Rev. vii. 10, xii. 10, xix. 1.

For εἶναι ἐκ compare i. 46, note, vii. 22, 52, (x. 16). The thought is expressed in a symbol in Rev. xii. 5, and in detail in Rom. ix. 4 f.

23. ἀλλά . . .] The old differences of more and less perfect knowledge were to be done away with.

ἐρχ. ὥρα κ. νῦν ἐστ.] *an hour cometh, and now is.* The presence of Christ among men brought with it this result at once, though local worship (*v.* 21) was not yet

that which ye know not: we worship that which we
23 know: for the salvation is from the Jews. But an
hour cometh, and now is, when the true worshippers
shall worship the Father in spirit and truth: for such

abolished. Compare v. 25, as
contrasted with v. 28. In each
case the subtle contrast between
the immediate and ultimate
issues which are pointed to is
most significant and characteristic of the exact circumstances
to which the words belong. See
also xvi. 25, 32.

Origen recognises the difference
of the two thoughts : Οἶμαι τὸ μὲν
πρότερον δηλοῦν τὴν ἔξω σωμάτων
προσκύνησιν ἐνστησομένην κατὰ τὴν
τελειότητα· τὸ δὲ δεύτερον τὴν τῶν
ἐν βίῳ τούτῳ ὡς ἐνδέχεται κατὰ
ἀνθρωπίνην φύσιν προκοπὴν τελειου-
μένων.

οἱ ἀληθινοὶ προσκυνηταί] veri
adoratores v. ; the true worshippers. The term ἀληθινός describes that which is not only
truly but also completely what
it professes to be. Thus it is
used in connexion with those
material objects under which
Christ represents Himself. See
i. 9, vi. 32, vii. 28, viii. 16, xv.
1, note, xvii. 3, xix. 35. The
popular sense of the word "i-
deal" — fulfilling the complete
conception—comes near to this
usage.

ἐν πν. καὶ ἀληθ.] in spiritu et
veritate v.; in spirit and truth.
The words describe the characteristics of worship in one complex phrase, and not in two
co-ordinate phrases. Worship
involves an expression of feeling
and a conception of the object
towards whom the feeling is
entertained. The expression is
here described as made in spirit:

the conception as formed in
truth. Judaism (speaking generally) was a worship of the letter
and not of spirit (to take examples
from the time): Samaritanism
was a worship of falsehood and
not of truth. By the Incarnation men are enabled to have
immediate communion with God,
and thus a worship in spirit has
become possible : at the same
time the Son is a complete
manifestation of God for men,
and thus a worship in truth has
been placed within their reach.
These two characteristics answer
to the higher sense of the second
and third commandments, the
former of which tends to a
spiritual service, and the latter
to a devout regard for the
"name" of God, that is, for
every revelation of His Person
or attributes or action.

"The first strikes at hypocrisy,
the last at idolatry."

πνεύματι] In biblical language,
that part of man's nature which
holds, or is capable of holding,
intercourse with the eternal order,
is the spirit (1 Thess. v. 23).
The spirit in man responds to the
Spirit of God. Compare vi. 63.
The sphere of worship was therefore now to be that highest
region where the divine and
human meet, and not, as in an
earlier period of discipline, material or fleshly. Comp. Rom. i. 9.
Forms and words are (as it were)
the body of worship, and are
necessary for us.

"In templo vis orare? in te

24 πνεῦμα ὁ θεός, καὶ τοὺς προσκυνοῦντας αὐτὸν [1] ἐν πνεύματι
25 καὶ ἀληθείᾳ δεῖ προσκυνεῖν. λέγει αὐτῷ ἡ γυνή Οἶδα
ὅτι Μεσσίας ἔρχεται, ὁ λεγόμενος Χριστός· ὅταν ἔλθῃ
26 ἐκεῖνος, ἀναγγελεῖ ἡμῖν ἅπαντα. λέγει αὐτῇ ὁ Ἰησοῦς

[1] Omit αὐτόν ℵ*D*.

ora. Sed prius esto templum Dei,
quia ille in templo suo exaudiet
orantem " (Aug. ad loc.).

ἀληθείᾳ] Worship is necessarily
limited by the idea of the being
worshipped.   A true idea of
God, even if still διὰ κατόπτρου, is
essential to a right service of
Him. Comp. Heb. viii. 5, x. 1.

καὶ γάρ] nam et v. The phrase
is remarkable.   It alleges a
reason which is assumed to be
conclusive from the nature of
the case : for the Father also on
His part, which is expressed
fairly by for in fact, for indeed.
Comp. Matt. viii. 9 and parallel,
xxvi. 73 and parallels ; Mark
x. 45 ; Luke vi. 32 ff., xi. 4, xxii.
37 ; Acts xix. 40 ; Rom. xi. 1,
and not infrequently in St.
Paul.

τοι. ζ. τ. προσκ.] seeks such for
his worshippers, or seeks his worshippers in such.   The Father
seeks those who have this character, and finds them.   The
search is for a character essentially formed, and not for a character aimed at ("seeketh his
worshippers to be such "). There
appears to be no parallel for such
a use of ζητεῖν.

ζητεῖ] There is a real correspondence between the true
worshipper and God. Compare
i. 43 (εὑρίσκει), note. The true
(ἀληθινός) worshipper answers to
the true (ἀληθινός) God (xvii. 3).

Εἰ ζητεῖ ὁ πατὴρ διὰ τοῦ υἱοῦ
ζητεῖ τοῦ ἐληλυθότος ζητῆσαι καὶ

σῶσαι τὸ ἀπολωλός (Orig. tom.
xiii. 20).

24. πνεῦμα ὁ θεός] spiritus est
deus v. ; God is Spirit, absolutely
free from all limitations of space
and time. The nature and not
the personality of God is described, just as the phrases God
is light (1 John i. 5), or God is
love (1 John iv. 8). This premiss
is drawn from a true interpretation of the old revelation (Isa.
xxxi. 3), but the conclusion which
follows belongs to the new. The
declaration in its majestic simplicity is unique ; though St.
John implies in the two other
revelations of God's being which
he has given (ll. cc.) the truth
which is declared by it. See 1
John iv. 8, Additional Note.

ἐν πν. κ. ἀληθ.] Comp. 1 John
iii. 18. The revelation, xiv. 6,
ἐγώ εἰμι ἡ ἀλήθεια, reconciles the
two requirements.

So Rupert applies the words :
" Patrem in spiritu adorare
quid est nisi spiritum adoptionis
filiorum accepisse in quo cla-
mamus Abba, Pater ? Quid est
adorare Patrem in veritate nisi
in filio ejus manendo qui dicit
Ego sum veritas ? "

25. The woman's answer to
the declaration made to her helps
us to understand why it was
made. She had acknowledged
the Lord as a prophet, but she
felt that such truths could be
affirmed only by one who was
more than a prophet, and for

24 doth the Father seek to be his worshippers. God is Spirit: and they that worship him must worship in 25 spirit and truth. The woman saith unto him, I know that Messiah cometh (which is called Christ): when 26 he cometh, he will declare unto us all things. Jesus

such a one she looked. In her hope Messiah was the perfect lawgiver and not the conqueror. Truth and not dominion was the blessing she connected with His mission. The confession, like the revelation by which it was followed, is unique in the Gospels.

Οἶδα] Compare iii. 2, οἴδαμεν. The object and the ground of knowledge are characteristically different.

Μεσσίας] i. 41, εὑρήκαμεν τὸν Μ. The absence of the article. here gives the title the form of a simple proper name. Compare Χριστός and ὁ χριστός.

ὁ λεγ. Χρ.] The words may be part of the speech of the woman, in which case they imply that the Greek title was that which was popularly current (cf. v. 29). At least, the different form in which the interpretation is given in i. 41 must be noticed. This exact form is used as part of a title elsewhere, xi. 16, xx. 24, xxi. 2 (cf. Luke xxii. 1).

For the Samaritan conceptions of Messiah, see *Introd. to Study of the Gospels*, pp. 159 f.

ὅταν ἔλθῃ ἐκ.] *when he comes.* The pronoun is emphatic, and fixes the attention on Messiah as contrasted with, and standing apart from, all other teachers.

ἀναγγ. ἡ. ἅπαν.] *nobis adnuntiabit omnia* v.; *he will announce all things unto us.* The word ἀναγγέλλω is used of the fresh

and authoritative message of the Advocate, xvi. 13 ff. The teaching so given would be absolute and complete. At the same time the woman implies that no less authority could solve the problem.

26. The woman was prepared to welcome Messiah in His prophetic dignity, and in this He makes Himself known to her. Compare ix. 35 ff. In each case the revelation answers to the faith of the recipient. With these acknowledgements prompted by grace contrast the acknowledgement yielded to legal authority, Matt. xxvi. 63, 64.

"Alienigenæ seipsum credidit quem Judæis non crediderat . . . Honoratus est enim ab his alienigenis Samaritanis ubi Christum se esse dixit; inhonoratus est et crucifixus a contribulibus suis ubi signa et prodigia fecit in eis quæ nemo alius fecit " (Rupert).

ἐγ. εἰμ.] The phrase ἐγώ εἰμι is used with different shades of meaning. Sometimes it is equivalent to "I am the Christ" (Mark xiii. 6; Luke xxi. 8). Sometimes it simply identifies the person : "It is I " (Matt. xiv. 27; John vi. 20; Luke xxiv. 39; John xviii. 5, 6, 8). In both these cases the common idea is "I am He to whom your thoughts are turned " (comp. Mark xiv. 62; Luke xxii. 70). But sometimes again the sense seems to be more absolute:

11

27 Ἐγώ εἰμι, ὁ λαλῶν σοι. Καὶ ἐπὶ τούτῳ ἦλθαν οἱ μαθηταὶ
αὐτοῦ, καὶ ἐθαύμαζον ὅτι μετὰ γυναικὸς ἐλάλει· οὐδεὶς
28 μέντοι εἶπεν Τί ζητεῖς; ἢ Τί λαλεῖς μετ᾽ αὐτῆς; ἀφῆκεν
οὖν τὴν ὑδρίαν αὐτῆς ἡ γυνὴ καὶ ἀπῆλθεν εἰς τὴν πόλιν
29 καὶ λέγει τοῖς ἀνθρώποις Δεῦτε ἴδετε ἄνθρωπον ὃς εἶπέ μοι
30 πάντα ἃ ἐποίησα· μήτι οὗτός ἐστιν ὁ χριστός; ¹ ἐξῆλθον

¹ Insert καί CD.

"I am," with sovereign, supreme being (viii. 24, 28, 58, xiii. 19).

This is the first occasion on which the Lord is recorded to have used the phrase, or to have directly revealed Himself. Hitherto He had spoken of Himself indirectly (i. 51, ii. 16, iii. 13 f.).

Afterwards He makes Himself known in a series of declarations:

vi. 35, 41, 48, 51, ὁ ἄρτος.

viii. 12, τὸ φῶς τοῦ κόσμου. Cf. xii. 46.

x. 7, ἡ θύρα.

x. 11, 14, ὁ ποιμὴν ὁ καλός.

xi. 25, ἡ ἀνάστασις.

xiv. 6, ἡ ὁδός, κ. ἡ ἀλήθεια κ. ἡ ζωή.

xv. 1, 5, ἡ ἄμπελος.

ὁ λαλῶν] qui loquor v.; I that talk. The word suggests the notion of free, familiar conversation, which is brought out in the next verse. It was by this intercourse of loving and searching sympathy, that Christ revealed Himself as the hope of men. Comp. ix. 37, note.

27—30. The conversation being ended, its immediate effects are noticed. The disciples reverently wonder. The woman is filled with a hope beyond hope. Her countrymen are moved by her enthusiasm. The whole picture is full of life.

27. Καί . . . ἦλθαν . . . καὶ ἐθαύμαζον] And . . . came . . .;

and they marvelled. The change of tense, which marks the pause of wonder, requires the insertion of the pronoun.

ὅτι μ. γ. ἐλάλει] quia cum muliere loquebatur v.; that he was talking with a woman, against the custom of the doctors, by whom it was said that "a man should not salute a woman in a public place, not even his own wife," and that it was "better that the words of the law should be burnt than delivered to women." Compare Aboth, i. 5 (Taylor); and Buxtorf, Lex. Rabb., p. 1146; and contrast Gal. iii. 28. One of the thanksgivings in the daily service of the Synagogue is: "Blessed art Thou, O Lord, . . . who hast not made me a woman."

A double question arose in the minds of the disciples. Could their Master require a service from a woman? or could He wish to commune with her as a teacher? Yet they were content to wait. In due time He would remove their doubts. Even thus early they had learnt to abide His time.

Cyril refers well to Luke xii. 42: the flame was kindled.

28. ἀφῆκεν οὖν . . . καὶ ἀπῆλθεν . . .] so the woman left . . . went away. . . This time the woman's answer is in action. She had received the message which she

27 saith unto her, I that talk unto thee am *he*. And upon this came his disciples; and they marvelled that he was talking with a woman; yet no man said, What seekest thou? or, Why speakest thou 28 with her? So the woman left her waterpot, and 29 went away into the city, and saith to the men, Come, see a man, which told me all things that I did: can 30 this be the Christ? They went out of the city, and

required. " Posteaquam audivit hoc : *Ego sum qui loquor tecum, jam ultra quid diceret . . .?* " (Bede). The Lord had set aside His own want: she set aside her own purpose. But she showed that her absence was to be but for a brief space, by " leaving her water-pot " (" Onere abjecto cucurrit ad civitatem " [Bede]). And meanwhile the message which she bore to the city was for all, for *the men* (τοῖς ἀνθρώποις), the inhabitants generally, and not for her "husband" only.

29. The Samaritan woman, like the first disciples (i. 41, 45), at once tells what she has found, and with just the same appeal : *Come, see* (i. 46). She becomes an " apostle" commissioned by faith. Κατὰ τὴν ἰδίαν δύναμιν ὅπερ οἱ ἀπόστολοι ἐποίησαν καὶ αὐτὴ πεποίηκε μειζόνως (Chrys.). Ἀπόστολος γίνεται ὑπὸ τῆς τὴν καρδίαν αὐτῆς περιλαβούσης πίστεως χειροτονηθεῖσα (Theophylact).

Δεῦτε ἴδετε . . .] *Venite, videte* . . . v. See Matt. xxviii. 6. The word δεῦτε is found again in xxi. 12 (Rev. xix. 17). It occurs also in St. Matthew and St. Mark, and not infrequently in the LXX. (chiefly for לְכוּ). It expresses an immediate, personal (δεῦτε) urgency of call.

πάντα ἃ ἐποι.] *all things that I did.* The words here and in v. 39 are definite in form, and the truth of the exaggerated phrase lies in the effect which Christ's words had upon the woman's conscience (18 ff.). She was convinced that He knew all, and in the revelation which He made she seemed to feel that He had told her all, because He had by that called up all before her eyes. All thought of self had gone in the thought of Him. Ἐνῆν εἰπεῖν ἑτέρως Δεῦτε, ἴδετε προφητεύοντα· ἀλλ' ὅταν πυρωθῇ ψυχὴ τῷ πυρὶ τῷ θείῳ πρὸς οὐδὲν τῶν ἐν τῇ γῇ λοιπὸν ὁρᾷ, οὐ πρὸς δόξαν, οὐ πρὸς αἰσχύνην, ἀλλ' ἑνός ἐστι μόνου, τῆς κατεχούσης αὐτὴν φλογός (Chrys.).

μ. οὐ. ἐ. ὁ χρ.;] *numquid ipse est Christus?* v. ; *can this be the Christ?* Is it possible to believe that the highest blessing has suddenly been given to us ? The words suggest the great conclusion as something beyond hope. The form of the sentence grammatically suggests a negative answer (v. 33), but hope bursts through it. Compare Matt. xii. 23. The same phrase occurs Matt. xxvi. 22, 25; John viii. 22, xviii. 35; James iii. 11, etc.

ἐξῆλθον ἐκ . . .] The result of

31 ¹ ἐκ τῆς πόλεως καὶ ἤρχοντο πρὸς αὐτόν. Ἐν τῷ μεταξὺ
32 ἠρώτων αὐτὸν οἱ μαθηταὶ λέγοντες Ῥαββεί, φάγε. ὁ δὲ
εἶπεν αὐτοῖς Ἐγὼ βρῶσιν ἔχω φαγεῖν ἣν ὑμεῖς οὐκ
33 οἴδατε. ἔλεγον οὖν οἱ μαθηταὶ πρὸς ἀλλήλους Μή τις
34 ἤνεγκεν αὐτῷ φαγεῖν; λέγει αὐτοῖς ὁ Ἰησοῦς Ἐμὸν
βρῶμά ἐστιν ἵνα ποιήσω τὸ θέλημα τοῦ πέμψαντός με
35 καὶ τελειώσω αὐτοῦ τὸ ἔργον. οὐχ ὑμεῖς λέγετε ὅτι Ἔτι
τετράμηνός ² ἐστιν καὶ ὁ θερισμὸς ἔρχεται; ἰδοὺ λέγω

¹ Insert οὖν ℵΛ 69.   ² τετράμηνος ℵABCDLT᙮ΓΔ; τετράμηνον H.

the woman's message is given abruptly. The trust of the hearers is the measure of her zeal.

ἤρχοντο] *They went out of the city, and came on their way towards him* (Vulg. *exierunt et veniebant*). The tense is vividly descriptive. The villagers started on their journey, and are seen, as it were, pursuing it. Comp. *v.* 35. Cf. vi. 17, xix. 3, xx. 3.

31—38. The deeper lessons of the incident are unfolded when the Lord was left alone with His disciples. Their natural and loving request leads Him to point to wants more truly imperious than those of the body, thus carrying on the teaching of the act and word just given to and by the woman (31—34). The actual, unexpected condition of the Samaritans is used to illustrate the urgency and the fruitfulness of the work to which the apostles were called.

31. ἠρώτων] *rogabant* v.; *the* (*disciples*) *asked* (begged). See *vv.* 40, 47, xii. 21, etc. The love of the disciples overpowered their wonder. They strive to satisfy the wants of their Master and not their own curiosity (*v.* 27). The retention of the Hebrew term *Rabbi* is expressive.

32. ἣν ὑμεῖς οὐκ οἴδ.] *that ye know not;* that is, meat of which ye—ye in your present state of imperfect discipline—know not the virtue and power. Comp. *v.* 22. For the image, see vi. 27.

33. πρὸς ἀλλ.] *one to another*, not venturing to ask more from their Lord. Comp. xvi. 17, xxi. 12.

Μή τις . . .;] *Can it be that anyone . . .?* Comp. *v.* 29.

34. ἵνα ποιήσω . . . καὶ τελειώσω . . .] *ut faciam . . . et perficiam* v.; *to do . . . and to finish . . .* The form of the expression (ἵνα π.) emphasises the *end* and not the *process*, not *the doing . . . and finishing*, but *that I may do . . . and finish.* Comp. vi. 29, xv. 8, xvii. 3; 1 John iii. 11, v. 3.

Rupert remarks that the Lord alone could use the words in their fullest sense: "Sancti omnes quamdiu hic exsulant . . . quamlibet voluntarie quantolibet cum amore quod bonum est ad omnes operentur . . . nemo tamen illorum recte dicit: Meus cibus est ut faciam voluntatem Dei, solus autem ille qui non aliunde mercedem sperabat . . . Nostra . . . qualiacunque bona opera, nostra fides et dilectio, ceteraque talia,

31 were coming to him.   In the mean while the disciples
32 prayed him, saying, Rabbi, eat.   But he said unto
33 them, I have meat to eat that ye know not.   The
disciples therefore said one to another, Hath any
34 man brought him *aught* to eat?   Jesus saith unto
them, My meat is to do the will of him that sent me,
35 and to accomplish his work.   Say not ye, There are
yet four months, and *then* cometh the harvest?   behold,

nunc interdum cibus ejus sunt, postmodum vero noster cibus erit visio ejus ubi implebit quod promittere dignatus est ' ut edatis,' inquit, ' et bibatis super mensam meam in regno meo'" (Luke xxii.).

τοῦ πεμψ. με] Comp. v. 36 f.

τελειώσω] *accomplish.* The word is remarkable.   It expresses not merely "finishing," "bringing to an end," but "bringing to the true end," "perfecting."   It is characteristic of St. John, and of the Epistle to the Hebrews: ch. v. 36, xvii. 4, 23, xix. 28; 1 John ii. 5, iv. 12, 17 f.; Heb. ii. 10, v. 9, vii. 28, etc.   Christ came to fulfil the destiny of man, though fallen, and to crown creation.   Theophylact expresses this thought partly as an alternative explanation: Τάχα δέ μοι νόει θεοῦ ἔργον τὸν ἄνθρωπον, ὃν ἐτελείωσε μόνος ὁ υἱὸς τοῦ θεοῦ, ἐν ἑαυτῷ ἀναμάρτητον ἀποδείξας τὴν φύσιν ἡμῶν καὶ ἐν παντὶ ἔργῳ ἀγάθῳ διὰ τῆς ἐν σαρκὶ θείας πολιτείας τετελειωμένην καὶ ἀπηρτισμένην ἀποφήνας καὶ ἄχρι τέλους νικήσας τὸν κόσμον.

αὐτ. τ. ἐργ.] Comp. v. 19, note.

34 ff. The train of thought in these verses appears to be this. "My true food lies in working for the fulfilment of my Father's will, and the partial

accomplishment of this end is even now before my eyes.   You, as you traverse these corn plains, anticipate without doubt the coming harvest.   And the labour of the sower is a parable of all spiritual labour.   The issue of that labour is not less certain than the issue of this.   Nay, further: the spiritual harvest, of which that natural harvest is a figure, is even now ready for the sickle.   In this sense, the reaper already has his reward and the sower through him.   For the work of these two is essentially separate.   In spiritual labour the homely proverb is fulfilled: He who reaps sows not what he reaps, he who sows reaps not what he sows.   Still the joy of the reaper crowns the toil of the sower; and these first-fruits of Samaria, the first-fruits of a spiritual harvest, crown my joy."   Comp. Matt. ix. 37, 38.

35. οὐχ ὑμ. λεγ. . . . θερισμός] *say not ye . . . harvest.* These words have been understood in two ways, either (1) as a proverbial saying, marking roughly the interval between some familiar date (seedtime), or the first appearance of the blade, and harvest; or (2) as a description

ὑμῖν, ἐπάρατε τοὺς ὀφθαλμοὺς ὑμῶν καὶ θεάσασθε τὰς
36 χώρας ὅτι λευκαί εἰσιν πρὸς θερισμόν· ἤδη ὁ θερίζων
μισθὸν λαμβάνει καὶ συνάγει καρπὸν εἰς ζωὴν αἰώνιον,
37 ἵνα ὁ σπείρων ὁμοῦ χαίρῃ καὶ ὁ θερίζων. ἐν γὰρ τούτῳ
ὁ λόγος ἐστὶν ἀληθινὸς ὅτι ἄλλος ἐστὶν ὁ σπείρων καὶ
38 ἄλλος ὁ θερίζων· ἐγὼ ἀπέστειλα ὑμᾶς θερίζειν ὃ οὐχ
ὑμεῖς κεκοπιάκατε· ἄλλοι κεκοπιάκασιν, καὶ ὑμεῖς εἰς τὸν

of the actual state of things at the time, so that when the words were spoken there were four months to the harvest. The emphatic " ye," which appears to indicate men's clear calculation of natural events, favours the first interpretation ; but the form of the sentence (*there are yet . . .*) and the period named, which is less than the interval between seedtime and harvest, favour the second. If this latter view be adopted, we have an approximate date for the narrative. The harvest began about the middle of April, and lasted to the end of May (Tristram, *The Land of Israel,* pp. 583 f.). The conversation therefore might be placed about the end of January (or early in February). By this time the fields would be already green. Dr. Tristram found the wheat and barley near Jerusalem, sown just after Christmas, four inches high on February 20 (*l.c.,* p. 399). But on this supposition, it would follow from this passage, compared with ii. 13 and iv. 3, that the Lord must have continued about ten months in Judæa, a supposition which seems to be inconsistent with iv. 45. See Additional Note on v. 1.

ἐπάρατε τ. ὀφθ.] *levate oculos* v. ; *lift up your eyes.* Compare Isa.

xlix. 18. This prophetic passage offers a striking parallel in thought and language.

τ. χώρας] *regiones* v. ; *the fields.* At the present time the plain at the foot of Gerizim is fertile corn-land (Stanley, *Sin. and Pal.* 233 ff.). The detail has the truth of life in it. The disciples saw the promise of rich crops : but Christ saw the spiritual harvest, of which the fields were the image (Matt. xiii. 3 ff., etc.), even now come in its first-fruits, as the people from the city approached.

ὅτι . . .] *Look on* (i. 38) *the fields,* and observe *that . . .* The woman, we may suppose, with the Samaritans (*v.* 30), was seen returning to the well.

" Videte non regionem unam, non Judæam solam, patriam meam, in qua ego Domini aut possessoris honorem habiturus non sum, sed videte plures regiones gentium, regiones omnium nationum quam albæ sunt jam ad messem " (Rupert).

35, 36. The punctuation and reading at the end of verse 35 are uncertain, but it seems best to omit ἤδη at the close of it, and to substitute it for καί at the beginning of *v.* 36 : *Already he that reapeth . . .* The harvest was strangely anticipated in this first welcome of the Word beyond the limits of Judaism.

I say unto you, Lift up your eyes, and look on the
36 fields, that they are white unto harvest. Already he
that reapeth receiveth wages, and gathereth fruit unto
life eternal; that he that soweth and he that reapeth
37 may rejoice together. For herein is the saying true,
38 One soweth, and another reapeth. I sent you to
reap that whereon ye have not laboured: others
have laboured, and ye are entered into their labour.

36. μισθ. λαμβ. . . . ἵνα . . .]
receiveth wages . . . that he . . .
There is even now work for him
to do, which has an immediate
reward, and he *gathereth fruit*
which shall not perish or be consumed, but endure *unto life eter-*
nal. Comp. *v.* 14, vi. 27, xii. 25.
There, in that higher order, the
sower shall "see of his travail"
and be glad: the forerunner
who has long passed away shall
meet him who has received the
harvest of his earlier work and
share his joy. The application
seems to be to lawgiver and
priest and prophet, and all who
"went before" Christ's coming
in old times, and even now go
before Him. Christ Himself
stands as the Lord of the Harvest (*v.* 38) and not here as the
Sower.

37. ἐν γὰρ τουτ. ὁ λογ. . . .]
for herein is the saying . . .
"Herein," *i.e.* in the fact that
you are reaping already (*v.* 36)
what others sowed. And the
principle was to find application
in their labours also. "I say
this," so the words imply, "to
prepare you by the lesson of
your immediate success for future disappointment; for in this
spiritual sowing and harvest-
ing the common proverb finds

its complete, ideal fulfilment
(ἀληθινός) : *one soweth and an-*
other reapeth."

38. ἐγὼ ἀπεστ. . . . . ὃ οὐχ ὑμ.
κεκοπ. . . .] *I sent you . . . ye*
have not laboured . . . The words
probably point to the successful labours of the apostles in
Judæa (*v.* 2). At the same time
their whole mission was included
in their call.

ἄλλοι κεκοπιάκασιν, καὶ ὑμεῖς
. . .] *others have laboured . . . in-*
to their labour. The reference,
as in the case of the sower, is
to all who had in any manner
prepared the way for Christ.
Even in Samaria, there had
been those who, in unexpected
ways, had made ready for Him.
The lesson could not but come
with singular force in such a
place. Christ Himself revealed
and used their work. He was,
as has been said, like Joshua,
who brought his own people to
"a land for which they did not
labour" (Joshua xxiv. 13); and
it is possible that the words may
contain a reference to that passage of the Old Testament. The
result is identified with the effort
(*that which you have not wrought*
by your labour, ὃ οὐ κεκοπ., Vulg.
quod non laborastis). Compare
Ecclus. xiv. 15.

39 κόπον αὐτῶν εἰσεληλύθατε. Ἐκ δὲ τῆς πόλεως ἐκείνης
πολλοὶ ἐπίστευσαν εἰς αὐτὸν τῶν Σαμαρειτῶν διὰ τὸν
λόγον τῆς γυναικὸς μαρτυρούσης ὅτι Εἶπέν μοι πάντα
40 ἃ ἐποίησα. ὡς οὖν ἦλθον πρὸς αὐτὸν οἱ Σαμαρεῖται,
ἠρώτων αὐτὸν μεῖναι παρ᾽ αὐτοῖς· καὶ ἔμεινεν ἐκεῖ δύο
41 ἡμέρας. καὶ πολλῷ πλείους ἐπίστευσαν διὰ τὸν λόγον
42 αὐτοῦ, τῇ τε γυναικὶ ἔλεγον [ὅτι] Οὐκέτι διὰ τὴν σὴν
λαλιὰν πιστεύομεν· αὐτοὶ γὰρ ἀκηκόαμεν, καὶ οἴδαμεν
ὅτι οὗτός ἐστιν ἀληθῶς ὁ σωτὴρ τοῦ κόσμου [1].

[1] Insert ὁ χριστός AC³DLΓΔ.

"[Abraham, Moyses, et omnes sancti prophetæ] credentes et sperantes . . . seminaverunt euntes et flentes . . . flendo et seminando profitentes quod peregrini essent et advenæ super terram (Ps. cxxv. 7), et non haberent hic manentem civitatem sed futuram inquirerent (Heb. xiii. 14). Hoc modo laboriosam hiemem passi seminaverunt et non messuerunt " (Rupert).

THE WORK IN SYCHAR (39—42)

39—42. The ready faith of the woman was found also among her countrymen. As she had looked for a religious teacher in the Christ, they acknowledged in Him "the Saviour of the world."

39. Ἐκ δὲ τ. π. ἐκ.] The words go back to v. 30, ἐκ τῆς π.

διὰ τὸν λόγον] propter verbum v.; because of the word (v. 41), the narrative, and not the simple statement only, of the woman as (or while) she (earnestly, constantly, and not once for all) testified. The mention of the ground of the belief of the Samaritans places them in contrast with the people at Jerusalem who "believed [on the name of Christ],

beholding the signs which he did" (ii. 23). Comp. vv. 45, 48.

40. ὡς οὖν ἦλθ.] so when . . . came . . . Their belief went thus far, that they wished to hear more of His teaching. Rupert of Deutz remarks that it is never related that the Lord stayed in Jerusalem. Contrast Luke xxi. 37.

μεῖναι] to abide (i. 38, 39), as in the second clause.

41. πολλῷ πλείους] multo plures v.; far more. The phrase is comparative (in reference to v. 39), and not positive. This isolated notice is an instructive illustration of our fragmentary knowledge of the Lord's whole work.

διὰ τ. λογ. αὐτ.] Comp. v. 39.

42. Οὐκέτι διὰ τ. σ. λαλ. . . .] No longer is it because of thy speech that we believe, for we have heard for ourselves. The order is remarkable. The word λαλιά corresponds with λαλεῖν in vv. 26, 27. It occurs elsewhere in the New Testament only ch. viii. 43; Matt. xxvi. 73 (Mark xiv. 70). It does not appear that the Samaritans asked for signs like the Jews (comp. v. 48), or that

₃₉ And from that city many of the Samaritans believed on him because of the word of the woman, as ₄₀ she testified, He told me all things that I did. So when the Samaritans came unto him, they besought him to abide with them: and he abode there two ₄₁ days. And many more believed because of his word; ₄ and they said to the woman, No longer is it because of thy speech that we believe: for we have heard for ourselves, and know that this is indeed the Saviour of the world.

any outward miracles were wrought among them.

ὁ σωτὴρ τοῦ κόσμου] *salvator mundi* v.; *the Saviour of the world.* The words *the Christ* (A.V.) must be omitted, in accordance with an overwhelming concurrence of ancient authorities. The simple title, *the Saviour of the world*, is found once again in 1 John iv. 14, note; and it is a significant fact that this magnificent conception of the work of Christ was first expressed by Samaritans, for whom the hope of a Deliverer had not been shaped to suit national ambition. When a "Jew" appealed to the fount of their spiritual brotherhood through one Father, the conception naturally took shape. So at last faith rose to the level of the promise, *v.* 21. The "salvation" (*v.* 22) sprang from the Jews, and was recognised by Samaritans.

Comp. iii. 17, xii. 47, and contrast xii. 19.

"Audierunt veritatem docentis, mansuetudinem ad credendum invitantis, justitiam non accipientis personam Judæi sive Samaritani, neminem asper-

nandum velut minuendum judicantis quacunque ex gente sit" (Rupert).

3. THE WORK IN GALILEE (43—54)

This notice of Christ's Galilæan work consists of a general account of the welcome which He found (*vv.* 43—45), followed by the narrative of a second "sign" (*vv.* 46—54).

It seems probable that the earlier part of the Synoptic narratives (Mark i. 14—ii. 14 and parallels) must be placed in the interval which extended from iv. 43—v. 1. So far there are no signs of the special hostility which seems to have been called out by the healing on the Sabbath wrought on the next visit to Jerusalem.

The contents of the section are peculiar to St. John. It has indeed been questioned whether "the healing of the officer's son" is not identical with "the healing of the centurion's servant" recorded by St. Matthew (viii. 5 ff.) and St. Luke (vii. 2 ff.). Both miracles were wrought at Capernaum, and wrought in the same manner at

43 Μετὰ δὲ τὰς δύο ἡμέρας ἐξῆλθεν ἐκεῖθεν¹ εἰς τὴν
44 Γαλιλαίαν· αὐτὸς γὰρ Ἰησοῦς ἐμαρτύρησεν ὅτι προφήτης
45 ἐν τῇ ἰδίᾳ πατρίδι τιμὴν οὐκ ἔχει. ὅτε οὖν ἦλθεν εἰς
τὴν Γαλιλαίαν, ἐδέξαντο αὐτὸν οἱ Γαλιλαῖοι, πάντα ἑωρακότες ὅσα ἐποίησεν ἐν Ἱεροσολύμοις ἐν τῇ ἑορτῇ, καὶ
46 αὐτοὶ γὰρ ἦλθον εἰς τὴν ἑορτήν. Ἦλθεν οὖν πάλιν εἰς
τὴν Κανὰ τῆς Γαλιλαίας, ὅπου ἐποίησεν τὸ ὕδωρ οἶνον.

¹ Insert καὶ ἀπῆλθεν ΑΓΔ.

a distance. But in all other respects the incidents are characteristically unlike, as to

(1) *Place.* The request was
made here at Cana, there at Capernaum.

(2) *Time.* Here immediately
after the return to Galilee, there
after some time had elapsed.

(3) *Persons.* Here the subject
was a son, there a slave: here
the petitioner was probably a
Jew, there a heathen soldier.

(4) *Character.* Here the faith
of the father, as interpreted by
the Lord, is weak; there the
faith of the centurion is exceptionally strong.

(5) *Manner.* Here the request
is granted in a way opposed to
the prayer, there in accordance
with it: here the Lord refuses
to go, there He offers to go to
the sufferer.

The two miracles are in fact
complementary. In the one,
weak faith is disciplined and
confirmed: in the other, strong
faith is rewarded and glorified.
The fame of the former miracle
may easily have encouraged the
centurion to appeal to the Lord
in his distress.

In one other case the Lord is
recorded to have exercised His
power at a distance: Matt. xv.
22 and parallels.

43. Μετὰ δὲ τὰς δύο ἡμέρας]
After the two days (mentioned in
v. 40).

44. αὐτὸς γὰρ Ἰησοῦς] *ipse enim
Jesus* v. The testimony of Christ
was the same as the testimony
of the apostles after the fall of
Jerusalem.

ἐμαρτ. . . . πατρίδι] The general
meaning of this clause depends
upon the sense given to ἡ ἰδία
πατρίς (*sua patria* v.). This has
been understood to be (1) Galilee generally, (2) Nazareth, (3)
Lower Galilee, in which Nazareth was situated, as distinguished from Upper Galilee, in
which was Capernaum, (4) Judæa.
Against the first three lies the
fatal objection, that it seems
impossible that St. John should
speak of Galilee in this connexion as Christ's "own country"
(compare vii. 41, 42). Both by
fact and the current interpretation of prophecy, Judæa alone
could receive that title (comp.
Origen, tom. xiii. 54). Moreover, Judæa is naturally suggested by the circumstances.
The Lord had not been received
with due honour at Jerusalem.
His Messianic claim had not
been welcomed. He did not
trust Himself to the Jews there.
He was forced to retire. If
many followed Him, they were

43 And after the two days he went forth from thence
44 into Galilee. For Jesus himself testified, that a
45 prophet hath no honour in his own country. So
when he came into Galilee, the Galilæans received
him, having seen all the things that he did in Jerusalem at the feast: for they also went unto the feast.
46 He came therefore again unto Cana of Galilee,
where he made the water wine. And there was a

not the representatives of the people, and their faith reposed on miracles. No apostle was a Jew in this narrower sense. Nothing then can be more appropriate than to mark this outward failure of the appeal to Judæa by an application of the common proverb (comp. Matt. xxiii. 37; Luke xiii. 34), followed by the notice of the ready welcome given to Christ by Galilæans (v. 45).

If this interpretation of "his own country" be accepted, it will be enough simply to notice the other interpretations which have found favour. Thus the words have been supposed to mean, (1) Jesus departed into Upper Galilee (or Capernaum), for He testified that a prophet hath no honour in his own country (Lower Galilee or Nazareth). (2) Jesus departed into Galilee, ennobled by the fame which He had gained in Jerusalem, and which He could not have gained in Galilee, for He testified that a prophet hath no honour in his own country, and therefore must win it in some strange place. (3) Jesus departed into Galilee to meet what He knew would be a hopeless conflict; or to seek there rest from labour,

It may be noticed that the emphatic epithet ἰδία distinguishes the phrase used here from that found in Matt. xiii. 57 (where ἰδίᾳ is inserted by some copies) and in Luke iv. 23, 24. The addition indicates the special force which the Evangelist attached to the words.

45. ὅτε οὖν ἠλθ. . . .] *so when he came* . . . The issue justified the proverb. In Galilee, which was not Messiah's country, not even in popular estimation a prophet's home (vii. 52), Jesus found a ready reception. His works at Jerusalem, which had produced no permanent effect upon the spot, impressed the Galilæans more deeply; and it is not unlikely that Galilæan pilgrims formed the greater part of the "many" who "believed on his name" at the Passover (ii. 23). ἐδέξαντο] *exceperunt* v. See iii. 27, note.

καὶ αὐτ. γ. ἠλθ. . . .] and therefore, if in one sense they were strangers, yet they were not religious aliens.

46. Ἠλθεν οὖν πάλιν] *Venit ergo iterum* v.; *He came therefore again.* In consequence of the welcome which He received, He went on to Cana, where He had first "manifested his glory" (ii. 11).

βασιλικός] *regulus* v.; *officer in*

Καὶ ἦν τις βασιλικὸς¹ οὗ ὁ υἱὸς ἠσθένει ἐν Καφαρναούμ.
47 οὗτος ἀκούσας ὅτι Ἰησοῦς ἥκει ἐκ τῆς Ἰουδαίας εἰς τὴν
Γαλιλαίαν ἀπῆλθεν πρὸς αὐτὸν καὶ ἠρώτα ἵνα καταβῇ
καὶ ἰάσηται αὐτοῦ τὸν υἱόν, ἤμελλεν γὰρ ἀποθνήσκειν.
48 εἶπεν οὖν ὁ Ἰησοῦς πρὸς αὐτόν Ἐὰν μὴ σημεῖα καὶ
49 τέρατα ἴδητε, οὐ μὴ πιστεύσητε. λέγει πρὸς αὐτὸν
ὁ βασιλικός² Κύριε, κατάβηθι πρὶν ἀποθανεῖν τὸ παιδίον
50 μου. λέγει αὐτῷ ὁ Ἰησοῦς Πορεύου· ὁ υἱός σου ζῇ. ³
ἐπίστευσεν ὁ ἄνθρωπος τῷ λόγῳ ὃν εἶπεν αὐτῷ ὁ Ἰησοῦς
51 καὶ ἐπορεύετο. ἤδη δὲ αὐτοῦ καταβαίνοντος οἱ δοῦλοι
αὐτοῦ⁴ ὑπήντησαν αὐτῷ λέγοντες ὅτι ὁ παῖς αὐτοῦ ζῇ.
52 ἐπύθετο οὖν τὴν ὥραν παρ᾽ αὐτῶν ἐν ᾗ κομψότερον ἔσχεν·

¹ βασιλίσκος D.   ² βασιλίσκος D.   ³ Insert καί ΑΓΔ.   ⁴ Omit αὐτοῦ אDL.

the service of the king, i.e. Herod
Antipas, tetrarch of Galilee, who
was popularly known as "king":
Matt. xiv. 9. The word is used
by Josephus (e.g. Bel. J. I. xiii.
(xi.) 1) for any person employed
at court. The Vulgate, following an early but false reading
(βασιλίσκος), gives regulus, "a
petty king," "a chieftain." Some
have conjectured that this officer
was Chuza, "Herod's steward"
(Luke viii. 3), or Manaen, his
foster-brother (Acts xiii. 1).
Καφαρν.] See ii. 12, note.
47. ἀπηλ.] abiit v.; went away.
The word emphasises the thought
that the father left his son for
the time.
ἵνα καταβῇ] ut descenderet v.
Comp. ii. 12.
ἤμελλ. . . . ἀποθν.] he was at
the point of death. The Vulgate
rendering is worthy of notice:
incipiebat mori. Comp. Acts xxvii.
33. Contrast xii. 33, esset mori-
turus.
48. εἰπ. οὖν ὁ Ἰησ. . . .] Jesus
therefore said . . . The Lord read

the character of the petitioner
even through a petition which
might seem to show faith.
σημεῖα κ. τέρατα] signa et prodigia v.; signs and wonders.
The two words are combined,
Matt. xxiv. 24; Mark xiii. 22;
Acts (ii. 19), ii. 22, 43, iv. 30,
v. 12, vi. 8, vii. 36, viii. 13, xiv. 3,
xv. 12; Rom. xv. 19; 2 Cor. xii.
12; (2 Thess. ii. 9); Heb. ii. 4.
They severally mark the two
chief aspects of miracles: the
spiritual aspect, whereby they
suggest some deeper truth than
meets the eye, of which they
are in some sense symbols and
pledges; and the external aspect,
whereby their strangeness arrests
attention. Σημεῖον and ἔργον
(see v. 20) are the characteristic
words for miracles in St. John.
The word τέρας is never used
by itself in the New Testament.
ἴδητε] Comp. xx. 29. His faith
required the support of sight.
οὐ μὴ πιστεύσητε] non creditis
v.; ye will in no wise believe.

certain officer in the service of the king, whose son
47 was sick at Capernaum. When he heard that Jesus
was come out of Judæa into Galilee, he went unto
him, and besought *him* that he would come down,
and heal his son; for he was at the point of death.
48 Jesus therefore said unto him, Except ye see signs
49 and wonders, ye¹ will in no wise believe. The officer
saith unto him, Sir, come down ere my child die.
50 Jesus saith unto him, Go thy way; thy son liveth.
The man believed the word that Jesus spake unto
51 him, and he went his way. And as he was now
going down, his servants met him, saying that his
52 boy liveth. So he inquired of them the hour when

¹ *or* will ye in no wise believe?

The plural marks the officer as the representative of a class, to whom miracles were the necessary support of a faith which was not reluctant but feeble. The negative phrase does not express the simple fact, but in some degree connects it with the state of things of which it is the result: "There is no likelihood—no possibility—that ye should believe." Perhaps, however, the phrase is better taken as an interrogation: *Will ye in no wise believe?* Comp. ch. xviii. 11; (Rev. xv. 4). Luke xviii. 7 (οὐ μὴ ποιήσῃ).

The temper of the Galilæans is placed in sharp contrast with that of the Samaritans.

49. Κύριε, κατάβηθι] *Sir, come down.* The faith, however imperfect, which springs out of fatherly love is unshaken. It clings to what it can grasp. Comp. Mark ix. 24, which offers a complete spiritual parallel.

τὸ παιδίον] *filius* v.; *child.* The diminutive is used significantly here; not "son" (*v.* 47) or "boy" (*v.* 51). Comp. Mark v. 23, 35.

50. Πορεύου ὁ υἱ. σ. ζῇ] *Vade; filius tuus vivit* v.; *Go thy way; thy son liveth.* The assurance thus given is the final test, and it is sustained. So far the father endured without seeing. The crisis of life and death was present; hence it is enough to say "liveth" (*v.* 51) and not "is healed." Comp. Mark v. 23.

51. ὑπήντ. αὐτ. λεγ. ὅτι . . . ζῇ] *occurrerunt ei, et nuntiaverunt dicentes . . .* v.; *met him, saying that his boy liveth.* Here only (according to the true reading) St. John uses the oblique form, and not, as in the A.V., the direct ("Thy son liveth").

52. κομψότερον ἔσχεν] *melius habuerit* v.; *he began to amend.* The phrase is remarkable, and appears to have been used in familiar conversation, as we

εἶπαν οὖν αὐτῷ ὅτι Ἐχθὲς ὥραν ἑβδόμην ἀφῆκεν αὐτὸν
53 ὁ πυρετός. ἔγνω οὖν ὁ πατὴρ ὅτι ἐκείνῃ τῇ ὥρᾳ ἐν
ᾗ εἶπεν αὐτῷ ὁ Ἰησοῦς Ὁ υἱός σου ζῇ, καὶ ἐπίστευσεν
54 αὐτὸς καὶ ἡ οἰκία αὐτοῦ ὅλη. Τοῦτο πάλιν δεύτερον
σημεῖον ἐποίησεν ὁ Ἰησοῦς ἐλθὼν ἐκ τῆς Ἰουδαίας εἰς
τὴν Γαλιλαίαν.

might say " he begins to do nicely " or " bravely." The closest parallel is in Arrian: " When the doctor comes in, you must not be afraid as to what he will say; nor if he says ' You are doing bravely' (κόμψως ἔχεις), must you give way to excessive joy " (*Dissert. Epict.* iii. x. 13; comp. *Dissert.* ii. xviii. 14).

Ἐχθὲς ὥραν ἑβδόμην] *Heri hora septima* v.; *Yesterday in the seventh hour, i.e.* 7 *p.m.* See note on ch. xix. Such a phrase could scarcely be used of one o'clock in the afternoon in the evening of the same natural day. The case expresses duration of time, and not a point of time.

53. ἐπίστευσεν] *believed* that Jesus was the Christ. Comp. iii. 15, note. The belief in *v.* 50 is simply belief in the specific promise.

54. Τοῦτο παλ. . . . ἐλθών . . .] *This did Jesus again as a second sign, having come (after he came)* . . . The point lies in the relation of the two miracles as marking two visits to Cana, separated by a visit to Jerusalem. The form of the phrase corresponds with that in ii. 11.

In looking back over this section (ii. 13—iv. 54), the signs of harmonious progress in the development of the Lord's work are obvious. At first He stands before men with words and deeds of power, and they interpret and misinterpret His character, yet so that He cannot enter upon His kingdom by the way of a universal welcome from the ancient theocracy (ii. 13—25). Then follows the beginning of the direct revelation of a divine presence, which is shown at once to have a larger significance than for Israel. Christ sets Himself forth in two representative scenes as satisfying the hope of men, yet otherwise than they had expected (iii., iv.). He acknowledges that He is the Messiah in the sense of the woman of Samaria; but the higher teaching which He addressed to Nicodemus is veiled in riddles. At the same time a new confession is added to those of the first chapter (i. 51, note). The Samaritans acknowledge Christ to be " the Saviour of the world" (iv. 42, note).

ADDITIONAL NOTES ON CHAP. IV

THE WORK OF CHRIST IN SAMARIA

After the last testimony of the Baptist, which arose out of the mistaken jealousy of his disciples, the scene of the Lord's ministry was again changed. From Jerusalem, where He had offered Himself for recognition (ii. 13 ff.), He first retired to he began to amend. They said therefore unto him, Yesterday in the seventh hour the fever left him. 53 So the father knew that *it was* at that hour in which Jesus said unto him, Thy son liveth: and himself 54 believed, and his whole house. This did Jesus again as a second sign, having come out of Judæa into Galilee.

Judæa (iii. 22); and now *he left Judœa, and departed again into Galilee* (iv. 3). This withdrawal to the northern province was made in order to avoid a premature conflict with the Jewish leaders (iv. 1); and the word which is used to describe it (ἀφῆκε) suggests the thought of an abandonment of the Holy Land to its self-chosen fate.

The withdrawal to Galilee led to a visit to the people who stood spiritually in the sharpest opposition to the Jews (comp. viii. 48): [Jesus] *must needs go through Samaria* (v. 4). Perhaps the necessity of a quick return made it requisite for the Lord to take the most direct route (compare Jos. *Ant.* xx. v. 3; *Vit.* 52; Luke ix. 51 ff.).

Or we may suppose that the "necessity" lay in the spiritual circumstances of the case. There was at least a divine fitness that the Lord Himself should lay the foundation of His Church outside Israel (Acts i. 8). This He did, using an opportunity given by the hostility of the Jews, and not seeking the Samaritans on a special mission (Matt. x. 5). Compare Matt. xv. 2.

This thought is well expressed by Rupert of Deutz: "Dicis... Ad quid eum illo transire oportebat? Ad hæc inquam, Pro magno negotio oportebat, pro magnæ rei experimento oportebat. ... Si recte attendis (*v.* 44), liquet profecto quod utiliter et opportune per Samariam, per illam patriam non suam transire voluerit et ... honorem sibi ab eis impensum pro experimento testimonii sui admiserit."

At any rate, this passage through Samaria gave occasion for two representative interviews and two representative confessions. A single woman and the inhabitants of a village listen to the teachings of Christ and acknowledge Him in different forms. Thus the record corresponds closely with that of the general ministry to the people at Jerusalem (ii. 23 ff.) and the conversation with Nicodemus. In both cases the Lord deals with the society generally and with a single representative, but in a different order and with different results. At Jerusalem He speaks to the people first, as the people of God, and then is sought by a "teacher of Israel"; in Samaria the people are brought to Him by the sympathetic testimony of a woman to whom He made Himself known.

The correspondence of the conversation with the Samaritan woman to that with Nicodemus is singularly close and instructive.

In both cases the teaching is given through natural images, the wind and the water; in both cases the first confession is of the presence of prophetic power (iii. 2, iv. 19), based upon the interpretation of experience (iii. 2, οἴδαμεν ὅτι . . .; iv. 19, θεωρῶ); in both the partial acknowledgement is set aside to make way for the exposition of spiritual truth (iii. 3, ἀμὴν ἀμήν . . .; iv. 21, πίστευέ μοι . . .); in both the highest privilege, the life and the energy of life, is referred absolutely to the grace of God, the new birth (iii. 3 f.) and the gift of Christ (iv. 10).

But the points of contrast in the two incidents are as striking as the points of agreement. Nicodemus, "the ruler of the Jews," "the Pharisee," represents Israel, "the people of God." The woman, an alien and dishonoured, represents the outcasts from Israel. Nicodemus comes to Jesus confident in the intellectual deductions which he had drawn. Jesus Himself approaches the woman (iv. 7 ff.), and stirs in her the sense of His power even through the revelation of her shame. In the one case the boldness of assumed superiority is met by the declaration of overwhelming mysteries, of which account must be taken in thought (iv. 3 ff.); in the other, the frankness of sympathetic self-surrender is met by the first direct self-revelation of the Lord. The one conversation begins with a word of confidence; the other closes with a faithful word of self-distrust (iv. 29, μήτι . . . ;).

To Nicodemus, who expresses the claims of reason, the Lord laid open the new elements which belong to the kingdom, the new birth and the new order, revealed in His Person and His Work; to the woman who confessed failure and want He disclosed the personal essence of worship, the direct intercourse of spirit with spirit. The master of Israel is made to feel the necessity of redemption : the receptive woman is pointed to the law of conduct. In the one discourse we have, to speak generally, the revelation of the Son of man, and in the other the revelation of the Father.

Chrysostom touches on another question of general interest in connexion with the narrative. "Why is it," he asks, "that the Lord commonly uses in His teaching familiar illustrations from common life?" He replies for two reasons : in the first place, that His exposition may be more expressive and vivid; and secondly, that the impression may be more permanent, inasmuch as it is more pleasing (*Hom.* xxxiv. 2). We may, I think, see something more. The force of the correspondences suggests deeper connexions between the several regions of creation than we have yet realised.

The episode is unique in its character. In the strange land the Lord is met by an unexampled welcome on both sides, from His first hearer and from her countrymen. He begins in joy to gather the first-fruits of a universal Church. As He had found a circle of disciples in those who had been prepared by the Baptist (ch. i.), so now He finds in Samaria, outside the pale of the chosen people, those who had been made ready for Him in unknown ways. When He was forced to leave Judæa, where the issue of His work is passed over in silence, He was met by the assurance of a larger field ready for the spiritual harvest.

The narrative has interesting points of connexion both with the Synoptic narratives and with Old Testament history. The moral sensibility of the Samaritans finds a good illustration in the Gospel of St. Luke: x. 33, xvii. 16 (compare Acts viii. 12 ff.); and it may be added, that even when the inhospitality of Samaritans provoked the indignant condemnation of the disciples, they found shelter in "another village" (Luke ix. 52 ff.). So again are the larger views of the nature of the divine worship and character well indicated in Matt. xii. 7. On the other hand, the rest by the well could not fail to reveal to readers familiar with the Pentateuch memorable scenes in patriarchal history : Eliezer standing by the well, and waiting for the sign which should mark the bride of the heir of Abraham (Gen. xxiv.); and Jacob at the well meeting Rachel (Gen. xxix.), the future mother of Joseph, from whom the Samaritans claimed descent.

Each detail naturally admits a typical application. Philo gives a definite interpretation of the symbolism of wells in connexion with the history of Jacob (Gen. xxviii.): Ἐμοὶ δοκεῖ σύμβολον εἶναι τὸ φρέαρ ἐπιστήμης. οὐ γάρ ἐστιν ἐπιπόλαιος αὐτῆς ἡ φύσις ἀλλὰ πάνυ βαθεῖα· οὐδ᾽ ἐν φανερῷ πρόκειται ἀλλ᾽ ἐν ἀφανεῖ που κρύπτεσθαι φιλεῖ· οὐδὲ ῥᾳδίως ἀλλὰ μετὰ πολλῶν πόνων καὶ μόλις ἀνευρίσκεται (De Somn. i. § 2 ; i. 621 M; compare Quest. in Gen. iv. § 191). Else-

where he speaks of the "mist (LXX. πηγή) which watered the whole face of the earth" (Gen. ii. 6) as a symbol of "the word of God": Ὁ θεοῦ λόγος ποτίζει τὰς ἀρετάς· ἀρχὴ γὰρ καὶ πηγὴ καλῶν πράξεων οὑτοσί (De Poster. Cain, § 37 ; i. 249 M).

The marriage relation is the peculiar figure of the connexion of Israel with Jehovah ; and many commentators have found in the personal traits of the woman's unhappy history a reflection of the religious history of the people which added to the worship of the gods of five nations an imperfect service to the God of Israel (2 Kings xvii. 24, 30 ff.).

It is not surprising that many allegorical interpretations of the narrative have been suggested. Thus Origen thinks that the woman represents a soul which has given itself to a false law, and which Christ, as the true Bridegroom, wins back to Himself. But whatever significant correspondences may be traced between the record and the experiences of social or personal life, the simple reality of the facts must be carefully guarded.

ON THE TITLES "THE FATHER," "MY FATHER," IN ST. JOHN

Very much of the exact force of St. John's record of the Lord's words appears to depend upon the different conceptions of the two forms under which the Fatherhood of God is described. God is spoken of as "the Father" and as "my Father." Generally it may be said that the former title expresses the original relation of God to being and specially to humanity, in virtue of man's creation in the divine

12

image, and the latter more particularly the relation of the Father to the Son Incarnate, and so indirectly to man in virtue of the Incarnation. The former suggests those thoughts which spring from the consideration of the absolute moral connexion of man with God: the latter, those which spring from what is made known to us through revelation of the connexion of the Incarnate Son with God and with man. "The Father" corresponds, under this aspect, with the group of ideas gathered up in the Lord's titles, "the Son," "the Son of man": and "my Father" with those which are gathered up in the title "the Son of God," "the Christ."

The two forms are not infrequently used in close succession. Thus, for example, we read:

v. 43. I have come in the name of *my Father*.

v. 45. Do not think that I will accuse you to *the Father*.

The coming of Christ was a new revelation: the accusation of the unbelieving lies already in the primal constitution of things.

vi. 27. Which the Son of man will give you, for him *the Father* sealed, even God.

vi. 32. *My Father* giveth you the true bread from heaven.

In the one place the Lord appears as satisfying the wants of humanity: in the other, the New Dispensation is contrasted with the Old.

x. 17. Therefore doth *the Father* love me, because I lay down my life.

x. 18. This commandment received I from *my Father*.

The one statement rests on the conception of true self-sacrifice:

the other deals with the mission of Christ.

Other instructive examples will be found: viii. 18 f., x. 29 ff., 36 ff., xiv. 6—10, xv. 8—10, 15 f., 23—26. In many cases it will be seen that the absolute conception of Fatherhood is that on which the main teaching of a passage really depends: iv. 21 ff., vi. 45 f., xvi. 23 ff., and to such pregnant sentences as x. 30, xx. 21, the title "*the Father*" gives a singular depth of meaning. Of the two phrases, *the Father* is by far the more common, and yet in many places *my Father* has been substituted for it in the later texts, to express a more obvious sense: vi. 65, viii. 28, 38, x. 29, 32, xv. 10, xvi. 10.

The form *my Father* is the true reading in the following passages: ii. 16, v. 17, 43, vi. 32, 40, viii. 19, 49, 54, x. 18, 25, 29, 37, xiv. 2, 7, 20, 21, 23, xv. 1, 8, 15, 23 f., xx. 17.

It may be added that St. John never uses the phrase "our Father," which is not infrequent in St. Paul, nor yet the phrase "your Father," except xx. 17. Nor does he use πατήρ without the article by itself (compare 2 John 3) of God, except (of course) in the vocative case: xi. 41, xii. 27 f., xvii. 1, 5, (11), 21, 24, (25). Comp. i. 14, note.

[CHAP. IV. 35. *The translation of* τετράμηνος. Bishop Westcott had placed inside the pages of his copy of St. John's Gospel a letter published in *The Tablet* (Dec. 23, 1899) on "A new translation of John iv. 35." The writer says:

"As to τετράμηνος and its translation, four main sources of information were open to me: (1) The Septuagint, (2) The Greek

N.T., (3) the Greek Fathers, (4) Greek classics. These lines of research I have pursued. . . . The scope of the inquiry took in *all* compounds of a numeral with μήν.

" The conclusions drawn therefrom may be thus briefly summarised :

I. As to τετράμηνον.
(*a*) It is a substantive.
(*b*) It always and necessarily means *four-months-time.*
(*c*) The form is especially Biblical.

" I add that it has been finally dislodged by critics from the text of St. John, never to reappear.

II. As to τετράμηνος.
(*a*) *Standing by itself* (John iv. 35).
(a) It is an adjective.
(β) Always and in all cases, it means *four-months-long,* or *four-months-old.*
(*b*) *Standing with the article* ὁ or ἡ.
(a) Some word must be understood, such as παῖς or ὥρα.
(β) χρόνος is rarely the word to be supplied.
(γ) It has precisely the same meaning as above.

" My contention is, not that the new translation is possible or allowable, but that *if Greek is to be construed as Greek,* the disciples must have remarked that the crop before their eyes was *four-months-old,* and the harvest coming."

From the fact that Dr. Westcott preserved the letter, it may be concluded that he considered the " new translation " worthy of consideration. It may be added that the " proverbial saying " is, in rhythmical form, as has been pointed out to me, a " good comic Iambic senarius." Omit-

ting the ἔτι, which Griesbach omits on very fair authority, including the MSS. D and L, the quotation runs :

τετράμηνός ἐστιν χὠ θερισμὸς ἔρχεται.

The rhythmical structure may be purely accidental, but in an acknowledged quotation is certainly interesting.—A. W.]

NOTE ON READINGS IN CHAP. iv. 1

(The following note is taken from Vol. II. of the Westcott & Hort Greek Testament.—A. W.)
iv. 1 (†) ὡς . . . βαπτίζει [ἢ] Ἰωάνης] < ἢ AB*LGΓ cuᵖ Or. Jo Epiph. *Haer.* 480 Dindorf (the passage is wanting in earlier editions) : not אBᵃCD vv.omn Cyr.al.*loc.* For ὁ κύριος the Western text, with all the earlier vv, has ὁ Ἰησοῦς; so אD(Λ) 1-118-209 22 61 81 alᵐᵘ lat. afr-eur-vg syr. vt-(vg)-hl.txt me arm Chr. Λ cuᵖ syr.vg omitting the subsequent Ἰησοῦς : while ὁ κύριος is attested only by lat.it syr hl.mg aeth and the Syrian Greek text in addition to ABCLTᵦ.

The Western change is doubtless due to the apparent awkwardness of the combination ὁ κύριος . . . Ἰησοῦς : but the difficulty lies rather in the absence of any perceptible force in the double naming; the most probable explanation being that ὅτι is ' recitative,' and that Ἰησοῦς . . . Ἰωάνης are in *oratio recta* as the very words of the report.[1]]

[1] Dr. Hort adds to the above a further note, which concludes with the words, " On the whole the text of the verse cannot be accepted as certainly free from doubt."—A. W.

5 Μετὰ ταῦτα ἦν ¹ ἑορτὴ τῶν Ἰουδαίων, καὶ ἀνέβη
2 Ἰησοῦς εἰς Ἱεροσόλυμα. Ἔστιν δὲ ἐν τοῖς Ἱεροσολύμοις
ἐπὶ τῇ προβατικῇ κολυμβήθρα ἡ ἐπιλεγομένη Ἑβραϊστὶ

¹ Insert ἡ ΝCEFLΔ.

THE CONFLICT (v. 1—xii. 50)

Up to the present time the
Lord has offered Himself to
typical representatives of the
whole Jewish race at Jerusalem,
in Judæa, in Samaria, and in
Galilee, in such a way as to
satisfy the elements of true faith.
Now the conflict begins which
issues in the Passion. Step by
step faith and unbelief are called
out in a parallel development.
The works and words of Christ
become a power for the revelation of men's thoughts. The
main scene of this saddest of all
conceivable tragedies is Jerusalem. The crises of its development are the national Festivals.
And the whole controversy is
gathered around three miracles.

(1) *The healing of the impotent
man at Bethesda* (v.).

(2) *The healing of the man born
blind* (ix.).

(3) *The raising of Lazarus*
(xi.).

The sixth chapter is a Galilæan
episode, marking the crisis of
faith and unbelief outside Judæa
proper.

The unity of the record is
marked by the symptoms of the
earlier conflict which appear at
the later stages, *e.g.* vii. 19 ff.,
compared with v. 18 ff.; x. 27 ff.,
compared with x. 1 ff. xi. 47 ff.

With the exception of parts
in ch. vi., the contents of this
division of the Gospel are peculiar to St. John.

The narrative falls into two
parts : THE PRELUDE (v., vi.),
and THE GREAT CONTROVERSY
(vii.—xii.).

I. THE PRELUDE (v., vi.)

The Prelude consists of two
decisive incidents, with their
immediate consequences ; one at
Jerusalem (ch. v.), the other in
Galilee (ch. vi.). In the first
we have Christ's revelation of
Himself in answer to false views
of His relation to God (v. 18) ;
in the other, His revelation of
Himself in answer to false views
of His work for men (vi. 15, 26).
In the first case the revelation is
indirect ("the Son"; compare
vv. 24, 30, 31 ff.) ; in the second
case the revelation is predominantly direct ("I am"; yet see
vv. 40, 53).

The section closes with the
first division in the circle of the
disciples (vi. 66), and the foreshadowing of the end (vi. 70 f.).

i. THE SON AND THE FATHER
(ch. v.)

The record of the healing (*vv.*
2—9 *a*), and of the immediate
sequel to it (*vv.* 9 *b*—18), is
followed by a long discourse
addressed by "the Lord" to "the
Jews," in answer to their charge
that "He spake of God as His
own Father, as His Father in a
sense wholly unique (πατὴρ ἴδιος)."
This discourse consists of two
main divisions.

5   After these things there was a feast of the Jews;
2 and Jesus went up to Jerusalem. Now there is in
Jerusalem by the sheep *gate* a pool, which is called

(*a*) *The nature and prerogatives of the Son* (*vv.* 19—29).
(*β*) *The witness to the Son, and
the ground of unbelief* (*vv.* 31—
47).

v. 30 serves as a connecting
link between the two parts.

The contents of these two sections form the foundation of all
the later teaching in the Gospel.

The discourse appears to have
been addressed to a small
(official) gathering: perhaps to
the Sanhedrin, and certainly not
to the multitude (comp. *vv.* 33,
39). Perhaps there is a reference to it in vii. 26 (ἔγνωσαν).

The sign (*vv.* 2—9 *a*)

The healing of the impotent
man was a work wrought by the
Lord spontaneously. He chose
both the object of it and the
occasion. The malady of the
sufferer was not urgent in such
a sense that the cure could not
have been delayed. The cure
therefore was not wrought on
a Sabbath although it was a
Sabbath, but because it was
Sabbath, with the view of bringing out a deeper truth (comp.
vii. 21 ff.).

For other healings on Sabbaths
see Matt. xii. 9 ff. and parallels;
Luke xiii. 10 ff., xiv. 1 ff.

CHAP. V. 1. Μετὰ ταῦτα] There
is a slight difference between
μετὰ τοῦτο (ii. 12, xi. 7, 11, xix.
28 [Heb. ix. 27]) and μετὰ ταῦτα
(*v.* 14, iii. 22, vi. 1, xiii. 7, xix.
38, xxi. 1, etc.). The former
implies a connexion of some kind

(of time or dependence) between
the preceding and subsequent
events, which is not suggested
by the latter.

ἑορτή] *dies festus* v.; *a feast.*
The evidence for the identification of this unnamed feast is very
slight. The tradition of the
early Greek Church identified it
with Pentecost. Most modern
commentators suppose it to be
the Feast of Purim (March),
from a comparison of iv. 35 and
vi. 4. But see Additional Note.

ἀνέβη . . . εἰς Ἱεροσ.] If the
feast were that of Purim, this
journey was not of obligation;
but compare x. 22 (the Feast of
Dedication).

2. Ἔστιν δέ . . . .] The use of
the present tense does not prove
that the narrative was written
before the destruction of Jerusalem. It is quite natural that
St. John in recalling the event
should speak of the place as he
knew it. It has indeed been
conjectured that a building used
for a benevolent purpose might
have been spared in the general
ruin, but this explanation of the
phrase is improbable.

ἐπὶ τῇ προβατ.] *super probatica*
v.; *by the sheep gate,* which lay
near the temple, on the east of
the city (Neh. iii. 1, 32, xii. 39),
though it cannot now be certainly
fixed (*Dictionary of Bible, s.v.*).
The ellipsis, which is most naturally supplied by *gate,* is (apparently) without parallel.

κολυμβ.] *piscina* v.; *a pool.*
This has been identified by some

3 Βηθζαθά¹, πέντε στοὰς ἔχουσα· ἐν ταύταις κατέκειτο
5 πλῆθος τῶν ἀσθενούντων, τυφλῶν, χωλῶν, ξηρῶν ². ἦν
δέ τις ἄνθρωπος ἐκεῖ τριάκοντα [καὶ] ὀκτὼ ἔτη ἔχων ἐν
6 τῇ ἀσθενείᾳ αὐτοῦ· τοῦτον ἰδὼν ὁ Ἰησοῦς κατακείμενον,
καὶ γνοὺς ὅτι πολὺν ἤδη χρόνον ἔχει, λέγει αὐτῷ Θέλεις
7 ὑγιὴς γενέσθαι; ἀπεκρίθη αὐτῷ ὁ ἀσθενῶν Κύριε, ἄνθρωπον οὐκ ἔχω ἵνα ὅταν ταραχθῇ τὸ ὕδωρ βάλῃ με
εἰς τὴν κολυμβήθραν· ἐν ᾧ δὲ ἔρχομαι ἐγὼ ἄλλος πρὸ

¹ Βηθζαθά אL; Βελζεθά D; Βηθσαιδά B; Βηθεσδά ACΓΔ.
² Insert ἐκδεχομένων τὴν τοῦ ὕδατος κίνησιν A²C³DΓΔ. See note. Insert
v. 4, which according to best text (singula verba vehementer fluctuant—Tisch.)
reads: ἄγγελος γὰρ κατὰ καιρὸν κατέβαινεν ἐν τῇ κολυμβήθρᾳ καὶ ἐτάρασσε τὸ ὕδωρ·
ὁ οὖν πρῶτος ἐμβὰς μετὰ τὴν ταραχὴν τοῦ ὕδατος ὑγιὴς ἐγίνετο, ᾧ δήποτε κατείχετο
νοσήματι AC³EFGLΓΔ. See note.

with an intermittent spring, known as the *Fountain of the Virgin*, in the Valley of Kidron. The traditional site is the *Birket Israil*, by the modern gate of St. Stephen, on the north-east of the city. But neither spot fully answers to the conditions of the pool.

Ἑβραϊστί] *in the Hebrew*, that is, in the language "of those beyond the river" brought from Babylon, and not in the classical language of the Old Testament. Compare Lightfoot *ad loc.*

Βηθζαθά] The original reading and the meaning of the name are both very uncertain. The common interpretation of the form Bethesda is *House of mercy* (בית חסדא); but this is open to objection on the ground of the usage of חסדא, and it has been supposed to represent the *House of the portico* (בית אסטיו, οἶκος στοῆς). See Delitzsch, *Ztschr. für Luth. Theol.*, 1856, 622 f. The true reading appears to contain the element -*zatha* (-*saida*), which suggests בית זיתא, the

House of the olive. The pool is not mentioned by any Jewish writer.

πεν. στοάς] *quinque porticus* v.; *five porches.* Cloisters, or covered spaces around the pool, such as are commonly found by tanks in India.

3. ἐν ταύταις κατεκ. πλῆθος τ. ἀσθεν.] *in his jacebat multitudo magna languentium* v.; *in these were lying a multitude of sick folk.* The healing properties of the pool may have been due to its mineral elements. Eusebius (*De Situ et Nom.*, *s.v.*) describes the waters of the pool identified with it in his time as "marvellously red," *i.e.* probably from deposits of iron on the stones. A chalybeate spring would be efficacious generally in cases of weakness.

A similar scene is still presented by the hot sulphureous springs near Tiberias (*Hammath*, Joshua xix. 35): Tristram, *Land of Israel*, 416.

3, 4. The words ἐκδεχομένων . . . νοσήματι (*waiting for . . . he*

3 in Hebrew Bethzatha, having five porches. In these
were lying a multitude of them that were sick,
5 blind, halt, withered. And a certain man was there,
which had been thirty and eight years in his
6 infirmity. When Jesus saw him lying, and knew
that he had been now a long time *in that case*, he
saith unto him, Wouldest thou be made whole?
7 The sick man answered him, Sir, I have no man,
when the water is troubled, to put me into the pool:
but while I am coming, another steppeth down

had, A.V.) are not part of the
original text of St. John, but
form a very early note added to
explain *v.* 7, while the Jewish
tradition with regard to the pool
was still fresh. Some authorities
add the last clause of *v.* 3 only ;
others *v.* 4 only ; others add
both, but with considerable verbal variations. See Additional
Note.

5. τριακ. [κ.] ὀκτ. ἔτη] This period
of time, corresponding with the
period of the punishment of the
Israelites in the wilderness, has
led many, from a very early
date, to regard the man as a
type of the Jewish people paralysed by faithlessness at the time
of Christ's coming. The detail
may, however, be added simply
to mark the inveteracy of the
disease (ix. 1, *blind from his
birth*).

6. ἰδών . . . κατακειμ. κ. γνούς]
cum vidisset . . . et cognovisset v. ;
saw him lying and knew, by the
information of bystanders, or
(more probably) by His divine
intuition (see Additional Note on
ii. 11). The life of this sick man
was open to Him (*v.* 14), just as
the life of the Samaritan woman

(iv. 18). It is to be noticed
that all the miracles recorded
by St. John, except the healing
of the officer's son, were wrought
spontaneously by Christ. But
the question with which this
work is prefaced is a peculiar
feature.

Θέλεις] *Vis* v. ; *Wilt thou, i.e.*
hast thou the will ? desirest
thou ? The English rendering
is often ambiguous, as (for example) v. 40, vi. 11, 67, vii. 17,
viii. 44, ix. 27. The question was
suggested by the circumstances of
the man's case. It might seem
that he acquiesced in his condition, and was unwilling to
make any vigorous effort to gain
relief. If it was so, the words
were fitted to awaken attention,
hope, effort in one who had
fallen into apathy. Comp. Acts
iii. 4.

7. ὁ ἀσθ.] *languidus* v. ; *the
sick man.* The sufferer answers
the thought which underlay the
inquiry. The delay in his healing was due, as he explains, not
to want of will but to want of
means.

ταραχθῇ] *turbata fuerit* v.
The popular explanation of the

8 ἐμοῦ καταβαίνει. λέγει αὐτῷ ὁ Ἰησοῦς Ἔγειρε ἆρον
9 τὸν κράβαττόν σου καὶ περιπάτει. καὶ εὐθέως¹ ἐγένετο
ὑγιὴς ὁ ἄνθρωπος, καὶ ἦρε τὸν κράβαττον αὐτοῦ καὶ
περιεπάτει. Ἦν δὲ σάββατον ἐν ἐκείνῃ τῇ ἡμέρᾳ.
10 ἔλεγον οὖν οἱ Ἰουδαῖοι τῷ τεθεραπευμένῳ Σάββατόν
11 ἐστιν, καὶ οὐκ ἔξεστίν σοι ἆραι τὸν κράβαττον². ὃς δὲ³
ἀπεκρίθη αὐτοῖς Ὁ ποιήσας με ὑγιῆ ἐκεῖνός μοι εἶπεν
12 Ἆρον τὸν κράβαττόν σου καὶ περιπάτει. ἠρώτησαν⁴
αὐτόν Τίς ἐστιν ὁ ἄνθρωπος ὁ εἰπών σοι Ἆρον καὶ
13 περιπάτει; ὁ δὲ ἰαθεὶς⁵ οὐκ ᾔδει τίς ἐστιν, ὁ γὰρ Ἰησοῦς
14 ἐξένευσεν ὄχλου ὄντος ἐν τῷ τόπῳ. Μετὰ ταῦτα εὑρίσκει

¹ Omit εὐθέως אＮ*D.   ² Insert σου אC*DL.   ³ Omit ὃς δέ C³DEFΓ.
⁴ Insert οὖν ACLΓΔ.   ⁵ ἰαθείς אABCLΓΔ; ἀσθενῶν D.

phenomenon of an intermittent spring.

βάλῃ] *mittat* v.; *put.* The word βάλλειν is commonly translated *cast*. In late Greek it is used very widely (*e.g.* xiii. 2, xviii. 11, xx. 25, 27), but it may express the necessary haste of the movement according to the gloss in *v.* 4.

8. The three features of the complete restoration are to be noticed (*rise, take up thy bed, walk*). The phrase occurs Mark ii. 9.

κράβαττον] *grabattum* v.; *bed.* This word is said to be of Macedonian origin. It occurs Mark ii. 4 ff., vi. 55; Acts v. 15, ix. 33. It describes technically the bed of the poor—"a pallet."

The immediate sequel of the sign
(9 b—18)

In this section the various elements of the coming conflict are brought out distinctly; the significance of the cure as a work of power and judgement (*v.* 14), the accusations of the Jews

(*vv.* 10, 16, 18), the self-vindication of Christ (*v.* 17).

9. Ἦν δὲ σαββ. ...] A new paragraph begins with these words: *Now on that day was a sabbath,* which prepares the way for the subsequent discourse. The form of the phrase is very remarkable (comp. ix. 14, xix. 31), and suggests the idea that the sabbath was a day of rest other than the weekly sabbath.

10. οἱ Ἰουδ.] See Introd.

τῷ τεθεραπευ.] The word and tense are contrasted with those found in *v.* 13.

Σαββ. ... κραβ.] The objectors would refer to such passages as Jer. xvii. 21 f. "If any one carries anything from a public place to a private house on the sabbath ... intentionally, he renders himself liable to the punishment of premature death (כרת) and stoning" (*Sabb.* 6 a, quoted by Wünsche).

11. ὃς δέ ...] *but he* ... The authority of One who had wrought the miracle seemed to

8 before me. Jesus saith unto him, Arise, take up
9 thy bed, and walk. And straightway the man was
made whole, and took up his bed and walked.
10 Now on that day was a sabbath. So the Jews
said unto him that had been cured, It is the sabbath,
and it is not lawful for thee to take up thy bed.
11 But he answered them, He that made me whole,
even he said unto me, Take up thy bed, and walk.
12 They asked him, Who is the man that said unto
13 thee, Take up, and walk? But he that was healed
wist not who it was: for Jesus withdrew, a multitude
14 being in the place. After these things Jesus findeth

him to outweigh any legal en-
actment. He felt instinctively
the presence of that which was
greater than the sabbath.

ἐκεῖνος] *even he*, with a marked
emphasis on the pronoun. This
usage is characteristic of St.
John : i. 18, 33, ix. 37, x. 1, xii.
48, xiv. 21, 26. Compare also
Mark vii. 15, 20; Rom. xiv. 14;
2 Cor. x. 18.

12. Τίς ἐστιν ὁ ἄνθρωπος . . .;]
Who is the man that said . . .?
The introduction of ὁ ἄνθρωπος
marks the spirit of the inquiry,
and suggests the contrast between the Divine Law and this
(assumed) human teacher, who
claimed to deal with it by his own
power. Moreover, as the sufferer
had spoken of his healing, these
speak only of the technical offence,
and pass by that work of power
and mercy. Comp. *v.* 15.

Ἀρ. κ. περιπ.] The words are
given with great naturalness in
an abrupt form.

13. ὁ γὰρ Ἰησοῦς ἐξένευσεν]
Jesus enim declinavit turba v. ;
for Jesus retired — withdrew —

silently and unperceived, from a
place where He might be exposed
to embarrassment ; for this
appears to be the force of the
reference to the multitude, and
not that the crowd made escape
easier. The word ἐκνεύειν (which
occurs only here in the New
Testament) expresses literally,
" to bend the head aside, to
avoid a blow." Comp. Judges
iv. 18, xviii. 26; 2 Kings ii.
24, xxiii. 16; 3 Macc. iii. 22
(LXX.); Jos. *Ant.* VII. iv. 2.

14. Μετὰ ταῦτα] Compare *v.* 1,
note.

εὑρίσκει] The healing was incomplete till its spiritual lesson
was brought out clearly. Though
Christ had withdrawn from the
multitude He sought (compare
i. 43, ix. 35) the object of His
mercy; and so much at least the
man had already learnt, that he
repaired to the temple, as we
must suppose, to offer thanks
there for his restoration directly
after his cure.

μηκέτι ἁμάρτανε] *jam noli pec-
care* v. ; *no longer continue to sin*

αὐτὸν [ὁ] Ἰησοῦς ἐν τῷ ἱερῷ καὶ εἶπεν αὐτῷ Ἴδε ὑγιὴς
γέγονας· μηκέτι ἁμάρτανε, ἵνα μὴ χεῖρόν σοί τι γένηται.
15 ἀπῆλθεν ὁ ἄνθρωπος καὶ εἶπεν τοῖς Ἰουδαίοις ὅτι Ἰησοῦς
16 ἐστιν ὁ ποιήσας αὐτὸν ὑγιῆ. καὶ διὰ τοῦτο ἐδίωκον οἱ
17 Ἰουδαῖοι τὸν Ἰησοῦν¹ ὅτι ταῦτα ἐποίει ἐν σαββάτῳ. ὁ
δὲ² ἀπεκρίνατο αὐτοῖς Ὁ πατήρ μου ἕως ἄρτι ἐργάζεται,
18 κἀγὼ ἐργάζομαι. διὰ τοῦτο οὖν μᾶλλον ἐζήτουν αὐτὸν

¹ Insert καὶ ἐζήτουν αὐτὸν ἀποκτεῖναι ΑΓΔ.   ⁹ Insert Ἰησοῦς ACDL.

(comp. 1 John iii. 6, 9). How his sickness was connected with his sin must remain undefined ; but the connexion is implied, yet in no such way as to lend colour to the belief in the direct connexion of all suffering with personal sin which is corrected in ix. 3.

χεῖρον] *deterius* v. ; *a worse thing* even than the sickness of thirty-eight years, by which the greater part of his life had been saddened.

15. ἀπῆλθεν . . .] It is difficult to understand the motive of the man in conveying this information to the Jews, since he knew the hostile spirit in which they regarded the cure. He was certainly not ungrateful, for he still speaks of Jesus as having cured him (*which had made him whole*, v. 11, and not *which had told him to take up his bed*, v. 12). He may have wished to leave the responsibility of his illegal act on the sabbath with One who had power to answer for it ; or it may be simplest to suppose that he acted in obedience to the instructions of those whom, as a Jew, he felt bound to obey.

16. διὰ τοῦτο] *for this cause.* This is the first open declaration of hostility to Christ, and it is based upon the alleged violation of the letter of the Law with regard to the sabbath, as in the other Gospels, Matt. xii. 2 ff. and parallels. The miracle just recorded called out the settled enmity of the Jews, but the phrase *because he was in the habit of doing* (ἐποίει) *these things* (acts of mercy which involved offences against the traditional interpretations of the Law) *on a sabbath,* shows that the feeling was not due to a solitary act, but to an obvious principle of action.

17. Ὁ πατήρ μου ἕως ἄρτι ἐργ. . . .] *pater meus usque modo operatur* . . . v. The answer (see *v.* 19, note) of Christ contains in the briefest possible space the exposition of His office : *My Father* (ii. 16, xx. 17) *worketh even until now, and I work.* That is to say, the rest of God after the creation, which the sabbath represents outwardly, and which I am come to realise, is not a state of inaction, but of activity, and man's true rest is not a rest *from* human earthly labour, but a rest *for* divine heavenly labour. Thus the merely negative, traditional observance of the sabbath is placed

him in the temple, and said unto him, Behold, thou
art made whole: no longer continue to sin, lest a
15 worse thing befall thee. The man went away, and
told the Jews that it was Jesus which had made him
16 whole. And for this cause did the Jews persecute
Jesus, because he did these things on the 'sabbath.
17 But Jesus answered them, My Father worketh even
18 until now, and I work. For this cause therefore

in sharp contrast with the positive, final fulfilment of spiritual
service, for which it was a preparation. The works of Christ
did not violate the Law, while
they brought out the truth to
which that tended. Cf. Matt.
xii. 1 ff. and parallels. By the
"work" of the Father we must
understand at once the main-
tenance of the material creation
and the redemption and restoration of all things, in which the
Son co-operated with Him (Heb.
i. 3 ; Eph. i. 9 f.).

The form of the sentence is
remarkable. Christ places His
work as co-ordinate with that of
the Father, and not as dependent
on it. Comp. Mark ii. 27, 28
(κύριός ἐστ. ὁ υἱὸς τ. ἀνθρώπου καὶ
τ. σαββάτου).

The question of the action of
God upon the sabbath was much
debated in the Jewish schools.
"Why does not God," said a
caviller, "keep the sabbath?"
"May not a man," was the
answer, "wander through his
own house on the sabbath? The
house of God is the whole realm
above and the whole realm below" (*Shem. R.* xxx.). Compare
Philo, *Leg. Alleg.* i. p. 46 м.

ἕως ἄρτι] The work of Christ
which had excited the hostility
of the Jews was, however little
they could see it, really coincident
with a working of God which
knows no interruption.

18. The Jews rightly interpreted the words of the Lord. They
saw that He claimed the power
of abrogating the law of the
sabbath in virtue of His absolutely special relation to God :
πατέρα ἴδιον ἔλεγε τ. θεόν, *he
called God his own Father* (*patrem
suum* v.) (Rom. viii. 32)—His
Father in a peculiar sense—
making himself equal with God,
by placing His action on the
same level with the action of
God. Compare x. 33. *For this
reason the more they* (not only
persecuted Him, *v.* 16, but)
sought to kill him. Comp. Matt.
xii. 14 and parallels. Matt.
xxvi. 65, note. Comp. viii. 59,
x. 33 ; Mark ii. 7.

ἔλυε] *solvebat* v.; *he was loosing, i.e.* he declared that the law
of the sabbath was not binding.
The word λύω expresses not the
violation of the sanctity of the
day in a special case, but the
abrogation of the duty of observance. Comp. Matt. v. 19, xviii.
18. A prophet might absolve
from the obligation of the law in
a particular instance, but not
generally.

οἱ Ἰουδαῖοι ἀποκτεῖναι ὅτι οὐ μόνον ἔλυε τὸ σάββατον
ἀλλὰ καὶ πατέρα ἴδιον ἔλεγε τὸν θεόν, ἴσον ἑαυτὸν ποιῶν
19 τῷ θεῷ. Ἀπεκρίνατο οὖν [ὁ Ἰησοῦς]¹ καὶ ἔλεγεν αὐτοῖς
Ἀμὴν ἀμὴν λέγω ὑμῖν, οὐ δύναται ὁ υἱὸς ποιεῖν ἀφ' ἑαυτοῦ
οὐδὲν ἂν μή τι βλέπῃ τὸν πατέρα ποιοῦντα· ἃ γὰρ ἂν
20 ἐκεῖνος ποιῇ, ταῦτα καὶ ὁ υἱὸς ὁμοίως ποιεῖ. ὁ γὰρ

¹ Omit ὁ Ἰησοῦς B.

*The Nature and Prerogatives of
the Son* (19—29)

The first part of the comprehensive answer of the Lord to
the Jews deals with His Nature
and prerogatives (1) in relation
to the Father (19—23), and (2)
in relation to men (24—29).

The fact that the discourse
was addressed to a small, trained
audience (see preliminary note)
explains the close brevity of the
reasoning.

vv. 19—23. The action and
honour of the Son are coincident
with the action and honour of
the Father. It is through the
action of the Son that men see
the action of the Father, and it
is by honouring the Son that
they honour the Father.

The   exposition   of   these
thoughts is made in a series of
statements bound together by
"for" (γάρ) four times repeated.

The Son doeth nothing self-
determined of Himself, which
would be impossible (19 *a*) ;

for His action is absolutely coincident in range with that of
the Father (19 *b*) ; and this
can be ;

for His Father shows Him His
widening counsels, which ex-
tend to the exhibition of
greater works than healing
(20) ;

for it is the prerogative of the

Son to give life (21), as is
shown to be the case ;

for all judgement is given to
Him, and men can see that
He exerts this power (22).

Hence it follows that men
should honour the Son even as
they honour the Father (23).

19. Ἀπεκριν. οὖν . . .] *Jesus
therefore answered* . . . He met
their thoughts and their actions
(comp. ii. 18, note) by a justification of His own works and His
divine claims as Messiah. This
"answer" is not to be placed in
immediate temporal connexion
with what precedes.

Ἀμὴν ἀμήν] See i. 51, note.
The teaching is "with authority"
(Matt. vii. 28 f.).

ὁ υἱός] See iii. 35. The idea is
simply that of the absolute relation of the Divine Persons, of
the Son to the Father, and
consequently this term is used
(19—23), and not (as below *vv.*
30 ff.) " I "—the Christ whom
you reject—or " the Son of God "
(*v.* 25), or " Son of man " (*v.* 27),
which emphasise the divine or
human nature of the Lord relatively to man. At the same
time the Son is regarded as
" sent " (*vv.* 23 f.), and therefore
as Incarnate. But this idea lies
in the background here, where
the immediate point is the justification of the statement in *v.* 17

the Jews sought the more to kill him, because he
not only brake[1] the sabbath, but also called God
his own Father, making himself equal with God.
19 Jesus therefore answered and said unto them, Verily,
verily, I say unto you, The Son can do nothing
of himself, except he see the Father doing it:
for what things soever he doeth, these also the
20 Son doeth in like manner. For the Father loveth

[1] *lit.* was loosing.

from the essential relation of the Son to the Father. The argument is conducted by the Lord without a direct personal reference to Himself in such a way as to arrest the attention of the Jews, and not to drive them away at once. Perfect Sonship involves perfect identity of will and action with the Father. Οὐ δύναται ὁ υἱὸς ποιεῖν ἀφ᾽ ἑαυτοῦ οὐδέν . . . *The Son can do nothing of himself,* self-determined, without the Father, nothing, that is, *except he see the Father doing it.* Separate action on His part is an impossibility, as being a contradiction of His unity with the Father (comp. v. 30 and xvi. 13). The limitation (*except he see . . .*) refers to *can do nothing,* and not to the last words (*of himself*); and the coincidence of the action of the Father and of the Son is brought out by the exact turn of the phrase—*see the Father doing,* and not *do.*

οὐ δύναται . . .] The eternal law of right is (in human language) the definition of divine power. The words do not convey any limitation of the Son's working, but explain something as to its character. Comp. *v.* 30, iii. 27 ; Mark vi. 5 ; (Gen. xix. 22).

For another aspect of this "cannot" see vii. 7, note.

ἀφ᾽ ἑαυτ.] *a se* v. See *v.* 30, note ; Num. xvi. 28 (LXX.). The truth lies in the very idea of Sonship.

ἃ γὰρ ἄν . . .] The negative statement is supplemented by a positive one . . . *The Son can do nothing . . . for* . . . His action is not only coincident but coextensive with the action of the Father: *what things soever he doeth, these also the Son doeth in like manner,* not in imitation, but in virtue of His sameness of nature.

20. ὁ γὰρ πατήρ . . .] The action of the Son, as coincident and coextensive with that of the Father, depends upon the continuous revelation which the Father makes to Him in accordance with His eternal love : *for the Father loveth the Son ;* . . . and this revelation, regarded under the limitations of human existence, is progressive, and signs of healing are only preparatory to *greater works ; for as the Father . . . quickeneth, even so the Son also quickeneth whom he will.*

Thus we can see that there is a divine coherence, a divine meaning, in all nature and all history. The Son *sees* all, for

πατὴρ φιλεῖ τὸν υἱὸν καὶ πάντα δείκνυσιν αὐτῷ ἃ αὐτὸς
ποιεῖ, καὶ μείζονα τούτων δείξει αὐτῷ ἔργα, ἵνα ὑμεῖς
21 θαυμάζητε. ὥσπερ γὰρ ὁ πατὴρ ἐγείρει τοὺς νεκροὺς
22 καὶ ζωοποιεῖ, οὕτως καὶ ὁ υἱὸς οὓς θέλει ζωοποιεῖ. οὐδὲ
γὰρ ὁ πατὴρ κρίνει οὐδένα, ἀλλὰ τὴν κρίσιν πᾶσαν

the Father *shows* all to Him; and we also can see parts at least in Him. Comp. Matt. xi. 27.

φιλεῖ] *diligit* v.; *loveth.* The word φιλεῖν marks personal affection, based upon a special relation (xi. 3, 36; comp. Matt. x. 37), and not the general feeling of regard, esteem, consideration (ἀγαπᾶν) which comes from reflection and knowledge: the former feeling answers to nature, the latter to experience and judgement (iii. 35, x. 17), and so is specially appropriate to spiritual relations. This love expresses (so to speak) the moral side of the essential relation of the Father to the Son. And so it is through the Son that the personal love of God is extended to believers: xvi. 27; comp. Rev. iii. 19.

The sign of love is the perfect revelation of thought and feeling: xv. 15.

μείζονα τούτων δείξει αὐτῷ ἔργα] *greater works* (comp. xiv. 12) *than these will he show* (comp. x. 32) *him;* and He (so it is implied, v. 19) when He seeth them will do them in like manner, *that ye may marvel.* It cannot but appear strange at first sight that wonder is given as the object of Christ's works. The difficulty is removed by taking account of the pronoun: that *ye* who question My authority and are blind to My divine Sonship *may marvel.* Till Christ was recog-

nised His works could at the most appear only to be prodigies: their effect would be astonishment, not belief. But wonder might give occasion for faith. Under this aspect "wonder" is presented in two remarkable traditional sayings of the Lord preserved by Clement of Alexandria (*Strom.* II. ix. 45): "He that wonders shall reign, and he that reigns shall rest": "Wonder at that which is before you." This partial object of wonder, however, is contrasted with the general object in *v.* 23. Works — outward signs — may produce wonder, but judgement completed enforces honour. Comp. Plato, *Theæt.* p. 155 D.

δείξει] *demonstrabit* v. See x. 32. The divine works require the interpretation of sympathy. Such sympathy the Son has absolutely.

ἔργα] *opera* v. This is a characteristic term in St. John (compare Matt. xi. 2), in which Christ includes under the same category the manifold forms of His action. His "works" were fragments contributing to "the work" which He came to finish (iv. 34, xvii. 4), and these He must needs work while it was day (ix. 4). Miracles from this point of view are regarded on the same level with the other works of Christ, though "miraculous" works may in a peculiar sense move to faith (v. 36, x. 25, 32, xiv. 10, 12, xv. 24). All

the Son, and showeth him all things that himself
doeth : and greater works than these will he show
21 him, that ye may marvel. For as the Father raiseth
the dead and quickeneth them, even so the Son also
22 quickeneth whom he will. For not even doth the
Father judge any man, but hath given all judgement

works alike are designed to contribute to the redemption of the
world (comp. ch. xvii. 21, note).
See *v.* 36, note.

21. The progress in the dignity
of the works of the Son follows
from the extent of their sphere,
ὥσπερ γὰρ ὁ πατήρ . . . οὕτως καὶ
ὁ υἱός . . . The restoration of
an impotent man is then but a
beginning of that giving of life of
which it was a sign. The vivifying
power of the Father is described
in its twofold physical aspect,
. . . ἐγείρει τοὺς νεκροὺς καὶ ζωοποιεῖ : that of the Son in reference to its moral law, οὓς θέλει
ζωοποιεῖ. The " quickening " as
it stands in the second clause is
necessarily coextensive with the
raising the dead and quickening
in the first, which is not to be
limited to any isolated " miraculous " acts, but extends to all
communication of life, natural
and spiritual. The main forms
of "quickening" are distinguished
afterwards, *vv.* 25, 28.

The definition οὓς θέλει marks
(1) the efficacy of Christ's power,
and (2) connects this communication of higher life with the
counsels of infinite wisdom and
love, and (3) shows its independence of outward descent (as
from Abraham). There is no
emphasis on the personal will of
the Son, as in *v.* 20 (ἃ αὐτὸς ποιεῖ).

The full significance of this

claim of Christ to " quicken
whom He will " is illustrated
by the second of the *Shemoneh
Esreh*, the " Eighteen [Benedic-
tions]," of the Jewish Prayer
Book. It is probable that this
thanksgiving was used in substance in the apostolic age :
" Thou, O Lord, art mighty for
ever : Thou quickenest the dead :
Thou art strong to save. Thou
sustainest the living by Thy
mercy : Thou quickenest the dead
by Thy great compassion. Thou
. . . makest good Thy faithfulness to them that sleep in the
dust . . . Thou art faithful to
quicken the dead. Blessed art
Thou, O Lord, who quickenest
the dead."

22. The fact that the Son
possesses and exercises this quickening power is established by the
fact that He has a still more
awful prerogative. The quickening of men is contrasted with
the judgement of men, which is
the correlative of sin (iii. 17 ff.).
And this judgement belongs to
the Son (as *Son of man, v.* 27).

οὐδὲ γὰρ ὁ πατήρ . . . τὴν κρίσιν πᾶσαν . . .] *for not even doth
the Father judge any man, but
hath given all judgement* (or literally, *the judgement* which comes
and will come, *wholly, in all its
parts,* now in its first beginning
and hereafter in its complete
accomplishment) *unto the Son.*

23 δέδωκεν τῷ υἱῷ, ἵνα πάντες τιμῶσι τὸν υἱὸν καθὼς τιμῶσι
τὸν πατέρα. ὁ μὴ τιμῶν τὸν υἱὸν οὐ τιμᾷ τὸν πατέρα
24 τὸν πέμψαντα αὐτόν. Ἀμὴν ἀμὴν λέγω ὑμῖν ὅτι ὁ τὸν
λόγον μου ἀκούων καὶ πιστεύων τῷ πέμψαντί με ἔχει
ζωὴν αἰώνιον, καὶ εἰς κρίσιν οὐκ ἔρχεται ἀλλὰ μετα-
25 βέβηκεν ἐκ τοῦ θανάτου εἰς τὴν ζωήν. ἀμὴν ἀμὴν λέγω
ὑμῖν ὅτι ἔρχεται ὥρα καὶ νῦν ἐστιν ὅτε οἱ νεκροὶ ἀκού-

οὐδὲ γὰρ ὁ πατήρ . . . οὐδένα]
The phrase marks a climax : *not
even doth the Father*—to whom
this office might seem to pertain
—*judge any man.*

δέδωκεν] This word is constantly used of the privileges
and office of the Son: *v.* 36, iii.
35, vi. 37, 39, x. 29, xvii. 2, 4 ff.,
22 ff. See *v.* 36, note.

23. The Son has received the
prerogative of judgement, and it
is through the exercise of this
power that men come to perceive
His true majesty. For it was
committed to Him for this end,
ἵνα πάντες τιμῶσι (*ut omnes
honorificent* v.) τὸν υἱὸν καθὼς
τιμῶσι τὸν πατέρα (x. 37, 38).
Sooner or later, in loss or in
sorrow, this must be. And
there is also a converse form of
the Truth. It is by honouring
the Son that we can honour the
Father; and *he that honoureth not
the Son honoureth not the Father
which sent him* (compare 1 John
iv. 20 ; ch. xv. 24).

τ. πεμψ. αὐτ.] *qui misit illum
v.* These words mark the transition from the conception of *the
Son* essentially to that of the
Son revealed by the Incarnation.
The phrase ὁ πέμψας με is peculiar to St. John (compare Rom.
viii. 3). It is used only by the
Lord absolutely of the Father, iv.
34, *vv.* 24, 30, vi. 38, 39, vii. 16,

28, 33, viii. 26, 29, ix. 4, xii. 44,
45, xiii. 20, xv. 21, xvi. 5. Elsewhere the full form, ὁ πέμψας με
πατήρ, occurs, v. 37, vi. 44, viii.
16, 18, xii. 49, xiv. 24. Comp.
i. 33 (ὁ πέμψας με βαπτίζειν).

24—29. In these verses we
pass from the consideration of
the relation of the Son to the
Father to that of the relation of
Christ to men. The conception
of the "greater works" of the
Son, the quickening and the
judgement of men, is defined more
exactly in connexion with the
Son as revealed by the Incarnation. At the same time, though
the oblique form is generally
preserved, the work and the mission of Christ are referred to
directly (τὸν λόγον μου . . . τῷ πέμψαντί με, v. 24). In v. 24 the
general ideas of all life and all
judgement in connexion with the
Son (21, 22) are restated : in vv.
25, 26 they are applied to the
present order ; in 28, 29 they
are applied to the future order.

24. Ἀμὴν ἀμήν] See vv. 19, 25.
Comp. i. 51, note.

ὁ τ. λόγον . . . εἰς τ. ζωήν] *he
that heareth my word and believeth
him that sent me hath life
eternal and cometh not into
judgement, but is passed out of
death* (*the* death that is truly
death) *into life* (*the* life that is
truly life). (Compare 1 John

23 unto the Son; that all may honour the Son, even
as they honour the Father. He that honoureth not
the Son honoureth not the Father which sent him.
24 Verily, verily, I say unto you, He that heareth my
word, and believeth him that sent me, hath life
eternal, and cometh not into judgement, but hath
25 passed out of death into life. Verily, verily, I say
unto you, The hour cometh, and now is, when the

iii. 14.) The two conditions of
eternal life are (1) knowledge of
the revelation made by the Son,
and (2) belief in the truth of it,
that is, belief in the word of the
Father who speaks through the
Son. Compare xvii. 3. He who
knows the gospel, and knows
that the gospel is true, cannot
but *have* life. Eternal life is
not future but present, or rather
it *is*, and so is above all time.
Compare iii. 18 f. For him who
hath this life judgement is impossible. He has already gone
beyond it. Comp. 1 John ii. 28,
iv. 17.

πιστεύων τῷ π. . . . .] *believeth
him* . . . The difference between
" believing a person or statement" (πιστεύειν τινί) and " believing on a person " (πιστεύειν
εἰς τινά) is as clearly marked in
Greek as in English, though it is
destroyed here in A. V. and in
viii. 31 ; Acts xvi. 34, xviii. 8 ;
Tit. iii. 8 ; while it is preserved
vv. 38, 46, viii. 45, 46 ; Rom. iv.
3 ; Acts xxvii. 25. The two
phrases are contrasted in vi. 29,
30, viii. 30, 31 ; 1 John v. 10.
To believe God or to believe the
Lord is to acknowledge as true
the message which comes from
Him or the words which He
speaks. It is assumed that the

message does come from Him, and
therefore to believe the message
is to believe Him. So here Christ
refers His word to the authority
of the Father : compare *v*. 37.

κρίσιν] *judgement.* Compare
Introd.

οὐκ ἔρχεται] *cometh not.* The
issues of action are regarded in
their potential accomplishment
in the present.

ἐκ τ. θαν. εἰς τ. ζω.] *a morte in
vitam* v. ; *out of death into life.*
1 John iii. 14. In his Epistle
St. John speaks of " love to the
brethren " as the personal proof
of this transition. Such love
flows from an acceptance in
faith of Christ's word (1 John ii.
7, iii. 11). Death and life are,
as it were, two spheres of existence, like darkness and light :
1 John v. 19, 20 ; ch. viii. 31, note.

25. The present manifestation
of Christ's vivifying power in
the spiritual resurrection (ἔρχεται
. . . κ. νῦν ἐστιν) is stated in
contrast with the future manifestation in the general resurrection (ἔρχεται, *v*. 28). See iv.
23, 21. The hour was " coming,"
so far as the Christian Dispensation truly began with the gift of
Pentecost : but it " was " already
while Christ openly taught
among men.

13

σουσιν τῆς φωνῆς τοῦ υἱοῦ τοῦ θεοῦ καὶ οἱ ἀκούσαντες
26 ζήσουσιν[1]. ὥσπερ γὰρ ὁ πατὴρ ἔχει ζωὴν ἐν ἑαυτῷ,
27 οὕτως καὶ τῷ υἱῷ ἔδωκεν ζωὴν ἔχειν ἐν ἑαυτῷ· καὶ
ἐξουσίαν ἔδωκεν αὐτῷ[2] κρίσιν ποιεῖν, ὅτι υἱὸς ἀνθρώπου
28 ἐστίν. μὴ θαυμάζετε τοῦτο, ὅτι ἔρχεται ὥρα ἐν ᾗ πάντες
29 οἱ ἐν τοῖς μνημείοις ἀκούσουσιν τῆς φωνῆς αὐτοῦ καὶ
ἐκπορεύσονται οἱ τὰ ἀγαθὰ ποιήσαντες εἰς ἀνάστασιν
ζωῆς, οἱ τὰ φαῦλα πράξαντες εἰς ἀνάστασιν κρίσεως.
30 Οὐ δύναμαι ἐγὼ ποιεῖν ἀπ᾽ ἐμαυτοῦ οὐδέν· καθὼς ἀκούω

---

[1] ζήσουσιν ℵBDL; ζήσονται ΑΓΔ.　　　[2] Insert καὶ ΔΓΔ.

οἱ νεκροί] *the dead*, the spiritually dead : this is the predominant idea ; but at the same time we cannot exclude the outward signs of it, as in the raising of Lazarus : compare xi. 23 ff. For this use of the word see Matt. viii. 22 ; Luke xv. 24, 32 ; Rom. vi. 11 ; Eph. v. 14. It will be observed that the voice of power is attributed to the *Son of God*. Comp. xi. 4 ; contrast ix. 35.

οἱ ἀκουσαν.] *qui audierint* v. ; *they that hear*. This phrase is not co-extensive with οἱ νεκροί. The voice is addressed to the whole class : those who receive it shall live. As yet the thought is of *life* only, and not of judgement, except so far as that is expressed in the want of life.

26. ὥσπερ . . . οὕτως] The particles mark the *fact* of the gift and not the *degree* of it. Comp. v. 21 ; Matt. xiii. 40, etc.

οὔτ. κ. . . . ἔδωκ. . . .] *so gave he also* . . . The Son has not life only as given, but life *in himself* as being a spring of life. "Nos non habemus vitam in nobis ipsis, sed in Deo nostro. Ille autem Pater vitam in semetipso habet ; et talem genuit Filium qui haberet vitam in

semetipso ; non fieret vitæ particeps, sed ipse vita esset, cujus nos vitæ participes essemus " (Augustine, *Serm.* cxxvii. 9). The tense carries us back beyond time ; and yet it has a further application to the Incarnation, wherein the Son became also the Son of man (*v.* 27). The sovereignty of life is followed by the authority to judge, as in *vv.* 21, 22. Comp. vi. 57 ; Rev. i. 17.

27. ἐξουσ. ἔδωκ. αὐτ. . . . υἱὸς ἀνθρ. ἐστ.] *potestatem dedit ei et judicium facere, quia filius hominis est* v. ; *gave him . . . judgement because he is Son of man*, or *a son of man*. The prerogative of judgement is connected with the true humanity of Christ (*Son of man*), and not with the fact that He is the representative of humanity (*the Son of man*). The Judge, even as the Advocate (Heb. ii. 18), must share the nature of those who are brought before Him. The omission of the article concentrates attention upon the nature and not upon the personality of Christ. Comp. i. 1 ; Heb. i. 1, 2 (ἐν τοῖς προφήταις . . . ἐν υἱῷ, in One who was a Son). The phrase (υἱὸς ἀνθρ.) is found here only in the Gospel,

dead shall hear the voice of the Son of God; and
26 they that hear shall live. For as the Father hath
life in himself, even so gave he also to the Son to
27 have life in himself: and he gave him authority
to execute judgement, because he is Son of man.[1]
28 Marvel not at this: for the hour cometh, in which
29 all that are in the tombs shall hear his voice, and
shall come forth; they that wrought good, unto the
resurrection of life ; and they that did ill, unto
30 the resurrection of judgement. I can of myself do

[1] *or* a son of man.

but it occurs also Rev. i. 13, xiv.
14: ὁ υἱὸς τ. ἀνθρ. occurs i. 51,
iii. 13, 14, vi. 27, 53, 62, as often
in the other Gospels. Comp. i.
51, Additional Note.

28. μὴ θαυμ. . . . ὅτι . . .] The
partial spiritual quickening and
judgement is consummated in an
universal quickening and judgement. There is a marked contrast between the corresponding
clauses of *vv.* 25, 28 : οἱ νεκροί
(*v.* 25), πάντες οἱ ἐν τ. μνημ.
(*omnes qui in monumentis sunt* v.)
(*v.* 28) : ἔρχ. κ. νῦν ἐστ. (*v.* 25),
ἔρχεται (*v.* 28). Here the quickening is the inevitable result of the
divine action (πάντες . . . ἀκουσ.) ;
before it followed from the concurrence of faith with the divine
message (οἱ ἀκουσαντ. ζησ.).

μὴ θαυμάζετε . . .] Comp. *v.* 20.
Wonder is at most only a stage
of transition. Each manifestation of Christ's power is a preparation for something greater.

29. It will be observed that
there is a contrast between the
one result of the present action
of the Son, ζήσουσι (*v.* 25), and
the complex result of His future
action : ἐκπορεύσονται . . .

οἱ τὰ ἀγ. ποιήσαντες . . .] *qui
bona fecerunt* . . . v. ; *they that
wrought good.* . . . The "doing"
of good is described as issuing in
a definite production, while in
the second member, οἱ τὰ φαῦλα
πραξ. (*qui . . . mala egerunt* v.),
the "doing" is regarded simply
in the moral character of the
action. The same words (ποιεῖν,
πράσσειν) are contrasted, ch. iii.
20, 21, note ; Rom. i. 32, vii. 15,
19, xiii. 4. The distinction is
well preserved in the Vulgate.

For the contrast of *a resurrection of life* (2 Macc. vii. 14) and
a resurrection of judgement, see *v.*
24. In one case the resurrection
is accompanied by the full fruition
of life, judgement being past : in
the other, resurrection issues in
judgement.

κρίσεως] *of judgement.* Comp.
iii. 17 ff.

30. This verse forms a transition from the first section of the
discourse to the second. At the
same time it marks the passage
from the indirect (*the Son*) to the
personal (*I*) revelation of Christ.
The truth of the divine Sonship,
with which the discourse opened,

κρίνω, καὶ ἡ κρίσις ἡ ἐμὴ δικαία ἐστίν, ὅτι οὐ ζητῶ
τὸ θέλημα τὸ ἐμὸν ἀλλὰ τὸ θέλημα τοῦ πέμψαντός με¹.
31 Ἐὰν ἐγὼ μαρτυρῶ περὶ ἐμαυτοῦ, ἡ μαρτυρία μου οὐκ
32 ἔστιν ἀληθής· ἄλλος ἐστὶν ὁ μαρτυρῶν περὶ ἐμοῦ, καὶ
οἶδα² ὅτι ἀληθής ἐστιν ἡ μαρτυρία ἣν μαρτυρεῖ περὶ
33 ἐμοῦ. ὑμεῖς ἀπεστάλκατε πρὸς Ἰωάνην, καὶ μεμαρτύρηκε

¹ Insert πατρός EGΓ.   ² οἶδα ℵᶜABL; οἴδατε ℵ*D.

is first repeated in a new form, *I
(ἐγώ) can of mine own self do
nothing;* and then the principle
of Christ's judgement is laid down
(*as I hear, I judge*), which is the
ground of all true judgement.

Οὐ δύν. ἐγώ . . . οὐδέν] Comp.
v. 19, note.

ἀπ᾽ ἐμαυτ.] *a me ipso* v. Comp.
vii. 17 f., 28, viii. 28, 42 (xii.
49, ἐξ ἐμ.), xiv. 10 (xi. 51), xv.
4, note, xvi. 13. The very idea
of Sonship involves (in some
sense) that of dependence. There
is but one "fountain" of Deity.
But under another aspect the
Son "lays down His life of Himself" (x. 18).

καθὼς ἀκούω κρίνω] *as I hear, I
judge.* The judgement of the Son
is based upon the perfect knowledge of the thoughts of the
Father, as the action of the Son
is based upon the perfect vision
of His works. The "hearing"
in this verse with regard to
judgement corresponds with the
"seeing" in *v.* 19 with regard to
action.

ὅτι οὐ . . . τὸ θέλημα τοῦ πεμψ.
με] *because I seek . . . the will of
him that sent me* (iv. 34, vi. 38,
39). The two conditions of absolute justice are (1) negative:
absence of all respect to self; and
(2) positive: devotion to the will
of the Father. In both these

respects the just judgement of the
Son is contrasted with the false
judgement of the Jews, *vv.* 41
—44.

The connexion between the
obedience rendered by the Son,
and the honour rendered to the
Son (*v.* 23), must be noticed.

It will be observed that the
" will " of Christ corresponds
with His one unchanged personality (ἐγώ). Comp. Matt. xxvi.
39, and parallels. The thought
of the verse is partially illustrated by a noble saying of R.
Gamaliel: " Do His will as if it
were thy will, that He may do
thy will, as if it were His will."
But he continues: "Annul thy
will before His will, that He may
annul the will of others before
thy will" (*Aboth*, xi. 4).

*The witness to the Son and the
ground of unbelief* (31—47)

This second main division of
the discourse consists, like the
first, of two parts. The witness
to the Son is first laid open (31—
40), and then the rejection of
the witness in its cause and end
(41—47).

31—40. Christ appeals to a
witness separate from His own,
and yet such that He has immediate knowledge of its truth.
Such witness is partly provisional

nothing: as I hear, I judge: and my judgement is righteous; because I seek not mine own will, but 31 the will of him that sent me. If I bear witness 32 concerning myself, my witness is not true. It is another that beareth witness of me; and I know that the witness which he witnesseth of me is 33 true. Ye have sent unto John, and he hath borne

and partly final. Of the former kind that of John the Baptist is the type (33—35). The latter lies in the witness of "works" leading up to the witness of the Father (36 —40).

31. Ἐὰν ἐγώ . . .] The stress lies on the pronoun, "If I alone and in fellowship with no other . . ." Comp. viii. 14.

οὐκ . . . ἀληθής] The words anticipate an objection, and define the amount of truth which it contains. According to legal usage the testimony of a witness was not received in his own case. This principle the Jews might urge against Christ; and He acknowledges the deeper meaning which lay beneath it. If He asserted His claims self-prompted (*of Himself*) He would violate the absolute trust which the Son owed to the Father; though there was a sense in which He could bear witness of Himself (viii. 12 ff.) when the Father spoke through Him (viii. 18).

32. ἄλλος ἐστ.] In due time and in due manner another bears witness. The whole scope of the statement decides that this other is "the Father" and not the Baptist. In the verses which follow the testimony of the Baptist is treated as provisional, and as being in a certain degree an accommodation. The testimony of

the Father is that upon which the Son rests, v. 37, viii. 18.

ὁ μαρτυρῶν . . . μαρτυρεῖ] The action is present and continuous.

οἶδα . . .] In the certainty of this knowledge Christ could repose. Such witness could not but produce its true effect. The absolute knowledge spoken of here is to be distinguished from the knowledge of experience (ἔγνωκα) in v. 42.

ἡ μαρτ. ἣν μαρτυρεῖ] This full form of expression, as distinguished from "his witness," emphasises the idea of the continuity of the witness as a matter of actual experience.

33. ὑμ. ἀπεστάλκ. . . . κ. με- μαρτ. . . .] *Ye have sent . . . and he hath borne. . . .* The mission and the testimony are spoken of as abiding in their results. The prominent idea is not the historic fact (i. 32), but the permanent and final value of the witness (i. 34, iii. 26, v. 37, xix. 35).

The emphatic pronoun marks a contrast between the standard of authority which the Jews set and that which Christ admitted (*v.* 34). At the same time the reference to John follows naturally after the mysterious reference to "another" in whom some might think that they recognised him.

34 τῇ ἀληθείᾳ· ἐγὼ δὲ οὐ παρὰ ἀνθρώπου τὴν μαρτυρίαν
35 λαμβάνω, ἀλλὰ ταῦτα λέγω ἵνα ὑμεῖς σωθῆτε. ἐκεῖνος
ἦν ὁ λύχνος ὁ καιόμενος καὶ φαίνων, ὑμεῖς δὲ ἠθελήσατε
36 ἀγαλλιαθῆναι πρὸς ὥραν ἐν τῷ φωτὶ αὐτοῦ· ἐγὼ δὲ ἔχω
τὴν μαρτυρίαν μείζω τοῦ Ἰωάνου, τὰ γὰρ ἔργα ἃ δέδωκέν
μοι ὁ πατὴρ ἵνα τελειώσω αὐτά, αὐτὰ τὰ ἔργα ἃ¹ ποιῶ,
37 μαρτυρεῖ περὶ ἐμοῦ ὅτι ὁ πατήρ με ἀπέσταλκεν, καὶ
ὁ πέμψας με πατὴρ ἐκεῖνος² μεμαρτύρηκεν περὶ ἐμοῦ·

¹ Insert ἐγώ ΓΔ. ² ἐκεῖνος אBL ; αὐτός ΑΓΔ.

34. ἐγὼ δὲ οὐ παρ. ἀνθρ. τ. μαρτ. λαμβ.] *But* though the witness of John was decisive according to your view, *I* (emphatic as distinguished from *you*) *receive not my witness* (*the witness* which characterises the reality of my work and answers to it) *from a man* (even though he be a prophet), *but these things I say*—I appeal even to this imperfect witness, I urge every plea which may be expected to prevail with you— *that ye*—even ye—*may be saved.*

35. ἐκεῖνος ἦν ὁ λυχν. ὁ καιομ. κ. φαίνων] *ille erat lucerna ardens et lucens* v. *He was*—though now his work is ended by imprisonment or death—*the lamp that burneth and shineth.* . . . The phrase may also be rendered, *the lamp that is kindled and shineth,* by the analogy of Matt. v. 15; but Luke xii. 35, Rev. iv. 5, viii, 10, are strongly against this interpretation. John the Baptist was the *lamp,* the derivative and not the self-luminous light (i. 8). Comp. Matt. vi. 22 ; 2 Pet. i. 19 ; but the word is used also of the Lamb, Rev. xxi. 23, where the glory of God, as the source of light, is placed in connexion with the Lamb, through whom (as the lamp of this vast

temple) the light is conveyed in the city of God. The definite article (*the* lamp) simply marks the familiar piece of household furniture (comp. Mark iv. 21 ; Luke xi. 36). The epithets complete the image. The lamp is exhausted by shining; its illuminating power is temporary, and sensibly consumed. John the Baptist necessarily decreased (iii. 30). The title is eminently appropriate to the Baptist in his relation to Christ (τὸ φῶς) ; but there is no evidence to show that it was given to the herald of Messiah by tradition, though it was applied to several distinguished teachers. Compare Buxtorf, *Lex. s.v.* בוּצִינָא, p. 338. But while his glory lasted the Jews (*ye* emphatic) *were willing for a season* (*an hour,* 2 Cor. vii. 8 ; Gal. ii. 5 ; Philem. 15) *to rejoice* (ἀγαλλιασθῆναι) *in his light.* This exulting joy, however, showed their real misunderstanding of his mission. They welcomed his power, but disregarded the solemn warning of his preaching of repentance. His stern presence became a mere spectacle. Comp. Luke vii. 24 ff.

36, 37a. ἐγὼ δὲ ἔχω τ. μαρτ. μείζω τ. Ἰωαν. . . .] *ego autem*

34 witness unto the truth. But the witness which I receive is not from a man : howbeit I say these 35 things, that ye may be saved. He was the lamp that burneth[1] and shineth : and ye were willing to 36 rejoice for a season in his light. But the witness which I have is greater than *that of* John[2] : for the works which the Father hath given me to accomplish, the very works that I do, bear witness of me, that 37 the Father hath sent me. And the Father which

[1] *or* is kindled.　　　　[2] *or* than John.

habeo testimonium majus Johanne v. . .; *But the witness which I have is greater* (more conclusive) *than that of John* (or *than John*), *for* . . . *the very works that I do bear witness of me . . . and the Father which sent me, He hath borne witness.* The one witness was even then being given ; the other was complete. The revelation made in Christ, and especially in His works of power, was a proof developed before the eyes of men. The historical revelation of the Old Testament consummated at the Baptism was already a finished whole, and recorded in the preparatory Scriptures of the old Covenant.

τ. γὰρ ἐργ. ἃ δεδ. . . .] "The works" of Messiah from the divine side were a complete whole (δέδωκεν) ; but they were gradually wrought out on earth (ἵνα τελειώσω, v. 34) ; and this accomplishment was the end proposed in the divine gift (ἵνα).

τὰ ἔργα] This phrase is used, as generally in St. John's Gospel (v. 20, note), to describe the whole outward manifestation of Christ's activity, both those acts which we call supernatural and those which we call natural. All alike are wrought in fulfilment of one plan and by one power. The many "works" (vii. 3, ix. 3, x. 25, 32, 37 f., xiv. 10 ff., xv. 24) are parts of the one "work" (iv. 34, xvii. 4). The phrase occurs elsewhere in Matt. v. 16.

δέδωκεν] The declaration of this relation of the Father to the Son (Incarnate) is characteristic of St. John. The Father hath given all things in His hand (iii. 35, xiii. 3) ; He hath given Him all judgement (vv. 22, 27) ; He gave Him to have life in Himself (v. 26) ; He hath given Him a company of faithful servants (vi. 39 ; comp. vi. 65, xvii. 2, 6, 9, 12, 24, xviii. 9) ; He hath given Him commandment what to say (xii. 49) and to do (xiv. 31, xvii. 4 ; comp. xvii. 7 f.). He gave Him authority over all flesh (xvii. 2) ; He hath given Him His name (xvii. 11 f.) and glory (xvii. 24 ; comp. v. 22).

τελειώσω] Comp. iv. 34, note.

ἃ ποιῶ] The pronoun ἐγώ, which is inserted in the common text must be omitted. It stands in x. 25, xiv. 12, and xiii. 7.

37. ὁ . . . πατὴρ ἐκεῖνος . . .] *the Father . . . He hath borne*

οὔτε φωνὴν αὐτοῦ πώποτε ἀκηκόατε οὔτε εἶδος αὐτοῦ
38 ἑωράκατε, καὶ τὸν λόγον αὐτοῦ οὐκ ἔχετε ἐν ὑμῖν μένοντα,
ὅτι ὃν ἀπέστειλεν ἐκεῖνος τούτῳ ὑμεῖς οὐ πιστεύετε.
39 ἐραυνᾶτε τὰς γραφάς, ὅτι ὑμεῖς δοκεῖτε ἐν αὐταῖς ζωὴν
αἰώνιον ἔχειν· καὶ ἐκεῖναί εἰσιν αἱ μαρτυροῦσαι περὶ

witness . . . Side by side with
the continuous witness of the
Father (v. 32) there is a witness
which is complete. This was
given, in its outward form, in
the prophetic teaching of the
Old Testament closed by the
work of the Baptist; and in its
spiritual form, in the constitution of man whereby he recognises in Christ the fulfilment of
the providential teaching of God.
Comp. Introd.

37 b, **38.** But still the double
witness was unavailing. The
words and visions of the Old
Testament were fulfilled in Christ
(i. 17). If He was rejected at
His coming, they were inarticu-
late and unreal to the faithless.
So too it was with the last witness at the Baptism (i. 32 ff.).
Since, therefore, it is only through
the Son that men can hear or
see God (xiv. 9), the Jews by
their disbelief of Christ failed
to hear and see Him (ye is unemphatic); nor was His word,
which answers from within to
the revelation without, abiding
in them (1 John ii. 14). This
all follows from the words which
are emphasised by their position:
ὃν ἀπέστειλεν ἐκεῖνος τούτῳ ὑμεῖς
οὐ πιστεύετε.

The passage is a summary of
the mode and conditions of revelation. The teaching and the
character of God can be discovered in nature and history,
but His Word must be welcomed

and kept in the soul in order
that that which is without may
be intelligible.

φωνήν . . . εἶδος . . .] vocem
. . . speciem . . . v.; his voice . . .
shape . . . Comp. Luke iii. 22
(εἶδει, φωνήν), ix. 35. Comp. ch.
xii. 28; Acts vii. 31, ix. 4, x. 13.

38. τ. λογ. αὐτ.] verbum ejus,
v.; compare xvii. 6 ff.; 1 John
i. 10, ii. 14 (Heb. iv. 12). The
word of God is a power within
man, speaking to and through
his conscience; not simply the
sum of the earlier revelation
under the old Covenant as an
outward power; nor yet an independent illumination; but the
whole teaching of Providence felt
to be a divine message.

ὅτι . . .] because . . . This is
not alleged as the ground, but as
the sign of what has been said.
Comp. Luke vii. 47; 1 John iii. 14.

ἀπεστ.] Comp. xx. 21, note.

39, 40. From the essential
elements of revelation, external
(εἶδος, φωνήν) and internal (λόγον),
the Lord passes to the record of
Revelation in Scripture. This
the Jews misused.

39. ἐραυνᾶτε τ. γραφάς] scruta-
mini scripturas v.; Ye search
the Scriptures . . . The original
word may be either imperative
(A.V.) or indicative. The indicative rendering is strongly
recommended by (1) the immediate connexion, ye search . . .
and they . . .; (2) the sense of for
in them ye think . . ., which

sent me, he hath borne witness of me. Ye have
neither heard his voice at any time, nor seen his
38 form. And ye have not his word abiding in you:
39 because whom he sent, him ye believe not. Ye
search the scriptures, because ye think that in them
ye have eternal life; and these are they which bear

rather explains a practice than recommends a precept; (3) the general form of the passage : *ye have . . . ye have not . . . ye will not;* (4) the character of the Jews who reposed in the letter of the Old Testament instead of interpreting it by the help of the living Word. On the other side the position of the verb at the beginning of the sentence, and the omission of the pronoun, which occurs in the second clause, are in favour of the imperative rendering. But on the whole, the former view is the more probable. The insertion of the pronoun would weaken the stress which is laid on the idea of *searching*, and this is the central thought. The intense, misplaced diligence of search is contrasted with the futile result.

ἐραννᾶτε] ch. vii. 52; 1 Pet. i. 11. Comp. Rom. viii. 27; 1 Cor. ii. 10; Rev. ii. 23. The word ἐραννᾷν describes that minute, intense investigation of Scripture (דרש) which issued in the allegorical and mystical interpretations of the *Midrash*. A single example of the stress laid upon the written word will suffice : "Hillel used to say . . . more Thorah (Law), more life (Prov. iii. 1 f.) . . . He who has gotten to himself words of Thorah, has gotten to himself the life of the world to come"

(*Aboth*, ii. 8. Compare *Perek R. Meir* throughout; Taylor, *Sayings of the Fathers*, pp. 113 ff.). The knowledge of God, it was thought, without repentance brought forgiveness of sins (Just. M. *Dial.* § 141).

τ. γραφάς] the book as distinguished from the living word (*v.* 38).

ὅτι ὑμ. δοκεῖτε] *because ye think* because you for your part, following your vain fancies, think falsely and superstitiously that in them—in their outward letter —ye have eternal life, without penetrating to their true, divine meaning. You repose where you should be moved to expectation. You set up your theory of Holy Scripture against the divine purpose of it.

κ. ἐκεῖναι . . . κ. οὐ θελ. . . .] The words mark a double failure. The scriptures witnessed of One whom the Jews rejected; they pointed to life which the Jews would not seek. There is deep pathos in the simple co-ordination : καί . . . καί . . .

ἐκεῖναι . . .] those very scriptures which you idolise. Comp. i. 18, note.

αἱ μαρτυροῦσαι] *which testify* still and always. Comp. *v.* 32. The teaching of the Old Testament is never exhausted. As we know more of Christ it reveals more to us concerning Him.

40 ἐμοῦ· καὶ οὐ θέλετε ἐλθεῖν πρός με ἵνα ζωὴν ἔχητε.
41
42 Δόξαν παρὰ ἀνθρώπων οὐ λαμβάνω, ἀλλὰ ἔγνωκα ὑμᾶς
43 ὅτι τὴν ἀγάπην τοῦ θεοῦ οὐκ¹ ἔχετε ἐν ἑαυτοῖς. ἐγὼ
ἐλήλυθα ἐν τῷ ὀνόματι τοῦ πατρός μου καὶ οὐ λαμ-
βάνετέ με· ἐὰν ἄλλος ἔλθῃ ἐν τῷ ὀνόματι τῷ ἰδίῳ,
44 ἐκεῖνον λήμψεσθε. πῶς δύνασθε ὑμεῖς πιστεῦσαι, δόξαν
παρ᾽ ἀλλήλων λαμβάνοντες, καὶ τὴν δόξαν τὴν παρὰ
45 τοῦ μόνου [θεοῦ]² οὐ ζητεῖτε; μὴ δοκεῖτε ὅτι ἐγὼ κατη-

¹ Transpose οὐκ ἔχετε to before τὴν ἀγάπην ℵ*D.   ² Omit θεοῦ B.

40. καί...] *And* still, even with this testimony before you, the personal act of faith fails, *ye will not* (ye have no will to) *come unto me* (comp. Matt. xxiii. 37, ch. iii. 19) *that ye may have life*— "life" in its simplest form, the condition of all else (iii. 36, xx. 31), not qualified even as "eternal life" (*v.* 39).

οὐ θέλετε] *non vultis* v. ; *ye will not*. Man has that freedom of determination which makes him responsible. This truth is expressed in various forms in St. John's Gospel (comp. vii. 17, viii. 44, vi. 67) side by side with the affirmation of the divine action through which the will is effective for good (vi. 44).

41—47. In this section Christ, starting from the fact of a want of will to believe in His hearers, unfolds the cause (41—44) and the end (45—47) of their rejection of Himself.

The ground of rejection (41—44) lies in a want of divine love in the Jews (*v.* 42), which is shown by their inability to recognise Christ's self-sacrifice (*v.* 43), while they themselves pursued selfish ends (*v.* 44).

41. The connexion of thought with what precedes appears to lie in the anticipation of a natural objection. The condemnation which Christ pronounced might be referred to disappointed hope. It is, He replies, your spiritual life and not my own glory that I seek. I want nothing for myself, but I see a fatal defect in you. "Glory from men I receive not"—the order is emphatic, and contrasted with that in *v.* 34—"but I know you, that ye have not the love of God in you."

Δόξαν παρ. ἀνθρ.] *claritatem ab hominibus* v. ; *glory from men*. The glory of Messiah lies in His perfect fellowship with the Father (comp. i. 14, ii. 11, xii. 41); and men show their sympathy with Him by "the love of God." This the Jews had not, and their rejection of Christ was the sign of the fatal defect.

42. ἔγνωκα] *I know* by the knowledge of experience. Comp. ii. 24, note.

τ. ἀγ. τ. θεοῦ] *dilectionem dei* v. ; The phrase occurs elsewhere in the Gospels only in Luke xi. 42. Comp. 1 John iii. 5, iii. 17, iv. 7, 9, v. 3; Rom. v. 5; 2 Cor. xiii. 14; 2 Thess. iii. 5; Jude 21. God is at once the Author and the Object of this love; and it

40 witness of me; and ye will not come to me, that
41 ye may have life. Glory from men I receive not.
42 But I know you, that ye have not the love of God
43 in yourselves. I am come in the name of my Father,
and ye receive me not: if another shall come in his
44 own name, him ye will receive. How can ye believe,
seeing that ye receive glory one of another, and the
glory that *cometh* from the only God ye seek not?
45 Think not that I will accuse you to the Father:
there is one that accuseth you, *even* Moses, on whom

is frequently difficult to determine whether the words express the quickening love of God towards man, or the responsive love of man towards God.

οὐκ ἔχ. ἐν ἑαυτοῖς] Comp. *v.* 26, vi. 53; 1 John v. 10; Mark iv. 17.

43. The utter want of fellowship with God on the part of the Jews is exhibited in its contrasted results: *I* (emphatic) *am come in the name of my Father*, revealing God to you in this character, *and ye receive me not: if another shall come in his own name*, giving expression to his own thoughts, his own desires, which are in harmony with your own, *him ye will receive.*

ἐν τ. ὀν. τ. πατρ. μου] ch. x. 25, that is, resting absolutely in Him who is my Father and whom I make known to you as such; not simply "as representing" or "by the authority of" my Father, though these ideas are included in that deeper and more comprehensive one. Comp. xiv. 13 f., xv. 16, xvi. 23 f., 26, xvii. 11, 12, xx. 31.

44. The Jews offered a complete contrast to Christ (*v.* 30);

for they made the judgement of men their standard. Hence the cause of their faithlessness is summed up in the question which represents faith as an impossibility for them: *How can ye* (emphatic) *believe, seeing that ye receive glory* (the highest reward of action) *one of another* (comp. Matt. xxiii. 5); *and the glory that* cometh *from the only God ye seek not? The only God,* the one source of all glory, absolutely one in nature, stands in opposition to the "gods many" and to the many common dispensers of praise; to regard these in themselves is idolatry (comp. xii. 42, 43). The change of construction is remarkable, from the causal participle (λαμβάνοντες) to the finite verb (ζητεῖτε). The first clause gives the sufficient reason of unbelief; the second an accompanying fact. Comp. i. 32.

45—47. The rejection of Christ carries condemnation with it. The accuser is found in the supposed advocate (*v.* 45); and unbelief in the vaunted belief (*v.* 47).

μὴ δοκεῖτε . . .] *nolite putare*

γορήσω ὑμῶν πρὸς τὸν πατέρα· ἔστιν ὁ κατηγορῶν
46 ὑμῶν Μωυσῆς, εἰς ὃν ὑμεῖς ἠλπίκατε. εἰ γὰρ ἐπιστεύετε
Μωυσεῖ, ἐπιστεύετε ἂν ἐμοί, περὶ γὰρ ἐμοῦ ἐκεῖνος
47 ἔγραψεν. εἰ δὲ τοῖς ἐκείνου γράμμασιν οὐ πιστεύετε,
πῶς τοῖς ἐμοῖς ῥήμασιν πιστεύσετε ;

. . . v. Though I lay bare the cause and nature of your unbelief, *do not think that I will accuse you to the Father* (not *my Father*) ; there is one *that accuseth you, even Moses on whom you have set your hope.* Disbelief in me is disbelief in him, in the record of the promises to the patriarchs (viii. 56), in the types of the deliverance from Egypt (iii. 14), in the symbolic institutions of the Law, in the promise of a prophet like to himself ; *for it was of me* (the order is emphatic) *he wrote.* If ye were now at this very time his faithful disciples, you would be mine also. Christ was the essential subject of the Law as of the Prophets ; and so of the permanent records of the earlier Dispensation.

εἰς ὃν ὑμεῖς ἠλπίκατε] *in quo vos speratis* v. ; *on whom ye have set your hope.* Comp. 2 Cor. i. 10 ; 1 Tim. iv. 10, v. 5.

47. The converse of *v.* 46

also holds true. Disbelief in Moses involved disbelief in Christ. *If ye believe not his writings,* the testimony which he has given formally, solemnly, and which you profess to accept as authoritative, *how shall ye believe my words,* my sayings (iii. 34), which come to you without the recommendation of use and age ? The essence of the disbelief which the Jews showed to Moses lay in refusing to regard the Law as transitory. They failed to seize the principle of life by which it was inspired, and petrified the form. If they thus allowed their pride to interfere with their acceptance of the real teaching of Moses, they could much less admit the teaching of Christ. Outward zeal became spiritual rebellion.

γράμμασιν] *writings.* The word γράμματα appears to mark the specific form rather than the general scope of the record (γραφαί). Comp. 2 Tim. iii. 15 f.

ADDITIONAL NOTES ON CHAP. V. 1, 3

The evidence for the identification of the unnamed feast in *v.* 1 is obscure and slight. The feast has in fact been identified with each of the three great Jewish festivals—the *Passover* (Irenæus, Eusebius, Lightfoot, Neander, Greswell, etc.), *Pentecost* (Cyril, Chrysostom, Calvin, Bengel, etc.), and the feast of

Tabernacles (Ewald, etc.). It has also been identified with the Day of *Atonement* (Caspari), the feast of *Dedication* (Petavius ?), and more commonly in recent times with the feast of *Purim* (Wieseler, Meyer, Godet, etc.).

The difficulty was felt at a very early time. The definite article (ἡ ἑορτή) was added as

46 ye have set your hope.   For if ye believed Moses,
47 ye would believe me; for it was of me he wrote.   But
if ye believe not his writings, how shall ye believe
my words?

soon as the second century, and is found in a large number of copies, among which are ℵ, C, L, and the early Egyptian versions. It is, however, omitted by ABD, Origen, and a large number of later copies; and this combination of authorities is of far greater weight in such a case than the former.   We may therefore safely conclude that the Evangelist speaks of "a feast," not of "the feast."   If the definite article were authentic the reference would be to the Feast of Tabernacles, which was emphatically "the Feast of the Jews" (comp. Browne, *Ordo Sæclorum*, p. 87), and not, as is commonly said, to the Passover. One MS., it may be added, inserts "of unleavened bread," and another "the Feast of Tabernacles."

The determination of the event, if it can be reached, has a decisive bearing both upon the chronology of St. John's narrative, and upon the relation of St. John's narrative to that of the Synoptists.

The fixed points between which the Feast lies are the Passover (ii. 23) and the Feeding of the Five Thousand; the latter event taking place, according to the universal testimony of MSS. and versions, "when the Passover was near at hand" (vi. 4).

The following details in St. John bear more or less directly upon the date.

1.   After leaving Jerusalem at the conclusion of the Passover (iii. 22), the Lord "tarried" in Judæa.   This stay was sufficiently long to lead to results which attracted the attention of the Baptist's disciples (*l. c.*) and of the Pharisees (iv. 1).

2.   On the other hand, the interval between the Passover and the Lord's return to Galilee was such that the memory of the events of that Feast was fresh in the minds of those who had been present at it (iv. 45); and from the mention of "the Feast" it is unlikely that any other great Feast had occurred since.

3.   The ministry of the Baptist who was at liberty after the Passover (iii. 26 ff.), is spoken of as already past at the unnamed Feast (*v.* 35).

4.   To this it may be added that the language in which the Lord's action in regard to the Sabbath is spoken of, implies that His teaching on this was now familiar to the leaders of the people (*v.* 18, ἔλυε).

5.   The phrase used in iv. 35 has special significance if the conversation took place either shortly after seedtime or shortly before harvest.

6.   The circumstances of the conversation in ch. iv. suit better with summer than with early spring.

7.   At the time when the healing took place the sick lay

in the open air, under the shelter of the porches.

8. From vii. 21 ff. it appears that the Lord had not visited Jerusalem between this unnamed Feast and the Feast of Tabernacles, and that the incident of *vv.* 1 ff. was fresh in the minds of the people at the later visit.

9. It is improbable that the Feast was one of those which St. John elsewhere specifies by name (the *Passover*, ii. 13, vi. 4, xi. 55; the *Tabernacles*, vii. 2; the *Dedication*, x. 22).

A consideration of these data seems to leave the choice between *Pentecost, the Feast of Trumpets, (the Day of Atonement)* and *Purim.*

Purim (March) would fall in well with the succession of events; but the character of the discourse has no connexion with the thoughts of the Festival; and the Festival itself was not such as to give a natural occasion for such teaching.

Pentecost would suit well with the character of the discourse, but the interval between the Passover of ch. ii. and the Pentecost of the same year would scarcely leave sufficient time for the events implied in ch. iii., iv.; while to regard it as the Pentecost of the year after (McClellan) seems to make the interval too great.

It is scarcely likely that the *Day of Atonement* would be called simply " a festival," though Philo (*de septen.* § 23) speaks of it as " a festival of a fast " (νηστείας ἑορτή), but *the Feast of Trumpets* (the new moon of September), which occurs shortly before, satisfies all the conditions which are required. This " beginning of the year," " the day

of memorial," was in every way a most significant day. It had, according to the contemporary interpretation of Philo, a double significance, national and universal : national in memory of the miraculous giving of the Law with the sound of the trumpet ; and universal as calling men to a spiritual warfare in which God gives peace (*l. c.* § 22). On this day, according to a very early Jewish tradition, God holds a judgement of men (Mishnah, *Rosh Hashanah,* § 11 and notes) ; as on this day He had created the world (Suren. on Mishnah, *Rosh Hashanah,* § 1, 11, pp. 306, 313). Thus many of the main thoughts of the discourse, creation, judgement, law, find a remarkable illustration in the thoughts of the Festival, as is the case with the other Festival discourses in St. John. These find expression in the ancient prayer attributed to Rav (second century), which is still used in the Synagogue service for the day : " This is the day of the beginning of Thy works, a memorial of the first day . . . And on the provinces is it decreed thereon, ' This one is for the sword,' and ' This for peace ;' ' This one is for famine,' and ' This for plenty.' And thereon are men (creatures) visited, that they be remembered for life and for death. Who is not visited on this day ? for the remembrance of all that hath been formed cometh before Thee. . . ." (*Additional Service for the New Year,* אתה זוכר). And again, shortly after (comp. *vv.* 37 f.): " Thou didst reveal Thyself in the cloud of Thy glory unto Thy holy people, to speak with them ; from the heavens didst Thou make them to hear Thy voice, and Thou didst reveal Thyself to them in a dense bright cloud. Yea the whole world trembled at Thy presence, and the creatures of Thy making trembled because of Thee, when Thou, our King, didst reveal Thyself on Mount Sinai, to teach Thy people Thy Law and Thy commandments" (id. אתה נגלית).

Note on the Reading in v. 3 ff.

The various readings in vv. 3, 4 are very instructive. The last clause of v. 3 and the whole of v. 4 (ἐκδεχομένων . . . νοσήματι) is omitted by אBC*, Memph., Theb., Syr. vt., and one Latin copy (q).

The last clause of v. 3 (ἐκδεχομένων . . . κίνησιν) is omitted by A*L; while it is contained in D, 1, 33, (Latt.), (Syrr.), and the great mass of later authorities.

The whole of v. 4 is omitted by D, 33, and by some Latin copies, and is marked as spurious in very many MSS.; while it is contained in AL, (Latt.), (Syrr.), and the great mass of later authorities. The passage is not referred to by any writer except Tertullian (see below) earlier than Chrysostom, Didymus and Cyril of Alexandria.

Thus the whole passage is omitted by the oldest representatives of each great group of authorities. And, on the other hand, the whole passage is not contained in any authority, except Latin, which gives an ante-Nicene text. It is also to be noticed that the passage is inserted in the later texts of the Memph. and Arm., which omit it, wholly or in part, in their earliest form.

The earliest addition to the original text was the conclusion of v. 3. This was a natural gloss suggested by v. 7, which is undisturbed.

The gloss in v. 4 probably embodied an early tradition; and Tertullian was acquainted with it (de Bapt. 5).

The glosses (though longer and more important) are like many which are found in אD, Syr. vt. and Lat. vt., and the fact that they are not found in א, Syr. vt., and only partly in D, shows that they were for a time confined to North Africa.

It is obvious that there could be no motive for omitting the words, if they originally formed part of St. John's text; nor could any hypothesis of arbitrary omission explain the partial omissions in the earliest authorities which omit; while all is intelligible if the words are regarded as two glosses. The most ancient evidence and internal probability perfectly agree.

6   Μετὰ ταῦτα ἀπῆλθεν ὁ Ἰησοῦς πέραν τῆς θαλάσσης
2 τῆς Γαλιλαίας τῆς Τιβεριάδος.   ἠκολούθει δὲ αὐτῷ ὄχλος
πολύς, ὅτι ἐθεώρουν τὰ σημεῖα ἃ ἐποίει ἐπὶ τῶν ἀσθε-

ii. CHRIST AND MEN (ch. vi.)

The record of a critical scene in Christ's work in Galilee follows the record of the critical scene at Jerusalem. At Jerusalem Christ revealed Himself as the Giver of life; here He reveals Himself as the Support and Guide of life. In the former case the central teaching was upon the relation of the Son to the Father; in this case it is on the relation of Christ to the believer. The divine authority of the Son is declared in the Holy City; the redemptive work of the Son, through His atoning Death, in Galilee.

This episode contains the whole essence of the Lord's Galilæan ministry. It places in a decisive contrast the true and false conceptions of the Messianic Kingship, the one universal and spiritual, the other local and material.

The record consists of three parts: *the signs* (vv. 1—21); *the discourses* (vv. 22—59); *the issue* (vv. 60—71).

The Signs on the Land and on the Lake (1—21)

The two signs, *the Feeding of the Five Thousand* (1—15), and *the Walking on the Sea* (15—21), combine to show Christ as the support of life and as the guide and strengthener of the toiling. Through His disciples He first satisfies the multitudes, and then He Himself, at first unseen and unrecognised, brings His labouring disciples to the haven of rest.

1—15. *The sign on the land, the Feeding of the Five Thousand.*

The feeding of the five thousand is the only incident in the Lord's life, before His last visit to Jerusalem, which is recorded by all four Evangelists. The variations of detail in the four narratives are therefore of the deepest interest (Matt. xiv. 13—21; Mark vi. 30—44; Luke ix. 10—17; John vi. 1—15).

Generally it may be said that the Synoptic narratives are given in broad outline, as part of a prolonged ministry. St. John's narrative is part of an isolated episode, but at the same time individual in detail. The actors in the former are the Lord and "the disciples," or the "twelve": "the disciples say to Him," "He saith to them"; in the latter, the Lord, and Philip, and Andrew. As a natural consequence the conversation, of which St. John has preserved characteristic fragments, is condensed into a simple form by the first three Evangelists; and, on the other hand, the circumstances which led up to the event are to be found only in the Synoptists, though we may detect traces of their influence in St. John's record.

It follows that the two narratives are derived from two distinct sources; for it is not possible that the narrative of St. John could have been derived from any one of the Synoptists, or

6   After these things Jesus went away to the other
side of the sea of Galilee, which is *the sea* of Tiberias.
2 And a great multitude followed him, because they

from the common original from
which they were finally derived.

The chronology of the event
cannot be determined with absolute certainty. Some have
supposed that the words τὸ πάσχα
(*v.* 4) are a very early and
erroneous gloss (1); and others
again have suggested that chh. v.
and vi. were transposed acciden-
tally, perhaps at the time when
chh. vi., xxi.—episodes of the
Galilæan lake—were added on
the last review of the Gospel (2).

Against (1) (Browne, *Ordo
Sæclorum*, pp. 84 ff.) it must be
urged that all direct documentary
evidence whatever supports the
disputed words. The ground for
suspecting them is derived indirectly from patristic citations,
and it is by no means clear that
there is not in the passages
quoted a confusion between vi. 4
and vii. 2. Irenæus (ii. 22, § 3)
appears to interpret nigh (vi. 4,
ἐγγύς) retrospectively. Comp.
Mark vi. 39, note).

The transposition (2) (Norris,
Journal of Philology, 1871,
pp. 107 ff.) would give a simple
connexion of events, but in the
absence of all external evidence
it cannot be maintained.

Our knowledge of the details
of the Lord's life is far too
fragmentary to justify us in the
endeavour to make a complete
arrangement of those which have
been recorded. The very abruptness of the transition in vi. 1
is characteristic of St. John;
comp. iii. 22, x. 22, xii. 1.

CHAP. VI. 1. Μετὰ ταῦτα.]
See v. 1, note.

ἀπῆλθεν] *abiit* v.; *went away*,
that is from the scene of His
ministry at the time, which is
left undetermined, and not from
Jerusalem, as if this verse stood
in immediate connexion with
ch. v. There was probably an
interval of many months. Comp.
iv. 3; x. 40; xi. 54; xv. 36.
" Ecce palam est quia *abiit*, quia
reliquit domum suam, dimisit
hæreditatem suam"(Rupert). Cf.
Matt. xiii. 54 ff. The abruptness with which the narrative
is introduced is most worthy of
notice. All we read is that
the departure "over the sea of
Galilee" (*i.e.* to the east side of
it) took place at some time after
the visit to Jerusalem, which,
as we have seen, probably took
place at the feast of the New
Year. The Passover also was
near, if the present text in *v.* 4
is correct; but we learn nothing
from St. John as to the facts by
which the incident was immediately preceded. This information must be sought from
the other Gospels. And it is
very significant that the Synoptists set the withdrawal of the
Lord in connexion with two
critical events. They all agree
in stating that it followed upon
tidings brought from without.
St. Matthew makes it consequent
upon the account of the death
of the Baptist brought by his
disciples (xiv. 13). St. Luke
places it immediately after the

14

3 νούντων. ἀνῆλθεν δὲ εἰς τὸ ὄρος Ἰησοῦς, καὶ ἐκεῖ
4 ἐκάθητο μετὰ τῶν μαθητῶν αὐτοῦ. ἦν δὲ ἐγγὺς τὸ¹
5 πάσχα, ἡ ἑορτὴ τῶν Ἰουδαίων. ἐπάρας οὖν τοὺς ὀφθαλμοὺς ὁ Ἰησοῦς καὶ θεασάμενος ὅτι πολὺς ὄχλος ἔρχεται

¹ Omit τὸ πάσχα "apparently some Fathers and other ancient writers, though
it stands in all extant Greek MSS. and VV." (See Appendix, W. H.)

return of the twelve from their mission, but without any definite combination of the two events (ix. 10). St. Mark brings out more clearly that at least one object of the retirement was rest from exhausting labour (vi. 30, 31). These indications of a concurrence of motives exactly correspond with the fulness of life. And St. Luke has preserved the link which combines them. "Herod," he says, "sought to see [Jesus]," troubled by the thought of a new John come to take the place of him whom he had murdered (ix. 9). The news of the death of the Baptist, of the designs of Herod, of the work of the twelve, coming at the same time, made a brief season of quiet retirement, and that outside the dominions of Herod, the natural counsel of wisdom and tenderness. St. Luke alone gives the name of the place which was chosen for this object, "a city called Bethsaida" (ix. 10), that is the district of Bethsaida Julias in Gaulonitis, at the N.-E. of the lake (Jos. *Ant.* XVIII. ii. 1). This second city of the same name was probably present to the mind of St. John when he spoke of "Bethsaida of *Galilee*" (xii. 21 ; but not i. 44) as the home of Philip. Perhaps we may add, that this withdrawal for calm devotion would be still more necessary, if it was intended

to cover the period of the Passover, which the Lord could not celebrate at Jerusalem owing to the hostility shown towards Him there not long before.

πέραν] (*vv.* 17, 22, 25) implies their coming from Capernaum or neighbourhood (Matt. xiv. 22; Mark v. 1, 21).

τ. θαλ. . . . . τ. Τιβερ.] *the sea of Tiberias.* This is the name by which the lake was known to classical writers (Paus. v. 7, p. 391, λίμνη Τιβεριάς). The title occurs only here and in ch. xxi. 1 in the New Testament; and it will be noticed that in xxi. 1 no second name is given. The later incident was not contained in the common basis of the Synoptic accounts, and was not therefore connected with the Synoptic title of the lake. St. Luke never speaks of the "sea " but of the "lake " (5 times). The name of Tiberias, the splendid but unholy capital which Herod the tetrarch had built for himself, is not mentioned in the New Testament except in these two places and in *v.* 23.

2. ἠκολούθει] *followed ;* not simply on this occasion but generally. The verse describes most vividly the habitual work and environment and influence of Christ. Τοσαύτης διδασκαλίας ἀπολαύσαντες ἀπὸ τῶν σημείων ἐνήγοντο μᾶλλον· ὁ παχυτέρας γνώμης ἦν (Chrys. But notice

beheld the signs which he did on them that were
3 sick.   And Jesus went up into the mountain, and
4 there he sat with his disciples.   Now the passover,
5 the feast of the Jews, was at hand.   Jesus therefore
having lifted up his eyes, and seen that a great mul-

Matt. vii. 28 f.).   The tense
stands in contrast with that in
Matt. xiv. 13; Luke ix. 11.

ἐθεώρουν] *beheld*, v. 19. See
ii. 23, note.

ἐποίει] *faciebat* v. This verb,
like those which precede, marks
a continued ministry.

3. εἰς τ. ὄρ.] *into the mountain.*
So *v.* 15. The use of the definite
article implies an instinctive
sense of the familiar landscape,
the mountain range closing round
the lake. This use is found
also in the Synoptic narrative,
Matt. v. 1, xiv. 23, xv. 29;
Mark iii. 13, vi. 46; Luke vi. 12,
ix. 28. St. Matthew adds that
it was "a desert spot" (xiv. 13).

ἐκαθ.] *sedebat* v.; *was sitting.*
The word has a life-like distinctness when taken in connexion
with *v.* 5. Comp. Matt. xiii. 1,
xv. 29; Mark x. 46; Acts xiv. 8.
"Dominus in monte: multo
magis intelligamus quia Dominus
in monte Verbum est in alto"
(Aug.).

4. ἦν δ. ἐγ. τ. πασχ.] *erat autem
proximum pascha* v.; *now the passover . . . was nigh*, i.e. "near
at hand" (ii. 13, vii. 2, xi. 55),
and not as Irenæus (?) and some
moderns have taken it, "lately
past." The notice of the feast
is probably designed to give a
clue to the understanding of the
spiritual lessons of the miracle
which are set forth in the discourse which followed (1 Cor. v. 7);
and at the same time it serves

to explain how trains of pilgrims
on their way to Jerusalem may
have been attracted to turn aside
to the new Teacher, in addition
to "the multitude" who were
already attached to Him.

ἡ ἑορτ. τ. Ἰουδ.] *the feast of
the Jews*; i.e. "the well-known
feast." The phrase when it
stands alone signifies the Feast
of Tabernacles, "the one great
national feast." Compare vii. 2
(where the order is different),
and v. 1, note. Οὐ γὰρ τοῦ χριστοῦ ἦν ἑορτή . . . ἀλλὰ μόνων τῶν
Ἰουδαίων (Theophylact).

5. ἐπαρ. οὖν τ. ὀφθ. . . . θεασ.
. . .] iv. 35 (i. 38). Comp.
Luke vi. 20; Matt. xvii. 8. The
Lord sees the harvest as He
showed it to His disciples.

ἔρχεται] Jesus and His disciples
sailed across the lake (Matt.
xiv. 13), but "the multitudes"
observed their departure and
reached Bethsaida on foot (Mark
vi. 33). The point of time here
is evidently the first arrival of
the people. A day of teaching
and healing must be intercalated
before the miracle of feeding was
wrought (Matt. xiv. 14; Mark
vi. 34; Luke ix. 11). St. John
appears to have brought together
into one scene, as we now regard it, the first words spoken
to Philip on the approach of the
crowd, and the words in which
they were afterwards taken up
by Andrew, when the disciples
themselves at evening restated

πρὸς αὐτὸν λέγει πρὸς Φίλιππον Πόθεν ἀγοράσωμεν
6 ιρτους ἵνα φάγωσιν οὗτοι ; τοῦτο δὲ ἔλεγεν πειράζων
7 αὐτόν, αὐτὸς γὰρ ᾔδει τί ἔμελλεν ποιεῖν. ἀπεκρίθη
αὐτῷ Φίλιππος Διακοσίων δηναρίων ἄρτοι οὐκ ἀρκοῦσιν
8 αὐτοῖς ἵνα ἕκαστος βραχὺ λάβῃ. λέγει αὐτῷ εἷς ἐκ
τῶν μαθητῶν αὐτοῦ, Ἀνδρέας ὁ ἀδελφὸς Σίμωνος Πέτρου
9 Ἔστιν παιδάριον¹ ὧδε ὃς ἔχει πέντε ἄρτους κριθίνους
καὶ δύο ὀψάρια· ἀλλὰ ταῦτα τί ἐστιν εἰς τοσούτους ;
10 εἶπεν ὁ Ἰησοῦς Ποιήσατε τοὺς ἀνθρώπους ἀναπεσεῖν.
ἦν δὲ χόρτος πολὺς ἐν τῷ τόπῳ. ἀνέπεσαν οὖν οἱ ἄνδρες

¹ Insert ἕν ΑΓΔ. See note.

the difficulty (Matt. xiv. 15 ;
Mark vi. 35 ; Luke ix. 12). If
this view be true, so that the
words addressed to Philip with
his answer preceded the whole
day's work, then the mention of
"two hundred pennyworth of
bread" made by the disciples in
St. Mark (vi. 37) gains great
point, and so too the phrase
"what he was about to do"
(v. 6), which otherwise appears
to be followed too quickly by its
fulfilment. We may not unnatur-
ally suppose a break after v. 7.
It appears also from v. 15 that
the Lord came down from the
mountain before the miracle was
wrought.

Φίλιππον] i. 44 ff., xii. 21 f.,
xiv. 8 f.

Πόθεν ἀγορασ. . . .] *unde eme-
mus . . .* v. The words are a
spontaneous expression of the
feeling of tender compassion
noticed by the Synoptists (Matt.
xiv. 14 ; Mark vi. 34).

6. πειράζων] *temtans* v.; *trying*
him, to see whether he could
meet the difficulty. Comp. 2
Cor. xiii. 5 ; Rev. ii. 2. Δοχιμώ-
τερον αὐτὸν εἰργάζετο (Chrys.).

Θέλων αὐτὸν γνώριμον καταστῆσαι
τίνα πίστιν ἔχει (Theophylact). As
Rupert puts the case, he asked
"ut manu inquisitionis suæ ten-
tando et per vocem responsionis
eliciendo ignorantiam ejus ipsi
ostenderet, quomodo benevolus cu-
jusque artis præceptor, interdum
discipulum interrogat non quod
de ignorantia illius dubitet sed
ut ad interrogationem evigilet."
Philip had already at his first
call made a noble confession of
Christ (i. 45). The word does
not necessarily carry with it (as
these passages show) the secondary idea of temptation (comp.
also Matt. xxii. 35 ; Mark xii.
15) ; but practically in the case
of men such trial assumes for
the most part this form, seeing
that it leads to failure, either
as designed by him who applies
it (Matt. xvi. 1, xix. 3, xxii. 18,
etc.), or consequent upon the
weakness of him to whom it is
applied (Heb. xi. 17 ; 1 Cor. x.
13). Comp. Deut. xiii. 3.

αὐτ. γ. ᾔδ. . . .] *for he himself
knew* . . . Throughout the Gospel
the Evangelist speaks as one
who had an intimate knowledge

titude cometh unto him, saith unto Philip, Whence
6 are we to buy bread, that these may eat? And this
he said trying him: for he himself knew what he
7 was about to do. Philip answered him, Two hundred
pennyworth of bread is not sufficient for them, that
8 every one may take a little. One of his disciples,
9 Andrew, Simon Peter's brother, saith unto him, There
is a lad here, which hath five barley loaves, and two
10 fishes: but what are these among so many? Jesus
said, Make the people sit down. Now there was
much grass in the place. So the men sat down, in

of the Lord's mind. He reveals
both the thoughts which belong
to his own internal, absolute
knowledge (εἰδέναι, vv. 61, 64,
xiii. 3, xviii. 4, xix. 28), and also
those which answered to actual
experience and insight (γινώσκειν,
v. 15, iv. 1, v. 6, xvi. 19).

7. *Two hundred pennyworth*]
i.e. between six and seven pounds
worth. See Mark vi. 37. We
cannot tell by what calculation
this exact sum was reached.
The reference may be to some
unrecorded fact. The denarius,
which was the ordinary day's
wages (Matt. xx. 2), in ordinary
times could purchase eight chœ-
nixes of wheat. A chœnix was
the bare allowance of food for
a day. The price of barley was
one-third that of wheat (Rev.
vi. 6). Two hundred denarii
would therefore provide 4,800
quarts of barley, or 1,600 quarts
of wheat. The latter quantity
would provide "a little" for the
whole number.

Rupert gives an applica-
tion of the words to Christian
teachers. This is, he remarks, as
though we said "all the teaching

of the old masters and the new
is not enough that this dull
people should each receive a
little Christian faith."

8. 'Ανδρ.] He appears elsewhere in connexion with Philip,
i. 44, xii. 22.

9. ἀρτ. κριθ.] *panes hordiacios*
v. v. 13. The detail is peculiar
to St. John. Comp. 2 Kings iv.
42. Barley bread was the food
of the poor. Wetstein (*ad loc.*)
has collected a large number of
passages to show the small account in which it was held. See
Judges vii. 13 f.; Ezek. xiii. 19.

δύο ὀψάρ.] *duos pisces* v.; *two
fishes.* It is worthy of remark
that the word ὀψάριον is found in
the New Testament only in this
passage and in ch. xxi. It may
have been a familiar Galilæan
word locally used by fishermen.
Comp. Numb. xi. 22 ὄψον (LXX.).

10. τ. ἀνθρωπ. . . . . οἱ ἀνδρ. . . .
ὡς πεντακισχ.] *homines . . . viri*
v.; *the people . . . the men . . .
about five thousand.* The change
of word in the latter case implies the remark added by St.
Matthew (xiv. 21) *beside women
and children.*

11 τὸν ἀριθμὸν ὡς πεντακισχίλιοι. ἔλαβεν οὖν¹ τοὺς ἄρτους
ὁ Ἰησοῦς καὶ εὐχαριστήσας διέδωκεν τοῖς ἀνακειμένοις,
12 ὁμοίως καὶ ἐκ τῶν ὀψαρίων ὅσον ἤθελον. ὡς δὲ ἐνεπλήσθησαν λέγει τοῖς μαθηταῖς αὐτοῦ Συναγάγετε τὰ
13 περισσεύσαντα κλάσματα, ἵνα μή τι ἀπόληται. συνή-
γαγον οὖν, καὶ ἐγέμισαν δώδεκα κοφίνους κλασμάτων
ἐκ τῶν πέντε ἄρτων τῶν κριθίνων ἃ ἐπερίσσευσαν τοῖς
14 βεβρωκόσιν. Οἱ οὖν ἄνθρωποι ἰδόντες ἃ² ἐποίησεν

¹ οὖν אᶜABDL; δέ א*ΓΔ.
² ἃ ἐποίησεν σημεῖα B; ὃ ἐποίησεν σημεῖον אADLΓΔ.

χορτ. πολ.] *fœnum multum* v.
See Mark vi. 39. The difference
of the form in which the detail
is introduced marks apparently
the testimony of two eye-witnesses. This detail corresponds
with the date, which is fixed
(vi. 4) in the early spring. In
this sign the Lord uses the
supply which was present and
blesses it.

11. ἔλαβ. οὖν ... ὁ Ἰησ.] *Jesus
therefore* . . ., answering the
obedience of faith.

εὐχαριστήσας] *cum gratias egis-
set* v. ; *when he had given thanks*
(*v.* 23). By this act the Lord
takes the place of the head of
the family (comp. Luke xxiv.
30). The word itself is found
elsewhere in St. John only, xi.
41. This second passage suggests that the thanksgiving was
rendered in acknowledgement of
the revelation of the Father's
will in accordance with which
the miracle was wrought. In the
parallels the word is εὐλόγησεν
(yet comp. Matt. xv. 36; Mark
viii. 6). The two words preserve
the two aspects of the action in
relation to the source and in
relation to the mode of its accomplishment. Compare in this

connexion Matt. xxvi. 26 f. ;
Mark xiv. 22 f.

In the ordinary Jewish
"graces" the word "bless" is
referred to God as the expression of thankful adoration (*Daily
Prayers*, i. 270 ff.), and this
appears to be the sense of the
word when it is used absolutely
in the New Testament; 1 Cor.
xiv. 16; Matt. xxvi. 26 and parallels. (Comp. εὐλ. τὸν θεόν. Luke
i. 62, ii. 28; James iii. 9).
Yet it must be noticed that in
St. Luke's Gospel (ix. 16) in the
phrase parallel to Matt. xiv. 19 ;
Mark vi. 41, and in two other
places of the New Testament
(Mark viii. 7 (*v.l.*); 1 Cor. x. 16)
a material object is definitely
added.

Once also in the Old Testament man is said to bless a thing,
1 Sam. ix. 13 (εὐλ. τὴν θυσίαν).
The word is used of God blessing "the seventh day" (Gen.
ii. 3; Ex. xx. 11); "the field"
(Gen. xxvii. 27); bread (Exod.
xxiii. 25); substance (Deut. xxxiii.
11); the end of Job (Job xlii.
12). Comp. Ps. lxiv. 12 (LXX.).

The blessing passes (if we may
so speak) from the recognition
of God's majesty and love to

11 number about five thousand. Jesus therefore took the loaves; and having given thanks, he distributed to them that were set down; likewise also of the 12 fishes as much as they would. And when they were filled, he saith unto his disciples, Gather up the broken pieces which remain over, that nothing be 13 lost. So they gathered them up, and filled twelve baskets with broken pieces from the five barley loaves, which remained over unto them that had 14 eaten. When therefore the people saw the sign which

that in connexion with which His goodness is contemplated. So we read, ἀπὸ τοῦ εὐχαριστη-θέντος ἄρτου καὶ οἴνου καὶ ὕδατος (Just. M. *Ap.* i. 65); ἡ δι᾽ εὐχῆς λόγου τοῦ παρ᾽ αὐτοῦ εὐχαριστη-θεῖσα τροφή (ch. 66).

Comp. Iren. i. 13, 2, and ὕδωρ εὐχαριστεῖν (Clem. Al. *Strom.* i. §96 (f. 375)).

διεδ. τ. ἀνακειμ . . .] *he distributed to . . . them that . . . were set down.* The words *to the disciples and the disciples* of A.V. must be omitted. They are an obvious gloss introduced from St. Matthew xiv. 19. What the Lord did through the disciples He did. Comp. iv. 1.

12. τὰ περισσ.] *quæ superaverunt* v. The increase takes place in the use and for use, but that which was provided is more than enough. The manna was not kept.

κλάσματα] *fragmenta* v.; *i.e. the broken pieces* for distribution (Ezek. xiii. 19). The word is used of the bread in Holy Communion in the *Teaching*, ix. 3 f. Comp. 1 Cor. x. 16. The command to collect these is preserved by St. John only.

13. συνήγαγον] *gathered . . . up,* as in *v.* 12. The simple repetition gives character to the narrative.

δώδεκα] The number implies that the work was given to the apostles, though they have not been specially mentioned. Comp. *v.* 70.

κοφίνους] *cophinos* v. The stout wicker baskets (Οἱ κόφινοι ἐκ βαΐων φοινικίνων. Theophylact) as distinguished from the soft, flexible "frails" (σφυρίδες, Matt. xv. 37; Mark viii. 8). Juv. *Sat.* III. 14, VI. 542.

Notice that the description "barley loaves" is repeated.

Chrysostom says: Οὐκ ἐπίδειξις ἦν τοῦτο περιττὴ ἀλλ᾽ ὥστε μὴ φαντασίαν νομισθῆναι τὸ πρᾶγμα.

14, 15. This incident is peculiar to St. John, but St. Luke has preserved a detail which illustrates it. He notices that Christ spoke to the multitudes "concerning the kingdom of God" (ix. 11); and it is natural to suppose that the excitement consequent upon the death of the Baptist, which in part led to the Lord's retirement, may have moved many to believe that He would place Himself at the head

σημεῖα [1] ἔλεγον ὅτι   Οὗτός ἐστιν ἀληθῶς ὁ προφήτης
15 ὁ ἐρχόμενος εἰς τὸν κόσμον.   Ἰησοῦς οὖν γνοὺς ὅτι
μέλλουσιν ἔρχεσθαι καὶ ἁρπάζειν αὐτὸν ἵνα [2] ποιήσωσιν
βασιλέα ἀνεχώρησεν [3] πάλιν εἰς τὸ ὄρος αὐτὸς μόνος.
16 Ὡς δὲ ὀψία ἐγένετο κατέβησαν οἱ μαθηταὶ αὐτοῦ ἐπὶ

[1] Insert ὁ Ἰησοῦς ΑΓΔ.
[2] ἵνα ποιήσωσιν βασιλέα ℵ°ABL; καὶ ἀναδεικνύναι βασιλέα ℵ*.
[3] ἀνεχώρησεν ℵ°ABDLΓΔ; φεύγει ℵ*.   See note.

of a popular rising to avenge
the murder.

14. ὁ προφ. ὁ ἐρχ.] *the prophet
that cometh*. . . . Comp. i. 21, 25,
vii. 40.   The phrase is peculiar
to St. John.   Yet see Matt. xxi.
11, and Acts vii. 37.   " Erat
autem ille Dominus prophetarum,
Empletor prophetarum, Sancti-
ficator prophetarum, sed et pro-
pheta ; nam et Moysi dictum est,
*Suscitabo eis prophetam similem
tui*, similem secundum carnem,
non secundum majestatem "
(Aug.).

15. Ἰησοῦς οὖν] This was the
consequence which the Lord saw
in the false interpretation which
the people put on their conclusion.

μέλλουσιν . . . ἁρπάζειν . . .] *ut
raperent* v. ; *were about to . . .
take him by force.*   Comp. Acts
xxiii. 10 ; (Judg. xxi. 21, LXX.);
Matt. xi. 12.   The multitude
wished to use Christ to fulfil their
own ends even against His will.
In this lies the foreshadowing of
the sin of Judas, ch. xviii. 6.

ἵνα ποιησ. βασιλ.] " Vix quæ-
ritur Jesus propter Jesum " (Aug.
and Bede).

" Regem enim facere Patris
erat, non populi ; neque adhuc
tempus erat " (Bengel).

" Quid enim ? non erat rex qui
timebat fieri rex ? Erat omnino,
nec talis rex qui ab hominibus

fieret, sed talis qui hominibus
regnum daret.   Numquid forte
et hic aliquid significat nobis
Jesus cujus facta verba sunt ? . . .
An forte hoc erat rapere eum,
prævenire velle tempus regni
ejus ? " (Aug., followed by Bede).

The multitude recognise the
Lord as " the prophet," not
simply as " a prophet."   He is
acknowledged as the second
Moses : Deut. xviii. 15.

But they are unwilling to place
themselves absolutely under His
guidance.   They seek to use Him
for the fulfilment of their own
designs : ch. viii. 31 ff.

With Judas-like faithlessness
they will force Him to exert His
power.   If they can make Him
a King He must (so they would
argue) vindicate His rightful
dignity.

The circumstances, as we have
seen, stimulated such feelings.
The death of John the Baptist
(Matt. xiv. 12 f.) seemed to call
for decisive action.   The preaching of the Kingdom by the Twelve
(Luke ix. 11) admitted a superficial and selfish interpretation
(comp. Acts xvii. 7).

Something of the same feeling
was seen in the triumphal entry
into Jerusalem.   Then the Lord
accepted the title of King, because He was about to give
Himself for His people.

he did, they said, This is of a truth the prophet that
15 cometh into the world.   Jesus therefore perceiving
that they were about to come and take him by
force, to make him king, withdrew again into the
16 mountain himself alone.   And when evening came, his

ἀνεχώρησεν] *fugit* v.; *withdrew.*
Rupert remarks: "Qui Christum
propter aliud quam propter
ipsum sequuntur, fugit ab eis
Christus, fugit veritatis Spiritus."
Comp. Matt. ii. 12 ff., xiv. 13,
xv. 21, etc.; Acts xxiii. 19.

πάλιν] It follows (*v.* 3) that
He had descended towards the
shore when the miracle took
place.

αὐτ. μον.] to pray, as is added
in the parallel narratives (Matt.
xvi. 23; Mark vi. 46). The dis-
missal of the apostles mentioned
in Matt. xiv. 22; Mark vi. 45,
is involved in these words (contrast *v.* 3). The apostles were
first withdrawn from the influence of the multitude, and the
mass of the people were then
sent away; but some (*v.* 22) still
lingered with vain hopes till the
morning.

Though the other Evangelists
do not notice the attempt of the
multitude, they specially notice
the care of the Lord to remove
the disciples from their influence
(ἠνάγκασεν).

Bede (following Augustine)
sees in the " ascent to the mountain" a figure of the Ascension,
and adds: " Videamus illo intra
velum cælestis altitudinis morante
(Heb. ix.), quid discipuli in
navicula patiebantur. Quid est
navicula quæ a fluctibus jactatur
nisi ecclesia quæ persecutionibus
fatigatur et foris et intus? Foris
a paganis aperta persecutione,

intus a falsis fratribus occulta
seditione."

16—21. *The Sign upon the Lake*

This incident is related also by
St. Matthew (xiv. 22 ff.) and by
St. Mark (vi. 45 ff.). The change
in time, scene, persons, belongs
to the significance of the sign.

The miracle stands alone.

It may be compared with the
Transfiguration. Like that event,
it anticipates some of the consequences of the Resurrection.

It is a revelation of the sovereignty of humanity in Christ
over the material conditions of
present existence. We must
not think of law suspended,
but of a new force called into
exercise.

It carries forward the lesson
of the former sign. The Lord's
supporting power is not limited
by earthly supply. The Lord's
presence with His people is not
limited by sensible obstacles.
And when His presence is welcomed, toiling believers reach
their end through fellowship
with Him.

This sign is given to the
apostles and not to the multitude. They specially needed the
encouragement in the fulfilment
of their work. The image of
the ship and the stormy waters
is a significant and universal
symbol of the Church in the
world. The Lord on the mountain in communion with the

17 τὴν θάλασσαν, καὶ ἐμβάντες εἰς πλοῖον ἤρχοντο πέραν
τῆς θαλάσσης εἰς Καφαρναούμ. καὶ¹ σκοτία ἤδη ἐγεγόνει
18 καὶ οὔπω² ἐληλύθει πρὸς αὐτοὺς ὁ Ἰησοῦς, ἥ τε θάλασσα
19 ἀνέμου μεγάλου πνέοντος διεγείρετο. ἐληλακότες οὖν ὡς
σταδίους εἴκοσι πέντε ἢ τριάκοντα θεωροῦσιν τὸν Ἰησοῦν
περιπατοῦντα ἐπὶ τῆς θαλάσσης καὶ ἐγγὺς τοῦ πλοίου
20 γινόμενον, καὶ ἐφοβήθησαν. ὁ δὲ λέγει αὐτοῖς Ἐγώ
21 εἰμι, μὴ φοβεῖσθε. ἤθελον οὖν λαβεῖν αὐτὸν εἰς τὸ

¹ καὶ σκοτία ἤδη ἐγεγόνει ABLΓΔ; κατέλαβεν δὲ αὐτοὺς ἡ σκοτία ΝD.
² οὔπω ΝBDL; οὐκ ΑΓΔ.

Father; the disciples struggling
in darkness and storm. The
trials of first age, "Illo in altis
constituto navicula illa Eccle-
siam prosignabat" (Aug.). "La-
borat (Ecclesia) sed non mergitur.
Christum expectat quando per
eum ad portum perveniat tran-
quillitatis" (Bede).
Compare the stilling of the
storm : Mark iv. 36 ff. and parallels; and a curious imitation of
the two narratives in *Test. XII
Patr.*, Napth. c. 6.
16. Comp. Matt. xiv. 22 ff.;
Mark vi. 45 ff.
Ὡς δ. ὀψ. ἐγεν.] The "second
evening," from sunset till dark.
Comp. Matt. xiv. 15, 23.
17. ἤρχοντο . . . εἰς . . .] *set out
on their way to* . . . Comp. iv.
30. This continuous toil is contrasted by the tense with the
simple act which preceded it
(κατέβησαν, ἐμβάντες, ἤρχοντο).
εἰς Καφ.] Mark vi. 45, πρὸς
Βηθσαιδάν.
οὔπω ἐληλ. . . .] *was not yet
come* . . . at the time when
they finally left the shore, along
which they may have kept for a
time. It appears that some incidents are here omitted. Probably Jesus had directed the

apostles to wait for Him at
some point on the eastern shore
on their way to Capernaum,
but not beyond a certain time.
The phrase "not yet" implies
that He had led them to expect
that He would be with them,
and that they clung in some
way to the expectation even in
their disappointment.
18. The singular vividness of
the description is to be noticed.
Comp. Jonah i. 13 (LXX.).
19. σταδίους εἰκ. πέντε . . .]
five and twenty . . . furlongs. The
lake is at its broadest about
forty stades ("furlongs"), or six
miles. Thus they were "in the
middle" of the lake (Mark vi.
47), having for a time kept to
the shore.
θεωρ.] *behold.* The word marks
the arrested, absorbed attention
of the disciples (v. 2). Comp.
Acts xxvii. 23 f.
ἐπὶ τ. θαλ.] *super mare* v.; *on
the sea.* The words might mean
(as xxi. 1) "on the sea-shore,"
but the context and parallels
determine the sense here. Comp.
Job ix. 8 (LXX.). The fact is
mentioned without any expression of surprise or explanation.
All is "neutral."

17 disciples went down unto the sea; and they entered
into a boat, and were going over the sea unto
Capernaum. And it was now dark, and Jesus had
18 not yet come to them. And the sea was rising by
19 reason of a great wind that blew. When therefore
they had rowed about five and twenty or thirty furlongs, they behold Jesus walking on the sea, and
drawing nigh unto the boat: and they were afraid.
20
21 But he saith unto them, It is I; be not afraid. They
were willing therefore to receive him into the boat:

The other Evangelists fix the
time περὶ τετάρτην φυλακὴν τῆς
νυκτός. Comp. Ex. xiv. 24, in
the morning watch.

ἐφοβήθησαν] Comp. Matt. xiv.
26; Mark vi. 49; Luke xxiv. 37.
See also Luke v. 8 f.; Isa. lx. 5.

20. Ἐγώ εἰμι] *It is I.* Comp.
iv. 26, viii. 24, 28, 58 (ix. 9),
xiii. 19, xviii. 5, 6, 8; Mark
xiii. 6; Luke xxi. 8.

The words ἐγώ εἰμι, μὴ φοβεῖσθε
are preserved in the three accounts. St. Matthew and St.
Mark add before them, θαρσεῖτε.
"Venit Jesus et venit quomodo?
Calcans fluctus: omnes tumores
mundi sub pedibus habens, omnes
celsitudines sæculi premens. Hoc
agitur quantum additur tem-
pori, et quantum accedit ætas
sæculi. Augentur in mundo
tribulationes, augentur mala,
augentur contritiones, exaggeran-
tur hæc omnia. Jesus transit,
calcans fluctus . . .
"Christo fluctus calcante,
sæculi ambitiones et altitudines
deprimente, expavescit Christianus" (Aug.).

21. ἤθελον . . . λαβεῖν] *voluerunt
accipere* v.; *they were willing to
take.* The imperfect expresses

a continuous state of feeling as
distinguished from an isolated
wish. It is commonly used of
a desire which is not gratified
(vii. 44, xvi. 19; Mark vi. 19,
48; Gal. iv. 20, etc.), but this
secondary idea does not necessarily lie in the word. In
Mark vi. 48 the same word is
used of the supposed purpose of
the Lord to "pass by" (ἤθελεν
παρελθεῖν) the disciples, which
was not fulfilled. Comp. Mark
xii. 38; Luke xii. 46. Fear
passed into joy. Comp. Luke
xxiv. 37 with John xx. 20.

ἐπὶ τ. γῆς] *ad terram* v. This
phrase may mean *in the direction
of the land,* that is, "moving
straight towards the land"; but
it more probably means *on the
land,* being used of the vessel
run up on the beach, so contrasted with ἐπὶ τῆς θαλάσσης.
Comp. Ps. cvii. (cvi.) 30. The
Synoptists notice that the opposing forces were removed
(Matt. xiv. 32; Mark vi. 51,
ἐκόπασεν ὁ ἄνεμος); St. John that
the desired end was gained. Both
results followed at once from the
presence of Christ welcomed.

ὑπῆγον] *ibant* v. The word is

πλοῖον, καὶ εὐθέως ἐγένετο τὸ πλοῖον ἐπὶ τῆς γῆς εἰς
ἦν ὑπῆγον.

22 Τῇ¹ ἐπαύριον ὁ ὄχλος ὁ ἑστηκὼς πέραν τῆς θαλάσσης
εἶδον ὅτι πλοιάριον ἄλλο οὐκ ἦν ἐκεῖ εἰ μὴ ἕν, καὶ ὅτι
οὐ συνεισῆλθεν τοῖς μαθηταῖς αὐτοῦ ὁ Ἰησοῦς εἰς τὸ
23 πλοῖον ἀλλὰ μόνοι οἱ μαθηταὶ αὐτοῦ ἀπῆλθον· ἀλλὰ

¹ For readings of א* in *vv.* 22—24 (*Inprimis memorabile est ἐπελθόντων,*
v. 23), see Tischendorf.

somewhat remarkable. Comp.
v. 67, vii. 33, note, xii. 11,
xviii. 8. The idea of "with-
drawing from," "leaving" something, seems to underlie it.

"Factus est finis ad terram ;
de humido ad solidum, de tur-
bato ad firmum, de itinere ad
finem" (Aug.).

It will be obvious that these
two "signs" are introductory
to the discourse which follows.
Both correct limited views springing out of our material conceptions. Effects are produced at
variance with our ideas of quantity and quality. That which is
small becomes great. That which
is heavy moves on the surface of
the water. Contrary elements
yield at a divine presence. Both
"signs," in other words, prepare
the way for new thoughts of
Christ, of His sustaining, preserving, guiding power, and exclude deductions drawn from
corporeal relations only. He
can support men, though visible
means fall short. He is with His
disciples, though they do not recognise or see Him. And in both cases
also the powers and action of men
are needed. They receive and
assimilate the food which is given;
they take Christ into their boat
before they reach their haven.

The remarks with which Au-

gustine opens his explanation
of the narrative are of permanent value. "Miracula quæ
fecit Dominus noster Jesus
Christus sunt quidem divina
opera et ad intellegendum Deum
de visibilibus admonent huma-
nam mentem . . . Nec tamen
sufficit hæc intueri in miraculis
Christi. Interrogemus ipsa miracula, quid nobis loquantur de
Christo : habent enim si intelle-
gantur linguam suam. Nam
quia ipse Christus Verbum Dei
est, etiam factum Verbi verbum
nobis est" (August. *In Johann.*
Tract. xxiv. i. 2).

The Discourses at Capernaum
(22—59)

The discourses which followed
the feeding of the five thousand
serve in part as an answer to
the mistaken expectations of the
multitude (*vv.* 14, 15), while they
unfold those views of Christ's
Person and work which became
a decisive trial for the faith of
the disciples who were already
attached to Him. The short
absence had been sufficient to
remove the fear of immediate
violence on the part of Herod ;
though it appears that the Lord
withdrew not long afterwards to
"the coasts of Tyre and Sidon"
(Matt. xv. 21 ff.).

and straightway the boat was on[1] the land whither they were going.

22 The next day the multitude which stood on the other side of the sea saw that there was none other boat there, save one, and that Jesus entered not with his disciples into the boat, but *that* his disciples went
23 away alone (howbeit there came boats from Tiberias

[1] *or* in the direction of.

The discourses fall into three groups: *vv.* 25—40, *vv.* 41—51, *vv.* 52—58. Each group is introduced by some expression of feeling on the part of those to whom the words are addressed, a simple question (*v.* 25), a murmuring (*v.* 41), a contention among themselves (*v.* 52). The thoughts successively dealt with are distinct: (1) the search after life, (2) the relation of the Son to the Father and to man, (3) the appropriation by the individual of the Incarnate Son; and it appears that the audience and place do not remain the same. There are evident breaks after *v.* 40, and *v.* 51. The "Jews" are introduced in *vv.* 41, 52, but not before. The last words were spoken "in synagogue" (*v.* 59), but it is scarcely conceivable that the conversation began there.

22—24. This long sentence is complicated and irregular in construction. The irregularity is due to the mention of two facts which are intercalated between the beginning and end of the sentence. The narrative would naturally have run: Τῇ ἐπαύριον ὁ ὄχλος ... ὅτε ... εἶδον (*v.* 24) ... ὅτι Ἰησ. οὐκ ἐστ. ἐκεῖ ... ἐνέβησαν ...; but St. John has inserted two explanatory clauses, the first to explain why they

still lingered on the eastern shore in the hope of finding Jesus: Τῇ ἐπαύριον ὁ ὄχλος ... εἶδον ὅτι πλοιαρ. ... εἰ μὴ ἓν καὶ ὅτι οὐ συνηλθ. Ἰησ. ... ἀλλὰ μον. οἱ μαθ. ...; and the second to explain how they were themselves able to cross over: ἀλλὰ ἦλθ. πλοῖα ἐκ Τιβερ. ... As a consequence he begins the sentence again in *v.* 24, ὅτε οὖν εἶδεν ὁ ὄχλος ..., where the εἶδεν is not a simple resumption of the εἶδον in *v.* 22, but the result of later observation.

22. ὁ ὄχλ. ὁ ἑστηκ.] *turba quæ stabat* v.; *the multitude which stood* ... , some, that is, who still lingered when the rest were dismissed (Matt. xiv. 23), the more eager zealots, as it seems, who wished still to make Christ fulfil their designs. They were not more than could cross the lake in the boats which came over (*v.* 23).

23. ἀλλὰ ἦλθεν πλοῖα] *aliæ vero supervenerunt naves.* .. v. These boats, perhaps, were driven by the "contrary wind" (Matt. xiv. 24) across the lake. Their coming probably explains the reference to the "disciples" in *v.* 24. At first the multitude might have supposed that they had returned in one of them from some brief mission to the other side.

ἦλθεν πλοῖα ἐκ Τιβεριάδος ἐγγὺς τοῦ τόπου ὅπου ἔφαγον
24 τὸν ἄρτον εὐχαριστήσαντος τοῦ κυρίου. ὅτε οὖν εἶδεν
ὁ ὄχλος ὅτι Ἰησοῦς οὐκ ἔστιν ἐκεῖ οὐδὲ οἱ μαθηταὶ
αὐτοῦ, ἐνέβησαν αὐτοὶ εἰς τὰ πλοιάρια καὶ ἦλθον εἰς
25 Καφαρναοὺμ ζητοῦντες τὸν Ἰησοῦν. καὶ εὑρόντες αὐτὸν
πέραν τῆς θαλάσσης εἶπον αὐτῷ Ῥαββεί, πότε ὧδε
26 γέγονας; ἀπεκρίθη αὐτοῖς ὁ Ἰησοῦς καὶ εἶπεν Ἀμὴν
ἀμὴν λέγω ὑμῖν, ζητεῖτέ με οὐχ ὅτι εἴδετε σημεῖα
27 ἀλλ᾽ ὅτι ἐφάγετε ἐκ τῶν ἄρτων καὶ ἐχορτάσθητε· ἐργάζεσθε μὴ τὴν βρῶσιν τὴν ἀπολλυμένην ἀλλὰ τὴν βρῶσιν

ἐγγ. τ. τοπ.] that is, to some unfrequented part of the shore, as driven by stress of weather.

εὐχαριστ. τοῦ κ.] gratias agente domino v. The significant act lived in the memory of those who saw it. For the use of ὁ κύριος comp. iv. 1, xi. 2, xxi. 7.

24. αὐτοί] they themselves. The force of the word is that they also did what they found the disciples had done.

25—40. The search after life.— The first part of the discourses consists of answers to successive questions (vv. 25, 28, 30, 34). The conversation is natural and rapid. It may be thus summarised:

25—27. The end of man spiritual. Man's effort, God's gift. The giver, true man.

28—29. The work of God— man's true service—is faith in a Person (the Son of man).

30—33. A new temptation. Establish your claim. The sign is in the gift itself. The gift is life and not support only.

34—35. The gift is the Giver: the perfect source of strength and joy.

36—40. The will of the Father

is fulfilled even in the face of unfaithfulness. This will is Life and Resurrection.

25. Ῥαββεί] i. 38, 50; iii. 2; iv. 31; ix. 2; xi. 8.

πότε;] "tam brevi tempore, tam longa via" (Bengel). The idea suggested by when, as contrasted with the more natural how, is that of the separation from Christ; as if the people had pleaded, "We sought thee long and anxiously on the other side. Could it be that even then thou hadst left us?" If this turn is given to the words the connexion is obvious: "It is not me ye seek, but my gifts."

The phrase ὧδε γέγονας (paraphrased by D. Latt, etc., ὧδε ἐλήλυθας) is remarkable. Comp. Acts xx. 16, xxi. 17, xxv. 15 γεν. εἰς.

26. ἀπεκρίθη] iv. 10 n.

ἀμὴν ἀμήν] * The phrase occurs again in this chapter, vv. 32, 47, 53. Each time it marks a critical revelation: (1) The right object of human endeavour is spiritual; (2) The true support of life is God's gift; (3) This

* Bp. Westcott has written "consider" at margin of this note.—A. W.

nigh unto the place where they ate the bread after
24 the Lord had given thanks): when the multitude
therefore saw that Jesus was not there, neither his
disciples, they themselves got into the boats, and
25 came to Capernaum, seeking Jesus. And when they
found him on the other side of the sea, they said
26 unto him, Rabbi, when camest thou hither? Jesus
answered them and said, Verily, verily, I say unto
you, Ye seek me, not because ye saw signs, but
27 because ye ate of the loaves, and were filled. Work
not for the meat which perisheth, but for the meat

support is Christ; (4) His life must be incorporated and assimilated by the believer.

οὐχ ὅτι εἰδ. σημ. . . .] *not because ye saw signs . . .*, not because my manifold works of healing (*v.* 2) and sustaining led you to look for other manifestations of spiritual glory. That one last miracle—a speaking sign—was to you a gross material satisfaction, and not a pledge, a parable of something higher. You failed to see in it the lesson which it was designed to teach, that I am waiting to relieve the hunger of the soul.

"Quæritis me propter aliud, quærite me propter me" (Aug.).

"Ad cor suum quisque nostrum redeat et interroget semetipsum, qua mente ad thronum vel mensam eius adeat, id est, quid desiderans ad sanctum eius altare accedat" (Rup.).

ἐχορτάσθητε] *saturati estis* v.; *were filled.* Literally, "were satisfied with food as animals with fodder." The word is different from that used in *v.* 12 (ἐνεπλήσθησαν). It is, however, used in connexion with the narrative in the other

Gospels (Matt. xiv. 20, and parallels) without any disparaging sense; and it is not therefore possible to press the material idea which predominates in it (Luke xv. 16, xvi. 21). See Matt. v. 6; Luke vi. 21.

27. ἐργαζ. μή . . .] *operamini non* . . . v.; *Work not for. . . .* The verb stands emphatically at the head of the sentence. "Work, yea win by work, not. . . ." Thus perhaps there is a contrast between "seeking" and "working." Comp. Isa. lv. 1 ff. The charge is present and personal (ἐργάζεσθε) and not general.

ἐργ. . . . δωσ.] The contrast of these verbs is essential to the sense of the passage. The believer's work does not earn a recompense at the last, but secures a gift. Even common work may bring more than its natural result, "the meat which perisheth." And no work brings more than the possibility of blessings to be used. Comp. i. 12 f., note.

τ. βρωσ. τ. ἀπολλ.] *cibum qui perit* v.; *the meat which perisheth;* that food which belongs to our

τὴν μένουσαν εἰς ζωὴν αἰώνιον, ἣν ὁ υἱὸς τοῦ ἀνθρώπου
ὑμῖν¹ δώσει, τοῦτον γὰρ ὁ πατὴρ ἐσφράγισεν ὁ θεύς.
28 εἶπον οὖν πρὸς αὐτόν Τί ποιῶμεν ἵνα ἐργαζώμεθα τὰ
29 ἔργα τοῦ θεοῦ; ἀπεκρίθη ὁ Ἰησοῦς καὶ εἶπεν αὐτοῖς
Τοῦτό ἐστιν τὸ ἔργον τοῦ θεοῦ ἵνα πιστεύητε εἰς ὃν
30 ἀπέστειλεν ἐκεῖνος. εἶπον οὖν αὐτῷ Τί οὖν ποιεῖς σὺ
σημεῖον, ἵνα ἴδωμεν καὶ πιστεύσωμέν σοι; τί ἐργάζῃ;

¹ ὑμῖν δώσει ABΓΔ ; δίδωσιν ὑμῖν ℵD.

material life; which supports life only by undergoing change; for material life is truly a process of death (comp. 1 Cor. vi. 13). It is possible too that there may be even at this point a reference to the manna: Exod. xvi. 20.

τ. βρωσ. τ. μεν. εἰς ζω. αἰων.] *qui permanet in vitam æternam* v.; *the meat which abideth unto eternal life*; that food which suffers no change, but remains in the man as a principle of power issuing in eternal life. Comp. iv. 14.

ὁ υἱ. τ. ἀνθρ.] This title suggests the thought which underlies the whole discourse. Christ is speaking of His relation to men in virtue of His perfect humanity. He, as the absolute representative of mankind, will give this food of the higher life—the life also being His gift, v. 25—*for Him the Father* (not *my Father, v.* 32), His Father and the Father of men, *sealed, even God* (ch. x. 36. See also v. 36 ff.). The title has not occurred in the Gospel since iii. 14.

δώσει] as the issue of His work (v. 51); or perhaps as the crown of your work of faith in Him. The issue is future. Comp. iv. 14 δώσω.

τοῦτον γάρ . . .] The assurance of the gift lies in the attestation

rendered to the Person of the Son.

ὁ πατ. . . . ὁ θεός] *The Father . . . even God.* The addition of the divine name at the close of the sentence emphasises the identification of God with "the Father" of "the Son of man." Comp. viii. 19.

ἐσφραγ.] *signavit* v.; *sealed*, solemnly set apart for the fulfilment of this charge and authenticated by intelligible signs. Comp. iii. 33, note. In the Jewish ritual the victims were examined and sealed if perfect (Mishn. *Shek.* i. 5). Perhaps the thought of Christ as an accepted sacrifice is already indicated by the term.

"Quo signo hunc signavit? Magno plane et reverendo signo, scilicet nomine suo. Dixit enim de hoc pane vivo et est nomen meum in illo" (Ex. xxiii. 21). (Rup.)

Theophylact develops the thought which is indicated by Rupert: Ἐπεὶ καὶ εἰκών ἐστι τοῦ πατρὸς ὁ υἱὸς καὶ σφράγισμα καὶ χαρακτήρ, νόει παρ᾽ αὐτοῦ σφραγισθῆναι τοῦτον καθ᾽ ὃ εἰκὼν καὶ σφράγισμά ἐστι.

"Sic filius hominis sum ut non sim unus ex vobis: sic sum filius hominis ut Deus pater me signaret. Quid est signare? pro-

which abideth unto eternal life, which the Son of
man shall give unto you : for him the Father sealed,
28 *even* God.   They said therefore unto him, What must
29 we do, that we may work the works of God?   Jesus
answered and said unto them, This is the work of
God, that ye believe on him whom he hath sent.
30 They said therefore unto him, What then doest thou

prium aliquid mihi dare, quo
non confunderer cum genere
humano sed per quem liberaretur
genus humanum" (Bede after
Aug.).   Οὐδέν ἐστιν ἄλλο τὸ
Ἐσφράγισεν ὁ πατήρ, ἀλλ' ἢ
ἀπέδειξεν, ἐξεκάλυψε διὰ τῆς αὐτοῦ
μαρτυρίας (Chrys.).

28. εἶπον οὖν ... Τί ...] The
questioners appear to admit in
word the necessity of the higher
aim of work, and inquire as to
the method of reaching it ; but
the phrase *work the works of
God*, when connected with something to be done—some visible
result—marks the external conception of the service of God
to which they still clung.   The
works of God—works which He
requires—are assumed to be the
one condition of obtaining the
spiritual food.

The phrase occurs in a different
sense c. ix. 3.

Τί ποιῶμεν] Contrast Τί ποιοῦ
μεν; xi. 47.

29. The Lord deals with the
error and the truth in the
question which was put to Him.
He substitutes " work " for
" works."   In the one work
which God requires of man and
man owes to God, all fragmentary
and partial works are included.
It is a true work as answering
to man's will, but it issues in
that which is not a work.   *This*

*is the work of God, that ye believe
on.* . . .   Comp. 1 John iii. 23 (*his
commandment*).

ἵνα πιστεύητε εἰς . . .] The
phrase marks not only the simple
fact of believing (τὸ πιστεύειν),
but the effort directed to and
issuing in this belief.   Here for
the first time in the Lord's words
is the phrase πιστ. εἰς used (not
iii. 15).   Comp. iv. 34, note.
And again it expresses not the
single decisive act (ἵνα πιστεύσητε,
xiii. 19), but the continuous state
of faith.

This simple formula contains
the complete solution of the relation of faith and works.   Faith
is the life of works ; works are
the necessity of faith.   The teaching of St. James and St. Paul is
thus brought to a full harmony.

It may be added, though the
connexion does not admit this
thought here, that there is a
true sense in which this " work "
is " a work of God," as inspired
and sustained by Him (Rom. xiv.
29) : " Noluit discernere ab opere
fidem . . . nec dixit *Hoc est opus
vestrum* sed *Hoc est opus Dei* . . .
ut qui gloriatur in Domino
glorietur " (Aug.).

30. εἰπ. οὖν . . .] *They said
therefore* . . . ; as recognising the
claim which Christ preferred, and
seeking an authentication of it.
The question becomes, as it were,

15

31 οἱ πατέρες ἡμῶν τὸ μάννα ἔφαγον ἐν τῇ ἐρήμῳ, καθώς
ἐστιν γεγραμμένον Ἄρτον ἐκ τοῦ οὐρανοῦ ἔδωκεν αὐτοῖς
32 φαγεῖν. εἶπεν οὖν αὐτοῖς ὁ Ἰησοῦς Ἀμὴν ἀμὴν λέγω
ὑμῖν, οὐ Μωυσῆς ἔδωκεν¹ ὑμῖν τὸν ἄρτον ἐκ τοῦ οὐρανοῦ,
ἀλλ᾽ ὁ πατήρ μου δίδωσιν ὑμῖν τὸν ἄρτον ἐκ τοῦ οὐρανοῦ

¹ ἔδωκεν BDL; δέδωκεν ℵΑΤΓΔ.

a new temptation, a suggestion for the exercise of power to justify the claim of "the prophet."

Τί οὖν ποιεῖς σὺ σ.;] *What then doest thou as a sign . . . ?* thou, with thy commands to us, peremptory as a second Moses? Moses, it is implied, imposed upon the fathers the yoke of the Law, but he justified his authority indeed. What then doest *thou*? Christ had charged the questioners with misunderstanding His signs before (*v.* 26); they ask therefore for some clear attestation of His claims. And in this there is nothing inconsistent with the effect which the feeding of the multitude had produced on some. Great as that work was, their history taught them to look for greater. They ask, as in the Synoptists, for "a sign from heaven" (Matt. xvi. 1).

ἵνα ἴδ. κ. πιστ.] In these words faith is treated as equivalent to simple belief in the truth of a message, and grounded upon the testimony of the senses. The "believing on Christ" (*v.* 29) is reduced to "believing Christ." Comp. viii. 30, 31, note.

τί ἐργάζῃ;] The words take up the demand made on themselves. There is a work, they plead, for the teacher as well as for the hearer. Thy claims on us are large and peremptory, but *what workest thou?* The question expresses what was suggested by the emphatic pronoun just before. Words must be justified by works. On what is the faith which you require to be rationally grounded?

"Attendebant eum plus promittentem et nondum videbant majora facientem" (Aug.).

"Tu promittis cibum . . . qui permanet in vitam æternam, et non talia operaris qualia Moyses. Panes hordeaceos ille non dedit sed manna de cælo" (Aug.).

31. τ. μάννα] *the manna* [Ps. lxxvii. (lxxviii.) 24.] The miracle which Christ had wrought suggested the greater miracle of Moses, by which the people were sustained for forty years. There was a tradition (*Midrash Koheleth*, p. 73, quoted by Lightfoot and Wünsche) that "as the first Redeemer caused the manna to fall from heaven, even so should the second Redeemer (גואל אחרון) cause the manna to fall." For this sign, then, or one like this, the people looked from Him whom they were ready to regard as Messiah. Compare Matt. xvi. 1; Mark viii. 11. The manna was a favourite subject with Jewish expositors. A single passage from Philo (*de Profugis*, § 25, p. 566) may serve as an example of their interpretations: "[When the people] sought what it is which feeds the soul, for they did not, as Moses says, know

as a sign, that we may see, and believe thee? what
31 workest thou? Our fathers ate the manna in the
wilderness; as it is written, He gave them bread out
32 of heaven to eat. Jesus therefore said unto them,
Verily, verily, I say unto you, It was not Moses that
gave you the bread out of heaven; but my Father

what it was, they discovered by learning that it is the utterance (ῥῆμα) of God and the divine word (θεῖος λόγος) from which all forms of instruction and wisdom flow in a perennial stream. And this is the heavenly food which is indicated in the sacred records under the Person of the First Cause (τοῦ αἰτίου) saying, Behold I rain on you bread (ἄρτους) out of heaven (Exod. xvi. 4). For in very truth God distils from above the supernal wisdom on noble and contemplative minds; and they when they see and taste, in great joy, know what they experience, but do not know the Power which dispenses the gift. Wherefore they ask, What is this which is sweeter than honey and whiter than snow? But they shall be taught by the prophet that this is the bread which the Lord gave them to eat" (Exod. xvi. 15). Comp. Siegfried, *Philo v. Alex.* s. 229. The reference to the manna shows the continued expectation of some material gift.

ἐκ τ. οὐρ.] *out of heaven* (33, 38, 50, 51, 58. Comp. 62), which came out of the heavenly treasures, and did not simply descend from a higher region.

"Majus fuit quod patres nostri manducaverunt manna in deserto, non panem de terra creatum sed de cælo datum, non quatuor aut quinque millia hominum sed exceptis parvulis et mulieribus sexcenta millia pugnatorum, non semel aut bis, sed totis quadraginta annis" (Rup.).

32. Ἀμὴν ἀμήν] *v.* 26.

οὐ Μωυσ. ἐδ. ὑμῖν τ. ἀρτ.] *Moses gave . . . not the bread.* There is a double contrast. It was not Moses but God revealing Himself through Moses who gave the manna (Exod. xvi.. 4, 15); and again the manna—the perishable bread — was not in the highest sense "bread from heaven," but rather the symbol of spiritual food.

The Jews had made no direct reference to Moses. The Lord meets the parallel which they had implicitly drawn.

ἔδωκεν ὑμ.] The people are identified with their ancestors. If the reading δέδωκεν be adopted, then the present realisation of what Moses gave in a symbol is assumed.

ὁ πατ. μ. δίδωσιν . . .] not in one miraculous act only, but now and at all times. Chrysostom contrasts the language with iv. 14: Οὐχ ὅτε τῇ Σαμαρείτιδι ὑπισχνεῖ τὸ δώσειν τὸ ὕδωρ ἐμνημόνευσε τοῦ πατρός . . .¹ ἐνταῦθα δὲ τοῦ πατρὸς| μέμνηται ἵνα μάθῃς πόση μὲν τῆς Σαμαρείτιδος ἡ πιστις πόση δὲ τῶν Ἰουδαίων ἡ ἀσθένεια.

τ. ἀρτ. . . . . τ. ἀληθινόν] that which fulfils absolutely, ideally,

33 τὸν ἀληθινόν· ὁ γὰρ ἄρτος τοῦ θεοῦ ἐστιν ὁ καταβαίνων
34 ἐκ τοῦ οὐρανοῦ καὶ ζωὴν διδοὺς τῷ κόσμῳ. εἶπον οὖν
πρὸς αὐτόν Κύριε, πάντοτε δὸς ἡμῖν τὸν ἄρτον τοῦτον.
35 εἶπεν ¹ αὐτοῖς ὁ Ἰησοῦς Ἐγώ εἰμι ὁ ἄρτος τῆς ζωῆς·
ὁ ἐρχόμενος πρὸς ἐμὲ οὐ μὴ πεινάσῃ, καὶ ὁ πιστεύων
36 εἰς ἐμὲ οὐ μὴ διψήσει πώποτε. ἀλλ᾽ εἶπον ὑμῖν ὅτι

¹ Insert δέ ΑΔ.   Insert οὖν ΝΔΓ.

the highest conception of sustaining food. Compare iv. 23, note. The exact form of the phrase is emphatic : *the bread out of heaven, the true* bread.

Λέγει δὲ ἑαυτὸν ἀληθινὸν ἄρτον οὐχ ὡς τοῦ μάννα ψευδοῦς ὄντος ἀλλ᾽ ἐπειδὴ ἐκεῖνος τύπος ἦν καὶ σκία καὶ οὐκ αὐτοαλήθεια (Theophylact).

33. ὁ ἀρτ. τ. θεοῦ] *the bread of God*, the bread which God gives directly ; not simply that which He gives by the hand of His servants. Comp. i. 29 (*the Lamb of God*), note.

ὁ καταβαιν.] *that which cometh down* . . . The support of the heavenly life must be itself of heaven. Christ does not identify Himself with "the bread" till the next answer ; and the request of the multitude which follows shows that nothing more than the notion of heavenly bread was present to them (comp. *vv.* 41, 50). This new manna was distinguished from the old in that it was continuous in its descent and not for a time ; and again it was not confined to one people, but was for the world.

καταβαιν.] The phrase prepares the way for the interpretation which follows, *vv.* 38, 41.

Οὐκ εἶπεν ἁπλῶς τροφὴν ἀλλὰ ζωήν (Chrys.). Men required

not only nourishment but quickening.

τ. κόσμῳ] *unto the world* and not to a fugitive race. Οὐκ Ἰουδαίοις μόνον ἀλλὰ καὶ πάσῃ τῇ οἰκουμένῃ (Chrys.). Without the Word, without Christ, the world can have no life. He makes the blessing, which was national, universal.

34. εἰπ. οὖν . . .] The multitude see in the words of Christ a mysterious promise which they cannot understand ; but they interpret it according to their material hopes. *Lord, evermore*, not on one rare occasion (Οὐ μίαν ἡμέραν οὐδὲ δύο. Theophylact), but always, *give us this bread.* They acknowledge that the gift must be continuous (1 Thess. v. 15, πάντοτε), though its effects are lasting, and they no longer address the new prophet as Rabbi (*v.* 25) but "Lord." Comp. iv. 15.

35. εἰπ. . . . . ὁ Ἰησ. . . .] *Jesus said* . . . The multitude asked for something from Christ : He offers them Himself. The great gift, if only it were rightly perceived, was already made.

Ἐγώ εἰμι . . .] This form of expression is not found in the Synoptists. It occurs not infrequently in St. John's Gospel, and the figures with which it is connected furnish a complete

33 giveth you the true bread out of heaven. For the bread of God is that which cometh down out of 34 heaven, and giveth life unto the world. They said therefore unto him, Lord, evermore give us this 35 bread. Jesus said unto them, I am the bread of life: he that cometh to me shall not hunger, and 36 he that believeth on me shall never thirst. But I

study of the Lord's work. Comp. vv. 41, 48, 51, viii. 12 (the Light of the world), x. 7, 9 (the Door), x. 11, 14 (the good Shepherd), xi. 25 (the Resurrection and the Life), xiv. 6 (the Way, the Truth, and the Life), xv. 1, 5 (the true Vine).

ὁ ἀρτ. τ. ζω.] *panis vitæ* v.; *the bread of life*; the food which supplies life: of which life is not a quality only (*v.* 51, ὁ ἀρτ. ὁ ζῶν), but (so to speak) an endowment which it is capable of communicating. Compare *the tree of life* (Gen. ii. 9, iii. 22, 24; Prov. iii. 18, xi. 30, xiii. 12, xv. 4; Rev. ii. 7, xxii. 2, etc.); *the water of life* (Rev. xxi. 6, xxii. 1, etc. Comp. Ps. xxxvi. (xxxv.) 9; Prov. x. 11, xiii. 14, xiv. 27, xvi. 22, fountain of life). The phrases "words (distinct utterances, sayings, ῥήματα) of life" (*v.* 68), and "the word (the whole revelation, λόγος) of life" (1 John i. 1) are nearly connected.

ὁ ἐρχ. . . . ὁ πιστ. . . .] The first word presents faith in deed as active and outward; the second presents faith in thought as resting and inward. Each element is, it is true, implied in the other, but they can be contemplated apart. For *coming to me* see v. 40, vv. (37), 44 f., 65, vii. 37.

οὐ μὴ πειν. . . . οὐ μὴ διψ.] *non esuriet . . . non sitiet unquam* v.; *shall never hunger . . . shall never thirst.* The double image, suggested it may be by the thought of the Passover, extends the conception of the heavenly food, and prepares the way for the double form under which it is finally described (*v.* 53). The gift of strength corresponds with the effort to reach to Christ; the gift of joy with the idea of repose in Christ.

οὐ μὴ διψήσει πώποτε] The exact form of expression is remarkable and irregular. (Contrast iv. 14, οὐ μὴ διψήσει εἰς τὸν αἰῶνα). Perhaps it suggests the image of Christ present in all time and regarding the unfailing satisfaction of those who come to Him as distinguished from a simple future.

πώποτε] i. 18, v. 37, viii. 33; 1 John ii. 12, Luke xix. 30. It is used again with future in 1 Sam. xxv. 28 (the only place in LXX.). Comp. [Dem.] p. 1115, 10 (MSS.). Thuc. ii. 12 (πώ).

36. ἀλλ᾽ . . .] The gift was indeed made, but the presence of the gift was unavailing, for the condition required of those who should receive it was unfulfilled.

εἶπον ὑμ. . . .] The thought is contained in *v.* 26, and the reference may be to those words;

37 καὶ ἑωράκατέ [με]¹ καὶ οὐ πιστεύετε. Πᾶν ὃ δίδωσίν
μοι ὁ πατὴρ πρὸς ἐμὲ ἥξει, καὶ τὸν ἐρχόμενον πρός με
38 οὐ μὴ ἐκβάλω ἔξω², ὅτι καταβέβηκα ἀπὸ³ τοῦ οὐρανοῦ
οὐχ ἵνα ποιῶ τὸ θέλημα τὸ ἐμὸν ἀλλὰ τὸ θέλημα τοῦ
39 πέμψαντός με· τοῦτο δέ ἐστιν τὸ θέλημα τοῦ πέμψαντός
με⁴ ἵνα πᾶν ὃ δέδωκέν μοι μὴ ἀπολέσω ἐξ αὐτοῦ ἀλλὰ
40 ἀναστήσω αὐτὸ⁵ τῇ ἐσχάτῃ ἡμέρᾳ. τοῦτο γάρ ἐστιν

¹ Omit με אA.   ² Omit ἔξω א*D.   ³ ἀπό ABLT ; ἐκ אΓΔ.
⁴ Insert πατρός ΓΔ.   ⁵ αὐτό אABCDKLᵖT ; αὐτόν EGL*ΓΔ.

but more probably the reference is to other words like them spoken at some earlier time.

ὅτι καὶ ἑωρακ. . . . καί . . .] The first καί emphasises the fact : *that ye have indeed seen and . . .* Comp. ix. 37. The Lord returns to the words in *v.* 30 (ἰδ. πιστ.), now that the question in *v.* 34 has been answered. He Himself was the sign which the Jews could not read. No other more convincing could be given.

37. There is a pause in the discourse before this verse. The unbelief of the people was not a proof that the purpose of God had failed. Rather it gave occasion for declaring more fully how certainly the Son carried out the Father's will.

Πᾶν ὅ . . . τ. ἐρχομ . . .] *omne quod . . . eum qui venit . . .* v.; *All that which . . . him that cometh . . .* The first clause is a general and abstract statement; the second gives the concrete and individual realisation of it. Believers are first regarded as forming a whole complete in its several parts, a gift of the Father; and then each separate believer is regarded in his personal relation to the Son. In the first case stress is laid upon

the successful issue of the coming, the arrival (ἥξει, *shall reach me*; comp. Matt. viii. 4 ; Heb. x. 37 ; Rev. iii. 3, xv. 4, xviii. 8) ; in the second case on the process of the coming (τὸν ἐρχόμενον, not τὸν ἐλθόντα) and the welcome.

The same contrast between the abstract conception and the concrete fulfilment of it is found in *vv.* 39 f. and xvii. 2. Comp. also the use of the abstract form, 1 John v. 4 contrasted with v. 5, 18 ; and ch. iii. 6 contrasted with iii. 8.

δίδωσίν] Compare xvii. 2, 6, 9, 12, 24, xviii. 9.

οὐ μή . . .] *in no wise . . .* The stern words to the Galilæans might have seemed to be a casting out, but the Lord shows that, on the contrary, they were not truly coming to Him.

ἐκβάλω] *ejiciam foras* v.; *cast out* ; from the house of God, the house of wisdom, Prov. ix. 1. Comp. xii. 31, ix. 34 f.

"Quale est intus illud unde non exitur foras ? Magnum penetrale et dulce secretum" (Aug., Bede).

38. ὅτι] *Because* this is the Father's will, as is implied in the gift (*v.* 39), and *I am come down . . .* (Contrast γάρ *v.* 40).

said unto you, that ye have seen me, and yet believe
37 not. All that which the Father giveth me shall come
unto me; and him that cometh to me I will in no
38 wise cast out. For I am come down from heaven,
not to do mine own will, but the will of him that
39 sent me. And this is the will of him that sent me,
that of all that which he hath given me I should
lose nothing, but should raise it up at the last day.
40 For this is the will of my Father, that every one
that beholdeth the Son, and believeth on him, should

καταβέβηκα] *I am come down to earth.* Comp. iii. 13; (Eph. iv. 9 f. ?). With these exceptions the word is used of Christ's descent only in this discourse.

ἀπὸ τ. οὐρ.] *from heaven.* In this verse the preposition (according to the true reading) expresses the idea of leaving, in *v.* 42 (as iii. 13) of proceeding out of (ἐκ). In the one case the thought is that of sacrifice; in the other that of divinity.

τὸ θελ. τὸ ἐμ.] See *v.* 19 ff. For the form see xv. 9, note.

39. ἵνα πᾶν . . .] *that of all* . . . The construction is broken: "that *as for all that which he has given me I should not lose of it.* . . ." Comp. vii. 38, (1 John ii. 24, 27), Luke xxi. 6.

δέδωκέν] The present used in *v.* 37 is here changed into the past when the gift is looked at in relation to the will of the Father, and not to the waiting of the Son.

μὴ ἀπολ. ἐξ αὐτ. ἀλ. ἀναστήσω] *non perdam ex eo sed resuscitem* v.; *should lose nothing, but should raise it up;* filled with a new life, transfigured and glorified. This is the issue of the communi-

cation of Christ to the Church. In this place the effect is represented as dependent on the Father's will; but when the words are repeated (*vv.* 40, 44, 54)—once in each great division of the discourses—the effect is referred to the will of the Son (*and I will raise him up*). Comp. xii. 24.

ἐν ἐσχ. ἡμ.] *in novissimo die* v.; *at the last day.* The phrase is found only in St. John, *vv.* 40, 44, 54, xi. 24, xii. 48. Comp. 1 John ii. 18. The plural occurs Acts ii. 17; James v. 3; 2 Tim. iii. 1. Comp. *v.* 28 (ὥρα).

40. τοῦτο γὰρ ἐστ. τ. θελ. τ. πατ. μ.] The general fulfilment of the will of the Father passes into this further truth, that the contemplation of the Son and belief on Him brings with it eternal life.

ὁ θεωρ. τ. υἱ.] *that beholdeth the Son.* Comp. xii. 45, xiv. 19, xvi. 10, 16, 19. The act of contemplation and faith is not momentary or past, but continuous.

"Non dixit Vidit Filium et credit in Patrem. Hoc est enim credere in Filium quod et in Patrem" (Bede).

τὸ θέλημα τοῦ πατρός μου¹ ἵνα πᾶς ὁ θεωρῶν τὸν υἱὸν
καὶ πιστεύων εἰς αὐτὸν ἔχῃ ζωὴν αἰώνιον, καὶ ἀναστήσω
41 αὐτὸν ἐγὼ τῇ ἐσχάτῃ ἡμέρᾳ. Ἐγόγγυζον οὖν οἱ Ἰουδαῖοι
περὶ αὐτοῦ ὅτι εἶπεν Ἐγώ εἰμι ὁ ἄρτος ὁ καταβὰς ἐκ
42 τοῦ οὐρανοῦ, καὶ ἔλεγον Οὐχὶ² οὗτός ἐστιν Ἰησοῦς ὁ
υἱὸς Ἰωσήφ, οὗ ἡμεῖς οἴδαμεν τὸν πατέρα καὶ τὴν

¹ τοῦ πατρός μου ℵBCDLT; τοῦ πέμψαντός με AEGΓΔ.
² οὐχί BT; οὐχ ℵACDLΓΔ.

ἐχ. ζω. αἰων.] have eternal life;
not as future, but as present
already as a divine power before
resurrection. Comp. v. 47, xvii. 3.

The possession of eternal life
is followed by the crowning action
of the Son : and I—I the Incarnate Son—will raise him up.
" Reddam quod sperat : videbit
quod adhuc non videndo credidit."
Eternal life is consummated in
the restoration to the believer
of a transfigured manhood. So
far from the doctrine of the
Resurrection being, as has been
asserted, inconsistent with St.
John's teaching on the present
reality of eternal life, it would
be rather true to say that this
doctrine makes the necessity of
the Resurrection obvious. He
who feels that life is now, must
feel that after death all that belongs to the essence of its present
perfection must be restored, however much ennobled under new
conditions of manifestation.

" Ille Deus factus est homo :
tu, homo, cognosce quia es homo :
tota humilitas tua ut cognoscas
te " (Aug.).

2. The union of the Son with the
Father and with man (41—51)

The second part of the discourses, which deals with the
relation of Christ to God and to
man, is directly connected both
with the first and with the third
part : with the first by the
reiteration of the office of the
Son (v. 44), and with the third
by the reference to Christ's
" flesh " (v. 51). It touches on
the greatest mysteries of Christ's
life, the Incarnation and the
Atonement (vv. 42, 51), and the
greatest mysteries of man's life,
the concurrence of the divine and
human will, and the permanence
of life (vv. 44, 45, 47 ff.). It is
briefly an answer to the question,
How can the spring and support
of life be in Christ, who is truly
man ?

It may be summarised as
follows :

41, 42. The difficulty. How
can He who is man be the source
and support of life ? unite heaven
and earth ?

43, 44. The solution can be
received only through spiritual
fellowship. There are higher
than human relationships.

45, 46. This truth is recognised
in the Old Testament, and fulfilled in the Son of man, through
whom alone the answer comes.

47—50. The answer repeated
and enlarged. . . . Man has a
work. Man himself must co-
operate and receive by faith the
divine gift.

have eternal life; and I will raise him up at the
41 last day. The Jews therefore murmured concerning
him, because he said, I am the bread which came
42 down out of heaven. And they said, Is not this
Jesus, the son of Joseph, whose father and mother
we know? how doth he now say, I am come down

51. The gift of Christ is life:
life through His "flesh," the
fulness of His humanity.

41. This verse seems to mark
the presence of new persons and
a new scene, as well as a new
stage in the history. The verses
37—40 were probably addressed
specially to the immediate circle
of the disciples. Thus we can
understand how the Jews dwelt
on the words in which Christ
identified Himself with the true
spiritual food of the world, while
they took no notice of the loftier
prerogatives which followed from
this truth, since the exposition
of these was not directed to
them.

Ἐγόγγυζον οὖν οἱ Ἰουδ.] *murmur-
abant ergo Judaei* v.; *The Jews
therefore . . .*, the representatives
of the dominant religious party,
full of the teaching of the schools,
murmured concerning him, half
in doubt (vii. 32, [12]) and half
in dissatisfaction (*v.* 61; Luke v.
30). These murmurings probably
found expression for some little
time before they were answered.
There is nothing to show that
they were first uttered in Christ's
presence.

Ἐγώ εἰμ. ὁ ἄρτ. ὁ καταβ. ἐκ τ.
οὐρ.] The exact phrase does not
occur in the previous record;
but it is a fair combination of
the three phrases in which the
Lord had described Himself: *the*

bread of God is that which cometh
down from heaven (*v.* 33); *I am
the bread of life* (*v.* 35); *I have
come down from heaven* (*v.* 38).

42. Οὐχὶ οὗτος . . .;] There is
perhaps a tinge of contemptuous
surprise in the pronoun as in
v. 52, vii. 15, iii. 26, though it
does not necessarily lie in the
word, iv. 14, ix. 33, etc.

ὁ υἱ. Ἰωσ.] i. 46. Comp.
Luke iv. 22; Matt. xiii. 54 ff.

ἡμ. οἴδ.] The pronoun is emphatic: *whose father we*, directly
in the way of our ordinary life
without any further inquiry
(comp. vii. 27), *know* . . . There
was (so they argue from their
point of view) no room for mistake upon the matter. The word
know expresses simply acquaintance with the fact that Joseph
was in popular esteem the father
of Jesus, and not personal acquaintance with him as still
living.

πῶς νῦν λέγει;] *quomodo ergo
dicit?* v.; *how doth he now say—
now*, at last, when for so long
he has lived as one of ourselves?
For πῶς; see iii. 4, 9, vi. 52,
xii. 34. Ὅταν ἡ ζήτησις τοῦ πῶς
εἰσέλθῃ συνεισέρχεται καὶ ἡ ἀπιστία
(Ammon *ap.* Cr. *Cat.*).

Ἐκ τ. οὐρ. καταβέβ.] See *v.* 38,
note.

The order of the words is
changed, and the emphasis is
thrown on "out of heaven." This

μητέρα; πῶς νῦν¹ λέγει² ὅτι Ἐκ τοῦ οὐρανοῦ κατα-
43 βέβηκα; ἀπεκρίθη Ἰησοῦς καὶ εἶπεν αὐτοῖς Μὴ
44 γογγύζετε μετ' ἀλλήλων. οὐδεὶς δύναται ἐλθεῖν πρός
με³ ἐὰν μὴ ὁ πατὴρ ὁ πέμψας με ἑλκύσῃ αὐτόν, κἀγὼ
45 ἀναστήσω αὐτὸν ἐν⁴ τῇ ἐσχάτῃ ἡμέρᾳ. ἔστιν γεγραμμένον ἐν τοῖς προφήταις Καὶ ἔσονται πάντες διδακτοὶ

¹ νῦν BCT; οὖν אADLΓΔ.   ³ ἐμέ BEΔ.
² Insert οὗτος אAΓΔ.   ⁴ Omit ἐν אΔ.

order, which has not occurred before, is preserved afterwards: 50, 51, 58 (contrast 33, 41).

43. ἀπεκρ. Ἰησ.] The answer corresponds in some way with that given to Nicodemus (iii. 3). The false claim to knowledge, and the assertion of unsubstantial objections, are both met in the same manner. The Jews were unable to understand the divine descent of the Lord, which seemed irreconcilable with His actual circumstances. He replies that a spiritual influence is necessary before His true Nature can be discerned, and that such influence was promised by the prophets as one of the characteristic blessings of the Messianic age.

μετ' ἀλλήλων] We must turn to some higher authority for the solution of such questions. As long as men keep within their own circle they can find no satisfaction.

44. οὐδ. δυν. . . . ἐὰν μὴ ὁ πατ. . . . ἑλκ.] Comp. v. 40, οὐ θελ. ἐλθ. πρός με. The objection which was drawn from assumed human fatherhood is such suggestively. The Lord leads His opponents to consider higher relations : "Hoc plane majus est quam Joseph . . . Immo et omni homine hoc majus est" (Rup.). But he speaks of "the Father" and not directly of "my Father."

As in all similar cases, this "coming to Christ" may be regarded from its human side, as dependent on man's will; or from its divine side, as dependent on the power of God. So St. Bernard remarks in connexion with these words: "nemo quippe salvatur invitus" (de Grat. et Lib. Act. xi.). Yet even the will itself comes from a divine nature, a divine gift (ch. i. 12 f., iii. 7 ff., viii. 47, vi. 65). The "drawing" of the Father is best illustrated by the "drawing" of the Son, xii. 32. The constraining principle is love stirred by self-sacrifice, a love which calls out, and does not destroy, man's freedom and issues in self-sacrifice. The mission of the Son by the Father (ὁ πέμψας με), the sovereign act of love (iii. 16), is thus brought into close connexion with the power exerted by the Father on men. Augustine (ad loc.) puts the thought most forcibly : "Noli te cogitare invitum trahi: trahitur animus et amore. . . . 'Trahit sua quemque voluptas;' non trahit revelatus Christus a Patre? Quid enim fortius desiderat anima quam veritatem?" Comp. v. 68.

"Attrahi ad Christum panem vivum et verum id est esurire et sitire justitiam . . ." (Rup.)

43 out of heaven?   Jesus answered and said unto them,
44 Murmur not among yourselves.   No man can come
to me, except the Father which sent me draw him:
45 and I will raise him up in the last day.   It is written
in the prophets, And they shall all be taught of God.
Every one that hath heard from the Father, and

" Hæc attractio non minus Filii quam Patris gratiæ opus est": xii. 32 (Rup.).

οὐδεὶς δυν.] This divine impossibility is the expression of a moral law. It is not anything arbitrary, but inherent in the very nature of things; it does not limit but it defines the nature of human power. Comp. v. 19 (note), 30 (of the Son), xii. 39, note.

ἐλθεῖν] Here and in v. 65 the "coming" is regarded as complete, and not in progress as in v. 37, vii. 37 (ἐρχέσθω).

ἐλκύσῃ] traxerit v. Comp. Jer. xxxviii. (xxxi.) 3 (LXX.).

κἀγώ . . .] The Son takes up and completes what the Father has begun. The believer is brought to the Son by the action of the Father; and the Son brings him to the end of his redeemed manhood. The change in the position of the pronoun slightly modifies the force of this repeated clause. In v. 40 the believer and Christ are placed in remarkable juxtaposition (ἀναστήσω αὐτὸν ἐγώ, him, I); here the I stands first with a reference to the whole preceding clause (καὶ ἐγὼ ἀναστήσω αὐτόν).

45. The "drawing" of the Father is illustrated by a prophetic promise. And under this new image of "teaching" the power is seen in its twofold as-

pect; the divine and human elements are combined. The "hearing" brings out the external communication, the learning the internal understanding of it. "Nisi ergo revelet ille qui intus est, quid dico aut quid loquor? Exterior cultor arboris, interior est Creator. . . . Videte quomodo trahit Pater: docendo delectat non necessitatem imponendo" (Aug.).

"In the present world the Torah is given to men for their own study; in the world to come God Himself will teach it to all Israel and they shall no more forget it" (Pesikta 107a; comp. Weber, p. 360).

Comp. Barn. xiv., and xx. 22, note.

ἔστιν γεγρ.] v. 31, xii. 14, x. 34, xx. 30 (οὐκ ἔστι γεγρ.); ii. 17, γεγρ. ἐστίν; γέγραπται viii. 17.

ἐν τ. προφ.] in the prophets, i.e. in the division of the Scriptures which is so called. Comp. Acts xiii. 40, vii. 42 (Βίβλον τ. προφητῶν); ch. i. 45, note. The phrase is found substantially in Isa. liv. 13; and the central idea of it is the promise of direct divine teaching. Thus the emphasis lies on "taught of God" and not on "all." This teaching lies for us in the Person and Work of Christ interpreted by the Spirit.

θεοῦ· πᾶς ὁ ἀκούσας παρὰ τοῦ πατρὸς καὶ μαθὼν
46 ἔρχεται πρὸς ἐμέ¹. οὐχ ὅτι τὸν πατέρα ἑώρακέν τις εἰ
μὴ ὁ ὢν παρὰ [τοῦ]² θεοῦ, οὗτος ἑώρακεν τὸν πατέρα.
47 ἀμὴν ἀμὴν λέγω ὑμῖν, ὁ πιστεύων³ ἔχει ζωὴν αἰώνιον.
48/49 ἐγώ εἰμι ὁ ἄρτος τῆς ζωῆς· οἱ πατέρες ὑμῶν ἔφαγον
50 ἐν τῇ ἐρήμῳ τὸ μάννα καὶ ἀπέθανον· οὗτός ἐστιν ὁ
ἄρτος ὁ ἐκ τοῦ οὐρανοῦ καταβαίνων ἵνα τις ἐξ αὐτοῦ
51 φάγῃ καὶ μὴ ἀποθάνῃ⁴· ἐγώ εἰμι ὁ ἄρτος ὁ ζῶν ὁ ἐκ

¹ θεόν א*D.   ² Omit τοῦ B.   ³ Insert εἰς ἐμέ ACDΓΔ.   ⁴ ἀποθνήσκῃ B.

διδακτοὶ Θεοῦ] *docibiles Dei* v.
Comp. 1 Cor. ii. 13 ; 1 Thess.
iv. 9 (θεοδίδακτοι). Barn. xxi. 6,
γίνεσθε δὲ θεοδίδακτοι. The phrase
describes not only one divine
communication, but a divine relationship. Believers are lifelong pupils in the school of God
("ה ידומל, Isaiah, *l.c.* Comp. Isa.
viii. 16).

πᾶς ὁ ἀκουσ. . . . . κ. μαθών]
Every one that heareth . . . *and
learneth* . . . The fulfilment of
the promise is followed by its
proper consequence. The message is given and it is apprehended. Both the divine and
the human elements are recognised. The "hearing" and
"learning" are presented as
single events corresponding with
a definite voice and revelation.
The call is obeyed at once, though
it may be fulfilled gradually ; the
fact of the revelation is grasped
at once, though it may be apprehended in detail little by little.

παρὰ τ. πατ.] the message which
comes *from the Father.* Comp.
i. 40, vii. 51, viii. 26, 40, xv. 15.

46. But there is a danger of
a limited and material interpretation of the prophetic word.
Though the revelation made by
the Father is direct in one sense,

yet it must not be understood to
be immediate. "Hearing" and
"learning" fall short of seeing.
The Father is seen only by the
Son (i. 18. Comp. Matt. xi. 27,
and parallels). He alone who
is truly God can naturally see
God. The voice of God came to
men under the Old Covenant, but
in Christ the believer can now
see the Father (xiv. 9) in part,
and will hereafter see God as He
is (1 John iii. 2).

ὁ ὢν παρά . . .] *he which is
from.* Comp. vii. 29, ix. 16, 33
(Contrast ἦν πρός). The phrase
implies not only mission (xvi.
27 f. παρὰ τ. πατ. ἐξῆλθον), but
also a present relation of close
dependence.

ἑώρακεν] *he hath seen,* when
He was "with God" (i. 1) before
He "became flesh." The words
mark emphatically the un-
changed personality of Christ
before and after the Incarnation. The substitution τ. θεόν
for τ. πατέρα in some early texts
(א*D) is a kind of gloss which
is not infrequent in the group.

47. At this point the discourse
takes a fresh start. Ἀμὴν ἀμήν
(*v.* 26, note). The objection of
the Jews has been met, and the
Lord goes on to develop the

46 hath learned, cometh unto me. Not that any man
hath seen the Father, save he which is from God,
47 he hath seen the Father. Verily, verily, I say unto
48 you, He that believeth hath eternal life. I am the
49 bread of life. Your fathers did eat the manna in
50 the wilderness, and they died. This is the bread
which cometh down out of heaven, that a man may
51 eat thereof, and not die. I am the living bread

idea set forth in *vv.* 35, 36, taking up the last word: *He that believeth* (omit *on me*, the phrase stands absolutely) *hath eternal life.* The actual existence of true faith implies the right object of it. Comp. iii. 3, note.

ἔχει] See *v.* 40, note.

"Compendio dicere potuit, Qui credit in me habet me" (Aug.).

48—51. There is a close parallelism and contrast between *vv.* 48—50 and 51. *The bread of life: the living bread—which cometh down . . . that: which came down; if . . . may . . . not die: shall live for ever.* In the first case the result is given as part of the divine counsel (*that cometh down, that* [ἵνα] . . .); in the second as a simple historical consequence (*came down . . . if a man . . .*).

48. ἐγώ εἰμι . . .] See *v.* 35, note.

49. οἱ πατ. ὑμ. ἔφαγ . . . κ. ἀπέθανον] *Your fathers ate the manna . . . and died.* The words are quoted from the argument of the Jews, *v.* 31. The heavenly food under the Old Dispensation could not avert death. This then was not *bread of life*, even in the sphere to which it belonged. Comp. iv. 13.

Τὸ ἐν τῇ ἐρήμῳ οὐχ ἁπλῶς τέθεικεν ἀλλ᾽ αἰνιττόμενος ὅτι οὐδὲ ἐξετάθη ἐπὶ χρόνον πολὺν οὐδὲ συν-

εισῆλθεν εἰς τὴν τῆς ἐπαγγελίας γῆν (Chrys.).

Philo, *Leg. Alleg.* iii. § 60 (i. p. 121): Ἡ ψυχὴ γανωθεῖσα πολλάκις εἰπεῖν οὐκ ἔχει τί τὸ γανῶσαν αὐτήν ἐστι διδάσκεται δὲ ὑπὸ τοῦ ἱεροφάντου καὶ προφήτου Μωϋσέως, ὃς ἐρεῖ οὗτός ἐστιν ὁ ἄρτος, ἡ τροφὴ ἣν ἔδωκεν ὁ θεὸς τῇ ψυχῇ (Ex. xvi. 15), προσενέγκασθαι τὸ ἑαυτοῦ ῥῆμα καὶ τὸν ἑαυτοῦ λόγον· οὗτος γὰρ ὁ ἄρτος ὃν δέδωκεν ἡμῖν φαγεῖν, τοῦτο τὸ ῥῆμα.

50. οὗτός ἐστ. ὁ ἄρτ. ὁ . . . καταβαιν. ἵνα . . .] *hic est panis . . . descendens ut . . .* v.; *This* bread —the true manna—*is the bread which cometh . . . that.* . . . It is best to take *this* [*bread*] as the subject (*v.* 48, *I am the bread of life,* further defined in *v.* 51), and *the bread which cometh down from heaven* as the predicate; compare *vv.* 33, 58. The interpretation which makes οὗτός the predicate (*the bread which cometh . . . is this,* that is, is of such a nature, *that* . . .) appears to destroy the connexion.

μὴ ἀποθάνῃ] Comp. viii. 51, note; Gen. iii. 22.

51. ἐγώ εἰμι. ὁ ἄρτ. ὁ ζῶν] *ego sum panis vivus* v.; *I am the living bread,* able to communicate the life which I possess. He therefore who receives me receives a principle of life. Cf.

τοῦ οὐρανοῦ καταβάς· ἐάν τις φάγῃ ἐκ τούτου τοῦ
ἄρτου ζήσει εἰς τὸν αἰῶνα, καὶ ὁ ἄρτος δὲ ὃν ἐγὼ
δώσω ἡ σάρξ μου ἐστὶν¹ ὑπὲρ² τῆς τοῦ κόσμου ζωῆς.
52 Ἐμάχοντο οὖν πρὸς ἀλλήλους οἱ Ἰουδαῖοι λέγοντες
Πῶς δύναται οὗτος ἡμῖν δοῦναι τὴν σάρκα [αὐτοῦ]³

¹ Insert ἣν ἐγὼ δώσω ΓΔ.
² ℵ transposes ὑπ. τ. τ. κοσ. ζω. to after δώσω. See note.
³ Omit αὐτοῦ ℵCDLΓΔ.

iv. 10 f. τὸ ὕδωρ τὸ ζῶν; Acts vii.
38 λόγια ζῶντα; Rom. xii. 1
θυσίαν ζῶσαν; 1 Peter i. 3 εἰς
ἐλπίδα ζῶσαν, ii. 4 λίθον ζ. (Heb.
iv. 12).

ὁ ἐκ τ. οὐρ. κατ.] iii. 13. With
this exception the phrase, as
applied to the Lord, is peculiar
to this chapter (comp. Eph. iv. 9).

ζησ. εἰς τὸν αἰ.] vivet in œ-
ternum v. The phrase only occurs
here and in v. 58. Comp. Rev.
iv. 9 f.; x. 6; xv. 7.

καί ... δέ] yea and (and in fact)
the bread. . . .   Comp. viii. 16 f.,
xv. 27; 1 John i. 3.

ὁ ἄρτ. . . . ὃν ἐγὼ δώσω] The
pronoun is emphatic, and brings
out the contrast between Christ
and Moses. At the same time
a passage is made from the
thought of Christ as the living
bread (ἐγὼ εἰμι) to the thought
of the participation in Him
(δώσω). This participation is
spoken of as still future, since
it followed in its fulness on the
completed work of Christ. There
is also a difference indicated here
between that which Christ is
and that which He offers. He is
truly God and truly man (ἐγώ);
He offers His "flesh," His perfect
humanity, for the life of the
world.

ἡ σάρξ μου] caro mea v.; my
flesh. "Flesh" describes human
nature in its totality regarded

from its earthly side. Comp. i.
14. See also i. 13, iii. 6, vi. 63,
viii. 15, xvii. 2; 1 John ii. 16,
iv. 2; 2 John 7; Rom. viii. 3;
1 Tim. iii. 16; Heb. v. 7. The
thought of death lies already in
the word, but that thought is
not as yet brought out, as afterwards by the addition of αἷμα.
Comp. Eph. ii. 14 ff.; Col. i. 22;
1 Pet. iii. 18.

The life of the world in the
highest sense springs from the
Incarnation and Resurrection of
Christ. By His Incarnation
and Resurrection the ruin and
death which sin brought in are
overcome. The thought here is
of support and growth, and not
of atonement (I lay down my life
for . . . x. 11, 15, note). The
close of the earthly life, the end
of the life which is, in one aspect,
of self for self, opens wider relations of life. Comp. xii. 24.
At this point no more than the
general truth is stated. It is
not yet indicated how the "flesh"
of Christ, the virtue of His
humanity, will be communicated
to and made effectual for mankind or men. That part of the
subject is developed in the last
division of the whole argument.

ἡ σάρξ μου ... ὑπὲρ τ. ... ζωῆς]
my flesh for the life ... For this
shortened form compare 1 Cor.
xi. 24. The omission of the

which came down out of heaven: if any man eat
of this bread, he shall live for ever: yea and the
bread which I will give is my flesh, for the life
52 of the world. The Jews therefore strove one with
another, saying, How can this man give us his flesh

clause (ὅν (א) ἤν (ΓΔ) ἐγω δώσω)
which I will give turns the attention to the general action of
Christ's gift rather than to the
actual making of it. The special
reference to the future Passion
would distract the thought at
this point, where it is concentrated upon the Incarnation and
its consequences generally. See
Additional Note.

τοῦ κόσμου] iii. 17, iv. 42.

"O sacramentum pietatis! O
signum unitatis! O vinculum
caritatis! Qui vult vivere habet
ubi vivat, habet unde vivat. Accedat, credat: incorporetur ut
vivificetur. . . . Vivat Deo de
Deo. Nunc laboret in terra ut
postea regnet in cælo" (Aug.).

3. *The personal appropriation of the Incarnate Son* (52—59)

This last section of the teaching on "the true bread from
heaven" carries forward the conceptions given in *vv.* 41—51 to
a new result. The question
before was as to the Person of
the Lord: "Is not this the son
of Joseph?" The question now
is as to the communication of that
which He gives: "How can this
man give us his flesh to eat?"
How can one truly man impart
to others his humanity, so that
they may take it to themselves
and assimilate it? The answer
is in this case also not direct but
by implication. The fact, and
the necessity of the fact, dispense

with the need for further inquiry.
The life is a reality.

The whole section may be thus
summarised:

52. New difficulty. How can
one man give himself to another?

53—55. The gift is necessary,
and life can be given through
death. So the Lord's humanity
is made available and becomes
efficacious.

56, 57. By sharing Christ's
humanity the believer has perfect
fellowship with Him. The relation of the believer to the Son
corresponds with the relation of
the Son to the Father.

58. Here, then, the sign of the
Exodus finds fulfilment. Men
have the food which is life.

52. Ἐμαχ. οὖν πρὸς ἀλληλ. οἱ
Ἰουδ.] *The Jews* (*v.* 41, note) . . .
strove one with another (iv. 33,
xvi. 17). They did not all reject
at once the teaching of Christ.
There were divisions among them;
and they discussed from opposite
sides the problem raised by the
last mysterious words which they
had heard (comp. vii. 12, 40 ff.,
x. 19 ff.). It is important to
notice how the Evangelist records
the varying phases of contemporary feeling. "The Jews"
were not yet all of one mind.

Ἐμάχοντο] *Litigabant* v.; 2
Tim. ii. 24; James iv. 2. So
μάχη, 2 Tim. ii. 23, etc.

Πῶς δυν. . . . ;] The old question (iii. 4, 9), which is again
left without an explicit answer.

53 φαγεῖν ; εἶπεν οὖν αὐτοῖς [ὁ]¹ Ἰησοῦς Ἀμὴν ἀμὴν
λέγω ὑμῖν, ἐὰν μὴ φάγητε τὴν σάρκα τοῦ υἱοῦ τοῦ
ἀνθρώπου καὶ πίητε αὐτοῦ τὸ αἷμα, οὐκ ἔχετε ζωὴν ἐν
54 ἑαυτοῖς. ὁ τρώγων μου τὴν σάρκα καὶ πίνων μου τὸ
αἷμα ἔχει ζωὴν αἰώνιον, κἀγὼ ἀναστήσω αὐτὸν τῇ

¹ Omit ὁ B.

The simple reassertion of the fact is opposed both in a negative (v. 53) and in a positive statement to the difficulty as to the manner.

ἡμῖν] us who are living with Him, men as He is man. For the order see xiv. 22, xviii. 31; 1 John iii. 24.

φαγεῖν] ad manducandum v. The Jews transfer directly to "the flesh" what hitherto, as far as our record goes, has been said only of "the bread," now identified with it. There is no gross misunderstanding on their part, but a clear perception of the claim involved in the Lord's words. Comp. iii. 4, iv. 15, viii. 33. See also Num. xi. 13.

Compare Philo, Leg. Alleg. i. 31 (i. p. 63): Τὸ φαγεῖν σύμβολόν ἐστι (referring to Gen. ii. 16) τροφῆς ψυχικῆς· τρέφεται δὲ ἡ ψυχὴ ἀναλήψει τῶν καλῶν καὶ πράξει τῶν κατορθωμάτων.

53. The thought indicated in v. 51 is now developed in detail. The "flesh" is presented in its twofold aspect as "flesh" and "blood," and by this separation of its parts the idea of a violent death is presupposed. Further "the flesh" and "the blood" are described as "the flesh" and "the blood" "of the Son of man," by which title the representative character of Christ is marked in regard to that

humanity which He imparts to the believer. And once again both elements are to be appropriated individually ("eat," "drink"). By the "flesh" in this narrower sense we must understand the virtue of Christ's humanity as living for us; by the "blood" the virtue of His humanity as subject to death. The believer must be made partaker in both. The Son of man lived for us and died for us, and communicates to us the effects of His life and death as perfect man. Without this communication of Christ men can have "no life in themselves." But Christ's gift of Himself to a man becomes in the recipient a spring of life within. Comp. iv. 14.

εἰπ. οὖν . . . ὁ Ἰησ. . . .] Meeting the difficulty which was raised by an appeal to what is really a fact of experience. He draws out in its fulness what they had expressed generally. The believer must not "eat the flesh" only, which was the difficulty raised, but he must "drink the blood" of the Son of man. By this addition the Lord indicates generally how one man can give himself for another, by dying for him.

φαγ. . . . πιη. . . .] To "eat" and to "drink" is to take to oneself by a voluntary act that which is external to oneself, and

53 to eat ?   Jesus therefore said unto them, Verily,
verily, I say unto you, Except ye eat the flesh of
the Son of man and drink his blood, ye have not
54 life in yourselves.   He that eateth my flesh and
drinketh my blood hath eternal life ; and I will raise

then to assimilate it and make
it part of oneself. It is, as it
were, faith regarded in its converse action. Faith throws the
believer upon and into its object;
this spiritual eating and drinking
brings the object of faith into
the believer.

πιη. αὐτ. τ. αἰ.] The phrase is
unique in the New Testament.
To Jewish ears it could not but
be full of startling mystery. The
thought is that of the appropriation of "life sacrificed."
St. Bernard expresses part of it
very well when he says . . . hoc
est si compatimini conregnabitis
(*De dil. Deo*, IV.). Compare
In Psalm. III. 3, "Quid autem
est manducare eius carnem et
bibere sanguinem nisi communi-
care passionibus eius et eam
conversationem imitari quam
habuit in carne ? "

ἐν ἑαυτ.] *in vobis* v. ; *in yourselves.* Compare v. 26; Matt. xiii.
21. Without the Son men have
no life ; for in men themselves
there is no spring of life. Even
to the last their life is "in Christ"
and not "in themselves."

"Hujus rei sacramentum, id
est, unitatis corporis et sanguinis
Christi alicubi quotidie, alicubi
certis intervallis dierum in dominica mensa præparatur, et de
mensa dominica sumitur, quibusdam ad vitam, quibusdam
ad exitium : res vero ipsa cujus
sacramentum est omni homini
ad vitam, nulli ad exitium, qui-

cunque ejus particeps fuerit "
(Aug.).

54. ὁ τρωγ.] *qui manducat* v.
The verb τρώγειν expresses not
only the simple fact of eating
but the process as that which is
dwelt upon with pleasure (Matt.
xxiv. 38. Comp. ch. xiii. 18). So
also the tense (ὁ τρώγων, contrast
v. 45, ὁ ἀκούσας) marks an action
which must be continuous and
not completed once for all.

ἐχ. ζω. αἰων. . . . .] Compare *v.*
40, note. Note the contrast
between the present (ἔχει) which
is the beginning, and the future
(ἀναστήσω) which is the consummation. Col. iii. 3 f. ; 1 John
iii. 2. Comp. Iren. iv. 38, 1.

Origen, when speaking of the
Christian Passover (referring to
v. 54), writes : "Hoc quod modo
loquimur carnes sunt Verbi Dei,
si tamen non quasi infirmis olera
aut quasi pueris lactis alimoniam
proferamus. Si perfecta loquimur, si robusta, si fortiora,
carnes vobis Verbi Dei apponimus
comedendas. Ubi enim mysticus
sermo, ubi dogmaticus et Trini-
tatis fide repletus profertur ac
solidus, ubi futuri sæculi amoto
velamine litteræ legis spiritalis
sacramenta panduntur . . . hæc
omnia carnes sunt Verbi Dei,
quibus qui potest perfecto in-
tellectu vesci et corde purificato,
ille vere festivitatis Paschæ im-
molat sacrificium et diem festum
agit cum Deo et angelis ejus "
(*Hom. in Num.* xxiii. 6).

16

242   GOSPEL ACCORDING TO ST. JOHN   [CH. VI

⁵⁵ ἐσχάτῃ ἡμέρᾳ· ἡ γὰρ σάρξ μου ἀληθής¹ ἐστι βρῶσις,
⁵⁶ καὶ τὸ αἷμά μου ἀληθής¹ ἐστι πόσις. ὁ τρώγων μου
τὴν σάρκα καὶ πίνων μου τὸ αἷμα ἐν ἐμοὶ μένει κἀγὼ
⁵⁷ ἐν αὐτῷ.²   καθὼς ἀπέστειλέν με ὁ ζῶν πατὴρ κἀγὼ ζῶ

¹ ἀληθῶς ℵ*DΓΔ.
² D inserts (after ἐν αὐτῷ) καθὼς ἐν ἐμοὶ ὁ πατὴρ κἀγὼ ἐν τῷ πατρί. ἀμὴν ἀμὴν
λέγω ὑμῖν, ἐὰν μὴ λάβητε τὸ σῶμα τοῦ υἱοῦ τοῦ ἀνθρώπου ὡς τὸν ἄρτον τῆς ζωῆς,
οὐκ ἔχετε ζωὴν ἐν αὐτῷ.

55. ἡ γὰρ σάρξ μου . . .] The
possession and the highest manifestation of life follow necessarily
from participation in Christ's
" flesh " and " blood " : such is
their power. His " flesh " and
" blood " naturally support the
life which they communicate.
They are "true meat" and "true
drink." They stand in the same
relation to man's whole being,
as food does to his physical being.
They must first be taken, and
then they must be assimilated.

Origen interprets the thought
so as to suggest that the Christian
teacher is, in a subordinate sense,
the food of his people : " Jesus
quia totus ex toto mundus est,
tota eius caro cibus est, et totus
sanguis eius potus est ; quia
omne opus eius sanctum est et
omnis sermo eius verus est. Prop-
terea ergo et caro eius verus est
cibus et sanguis eius verus est
potus. Carnibus enim et san-
guine verbi sui tanquam mundo
cibo ac potu potat et reficit
omne hominum genus   Secundo
in [hoc] loco post illius carnem
mundus cibus est Petrus, et
Paulus et omnes apostoli. Tertio
loco discipuli eorum . . ." (Hom.
in Lev. vii. 5).

56. The truth of v. 54 is traced
to its necessary foundation. In
virtue of Christ's impartment of
His humanity to the believer,

the believer may rightly be said
to " abide in Christ " and Christ
to " abide in the believer." The
believer has therefore " eternal
life," and in that, the certainty
of a resurrection, a restoration
in glory of the fulness of his
present powers.

ἐν ἐμ. μέν. κἀγ. ἐν αὐτ.] There is,
so to speak, a double personality.
The believer is quickened by
Christ's presence, and he is
himself incorporated in Christ.
Compare xv. 4, xvii. 23 ; 1 John
iii. 24, iv. 15 f., note. This
twofold aspect of the divine
connexion is illustrated by the
two great images of the " body "
and the "temple." " Manemus
in illo cum sumus membra eius :
manet autem ipse in nobis cum
sumus templum eius " (Aug. In
Joh. XXVII. 6).

Some early authorities (D (aff'
in a positive form)) add a remarkable gloss at the end of the
verse : *even as the Father is in
me and I in the Father. Verily,
verily, I say unto you, unless ye
receive* (λάβητε) *the body of the
Son of man as the bread of life
ye have not life in him.*

"Dominus noster Jesus Christus
corpus et sanguinem suum in eis
rebus commendavit quæ ad unum
rediguntur ex multis. Namque
aliud in unum ex multis granis
confit : aliud in unum ex multis

₅₅ him up at the last day.   For my flesh is true meat,
₅₆ and my blood is true drink.   He that eateth my
flesh and drinketh my blood abideth in me, and I in
₅₇ him.   As the living Father sent me, and I live

alienis confluit" (Aug. and Bede).

"In sanctificando calice Domini offerri aqua sola non potest, quomodo nec vinum solum potest. Nam si vinum tantum quis offerat sanguis Christi incipit esse sine nobis : si vero aqua sola, plus incipit esse sine Christo . . . Sic vero calix Domini non est aqua sola aut vinum solum, nisi utrumque sibi misceatur, quomodo nec corpus Domini potest esse farina sola aut aqua sola, nisi utrumque adunatum fuerit et copulatum et panis unius compage solidatum. Quo et ipso sacramento populus noster ostenditur adunatus ; ut quemadmodum grana multa in unum collecta et commolita et commixta panem unum faciunt, sic in Christo qui est panis cælestis unum sciamus esse corpus cui conjunctus sit noster numerus et adunatus" (Cypr. ad Cæcil. ep. lxiii. 13).

"Quando Dominus corpus suum panem vocat de multorum granorum adunatione congestum, populum nostrum quem portabat indicat adunatum ; et quando sanguinem suum vinum appellat de botris atque acinis plurimis expressum atque in unum coactum gregem item nostrum significat commixtione adunatæ multitudinis copulatum" (Cypr. ad Magn. ep. lxxvi. 6).

μένει] manet v. ; abideth, as the word is commonly rendered. See also xiv. 10, 17 ; 1 John iii. 17, 24, iv. 12, 13, 15, 16. The word is singularly frequent in

St. John (Gospel, Epistles), and the phrases " abide in [Christ] " and the like are peculiar to him (yet compare 1 Tim. ii. 15 ; 2 Tim. iii. 14).

57. καθώς . . . καί] The same combination occurs xiii. 15 ; 1 John ii. 6, iv. 17.

καθ. ἀπεστ. . . .] The introduction of these words marks the fact that Christ speaks of His vital fellowship with the Father not as the Word only, but as the Son Incarnate, the Son of man. Comp. v. 23. And thus the acceptance of the divine mission by the Son, and His dependence in His humanity on the Father, are placed in some sense in correlation with the appropriation of the Incarnate Son (*he that eateth me*) by the Christian ; so that the relation of the believer to Christ is prefigured in the relation of the Son to the Father. Comp. x. 14, 15, note.

ὁ ζῶν πατ.] *vivens pater* v. The title is unique. Comp. the phrase τ. θεοῦ τ. ζῶντος, Matt. xvi. 16 ; 2 Cor. vi. 16 ; Heb. vii. 25, etc.

διὰ τὸν π. . . . δι' ἐμέ] *propter patrem . . . propter me* v. ; *because of the Father . . . because of me* . . . The phrase is a very remarkable one. Διά with acc. may be rendered generally *because of, on account of*, as expressing the ground and not the end, the fact that something is which influences action or judgement and not the aim that something may be. Thus "the

διὰ τὸν πατέρα, καὶ ὁ τρώγων με κἀκεῖνος ζήσει δι᾽
58 ἐμέ. οὗτός ἐστιν ὁ ἄρτος ὁ ἐξ οὐρανοῦ καταβάς, οὐ
καθὼς ἔφαγον οἱ πατέρες¹ καὶ ἀπέθανον· ὁ τρώγων
59 τοῦτον τὸν ἄρτον ζήσει εἰς τὸν αἰῶνα. Ταῦτα εἶπεν

¹ Insert ὑμῶν DΔ.

sabbath was made διὰ τὸν ἄνθρωπον" "for the sake of man," seeing that he was of a particular constitution and in particular circumstances. And with persons the rendering "for the sake of" is commonly the simplest and best, the thought being that of consideration of what the person is rather than of service to be rendered on his behalf (ὑπέρ). Comp. vii. 43; xi. 15; xii. 42.

The preposition is used of the Father in this construction in two places besides this: Rom. viii. 20, οὐχ ἑκοῦσα ἀλλὰ διὰ τὸν ὑποτάξαντα; Heb. ii. 10, δι᾽ ὃν τὰ πάντα καὶ δι᾽ οὗ τὰ πάντα.

Both passages imply that the will, the counsel, the character of God—however we speak—is the absolute rule of all created beings. Creation is what it is because He is what He is.

So the word is used, though rarely, in connexion with the Lord: 1 Cor. iv. 10, ἡμεῖς μωροὶ διὰ χριστόν; Phil. iii. 7, ταῦτα ἥγημαι διὰ τὸν χριστὸν ζημίαν; 1 Pet. ii. 13, ὑποτάγητε . . . διὰ τὸν κύριον; 2 Cor. iv. 5 (κηρύσσομεν) ἑαυτοὺς δούλους ὑμῶν διὰ Ἰη.; 2 Cor. iv. 11, εἰς θάνατον παραδιδόμεθα διὰ Ἰησοῦν. Comp. John xii. 9, διὰ τὸν Ἰη.; 30 οὐ δι᾽ ἐμέ.

From a consideration of these passages it seems to follow that the sense of διὰ τὸν πατέρα here is, "because of the Father," that is, "because the Father is Father," and not simply "because the

Father lives" (ὅτι ζῇ ὁ πατήρ comp. xiv. 19). The Son lives because He is the Son of the Father. In the same way the believer lives because the Son is Son, in whom humanity is potentially gathered together and reunited to God. Comp. x. 14 f.

But the difference between the relation of the Son to the Father and that of men to the Son is clearly marked. The Son lives absolutely διὰ τὸν πατέρα, and so "has life in Himself" by the Father's gift (v. 26): the man who "eats" the Son lives because of the Son. "Est ergo dissimilitudo similis et similitudo dissimilis unici Filii multorumque filiorum Excelsi, dum hic vivit quia genitus est, illi autem vivunt quia manducant eum qui genitus est" (Rup.).

ὁ τρωγ. με] In this phrase we reach the climax of the revelation. The words eat of the bread (vv. 50, 51), eat the flesh of the Son of man and drink His blood (v. 53), rise at last to the thought of eating Christ. The appropriation of the food which Christ gives, of the humanity in which He lived and died, issues in the appropriation of Himself, and this appropriation is continuous (ὁ τρώγων) and not "one act at once" (ὁ φαγών).

κἀκεῖνος] The insertion of the emphatic pronoun immediately after the subject, which it repeats and emphasises, is most

because of the Father; so he that eateth me, he
58 also shall live because of me.   This is the bread
which came down out of heaven: not as the fathers
did eat, and died: he that eateth this bread shall
59 live for ever.   These things said he in a synagogue,

remarkable. It appears to lay stress upon that relation of dependence which constitutes the parallel between the disciples and the Son. Comp. xiv. 12.

ζήσει] *shall live,* not *liveth.* The fulness of the life was consequent upon the exaltation of Christ. Comp. xiv. 19.

58. These concluding words carry back the discourse to its commencement (*vv.* 33, 35). The fulfilment of the type of the manna in Christ, after it has been set forth in its complete form, is placed in direct connexion with the earlier event.

οὗτ. ἐστ. ὁ ἀρτ. ὁ . . . καταβάς] *This* bread, this heavenly food, which has been shown to be Christ Himself, and His "flesh" (*v.* 51), *is the bread which came* . . . Contrast *v.* 50: *This is the bread which cometh.* . . . Both aspects of Christ's work must be kept in mind. He came, and He comes.

οὐ καθ. ἔφαγ. οἱ πατ. . . . κ. ἀπέθ.] *not as the fathers did eat and died.* The construction is irregular. Naturally the sentence would have run: *This is the bread . . . heaven: he that eateth this bread . . .,* but the parenthetical clause expresses in a condensed form the contrast between the true and the typical manna. "The fact and the issue of the fact is *not as the fathers ate and died.*" Comp. 1 John iii. 12 (οὐ καθώς). The reference to

the "death" of "the generation in the wilderness" would have a fuller meaning if the tradition were already current that this generation "had no part in the world to come" (quoted by Lightfoot on *v.* 39).

οἱ πατ.] This title, as distinguished from the common text οἱ πατ. ὑμῶν (*patres vestri* v.), recognises the representative position which the early generation occupied.

οἱ πατ. . . . ὁ τρωγ. . . .] There appears to be significance in the passage from the plural to the singular. Throughout the discourses the believer is dealt with as exercising personal faith and not only as one of a society. Compare *vv.* 35, 37, 40, 45, 47, 50, 51, 54, 56.

ὁ τρωγ. . . .] *he that eateth,* as in *vv.* 54, 56. The construction in *vv.* 26, 50, 51, is different (φαγεῖν ἐκ).

59. ἐν συναγωγῇ] This is the only notice of the kind in St. John's Gospel, though the general custom is referred to, xviii. 20. The absence of the definite article in the original here and in xviii. 20, which leads to a form of expression not found elsewhere in the New Testament, seems to mark the character of the assemblage rather than the place itself: "when people were gathered for worship," "in time of solemn assembly" (comp. 1 Macc. xiv. 28). Comp. ἐν ἐκκλησίᾳ 1 Cor.

60 ἐν συναγωγῇ¹ διδάσκων ἐν Καφαρναούμ. Πολλοὶ οὖν
ἀκούσαντες ἐκ τῶν μαθητῶν αὐτοῦ εἶπαν Σκληρός ἐστιν
61 ὁ λόγος οὗτος· τίς δύναται αὐτοῦ ἀκούειν; εἰδὼς δὲ
ὁ Ἰησοῦς ἐν ἑαυτῷ ὅτι γογγύζουσιν περὶ τούτου οἱ
μαθηταὶ αὐτοῦ εἶπεν αὐτοῖς Τοῦτο ὑμᾶς σκανδαλίζει;
62 ἐὰν οὖν θεωρῆτε τὸν υἱὸν τοῦ ἀνθρώπου ἀναβαίνοντα
63 ὅπου ἦν τὸ πρότερον; τὸ πνεῦμά ἐστιν τὸ ζωοποιοῦν,

¹ Insert σαββάτῳ D.

xiv. 19, 35; 1 Cor. xi. 18 (ἐν
ἐκκλ.); 3 John 6. See also κατὰ
ἑορτήν, Matt. xxvii. 15; 2 Macc.
xiv. 5, προσκληθεὶς εἰς συνέδριον
בית דין. It is a fact of great
interest that among the ruins
which mark the probable site of
Capernaum (Tell Hûm) are the
remains of a handsome synagogue, of which Wilson says:
"On turning over a large block
[of stone] we found the pot of
manna engraved on its face"
(Warren's *Recovery of Jerusalem*,
pp. 344 ff.). This very symbol
may have been before the eyes
of those who heard the Lord's
words. It may be added that
the history of the manna (Exod.
xvi. 4—36) is appointed to be
read in the Synagogues at morning service.

διδάσκων] vii. 14 f., 28; viii.
20; xviii. 20. The phrase gives
a marked emphasis to the words
which have gone before. The
crisis corresponds in character
with that at Nazareth, Luke
iv. 16 ff. Comp. Matt. xi. 23.
Some early authorities (D. a ff')
add, what may be a true traditional gloss, "on a sabbath."

The Issue (60—71)

The discourses proved a trial
to the faith of the disciples.
The immediate effect was a

"murmuring" among them which
led to a clear affirmation of the
divine conditions of discipleship
(60—65). And this was followed
by a separation between the faithful and the unfaithful, both visibly
(66—69) and invisibly (70, 71).

60. Πολλ. οὖν] *many therefore*,
not only of the misunderstanding
multitude (28 ff.) and of the ill-
disposed Jews (41 ff.), but *of the
disciples* (v. 3) who had hitherto
followed Him, *when they heard
this*, found the new teaching of
life through death a burden too
heavy to be borne. See the
"woe" pronounced on Capernaum
(Matt. xi. 23 f.).

Σκληρός . . . ὁ λογ.] *durus . . .
sermo* v.; *hard saying*, that is,
difficult to receive, accept, appropriate. The idea is not that of
obscurity. The discourse was
offensive, and not unintelligible.
It made claims on the complete
submission, self-devotion, self-
surrender of the disciples. It
pointed significantly to death.
The same word occurs Jude 15,
in a somewhat similar connexion.
Compare Gen. xxi. 11, xlii. 7;
1 Kings xii. 13 (LXX.). Compare
also Eur. *Fragm.* 1023 (Stob. 13)
πότερα θέλεις σοι μαλθακὰ ψευδῆ
λέγω Ἢ σκλήρ' ἀληθῆ;

λόγος] *speech, discourse*. The
English representative of λόγος

⁶⁰ as he taught in Capernaum. Many therefore of his disciples, when they heard *this*, said, This is a hard ⁶¹ discourse; who can hear it? But Jesus knowing in himself that his disciples murmured at this, said unto ⁶² them, Doth this cause you to stumble? *What* then if ye should behold the Son of man ascending where ⁶³ he was before? It is the spirit that quickeneth; the

is not sufficiently elastic to give its sense in all cases.

αὐτ. ἀκούειν] *hear it*, listen to it with patience, as ready to admit it. See vii. 40, x. 3, 16, 27, xii. 47, xviii. 37. The pronoun may be taken as personal: *who can hear him?* but this is an unlikely rendering.

61. εἰδὼς δ. ὁ Ἰησ. ἐν ἑαυτ. . . .] See ii. 24, note.

γογγύζ.] *murmured* as the Jews. Compare *v.* 41, note.

σκανδαλίζει] Compare xvi. 1, note.

"Secretum Dei intentos debet facere non aversos" (Bede).

62. ἐὰν οὖν θεωρ. . . .] *What then if ye should behold.* . . . This incomplete question, which seems to leave open in some measure the alternatives of greater offence and possible victory, has been interpreted in two very different ways, by supplying in one case a negative answer: "Ye will not then be offended any more"; and in the other a positive: "Ye will then assuredly be still more offended." According to the first interpretation the "ascending up" is the Ascension as the final spiritualising of the Lord's Person, whereby the offence of the language as to His flesh would be removed by the apprehension of the truth as to His spiritual humanity ("Noli me

tangere"). In the second the "ascending up" is referred to the "elevation" on the Cross, and the offence caused by the reference to the death of Christ is regarded as increased by the death itself in its actual circumstances. Each of these two interpretations appears to contain elements of the full meaning. The whole context shows distinctly that the disciples were to be subjected to some severer trial. The turn of the sentence therefore must be: "If then ye see the Son of man ascending . . . ye will be, according to your present state, more grievously offended; for that trial you must still be disciplined." But, on the other hand, the Crucifixion alone could not be described as an "ascending up where Christ was before"; yet it was the first part of the Ascension, the absolute sacrifice of self which issued in the absolute triumph over the limitations of earthly existence. The Passion, the Resurrection, the Ascension, were steps in the progress of the "ascending up" through suffering, which is the great offence of the Gospel. The difficulty of accepting this completed fact is (though greater) of the same kind as the difficulty of accepting life only through the communicated humanity of the Incarnate

ἡ σὰρξ οὐκ ὠφελεῖ οὐδέν· τὰ ῥήματα ἃ ἐγὼ λελάληκα¹
64 ὑμῖν πνεῦμά ἐστιν καὶ ζωή ἐστιν· ἀλλὰ εἰσὶν ἐξ ὑμῶν
τινὲς οἳ οὐ πιστεύουσιν. Ἤιδει γὰρ ἐξ ἀρχῆς ὁ Ἰησοῦς²
τίνες εἰσὶν οἱ μὴ πιστεύοντες καὶ τίς ἐστιν ὁ παρα-
65 δώσων αὐτόν. καὶ ἔλεγεν Διὰ τοῦτο εἴρηκα ὑμῖν ὅτι

¹ λαλῶ ΓΔ. See note.   ² ἀπ' ἀρχῆς ὁ σωτήρ א.

Son. For other examples of "aposiopesis" see Luke xix. 42 ; Acts xxiii. 9 ; Phil. i. 22 (Ltft.). τ. υἱ. τ. ἀνθρ. ἀναβαιν. ὁπ. ἦν τ. προτ.] Compare viii. 58, xvii. 5, 24 ; Col. i. 17. No phrase could show more clearly the unchanged personality of Christ. As "the Son of man" He speaks of His being in heaven before the Incarnation. "Filius Dei et filius hominis unus Christus . . . Filius Dei in terra suscepta carne, filius hominis in cælo in unitate personæ" (Aug. ad loc.).

You are troubled, the Lord seems to say, by words which cannot be interpreted according to the laws of material, phenomenal existence. How then will you bear the last revelation of the Ascension, when that which is truly human will be seen to be transfigured and to rise beyond the conditions of earthly life? This will be at once the severest trial and the highest reward of faith. That "ascent" will serve to explain the "descent" (comp. Eph. iv. 9), and show the union of earth and heaven.

63. τ. πνεῦμα . . . ἡ σάρξ . . .] The same contrast occurs in iii. 6 (see note), 1 Peter iii. 18. Just as in man the *spirit* is that part of his nature by which he holds fellowship with the unseen eternal order, and *the flesh* that part of it by which he holds fellowship

with the seen temporal order, so the two words are applied to the working of Christ. Nothing can carry us beyond the limits of its own realm. The new life must come from that which belongs properly to the sphere in which it moves. Compare 1 Cor. xv. 45, (2 Cor. iii. 6). The truth is expressed in its most general form, and is not to be limited to the spiritual and carnal apprehension of Christ's Person ; or to the spiritual and external participation in the Holy Communion ; or even to the spiritual and historical manifestation of Christ. Each of these partial thoughts has its place in the whole conception. Compare 2 Cor. v. 16.

ζωοπ.] *qui vivificat* v. ; 1 Cor. xv. 45 ; 2 Cor. iii. 6 ; 1 Peter iii. 18.

τ. ῥήματα . . .] Here the definite utterances (Vulg. *verba*, *v.* 68) and not the whole revelation (λόγος, Vulg. *sermo*, *v.* 60). The reference is to the clear unfolding of the complete relation of man and humanity to the Incarnate Saviour. Hence a marked emphasis is laid on the pronoun *I* : the words that *I* (ἐγώ) and no prophet, not even Moses (*v.* 32) before me ; and on the tense : *the words that I have spoken* (λελάληκα, according to the true reading), which cause your present perplexity, and not generally *speak,*

flesh profiteth nothing : the words that I have spoken
64 unto you are spirit, and are life. But there are
some of you that believe not. For Jesus knew from
the beginning who they were that believed not, and
65 who it was that should betray him. And he said,

though in some sense all Christ's words are life-giving, as conveying something of this central truth.
For the exact sense of τὰ ῥήματα see iii. 34, viii. 47, xvii. 8.

πν. ἐστ. κ. ζω. ἐστ.] *are spirit, and are life,* that is, belong essentially to the region of eternal being, and so are capable of quickening an organization limited by the conditions of any particular order. Comp. *v.* 68; i. 3 f.

The flesh is, so to speak, the visible expression of the spirit. In itself it is nothing.

For of the soul the body form doth take,
For soul is form and doth the body make.

Note the power of "the word" as the expression of "the mind," xv. 3, διὰ τὸν λ., xvii. 17; Eph. v. 26 f. Our words are expressive of our minds—Christ "the word" is the perfect expression of the Father's mind: His words the perfect expression of Himself. Comp. Aug. *de Fid. et Symb.* 3, 4.

64. ἀλλά] *But,* even so, while "the words" have essentially this virtue, in the closest circle of my disciples there are some to whom they convey no vivifying influence, because the human condition is unfulfilled : *there are of you* (ἐξ ὑμῶν) *some who believe not,* who do not surrender yourselves without reason to their moulding, purifying force. "Per

fidem copulamur: per intellectum vivificamur. Prius hæreamus per fidem ut sit quod vivificetur per intellectum " (Aug.). For the order compare *v.* 70 (*of you one*); and for the use of πιστεύειν absolutely *v.* 47.

Ἤιδει γάρ . . .] Compare ii. 24, note.

ἐξ ἀρχῆς] *ab initio v.* Compare xvi. 4, (xv. 27). From the first moment when the public work of Christ began (1 John ii. 7, 24, iii. 11 ; Luke i. 2). The phrase must always be relative to the point present to the mind of the writer or speaker; and here that seems to be fixed by *v.* 70.

τίς ἐστ. ὁ παραδώσων] *quis traditurus esset* v. ; *who it was that should betray him.* This first allusion to the sin of Judas evidently stands in a significant connexion with the first unveiling of the Lord's Passion. The word παραδιδόναι means strictly *deliver up, to give into* the hands of another to deal with as he pleases (xviii. 30, 35 f., xix. 16 ; Matt. v. 25, etc.). The title of "traitor" is only once applied to Judas in the New Testament : Luke vi. 16 (προδότης). In other words his act is regarded in relation to the Lord's Passion, and not to his sin.

65. καὶ ἔλεγεν] not once only and on this occasion.

Διὰ τοῦτ. εἴρ. . . .] The divine condition of discipleship was clearly stated, because the dis-

οὐδεὶς δύναται ἐλθεῖν πρός με ἐὰν μὴ ἦ δεδομένον αὐτῷ
66 ἐκ τοῦ πατρός ¹. Ἐκ τούτου πολλοὶ ἐκ ² τῶν μαθητῶν
αὐτοῦ ἀπῆλθον εἰς τὰ ὀπίσω καὶ οὐκέτι μετ᾽ αὐτοῦ
67 περιεπάτουν. Εἶπεν οὖν ὁ Ἰησοῦς τοῖς δώδεκα Μὴ
68 καὶ ὑμεῖς θέλετε ὑπάγειν; ἀπεκρίθη ³ αὐτῷ Σίμων Πέτρος

¹ Insert μου C³ΓΔ.   ² Omit ἐκ אCDLΓΔ.   ³ Insert οὖν EFΓ.

ciples would have to bear the trial of treachery revealed in their midst, which might seem to be inconsistent with Christ's claims, and with what they thought that they had found in Him. His choice even of Judas was not made without full knowledge (xiii. 18).

ὅτι . . .] might be translated "because."

ἐλθ. πρός με] Judas then, though "chosen out" (v. 70) and called, had not come to Christ (v. 37). He remained still in himself; and now at this crisis he can keep silence.

ἦ δεδομ. αὐτ. ἐκ τ. πατ.] Comp. iii. 27. There is a sense in which all life is the unfolding of the timeless divine will. *The Father* (not *my Father*) here is looked upon as the source (ἐκ) from whom all flows. Comp. x. 32; 1 Cor. vii. 7; (2 Cor. ii. 2). It must be noticed likewise how here the divine and human elements are placed in close juxtaposition, *given*, *come*. The mystery must be left with the assertion of both the concurrent parts, the will of God and the will of man.

Μονονουχὶ τοῦτό φησιν Οὐ θορυβοῦσιν οὐδὲ ταράττουσιν οὐδὲ ξενίζουσί με οἱ μὴ πιστεύοντες· οἶδα τοῦτο ἄνωθεν πρὶν ἢ γενέσθαι· οἶδα τίσιν ἔδωκεν ὁ πατήρ (Chrys.).

66 ff. The "murmuring" issued in separation. This separation was partly open and partly

secret. The same teaching which led some disciples to desert Christ, appears to have called out in Judas that deeper antagonism of spirit which was shown at last in the betrayal.

66. Ἐκ τούτου] *ex hoc* v.; *upon this* (compare xix. 12), with the notion of dependence on what had now happened. The phrase is not simply temporal (ix. 1; Luke x. 20; Acts ix. 33, xxiv. 10, xxvi. 4), nor simply causal (Rom. i. 4; Rev. xxvi. 21, viii. 13). Augustine has preserved a singular tradition as to the number: "Septuaginta fere homines dixerunt Durus est hic sermo et recesserunt ab eo et remanserunt duodecim" (Aug. *In* 1 *Joh.* i. § 12). He appears also to have found an interpolated MS., for he writes: "Sic Evangelista loquitur *Et Dominus ipse remansit cum duodecim et illi ad eum* "*Domine ecce illi dimiserunt te.*" *Et ille* "*Numquid et vos vultis abire?*" (*In Joh. Tract.* xi. 5).

ἀπῆλθον εἰς τὰ ὀπίσω] *abierunt retro* v.; they not only left Christ, but gave up what they had gained with Him, and, so far as they could, reoccupied their old places, Phil. iii. 13. καλῶς ὁ εὐαγγελιστὴς οὐκ εἶπεν Ἀνεχώρησαν, ἀλλὰ Ἀπῆλθον εἰς τὰ ὀπίσω, δηλῶν ὅτι τῆς κατὰ ἀρετὴν ἐπιδόσεως ὑπετέμοντο, καὶ ὅτι ἦν εἶχον πάλαι πίστιν ἀπώλεσαν ἀποσχίσαντες ἑαυτούς (Chrys.).

For this cause have I said unto you, that no man
can come unto me, except it be given unto him of
66 the Father.   Upon this many of his disciples went
67 back, and walked no more with him.   Jesus said
68 therefore unto the twelve, Would ye also go?   Simon

ὁ δὲ κατὰ Παῦλον κολλώμενος
τῷ Κυρίῳ ἀεὶ τοῖς ἔμπροσθεν
ἐπεκτείνεται (Theophylact).

οὐκέτι μετ᾽ αὐτ. περιεπ.] jam
non cum illo ambulabant v.;
Compare vii. 1, xi. 54.   The
phrase gives a vivid portraiture
of the Lord's life.

67. Εἰπ. οὖν . . .] The test had
been applied to the mass—the
multitude, the Jews, the disciples
(v. 60, note)—and it was now
necessarily applied to the innermost circle of disciples.

τοῖς δώδεκα] These are spoken
of as known, though they have
not been mentioned before.   The
number is implied in v. 13.   In
the earlier part of the record
(chh. i.—iv.) no such chosen
company is noticed, a fact which
is a slight sign of the distinctness with which the course of
the work of Christ was impressed
on the apostle's mind.   He does
not record the call of the twelve,
yet it lies hidden and implied
in his narrative.   From another
side the reference shows that
St. John assumes that his readers
are familiar with the main facts
of the history.

Μὴ θέλετε] numquid vultis? v.;
will ye also . . .? The form of the
question implies that such desertion is incredible and yet to
be feared; but here the negation
is virtually assumed.   Compare
vii. 47, 52, xviii. 17, 25.

ὑπαγ. . . . ἀπελευσ. . . .] go . . .
go away . . . The first word sug-

gests the notion of the personal
act in itself; the second that of
separation.   See vii. 33, note.

68. Σιμ. Πετ.] St. Peter occupies the same representative
place in St. John's narrative as
in the others.   Compare xiii. 6 ff.,
24, 36, xviii. 10, xx. 2, xxi. 3.
He assumes that only a Person
(cf. xx. 15) could satisfy their
need.   His reply is the strong
confession that the apostles have
found in Christ all that they
could seek.   The thought is of
what Christ has, as they have
known, and not of Himself: *thou
hast* in thy spiritual treasury
ready to be brought forth according to our powers and necessities
(Matt. xiii. 52) *words of eternal
life*.   This phrase may mean either
(1) words—utterances (v. 63)—
concerning eternal life; or (2)
words bringing, issuing in, eternal
life (1 John i. 1).   The usage
of St. John is on the whole
decidedly in favour of the second
interpretation.   Thus we find *the
bread of life* (vv. 35, etc.), *the
light of life* (viii. 12), *the water
of life* (Rev. xxi. 6, xxii. 1, 17),
the tree of life (Rev. ii. 7, xxii. 2,
14).   St. Peter does not speak
of the completed Gospel ("the
word"), but of specific sayings
(ῥήματα, not τὰ ῥήματα) which
had been felt to carry life with
them.   He had recognised the
truth of what the Lord had
said v. 63 (τὰ ῥήματα).   Contrast
v. 39 f.

Κύριε, πρὸς τίνα ἀπελευσόμεθα; ῥήματα ζωῆς αἰωνίου
69 ἔχεις, καὶ ἡμεῖς πεπιστεύκαμεν καὶ ἐγνώκαμεν ὅτι σὺ
70 εἶ ὁ ἅγιος τοῦ θεοῦ¹. ἀπεκρίθη αὐτοῖς ὁ Ἰησοῦς Οὐκ
ἐγὼ ὑμᾶς τοὺς δώδεκα ἐξελεξάμην; καὶ ἐξ ὑμῶν εἷς διά-
71 βολός ἐστιν. ἔλεγεν δὲ τὸν Ἰούδαν Σίμωνος Ἰσκαριώ-

¹ ὁ χριστὸς ὁ υἱὸς τοῦ θεοῦ τοῦ ζῶντος ΓΔ. See note.

Philo contrasts "words" and "the word": Οὐκ ἐπ᾽ ἄρτῳ μόνῳ ζήσεται ὁ ἄνθρωπος [ὁ] κατ᾽ εἰκόνα ἀλλ᾽ ἐπὶ πάντι ῥήματι τῷ ἐκπορευομένῳ διὰ στόματος θεοῦ, τουτέστι καὶ διὰ παντὸς τοῦ λόγου τραφήσεται καὶ διὰ μέρους αὐτοῦ· τὸ μὲν γὰρ στόμα σύμβολον τοῦ λόγου τὸ δὲ ῥῆμα μέρος αὐτοῦ. τρέφεται δὲ τῶν μὲν τελειοτέρων ἡ ψυχὴ ὅλῳ τῷ λόγῳ, ἀγαπήσαιμεν δ᾽ ἂν ἡμεῖς εἰ καὶ μέρει τραφείημεν αὐτοῦ (Philo, Leg. Alleg. iii. 61, i. 122).

69. κ. ἡμεῖς] and we, who are nearest to Thee and have listened to Thee most devoutly, whatever may be the case with others.

πεπιστευκ. κ. ἐγνωκ.] have believed and have come to know. The vital faith which grasps the new data of the higher life precedes the conscious intellectual appreciation of them. "Non cognovimus et credidimus ... Credidimus enim ut cognosceremus; nam si prius cognoscere et deinde credere vellemus, nec cognoscere nec credere valeremus" (Aug. ad loc.). Comp. ch. x. 38; 2 Peter i. 5.

In 1 John iv. 16 the words stand in the inverted order, but it will be noticed from the construction there that the words πεπιστεύκαμεν qualify and explain, so to speak, ἐγνώκαμεν, but do not go closely with τ. ἀγάπην ἣν ἔχ. ὁ θεὸς ἐν ἡμῖν, which depends directly on ἐγνώκαμεν.

Chrysostom calls attention to the use of the plural: Ὅρα τὸν φιλάδελφον, τὸν φιλόστοργον, πῶς ὑπὲρ παντὸς ἀπολογεῖται τοῦ χοροῦ· οὐ γὰρ εἶπεν Ἔγνωκα ἀλλά Ἐγνώκαμεν.

ὁ ἅγιος τ. θεοῦ] According to the true reading (see Additional Note), the Holy One of God. Mark i. 24; Luke iv. 34. The knowledge of the demoniacs reached to the essential nature of the Lord. Comp. Rev. iii. 7; 1 John ii. 20. See also ch. x. 36, and v. 27 of this chapter.

With this confession of St. Peter that which is recorded in Matt. xvi. 16, which belongs to the same period but to different circumstances, must be compared. Here the confession points to the inward character in which the Apostles found the assurance of life; there the confession was of the public office and theocratic Person of the Lord. To suppose that the one confession is simply an imperfect representation of the other is to deny the fulness of the life which lies beyond both.¹ This confession must be

¹ Bishop Westcott had sketched a fuller note on this subject. He believed that St. Peter's confession in this Gospel differed from that recorded by the Synoptists "in place (apparently), in occasion, in scope, in circumstances." That recorded by St. John was "personal" "after desertion": that recorded by the Synoptists "official," "after partial confession."—A. W.

Peter answered him, Lord, to whom shall we go away? 69 thou hast words of eternal life. And we have believed and have come to know that thou art the Holy One 70 of God. Jesus answered them, Did not I choose you 71 the twelve, and of you one is a devil? Now he spake

compared with the confessions in ch. i. Here the confession is made after the disappointment of the popular hope, and reaches to the recognition of that absolute character of Christ which the demoniacs tried to reveal prematurely.

70. Even in those who still clung to Christ there was an element of unfaithfulness. Comp. xiii. 10 f.

ἀπ. αὐτοῖς ὁ 'I.] We can picture to ourselves how others by look and gesture made St. Peter's words their own; and the Lord answered not the one apostle but the body for whom he spoke (comp. i. 51 λέγει αὐτῷ . . . λέγω ὑμῖν). The reply is to the confident affirmation of St. Peter, who rested his profession of the abiding faithfulness of the apostles upon their perception of the Lord's nature. So far was this from leaving no ground for doubt that the Lord shows that even His own choice (*Did not I—even I—choose*) left room for a traitor among those whom He had chosen.

Οὐκ ἐγὼ ὑμ. τ. δωδ. ἐξελ.] *Did not I choose you the twelve?* you the marked representatives of the new Israel, the patriarchs of a divine people. The reference is not to the number of the apostles, but to their special position (ὑμᾶς τοὺς δώδεκα: comp. xx. 24).

ἐξελεξ.] *elegi* v.; xiii. 18, xv. 16 f.

Compare Luke vi. 13 ; Acts i. 2, 24; 1 Cor. i. 27 f. ; Eph. i. 4. On the choice of Judas see xiii. 18, note

ἐξ ὑμῶν εἷς . . .] Even out of this chosen body one is faithless. There is a tragic pathos in the order.

διάβολος] viii. 44, xiii. 2; 1 John iii. 8, 10 ; Rev. xii. 9, xx. 2. The fundamental idea seems to be that of turning good into evil (διαβάλλειν). The two great temptations are the characteristic works of " the devil." Hence Judas, by regarding Christ in the light of his own selfish views, and claiming to use His power for the accomplishment of that which he had proposed as Messiah's work, partook of that which is essential to the devil's nature. With this term applied to Judas we must compare that of *Satan* applied at no long interval to St. Peter (Matt. xvi. 23). Judas wished to pervert the divine power which he saw to his own ends ; St. Peter strove to avert what he feared in erring zeal for his Lord.

71. τ. 'Ιουδ. Σιμ. 'Ισκ.] *Judas the son of Simon Iscariot.* The true reading here marks Iscariot as certainly a local name : *a man of Kerioth (Karioth).* The place is commonly identified with *Kerioth,* a town of Judah (Josh. xv. 25), according to the A.V., so that Judas alone was strictly a Judæan. But it appears that the render-

τοῦ[1]· οὗτος γὰρ ἔμελλεν παραδιδόναι αὐτόν, εἷς ἐκ τῶν
δώδεκα.

[1] Ἰσκαριώτην ΓΔ; Σκαριώθ D; ἀπὸ Καρυώτου ℵ. See note.

ing there is incorrect, and that
Kerioth ought to be joined with
Hezron (Kerioth-hezron, R.V.).
May not the town be identified
with the Kerioth (Καριώθ) of
Moab mentioned in Jer. xlviii.
24 ?

ἔμελλεν παραδιδόναι . . .] Compare xii. 4; Luke xxii. 23. The

phrase in v. 64 is different
(ὁ παραδώσων).

εἷς ἐκ τ. δωδ.] The phrase is
slightly different from that in
Matt. xxvi. 14, 47 and parallels
(εἷς τ. δ.), and seems to mark the
unity of the body to which the
unfaithful member belonged.
Compare xx. 24.

ADDITIONAL NOTES ON CHAP. VI.[1]

26—58. A brief summary of
the argument of the three discourses furnishes the best clue
to their general interpretation
in view of the controversies
which have attached to parts of
them. Their central subject is
Christ, truly man, the source
and the support of life. They
deal, as we have seen, with three
questions in succession. How
can man gain fellowship with
God? How can one who is man
be the source and support of life?
How can the virtue of Christ's
humanity be imparted to and appropriated by others? Or, putting
the last two questions in their
final form : Can the Incarnation
be a fact? Can the Incarnate
Son of God communicate Himself
to men? They are, it is evident,
questions of universal moment,
which go to the very heart of
faith; and according as they are
answered bring separation or
closer union at all times between
Christ and His disciples.

1. The source of life.

Man's effort is combined and

contrasted with God's gift (26,
27).

The divine work of man is
faith in a Person (28, 29).

The attestation of the gift
which He brings lies in the gift
itself (30—33).

He is Himself the gift; and
even through apparent failure
He fulfils His work (34—38).

Belief in the Son is life now,
and will be followed by resurrection (39, 40).

2. But how can One who is
man thus unite earth and heaven?

The answer requires a spiritual
preparation in the hearer (43, 44).

But in part it is answered in
the promises of the Old Testament (45, 46).

In part too the believer must
himself co-operate (47—50).

Christ gives what He is: the
fulness of His humanity (51).

3. How again can men partake
in the virtues of another's being?

The answer lies deep in the
perception of the divine nature
of the Son of man.

Man lives only by the partici-

[1] Bishop Westcott apparently wished to re-model this note. A revised summary of the discourses is now included in the running commentary.—A. W.

· of Judas *the son* of Simon Iscariot, for he it was
that was about to betray him, *being* one of the twelve.

pation in the virtues of His life
and death (53—55).

This participation brings with
it a personal union between the
believer and Christ (56),

Which is the fulness of divine
life (57, 58).

From first to last the gift to
men on the part of God is set
forth as Christ "the Son of
man"; and the power by which
man makes the gift his own is
active "faith." The repetition
of the title "the Son of man"
three times in most significant
connexions brings out very clearly
the aspect of Christ's Person to
which the teaching specially
points (*vv.* 27, 53, 62). So also
the stress laid on believing (πιστεύειν εἰς, *vv.* 29, 35, 40, 47) keeps
in prominence the requirement
from man. In the last section
(52—58) "believing" is not
mentioned, but the same effect
is attributed to "eating the
flesh and drinking the blood" of
Christ as before to "believing"
absolutely (*vv.* 47, 54, ἔχει ζωὴν
αἰώνιον). (Here then the activity
of faith is presented in its com-
pletest energy in connexion with
the fullest description of the
divine gift.) The fundamental
antithesis of the human and
divine, which appears at the
opening of the discourses, is thus
distinctly expressed at the close.

It must not, however, be concluded that "eating the flesh of
the Son of man and drinking His
blood" is simply a metaphorical
expression for "believing on
Christ," or more specifically for
"believing on Christ as having
lived and died for men." It is

quite unnatural to suppose that
the earlier and plain words are
involved in dark figures by the
later phrases. On the contrary,
these figures indicate the effective
action and issue of faith, while
they preserve and recognise the
meeting together of the human
and divine in the highest consummation of the destiny of man.

The progress which underlies
the apparent monotony of the
discourses is most conspicuously
marked by the comparison of
the corresponding phrases "believing on the Son of man," and
"eating" the Son of man, and
is indicated also in the recurrent
forms of expression which seem
at first sight to be identical.
Thus *vv.* 33, 50, 58, which in
their general structure and elements are closely connected, are
yet found upon examination to
be clearly distinguished:

v. 33. The bread of God is that
which *cometh* down from heaven,
and *giveth* (διδούς) *life to the world.*

v. 50. This (bread) [*v.* 48,
I am the bread of life] is the
bread which *cometh* down from
heaven that *a man may eat of it*
(ἐξ αὐτοῦ φάγῃ) *and not die.*

v. 58. This (bread) [*i.e.* I (*v.* 57)]
is the bread which *came* down from
heaven: *he that eateth* (τρώγων) *this
bread shall live far ever.*

The general divine fact is
stated first; next the divine
purpose in connexion with man;
and then last the historic fact as it
is appropriated by individual men.

From what has been said it
will be seen that the discourses
spring naturally out of the position in which the Lord stood at

a critical moment towards His disciples and the people, and are perfectly intelligible as an answer to the questionings among them conveyed in such a parabolic form (Matt. xiii. 34) as was suggested partly by the miracle of feeding, and partly by the memories of the Passover. That which is outward is made the figure of the inward, and then, when the spiritual conception is fully developed, the outward imagery is again adopted in order to indicate fresh forms of the truth. The people had "eaten of the loaves" (v. 26); that which it was their highest blessing to do was to eat the Son of man (v. 57). This "eating" is essential for all, inasmuch as without it there is no life and no resurrection (v. 53). And further, this "eating" leads necessarily to life in the highest sense ; it has no qualification (such as eating "worthily"); it is operative for good absolutely.

It follows that what is spoken of "eating ($\phi\alpha\gamma\epsilon\hat{\iota}\nu$) of the bread which cometh down from heaven" (v. 51), "eating ($\phi\alpha\gamma\epsilon\hat{\iota}\nu$) the flesh of the Son of man" (v. 53), "eating ($\tau\rho\acute{\omega}\gamma\epsilon\iota\nu$) His flesh, and drinking His blood" (vv. 54, 56), "eating ($\tau\rho\acute{\omega}\gamma\epsilon\iota\nu$) Him" (v. 57), "eating ($\tau\rho\acute{\omega}\gamma\epsilon\iota\nu$) the bread which came down from heaven" (v. 58)—the succession of phrases is most remarkable—cannot refer primarily to the Holy Communion ; nor again can it be simply prophetic of that Sacrament. The teaching has a full and consistent meaning in connexion with the actual circumstances, and it treats essentially of spiritual realities with which no external act, as such, can be co-extensive. The well-known words of Augustine, *crede et manducasti,* "believe and thou hast eaten," give the sum of the thoughts in a luminous and pregnant sentence.

But, on the other hand, there can be no doubt that the truth which is presented in its absolute form in these discourses is presented in a specific act and in a concrete form in the Holy Communion ; and yet further that the Holy Communion is the divinely appointed means whereby men generally may realise the truth. Nor can there be a difficulty to any one who acknowledges a divine fitness in the ordinances of the Church, an eternal correspondence in the parts of the one counsel of God, in believing that the Lord, while speaking intelligibly to those who heard Him at the time, gave by anticipation a commentary, so to speak, on the Sacrament which He afterwards instituted. But that which He deals with is not the outward rite, but the spiritual fact which underlies it. To attempt to transfer the words of the discourse with their consequences to the Sacrament is not only to involve the history in hopeless confusion but to introduce overwhelming difficulties into their interpretation, which can only be removed by the arbitrary and untenable interpolation of qualifying sentences.

In this connexion two points require careful consideration. The words used here of the Lord's humanity are "flesh" and "blood," and not as in every case where the Sacrament is spoken of in Scripture "body" and "blood." And again St. John nowhere refers directly to the Sacraments of

Baptism and Holy Communion as outward rites.[1]

The second point need not cause any surprise. St. John living in the centre of the Christian society does not notice the institution of services which were

[1] Bishop Westcott had purposed to write a new note upon the "Absence of reference to the Institution of the Sacraments in St. John." He has roughly sketched in pencil the outline of the note, which I here place just as he left it.—A. W.

They are equally absent from his Epistles.

There can be no question that he was familiar with them.

They were from the first universal [Ign. *Smyr.* 7. Iren. iv. 18, 4 ff.].

We must then seek some explanation.

We must read the Gospel (as New Testament generally) in light of Christ's life.

St. John (as elsewhere) reveals the idea :

1. Of Baptism.
2. Of Holy Communion.
3. Of both in their relation to Christ living through death.

Notice specially how this thought —life through death—underlies the Sacraments.

1. Baptism—a new birth (c. iii) — not cleansing only. Therefore a death. Rom. vi. 4.

Symbolism of water—Spirit : not cleansing but quickening.

2. Holy Communion.

The participation in a life surrendered and accepted (1 Cor. xi. 26).

Symbolism of bread—manna—food from heaven. Food for our whole being.

3. The significance of sign: xix. 34 f.

The fulness of the teaching prepared by the two signs—

The outward feeding.

The unexpected presence.

ὁ ἄρτος ὁ ἐκ τοῦ οὐρανοῦ καταβαίνων καταβάς.

Notice the foot-washing : xiii. 3.

Life. Food. But failures?

The ministry of love in fellowship with Christ.

Generally St. John leads us to the idea of the transfiguration of all life, of which Sacraments are signs and pledges.

parts of the settled experience of Church life. He presupposes them ; and at the same time records the discourses in which the ideas clothed for us and brought near to us in the two Sacraments were set forth. He guards the Sacraments in this way from being regarded either as ends in themselves or as mere symbols. He enables us to see how they correspond with fundamental views of the relations of man to God ; how they are included in one sense in the first teaching of the Gospel ; how Christianity is essentially sacramental as Judaism is essentially typical ; how, through the Incarnation, the relations between things outward and inward, things seen and unseen, are revealed to us as real and eternal, and not superficial and transitory.

The first point is evidently of critical importance for the understanding of the relation between the discourses and the Sacrament. The "flesh" is (so to speak) the constituent element of the human organization ; the "body" is the organization itself. That which the believer must appropriate is, as we have seen, the virtue of Christ's humanity ; through this, in the unity of His Person, Christ unites him to God. That which Christ presents to His Church in the institution of Holy Communion is His "Body." The term "flesh" marks that which must be assimilated, and suggests the due co-operation of the individual recipient for an effect which is absolute. The term "body" answers to the outward rite, which is primarily social (1 Cor. x. 16 f.). Or, to put the idea in a somewhat different light, the "flesh" ex-

17

presses that which characterises the essential limitation of that humanity which "the Word became," capable of an indefinite variety of manifestations, while the "body" is a specific manifestation. The one suggests the conception of the principle of human life ; the other the unity of a particular form of human life. (The gloss in D on *v.* 56 shows how soon the distinction was neglected.)

Among early writers Augustine has expressed very clearly the relation of the discourse to the Sacrament, though he does not dwell on the difference of "flesh" and "body." "This food and drink," he writes, "Christ wishes to be understood as fellowship with His Body and members . . . The Sacrament of this thing, that is, of the unity of the Body and Blood of Christ, is prepared on the Lord's table (*in dominica mensa*) in some places daily, in other places at stated intervals, and is taken from the Lord's table, for some to life, for some to destruction (*ad exitium*); the thing itself, however, of which [that rite] is a sacrament, is for every man to life, to none to destruction, whoever partakes of it (*Tract. in Joh. XXVI.* 15) . . . This is therefore to eat that food (*escam*) and to drink that blood, to abide in Christ and to have Him abiding in oneself. And through this, he who does not abide in Christ and in whom Christ does not abide, doubtless does not eat His flesh (*procul dubio nec manducat carnem ejus,* the addition *spiritualiter* is a false gloss), nor drink His blood, although he eats and drinks the Sacrament of so great a thing to his own judgement" (*Id.* § 18, *etiamsi tantæ rei sacramentum ad*

judicium sibi manducet et bibat according to the MSS. The text as it is quoted in Art. xxix. has been interpolated from the commentary of Bede).

NOTES ON READINGS IN CHAP. VI.

There are several readings of considerable interest in chap. vi. which require notice as illustrating the history of the text.

9. The common text reads παιδάριον ἕν. This is supported by A, the mass of later uncial and cursive MSS., some copies of *vt. Lat., Vulg.,* the *Syriac* versions (except *Syr. vt.*), etc.

On the other hand, ἓν is omitted by אBDL and a fair number of later copies, including some very important cursives, the most important copies of *Lat. vt., Syr. vt.,* Origen, Cyril Alex., Chrysostom, etc. (C is defective). Here it will be observed that the oldest representatives of each class of authorities omit the word in dispute, the oldest Greek MSS., the oldest forms of the oldest versions, and the oldest father who quotes the passage.

There can then be no doubt that παιδάριον alone should be read.

15. In this verse א has one of those paraphrastic glosses which are characteristic of אD, *vt. Lat.* and *vt. Syr.* In place of ἵνα ποιήσωσιν [αὐτὸν] βασιλέα, which is read by all other authorities with one questionable exception, it reads καὶ ἀναδεικνύναι βασιλέα. This phrase is followed by φεύγει for ἀνεχώρησεν. This reading φεύγει is supported by other authorities of the same group, *vt. Lat., Vulg., Syr. vt.*; but such evidence only shows the wide extension of the gloss at a very early time.

Other examples of similar paraphrases in members of the same group occur in *v.* 17, κατέλαβεν δὲ αὐτοὺς ἡ σκοτία (for καὶ σκοτία ἤδη ἐγεγόνει) אD ; 46, ἐώρακεν τὸν θεόν (for ἑ. τὸν πατέρα) א*D *a b e* . . . 51, ἐκ τοῦ ἐμοῦ ἄρτου (for ἐκ τούτου τοῦ ἄρτου) א *a e* . . . 57, λαμβάνων (for τρώγων) D.

51. The last clause of this verse is found in three forms:

(1) . . . ὃν ἐγὼ δώσω ἡ σάρξ μου ἐστὶν ὑπὲρ τῆς τοῦ κόσμου ζωῆς, BCDLT, *Latt.*, *Syr. vt.*, *Theb.*, (Orig.), etc.

(2) . . . ὃν ἐγὼ δώσω ὑπὲρ τῆς τοῦ κόσμου ζωῆς ἡ σάρξ μου ἐστίν, א, (*m*).

(3) . . . ὃν ἐγὼ δώσω ἡ σάρξ μου ἐστὶν ἣν ἐγὼ δώσω ὑπὲρ τῆς τοῦ κόσμου ζωῆς. The mass of later MSS. (A is defective), *Syr. Pesh.* and *Hcl.*, *Memph.*, Clem. Al.

The insertion of the clause ἣν ἐγὼ δώσω in (3) is evidently an attempt to remove the harshness of the construction in (1), which is removed in (2) by a transposition. But the addition of such a clause as ὑπὲρ τ. τ. κ. ζ. to a sentence already grammatically complete in order to bring out a wider thought is completely in St. John's style.

63. The common reading λαλῶ is supported by the great mass of later MSS., but by no early evidence whatever ; all the oldest MSS., versions, and fathers reading λελάληκα, which at first sight seems to limit the statement unduly.

69. The words of St. Peter's confession offer a most instructive example of the manner in which a (supposed) parallel influences a reading.

The words are given in different authorities in the following forms : σὺ εἶ

(1) ὁ ἅγιος τοῦ θεοῦ אBC*DL (A and T are defective).

(2) ὁ χριστός, ὁ ἅγιος τοῦ θεοῦ, *Memph.*, *Theb.*

(3) ὁ υἱὸς τοῦ θεοῦ, 17, *b, Syr. vt.*

(4) ὁ χριστός, ὁ υἱὸς τοῦ θεοῦ, *Latt.*

(5) ὁ χριστός, ὁ υἱὸς τοῦ θεοῦ τοῦ ζῶντος, the mass of MSS. and *Syr.* (except *Syr. vt.*).

The last form (5) is identical with that in Matt. xvi. 16, in which the authorities (practically) do not vary. It is then scarcely to be questioned that the language in St. John has been brought into accord with St. Matthew and not changed from it. The stages of the assimilation are preserved in (2), (3), (4). Two changes were made separately at a very early time, the addition of ὁ χριστός (Egyptian versions) and the substitution of υἱός for ἅγιος. These two changes were then combined, and this is the reading preserved in the mass of Latin copies. And finally the complete phrase of St. Matthew was introduced by the addition of τοῦ ζῶντος.

71. The mass of later copies, with the Gothic and the later copies of the Vulgate, give the title Iscariot (Ἰσκαριώτην) to Judas, but the earlier MSS. (אᶜBC with some others) and the best copies of the Vulgate connect it with Simon (Ἰσκαριώτου). In D and some early Latin copies the reading is simply Σκαριώθ (*carioth*), for which א* and four other early authorities read (as D reads xii. 4, xiii. 2, 26, xiv. 22) ἀπὸ καρυώτου. In xii. 4, xiv. 22, the title undoubtedly belongs to Judas. Here and in xiii. 2, 26 it appears scarcely less certainly to belong to his father Simon. The natural conclusion is that it was a local name borne by father and son alike.

7 Καὶ¹ μετὰ ταῦτα περιεπάτει [ὁ]²Ἰησοῦς ἐν τῇ Γαλιλαίᾳ,
οὐ γὰρ ἤθελεν ἐν τῇ Ἰουδαίᾳ περιπατεῖν, ὅτι ἐζήτουν
2 αὐτὸν οἱ Ἰουδαῖοι ἀποκτεῖναι. ἦν δὲ ἐγγὺς ἡ ἑορτὴ
3 τῶν Ἰουδαίων ἡ σκηνοπηγία. εἶπον οὖν πρὸς αὐτὸν
οἱ ἀδελφοὶ αὐτοῦ Μετάβηθι ἐντεῦθεν καὶ ὕπαγε εἰς

¹ Omit καί ℵ*D.   ² Omit ὁ B.

II. THE GREAT CONTROVERSY (vii.—xii.)

The record of the great controversy at Jerusalem, during which faith and unbelief were fully revealed, falls into two parts. The first part (vii.—x.) contains the outline of the successive stages of the controversy itself ; the second the decisive judgement (xi., xii.).

i. THE RELATION OF FAITH AND UNBELIEF AT JERUSALEM (vii.—x.)

This central section of the whole Gospel contains events and discourses connected with two national festivals, *the Feast of Tabernacles* and *the Feast of Dedication*, which commemorated the first possession of Canaan and the great recovery of religious independence. Thus the festivals had a most marked meaning in regard to the life of the Jews, and this, as will be seen, influenced the form of the Lord's teaching.

There is a clear progress in the history. The discussions at the Feast of Tabernacles (vii., viii.) are characterised by waverings and questionings among the people. The discussions at the Feast of Dedication show the separation already consummated (ix., x.).

(1) *The Feast of Tabernacles* (vii., viii.)

No section in the Gospel is more evidently a transcript from life than this. It reflects a complex and animated variety of characters and feelings. Jerusalem is seen crowded at the most popular feast with men widely differing in hope and position : some eager in expectation, some immovable in prejudice. There is nothing of the calm solemnity of the private discourse, or of the full exposition of doctrine before a dignified body, such as has been given before. All is direct, personal encounter. The " brethren " of the Lord (vii. 3 ff.), " the Jews " (vii. 1, 11, 13, 15, 35, viii. 22, 48, 52, 57), " the multitudes " (vii. 12 f.), " the multitude " (vii. 12, 20, 31 f., 40 f., 43, 49), " the people of Jerusalem " (vii. 25), " the Pharisees " (vii. 32, 47, viii. 13), " the chief-priests (*i.e.* the Sadducean hierarchy) and Pharisees " (vii. 32, 45, for the first time), Nicodemus (vii. 50), " the Jews who believed him " (viii. 31), appear in succession in the narrative, and all with clearly marked individuality. Impatient promptings to action (vii. 3 ff.), vague inquiries (vii. 11), debatings (vii. 12, 40 ff), fear on this side and that (vii. 13, 30, 44),

7   And after these things Jesus walked in Galilee : for
he would not walk in Judæa, because the Jews sought
2 to kill him.   Now the feast of the Jews, the feast of
3 tabernacles, was at hand.   His brethren therefore said
unto him, Depart hence, and go into Judæa, that thy

wonder (vii. 15, 46), perplexity
(vii. 25 ff.), belief (vii. 31, viii. 30),
open hostility (vii. 32), unfriendly
criticism (vii. 23 ff., viii. 48 ff.),
selfish belief in Christ's Messianic
dignity (viii. 31 ff.), follow in
rapid alternation. All is full of
movement, of local colour, of
vivid traits of conflicting classes
and tendencies. There is a continuous revelation of thoughts
from the nearest to the most remote—the "brethren" (vii. 3 ff),
the "multitude" (12 ff.), "the
people of Jerusalem" (25 ff.),
"the rulers" (32 ff.).

The section is naturally divided
into several distinct scenes. The
circumstances of the visit (vii.
1—13). The discussions at "the
midst of the feast" (14—36).
The discussions on the last day
(37—52). The after-teaching
(viii. 12—20). The trial of true
and false faith (21—59).

1. *The circumstances of the visit
to the Feast of Tabernacles*
(vii. 1—13)

Chap. VII. **1—13**. In these
verses there is a lively picture
of the position which the Lord
held at the time. Continued
teaching in Judæa had become
impossible (*v.* 1). His brethren
impatiently pressed for some more
decisive public manifestation of
His power (*vv.* 3—9). The multitudes gathered at Jerusalem were
divided between faith and dis-

trust (*vv.* 11, 12). But the
dominant party kept down all
open discussion of His claims
(*v.* 13). The description brings
out distinctly various aspects of
a work and a Person not yet
fully revealed.

1. κ. μετ. ταυτ.] *And after these
things*, that is, the whole crisis
brought about by the miracle of
feeding.

περιεπ.] vi. 66, note, xi. 54.
The word is not so used in the
other Gospels.

οὐ γ. ἤθελ. ἐν τ. Ἰουδ. περιπ.]
would not walk in Judæa. The
words imply a previous work in
Judæa corresponding with that
now accomplished in Galilee.

ἀποκτεῖναι] See *v.* 18.

2. ἡ ἑορτ. τ. Ἰουδ. ἡ σκηνοπηγ.]
dies festus Judæorum scenopegia
v.; *the feast of the Jews, the feast
of Tabernacles.* This feast was
pre-eminent among the festivals
"as the holiest and greatest"
(Jos. *Ant.* VIII. iv. 1). It fell
on 15—22 Tisri (September,
October), and thus there is an
interval of six months after the
events of ch. vi., of which the
Evangelist records nothing. The
record of some details of this
period is given in Matt. xii.—
xvii., xxi.

3. οὖν] *therefore*, since Jesus had
not gone up to the last Passover.

οἱ ἀδελφ. αὐτ.] ii. 12. See
Lightfoot, Excursus ii. on *Galatians.* Perhaps we may conclude

τὴν Ἰουδαίαν, ἵνα καὶ οἱ μαθηταί σου θεωρήσουσιν
4 [σοῦ] τὰ ἔργα¹ ἃ ποιεῖς· οὐδεὶς γάρ τι ἐν κρυπτῷ ποιεῖ
καὶ ζητεῖ αὐτὸς² ἐν παρρησίᾳ εἶναι· εἰ ταῦτα ποιεῖς,
5 φανέρωσον σεαυτὸν τῷ κόσμῳ. οὐδὲ γὰρ οἱ ἀδελφοὶ
6 αὐτοῦ ἐπίστευον εἰς αὐτόν. λέγει οὖν³ αὐτοῖς ὁ Ἰησοῦς
Ὁ καιρὸς ὁ ἐμὸς οὔπω πάρεστιν, ὁ δὲ καιρὸς ὁ ὑμέτερος
7 πάντοτέ ἐστιν ἕτοιμος. οὐ δύναται ὁ κόσμος μισεῖν
ὑμᾶς, ἐμὲ δὲ μισεῖ, ὅτι ἐγὼ μαρτυρῶ περὶ αὐτοῦ ὅτι

¹ σου τὰ ἔργα B ; τὰ ἔργα σου אᶜLXΓΔ ; Omit σου א*DG.
² αὐτὸς אLXΓΔ ; αὐτό BD*.   ³ Omit οὖν א*D.

even from this notice, compared with Mark iii. 21, 31, that the brethren were elder brethren (i.e. sons of Joseph by a former marriage) who might from their age seek to direct the Lord.

κ. οἱ μαθ. σου θεωρ . . .] thy disciples also may behold . . .; not only those disciples who would be gathered from all parts to Jerusalem, but specially those who had been gained by earlier teaching in Judæa and Jerusalem, and who still remained there. From this notice it appears that miracles were wrought chiefly among strangers to arrest attention ; and also that the Lord was accompanied only by a small group of followers in His Galilæan circuits.

4. οὐδ. γ. τι ἐν κρυπτῷ ποι.] nemo quippe in occulto aliquid facit v. ; for no man doeth any thing in secret as Christ did, for His works in Galilee and even beyond the borders of Galilee were practically withdrawn (such is the argument) from the observation of those who could best judge of their worth.

κ. ζητ. αὐτ. ἐν παρρησίᾳ εἶναι] et quærit ipse in palam esse v. ; and seeketh to be known openly.

Literally, " to be in boldness," " to use full freedom of speech," to stand forth boldly as one urging his claims before the world without reserve or fear. Comp. Wisd. v. 1 ; Col. ii. 15. The words refer to the position claimed and not to the position gained ("to be publicly known"). The phrase, however (בפרהסיא), is not infrequent in Rabbinic writers in the sense of " in public " as opposed to " in secret," see Buxtorf, Lex. s.v.

εἰ . . . ποιεῖς] The words do not carry with them any definite denial of the fact (v. 3), but simply place the fact as the basis for the conclusion.

φανερ. σεαυτ.]manifesta te ipsum v. ; manifest thyself. The word φανερόω is characteristic of St. John. Comp. xxi. 1, note, i. 31, ix. 3, xvii. 6.

τ. κοσμ.] viii. 26. Comp. xiv. 22.

5. οὐδὲ γ. οἱ ἀδ. αὐτ. ἐπιστ.] for not even did his brethren believe in him. True, self-surrendering faith was so rare that not even those who were nearest to the Lord were inspired by it. Comp. Matt. xii. 46, and ||³. The phrase need not mean more than that

disciples also may behold thy works which thou doest. ⁴ For no man doeth anything in secret, and himself seeketh to be known openly. If thou doest these ⁵ things, manifest thyself to the world. For not even ⁶ did his brethren believe in him. Jesus therefore saith unto them, My time is not yet come ; but your time ⁷ is alway ready. The world cannot hate you ; but me it hateth, because I testify of it, that its works are

they did not sacrifice to absolute trust in Him all the fancies and prejudices which they cherished as to Messiah's office. Thus their belief could not be a constant power (οὐκ ἐπίστευον) influencing their whole mode of thinking. They ventured to advise and urge when Faith would have been content to wait.

ἐπιστ. εἰς . . .] Compare viii. 30, note.

6. Ὁ καιρὸς ὁ ἐμός] *my time,* the seasonable moment for the revelation of myself. The word καιρός occurs in St. John's Gospel only in this passage [*v.* 4 is a gloss]. As compared with ὥρα (viii. 20, note) καιρός appears to mark the fitness of time in regard to the course of human events, while ὥρα has reference to the divine plan. Comp. ii. 4, note. A short interval alters the whole relation.

ὁ δ. καιρ. ὁ ὑμ. παντ. ἐστ. ἕτοιμ.] Christ's brethren had no new thoughts to make known. What they had to say was in harmony with what others were feeling. Their *time was always ready.* They had no need to wait for a favourable moment or to avoid occasions of exceptional danger. They were in sympathy with the world ; while Christ was in

antagonism with the world. They risked nothing by joining in the festival pilgrimage; He kept back not only from the danger of open hostility, but also from the violence of mistaken zeal, lest some should "make Him a king" (vi. 15). The thought which underlies the verse corresponds with that in *v.* 17.

7. οὐ δυν. . . . μισεῖν] This "cannot" answers to the law of moral correspondence. It is of frequent occurrence in St. John's Gospel and in different relations. Thus it is used of the relation of "the Jews" to Christ (vii. 34, 36, viii. 21 f., 43 f., xii. 39), and of "the world" to the Paraclete (xiv. 17); and in another aspect of the relation of the believer to Christ, in his first approach (vi. 44, 65, iii. 3, 5), and in his later progress (xiii. 33, 36, xvi. 12); and yet again of the relation of the Son to the Father (*v.* 19, note). In each case the impossibility lies in the true nature of things, and is the other side of the divine "must" (xx. 9, note).

"... Dominus eos ut ordinate venirent ad patriam revocavit ad viam. Excelsa est enim patria, humilis via. Patria est vita Christi, via est mors Christi : patria est mansio Christi, via est

8 τὰ ἔργα αὐτοῦ πονηρά ἐστιν. ὑμεῖς ἀνάβητε εἰς τὴν
ἑορτήν· ἐγὼ οὔπω¹ ἀναβαίνω εἰς τὴν ἑορτὴν ταύτην, ὅτι
9 ὁ ἐμὸς καιρὸς οὔπω πεπλήρωται. ταῦτα δὲ εἰπὼν αὐτοῖς²
10 ἔμεινεν ἐν τῇ Γαλιλαίᾳ. Ὡς δὲ ἀνέβησαν οἱ ἀδελφοὶ
αὐτοῦ εἰς τὴν ἑορτήν, τότε καὶ αὐτὸς ἀνέβη, οὐ φανερῶς
11 ἀλλὰ ὡς³ ἐν κρυπτῷ. οἱ οὖν Ἰουδαῖοι ἐζήτουν αὐτὸν
12 ἐν τῇ ἑορτῇ καὶ ἔλεγον Ποῦ ἐστιν ἐκεῖνος; καὶ γογ-
γυσμὸς περὶ αὐτοῦ ἦν πολὺς ἐν τοῖς ὄχλοις· οἱ μὲν
ἔλεγον ὅτι Ἀγαθός ἐστιν, ἄλλοι [δὲ]⁴ ἔλεγον Οὔ, ἀλλὰ
13 πλανᾷ τὸν ὄχλον. οὐδεὶς μέντοι παρρησίᾳ ἐλάλει περὶ
αὐτοῦ διὰ τὸν φόβον τῶν Ἰουδαίων.

¹ οὔπω BLTXΓΔ; οὐκ ℵD.   ³ Omit ὡς ℵD.
² αὐτοῖς BD²TΓΔ; αὐτός ℵD*LX.   ⁴ Omit δέ ℵDLΓΔ.

passio Christi. Qui recusat viam, quid quærit patriam?" (Aug.)

8. ὑμεῖς ἀνάβητε] The pronoun is emphatic : *Do ye*, with your thoughts and hopes, *go up.*

ἐγ. οὔπω ἀναβαιν. εἰς τ. ἑορ. ταυτ.] *I go not up yet unto this feast.* The sense may be "I go not up with the great train of worshippers." Nor indeed did Christ go to the feast as one who kept it. He appeared during the feast (*v.* 14), but then as a prophet suddenly in the temple. Perhaps, however, it is better to give a fuller force to the "going up" and to suppose that the thought of the next paschal journey, when "the time was fulfilled," already shapes the words. The true reading οὔπω and also the exact phrase "this feast" give force to this interpretation. The Feast of Tabernacles was a festival of peculiar joy for work accomplished. At such a feast Christ had now no place.

Ὁ μακαρίζων τοὺς πενθοῦντας ἐπὶ

τοῦ παρόντος αἰῶνος ἀκολούθως καὶ νυνὶ φθέγγεται κοινόν τι καὶ εἰς ἅπαντας διαβαῖνον τοὺς ἁγίους ἐφ' ἑαυτοῦ λέγων τὸ μὴ εἶναι καιρὸν ἑορτῆς ἡμῖν ἐν μέσῳ τῶν παρουσῶν θλίψεων (*Apoll. ap. Cramer,* Cat.).

οὔπω πεπλήρωται] *nondum impletum est* v. ; *is not yet fulfilled.* Comp. Luke xxi. 24; Acts vii. 23 (ἐπληροῦτο); Eph. i. 10; Gal. iv. 4.

10. ἀλλ. ὡς ἐν κρυπτ.] *but as it were in secret*, hidden as one solitary stranger and not the centre of an expectant band. Contrast the visit in ii. 13 (in power), v. 1 (as a pilgrim), and here, when Christ was withdrawn from the pilgrim-company, with the final visit in triumph, xii. 12 f.

11. οἱ οὖν Ἰουδ. ἐζητ. αὐτ.] *the Jews therefore sought him*, in the parties of Galilæan worshippers, asking of them ποῦ ἐστιν ἐκεῖνος; *Where is he?* that famous teacher whom we saw, and of whom we have since heard (ix. 12)? The

8 evil. Go ye up unto the feast: I go not up yet unto
9 this feast; because my time is not yet fulfilled. And
having said these things unto them, he abode *still* in
10 Galilee. But when his brethren were gone up unto the
feast, then went he also up, not publicly, but as it
11 were in secret. The Jews therefore sought him at the
12 feast, and said, Where is he? And there was much
murmuring[1] among the multitudes concerning him:
some said, He is a good man; others said, Not so,
13 but he leadeth the multitude astray. Howbeit no
man spake boldly of him for fear of the Jews.

[1] *or* muttering.

question was asked half perhaps
in ill-will and half in curiosity.

Chrysostom writes too strongly
when he says: Ὑπὸ τοῦ πολλοῦ
μίσους καὶ τῆς ἀπεχθείας οὐδὲ ὀνο-
μαστὶ αὐτὸν καλεῖν ἐβούλοντο.

12. γογγυσμός] *murmur* v. ;
murmuring. Or perhaps here
muttering, as of men who did
not dare to speak plainly and
loudly what they felt. Comp. *v.*
32.

ἐν τ. ὄχλοις] *among the multitudes,* that is, among the different
groups of strangers who had come
up to the festival, and such as
consorted with them. This con-
fluence and separation will explain the occurrence of the plural
which is found here only in
St. John, as it occurs also once
only in St. Mark (x. 1).

οἱ μὲν ἐλεγ. . . . .] The omission
of the particle (*enim* v. ; A.V.
" for ") gives vividness to the
description.

Ἀγαθός] *a good man*, unselfish
and true. Compare Mark x. 17.

πλανᾷ τ. ὄχλ.] *seducit turbas*
v.; *leadeth the multitude astray*.
Comp. *v.* 47. The thought is of

practical and not of intellectual
error.

" De toto corpore Christi hoc
(sc. *seducit turbas*) dicitur . . .
Quod dictum est ergo de Domino,
valet ad consolationem de quocunque hoc dictum fuerit Christiano " (Aug., Bede).

13. οὐδείς] *no man*, whether
he thought well or ill of Christ,
spake boldly of him for fear—
an ill-pervading fear, τὸν φόβον—
of the Jews, the leaders of the
" national " party, who had as
yet not pronounced judgement
openly though their inclination
was plain.

παρρ.] *boldly*. The word παρρησία has a double sense. It
may mean either without reserve
or veil, giving free utterance to
every thought plainly (x. 24,
xi. 14, xvi. 25, 29, xviii. 20),
or without fear (xi. 54). Here,
and so probably in *v.* 26, it is
used in the latter sense.

Ὁρᾷς πανταχοῦ τὸ μὲν ἀρχικὸν
διεφθαρμένον τοὺς δὲ ἀρχομένους
ὑγιαίνοντας μὲν τῇ κρίσει οὐκ ἔχον-
τας δὲ ἀνδρίαν προσήκουσαν ἧς
μάλιστα τῷ πλήθει δεῖ (Chrys.).

14 Ἤδη δὲ τῆς ἑορτῆς μεσούσης ἀνέβη Ἰησοῦς εἰς τὸ
15 ἱερὸν καὶ ἐδίδασκεν. ἐθαύμαζον οὖν οἱ Ἰουδαῖοι λέγοντες
16 Πῶς οὗτος γράμματα οἶδεν μὴ μεμαθηκώς; ἀπεκρίθη
οὖν ¹ αὐτοῖς Ἰησοῦς καὶ εἶπεν Ἡ ἐμὴ διδαχὴ οὐκ ἔστιν
17 ἐμὴ ἀλλὰ τοῦ πέμψαντός με· ἐάν τις θέλῃ τὸ θέλημα
αὐτοῦ ποιεῖν, γνώσεται περὶ τῆς διδαχῆς πότερον ἐκ
18 τοῦ θεοῦ ἐστὶν ἢ ἐγὼ ἀπ' ἐμαυτοῦ λαλῶ. ὁ ἀφ' ἑαυτοῦ
λαλῶν τὴν δόξαν τὴν ἰδίαν ζητεῖ· ὁ δὲ ζητῶν τὴν δόξαν
τοῦ πέμψαντος αὐτὸν οὗτος ἀληθής ἐστιν καὶ ἀδικία ἐν

¹ Omit οὖν DLX.

2. *The discussions at the midst of the Feast* (vv. 14—36)

14—36. The discussions at "the midst of the feast" lay open thoughts of three groups of men : "the Jews" (14—24), "some of the inhabitants of Jerusalem" (25—31), the envoys of "the chief priests and the Pharisees" (32—36). Each discussion constitutes a separate scene. "The multitude" is swayed to and fro by conflicting fears and hopes (20, 31 f.). In dealing with the successive questioners the Lord indicates the authority of His teaching, His connexion with the Old Dispensation, the brief space of the people's trial.

14—24. In the first scene in the temple Christ shows the source and the test of His teaching (16—18) as against the false interpretations of the Law (v. 19), which were against the spirit and history of the Law itself (20—24).

14. τ. ἑορτ. μεσ.] *die festo mediante* v. The feast properly lasted seven days, but to these an eighth day was added as "the last day"

of the feast (v. 37), Lev. xxiii. 36; 2 Macc. x. 6.

εἰς τ. ἱερ. κ. ἐδίδ.] This is the first mention of the appearance of the Lord as a public teacher at Jerusalem. Compare vi. 59, vii. 28, viii. 20 (the case is different in x. 23), xviii. 20.

For ἐδίδασκε cf. Matt. vii. 29 (ἦν . . . διδάσκων).

15. ἐθαυμ.] Matt. xxii. 22 ; Luke iv. 22.

οἱ Ἰουδ.] v. 10. Introd.

γραμμ. οἶδ.] *litteras scit* v. Compare Acts xxvi. 24. The marvel was that Jesus showed Himself familiar with the literary methods of the time, which were supposed to be confined to the scholars of the popular teachers.

μὴ μεμαθ.] *cum non didicerit* v.; *having never learned*, though He has never studied in one of the great schools. Christ was in the eyes of the Jews a merely self - taught enthusiast. They marvelled at His strange success, while they did not admit His irregular claims.

16. ἀπεκρ. οὖν . . . Ἰησ. . . .] The Lord's reply meets the difficulty of the questioners. His teaching was not self-originated

14 But when it was now the midst of the feast Jesus
15 went up into the temple, and taught. The Jews therefore marvelled, saying, How knoweth this man letters,
16 having never learned? Jesus therefore answered them,
and said, My teaching is not mine, but his that sent
17 me. If any man willeth to do his will, he shall know
of the teaching, whether it be of God, or *whether* I
18 speak from myself. He that speaketh from himself
seeketh his own glory: but he that seeketh the glory
of him that sent him, the same is true, and no

(ἡ ἐμὴ διδαχὴ οὐκ ἔστιν ἐμή), but
derived from a divine Master; infinitely greater than the popular
Rabbis. And it had a twofold
attestation—an inward criterion
and an outward criterion; the
first from its essential character,
and the second from the character
of Him who delivered it. He
whose will was in harmony with
the will of God could not but
recognise the source of the teaching. And again, the absolute
devotion of Christ to Him who
sent Him was a sign of His
truth.

17. ἐάν τις θέλῃ τὸ θέλημα ποιεῖν]
si quis voluerit voluntatem facere
...v.; *if any man will do* . . . *i.e.*
if it be any man's will to do His
will. The force of the argument
lies in the moral harmony of
the man's purpose with the divine
law so far as this law is known
or felt. If there be no sympathy
there can be no understanding.
Religion is a matter of life and
not of thought only. The principle is universal in its application. The *will of God* is not to
be limited to the Old Testament
revelation, or to the claims of
Christ, but includes every mani-

festation of the purpose of God.
Comp. Ps. xl. 8 (Heb. x. 5).
A fine saying is attributed to
" Rabban Gamaliel, the son of
R. Jehudah ha-Nasi ": " Do His
will as if it were thy will, that
He may do thy will as if it were
His will" (*Aboth*, II. 4).

Μὴ κρύψω ἐγώ [φησί] ἀπὸ
Ἀβραὰμ τοῦ παιδός μου ἃ ἐγὼ
ποιῶ; εὖ σῶτερ, ὅτι τὰ σεαυτοῦ
ἔργα ἐπιδείκνυσαι τῇ ποθούσῃ τὰ
καλὰ ψυχῇ καὶ οὐδὲν αὐτὴν τῶν
σῶν ἔργων ἐπικέκρυψαι· τούτου
χάριν ἰσχύει φεύγειν κακίαν καὶ
ἐπικρύπτειν καὶ συσκιάζειν καὶ
ἀπολλύναι ἀεὶ τὸ βλαβερὸν πάθος
(Philo, *Leg. Alleg.* iii. § 8, i. 93).

ἀπ' ἐμαυτ. λαλ.] Compare v. 30,
note, xv. 4, note.

18. τ. δοξ. τ. ἰδ.] *gloriam pro-
priam* v. Compare v. 30, 41 ff.

ὁ δὲ ζητ. . . .] The second
part of the sentence is changed
in form so as to take a positive
shape, wrought out both in
relation to thought absolutely
(ἀληθής ἐστιν, *verax est* v.) and
action relating to others (ἄδικ. ἐν
αὐτ. οὐκ ἐστ.).

For the connexion of "falsehood" and "unrighteousness'"
see Rom. ii. 8; 1 Cor. xiii. 6

19 αὐτῷ οὐκ ἔστιν. οὐ Μωυσῆς ἔδωκεν¹ ὑμῖν τὸν νόμον;
καὶ οὐδεὶς ἐξ ὑμῶν ποιεῖ τὸν νόμον. τί με ζητεῖτε
20 ἀποκτεῖναι; ἀπεκρίθη ὁ ὄχλος² Δαιμόνιον ἔχεις· τίς σε
21 ζητεῖ ἀποκτεῖναι; ἀπεκρίθη Ἰησοῦς καὶ εἶπεν αὐτοῖς
22 ͣΕν ἔργον ἐποίησα καὶ πάντες θαυμάζετε. διὰ τοῦτο
Μωυσῆς δέδωκεν ὑμῖν τὴν περιτομήν,—οὐχ ὅτι ἐκ τοῦ
Μωυσέως ἐστὶν ἀλλ᾽ ἐκ τῶν πατέρων,—καὶ [ἐν]³ σαβ-
23 βάτῳ περιτέμνετε ἄνθρωπον. εἰ περιτομὴν λαμβάνει [ὁ]⁴

¹ ἔδωκεν BD; δέδωκεν אLTΓΔ.   ³ Omit ἐν B.
² Insert καὶ εἶπεν DΓΔ.   ⁴ Omit ὁ אDLTX.

2 Thess. ii. 12. Injustice is falsehood in deed.

19. The principle laid down is applied to the condemnation of the Jews. The words of Ps. xl. would naturally rise to the minds of the people, and they give the transition to the Law. The people professed unbounded devotion to Moses, "the Law of God was within their heart," and yet they broke the Law because they were estranged from its spirit. Their ignorance of the Law had at last grown so great that they were prepared to murder Him who came to fulfil the Law.

οὐ Μωυσ. ἐδωκ. . . . ;] The question is an appeal to their own proud boast. Then follows their condemnation by the Lord. τί με ζητ. ἀποκτ.] v. 1.

20. ὁ ὄχλος.] The multitude, made up chiefly of pilgrims, not the people of Jerusalem (v. 25), and therefore unacquainted with the full designs of the hierarchy.

δαιμον. ἐχ.] Compare Matt. xi. 18; Luke vii. 33, where the same phrase is used of John the Baptist, as one who sternly and, in men's judgement, gloomily and morosely withdrew himself from the cheerfulness of social life. So here perhaps the words mean no more than "thou art possessed with strange and melancholy fancies; thou yieldest to idle fears." In a different context they assume a more sinister force, viii. 48 f., 52, x. 20. Yet even in these cases the sense does not go beyond that of irrationality. The word δαιμόνιον is only found in this section in St. John's Gospel.

21. ἀπεκρ. Ἰησ. . . .] The point of the answer lies in the indication of the ground of the hostility which ended in murderous designs. All alike—"the Jews" and "the multitude"—marvelled at that which should have been an intelligible illustration of the Law. This wonder contained the germ of open misunderstanding and opposition which, if followed to its legitimate development, could not but end in deadly enmity. If men failed to see the inner significance of the Law they must persecute Christ who came to interpret it and offer its fulfilment in the Gospel.

ͣΕν ἐργ. ἐποιησ.] I did one work; ch. v. 1 ff. (Contrast x. 32.)

19 unrighteousness is in him. Did not Moses give you
the law, and none of you doeth the law? Why seek
20 ye to kill me? The multitude answered, Thou hast
21 a demon : who seeketh to kill thee? Jesus answered
and said unto them, I did one work, and ye all marvel.
22 For this cause hath Moses given you circumcision (not
that it is of Moses, but of the fathers); and on the
23 sabbath ye circumcise a man. If a man receiveth

This special healing on the
Sabbath is singled out of the
many which Christ wrought (ii.
23, iv. 45) from its exceptional
circumstances.

θαυμαζ.] To rest in wonder
is to lose the divine lesson ;
Luke ix. 43; Acts iii. 12. Yet
even wonder may be a first step
towards a truer apprehension of
the divine lesson. In this sense
Christ seeks to produce it. Compare v. 20.

22. διὰ τουτ. Μων. δεδ. . . .]
*For this cause Moses hath given
you circumcision,* that it may be
the sign and seal of the restoration of man's whole nature in
fellowship with God, as an abiding
ordinance. . . . The cause referred to is that which underlies
the restoration of the impotent
man, as it is brought out in
v. 23. Man in his present state
needs restoration that his destiny
(Gen. i. 26) may be reached.
Circumcision as the seal of the
Covenant was designed to give
assurance of this restoration. The
words διὰ τοῦτο certainly commence a new sentence, and do
not close *v.* 21. In this respect
the usage of St. John is decisive,
vi. 65, viii. 47.

οὐχ ὅτι . . .] The words are
parenthetical. The case was not
simply a conflict of two Mosaic

precepts. The law of circumcision was not in origin Mosaic ;
and thus in itself it carried men's
thoughts back to the great ideas
which the Mosaic Law was designed to embody. The Mosaic
Law of the Sabbath was, on the
other hand, new.

The connexion of διὰ τοῦτο
with οὐχ ὅτι appears to be against
the usage of the language (vi. 46);
2 Cor. i. 24, iii. 5; Phil. iv. 17 ;
2 Thess. iii. 9 : οὐχ ὅτι . . . ἀλλ' ;
yet see xii. 6 (where ὅτι is repeated) ; and against the argument, for the point in question
was not the origin of circumcision, though this furnished a
subsidiary thought, but the fact
of conflicting enactments in the
Law which were adjusted in a
particular manner.

ἐν σαββ.] *on a sabbath,* if that
happened to be the eighth day.
The principle is distinctly recognised in the Mishna, *Sabb.*
XIX. 1. R. Akiva said : " Every
work which can be done on the
eve of the Sabbath does not set
aside the Sabbath ; but circumcision, which cannot be done on
the eve of the Sabbath [if the
eve be the seventh day], sets
aside the Sabbath." Compare
Lightfoot and Wetstein, *ad loc.*

23. μὴ λυθῇ] *should not be
broken* by the violation of the

ἄνθρωπος ἐν σαββάτῳ ἵνα μὴ λυθῇ ὁ νόμος Μωυσέως,
ἐμοὶ χολᾶτε ὅτι ὅλον ἄνθρωπον ὑγιῆ ἐποίησα ἐν σαβ-
24 βάτῳ; μὴ κρίνετε κατ᾿ ὄψιν, ἀλλὰ τὴν δικαίαν κρίσιν
25 κρίνετε. Ἔλεγον οὖν τινὲς ἐκ τῶν Ἱεροσολυμειτῶν Οὐχ
26 οὗτός ἐστιν ὃν ζητοῦσιν ἀποκτεῖναι; καὶ ἴδε παρρησίᾳ
λαλεῖ καὶ οὐδὲν αὐτῷ λέγουσιν· μή ποτε¹ ἀληθῶς ἔγνω-
27 σαν οἱ ἄρχοντες ὅτι οὗτός ἐστιν² ὁ χριστός; ἀλλὰ
τοῦτον οἴδαμεν πόθεν ἐστίν· ὁ δὲ χριστὸς ὅταν ἔρχηται

¹ μήτι ℵD.   ² Insert ἀληθῶς ΓΔ.

commandment which enjoined circumcision on the eighth day. Comp. x. 35, v. 18, note.

χολᾶτε . . .] *indignamini* v. The contrast is between the effect of circumcision which made (as it were) one member sound, and that of the miracle which made the whole paralysed man sound. If then the Law itself ratified the precedence of this act of partial healing over the ceremonial observance of the Sabbath, how much more lawful was the complete healing.

"Circumcisio pertinet ad aliquod signum salutis, et non debent homines Sabbato vacare a salute. Ergo nec mihi irascamini quia salvum feci totum hominem in Sabbato " (Bede after Aug.).

The word χολάω is found here only in the New Testament. The more usual form χολοῦμαι is found in Symm., Ps. lxxvii. 21 and lxxxviii. 39 for הִתְעַבָּר. Cf. Just. M. *Dial.* 27.

ὅλον ἄνθρωπον ὑγιῆ] *totum hominem sanum* v. ; *a whole man sound. A whole man* regarded from the physical side, and not with the subordinate distinction of "soul and body." Comp. *v.* 14.

24. μὴ κριν. κατ᾿ ὄψ.] *nolite ju-*

dicare secundum faciem v. ; *judge not according to the appearance* superficially, by the external aspect, as the matter first presents itself. ὄψις—may be equivalent to πρόσωπον Mark xii. 14—Levit. xix. 15. Cf. viii. 15 κατὰ τ. σάρκα. Comp. Isa. xi. 3 Οὐ κατὰ τὴν δόξαν κρινεῖ (LXX.). Μὴ ἐπειδή, φησί, τὸν Μωυσῆ μείζονά μου εἶναι νομίζετε ἀπὸ τοῦ ἀξιώματος φέρετε τὴν ψῆφον ἀλλ᾿ ἀπὸ τῆς τῶν πραγμάτων φύσεως· τοῦτο γάρ ἐστι δικαίως κρῖναι (Theod. Heracl. ap. Cramer *Cat.*).

τ. δικ. κρισ.] Give the one true and complete decision of which the case admits. The truth is one.

25—31. In the second scene, which is still in the temple (*v.* 28), the Lord meets the popular objection which was urged against the belief that He was the Christ (*vv.* 25—27). He had perfect authority for His work, from Him whom the Jews "knew not" (*v.* 28 f.). So the people were divided by His words and works (*v.* 31).

25. Ἔλεγ. οὖν τιν. ἐκ τ. Ἱεροσ.] . . . *quidam ex Hierosolymis* v. ; *some therefore of them of Jerusalem said*, who were acquainted with

circumcision on a sabbath, that the law of Moses may
not be broken; are ye wroth with me, because I
24 made a man every whit whole on a sabbath? Judge
not according to appearance, but judge righteous
25 judgement. Some therefore of them of Jerusalem said,
23 Is not this he whom they seek to kill? And lo, he
speaketh openly, and they say nothing unto him. Can
it be that the rulers indeed know that this is the
27 Christ? Howbeit we know this man whence he is:
but when the Christ cometh, no one knoweth whence

the designs of the hierarchy,
and yet not committed to them.
Hence they are described by the
local name, which occurs elsewhere in New Testament only
in St. Mark i. 5 (Vulg. *Hiero-
solymitæ*). The chain of sequence
(οὖν) is that the Lord had taken
up the position of accuser when
He was Himself accused.

26. ἴδε παρρησ. λαλ.] *ecce palam
loquitur* v. Comp. *v.* 13.

μή ποτε ἀληθ. ἔγνωσ. οἱ ἀρχ. . . .
χριστός;] *Can it be that the rulers
indeed know . . . the Christ?* Can
it be that they have learnt, come
to know . . .? The words seem
to mark some point of transition,
as if a change might have passed
over the Sanhedrin. Possibly
(so the people argue) they have
examined the matter, and found
reason to decide in favour of
Him whom they before opposed.
Perhaps there is a reference to
the examination in ch. v. 19 ff.
For ἔγνωσαν cf. Luke xx. 19, and
for μήποτε (in oblique construction) Luke iii. 15, 2 Tim. ii. 25.

27. ἀλλά . . .] The suspicion is
at once set aside as impossible:
οἴδαμεν . . . οὐδεὶς γινώσκει. The
two words οἴδαμεν, γινώσκει offer

a contrast between the knowledge which is full and abiding,
and that which comes by progress
and observation. Compare xiv.
7, ii. 24, note. Contrast ix. 29.

πόθεν ἐστίν] *whence he is*—i.e.
we know His family and His
home (vi. 42). Yet even so they
thought of Nazareth and not of
Bethlehem, David's city, *v.* 42.
Compare Matt. xiii. 54 f. It
seems to have been expected that
Messiah would appear suddenly
(perhaps from Dan. vii. 13, or
from Isa. liii. 8), no one knew
whence, while Christ had lived
long among His countrymen in
obscurity and yet known to
them. According to a Jewish
saying (*Sanhedr.* 97 a, *Weber*,
p. 342), "three things come
wholly unexpected, Messiah, a
god-send, and a scorpion." According to another tradition,
Messiah would not even know
his own mission till he was
anointed by Elijah. Just. M.
Dial. § 8, p. 226 B.

ὁ δὲ χρ. ὅταν ἐρχ.] The exact
expression (contrasted with ὅταν
ἔλθῃ, *v.* 31) marks the actual
moment when the coming is
realised. The appearance is a

28 οὐδεὶς γινώσκει πόθεν ἐστίν. Ἔκραξεν οὖν ἐν τῷ ἱερῷ
διδάσκων [ὁ]¹ Ἰησοῦς καὶ λέγων Κἀμὲ οἴδατε καὶ
οἴδατε πόθεν εἰμί· καὶ ἀπ' ἐμαυτοῦ οὐκ ἐλήλυθα, ἀλλ'
ἔστιν ἀληθινὸς ὁ πέμψας με, ὃν ὑμεῖς οὐκ οἴδατε·
29 ἐγὼ οἶδα αὐτόν, ὅτι παρ' αὐτοῦ εἰμὶ κἀκεῖνός με ἀπέσ-
30 τειλεν². Ἐζήτουν οὖν αὐτὸν πιάσαι, καὶ οὐδεὶς ἐπέβαλεν
ἐπ' αὐτὸν τὴν χεῖρα, ὅτι οὔπω ἐληλύθει ἡ ὥρα αὐτοῦ.
31 Ἐκ τοῦ ὄχλου δὲ πολλοὶ ἐπίστευσαν εἰς αὐτόν, καὶ
ἔλεγον Ὁ χριστὸς ὅταν ἔλθῃ μὴ πλείονα σημεῖα ποιή-
32 σει ὧν οὗτος ἐποίησεν; Ἤκουσαν οἱ Φαρισαῖοι τοῦ

¹ Omit ὁ Bᵀ.   ² ἀπέστειλεν BLT; ἀπέσταλκεν אD.

surprise. The Christ is seen among men; but no one perceives whence He comes.

28. Ἔκραξ. οὖν ἐν τ. ἱερ. διδ. ὁ Ἰησ. κ. λεγ.] *Jesus therefore,* as being acquainted with their partial knowledge and the conclusions which they drew from it, *cried aloud in the temple, teaching and saying.* The testimony is given publicly and with solemn emphasis. Comp. *v.* 37, xii. 44, (i. 15). The word κράζω occurs only in these places in the Gospel (xii. 13, xix. 12, are false readings). In the Synoptists κράζω is used of Christ only in Matt. xxvii. 50.

The repetition of the words ἐν τ. ἱερῷ (comp. *v.* 14) seems to indicate a break of time between this scene and the last.

Κἀμὲ οἴδ. . . .] The claim of the people of Jerusalem is drawn out at length (ἐμέ, πόθεν εἰμί, perhaps only quoting words), and its superficial truth is conceded. So far as mere outward experience goes, Christ answers, Ye do know me and my origin: but that is not all. *I am not come of myself,* self-commissioned,

dependent on no other authority, *but there is one to whose mission I appeal: He that sent me is true,* is one who completely satisfies the conception of a sender (ἀληθινός); it is on Him I rely, and from Him I draw my strength; and Him *ye know not.*

κ. . . . οὐκ ἐληλ. . . .] The facts which the people knew and the facts which they did not know are simply set side by side. Comp. *v.* 30, viii. 20, ix. 30; Mark xii. 12.

ἀπ' ἐμαυτ.] Compare *v.* 30, note.

ἀληθινός] The word (compare iv. 23) retains its proper meaning. God is described as true not merely in so far as He gave a true message, but as one who really sent a messenger; a real Father, as it were, sending a real Son. The question was as to the authority of Christ.

ὑμ. οὐκ οἰδ] Comp. iv. 22. This fatal want of knowledge made their boast of knowledge vain. The words are a sad echo of the opening words. As they thought they knew Christ so they thought they knew God.

28 he is.   Jesus therefore cried aloud in the temple,
teaching and saying, Ye both know me, and know
whence I am; and I am not come of myself, but he
29 that sent me is true, whom ye know not.   I know
30 him; because I am from him, and he sent me.   They
sought therefore to take him: and no man laid his
hand on him, because his hour was not yet come.
31 But of the multitude many believed on him; and they
said, Will the Christ when he cometh do more signs
32 than those which this man did?   The Pharisees heard

29. ἐγὼ οἶδ. . . .] *I*—as opposed to you—*know him, because
I am from him.* Now as always
I rest upon Him, *and he sent
me.* The continuance of being
and the historic mission are set
side by side; and both are referred to God.

παρ᾽ αὐτοῦ εἰμί] vi. 46, ὁ ὢν π.
τ. θ. note. For πέμψας, ἀπέστειλεν,
see Additional Note on xx. 21.

30. Ἐζήτ. οὖν . . .] *They
sought therefore*—because of His
claim to be sent from God—*to
take him.* The subject is taken
from "some of them of Jerusalem" (*v.* 25), those among them
who are specially called "Jews."
Compare *vv.* 32, 44, (viii. 20, 59),
(x. 31), x. 39, xi. 57.

καὶ οὐδ. . . .] Compare *v.* 28,
note.

ἡ ὥρ. αὐτ.] Compare xiii. 1,
note.

31. Ἐκ τ. ὀχλ. δέ . . .] *de turba
autem* v.; *but of the multitude*—
in contrast with the leaders of
Jerusalem—*many believed on him,*
not only gave credence to what
He said ("believed Him") but
surrendered themselves to His
guidance. . It does not appear
that they yet definitely recognised

Him as Messiah, because He had
not yet openly asserted His
claim to the title (x. 24), though
they were prepared to do so.

Ὁ χρ. ὅτ. ἐλθ. μή . . .] *Christus
cum venerit numquid* . . . *v.*;
suggests the inference that Jesus
must be the Christ, though the
inference is not drawn.

ὅταν ἔλθῃ] iv. 25, xv. 26, xvi.
13, (xvi. 4); Matt. xxv. 31;
Luke ix. 26 (1 John ii. 28, n.
ἐάν).

πλείονα σημ. . . . ὧν οὗτ. ἐποιησ.]
They look back upon the "signs"
which Christ had wrought as a
whole, now seen dispassionately
far off.

Of these many signs St. John,
as Chrysostom notices, has only
related three: Καὶ μὴν τρία ἦν
σημεῖα, τὸ τοῦ οἴνου, καὶ τὸ τοῦ
παραλυτικοῦ, καὶ τὸ τοῦ υἱοῦ τοῦ
βασιλικοῦ· καὶ οὐδὲν διηγήσατο
πλέον ὁ εὐαγγελιστής.
Comp. ix. 16.

32—36. These verses describe
the third scene in the controversy. The wishes of Christ's
enemies (*v.* 30) soon found active
expression. The Sanhedrin sent
public officers to seize Him; and
in their presence for the first

18

ὄχλου γογγύζοντος περὶ αὐτοῦ ταῦτα, καὶ ἀπέστειλαν
οἱ ἀρχιερεῖς καὶ οἱ Φαρισαῖοι ὑπηρέτας ἵνα πιάσωσιν
33 αὐτόν. εἶπεν οὖν ¹ ὁ Ἰησοῦς Ἔτι χρόνον μικρὸν μεθ᾽
34 ὑμῶν εἰμὶ καὶ ὑπάγω πρὸς τὸν πέμψαντά με. ζητήσετέ
με καὶ οὐχ εὑρήσετέ με, καὶ ὅπου εἰμὶ ἐγὼ ὑμεῖς οὐ
35 δύνασθε ἐλθεῖν. εἶπον οὖν οἱ Ἰουδαῖοι πρὸς ἑαυτούς
Ποῦ οὗτος μέλλει πορεύεσθαι ὅτι ἡμεῖς οὐχ εὑρήσομεν

¹ Insert αὐτοῖς T.

time He announces His speedy
and irrevocable departure from
"the Jews" (vv. 33 f.), to their
bewilderment (vv. 35 f.).

32. Ἠκ. . . . . τ. ὄχλου γογγυζ.]
heard the multitude murmuring
these things, as being inwardly
dissatisfied and irresolute.

οἱ Φαρισ.] Comp. iv. 1.

οἱ ἀρχ. κ. οἱ Φαρ.] The combination occurs also in St.
Matthew : Matt. xxi. 45, xxvii.
62. The phrase probably describes the Sanhedrin under the
form of its constituent classes.
Comp. v. 45, note, xi. 47, 57,
xviii. 3.

ἀρχιερεῖς] principes v. The
title appears to be given not
only to those who had held the
office of high-priest, like Annas
(see ch. xviii. 13, note), and his
son Eleazar, and Simon the son
of Kamhit, and Ishmael the son
of Phabi, who may all have
been alive at the time, but also
to members of the hierarchical
families which were represented
by these men, alike infamous in
Jewish tradition. Comp. De-
renbourg, Histoire de Palestine, pp. 230 ff. Thus the title
describes rather a political faction than a definite office. Comp.
Acts iv. 6 (ὅσοι ἦσαν ἐκ γένους
ἀρχιερατικοῦ). See v. 45, xi. 47,

57, xii. 10, xviii. 3, (35), xix. 6,
15, 21.
Compare also Matt. xxvii. 1.
They are mentioned here for the
first time in St. John's Gospel.
In the other Gospels (except
Matt. ii. 4) they do not appear
till the last visit to Jerusalem.

ὑπηρέτας] ministros v. ; officers
clothed with legal authority and
obeying the instructions of the
Council. Comp. vv. 45 f., xviii.
3, 12, 18, 22, xix. 6; Acts v.
22, 26.

33. εἰπ. οὖν ὁ Ἰησ.] Jesus therefore said. The words have a
wider application than to the
officers.

χρον. μικρ.] modicum tempus
v. It was about six months to
the Last Passover.

μεθ᾽ ὑμ.] The "multitude,"
the "Jews," the "officers," are
all grouped together in one body.
Οὐκ εἶπεν ἁπλῶς "ἐνταῦθά εἰμι,"
ἀλλὰ "μεθ᾽ ὑμῶν εἰμι," τουτέστι,
κἂν διώκητε κἂν ἐλαύνητε οὐ παύσο-
μαι τὰ ὑπὲρ ὑμῶν οἰκονομῶν καὶ τὰ
πρὸς σωτηρίαν λέγων καὶ παραινῶν
ὑμῖν (Chrys.).

ὑπάγω . . .] vado v. Three
Greek words are translated "go"
in St. John, and two of them in
similar connexions. Each word
expresses a distinct aspect of
departure, and its special force

the multitude murmuring these things concerning him ;
and the chief priests and the Pharisees sent officers
33 to take him. Jesus therefore said, Yet a little while
34 am I with you, and I go unto him that sent me. Ye
shall seek me, and shall not find me : and where I
35 am, ye cannot come. The Jews therefore said among
themselves, Whither will this man go that we shall

must be taken into account in
the interpretation of the passage
in which it is found. The first
word, ὑπάγω, emphasises the personal act of going in itself, as
a withdrawal (viii. 14, 21 f.,
xiii. 3, 33, 36, xiv. 4 f., 28, xvi.
5, 10, 16 f.).

The second word, πορεύομαι,
marks the going as connected
with a purpose, a mission, an
end to be gained, a work to be
done (v. 35, xiv. 3, 12, 28, xvi. 7,
28).

The third word, ἀπέρχομαι,
expresses simple separation, the
point left (vi. 68, xvi. 7, *go
away*).

Their differences are very
clearly seen in a comparison of
xvi. 10 (ὑπάγω) with xiv. 28
(πορεύομαι), and the succession
of words in xvi. 7—10 (πορευθῶ,
ἀπέλθω, ὑπάγω).

πρ. τ. πεμψ. με] During the
discourses in this chapter the
reference is to the authority of
mission (*him that sent me*) and
not of nature (*the Father*). The
thought of *the Father* is added
in ch. viii. 16, 18. These words
themselves leave a riddle unsolved.

34. ζητησ. με] *Ye shall seek me*
. . . not in penitence nor yet in
anger, but simply in distress.
You shall recall my words and
works, and wish once again to

see if it might be that in me
there were deliverance. The
thought is not of the Christ
generally, but of the Lord Himself, whose power and love they
had experienced. Comp. Luke
xvii. 22. Contrast this ineffectual
seeking with Matt. vii. 7.

κ. ὅπ. εἰμ. ἐγώ . . .] The fact
of failure is referred to the cause
of failure. Christ is essentially
there whither He goes. The
stress in this place is laid upon
the difference of character (εἰμί)
which involves separation, and
not upon the simple historical
separation. Comp. viii. 21, xiii.
33 (ὑπάγω). The pronouns are
placed in emphatic juxtaposition
(εἰμὶ ἐγώ, ὑμεῖς . . .). Compare
xvii. 24.

35. εἰπ. οὖν οἱ Ἰουδ. . . .] Those
who claimed the monopoly of
religious privileges are separated
from the rest. Hence we have
among themselves (xii. 19) and
not *one to another*.

Ποῦ οὗτ. . . . .] *where will this
man*, this strange pretender, *go*?
The pronoun here carries an accent of surprise and contempt.
Comp. vi. 52.

ὅτι ἡμ. . . . .] *that we* who stand
in the closest connexion with all
the people of God *shall not find
him* (Amos viii. 12 ; Prov. i. 28).

εἰς τ. διασπ. τ. Ἑλλην.] *in dis-
persionem gentium* v. ; *unto the*

αὐτόν; μὴ εἰς τὴν διασπορὰν τῶν Ἑλλήνων μέλλει
36 πορεύεσθαι καὶ διδάσκειν τοὺς Ἕλληνας; τίς ἐστιν ὁ
λόγος οὗτος ὃν εἶπε Ζητήσετέ με καὶ οὐχ εὑρήσετέ με
καὶ ὅπου εἰμὶ ἐγὼ ὑμεῖς οὐ δύνασθε ἐλθεῖν;
37 Ἐν δὲ τῇ ἐσχάτῃ ἡμέρᾳ τῇ μεγάλῃ τῆς ἑορτῆς ἱστήκει
ὁ Ἰησοῦς, καὶ ἔκραξεν¹ λέγων Ἐάν τις διψᾷ ἐρχέσθω
38 πρός με καὶ πινέτω. ὁ πιστεύων εἰς ἐμέ, καθὼς εἶπεν ἡ

¹ ἔκραξεν ℵD.

dispersion among the Greeks, the Jews, that is, who are scattered among the heathen Greek-speaking nations. The Jews who were still separated from their own land after the Return were called by two strikingly significant terms: the "Captivity" (גלרת from גלה, he made bare, ἀποικία, μετοικεσία, αἰχμαλωσία), and the "Dispersion" (διασπορά), which has no distinct Hebrew correlative. The first marks their relation to their own land; the second their relation to the lands which they occupied. Their own land was stripped of them, and they were separated from their national privileges. On the other hand, they were so scattered among the nations as to become the seed of a future harvest. This thought is recognised in a striking comment on Hos. ii. 24, quoted by Wünsche: R. Eliezer said the Eternal has therefore scattered the Israelites among other nations that the heathen may attach themselves to them (Pesach. 87 b). Diaspora first occurs Deut. xxviii. 25 (LXX.) וּזֵעֲוָה. Comp. Isa. xlix. 6; Jer. xv. 7; 2 Macc. i. 27; 1 Pet. i. 1; James i. 1. For the genitive see 1 Pet. i. 1. This usage seems to be quite

decisive against the interpretation "the dispersed Greeks."

διδ. τ. Ἑλλην.] docturus gentes v.; and teach the Greeks, make these isolated groups of Jews the starting-point (as the apostles actually did) of teaching among the Gentiles. This is the climax of irrationality. No true Messiah, no one seriously claiming the title, could (it is argued) entertain such a plan.

36. τίς ἐστ. ὁ λογ. οὗτ.] What is this word . . . In spite of all, Christ's words cannot be shaken off. They are not to be explained away. A vague sense remains that there is in them some unfathomed meaning.

3. The discussions on the last day of the Feast (vv. 37—52)

The record of the circumstances of the last day of the Feast consists of a fragmentary utterance containing a most significant promise (37—39), together with its effect upon the multitude (40—44); and then more remotely upon the Sanhedrin (45—52).

37. Ἐν δ. τ. ἐσχ. ἡμ. τ. μεγ. τ. ἑορ.] in novissimo autem die magno festivitatis v. The peculiar greatness of the eighth day lay in the fact that it was the close

not find him? will he go unto the Dispersion among
36 the Greeks, and teach the Greeks? What is this word
that he said, Ye shall seek me, and shall not find
me: and where I am, ye cannot come?

37 Now on the last day, the great *day* of the feast,
Jesus was standing, and he cried, saying, If any man
38 thirst, let him come unto me, and drink. He that

of the whole festival and kept as a Sabbath (Lev. xxiii. 36). It has been conjectured that it was observed in memory of the entrance into Canaan. At present it is treated as a separate Festival. Comp. Lightfoot, *ad loc.*

ἱστήκει] *stabat* v. The phrase is singularly vivid: *Jesus was standing*, watching, as it might be, the procession of the people from their booths to the temple, *and* then, moved by some occasion, *he cried* . . . Comp. i. 35, note, xviii. 5, note.

Ἐάν τις διψ.] *si quis sitit* v. The image appears to have been occasioned by the libations of water brought in a golden vessel from Siloam which were made at the time of the morning sacrifice on each of the seven days of the feast while Isa. xii. 3 was sung. It is uncertain whether the libations were made on the eighth day. If they were not made, the significant cessation of the striking rite on this one day of the feast would give a still more fitting occasion for the words.

ἐρχ. . . . κ. πιν.] The two actions are continuous (contr. iv. 16; Matt. xiv. 29).

No prophet, as Cyril justly remarks, nor yet Moses, ever used such language.

πρός με] The satisfaction lies in the access to Christ. Comp. vi. 35.

The pouring out of the water (like the use of the great lights, viii. 12) was a commemoration of one conspicuous detail of the life in the wilderness typified by the festival. The water brought from the rock supplied an image of future blessing to the prophets: Ezek. xlvii. 1, 12; Joel iii. 18. And that gift is definitely connected with the Lord by St. Paul: 1 Cor. x. 4.

Christ therefore shows how the promise of that early miracle was completely fulfilled in Himself in a higher form. He who drank of that water thirsted again; but the water which He gave became a spring of water within. As in iv. 14 the thought passes at once from the satisfaction of personal wants to the satisfaction of the wants of others which follows on this.

Nothing can prove more clearly the intimate relation between the teaching recorded by St. John and the Old Testament, than the manner in which Christ is shown to transfer to Himself the figures of the Exodus (the brazen serpent, the manna, the water, the fiery pillar).

38. The connexion of the phrase ὁ πιστεύων εἰς ἐμέ, either with the words which precede (οἱ πιστεύσαντες), or with those which follow (καθὼς εἶπεν ἡ γραφή,

γραφή, ποταμοὶ ἐκ τῆς κοιλίας αὐτοῦ ῥεύσουσιν ὕδατος
30 ζῶντος. Τοῦτο δὲ εἶπεν περὶ τοῦ πνεύματος οὗ¹ ἔμελλον
λαμβάνειν οἱ πιστεύσαντες εἰς αὐτόν· οὔπω γὰρ ἦν
40 πνεῦμα², ὅτι Ἰησοῦς οὔπω ἐδοξάσθη. Ἐκ τοῦ ὄχλου
οὖν ἀκούσαντες τῶν λόγων τούτων ἔλεγον [ὅτι⁸] Οὗτός

¹ ὅ BE.
² Insert ἅγιον LXΓΔ ; insert τό and ἅγιον ἐπ' αὐτοῖς D ; insert ἅγιον
δεδομένον B. See note.
³ Omit ὅτι ℵLTX.

i.e. truly, in accordance with the divine word), is obviously against the spirit of the whole passage. The words are out of strict construction. Comp. vi. 39; (Rev. ii. 26, iii. 12, 21), xiv. 12; 1 John ii. 24.

The sense of thirst—personal want—comes first ; then with the satisfaction of this, the fulness of faith ; and then, the refreshing energies of faith.

καθ. εἰπ. ἡ γραφ.] The reference is not to any one isolated passage, but to the general tenor of such passages as Isa. lviii. 11; Zech. xiv. 8, taken in connexion with the original image (Exod. xvii. 6 ; Num. xx. 11).

ποτ. . . . ῥευσ.] *flumina . . . fluent* v. The reception of the blessing leads at once to the distribution of it in fuller measure. Compare the thought in iv. 14, vi. 57, v. 26. He who drinks of the Spiritual Rock becomes in turn himself a rock from within which the waters flow to slake the thirst of others.[1]

[1] Bishop Westcott had intended to consider the interpretation of this passage more fully, and has indicated that he "now inclines" to interpret αὐτοῦ of Christ. He refers to Lightfoot (? *Biblical Essays*, p. 77) and to Dr. E. G. King (*Yalkut on Zechariah*, p. 120 f.), as exponents of this view.—A. W.

He is not only satisfied himself : he overflows. The Christian, in some sense, becomes a Christ (1 John ii.).

As He is the light of the world (viii. 12), so are they (Matt. v. 14).

It seems more natural to regard the Spirit in the man as a fresh spring than as a gift simply.

There is a fine passage in Augustine's Commentary on this text as to the character of Christ's gifts (*In Joh. Tract.* xxxii. 9) :

"Quare ergo Dominus Spiritum cujus maxima beneficia sunt in nobis, quia caritas Dei per ipsum diffusa est in cordibus nostris, post resurrectionem suam dare voluit? quid significavit? . . . Vitam æternam promisit, ubi nihil timeamus, ubi non conturbemur, unde non migremus, ubi non moriamur ; ubi nec decessor plangatur, nec successor speretur. Quia ergo tale est quod nobis promisit amantibus et Spiritus sancti caritate ferventibus, ideo ipsum Spiritum noluit dare nisi cum esset glorificatus; ut in suo corpore ostenderet vitam, quam modo non habemus sed in resurrectione speramus."

39. Τουτ. δ. εἰπ. . . .] The inspired activity of the apostles did not commence till after Pentecost. Comp. Luke xxiv. 49,

believeth on me, as the scripture said, out of his belly
39 shall flow rivers of living water. But this spake he
of the Spirit, which they that believed on him were
about to receive : for the Spirit was not yet *given*;
40 because Jesus was not yet glorified. *Some* of the
multitude therefore, when they heard these words,

οἱ πιστευσ.] *credentes* v. The
thought of the Evangelist goes
back to the definite group of the
first disciples.

οὔπ. γ. ἦν πν.] *non enim erat
spiritus datus* v. ; *the Spirit was
not yet* given. The addition of
the word *given* expresses the true
form of the original. When
πνεῦμα occurs without the article,
it marks an operation, or manifestation, or gift of the Spirit,
and not the personal Spirit.
Compare i. 33, xx. 22 ; Matt. i.
18, 20, iii. 11, xii. 28 ; Luke i.
15, 35, 41, 67, ii. 25, iv. 1.

ὅτι . . .] Comp. xvi. 7, note,
xx. 17. The necessary limitations
of Christ's historical presence
with the disciples excluded that
realisation of His abiding presence which followed on the
Resurrection.

The gift of the Spirit answers
to the revelation of the transfigured human life.

It is impossible not to contrast
the mysteriousness of this utterance with the clear teaching of
St. John himself on the "unction"
(χρίσμα) of believers (1 John
ii. 20 ff.), which forms a commentary, gained by later experience, upon the words of the
Lord.

ἐδοξάσθη] *fuerat glorificatus* v.
This is the first distinct reference
to the Lord's "glorification."
The conception is characteristic
of St. John's Gospel (compare

i. 14, ii. 11 ; Introd.), and includes in one complex whole
the Passion with the Triumph
which followed. Thus St. John
regards Christ's death as a
Victory (compare xii. 32 f.,
note, xi. 4, 40), following the
words of the Lord who identified
the hour of His death with the
hour of His glorification (xii. 23f.).
In accordance with the same
thought Christ spoke of Himself
as already "glorified" when
Judas had gone forth to his work
(xiii. 31, note) ; and so He had
already received His glory by
the faith of His disciples before
He suffered (xvii. 10, note). In
another aspect His glory followed
after His withdrawal from earth
(xvii. 5, xvi. 14). By this use
of the phrase the Evangelist
brings out clearly the absolute
divine unity of the work of Christ
in His whole "manifestation"
(1 John iii. 5, 8, i. 2), which he
does not (as St. Paul) regard in
distinct stages as humiliation and
exaltation.

40. Ἐκ τ. ὀχλ. οὖν . . . τ. λόγων
τουτ.] *ex illa ergo turba . . . hos
sermones ejus* v. ; *some therefore
of the multitude . . . these words*,
that is, as it appears, all the
discourses at the festival, and
not those on the last day only.
Probably this judgement marks
the general opinion.

ἐλεγ.] *dicebant* v. The verb in
this verse and the next describes

41 ἐστιν ἀληθῶς ὁ προφήτης· ἄλλοι ἔλεγον Οὗτός ἐστιν
ὁ χριστός· οἱ δὲ ἔλεγον Μὴ γὰρ ἐκ τῆς Γαλιλαίας ὁ
42 χριστὸς ἔρχεται; οὐχ ἡ γραφὴ εἶπεν ὅτι ἐκ τοῦ σπέρματος Δαυείδ, καὶ ἀπὸ Βηθλεὲμ τῆς κώμης ὅπου ἦν
43 Δαυείδ, ἔρχεται ὁ χριστός; σχίσμα οὖν ἐγένετο ἐν τῷ
44 ὄχλῳ δι᾽ αὐτόν. τινὲς δὲ ἤθελον ἐξ αὐτῶν πιάσαι αὐτόν,
45 ἀλλ᾽ οὐδεὶς ἔβαλεν ἐπ᾽ αὐτὸν τὰς χεῖρας. ῏Ηλθον οὖν
οἱ ὑπηρέται πρὸς τοὺς ἀρχιερεῖς καὶ Φαρισαίους, καὶ
εἶπον αὐτοῖς ἐκεῖνοι Διὰ τί οὐκ ἠγάγετε αὐτόν; ἀπε-
46 κρίθησαν οἱ ὑπηρέται Οὐδέποτε ἐλάλησεν οὕτως¹ ἄν-
47 θρωπος. ἀπεκρίθησαν οὖν² [αὐτοῖς³] οἱ Φαρισαῖοι Μὴ
48 καὶ ὑμεῖς πεπλάνησθε; μή τις ἐκ τῶν ἀρχόντων ἐπί-
49 στευσεν⁴ εἰς αὐτὸν ἢ ἐκ τῶν Φαρισαίων; ἀλλὰ ὁ ὄχλος

¹ ὡς οὗτος λάλει D; ὡς οὗτος λάλει ὁ ἄνθρωπος א*; ὡς οὗτος ὁ ἄνθρωπος ΧΓΔ.
² Omit οὖν אD.   ³ Omit αὐτοῖς B.   ⁴ ἐπίστευεν א*D.

vividly a repeated expression of
opinion.

ὁ προφ.] Comp. i. 21, (Deut.
xviii. 15).

42. ἀπὸ Βηθλ. τ. κωμ. ὁπ. ...]
de Bethleem castello ubi . . . v.;
From Bethlehem the village where
. . . Comp. Isa. xi. 1; Jer. xxiii. 5;
Mic. v. 2. It seems strange that
any one should have argued from
this passage that the writer of
the Gospel was unacquainted
with Christ's birth at Bethlehem.
He simply relates the words of
the multitude who were unacquainted with it (comp. Luke
iv. 23); and there is a tragic
irony in the fact that the condition which the objectors ignorantly assumed to be unsatisfied
was actually satisfied. This is
the only reference to David in
St. John.

44. τινές . . . ἐξ αὐτ.] some of
them, of the multitude. Part

of "the common people" were
now dissatisfied with Christ, and
would have taken Him, as the
people of Jerusalem (v. 30) and
the Pharisees (v. 32) before.

πιάσαι] adprehendere v.; vv.
30, 32, ch. x. 39, xi. 57; not
elsewhere in this sense in the
Gospels (xxi. 3, 10); Acts xii. 4.

45. ᾽Ηλθ. οὖν οἱ ὑπηρ.] The
officers therefore came, because
they had found no opportunity
for fulfilling their mission.

πρὸς τ. ἀρχ. κ. Φαρ.] the chief
priests and Pharisees, regarded
now as one body, the Sanhedrin,
and not as the separate classes
composing it, as in v. 32 (οἱ ἀ. καὶ
οἱ Φ.). The day was a Sabbath
and yet the council was gathered.

εἶπ. . . . ἐκειν. Διὰ τί οὐκ ἠγ.
αὐτ. ...] they said . . . Why did
ye not bring him? The pronoun (ἐκεῖνοι) generally marks
the more remote subject (comp.

41 said, This is of a truth the prophet. Others said,
This is the Christ. But some said, Why, doth the
42 Christ come out of Galilee? Hath not the scripture
said that the Christ cometh of the seed of David, and
43 from Bethlehem, the village where David was? So
there arose a division in the multitude because of
44 him. And some of them would have taken him; but
45 no man laid hands on him. The officers therefore
came to the chief priests and Pharisees; and they said
46 unto them, Why did ye not bring him? The officers
47 answered, Never man so spake. The Pharisees there-
48 fore answered them, Are ye also led astray? Hath
any of the rulers believed on him, or of the Pharisees?
49 But this multitude which knoweth not the law are

Acts iii. 13). In the thought
of the apostle these enemies
of Christ fill up, as it were,
the dark background of his
narrative, ever present in the
distance.

46. Οὐδέποτ. ἐλαλ. . . .] Chrysostom remarks : Οὐκ εἶπον οὐδέποτε ἐθαυματούργησεν ἄνθρωπος
οὕτως, ἀλλὰ τί; οὐδέποτε ἐλάλησεν
οὕτως ἄνθρωπος.

47. ἀπεκρ. οὖν αὐτ. οἱ Φαρ.]
The Pharisees therefore specially
standing out from the whole body
answered them. The hostility of
opinion is stronger than that of
office.

Μὴ καὶ ὑμ. πεπλαν.] *Are ye
also*—whose simple duty it is to
execute our orders—*led astray*
(*v.* 12)? Their fault was in
action (*led astray*) rather than
in thought (*deceived*).

48. ἐκ τ. ἀρχ.] *of the rulers* :
of the members of the Sanhedrin (cf. *v.* 26, iii. 1, xii. 42),

whom you are bound to obey, or
of the Pharisees whose opinions
you are bound to accept. The
form of the phrase is significant : *Hath any one of the rulers
believed on him ; or,* to take a
wider range, *of the Pharisees ?*

49. ὁ ὄχλος οὗτ. . . . ἐπάρατοι]
sed turba hæc . . . maledicti v. ;
this multitude of whom we hear,
and by whose opinion you are
influenced, *are cursed. As knowing not the law* (for ὁ μὴ γιν.
see *Winer*, p. 610), they were
in the opinion of the wise "a
people of the earth," such that
he who gave them a morsel
merited divine chastisement. A
saying is given in *Aboth*, II. 6,
"No brutish man is sinfearing,
nor is one of the people of the
earth pious." Compare Wetstein,
ad loc. Men were divided into
"people of the earth" and
"fellows" (חברים), *i.e.* educated
men.

50 οὗτος ὁ μὴ γινώσκων τὸν νόμον ἐπάρατοί[1] εἰσιν. λέγει
Νικόδημος πρὸς αὐτούς, ὁ ἐλθὼν πρὸς αὐτὸν πρότερον[2],
51 εἷς ὢν ἐξ αὐτῶν Μὴ ὁ νόμος ἡμῶν κρίνει τὸν ἄνθρωπον
ἐὰν μὴ ἀκούσῃ πρῶτον παρ᾽ αὐτοῦ καὶ γνῷ τί ποιεῖ;
52 ἀπεκρίθησαν καὶ εἶπαν αὐτῷ Μὴ καὶ σὺ ἐκ τῆς Γαλιλαίας εἶ; ἐραύνησον καὶ ἴδε ὅτι ἐκ τῆς Γαλιλαίας
προφήτης οὐκ ἐγείρεται[3].

[1] ἐπικατάρατοι DLXΓΔ.
[2] Omit ὁ ἐλθὼν πρὸς αὐτὸν πρότερον ℵ; insert νυκτός and omit πρότερον
    EGΓΔ; insert νυκτός XD (νυκτὸς τὸ πρῶτον D).
[3] ἐγήγερται EGL.

50. εἷς ὢν ἐξ αὐτ.] *being one of them*, and therefore able to speak from a position of equality. So the question of v. 48 was answered.

51. Μὴ ὁ νομ. . . .] Those who pleaded for the law really broke the law. Compare Deut. i. 16; Exod. xxiii. 1.

τ. ἀνθρ.] *a man*; literally, "the man" in each case which comes before them. Cf. ii. 25; Matt. x. 36; Rom. vii. 1.

ἐὰν μὴ ἀκουσ. πρωτ. παρ᾽ αὐτ.] *except it first hear from himself*, i.e. "hear what he has to urge on his own side." The Law is personified. The true Judge is a living law.

γνῷ] *learn* by inquiry and observation.

52. Μὴ καὶ σὺ ἐκ τ. Γαλ.] *Art thou also of Galilee?* and therefore moved by local feeling. At the same time by the choice of this term to characterise Christ's followers, the questioners con-trast them contemptuously with the true Jews.

ἐραυν. κ. ἰδ. ὅτι . . .] *scrutare et vide quia* . . . v.; *Search and see that* . . . The particle ὅτι is ambiguous; but it seems on the whole better to give to it the sense "that" than "for."

ἐγείρεται] *ariseth*. The reference appears to be not so much to the past as to the future. Galilee is not the true country of the prophets; we cannot look then for Messiah to come thence. The words have that semblance of general truth which makes them quite natural in this connexion, though Jonah, Hosea, Nahum, and perhaps Elijah, Elisha, and Amos were of Galilee. Thus it was said by R. Jehuda in the name of Rab that "the law was maintained by the dwellers in Judæa (*Eruv.* 53, as quoted by Wünsche). Comp. Neubauer, *La Geogr. du Talmud*, pp. 183 f.

ADDITIONAL NOTE TO VII. 39

There is a singular and interesting variety of readings in the phrase which describes the gift of the Holy Spirit as yet future, though the sense is not materially affected by them.

⁵⁰ accursed. Nicodemus saith unto them (he that came
⁵¹ to him before, being one of them), Doth our law
judge a man, except it first hear from himself and
⁵² know what he doeth? They answered and said unto
him, Art thou also of Galilee? Search, and see that
out of Galilee ariseth no prophet.

(1) οὔπω γὰρ ἦν πνεῦμα, אT. The Egyptian Versions represent the same reading, though *Memph.* adds the article in its rendering.

(2) οὔπω γὰρ ἦν πνεῦμα ἅγιον, LX, Mass of authorities. (A is defective.)

(3) οὔπω γὰρ ἦν πν. δεδ. Syrr. Latt.

(4) οἴπω γὰρ ἦν τὸ πνεῦμα ἅγιον 'π' αὐτοῖς, D, (*f*).

(5) οὔπω γὰρ ἦν πνεῦμα ἅγιον δεδομένον, B e.

All the readings have early authority. But while (1) explains the others, it is not easy to see how it could have been derived from them. The simple addition of ἅγιον in (2) was a natural assimilation with xx. 22; and the glosses (3), (4), and (5), which appear to be of equal antiquity, express the sense truly, which might easily appear to be obscure in the bare (and original) text. The ungrammatical form in D marks the process of corruption.

END OF VOL. I

Printed in Great Britain
by Amazon